Pro Go

The Complete Guide to Programming Reliable and Efficient Software Using Golang

Adam Freeman

Apress®

Pro Go: The Complete Guide to Programming Reliable and Efficient Software Using Golang

Adam Freeman
London, UK

ISBN-13 (pbk): 978-1-4842-7354-8
https://doi.org/10.1007/978-1-4842-7355-5

ISBN-13 (electronic): 978-1-4842-7355-5

Managing Director, Apress Media LLC: Welmoed Spahr
Acquisitions Editor: Joan Murray
Development Editor: Laura Berendson
Editorial Operations Manager: Mark Powers

Cover designed by eStudioCalamar

Cover image designed by Freepik (www.freepik.com)

Distributed to the book trade worldwide by Apress Media, LLC, 1 New York Plaza, New York, NY 10004, U.S.A. Phone 1-800-SPRINGER, fax (201) 348-4505, e-mail orders-ny@springer-sbm.com, or visit www.springeronline.com. Apress Media, LLC is a California LLC and the sole member (owner) is Springer Science + Business Media Finance Inc (SSBM Finance Inc). SSBM Finance Inc is a **Delaware** corporation.

For information on translations, please e-mail editorial@apress.com; for reprint, paperback, or audio rights, please e-mail bookpermissions@springernature.com.

Apress titles may be purchased in bulk for academic, corporate, or promotional use. eBook versions and licenses are also available for most titles. For more information, reference our Print and eBook Bulk Sales web page at www.apress.com/bulk-sales.

Any source code or other supplementary material referenced by the author in this book is available to readers on GitHub. For more detailed information, please visit www.apress.com/source-code.

Printed on acid-free paper

Dedicated to my lovely wife, Jacqui Griffyth.
(And also to Peanut.)

Table of Contents

About the Author

Adam Freeman is an experienced IT professional who has held senior positions in a range of companies, most recently serving as chief technology officer and chief operating officer of a global bank. Now retired, he spends his time writing and long-distance running.

About the Technical Reviewer

Fabio Claudio Ferracchiati is a senior consultant and a senior analyst/developer using Microsoft technologies. He works for BluArancio (`www.bluarancio.com`). He is a Microsoft Certified Solution Developer for .NET, a Microsoft Certified Application Developer for .NET, a Microsoft Certified Professional, and a prolific author and technical reviewer. Over the past ten years, he's written articles for Italian and international magazines and coauthored more than ten books on a variety of computer topics.

PART I

■ ■ ■

Understanding the Go Language

CHAPTER 1

■ ■ ■

Your First Go Application

The best way to get started with Go is to jump right in. In this chapter, I explain how to prepare the Go development environment and create and run a simple web application. The purpose of this chapter is to get a sense of what writing Go is like, so don't worry if you don't understand all the language features that are used. Everything you need to know is explained in detail in later chapters.

Setting the Scene

Imagine that a friend has decided to host a New Year's Eve party and that she has asked me to create a web app that allows her invitees to electronically RSVP. She has asked for these key features:

>A home page that shows information about the party

>A form that can be used to RSVP, which will display a thank-you page

>Validation to ensure the RSVP form is filled out

>A summary page that shows who is coming to the party

In this chapter, I create a Go project and use it to create a simple application that contains all these features.

■ **Tip**   You can download the example project for this chapter—and for all the other chapters in this book—from https://github.com/apress/pro-go. See Chapter 2 for how to get help if you have problems running the examples.

Installing the Development Tools

The first step is to install the Go development tools. Go to https://golang.org/dl and download the installation file for your operating system. Installers are available for Windows, Linux, and macOS. Follow the installation instructions, which can be found at https://golang.org/doc/install, for your platform. When you have completed the installation, open a command prompt and run the command shown in Listing 1-1, which will confirm that the Go tools have been installed by printing out the package version.

© Adam Freeman 2022

A. Freeman, *Pro Go*, https://doi.org/10.1007/978-1-4842-7355-5_1

UPDATES TO THIS BOOK

Go is actively developed, and there is a steady stream of new releases, which means there may be a later version available by the time you read this book. Go has an excellent policy for maintaining compatibility, so you should have no issues following the examples in this book, even with a later release. If you do have problems, see the GitHub repository for this book, `https://github.com/apress/pro-go`, where I will post free updates that address breaking changes.

This kind of update is an ongoing experiment for me (and for Apress), and it continues to evolve—not least because I don't know what the future releases of Go will contain. The goal is to extend the life of this book by supplementing the examples it contains.

I am not making any promises about what the updates will be like, what form they will take, or how long I will produce them before folding them into a new edition of this book. Please keep an open mind and check the repository for this book when new versions are released. If you have ideas about how the updates could be improved, then email me at adam@adam-freeman.com and let me know.

Listing 1-1. Checking the Go Installation

```
go version
```

The current version at the time of writing is 1.17.1, which produces the following output on my Windows machine:

```
go version go1.17.1 windows/amd64
```

It doesn't matter if you see a different version number or different operating system details—what's important is that the go command works and produces output.

Installing Git

Some Go commands rely on the Git version control system. Go to `https://git-scm.com` and follow the installation instructions for your operating system.

Selecting a Code Editor

The only other step is to select a code editor. Go source code files are plain text, which means you can use just about any editor. Some editors, however, provide specific support for Go. The most popular choice is Visual Studio Code, which is free to use and has support for the latest Go language features. Visual Studio Code is the editor I recommend if you don't already have a preference. Visual Studio Code can be downloaded from `http://code.visualstudio.com`, and there are installers for all popular operating systems. You will be prompted to install the Visual Studio Code extensions for Go when you start work on the project in the next section.

If you don't like Visual Studio Code, then you can find a list of available options at https://github.com/golang/go/wiki/IDEsAndTextEditorPlugins. No specific code editor is required to follow the examples in this book, and all the tasks required to create and compile projects are performed at the command line.

Creating the Project

Open a command prompt, navigate to a convenient location, and create a folder named partyinvites. Navigate to the partyinvites folder and run the command shown in Listing 1-2 to start a new Go project.

Listing 1-2. Starting a Go Project

```
go mod init partyinvites
```

The go command is used for almost every development task, as I explain in Chapter 3. This command creates a file named go.mod, which is used to keep track of the packages a project depends on and can also be used to publish the project, if required.

Go code files have a .go extension. Use your chosen editor to create a file named main.go in the partyinvites folder with the contents shown in Listing 1-3. If you are using Visual Studio Code and this is your first time editing a Go file, then you will be prompted to install the extensions that support the Go language.

Listing 1-3. The Contents of the main.go File in the partyinvites Folder

```go
package main

import "fmt"

func main() {
    fmt.Println("TODO: add some features")
}
```

The syntax of Go will be familiar if you have used any C or C-like language, such as C# or Java. I describe the Go language in depth in this book, but you can discern a lot just by looking at the keywords and structure of the code in Listing 1-3.

Features are grouped into packages, which is why there is a package statement in Listing 1-3. Dependencies on packages are made using an import statement, which allows the features they use to be accessed in a code file. Statements are grouped in functions, which are defined with the func keyword. There is one function in Listing 1-3, which is named main. This is the *entry point* for the application, meaning that this is the point at which execution will begin when the application is compiled and run.

The main function contains a single code statement, which invokes a function named Println, which is provided by a package named fmt. The fmt package is part of the extensive standard library that Go provides, described in Part 2 of this book. The Println function prints out a string of characters.

Even though the details may not be familiar, the purpose of the code in Listing 1-3 is easy to figure out: when the application is executed, it will write out a simple message. Run the command shown in Listing 1-4 in the partyinvites folder to compile and execute the project. (Notice that there is a period after the word run in this command.)

Listing 1-4. Compiling and Executing the Project

```
go run .
```

The go run command is useful during development because it performs the compilation and execution tasks in one step. The application produces the following output:

```
TODO: add some features
```

If you received a compiler error, then the likely cause is that you didn't enter the code exactly as shown in Listing 1-3. Go insists on code being defined in a specific way. You may prefer opening braces to appear on their own line, and you may have formatted the code that way automatically, as shown in Listing 1-5.

Listing 1-5. Putting a Brace on a New Line in the main.go File in the partyinvites Folder

```
package main

import "fmt"

func main()
{
    fmt.Println("TODO: add some features")
}
```

Run the command shown in Listing 1-4 to compile the project, and you will receive the following errors:

```
# partyinvites
.\main.go:5:6: missing function body
.\main.go:6:1: syntax error: unexpected semicolon or newline before {
```

Go insists on a specific code style and deals with common code elements, such as semicolons, in unusual ways. The details of the Go syntax are described in later chapters, but, for now, it is important to follow the examples exactly as shown to avoid errors.

Defining a Data Type and a Collection

The next step is to create a custom data type that will represent the RSVP responses, as shown in Listing 1-6.

Listing 1-6. Defining a Data Type in the main.go File in the partyinvites Folder

```
package main

import "fmt"

type Rsvp struct {
    Name, Email, Phone string
    WillAttend bool
}
```

```go
func main() {
    fmt.Println("TODO: add some features");
}
```

Go allows custom types to be defined and given a name using the type keyword. Listing 1-6 creates a struct data type named Rsvp. Structs allow a set of related values to be grouped together. The Rsvp struct defines four fields, each of which has a name and a data type. The data types used by the Rsvp fields are string and bool, which are the built-in types for representing a string of characters and Boolean values. (The Go built-in types are described in Chapter 4.)

Next, I need to collect Rsvp values together. In later chapters, I explain how to use a database in a Go application, but for this chapter, it will be enough to store the responses in memory, which means that responses will be lost when the application is stopped.

Go has built-in support for fixed-length arrays, variable-length arrays (known as *slices*), and maps that contain key-value pairs. Listing 1-7 creates a slice, which is a good choice when the number of values that will be stored isn't known in advance.

Listing 1-7. Defining a Slice in the main.go File in the partyinvites Folder

```go
package main

import "fmt"

type Rsvp struct {
    Name, Email, Phone string
    WillAttend bool
}

var responses = make([]*Rsvp, 0, 10)

func main() {
    fmt.Println("TODO: add some features");
}
```

This new statement relies on several Go features, which are most readily understood by starting at the end of the statement and working backwards.

Go provides built-in functions for performing common operations on arrays, slices, and maps. One of those functions is make, which is used in Listing 1-7 to initialize a new slice. The last two arguments to the make function are the initial size and the initial capacity.

```go
...
var responses = make([]*Rsvp, 0, 10)
...
```

I specified zero for the size argument create an empty slice. Slices are resized automatically as new items are added, and the initial capacity determines how many items can be added before the slice has to be resized. In this case, ten items can be added to the slice before it has to be resized.

The first argument to the make method specifies the data type the slice will be used to store:

```go
...
var responses = make([]*Rsvp, 0, 10)
...
```

The square brackets, [ ], denote a slice. The asterisk, *, denotes a pointer. The Rsvp part of the type denotes the struct type defined in Listing 1-6. Put together, [ ]*Rsvp denotes a slice of pointers to instances of the Rsvp struct.

You may have flinched at the term *pointer* if you have arrived at Go from C# or Java, which do not allow pointers to be used directly. But you can relax because Go doesn't allow the types of operations on pointers that can get a developer into trouble. As I explain in Chapter 4, the use of pointers in Go determines only whether a value is copied when it is used. By specifying that my slice will contain pointers, I am telling Go not to create copies of my Rsvp values when I add them to the slice.

The rest of the statement assigns the initialized slice to a variable so that I can use it elsewhere in the code:

```
...
var responses = make([]*Rsvp, 0, 10)
...
```

The var keyword indicates that I am defining a new variable, which is given the name responses. The equal sign, =, is the Go assignment operator and sets the value of the responses variable to the newly created slice. I don't have to specify the type of the responses variable because the Go compiler will infer it from the value that is assigned to it.

Creating HTML Templates

Go comes with a comprehensive standard library, which includes support for HTML templates. Add a file named layout.html to the partyinvites folder with the content shown in Listing 1-8.

Listing 1-8. The Contents of the layout.html File in the partyinvites Folder

```html
<!DOCTYPE html>
<html>
<head>
    <meta name="viewport" content="width=device-width" />
    <title>Let's Party!</title>
    <link href=
        "https://cdnjs.cloudflare.com/ajax/libs/bootstrap/5.1.1/css/bootstrap.min.css"
            rel="stylesheet">
</head>
<body class="p-2">
    {{ block "body" . }} Content Goes Here {{ end }}
</body>
</html>
```

This template will be a layout that contains the content common to all of the responses that the application will produce. It defines a basic HTML document, including a link element that specifies a stylesheet from the Bootstrap CSS framework, which will be loaded from a content distribution network (CDN). I demonstrate how to serve this file from a folder in Chapter 24, but I have used the CDN for simplicity in this chapter. The example application will still work offline, but you will see HTML elements without the styles shown in the figures.

The double curly braces in Listing 1-8, {{ and }}, are used to insert dynamic content into the output produced by the template. The block expression used here defines placeholder content that will be replaced by another template at runtime.

To create the content that will greet the user, add a file named welcome.html to the partyinvites folder, with the content shown in Listing 1-9.

Listing 1-9. The Contents of the welcome.html File in the partyinvites Folder

```
{{ define "body"}}

    <div class="text-center">
        <h3> We're going to have an exciting party!</h3>
        <h4>And YOU are invited!</h4>
        <a class="btn btn-primary" href="/form">
            RSVP Now
        </a>
    </div>

{{ end }}
```

To create the template that will allow the user to give their response to the RSVP, add a file named form.html to the partyinvites folder with the content shown in Listing 1-10.

Listing 1-10. The Contents of the form.html File in the partyinvites Folder

```
{{ define "body"}}

<div class="h5 bg-primary text-white text-center m-2 p-2">RSVP</div>

{{ if gt (len .Errors) 0}}
    <ul class="text-danger mt-3">
        {{ range .Errors }}
            <li>{{ . }}</li>
        {{ end }}
    </ul>
{{ end }}

<form method="POST" class="m-2">
    <div class="form-group my-1">
        <label>Your name:</label>
        <input name="name" class="form-control" value="{{.Name}}" />
    </div>
    <div class="form-group my-1">
        <label>Your email:</label>
        <input name="email" class="form-control" value="{{.Email}}" />
    </div>
    <div class="form-group my-1">
        <label>Your phone number:</label>
        <input name="phone" class="form-control" value="{{.Phone}}" />
    </div>
    <div class="form-group my-1">
        <label>Will you attend?</label>
        <select name="willattend" class="form-select">
            <option value="true" {{if .WillAttend}}selected{{end}}>
                Yes, I'll be there
```

```
            </option>
            <option value="false" {{if not .WillAttend}}selected{{end}}>
                No, I can't come
            </option>
        </select>
    </div>
    <button class="btn btn-primary mt-3" type="submit">
        Submit RSVP
    </button>
</form>

{{ end }}
```

To create the template that will be presented to attendees, add a file named thanks.html to the partyinvites folder with the content shown in Listing 1-11.

Listing 1-11. The Contents of the thanks.html File in the partyinvites Folder

```
{{ define "body"}}

<div class="text-center">
    <h1>Thank you, {{ . }}!</h1>
    <div> It's great that you're coming. The drinks are already in the fridge!</div>
    <div>Click <a href="/list">here</a> to see who else is coming.</div>
</div>

{{ end }}
```

To create the template that will be presented when an invitation is declined, add a file named sorry.html to the partyinvites folder with the content shown in Listing 1-12.

Listing 1-12. The Contents of the sorry.html File in the partyinvites Folder

```
{{ define "body"}}

<div class="text-center">
    <h1>It won't be the same without you, {{ . }}!</h1>
    <div>Sorry to hear that you can't make it, but thanks for letting us know.</div>
    <div>
        Click <a href="/list">here</a> to see who is coming,
        just in case you change your mind.
    </div>
</div>

{{ end }}
```

To create the template that will show the list of attendees, add a file named list.html to the partyinvites folder with the content shown in Listing 1-13.

Listing 1-13. The Contents of the list.html File in the partyinvites Folder

```
{{ define "body"}}

<div class="text-center p-2">
    <h2>Here is the list of people attending the party</h2>
    <table class="table table-bordered table-striped table-sm">
        <thead>
            <tr><th>Name</th><th>Email</th><th>Phone</th></tr>
        </thead>
        <tbody>
            {{ range . }}
                {{ if .WillAttend }}
                    <tr>
                        <td>{{ .Name }}</td>
                        <td>{{ .Email }}</td>
                        <td>{{ .Phone }}</td>
                    </tr>
                {{ end }}
            {{ end }}
        </tbody>
    </table>
</div>

{{ end }}
```

Loading the Templates

The next step is to load the templates so they can be used to produce content, as shown in Listing 1-14. I am going to write the code to do this in stages, explaining what each change does as I go. (You may see error highlighting in your code editor, but this will be resolved as I add new code statements to later listings.)

Listing 1-14. Loading the Templates in the main.go File in the partyinvites Folder

```
package main

import (
    "fmt"
    "html/template"
)

type Rsvp struct {
    Name, Email, Phone string
    WillAttend bool
}

var responses = make([]*Rsvp, 0, 10)
var templates = make(map[string]*template.Template, 3)
```

```
func loadTemplates() {
    // TODO - load templates here
}

func main() {
    loadTemplates()
}
```

The first change is to the import statement and declares a dependency on the features provided by the html/template package, which is part of the Go standard library. This package provides support for loading and rendering HTML templates and is described in detail in Chapter 23.

The next new statement creates a variable named templates. The type of value assigned to this variable looks more complex than it is:

```
...
var templates = make(map[string]*template.Template, 3)
...
```

The map keyword denotes a map, whose key type is specified in square brackets, followed by the value type. The key type for this map is string, and the value type is *template.Template, which means a pointer to the Template struct defined in the template package. When you import a package, the features it provides are accessed using the last part of the package name. In this case, the features provided by the html/template package are accessed using template, and one of those features is a struct whose name is Template. The asterisk indicates a pointer, which means that the map using string keys that are used to store pointers to instances of the Template struct defined by the html/template package.

Next, I created a new function named loadTemplates, which doesn't do anything yet but which will be responsible for loading the HTML files defined in earlier listings and processing them to create the *template.Template values that will be stored in the map. This function is invoked inside the main function. You can define and initialize variables directly in code files, but the most useful language features can be done only inside functions.

Now I need to implement the loadTemplates function. Each template is loaded with the layout, as shown in Listing 1-15, which means that I don't have to repeat the basic HTML document structure in each file.

Listing 1-15. Loading the Templates in the main.go File in the partyinvites Folder

```
package main

import (
    "fmt"
    "html/template"
)

type Rsvp struct {
    Name, Email, Phone string
    WillAttend bool
}

var responses = make([]*Rsvp, 0, 10)

var templates = make(map[string]*template.Template, 3)
```

```
func loadTemplates() {
    templateNames := [5]string { "welcome", "form", "thanks", "sorry", "list" }
    for index, name := range templateNames {
        t, err := template.ParseFiles("layout.html", name + ".html")
        if (err == nil) {
            templates[name] = t
            fmt.Println("Loaded template", index, name)
        } else {
            panic(err)
        }
    }
}

func main() {
    loadTemplates()
}
```

The first statement in the loadTemplates folder defines variables using Go's concise syntax, which can be used only within functions. This syntax specifies the name, followed by a colon (:), the assignment operator (=), and then a value:

```
...
templateNames := [5]string { "welcome", "form", "thanks", "sorry", "list" }
...
```

This statement creates a variable named templateNames, and its value is an array of five string values, which are expressed using literal values. These names correspond to the names of the files defined earlier. Arrays in Go are a fixed length, and the array assigned to the templateNames variable can only ever hold five values.

These five values are enumerated in a for loop using the range keyword, like this:

```
...
for index, name := range templateNames {
...
```

The range keyword is used with the for keyword to enumerate arrays, slices, and maps. The statements inside the for loop are executed once for each value in the data source, which is the array in this case, and those statements are given two values to work with:

```
...
for index, name := range templateNames {
...
```

The index variable is assigned the position of the value in the array that is currently being enumerated. The name variable is assigned the value at the current position. The type of the first variable is always int, which is a built-in Go data type for representing integers. The type of the other variable corresponds to the values stored by the data source. The array being enumerated in this loop contains string values, which means that the name variable will be assigned the string at the position in the array indicated by the index value.

The first statement within the for loop loads a template:

```
...
t, err := template.ParseFiles("layout.html", name + ".html")
...
```

The html/templates package provides a function named ParseFiles that is used to load and process HTML files. One of the most useful—and unusual—features of Go is that functions can return multiple result values. The ParseFiles function returns two results, a pointer to a template.Template value and an error, which is the built-in data type for representing errors in Go. The concise syntax for creating variables is used to assign these two results to variables, like this:

```
...
t, err := template.ParseFiles("layout.html", name + ".html")
...
```

I don't need to specify the types of the variables to which the results are assigned because they are already known to the Go compiler. The template is assigned to a variable named t, and the error is assigned to a variable named err. This is a common pattern in Go, and it allows me to determine if the template has been loaded by checking whether the value of err is nil, which is the Go null value:

```
...
t, err := template.ParseFiles("layout.html", name + ".html")
if (err == nil) {
    templates[name] = t
    fmt.Println("Loaded template", index, name)
} else {
    panic(err)
}
...
```

If err is nil, then I add a key-value pair to the map, using the value of name as the key and the *template.Tempate assigned to t as the value. Go uses a standard index notation to assign values to arrays, slices, and maps.

If the value of err isn't nil, then something has gone wrong. Go provides a function named panic that can be called when an unrecoverable error happens. The effect of calling panic can vary, as I explain in Chapter 15, but for this application, it will have the effect of writing out a stack trace and terminating execution.

Compile and execute the project using the go run . command; you will see the following output as the templates are loaded:

```
Loaded template 0 welcome
Loaded template 1 form
Loaded template 2 thanks
Loaded template 3 sorry
Loaded template 4 list
```

Creating the HTTP Handlers and Server

The Go standard library includes built-in support for creating HTTP servers and handling HTTP requests. First, I need to define functions that will be invoked when the user requests the default URL path for the application, which will be /, and when they are presented with a list of attendees, which will be requested with the URL path /list, as shown in Listing 1-16.

Listing 1-16. Defining the Initial Request Handlers in the main.go File in the partyinvites Folder

```go
package main

import (
    "fmt"
    "html/template"
    "net/http"
)

type Rsvp struct {
    Name, Email, Phone string
    WillAttend bool
}

var responses = make([]*Rsvp, 0, 10)
var templates = make(map[string]*template.Template, 3)

func loadTemplates() {
    templateNames := [5]string { "welcome", "form", "thanks", "sorry", "list" }
    for index, name := range templateNames {
        t, err := template.ParseFiles("layout.html", name + ".html")
        if (err == nil) {
            templates[name] = t
            fmt.Println("Loaded template", index, name)
        } else {
            panic(err)
        }
    }
}

func welcomeHandler(writer http.ResponseWriter, request *http.Request) {
    templates["welcome"].Execute(writer, nil)
}

func listHandler(writer http.ResponseWriter, request *http.Request) {
    templates["list"].Execute(writer, responses)
}

func main() {
    loadTemplates()

    http.HandleFunc("/", welcomeHandler)
    http.HandleFunc("/list", listHandler)
}
```

The functionality for dealing with HTTP requests is defined in the net/http package, which is part of the Go standard library. Functions that process requests must have a specific combination of parameters, like this:

```
...
func welcomeHandler(writer http.ResponseWriter, request *http.Request) {
...
```

The second argument is a pointer to an instance of the Request struct, defined in the net/http package, which describes the request being processed. The first argument is an example of an interface, which is why it isn't defined as a pointer. Interfaces specify a set of methods that any struct type can implement, allowing code to be written to make use of any type that implements those methods, which I explain in detail in Chapter 11.

One of the most commonly used interfaces is Writer, which is used everywhere data can be written, such as files, strings, and network connections. The ResponseWriter type adds additional features that are specific to dealing with HTTP responses.

Go has a clever, if unusual, approach to interfaces and abstraction, the consequence of which is that the ResponseWriter that is received by the functions defined in Listing 1-16 can be used by any code that knows how to write data using the Writer interface. This includes the Execute method defined by the *Template type that I created when loading the templates, making it easy to use the output from rendering a template in an HTTP response:

```
...
templates["list"].Execute(writer, responses)
...
```

This statement reads the *template.Template from the map assigned to the templates variable and invokes the Execute method it defines. The first argument is the ResponseWriter, which is where the output from the response will be written, and the second argument is a data value that can be used in the expressions contained in the template.

The net/http package defines the HandleFunc function, which is used to specify a URL path and the handler that will receive matching requests. I used HandleFunc to register my new handler functions so they will respond to the / and /list URL paths:

```
...
http.HandleFunc("/", welcomeHandler)
http.HandleFunc("/list", listHandler)
...
```

I demonstrate how the request dispatch process can be customized in later chapters, but the standard library contains a basic URL routing system that will match incoming requests and pass them onto the handler function for processing. I have not defined all the handler functions needed by the application, but there is enough functionality in place to start processing requests with an HTTP server, as shown in Listing 1-17.

Listing 1-17. Creating an HTTP Server in the main.go File in the partyinvites Folder

```go
package main

import (
    "fmt"
    "html/template"
    "net/http"
)

type Rsvp struct {
    Name, Email, Phone string
    WillAttend bool
}

var responses = make([]*Rsvp, 0, 10)
var templates = make(map[string]*template.Template, 3)

func loadTemplates() {
    templateNames := [5]string { "welcome", "form", "thanks", "sorry", "list" }
    for index, name := range templateNames {
        t, err := template.ParseFiles("layout.html", name + ".html")
        if (err == nil) {
            templates[name] = t
            fmt.Println("Loaded template", index, name)
        } else {
            panic(err)
        }
    }
}

func welcomeHandler(writer http.ResponseWriter, request *http.Request) {
    templates["welcome"].Execute(writer, nil)
}

func listHandler(writer http.ResponseWriter, request *http.Request) {
    templates["list"].Execute(writer, responses)
}

func main() {
    loadTemplates()

    http.HandleFunc("/", welcomeHandler)
    http.HandleFunc("/list", listHandler)

    err := http.ListenAndServe(":5000", nil)
    if (err != nil) {
        fmt.Println(err)
    }
}
```

17

The new statements create an HTTP server that listens for requests on port 5000, which is specified by the first argument to the ListenAndServe function. The second argument is nil, which tells the server that requests should be processed using the functions registered with the HandleFunc function. Run the command shown in Listing 1-18 in the partyinvites folder to compile and execute the project.

Listing 1-18. Compiling and Executing the Project

```
go run .
```

Open a new web browser and request the URL http://localhost:5000, which will produce the response shown in Figure 1-1. (If you are using Windows, you may be prompted for approval by the Windows firewall before requests can be processed by the server. You will need to grant approval every time you use the go run . command in this chapter. Later chapters introduce a simple PowerShell script to address this issue.)

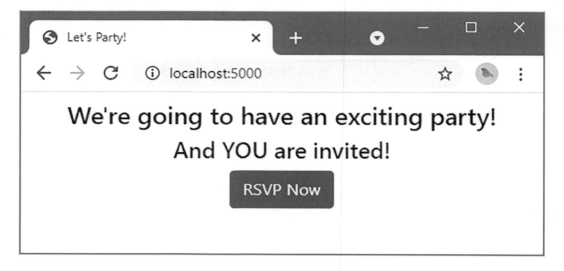

Figure 1-1. Handling HTTP requests

Press Ctrl+C to stop the application once you have confirmed that it can produce a response.

Writing the Form Handling Function

Clicking the RSVP Now button has no effect because there is no handler for the /form URL that it targets. Listing 1-19 defines the new handler function and starts implementing the features the application requires.

Listing 1-19. Adding the Form Handler Function in the main.go File in the partyinvites Folder

```
package main

import (
    "fmt"
    "html/template"
    "net/http"
)

type Rsvp struct {
    Name, Email, Phone string
    WillAttend bool
}

var responses = make([]*Rsvp, 0, 10)
var templates = make(map[string]*template.Template, 3)

func loadTemplates() {
    templateNames := [5]string { "welcome", "form", "thanks", "sorry", "list" }
    for index, name := range templateNames {
        t, err := template.ParseFiles("layout.html", name + ".html")
        if (err == nil) {
            templates[name] = t
            fmt.Println("Loaded template", index, name)
        } else {
            panic(err)
        }
    }
}

func welcomeHandler(writer http.ResponseWriter, request *http.Request) {
    templates["welcome"].Execute(writer, nil)
}

func listHandler(writer http.ResponseWriter, request *http.Request) {
    templates["list"].Execute(writer, responses)
}

type formData struct {
    *Rsvp
    Errors []string
}

func formHandler(writer http.ResponseWriter, request *http.Request) {
    if request.Method == http.MethodGet {
        templates["form"].Execute(writer, formData {
            Rsvp: &Rsvp{}, Errors: []string {},
        })
    }
}
```

```
func main() {
    loadTemplates()

    http.HandleFunc("/", welcomeHandler)
    http.HandleFunc("/list", listHandler)
    http.HandleFunc("/form", formHandler)

    err := http.ListenAndServe(":5000", nil)
    if (err != nil) {
        fmt.Println(err)
    }
}
```

The form.html template expects to receive a specific data structure of data values to render its content. To represent this structure, I have defined a new struct type named formData. Go structs can be more than just a group of name-value fields, and one feature they provide is support for creating new structs using existing structs. In this case, I have defined the formData struct using a pointer to the existing Rsvp struct, like this:

```
...
type formData struct {
    *Rsvp
    Errors []string
}
...
```

The result is that the formData struct can be used as though it defines the Name, Email, Phone, and WillAttend fields from the Rsvp struct and that I can create an instance of the formData struct using an existing Rsvp value. The asterisk denotes a pointer, which means that I don't want to copy the Rsvp value when I create the formData value.

The new handler function checks the value of the request.Method field, which returns the type of HTTP request that has been received. For GET requests, the form template is executed, like this:

```
...
if request.Method == http.MethodGet {
    templates["form"].Execute(writer, formData {
        Rsvp: &Rsvp{}, Errors: []string {},
    })
...
```

There is no data to use when responding to GET requests, but I need to provide the template with the expected data structure. To do this, I create an instance of the formData struct using the default values for its fields:

```
...
templates["form"].Execute(writer, formData {
        Rsvp: &Rsvp{}, Errors: []string {},
    })
...
```

Go doesn't have a new keyword, and values are created using braces, with default values being used for any field for which a value is not specified. This kind of statement can be hard to parse at first, but it creates a formData struct by creating a new instance of the Rsvp struct and creating a string slice that contains no values. The ampersand (the & character) creates a pointer to a value:

```
...
templates["form"].Execute(writer, formData {
        Rsvp: &Rsvp{}, Errors: []string {},
    })
...
```

The formData struct has been defined to expect a pointer to an Rsvp value, which the ampersand allows me to create. Run the command shown in Listing 1-20 in the partyinvites folder to compile and execute the project.

Listing 1-20. Compiling and Executing the Project

```
go run .
```

Open a new web browser, request the URL http://localhost:5000, and click the RSVP Now button. The new handler will receive the request from the browser and display the HTML form shown in Figure 1-2.

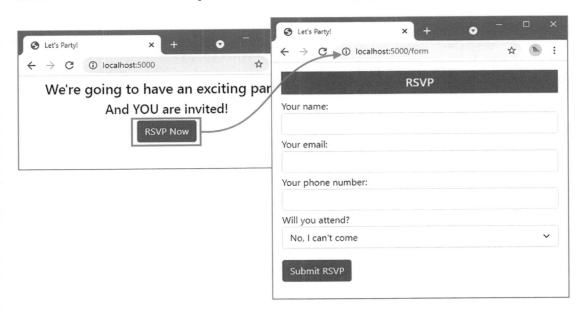

Figure 1-2. *Displaying the HTML form*

Handling the Form Data

Now I need to handle POST requests and read the data that the user has entered into the form, as shown in Listing 1-21. This listing shows only the changes to the formHandler function; the rest of the main.go file remains unchanged.

Listing 1-21. Handling Form Data in the main.go File in the partyinvites Folder

```
...
func formHandler(writer http.ResponseWriter, request *http.Request) {
    if request.Method == http.MethodGet {
        templates["form"].Execute(writer, formData {
            Rsvp: &Rsvp{}, Errors: []string {},
        })
    } else if request.Method == http.MethodPost {
        request.ParseForm()
        responseData := Rsvp {
            Name: request.Form["name"][0],
            Email: request.Form["email"][0],
            Phone: request.Form["phone"][0],
            WillAttend: request.Form["willattend"][0] == "true",
        }

        responses = append(responses, &responseData)

        if responseData.WillAttend {
            templates["thanks"].Execute(writer, responseData.Name)
        } else {
            templates["sorry"].Execute(writer, responseData.Name)
        }
    }
}
...
```

The ParseForm method processes the form data contained in an HTTP request and populates a map, which can be accessed through the Form field. The form data is then used to create an Rsvp value:

```
...
responseData := Rsvp {
    Name: request.Form["name"][0],
    Email: request.Form["email"][0],
    Phone: request.Form["phone"][0],
    WillAttend: request.Form["willattend"][0] == "true",
}
...
```

This statement demonstrates how a struct is instantiated with values for its fields, as opposed to the default values that were used in Listing 1-19. HTML forms can include multiple values with the same name, so the form data is presented as a slice of values. I know that there will be only one value for each name, and I access the first value in the slice using the standard zero-based index notation that most languages use.

Once I have created an Rsvp value, I add it to the slice assigned to the responses variable:

```
...
responses = append(responses, &responseData)
...
```

The append function is used to append a value to a slice. Notice that I use the ampersand to create a pointer to the Rsvp value I created. If I had not used a pointer, then my Rsvp value would be duplicated when it is added to the slice.

The remaining statements use the value of the WillAttend field to select the template that will be presented to the user.

Run the command shown in Listing 1-22 in the partyinvites folder to compile and execute the project.

Listing 1-22. Compiling and Executing the Project

```
go run .
```

Open a new web browser, request the URL http://localhost:5000, and click the RSVP Now button. Fill out the form and click the Submit RSVP button; you will receive a response selected based on which value you chose using the HTML select element. Click the link in the response to see a summary of the responses the application has received, as shown in Figure 1-3.

Figure 1-3. *Processing form data*

Adding Data Validation

All that's required to complete the application is some basic validation to ensure the user has filled out the form, as shown in Listing 1-23. This listing shows the changes to the formHandler function, and the rest of the main.go file remains unchanged.

Listing 1-23. Checking the Form Data in the main.go File in the partyinvites Folder

```
...
func formHandler(writer http.ResponseWriter, request *http.Request) {
    if request.Method == http.MethodGet {
        templates["form"].Execute(writer, formData {
            Rsvp: &Rsvp{}, Errors: []string {},
        })
    } else if request.Method == http.MethodPost {
        request.ParseForm()
        responseData := Rsvp {
            Name: request.Form["name"][0],
            Email: request.Form["email"][0],
            Phone: request.Form["phone"][0],
            WillAttend: request.Form["willattend"][0] == "true",
        }

        errors := []string {}
        if responseData.Name == "" {
            errors = append(errors, "Please enter your name")
        }
        if responseData.Email == "" {
            errors = append(errors, "Please enter your email address")
        }
        if responseData.Phone == "" {
            errors = append(errors, "Please enter your phone number")
        }
        if len(errors) > 0 {
            templates["form"].Execute(writer, formData {
                Rsvp: &responseData, Errors: errors,
            })
        } else {
            responses = append(responses, &responseData)
            if responseData.WillAttend {
                templates["thanks"].Execute(writer, responseData.Name)
            } else {
                templates["sorry"].Execute(writer, responseData.Name)
            }
        }
    }
}
...
```

The application will receive an empty string ("") from the request when the user doesn't provide a value for a form field. The new statements in Listing 1-23 check the Name, Email, and Phone fields and add a message to a slice of strings for each field that doesn't have a value. I use the built-in len function to get the number of values in the errors slice, and if there are errors, then I render the contents of the form template again, including the error messages in the data the template receives. If there are no errors, then the thanks or sorry template is used.

Run the command shown in Listing 1-24 in the partyinvites folder to compile and execute the project.

Listing 1-24. Compiling and Executing the Project

```
go run .
```

Open a new web browser, request the URL `http://localhost:5000`, and click the RSVP Now button. Click the Submit RSVP button without entering any values into the form; you will see warning messages, as shown in Figure 1-4. Enter some details into the form and submit it again, and you will see the final message.

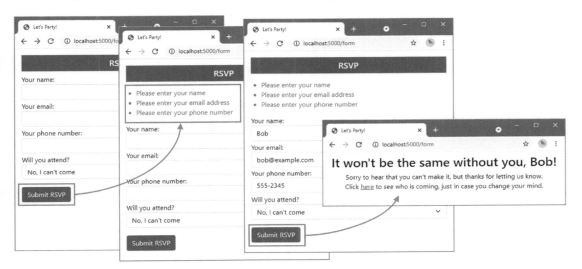

Figure 1-4. *Validating data*

Summary

In this chapter, I installed the Go package and used the tools it contains to create a simple web application using only a single code file and some basic HTML templates. Now that you have seen Go in action, the next chapter puts this book into context.

CHAPTER 2

Putting Go in Context

Go, often referred to as *Golang*, is a language originally developed at Google that has started to gain widespread use. Go is syntactically similar to C, but it has safe pointers, automatic memory management, and one of the most useful and well-written standard libraries I have encountered.

Why Should You Learn Go?

Go can be used for just about any programming task but is best suited to server development or system development. The extensive standard library includes support for most common server-side tasks, such as handling HTTP requests, accessing SQL databases, and rendering HTML templates. It has excellent threading support, and a comprehensive reflection system makes it possible to write flexible APIs for platforms and frameworks.

Go comes with a complete set of development tools, and there is good editor support, which makes it easy to create a good-quality development environment.

Go is cross-platform, which means you can write on Windows, for example, and deploy on Linux servers. Or, as I demonstrate in this book, you can package your application into Docker containers for easy deployment onto public hosting platforms.

What's the Catch?

Go can be difficult to learn and is an "opinionated" language, which can make it frustrating to use. These opinions range from the insightful to annoying. The insightful opinions make Go a fresh and pleasant experience, such as allowing functions to return multiple results so that a single value doesn't have to represent both successful and unsuccessful outcomes. There are some outstanding features in Go, including its intuitive support for threading, that many other languages would benefit from adopting.

The annoying opinions make writing Go feel like a drawn-out argument with the compiler, a sort of programming "and another thing..." dispute. If your coding style doesn't match the opinions of the Go designers, then you can expect to see a lot of compiler errors. If, like me, you have been writing code for a long time and have ingrained habits picked up from many languages, then you will develop new and innovative curse words to use when the compiler repeatedly rejects your code for expressions that would compile in every other mainstream programming language of the last 30 years.

Also, Go has a definite bias toward system programming and server-side development. There are packages that provide support for UI development, for example, but it is not an area in which Go shines, and there are better alternatives.

© Adam Freeman 2022
A. Freeman, *Pro Go*, https://doi.org/10.1007/978-1-4842-7355-5_2

Is It Really That Bad?

Don't be put off. Go is excellent and worth learning if you are working on system programming or server development projects. Go has features that are innovative and effective. An experienced Go developer can write complex applications with surprisingly little effort and code.

Learn Go knowing that it takes effort. Write Go knowing that when you and the language designers have differing opinions, then their preferences prevail.

What Do You Need to Know?

This is an advanced book written for experienced developers. This book does not teach programming, and you will need to understand adjacent topics such as HTML to follow all of the examples.

What Is the Structure of This Book?

This book is split into three parts, each of which covers a set of related topics.

Part 1: Understanding the Go Language

In Part 1 of this book, I describe the Go development tools and the Go language. I describe the built-in data types, show how custom types can be created, and cover features such as flow control, error handling, and concurrency. These chapters include some features from the Go standard library, where they are needed to support the explanation of the language features or where they perform tasks that are closely related to the language features being described.

Part 2: Using the Go Standard Library

In Part 2 of this book, I describe the most useful packages provided by the extensive Go standard library. You will learn about features for string formatting, reading, and writing data; creating HTTP servers and clients; using databases; and taking advantage of the considerable support for reflection.

Part 3: Applying Go

In Part 3 of this book, I use Go to create a custom web application framework, which is the foundation for an online store named SportsStore. This part of the book shows how Go and its standard library can be used together to solve the kinds of problems that arise in real projects. The examples in Part 1 and Part 2 of this book focus on a single feature at a time, and the purpose of Part 3 is to show features used in combination.

What Doesn't This Book Cover?

This book doesn't cover all the packages provided by the Go standard library, which, as already noted, is extensive. Also, there are some Go language features that I have omitted because they are not useful in mainstream development. The features that I have described in this book are the ones that most readers will need in most situations.

Please contact me and let me know if there is a feature that I didn't cover that you want to learn. I'll keep a list, and I'll include the most requested topics in a future edition.

What If You Find an Error in the Book?

You can report errors to me by email at adam@adam-freeman.com, although I ask that you first check the errata/corrections list for this book, which you can find in the book's GitHub repository at https://github.com/apress/pro-go, in case an issue has already been reported.

I add errors that are likely to confuse readers, especially problems with example code, to the errata/corrections file on the GitHub repository, with a grateful acknowledgment to the first reader who reported it. I also keep a list of less serious issues, which usually means errors in the text surrounding examples, and I use them when I write a new edition.

Are There Lots of Examples?

There are *loads* of examples. The best way to learn is by example, and I have packed as many of them as I can into this book. To help make the examples easier to follow, I have adopted a simple convention, which I follow whenever possible. When I create a new file, I list the complete contents, as shown in Listing 2-1. All code listings include the name of the file in the listing's header, along with the folder in which it can be found.

Listing 2-1. The Contents of the product.go File in the store Folder

```
package store

type Product struct {
    Name, Category string
    price float64
}

func (p *Product) Price(taxRate float64) float64 {
    return p.price + (p.price * taxRate)
}
```

This listing is taken from Chapter 13. Don't worry about what it does; just be aware that this is a complete listing, which shows the entire contents of the file, and the header tells you what the file is called and its location in the project.

When I make changes to the code, I show the altered statements in bold, as shown in Listing 2-2.

Listing 2-2. Defining a Constructor in the product.go File in the store Folder

```
package store

type Product struct {
    Name, Category string
    price float64
}

func NewProduct(name, category string, price float64) *Product {
    return &Product{ name, category, price }
}

func (p *Product) Price(taxRate float64) float64 {
    return p.price + (p.price * taxRate)
}
```

This listing is taken from a later example, which requires changes to the file created in Listing 2-1. To help you follow the example, the changes are marked in bold.

Some examples require a small change to a large file. So that I don't waste space listing the unchanged parts of the file, I just show the region that changes, as shown in Listing 2-3. You can tell this listing shows only part of a file because it starts and ends with an ellipsis (**...**).

Listing 2-3. A Mismatched Scan in the main.go File in the data Folder

```
...
func queryDatabase(db *sql.DB) {
    rows, err := db.Query("SELECT * from Products")
    if (err == nil) {
        for (rows.Next()) {
            var id, category int
            var name int
            var price float64
            scanErr := rows.Scan(&id, &name, &category, &price)
            if (scanErr == nil) {
                Printfln("Row: %v %v %v %v", id, name, category, price)
            } else {
                Printfln("Scan error: %v", scanErr)
                break
            }
        }
    } else {
        Printfln("Error: %v", err)
    }
}
...
```

In some cases, I need to make changes to different parts of the same file, in which case I omit some elements or statements for brevity, as shown in Listing 2-4. This listing adds new **using** statements and defines additional methods to an existing file, much of which is unchanged and has been omitted from the listing.

Listing 2-4. Using a Transaction in the main.go File in the data Folder

```
package main

import "database/sql"

// ...statements omitted for brevity...

func insertAndUseCategory(db *sql.DB, name string, productIDs ...int) (err error) {
    tx, err := db.Begin()
    updatedFailed := false
    if (err == nil) {
        catResult, err := tx.Stmt(insertNewCategory).Exec(name)
        if (err == nil) {
            newID, _ := catResult.LastInsertId()
```

```
        preparedStatement := tx.Stmt(changeProductCategory)
        for _, id := range productIDs {
            changeResult, err := preparedStatement.Exec(newID, id)
            if (err == nil) {
                changes, _ := changeResult.RowsAffected()
                if (changes == 0) {
                    updatedFailed = true
                    break
                }
            }
        }
    }
    if (err != nil || updatedFailed) {
        Printfln("Aborting transaction %v", err)
        tx.Rollback()
    } else {
        tx.Commit()
    }
    return
}
```

This convention lets me pack in more examples, but it does mean it can be hard to locate a specific technique. To this end, the chapters in this book begin with a summary table that describes the techniques it contains, and most of the chapters in Part 1 and Part 2 contain quick reference tables that list the methods used to implement a specific feature.

What Software Do You Need for the Examples?

The only software you need for Go development is described in Chapter 1. I install some third-party packages in later chapters, but these are obtained using the **go** command that you have already set up. I use the Docker container tools in Part 3, but this is optional.

What Platforms Will the Examples Run On?

All the examples have been tested on Windows and Linux (specifically Ubuntu 20.04), and all the third-party packages support these platforms. Go does support other platforms, and the examples should work on those platforms, but I am unable to offer help if you encounter problems with the examples in this book.

What If You Have Problems Following the Examples?

The first thing to do is to go back to the start of the chapter and begin again. Most problems are caused by accidentally skipping a step or not fully applying the changes shown in a listing. Pay close attention to the emphasis in the code listings, which highlights the changes that are required.

Next, check the errata/corrections list, which is included in the book's GitHub repository. Technical books are complex, and mistakes are inevitable, despite my best efforts and those of my editors. Check the errata list for the list of known errors and instructions to resolve them.

If you still have problems, then download the project for the chapter you are reading from the book's GitHub repository, `https://github.com/apress/pro-go`, and compare it to your project. I create the code for the GitHub repository by working through each chapter, so you should have the same files with the same contents in your project.

If you still can't get the examples working, then you can contact me at `adam@adam-freeman.com` for help. Please make it clear in your email which book you are reading and which chapter/example is causing the problem. A page number or code listing is always helpful. Please remember that I get a lot of emails and that I may not respond immediately.

Where Can You Get the Example Code?

You can download the example projects for all the chapters in this book from `https://github.com/apress/pro-go`.

Why Do Some of the Examples Have Odd Formatting?

Go has an unusual approach to formatting, which means that statements can be split onto multiple lines only at certain points. This isn't an issue in a code editor, but it causes problems for the printed page, which has a specific width. Some of the examples, especially in the later chapters, require long lines of code that are awkwardly formatted to make them suitable for a book.

How Do I Contact the Author?

You can email me at `adam@adam-freeman.com`. It has been a few years since I first published an email address in my books. I wasn't entirely sure that it was a good idea, but I am glad that I did it. I have received emails from around the world from readers working or studying in every industry, and—for the most part anyway— the emails are positive, polite, and a pleasure to receive.

I try to reply promptly, but I get many emails, and sometimes I get a backlog, especially when I have my head down trying to finish writing a book. I always try to help readers who are stuck with an example in the book, although I ask that you follow the steps described earlier in this chapter before contacting me.

While I welcome reader emails, there are some common questions for which the answers will always be "no." I am afraid that I won't write the code for your new startup, help you with your college assignment, get involved in your development team's design dispute, or teach you how to program.

What If I Really Enjoyed This Book?

Please email me at `adam@adam-freeman.com` and let me know. It is always a delight to hear from a happy reader, and I appreciate the time it takes to send those emails. Writing these books can be difficult, and those emails provide essential motivation to persist at an activity that can sometimes feel impossible.

What If This Book Has Made Me Angry and I Want to Complain?

You can still email me at `adam@adam-freeman.com`, and I will still try to help you. Bear in mind that I can only help if you explain what the problem is and what you would like me to do about it. You should understand that sometimes the only outcome is to accept I am not the writer for you and that we will have closure only when you return this book and select another. I'll give careful thought to whatever has upset you, but after 25 years of writing books, I have come to accept that not everyone enjoys reading the books I like to write.

Summary

In this chapter, I outlined the content and structure of this book. The best way to learn Go is by writing code, and in the next chapter, I describe the tools that Go provides for doing just that.

CHAPTER 3

Using the Go Tools

In this chapter, I describe the Go development tools, most of which were installed as part of the Go package in Chapter 1. I describe the basic structure of a Go project, explain how to compile and execute Go code, and show you how to install and use a debugger for Go applications. I also describe the Go linting and formatting tools.

■ **Tip** You can download the example project for this chapter—and for all the other chapters in this book—from https://github.com/apress/pro-go. See Chapter 2 for how to get help if you have problems running the examples.

Using the Go Command

The go command provides access to all the features needed to compile and execute Go code and is used throughout this book. The argument used with the go command specifies the operation that will be performed, such as the run argument used in Chapter 1, which compiles and executes Go source code. The Go command supports a large number of arguments; Table 3-1 describes the most useful ones.

Table 3-1. *Useful Arguments for the go Command*

Argument	Description
build	The go build command compiles the source code in the current directory and generates an executable file, as described in the "Compiling and Running Source Code" section.
clean	The go clean command removes the output produced by the go build command, including the executable and any temporary files that were created during the build, as described in the "Compiling and Running Source Code" section.
doc	The go doc command generates documentation from source code. See the "Linting Go Code" section for a simple example.
fmt	The go fmt command ensures consistent indentation and alignment in source code files, as described in the "Formatting Go Code" section.
get	The go get command downloads and installs external packages, as described in Chapter 12.

(cointinued)

© Adam Freeman 2022
A. Freeman, *Pro Go*, https://doi.org/10.1007/978-1-4842-7355-5_3

Table 3-1. (*continued*)

Argument	Description
install	The go install command downloads packages and is usually used to install tool packages, as demonstrated in the "Debugging Go Code" section.
help	The go help command displays help information for other Go features. The command go help build, for example, displays information about the build argument.
mod	The go mod command is used to create and manage a Go module, as demonstrated in the "Defining a Module" section, and is described in more detail in Chapter 12.
run	The go run command builds and executes the source code in a specified folder without creating an executable output, as described in the "Using the Go Run Command" section.
test	The go test command executes unit tests, as described in Chapter 31.
version	The go version command writes out the Go version number.
vet	The go vet command detects common problems in Go code, as described in the "Fixing Common Problems in Go Code" section.

Creating a Go Project

Go projects don't have an elaborate structure and are quick to set up. Open a new command prompt and create a folder named tools in a convenient location. Add a file named main.go to the tools folder with the content shown in Listing 3-1.

Listing 3-1. The Contents of the main.go File in the tools Folder

```
package main

import "fmt"

func main() {
    fmt.Println("Hello, Go")
}
```

I get into the details of the Go language in later chapters, but to get started, Figure 3-1 illustrates the key elements in the main.go file.

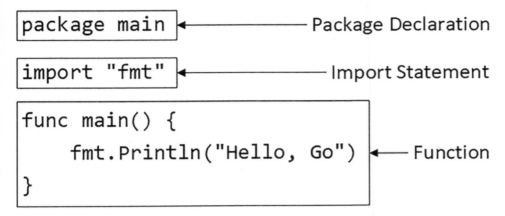

Figure 3-1. *The key elements in the code file*

Understanding the Package Declaration

The first statement is the package declaration. Packages are used to group related features, and every code file has to declare the package to which its contents belong. The package declaration uses the package keyword, followed by the name of the package, as shown in Figure 3-2. The statement in this file specifies a package named main.

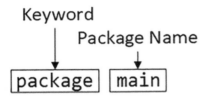

Figure 3-2. *Specifying the package for a code file*

Understanding the Import Statement

The next statement is the import statement, which is used to declare dependencies on other packages. The import keyword is followed by the name of the package, which is enclosed in double quotes, as shown in Figure 3-3. The import statement in Listing 3-1 specifies a package named fmt, which is the built-in Go package for reading and writing formatted strings (which I describe in detail in Chapter 17).

■ **Tip** A complete list of the built-in packages provided with Go is available at https://golang.org/pkg.

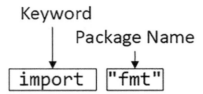

Figure 3-3. *Declaring a package dependency*

Understanding the Function

The remaining statements in the main.go file define a function named main. I describe functions in detail in Chapter 8, but the main function is special. When you define a function named main in a package named main, you create an *entry point*, which is where execution begins in a command-line application. Figure 3-4 illustrates the structure of the main function.

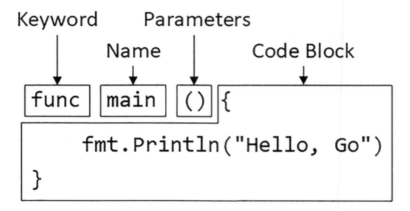

Figure 3-4. *The structure of the main function*

The basic structure of Go functions is similar to other languages. The func keyword denotes a function and is followed by the function's name, which is main in this example.

The function in Listing 3-1 defines no parameters, which is denoted by the empty parentheses and produces no result. I describe more complex functions in later examples, but this simple function is enough to get started with.

The function's code block contains the statements that will be executed when the function is invoked. Since the main function is the entry point, the function will be invoked automatically when the compiled output from the project is executed.

Understanding the Code Statement

The main function contains a single code statement. When you declare a dependency on a package with an import statement, the result is a package reference that provides access to the package features. By default, the package reference is assigned the name of the package so that the features provided by the fmt package, for example, are accessed through a fmt package reference, as shown in Figure 3-5.

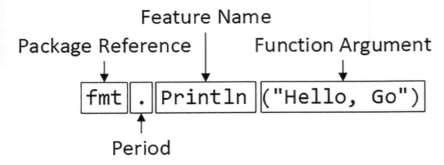

Figure 3-5. *Accessing package features*

This statement invokes a function named Println provided by the fmt package. This function writes a string to the standard out, which means it will be displayed on the console when the project is built and executed in the next section.

To access the function, the package name is used, followed by a period and then the function: fmt.Println. This function is passed one argument, which is the string that will be written.

USING SEMICOLONS IN GO CODE

Go has an unusual approach to semicolons: they are required to terminate code statements, but they are not required in source code files. Instead, the Go build tools figure out where the semicolons need to go as they process files, acting as though they had been added by the developer.

The result is that semicolons can be used in Go source code files but are not required and are conventionally omitted.

Some oddities arise if you don't follow the expected Go code style. For example, you will receive compiler errors if you attempt to put the opening brace for a function or for loop on the next line, like this:

```
package main

import "fmt"

func main()
{
    fmt.Println("Hello, Go")
}
```

The errors report an unexpected semicolon and a missing function body. This is because the Go tools have automatically inserted a semicolon like this:

```
package main

import "fmt"

func main();
{
    fmt.Println("Hello, Go")
}
```

39

The error messages make more sense when you understand why they arise, although it can be hard to adjust to the expected code format if this is your preferred brace placement.

I have tried to follow the no-semicolon convention throughout this book, but I have been writing code in languages that require semicolons for decades, so you may find the occasional example where I have added semicolons purely by habit. The go fmt command, which I describe in the "Formatting Go Code" section, will remove semicolons and adjust other formatting issues.

Compiling and Running Source Code

The go build command compiles Go source code and produces an executable. Run the command shown in Listing 3-2 in the tools folder to compile the code.

Listing 3-2. Using the Compiler

```
go build main.go
```

The compiler processes the statements in the main.go file and generates an executable file, which is named main.exe on Windows and main on other platforms. (The compiler will start creating files with more useful names once I introduce modules in the "Defining a Module" section.)

Run the command shown in Listing 3-3 in the tools folder to run the executable.

Listing 3-3. Running the Compiled Executable

```
./main
```

The project's entry point—the function named main in the package also named main—is executed and produces the following output:

```
Hello, Go
```

CONFIGURING THE GO COMPILER

The behavior of the Go compiler can be configured using additional arguments, although the default settings are sufficient for most projects. The two most useful are -a, which forces a complete rebuild even for files that have not changed, and -o, which specifies the name of the compiled output file. Use the go help build command to see the full list of options available. By default, the compiler generates an executable file, but there are different outputs available—see https://golang.org/cmd/go/#hdr-Build_modes for details.

Cleaning Up

To remove the output from the compilation process, run the command shown in Listing 3-4 in the tools folder.

Listing 3-4. Cleaning Up

```
go clean main.go
```

The compiled executable created in the previous section is removed, leaving only the source code file behind.

Using the Go Run Command

Most regular development is run using the go run command. Run the command shown in Listing 3-5 in the tools folder.

Listing 3-5. Using the Go Run Command

```
go run main.go
```

The file is compiled and executed in a single step, without creating the executable file in the tools folder. An executable file is created but in a temporary folder, from which it is then run. (It is this series of temporary locations that caused the Windows firewall to seek permission every time the go run command was used in Chapter 1. Each time the command was run, an executable was created in a new temporary folder, which appeared to be a completely new file to the firewall.)

The command in Listing 3-5 produces the following output:

```
Hello, Go
```

Defining a Module

The previous section demonstrated that you can get started just by creating a code file, but a more common approach is to create a Go module, which is the conventional first step when starting a new project. Creating a Go module allows a project to easily consume third-party packages and can simplify the build process. Run the command shown in Listing 3-6 in the tools folder.

Listing 3-6. Creating a Module

```
go mod init tools
```

This command adds a file named go.mod to the tools folder. The reason that most projects start with the go mod init command is that it simplifies the build process. Instead of specifying a particular code file, the project can be built and executed using a period, indicating the project in the current directory. Run the command shown in Listing 3-7 in the tools folder to compile and execute the code it contains without specifying the name of a code file.

Listing 3-7. Compiling and Executing a Project

```
go run .
```

The go.mod file has other uses—as later chapters demonstrate—but I start all the examples in the rest of the book with the go mod init command to simplify the build process.

Debugging Go Code

The standard debugger for Go applications is called Delve. It is a third-party tool, but it is well-supported and recommended by the Go development team. Delve supports Windows, macOS, Linux, and FreeBSD. To install the Delve package, open a new command prompt and run the command shown in Listing 3-8.

▪ **Tip** See https://github.com/go-delve/delve/tree/master/Documentation/installation for detailed installation instructions for each platform. Additional configuration may be required for your chosen operating system.

Listing 3-8. Installing the Debugger Package

```
go install github.com/go-delve/delve/cmd/dlv@latest
```

The go install command downloads and installs a package and is used to install tools such as debuggers. A similar command—go get—performs a similar task for packages that provide code features that are to be included in an application, as demonstrated in Chapter 12.

To make sure the debugger is installed, run the command shown in Listing 3-9.

Listing 3-9. Running the Debugger

```
dlv version
```

If you receive an error that the dlv command cannot be found, then try specifying the path directly. By default, the dlv command will be installed in the ~/go/bin folder (although this can be overridden by setting the GOPATH environment variable), as shown in Listing 3-10.

Listing 3-10. Running the Debugger with a Path

```
~/go/bin/dlv
```

If the package has been installed correctly, you will see the output similar to the following, although you may see a different version number and build ID:

```
Delve Debugger
Version: 1.7.1
Build: $Id: 3bde2354aafb5a4043fd59838842c4cd4a8b6f0b $
```

DEBUGGING WITH THE PRINTLN FUNCTION

I like debuggers like Delve, but I use them only for problems that I can't figure out using my go-to debugging technique: the Println function. I use Println because it is quick, simple, and reliable and because most bugs (at least in my code) are caused because a function didn't receive the value I expected or because a particular statement isn't being executed when I expect. These simple issues are easily diagnosed with a message writing to the console.

If the output from my Println messages doesn't help, then I fire up the debugger, set a breakpoint, and step through my code. Even then, once I get a sense of the cause of a problem, I tend to go back to Println statements to confirm my theory.

Many developers are reluctant to admit they find debuggers awkward or confusing and end up secretly using Println anyway. Debuggers *are* confusing, and there is no shame in using all the tools at your disposal. The Println function and the debugger are complementary tools, and what's important is that bugs get fixed, regardless of how that is done.

Preparing for Debugging

The main.go file doesn't contain enough code to debug. Add the statements shown in Listing 3-11 to create a loop that will print out a series of numeric values.

Listing 3-11. Adding a Loop in the main.go File in the tools Folder

```go
package main

import "fmt"

func main() {
    fmt.Println("Hello, Go")
    for i := 0; i < 5; i++ {
        fmt.Println(i)
    }
}
```

I describe the for syntax in Chapter 6, but for this chapter, I just need some code statements to demonstrate how the debugger works. Compile and execute the code with the go run . command; you will receive the following output:

```
Hello, Go
0
1
```

2
3
4

Using the Debugger

To start the debugger, run the command shown in Listing 3-12 in the tools folder.

Listing 3-12. Starting the Debugger

```
dlv debug main.go
```

     This command starts the text-based debugging client, which can be confusing at first but is extremely powerful once you get used to the way it works. The first step is to create a breakpoint, which is done by specifying a location in the code, as shown in Listing 3-13.

Listing 3-13. Creating a Breakpoint

```
break bp1 main.main:3
```

     The break command creates a breakpoint. The arguments specify a name for the breakpoint and a location. Locations can be specified in different ways, but the location used in Listing 3-13 specifies a package, a function within that package, and a line within that function, as illustrated by Figure 3-6.

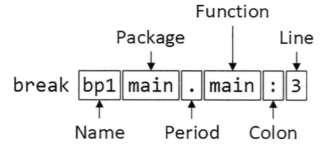

Figure 3-6. *Specifying a breakpoint location*

     The name for the breakpoint is bp1, and the location specifies the third line in the main function in the main package. The debugger displays the following confirmation message:

```
Breakpoint 1 set at 0x697716 for main.main() c:/tools/main.go:8
```

     Next, I am going to create a condition for the breakpoint so that execution will be halted only when a specified expression evaluates to true. Enter the command shown in Listing 3-14 into the debugger and press Return.

Listing 3-14. Specifying a Breakpoint Condition in the Debugger

```
condition bp1 i == 2
```

The arguments for the `condition` command specify a breakpoint and an expression. This command tells the debugger that the breakpoint named bp1 should halt execution only when the expression i == 2 is true. To start execution, enter the command shown in Listing 3-15 and press Return.

Listing 3-15. Starting Execution in the Debugger

```
continue
```

The debugger starts to execute the code, producing the following output:

```
Hello, Go
0
1
```

Execution is halted when the condition specified in Listing 3-15 is true, and the debugger displays the code and the point at which execution stops, which I have marked in bold:

```
> [bp1] main.main() c:/tools/main.go:8 (hits goroutine(1):1 total:1) (PC: 0x207716)
     3: import "fmt"
     4:
     5: func main() {
     6:        fmt.Println("Hello, Go")
     7:        for i := 0; i < 5; i++ {
=>   8:            fmt.Println(i)
     9:        }
    10: }
```

The debugger provides a full set of commands for inspecting and altering the state of the application, the most useful of which are shown in Table 3-2. (See https://github.com/go-delve/delve for the full set of commands supported by the debugger.)

Table 3-2. *Useful Debugger State Commands*

Command	Description
print <expr>	This command evaluates an expression and displays the result. It can be used to display a value (print i) or perform a more complex test (print i > 0).
set <variable> = <value>	This command changes the value of the specified variable.
locals	This command prints the value of all local variables.
whatis <expr>	This command prints the type of the specified expression such as whatis i. I describe the Go types in Chapter 4.

Run the command shown in Listing 3-16 to display the current value of the variable named i.

Listing 3-16. Printing a Value in the Debugger

```
print i
```

The debugger displays the response 2, which is the current value of the variable and matches the condition I specified for the breakpoint in Listing 3-16. The debugger provides a full set of commands for controlling execution, the most useful of which are shown in Table 3-3.

Table 3-3. *Useful Debugger Commands for Controlling Execution*

Command	Description
continue	This command resumes execution of the application.
next	This command moves to the next statement.
step	This command steps into the current statement.
stepout	This command steps out of the current statement.
restart	This command restarts the process. Use the continue command to begin execution.
exit	This command exits the debugger.

Enter the continue command to resume execution, which will produce the following output:

```
2
3
4
Process 3160 has exited with status 0
```

The condition I specified for the breakpoint is no longer met, so the program runs until it terminates. Use the exit command to quit the debugger and return to the command prompt.

Using a Delve Editor Plugin

Delve is also supported by a range of editor plugins that create a UI-based debugging experience for Go. The complete list of plugins can be found at https://github.com/go-delve/delve, but one of the best Go/Delve debugging experiences is provided by Visual Studio Code and is installed automatically when the language tools for Go are installed.

If you use Visual Studio Code, you can create breakpoints by clicking in the margin of the code editor and can start the debugger using the Start Debug command in the Run menu.

If you receive an error or you are prompted to select an environment, then open the main.go file for editing, click any code statement within the editor window, and select the Start Debug command again.

I am not going to describe the process for debugging using Visual Studio Code—or any editor—in detail, but Figure 3-7 shows the debugger after a conditional breakpoint has halted execution, re-creating the command-line example from the previous section.

Figure 3-7. *Using a Delve editor plugin*

Linting Go Code

A linter is a tool that checks code files using a set of rules that describe problems that cause confusion, produce unexpected results, or reduce the readability of the code. The most widely used linter for Go is called golint, which applies rules taken from two sources. The first is the Effective Go document produced by Google (https://golang.org/doc/effective_go.html), which provides tips for writing clear and concise Go code. The second source is a collection of comments from code reviews (https://github.com/golang/go/wiki/CodeReviewComments).

The problem with golint is that it provides no configuration options and will always apply all the rules, which can result in warnings you care about being lost in a long list of warnings for rules you don't care about. I prefer to use the revive linter package, which is a direct replacement for golint but with support for controlling which rules are applied. To install the revive package, open a new command prompt and run the command shown in Listing 3-17.

Listing 3-17. Installing the Linter Package

```
go install github.com/mgechev/revive@latest
```

THE JOY AND MISERY OF LINTING

Linters can be a powerful tool for good, especially in a development team with mixed levels of skill and experience. Linters can detect common problems and subtle errors that lead to unexpected behavior or long-term maintenance issues. I like this kind of linting, and I like to run my code through the linting process after I have completed a major application feature or before I commit my code into version control.

But linters can also be a tool of division and strife when rules are used to enforce one developer's personal preferences across an entire team. This is usually done under the banner of being "opinionated." The logic is that developers spend too much time arguing about different coding styles, and everyone is better off being forced to write in the same way.

My experience is that developers will just find something else to argue about and that forcing a code style is often just an excuse to make one person's preferences mandatory for an entire development team.

I didn't use the popular golint package in this chapter because in it individual rules cannot be disabled. I respect the strong opinions of the golint developers, but using golint makes me feel like I'm having an ongoing argument with someone I don't even know, which somehow feels worse than having an ongoing argument with the one developer on the team who gets upset about indentation.

My advice is to use linting sparingly and focus on the issues that will cause real problems. Give individual developers the freedom to express themselves naturally and focus only on issues that have a discernible impact on the project. This is counter to the opinionated ethos of Go, but my view is that productivity is not achieved by slavishly enforcing arbitrary rules, however well-intentioned they may be.

Using the Linter

The main.go file is so simple that it doesn't have any problems for the linter to highlight. Add the statements shown in Listing 3-18, which are legal Go code that does not comply with the rules applied by the linter.

Listing 3-18. Adding Statements in the main.go File in the tools Folder

```
package main

import "fmt"

func main() {
    PrintHello()
    for i := 0; i < 5; i++ {
        PrintNumber(i)
    }
}

func PrintHello() {
    fmt.Println("Hello, Go")
}
```

```
func PrintNumber(number int) {
    fmt.Println(number)
}
```

Save the changes and use the command prompt to run the command shown in Listing 3-19. (As with the dlv command, you may need to specify the go/bin path in your home folder to run this command.)

Listing 3-19. Running the Linter

```
revive
```

The linter inspects the main.go file and reports the following problem:

```
main.go:12:1: exported function PrintHello should have comment or be unexported
main.go:16:1: exported function PrintNumber should have comment or be unexported
```

As I explain in Chapter 12, functions whose names start with an uppercase letter are said to be *exported* and available for use outside of the package in which they are defined. The convention for exported functions is to provide a descriptive comment. The linter has flagged the fact that no comments exist for the PrintHello and PrintNumber functions. Listing 3-20 adds a comment to one of the functions.

Listing 3-20. Adding a Comment in the main.go File in the tools Folder

```
package main

import "fmt"

func main() {
    PrintHello()
    for i := 0; i < 5; i++ {
        PrintNumber(i)
    }
}

func PrintHello() {
    fmt.Println("Hello, Go")
}

// This function writes a number using the fmt.Println function
func PrintNumber(number int) {
    fmt.Println(number)
}
```

Run the revive command again; you will receive a different error for the PrintNumber function:

```
main.go:12:1: exported function PrintHello should have comment or be unexported
main.go:16:1: comment on exported function PrintNumber should be of the form
"PrintNumber ..."
```

Some of the linter rules are specific in their requirements. The comment in Listing 3-20 isn't accepted because Effective Go states that comments should contain a sentence that starts with the name of the function and should provide a concise overview of the function's purpose, as described by `https://golang.org/doc/effective_go.html#commentary`. Listing 3-21 revises the comment to follow the required structure.

Listing 3-21. Revising a Comment in the main.go File in the tools Folder

```go
package main

import "fmt"

func main() {
    PrintHello()
    for i := 0; i < 5; i++ {
        PrintNumber(i)
    }
}

func PrintHello() {
    fmt.Println("Hello, Go")
}

// PrintNumber writes a number using the fmt.Println function
func PrintNumber(number int) {
    fmt.Println(number)
}
```

Run the `revive` command again; the linter will complete without reporting any errors for the `PrintNumber` function, although a warning is still reported for the `PrintHello` function because it doesn't have a comment.

UNDERSTANDING GO DOCUMENTATION

The reason that the linter is so strict about comments is because they are used by the go doc command, which generates documentation from source code comments. You can see details of how the go doc command is used at `https://blog.golang.org/godoc`, but you can run the go doc -all command in the `tools` folder for a quick demonstration of how it uses comments to document a package.

Disabling Linter Rules

The `revive` package can be configured using comments in code files, disabling one or more rules for sections of code. In Listing 3-22, I have used comments to disable the rule that causes the warning for the `PrintNumber` function.

Listing 3-22. Disabling a Linter Rule for a Function in the main.go File in the tools Folder

```
package main

import "fmt"

func main() {
    PrintHello()
    for i := 0; i < 5; i++ {
        PrintNumber(i)
    }
}
```

// revive:disable:exported

```
func PrintHello() {
    fmt.Println("Hello, Go")
}
```

// revive:enable:exported

```
// PrintNumber writes a number using the fmt.Println function
func PrintNumber(number int) {
    fmt.Println(number)
}
```

The syntax required to control the linter is revive, followed by a colon, enable or disable, and optionally another colon and the name of a linter rule. So, for example, the revive:disable:exported comment prevents the linter from enforcing a rule named exported, which is the rule that has been generating warnings. The revive:enable:exported comment enables the rule so that it will be applied to subsequent statements in the code file.

You can find the list of rules supported by the linter at https://github.com/mgechev/revive#available-rules. Alternatively, you can omit the rule name from a comment to control the application of all rules.

Creating a Linter Configuration File

Using code comments is helpful when you want to suppress warnings for a specific region of code but still apply the rule elsewhere in the project. If you don't want to apply a rule at all, then you can use a TOML-format configuration file. Add a file named revive.toml to the tools folder with the content shown in Listing 3-23.

■ **Tip** The TOML format is intended specifically for configuration files and is described at https://toml.io/en. The full range of revive configuration options is described at https://github.com/mgechev/revive#configuration.

Listing 3-23. The Contents of the revive.toml File in the tools Folder

```
ignoreGeneratedHeader = false
severity = "warning"
confidence = 0.8
errorCode = 0
warningCode = 0

[rule.blank-imports]
[rule.context-as-argument]
[rule.context-keys-type]
[rule.dot-imports]
[rule.error-return]
[rule.error-strings]
[rule.error-naming]
#[rule.exported]
[rule.if-return]
[rule.increment-decrement]
[rule.var-naming]
[rule.var-declaration]
[rule.package-comments]
[rule.range]
[rule.receiver-naming]
[rule.time-naming]
[rule.unexported-return]
[rule.indent-error-flow]
[rule.errorf]
```

This is the default revive configuration described at https://github.com/mgechev/
revive#recommended-configuration, except that I have put a # character before the entry that enables the
exported rule. In Listing 3-24, I have removed the comments from the main.go file, which are no longer
required to satisfy the linter.

Listing 3-24. Removing Comments from the main.go File in the tools Folder

```
package main

import "fmt"

func main() {
    PrintHello()
    for i := 0; i < 5; i++ {
        PrintNumber(i)
    }
}

func PrintHello() {
    fmt.Println("Hello, Go")
}

func PrintNumber(number int) {
    fmt.Println(number)
}
```

To use the linter with the configuration file, run the command shown in Listing 3-25 in the tools folder.

Listing 3-25. Running the Linter with a Configuration File

```
revive -config revive.toml
```

There will be no output because the only rule that triggered an error has been disabled.

LINTING IN A CODE EDITOR

Some code editors support linting code automatically. If you are using Visual Studio Code, for example, linting is performed in the background, and the problems are flagged as warnings. The linter Visual Studio Code uses by default changes from time to time; it is staticcheck at the time of writing, which is configurable, but it was previously golint, which is not.

It is easy to change the linter to revive using the Preferences ➤ Extensions ➤ Go ➤ Lint Tool configuration option. If you want to use a custom configuration file, use the Lint Flags configuration option to add a flag with the value -config=./revive.toml, which will select the revive.toml file.

Fixing Common Problems in Go Code

The go vet command identifies statements likely to be mistakes. Unlike a linter, which will often focus on style issues, the go vet command finds code that compiles but that probably won't do what the developer intended.

I like the go vet command because it spots errors that other tools miss, although the analyzers don't spot every mistake and will sometimes highlight code that isn't a problem. In Listing 3-26, I have added a statement to the main.go file that deliberately introduces a mistake into the code.

Listing 3-26. Adding a Statement in the main.go File in the tools Folder

```
package main

import "fmt"

func main() {
    PrintHello()
    for i := 0; i < 5; i++ {
        i = i
        PrintNumber(i)
    }
}

func PrintHello() {
    fmt.Println("Hello, Go")
}
```

```
func PrintNumber(number int) {
    fmt.Println(number)
}
```

The new statement assigns the variable i to itself, which is allowed by the Go compiler but is likely to be a mistake. To analyze the code, use the command prompt to run the command shown in Listing 3-27 in the tools folder.

Listing 3-27. Analyzing Code

```
go vet main.go
```

The go vet command will inspect the statements in the main.go file and produce the following warning:

```
# _/C_/tools
.\main.go:8:9: self-assignment of i to i
```

The warnings produced by the go vet command specify the location in the code where a problem has been detected and provide a description of the issue.

The go vet command applies multiple analyzers to code, and you can see the list of analyzers at https://golang.org/cmd/vet. You can select individual analyzers to enable or disable, but it can be difficult to know which analyzer has generated a specific message. To figure out which analyzer is responsible for a warning, run the command shown in Listing 3-28 in the tools folder.

Listing 3-28. Identifying an Analyzer

```
go vet -json main.go
```

The json argument generates output in the JSON format, which groups warnings by analyzer, like this:

```
# _/C_/tools {
    "_/C_/tools": {
        "assign": [
            {
                "posn": "C:\\tools\\main.go:8:9",
                "message": "self-assignment of i to i"
            }
        ]
    }
}
```

Using this command reveals that the analyzer named assign is responsible for the warning generated for the main.go file. Once the name is known, the analyzer can be enabled or disabled, as shown in Listing 3-29.

Listing 3-29. Choosing Analyzers

```
go vet -assign=false
go vet -assign
```

The first command in Listing 3-29 runs all the analyzers except `assign`, which is the analyzer that produced the warning for the self-assignment statement. The second command runs only the `assign` analyzer.

WORKING OUT WHAT EACH ANALYZER DOES

It can be difficult to work out what each go `vet` analyzer is looking for. I find the unit tests that the Go team has written for the analyzers helpful because they contain examples of the types of problem that is being sought. The tests are at `https://github.com/golang/go/tree/master/src/cmd/vet/testdata`.

Some editors, including Visual Studio Code, display messages from go `vet` in the editor window, as shown in Figure 3-8, which makes it easy to benefit from the analysis without having to explicitly run a command.

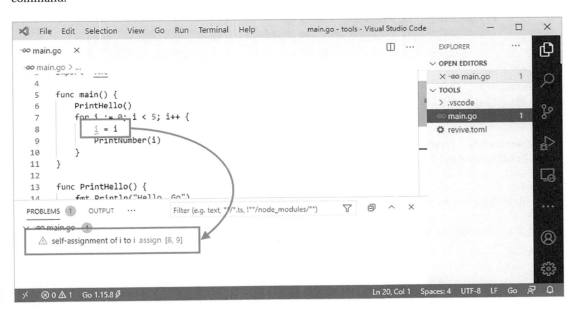

Figure 3-8. *A potential code issue in the code editor*

Visual Studio Code flags the error in the editor window and displays details in the Problems window. Analysis with go `vet` is enabled by default, you can disable this feature with the Settings ➤ Extensions ➤ Go ➤ Vet On Save configuration item.

Formatting Go Code

The go fmt command formats Go source code files for consistency. There are no configuration options to change the formatting applied by the go fmt command, which transforms code into the style specified by the Go development team. The most obvious changes are the use of tabs for indentation, the consistent alignment of comments, and the elimination of unnecessary semicolons. Listing 3-30 shows code with inconsistent indentation, misaligned comments, and semicolons where they are not required.

■ **Tip** You may find that your editor automatically formats code when it is pasted into the editor window or when the file is saved.

Listing 3-30. Creating Formatting Issues in the main.go File in the tools Folder

```
package main

import "fmt"

func main() {
    PrintHello ()
            for i := 0; i < 5; i++ { // loop with a counter
            PrintHello(); // print out a message
             PrintNumber(i); // print out the counter
    }
}

func PrintHello () {
      fmt.Println("Hello, Go");
}

func PrintNumber  (number int) {
  fmt.Println(number);
}
```

Run the command shown in Listing 3-31 in the tools folder to reformat the code.

Listing 3-31. Formatting Source Code

```
go fmt main.go
```

The formatter will remove the semicolons, adjust the indentation, and align the comments, producing the following formatted code:

```
package main

import "fmt"

func main() {
    PrintHello()
```

```
    for i := 0; i < 5; i++ { // loop with a counter
        PrintHello()    // print out a message
        PrintNumber(i) // print out the counter
    }
}

func PrintHello() {
    fmt.Println("Hello, Go")
}

func PrintNumber(number int) {
    fmt.Println(number)
}
```

I have not used go fmt for the examples in this book because the use of tabs causes layout issues on the printed page. I have to use spaces for indentation to ensure code appears as it should when a book is printed, and these are replaced with tabs by go fmt.

Summary

In this chapter, I introduced the tools that are used for Go development. I explained how to compile and execute source code, how to debug Go code, how to use a linter, how to format source code, and how to find common problems. In the next chapter, I start describing the features of the Go language, starting with the basic data types.

CHAPTER 4

■ ■ ■

Basic Types, Values, and Pointers

In this chapter, I begin to describe the Go language, focusing on the basic data types before moving on to how they are used to create constants and variables. I also introduce the Go support for pointers. Pointers can be a source of confusion, especially if you are coming to Go from languages such as Java or C#, and I describe how Go pointers work, demonstrate why they can be useful, and explain why they are not to be feared.

The features provided by any programming language are intended to be used together, which makes it difficult to introduce them progressively. Some of the examples in this part of the book rely on features that are described subsequently. These examples contain enough detail to provide context and include references to the part of the book where additional details can be found. Table 4-1 puts the basic Go features in context.

Table 4-1. *Putting the Basic Types, Values, and Pointers Features in Context*

Question	Answer
What are they?	The data types are used to store the fundamental values common to all programming, including numbers, strings, and true/false values. These data types can be used to define constant and variable values. Pointers are a special data type, which store a memory address.
Why are they useful?	The basic data types are useful in their own right to store values, but they are also the foundation on which more complex data types can be defined, as I explain in Chapter 10. Pointers are useful because they allow the programmer to decide whether a value should be copied when it is used.
How are they used?	The basic data types have their own names, such as int and float64, and can be used with the const and var keywords. Pointers are created using the address operator, &.
Are there any pitfalls or limitations?	Go does not perform automatic value conversion, except for a special category of values known as *untyped constants*.
Are there any alternatives?	There are no alternatives to the basic data types, which are used throughout Go development.

© Adam Freeman 2022
A. Freeman, *Pro Go*, https://doi.org/10.1007/978-1-4842-7355-5_4

Table 4-2 summarizes the chapter.

Table 4-2. *Chapter Summary*

Problem	Solution	Listing
Use a value directly	Use a literal value	6
Define a constant	Use the const keyword	7, 10
Define a constant that can be converted to a related data type	Create an untyped constant	8, 9, 11
Define a variable	Use the var keyword or use the short declaration syntax	12-21
Prevent compiler errors for unused variable	Use the blank identifier	22, 23
Define a pointer	Use the address operator	24, 25, 29–30
Follow a pointer	Use an asterisk with the pointer variable name	26–28, 31

Preparing for This Chapter

To prepare for this chapter, open a new command prompt, navigate to a convenient location, and create a directory named basicFeatures. Run the command shown in Listing 4-1 to create a go.mod file for the project.

Listing 4-1. Creating the Example Project

```
go mod init basicfeatures
```

Add a file named main.go to the basicFeatures folder, with the content shown in Listing 4-2.

■ **Tip**   You can download the example project for this chapter—and for all the other chapters in this book—from https://github.com/apress/pro-go. See Chapter 2 for how to get help if you have problems running the examples.

Listing 4-2. The Contents of the main.go File in the basicFeatures Folder

```
package main

import (
    "fmt"
    "math/rand"
)
```

```
func main() {
    fmt.Println(rand.Int())
}
```

Use the command prompt to run the command shown in Listing 4-3 in the basicFeatures folder.

Listing 4-3. Running the Example Project

```
go run .
```

The code in the main.go file will be compiled and executed, producing the following output:

```
5577006791947779410
```

The output from the code will always be the same value, even though it is produced by the random number package, as I explain in Chapter 18.

Using the Go Standard Library

Go provides a wide set of useful features through its *standard library*, which is the term used to describe the built-in API. The Go standard library is presented as a set of *packages* that are part of the Go installer used in Chapter 1.

I describe the way Go packages are created and used in Chapter 12, but some of the examples rely on the packages in the standard library, and it is important to understand how they are used.

Each package in the standard library groups together a set of related features. The code in Listing 4-2 uses two packages: the fmt package provides features for formatting and writing strings, and the math/rand package deals with random numbers.

The first step in using a package is to define an import statement. Figure 4-1 illustrates the import statement used in Listing 4-2.

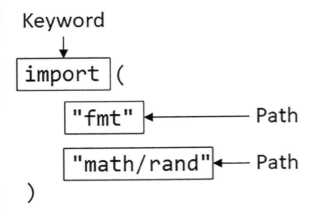

Figure 4-1. *Importing a package*

There are two parts to an import statement: the import keyword and the package paths. The paths are grouped with parentheses if more than one package is imported.

The import statement creates a package reference, through which the features provided by the package can be accessed. The name of the package reference is the last segment in the package path. The path for the fmt package has only one segment, so the package reference will be fmt. There are two segments in the math/rand path—math and rand—and so the package reference will be rand. (I explain how to select your own package reference name in Chapter 12.)

The fmt package defines a Println function that writes a value to the standard output, and the math/rand package defines an Int function that generates a random integer. To access these functions, I use their package reference, followed by a period and then the function name, as shown in Figure 4-2.

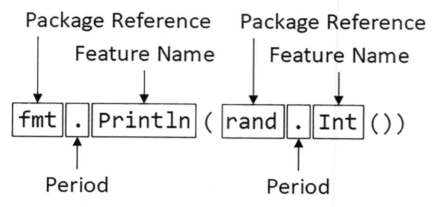

Figure 4-2. *Using a package reference*

■ **Tip** A list of the Go standard library packages is available at https://golang.org/pkg. The most useful packages are described in Part 2.

A related feature provided by the fmt package is the ability to compose strings by combining static content with data values, as shown in Listing 4-4.

Listing 4-4. Composing a String in the main.go File in the basicFeatures Folder

```
package main

import (
    "fmt"
    "math/rand"
)

func main() {
    fmt.Println("Value:", rand.Int())
}
```

The series of comma-separated values passed to the Println function are combined into a single string, which is then written to the standard output. To compile and execute the code, use the command prompt to run the command shown in Listing 4-5 in the basicFeatures folder.

Listing 4-5. Running the Example Project

```
go run .
```

The code in the main.go file will be compiled and executed, producing the following output:

```
Value: 5577006791947779410
```

There are more useful ways to compose strings—which I describe in Part 2 —but this is simple and a useful way for me to provide output in the examples.

Understanding the Basic Data Types

Go provides a set of basic data types, which are described in Table 4-3. In the sections that follow, I describe these types and explain how they are used. These types are the foundation of Go development, and many of the characteristics of these types will be familiar from other languages.

Table 4-3. *The Go Basic Data Types*

Name	Description
int	This type represents a whole number, which can be positive or negative. The int type size is platform-dependent and will be either 32 or 64 bits. There are also integer types that have a specific size, such as int8, int16, int32, and int64, but the int type should be used unless you need a specific size.
uint	This type represents a positive whole number. The uint type size is platform-dependent and will be either 32 or 64 bits. There are also unsigned integer types that have a specific size, such as uint8, uint16, uint32, and uint64, but the uint type should be used unless you need a specific size.
byte	This type is an alias for uint8 and is typically used to represent a byte of data.
float32, float64	These types represent numbers with a fraction. These types allocate 32 or 64 bits to store the value.
complex64, complex128	These types represent numbers that have real and imaginary components. These types allocate 64 or 128 bits to store the value.
bool	This type represents a Boolean truth with the values true and false.
string	This type represents a sequence of characters.
rune	This type represents a single Unicode code point. Unicode is complicated, but—loosely—this is the representation of a single character. The rune type is an alias for int32.

COMPLEX NUMBERS IN GO

As noted in Table 4-3, Go has built-in support for complex numbers, which have real and imaginary parts. I remember learning about complex numbers in school, and I promptly forgot about them until I started reading the Go language specification. I don't describe the use of complex numbers in this book because they are used only in specific domains, such as electrical engineering. You can learn more about complex numbers at `https://en.wikipedia.org/wiki/Complex_number`.

Understanding Literal Values

Go values can be expressed literally, where the value is defined directly in the source code file. Common uses for literal values include operands in expressions and arguments to functions, as shown in Listing 4-6.

■ **Tip**   Notice that I have commented out the `math/rand` package from the `import` statement in Listing 4-6. It is an error in Go to import a package that is not used.

Listing 4-6. Using Literal Values in the main.go File in the basicFeatures Folder

```
package main

import (
    "fmt"
    //"math/rand"
)

func main() {
    fmt.Println("Hello, Go")
    fmt.Println(20 + 20)
    fmt.Println(20 + 30)
}
```

The first statement in the main function uses a string literal, which is denoted by double quotes, as an argument to the `fmt.Println` function. The other statements use literal `int` values in expressions whose results are used as the argument to the `fmt.Println` function. Compile and execute the code, and you will see the following output:

```
Hello, Go
40
50
```

You don't have to specify a type when using a literal value because the compiler will infer the type based on the way the value is expressed. For quick reference, Table 4-4 gives examples of literal values for the basic types.

Table 4-4. *Literal Value Examples*

Type	Examples
int	20, -20. Values can also be expressed in hex (0x14), octal (0o24), and binary notation (0b0010100).
unit	There are no uint literals. All literal whole numbers are treated as int values.
byte	There are no byte literals. Bytes are typically expressed as integer literals (such as 101) or run literals ('e') since the byte type is an alias for the uint8 type.
float64	20.2, -20.2, 1.2e10, 1.2e-10. Values can also be expressed in hex notation (0x2p10), although the exponent is expressed in decimal digits.
bool	true, false.
string	"Hello". Character sequences escaped with a backslash are interpreted if the value is enclosed in double quotes ("Hello\n"). Escape sequences are not interpreted if the value is enclosed in backquotes (`Hello\n`).
rune	'A', '\n', '\u00A5', '¥'. Characters, glyphs, and escape sequences are enclosed in single quotes (the ' character).

Using Constants

Constants are names for specific values, which allows them to be used repeatedly and consistently. There are two ways to define constants in Go: typed constants and untyped constants. Listing 4-7 shows the use of typed constants.

Listing 4-7. Defining Typed Constants in the main.go File in the basicFeatures Folder

```
package main

import (
    "fmt"
    //"math/rand"
)

func main() {
    const price float32 = 275.00
    const tax float32 = 27.50
    fmt.Println(price + tax)
}
```

Typed constants are defined using the const keyword, followed by a name, a type, and a value assignment, as illustrated by Figure 4-3.

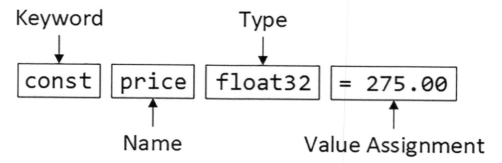

Figure 4-3. *Defining a typed constant*

This statement creates a `float32` constant named `price` whose value is 275.00. The code in Listing 4-7 creates two constants and uses them in an expression that is passed to the `fmt.Println` function. Compile and run the code, and you will receive the following output:

```
302.5
```

Understanding Untyped Constants

Go has strict rules about its data types and doesn't perform automatic type conversions, which can complicate common programming tasks, as Listing 4-8 demonstrates.

Listing 4-8. Mixing Data Types in the main.go File in the basicFeatures Folder

```
package main

import (
    "fmt"
    //"math/rand"
)

func main() {
    const price float32 = 275.00
    const tax float32 = 27.50
    const quantity int = 2
    fmt.Println("Total:", quantity * (price + tax))
}
```

The new constant's type is `int`, which is an appropriate choice for a quantity that can represent only a whole number of products, for example. The constant is used in the expression passed to the `fmt.Println` function to calculate a total price. But the compiler reports the following error when the code is compiled:

```
.\main.go:12:26: invalid operation: quantity * (price + tax) (mismatched types int and float32)
```

Most programming languages would have automatically converted the types to allow the expression to be evaluated, but Go's stricter approach means that int and float32 types cannot be mixed. The *untyped constant* feature makes constants easier to work with because the Go compiler will perform limited automatic conversion, as shown in Listing 4-9.

Listing 4-9. Using an Untyped Constant in the main.go File in the basicFeatures Folder

```go
package main

import (
    "fmt"
    //"math/rand"
)

func main() {
    const price float32 = 275.00
    const tax float32 = 27.50
    const quantity = 2
    fmt.Println("Total:", quantity * (price + tax))
}
```

An untyped constant is defined without a data type, as illustrated in Figure 4-4.

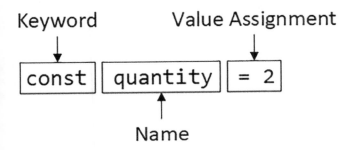

Figure 4-4. *Defining an untyped constant*

Omitting the type when defining the quantity constant tells the Go compiler that it should be more flexible about the constant's type. When the expression passed to the fmt.Println function is evaluated, the Go compiler will convert the quantity value to a float32. Compile and execute the code, and you will receive the following output:

```
Total: 605
```

Untyped constants will be converted only if the value can be represented in the target type. In practice, this means you can mix untyped integer and floating-point numeric values, but conversions between other data types must be done explicitly, as I describe in Chapter 5.

UNDERSTANDING IOTA

The `iota` keyword can be used to create a series of successive untyped integer constants without needing to assign individual values to them. Here is an `iota` example:

```
...
const (
    Watersports = iota
    Soccer
    Chess
)
...
```

This pattern creates a series of constants, each of which is assigned an integer value, starting at zero. You can see examples of `iota` in Part 3.

Defining Multiple Constants with a Single Statement

A single statement can be used to define several constants, as shown in Listing 4-10.

Listing 4-10. Defining Multiple Constants in the main.go File in the basicFeatures Folder

```
package main

import (
    "fmt"
    //"math/rand"
)

func main() {
    const price, tax float32 = 275, 27.50
    const quantity, inStock = 2, true
    fmt.Println("Total:", quantity * (price + tax))
    fmt.Println("In stock: ", inStock)
}
```

The const keyword is followed by a comma-separated list of names, an equal sign, and a comma-separated list of values, as illustrated by Figure 4-5. If a type is specified, all the constants will be created with this type. If the type is omitted, then untyped constants are created, and each constant's type will be inferred from its value.

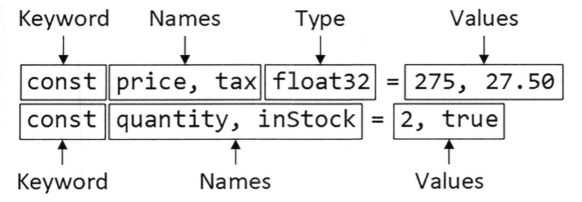

Figure 4-5. *Defining multiple constants*

Compiling and executing the code in Listing 4-10 produces the following output:

```
Total: 605
In stock:  true
```

Revisiting Literal Values

Untyped constants may seem like an odd feature, but they make working with Go a lot easier, and you will find yourself relying on this feature, often without realizing, because literal values are untyped constants, which means that you can use literal values in expressions and rely on the compiler to deal with mismatched types, as shown in Listing 4-11.

Listing 4-11. Using a Literal Value in the main.go File in the basicFeatures Folder

```go
package main

import (
    "fmt"
    //"math/rand"
)

func main() {
    const price, tax float32 = 275, 27.50
    const quantity, inStock = 2, true
    fmt.Println("Total:", 2 * quantity * (price + tax))
    fmt.Println("In stock: ", inStock)
}
```

The highlighted expression uses the literal value 2, which is an int value as described in Table 4-4, along with two float32 values. Since the int value can be represented as a float32, the value will be converted automatically. When compiled and executed, this code produces the following output:

```
Total: 1210
In stock:  true
```

Using Variables

Variables are defined using the var keyword, and, unlike constants, the value assigned to a variable can be changed, as shown in Listing 4-12.

Listing 4-12. Using Constants in the main.go File in the basicFeatures Folder

```
package main

import "fmt"

func main() {
    var price float32 = 275.00
    var tax float32 = 27.50
    fmt.Println(price + tax)
    price = 300
    fmt.Println(price + tax)
}
```

Variables are declared using the var keyword, a name, a type, and a value assignment, as illustrated in Figure 4-6.

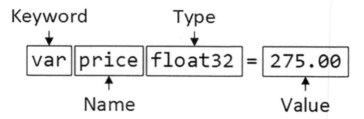

Figure 4-6. *Defining a Variable*

Listing 4-12 defines price and tax variables, both of which are assigned float32 values. A new value is assigned to the price variable using the equal sign, which is the Go assignment operator, as illustrated in Figure 4-7. (Notice that I can assign the value 300 to a floating-point variable. This is because the literal value 300 is an untyped constant that can be represented as a float32 value.)

Name   Value

price = 300

Figure 4-7. *Assigning a new value to a variable*

The code in Listing 4-12 writes two strings to the standard out using the fmt.Println function, producing the following output when the code is compiled and executed:

```
302.5
327.5
```

Omitting the Variable's Data Type

The Go compiler can infer the type of variables based on the initial value, which allows the type to be omitted, as shown in Listing 4-13.

Listing 4-13. Omitting a Variable's Type in the main.go File in the basicFeatures Folder

```
package main

import "fmt"

func main() {
    var price = 275.00
    var price2 = price
    fmt.Println(price)
    fmt.Println(price2)
}
```

The variable is defined using the var keyword, a name, and a value assignment, but the type is omitted, as illustrated by Figure 4-8. The value of the variable can be set using a literal value or the name of a constant or another variable. In the listing, the value of the price variable is set using a literal value, and the value of price2 is set to the current value of price.

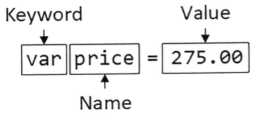

Keyword   Value

var price = 275.00

Name

Figure 4-8. *Defining a variable without specifying a type*

The compiler will infer the type from the value assigned to the variable. The compiler will inspect the literal value assigned to price and infer its type as float64, as described in Table 4-4. The type of price2 will also be inferred as float64 because its value is set using the price value. The code in Listing 4-13 produces the following output when compiled and executed:

```
275
275
```

Omitting a type doesn't have the same effect for variables as it does for constants, and the Go compiler will not allow different types to be mixed, as Listing 4-14 shows.

Listing 4-14. Mixing Data Types in the main.go File in the basicFeatures Folder

```go
package main

import "fmt"

func main() {
    var price = 275.00
    var tax float32 = 27.50
    fmt.Println(price + tax)
}
```

The compiler will always infer the type of literal floating-point values as float64, which doesn't match the float32 type of the tax variable. Go's strict type enforcement means that the compiler produces the following error when the code is compiled:

```
.\main.go:10:23: invalid operation: price + tax (mismatched types float64 and float32)
```

To use the price and tax variables in the same expression, they must have the same type or be convertible to the same type. I explain the different ways types can be converted in Chapter 5.

Omitting the Variable's Value Assignment

Variables can be defined without an initial value, as shown in Listing 4-15.

Listing 4-15. Defining a Variable Without an Initial Value in the main.go File in the basicFeatures Folder

```go
package main

import "fmt"

func main() {
    var price float32
    fmt.Println(price)
    price = 275.00
    fmt.Println(price)
}
```

Variables are defined using the var keyword followed by a name and a type, as illustrated by Figure 4-9. The type cannot be omitted when there is no initial value.

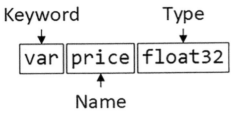

Figure 4-9. *Defining a variable without an initial value*

Variables defined this way are assigned the *zero value* for the specified type, as described in Table 4-5.

Table 4-5. *The Zero Values for the Basic Data Types*

Type	Zero Value
int	0
unit	0
byte	0
float64	0
bool	false
string	" " (the empty string)
rune	0

The zero value for numeric types is zero, which you can see by compiling and executing the code. The first value displayed in the output is the zero value, followed by the value assigned explicitly in a subsequent statement:

```
0
275
```

Defining Multiple Variables with a Single Statement

A single statement can be used to define several variables, as shown in Listing 4-16.

Listing 4-16. Defining Variables in the main.go File in the basicFeatures Folder

```
package main

import "fmt"

func main() {
    var price, tax = 275.00, 27.50
    fmt.Println(price + tax)
}
```

This is the same approach used to define constants, and the initial value assigned to each variable is used to infer its type. A type must be specified if no initial values are assigned, as shown in Listing 4-17, and all variables will be created using the specified type and assigned their zero value.

Listing 4-17. Defining Variables Without Initial Values in the main.go File in the basicFeatures Folder

```
package main

import "fmt"

func main() {
    var price, tax float64
    price = 275.00
    tax = 27.50
    fmt.Println(price + tax)
}
```

Listing 4-16 and Listing 4-17 both produce the same output when compiled and executed:

```
302.5
```

Using the Short Variable Declaration Syntax

The short variable declaration provides a shorthand for declaring variables, as shown in Listing 4-18.

Listing 4-18. Using the Short Variable Declaration Syntax in the main.go File in the basicFeatures Folder

```
package main

import "fmt"

func main() {
    price := 275.00
    fmt.Println(price)
}
```

The shorthand syntax specifies a name for the variable, a colon, an equal sign, and the initial value, as illustrated by Figure 4-10. The var keyword is not used, and a data type cannot be specified.

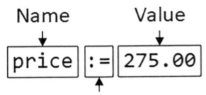

Shorthand Assignment

Figure 4-10. *The short variable declaration syntax*

The code in Listing 4-18 produces the following output when the code is compiled and executed:

```
275
```

Multiple variables can be defined with a single statement by creating comma-separated lists of names and values, as shown in Listing 4-19.

Listing 4-19. Defining Multiple Variables in the main.go File in the basicFeatures Folder

```
package main

import "fmt"

func main() {
    price, tax, inStock := 275.00, 27.50, true
    fmt.Println("Total:", price + tax)
    fmt.Println("In stock:", inStock)
}
```

No types are specified in the shorthand syntax, which means that variables of different types can be created, relying on the compiler to infer types from the values assigned to each variable. The code in Listing 4-19 produces the following output when compiled and executed:

```
Total: 302.5
In stock: true
```

The short variable declaration syntax can be used only within functions, such as the main function in Listing 4-19. Go functions are described in detail in Chapter 8.

Using the Short Variable Syntax to Redefine Variables

Go doesn't usually allow variables to be redefined but makes a limited exception when the short syntax is used. To demonstrate the default behavior, Listing 4-20 uses the var keyword to define a variable that has the same name as one that already exists within the same function.

Listing 4-20. Redefining a Variable in the main.go File in the basicFeatures Folder

```
package main

import "fmt"

func main() {
    price, tax, inStock := 275.00, 27.50, true
    fmt.Println("Total:", price + tax)
    fmt.Println("In stock:", inStock)

    var price2, tax = 200.00, 25.00
    fmt.Println("Total 2:", price2 + tax)
}
```

The first new statement uses the var keyword to define variables named price2 and tax. There is already a variable named tax in the main function, which causes the following error when the code is compiled:

```
.\main.go:10:17: tax redeclared in this block
```

However, redefining a variable is allowed if the short syntax is used, as shown in Listing 4-21, as long as at least one of the other variables being defined doesn't already exist and the type of the variable doesn't change.

Listing 4-21. Using the Short Syntax in the main.go File in the basicFeatures Folder

```
package main

import "fmt"

func main() {
    price, tax, inStock := 275.00, 27.50, true
    fmt.Println("Total:", price + tax)
    fmt.Println("In stock:", inStock)

    price2, tax := 200.00, 25.00
    fmt.Println("Total 2:", price2 + tax)
}
```

Compile and execute the project, and you will see the following output:

```
Total: 302.5
In stock: true
Total 2: 225
```

Using the Blank Identifier

It is illegal in Go to define a variable and not use it, as shown in Listing 4-22.

Listing 4-22. Defining Unused Variables in the main.go File in the basicFeatures Folder

```
package main

import "fmt"

func main() {
    price, tax, inStock, discount := 275.00, 27.50, true, true
    var salesPerson = "Alice"
    fmt.Println("Total:", price + tax)
    fmt.Println("In stock:", inStock)
}
```

The listing defines variables named discount and salesperson, neither of which is used in the rest of the code. When the code is compiled, the following error is reported:

```
.\main.go:6:26: discount declared but not used
.\main.go:7:9: salesPerson declared but not used
```

One way to resolve this problem is to remove the unused variables, but this isn't always possible. For these situations, Go provides the *blank identifier*, which is used to denote a value that won't be used, as shown in Listing 4-23.

Listing 4-23. Using the Blank Identifier in the main.go File in the basicFeatures Folder

```
package main

import "fmt"

func main() {
    price, tax, inStock, _ := 275.00, 27.50, true, true
    var _ = "Alice"
    fmt.Println("Total:", price + tax)
    fmt.Println("In stock:", inStock)
}
```

The blank identifier is the underscore (the _ character), and it can be used wherever using a name would create a variable that would not subsequently be used. The code in Listing 4-23 produces the following output when compiled and executed:

```
Total: 302.5
In stock: true
```

This is another feature that appears unusual, but it is important when using functions in Go. As I explain in Chapter 8, Go functions can return multiple results, and the blank identifier is useful when you need some of those result values but not others.

Understanding Pointers

Pointers are often misunderstood, especially if you have come to Go from a language such as Java or C#, where pointers are used behind the scenes but carefully hidden from the developer. To understand how pointers work, the best place to start is understanding what Go does when pointers are not used, as shown in Listing 4-24.

■ **Tip** The last example in this section provides a simple demonstration of why pointers can be useful, rather than just explaining how they are used.

Listing 4-24. Defining Variables in the main.go File in the basicFeatures Folder

```
package main

import "fmt"

func main() {

    first := 100
    second := first

    first++

    fmt.Println("First:", first)
    fmt.Println("Second:", second)
}
```

The code in Listing 4-24 produces the following output when compiled and executed:

```
First: 101
Second: 100
```

The code in Listing 4-24 creates two variables. The value of the variable named first is set using a string literal. The value of the variable named second is set using the first value, like this:

```
...
first := 100
second := first
...
```

Go copies the current value of first when creating second, after which these variables are independent of one another. Each variable is a reference to a separate memory location where its value is stored, as shown in Figure 4-11.

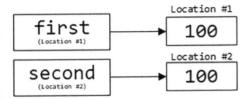

Figure 4-11. *Independent values*

When I use the ++ operator to increment the first variable in Listing 4-24, Go reads the value at the memory location associated with the variable, increments the value, and stores it at the same memory location. The value assigned to the second variable remains the same because the change affects only the value stored by the first variable, as shown in Figure 4-12.

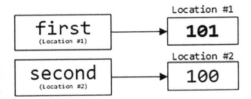

Figure 4-12. *Modifying a value*

UNDERSTANDING POINTER ARITHMETIC

Pointers have a bad reputation because of *pointer arithmetic*. Pointers store memory locations as numeric values, which means they can be manipulated using arithmetic operators, providing access to other memory locations. You can start with a location that points to an int value, for example; increment the value by the number of bits used to store an int; and read the adjacent value. This can be useful but can cause unexpected results, such as trying to access the wrong location or a location outside of the memory allocated to the program.

Go doesn't support pointer arithmetic, which means that a pointer to one location cannot be used to obtain other locations. The compiler will report an error if you try to perform arithmetic using a pointer.

Defining a Pointer

A pointer is a variable whose value is a memory address. Listing 4-25 defines a pointer.

Listing 4-25. Defining a Pointer in the main.go File in the basicFeatures Folder

```
package main

import "fmt"

func main() {

    first := 100
    var second *int = &first

    first++

    fmt.Println("First:", first)
    fmt.Println("Second:", second)
}
```

Pointers are defined using an ampersand (the & character), known as the *address operator*, followed by the name of a variable, as illustrated by Figure 4-13.

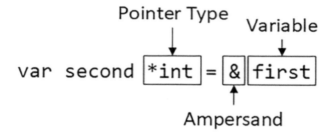

Figure 4-13. *Defining a pointer*

Pointers are just like other variables in Go. They have a type and a value. The value of the second variable will be the memory address used by Go to store the value for the first variable. Compile and execute the code, and you will see output like this:

```
First: 101
Second: 0xc000010088
```

You will see different output based on where Go has chosen to store the value for the first variable. The specific memory location isn't important, and it is the relationship between the variables that is of interest, illustrated by Figure 4-14.

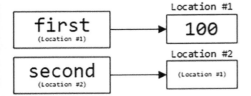

Figure 4-14. *A pointer and its memory location*

The type of a pointer is based on the type of the variable from which it is created, prefixed with an asterisk (the * character). The type of variable named second is *int, because it was created by applying the address operator to the first variable, whose value is int. When you see the type *int, you know it is a variable whose value is a memory address that stores an int variable.

A pointer's type is fixed, because all Go types are fixed, which means that when you create a pointer to an int, for example, you change the value that it points to, but you can't use it to point to the memory address used to store a different type, such as a float64. This restriction is important—in Go, pointers are not just memory addresses but, rather, memory addresses that may store a specific type of value.

Following a Pointer

The phrase *following a pointer* means reading the value at the memory address that the pointer refers to, and it is done using an asterisk (the * character), as shown in Listing 4-26. I have also used the short variable declaration syntax for the pointer in this example. Go will infer the pointer type just like it does with other types.

Listing 4-26. Following a Pointer in the main.go File in the basicFeatures Folder

```
package main

import "fmt"

func main() {

    first := 100
    second := &first

    first++

    fmt.Println("First:", first)
    fmt.Println("Second:", *second)
}
```

The asterisk tells Go to follow the pointer and get the value at the memory location, as illustrated by Figure 4-15. This is known as *dereferencing* the pointer.

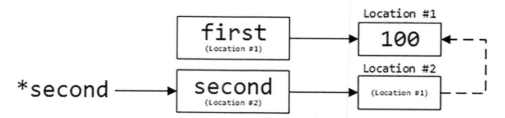

Figure 4-15. *Following a pointer*

The code in Listing 4-26 produces the following output when compiled and executed:

```
First: 101
Second: 101
```

A common misconception is that the first and second variables have the same value, but that's not what is happening. There are two values. There is an int value that can be accessed using the variable named first. There is also an *int value that stores the memory location of the first value. The *int value can be followed, which will access the stored int value. But, because the *int value is, well, a value, it can be used in its own right, which means that it can be assigned to other variables, used as an argument to invoke a function, and so on.

Listing 4-27 demonstrates the first use of the pointer. The pointer is followed, and the value at the memory location is incremented.

Listing 4-27. Following a Pointer and Changing the Value in the main.go File in the basicFeatures Folder

```
package main

import "fmt"

func main() {

    first := 100
    second := &first

    first++
    *second++

    fmt.Println("First:", first)
    fmt.Println("Second:", *second)
}
```

This code produces the following output when compiled and executed:

```
First: 102
Second: 102
```

Listing 4-28 demonstrates the second use of a pointer, which is to use it as a value in its own right and assign it to another variable.

Listing 4-28. Assigning a Pointer Value to Another Variable in the main.go File in the basicFeatures Folder

```
package main

import "fmt"

func main() {

    first := 100
    second := &first

    first++
    *second++

    var myNewPointer *int
    myNewPointer = second
    *myNewPointer++

    fmt.Println("First:", first)
    fmt.Println("Second:", *second)
}
```

The first new statement defines a new variable, which I have done with the var keyword to emphasize that the variable type is *int, meaning a pointer to an int value. The next statement assigns the value of the second variable to the new variable, meaning that the values of both second and myNewPointer are the memory location of the first value. Following either pointer accesses the same memory location, which means incrementing myNewPointer affects the value obtained by following the second pointer. Compile and execute the code, and you will see the following output:

```
First: 103
Second: 103
```

Understanding Pointer Zero Values

Pointers that are defined but not assigned a value have the zero-value nil, as demonstrated in Listing 4-29.

Listing 4-29. Defining an Uninitialized Pointer in the main.go File in the basicFeatures Folder

```
package main

import "fmt"

func main() {

    first := 100
    var second *int

    fmt.Println(second)
    second = &first
    fmt.Println(second)
}
```

The pointer second is defined but not initialized with a value and is written out using the fmt.Println function. The address operator is used to create a pointer to the first variable, and the value of second is written out again. The code in Listing 4-29 produces the following output when compiled and executed (ignore the < and > in the result, which is just to denote nil by the Println function):

```
<nil>
0xc000010088
```

A runtime error will occur if you follow a pointer that has not been assigned a value, as shown in Listing 4-30.

Listing 4-30. Following an Uninitialized Pointer in the main.go File in the basicFeatures Folder

```
package main

import "fmt"

func main() {

    first := 100
    var second *int

    fmt.Println(*second)
    second = &first
    fmt.Println(second == nil)
}
```

This code compiles but produces the following error when executed:

```
panic: runtime error: invalid memory address or nil pointer dereference
[signal 0xc0000005 code=0x0 addr=0x0 pc=0xec798a]
goroutine 1 [running]:
main.main()
    C:/basicFeatures/main.go:10 +0x2a
exit status 2
```

Pointing at Pointers

Given that pointers store memory locations, it is possible to create a pointer whose value is the memory address of another pointer, as shown in Listing 4-31.

Listing 4-31. Creating a Pointer to a Pointer in the main.go File in the basicFeatures Folder

```
package main

import "fmt"

func main() {

    first := 100
    second := &first
    third := &second

    fmt.Println(first)
    fmt.Println(*second)
    fmt.Println(**third)
}
```

The syntax for following chains of pointers can be awkward. In this case, two asterisks are required. The first asterisk follows the pointer to the memory location to get the value stored by the variable named second, which is an *int value. The second asterisk follows the pointer named second, which gives access to the memory location of the value stored by the first variable. This isn't something you will need to do in most projects, but it does provide a nice confirmation of how pointers work and how you can follow the chain to get to the data value. The code in Listing 4-31 produces the following output when compiled and executed:

```
100
100
100
```

Understanding Why Pointers Are Useful

It is easy to get lost in the detail of how pointers work and lose sight of why they can be a programmer's friend. Pointers are useful because they allow the programmer to choose between passing a value and passing a reference. There are lots of examples that use pointers in later chapters, but to finish this chapter, a quick demonstration is useful. That said, the listings in this section rely on features that are explained in later chapters, so you may want to return to these examples later. Listing 4-32 provides an example of when working with values is useful.

Listing 4-32. Working with Values in the main.go File in the basicFeatures Folder

```
package main

import (
    "fmt"
    "sort"
)
```

```go
func main() {

    names := [3]string {"Alice", "Charlie", "Bob"}

    secondName := names[1]

    fmt.Println(secondName)

    sort.Strings(names[:])

    fmt.Println(secondName)
}
```

The syntax may be unusual, but this example is simple. An array of three string values is created, and the value in position 1 is assigned to a variable called secondName. The value of the secondName variable is written to the console, the array is sorted, and the value of the secondName variable is written to the console again. This code produces the following output when compiled and executed:

```
Charlie
Charlie
```

When the secondName variable is created, the value of the string in position 1 of the array is copied to a new memory location, which is why the value isn't affected by the sorting operation. Because the value has been copied, it is now entirely unrelated to the array, and sorting the array does not affect the value of the secondName variable.

Listing 4-33 introduces a pointer variable to the example.

Listing 4-33. Using a Pointer in the main.go File in the basicFeatures Folder

```go
package main

import (
    "fmt"
    "sort"
)

func main() {

    names := [3]string {"Alice", "Charlie", "Bob"}

    secondPosition := &names[1]

    fmt.Println(*secondPosition)

    sort.Strings(names[:])

    fmt.Println(*secondPosition)
}
```

When the secondPosition variable is created, its value is the memory address used to store the string value in position 1 of the array. When the array is sorted, the order of the items in the array changes, but the pointer still refers to the memory location for position 1, which means that following the pointer returns the sorted value, producing the following output when the code is compiled and executed:

```
Charlie
Bob
```

A pointer means I can keep a reference to location 1 in a way that provides access to the current value, reflecting any changes that are made to the contents of the array. This is a simple example, but it shows how pointers provide the developer with a choice between copying values and using references.

If you are still unsure about pointers, then consider how the value versus reference issue is handled by other languages with which you are familiar. C#, for example, which I use a lot, supports both structs, which are passed by value, and classes, instances of which are passed as references. Go and C# both let me choose whether I want to use a copy or a reference. The difference is that C# makes me choose once when I create a data type, but Go lets me choose each time I use a value. The Go approach is more flexible but requires more consideration from the programmer.

Summary

In this chapter, I introduced the basic built-in types that Go provides, which form the building blocks for almost every language feature. I explained how constants and variables are defined, using both the full and short syntax; demonstrated the use of untyped constants; and described the use of pointers in Go. In the next chapter, I describe the operations that can be performed on the built-in data types and explain how to convert a value from one type to another type.

CHAPTER 5

■ ■ ■

Operations and Conversions

In this chapter, I describe the Go operators, which are used to perform arithmetic, compare values, and create logical expressions that produce true/false results. I also explain the process of converting a value from one type to another, which can be done using a combination of built-in language features and facilities provided by the Go standard library. Table 5-1 puts the Go operations and conversions in context.

Table 5-1. *Putting Operations and Conversions in Context*

Question	Answer
What are they?	The basic operations are used for arithmetic, comparisons, and logical evaluation. The type conversion features allow for a value in one type to be expressed as a different type.
Why are they useful?	The basic operations are required for almost every programming task, and it is difficult to write any code that doesn't use them. The type conversion features are useful because Go's strict type rules prevent values of different types from being used together.
How are they used?	The basic operations are applied using operands, which are similar to those used in other languages. Conversions are performed either by using the Go explicit conversion syntax or by using the facilities provided by the Go standard library packages.
Are there any pitfalls or limitations?	Any conversion process can be subject to a loss of precision and so care must be taken that converting a value doesn't produce a result with less precision than the task requires.
Are there any alternatives?	No. The features described in this chapter are fundamental to Go development.

Table 5-2 summarizes the chapter.

© Adam Freeman 2022
A. Freeman, *Pro Go*, https://doi.org/10.1007/978-1-4842-7355-5_5

Table 5-2. *Chapter Summary*

Problem	Solution	Listing
Perform arithmetic	Use the arithmetic operators	4–7
Concatenate strings	Use the + operator	8
Compare two values	Use the comparison operators	9–11
Combine expressions	Use the logical operators	12
Convert from one type to another	Perform an explicit conversion	13–15
Convert a floating-point value to an integer	Use the functions defined by the math package	16
Parse a string into another data type	Use the functions defined by the strconv package	17–28
Express a value as a string	Use the functions defined by the strconv package	29–32

Preparing for This Chapter

To prepare for this chapter, open a new command prompt, navigate to a convenient location, and create a directory named operations. Run the command shown in Listing 5-1 to initialize the project.

■ **Tip** You can download the example project for this chapter—and for all the other chapters in this book—from https://github.com/apress/pro-go. See Chapter 2 for how to get help if you have problems running the examples.

Listing 5-1. Initializing the Project

```
go mod init operations
```

Add a file named main.go to the operations folder, with the contents shown in Listing 5-2.

Listing 5-2. The Contents of the main.go File in the operations Folder

```
package main

import "fmt"

func main() {

    fmt.Println("Hello, Operations")
}
```

Use the command prompt to run the command shown in Listing 5-3 in the operations folder.

Listing 5-3. Running the Example Project

```
go run .
```

The code in the main.go file will be compiled and executed, producing the following output:

```
Hello, Operations
```

Understanding the Go Operators

Go provides a standard set of operators, and Table 5-3 describes those that you will encounter most often, especially when working with the data types described in Chapter 4.

Table 5-3. *The Basic Go Operators*

Operator	Description
+, -, *, /, %	These operators are used to perform arithmetic using numeric values, as described in the "Understanding the Arithmetic Operators" section. The + operator can also be used for string concatenation, as described in the "Concatenating Strings" section.
==, !=, <, <=, >, >=	These operators compare two values, as described in the "Understanding the Comparison Operators" section.
||, &&, !	These are the logical operators, which are applied to bool values and return a bool value, as described in the "Understanding the Logical Operators" section.
=, :=	These are the assignment operators. The standard assignment operator (=) is used to set the initial value when a constant or variable is defined, or to change the value assigned to a previously defined variable. The shorthand operator (:=) is used to define a variable and assign a value, as described in Chapter 4.
-=, +=, ++, --	These operators increment and decrement numeric values, as described in the "Using the Increment and Decrement Operators" section.
&, |, ^, &^, <<, >>	These are the bitwise operators, which can be applied to integer values. These operators are not often required in mainstream development, but you can see an example in Chapter 31, where the | operator is used to configure the Go logging features.

Understanding the Arithmetic Operators

The arithmetic operators can be applied to the numeric data types (float32, float64, int, uint, and the size-specific types described in Chapter 4). The exception is the remainder operator (%), which can be used only on integers. Table 5-4 describes the arithmetic operators.

Table 5-4. *The Arithmetic Operators*

Operator	Description
+	This operator returns the sum of two operands.
-	This operator returns the difference between two operands.
*	This operator returns the product of two operands.
/	This product returns the quotient of two operators.
%	This product returns the remainder, which is similar to the modulo operator provided by other programming languages but can return negative values, as described in the "Using the Remainder Operator" section.

The values used with the arithmetic operators must be of the same type (all int values, for example) or be representable in the same type, such as untyped numeric constants. Listing 5-4 shows the use of the arithmetic operators.

Listing 5-4. Using the Arithmetic Operators in the main.go File in the operations Folder

```
package main

import "fmt"

func main() {
    price, tax := 275.00, 27.40

    sum := price + tax
    difference := price - tax
    product := price * tax
    quotient := price / tax

    fmt.Println(sum)
    fmt.Println(difference)
    fmt.Println(product)
    fmt.Println(quotient)
}
```

The code in Listing 5-4 produces the following output when compiled and executed:

```
302.4
247.6
7535
10.036496350364963
```

Understanding Arithmetic Overflow

Go allows integer values to overflow by wrapping around, rather than reporting an error. Floating-point values overflow to positive or negative infinity. Listing 5-5 shows overflows for both data types.

Listing 5-5. Overflowing Numeric Values in the main.go File in the operations Folder

```
package main

import (
    "fmt"
    "math"
)

func main() {

    var intVal = math.MaxInt64
    var floatVal = math.MaxFloat64

    fmt.Println(intVal * 2)
    fmt.Println(floatVal * 2)
    fmt.Println(math.IsInf((floatVal * 2), 0))
}
```

Deliberately causing an overflow is most easily achieved using the math package, which is part of the Go standard library. I describe this package in more detail in Chapter 18, but for this chapter, I am interested in the constants provided for the smallest and largest values each data type can represent, as well as the IsInf function, which can be used to determine whether a floating-point value has overflowed to infinity. In the listing, I use the MaxInt64 and MaxFloat64 constants to set the value of two variables, which I then overflow in expressions passed to the fmt.Println function. The listing produces the following output when it is compiled and executed:

```
-2
+Inf
true
```

The integer value wraps around to produce a value of -2, and the floating-point value overflows to +Inf, which denotes positive infinity. The math.IsInf function is used to detect infinity.

Using the Remainder Operator

Go provides the % operator, which returns the remainder when one integer value is divided by another. This is often mistaken for the modulo operator provided by other programming languages, such as Python, but, unlike those operators, the Go remainder operator can return negative values, as shown in Listing 5-6.

Listing 5-6. Using the Remainder Operator in the main.go File in the operations Folder

```
package main

import (
    "fmt"
    "math"
)

func main() {
    posResult := 3 % 2
```

```
    negResult := -3 % 2
    absResult := math.Abs(float64(negResult))

    fmt.Println(posResult)
    fmt.Println(negResult)
    fmt.Println(absResult)
}
```

The remainder operator is used in two expressions to demonstrate that positive and negative results can be produced. The math package provides the Abs function, which will return an absolute value of a float64, although the result is also a float64. The code in Listing 5-6 produces the following output when it is compiled and executed:

```
1
-1
1
```

Using the Increment and Decrement Operators

Go provides a set of operators for incrementing and decrementing numeric values, as shown in Listing 5-7. These operators can be applied to integer and floating-point numbers.

Listing 5-7. Using the Increment and Decrement Operators in the main.go File in the operations Folder

```
package main

import (
    "fmt"
//    "math"
)

func main() {
    value := 10.2
    value++
    fmt.Println(value)
    value += 2
    fmt.Println(value)
    value -= 2
    fmt.Println(value)
    value--
    fmt.Println(value)
}
```

The ++ and - - operators increment or decrement a value by one. The += and -= increment or decrement a value by a specified amount. These operations are subject to the overflow behavior described earlier but are otherwise consistent with comparable operators in other languages, other than the ++ and - - operators, which can be only postfix, meaning there is no support for an expression such as - -value. The code in Listing 5-7 produces the following output when it is compiled and executed:

```
11.2
13.2
11.2
10.2
```

Concatenating Strings

The + operator can be used to concatenate strings to produce longer strings, as shown in Listing 5-8.

Listing 5-8. Concatenating Strings in the main.go File in the operations Folder

```go
package main

import (
    "fmt"
//    "math"
)

func main() {
    greeting := "Hello"
    language := "Go"
    combinedString := greeting + ", " + language

    fmt.Println(combinedString)
}
```

The result of the + operator is a new string, and the code in Listing 5-8 produces the following output when compiled and executed:

```
Hello, Go
```

Go won't concatenate strings with other data types, but the standard library does include functions that compose strings from values of different types, as described in Chapter 17.

Understanding the Comparison Operators

The comparison operators compare two values, returning the bool value true if they are the same and false otherwise. Table 5-5 describes the comparison performed by each operator.

Table 5-5. *The Comparison Operators*

Operator	Description
==	This operator returns true if the operands are equal.
!=	This operator returns true if the operands are not equal.
<	This operator returns true if the first operand is less than the second operand.
>	This operator returns true if the first operand is greater than the second operand.
<=	This operator returns true if the first operand is less than or equal to the second operand.
>=	This operator returns true if the first operand is greater than or equal to the second operand.

The values used with the comparison operators must all be of the same type, or they must be untyped constants that can be represented as the target type, as shown in Listing 5-9.

Listing 5-9. Using an Untyped Constant in the main.go File in the operations Folder

```
package main

import (
    "fmt"
//    "math"
)

func main() {

    first := 100
    const second = 200.00

    equal := first == second
    notEqual := first != second
    lessThan := first < second
    lessThanOrEqual := first <= second
    greaterThan := first > second
    greaterThanOrEqual := first >= second

    fmt.Println(equal)
    fmt.Println(notEqual)
    fmt.Println(lessThan)
    fmt.Println(lessThanOrEqual)
    fmt.Println(greaterThan)
    fmt.Println(greaterThanOrEqual)
}
```

The untyped constant is a floating-point value but can be represented as an integer value because its fractional digits are zeros. This allows the variable first and the constant second to be used together in comparisons. This would not be possible for a constant value of 200.01, for example, because the floating-point value cannot be represented as an integer without discarding the fractional digits and creating a different value. For this, an explicit conversion is required, as described later in this chapter. The code in Listing 5-9 produces the following output when compiled and executed:

```
false
true
true
true
false
false
```

PERFORMING TERNARY COMPARISONS

Go doesn't provide a ternary operator, which means that expressions like this cannot be used:

```
...
max := first > second ? first : second
...
```

Instead, one of the comparison operators described in Table 5-5 is used with an if statement, like this:

```
...
var max int
if (first > second) {
    max = first
} else {
    max = second
}
...
```

This syntax is less concise, but, like many Go features, you will quickly become used to working without ternary expressions.

Comparing Pointers

Pointers can be compared to see if they point at the same memory location, as shown in Listing 5-10.

Listing 5-10. Comparing Pointers in the main.go File in the operations Folder

```
package main

import (
    "fmt"
//    "math"
)

func main() {
```

```
    first := 100

    second := &first
    third := &first

    alpha := 100
    beta := &alpha

    fmt.Println(second == third)
    fmt.Println(second == beta)
}
```

The Go equality operator (==) is used to compare the memory locations. In Listing 5-10, the pointers named second and third both point to the same location and are equal. The pointer named beta points to a different memory location. The code in Listing 5-10 produces the following output when compiled and executed:

```
true
false
```

It is important to understand that it is the memory locations that are being compared and not the values they store. If you want to compare values, then you should follow the pointers, as shown in Listing 5-11.

Listing 5-11. Following Pointers in a Comparison in the main.go File in the operations Folder

```
package main

import (
    "fmt"
//    "math"
)

func main() {

    first := 100

    second := &first
    third := &first

    alpha := 100
    beta := &alpha

    fmt.Println(*second == *third)
    fmt.Println(*second == *beta)
}
```

These comparisons follow the pointers to compare the values stored at the referenced memory locations, producing the following output when the code is compiled and executed:

```
true
true
```

Understanding the Logical Operators

The logical operators compare bool values, as described in Table 5-6. The results produced by these operators can be assigned to variables or used as part of a flow control expression, which I describe in Chapter 6.

Table 5-6. *The Logical Operators*

Operator	Description
||	This operator returns true if either operand is true. If the first operand is true, then the second operand will not be evaluated.
&&	This operator returns true if both operands are true. If the first operand is false, then the second operand will not be evaluated.
!	This operator is used with a single operand. It returns true if the operand is false and false if the operand is true.

Listing 5-12 shows the logical operators being used to produce values that are assigned to variables.

Listing 5-12. Using the Logical Operators in the main.go File in the operations Folder

```
package main

import (
    "fmt"
//      "math"
)

func main() {

    maxMph := 50
    passengerCapacity := 4
    airbags := true

    familyCar := passengerCapacity > 2 && airbags
    sportsCar := maxMph > 100 || passengerCapacity == 2
    canCategorize := !familyCar && !sportsCar

    fmt.Println(familyCar)
    fmt.Println(sportsCar)
    fmt.Println(canCategorize)
}
```

Only bool values can be used with the logical operators, and Go will not attempt to convert a value to get a true or false value. If the operand for a logical operator is an expression, then it is evaluated to produce the bool result that is used in the comparison. The code in Listing 5-12 produces the following output when it is compiled and executed:

```
true
false
false
```

Go short-circuits the evaluation process when the logical operators are used, meaning that the smallest number of values is assessed to produce a result. In the case of the && operator, evaluation stops when a false value is encountered. In the case of the || operator, evaluation stops when a true value is encountered. In both cases, no subsequent value can change the outcome of the operation, so additional evaluations are not required.

Converting, Parsing, and Formatting Values

Go doesn't allow types to be mixed in operations and will not automatically convert types, except in the case of untyped constants. To show how the compiler responds to mixed data types, Listing 5-13 contains a statement that applies the addition operator to values of different types. (You may find your code editor automatically corrects the code in Listing 5-13, and you may have to undo the correction so the code in the editor matches the listing to see the compiler error.)

Listing 5-13. Mixing Types in an Operation in the main.go File in the operations Folder

```
package main

import (
    "fmt"
//    "math"
)

func main() {

    kayak := 275
    soccerBall := 19.50

    total := kayak + soccerBall

    fmt.Println(total)
}
```

The literal values used to define the kayak and soccerBall variables result in an int value and a float64 value, which are then used in the addition operation to set the value of the total variable. When the code is compiled, the following error will be reported:

```
.\main.go:13:20: invalid operation: kayak + soccerBall (mismatched types int and float64)
```

For such a simple example, I could simply change the literal value used to initialize the kayak variable to 275.00, which would produce a float64 variable. But types are rarely as easy to change in real projects, which is why Go provides the features described in the sections that follow.

Performing Explicit Type Conversions

An *explicit conversion* transforms a value to change its type, as shown in Listing 5-14.

Listing 5-14. Using an Explicit Conversion in the main.go File in the operations Folder

```
package main
```

```
import (
    "fmt"
//    "math"
)

func main() {

    kayak := 275
    soccerBall := 19.50

    total := float64(kayak) + soccerBall

    fmt.Println(total)
}
```

The syntax for explicit conversions is T(x), where T is the target type and x is the value or expression to convert. In Listing 5-14, I used an explicit conversion to produce a float64 value from the kayak variable, as shown in Figure 5-1.

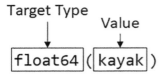

Figure 5-1. *Explicit conversion of a type*

The conversion to a float64 value means that the types in the addition operation are consistent. The code in Listing 5-14 produces the following output when compiled and executed:

```
294.5
```

Understanding the Limitations of Explicit Conversions

Explicit conversions can be used only when the value can be *represented* in the target type. This means you can convert between numeric types and between strings and runes, but other combinations, such as converting int values to bool values, are not supported.

Care must be taken when choosing the values to convert because explicit conversions can cause a loss of precision in numeric values or cause overflows, as shown in Listing 5-15.

Listing 5-15. Converting Numeric Types in the main.go File in the operations Folder

```
package main

import (
    "fmt"
//    "math"
)

func main() {
```

```
kayak := 275
soccerBall := 19.50

total := kayak + int(soccerBall)

fmt.Println(total)
fmt.Println(int8(total))

}
```

This listing converts the float64 value to an int for the addition operation and, separately, converts the int into an int8 (which is the type for a signed integer allocated 8 bits of storage, as described in Chapter 4). The code produces the following output when it is compiled and executed:

```
294
38
```

When converting from a floating-point to an integer, the fractional part of the value is discarded so that the floating-point 19.50 becomes the int value 19. The discarded fraction is the reason why the value of the total variable is 294 instead of the 294.5 produced in the previous section.

The int8 used in the second explicit conversion is too small to represent the int value 294 and so the variable overflows, as described in the earlier "Understanding Arithmetic Overflow" section.

Converting Floating-Point Values to Integers

As the previous example demonstrated, explicit conversions can produce unexpected results, especially when converting floating-point values to integers. The safest approach is to convert in the other direction, representing integers and floating-point values, but if that isn't possible, then the math package provides a set of useful functions that can be used to perform conversions in a controlled way, as described in Table 5-7.

Table 5-7. *Functions in the math Package for Converting Numeric Types*

Function	Description
Ceil(value)	This function returns the smallest integer that is greater than the specified floating-point value. The smallest integer that is greater than 27.1, for example, is 28.
Floor(value)	This function returns the largest integer that is less than the specified floating-point value. The largest integer that is less than 27.1, for example, is 28.
Round(value)	This function rounds the specified floating-point value to the nearest integer.
RoundToEven(value)	This function rounds the specified floating-point value to the nearest even integer.

The functions described in the table return float64 values, which can then be explicitly converted to the int type, as shown in Listing 5-16.

Listing 5-16. Rounding a Value in the main.go File in the operations Folder

```
package main

import (
    "fmt"
```

102

```
    "math"
)

func main() {

    kayak := 275
    soccerBall := 19.50

    total := kayak + int(math.Round(soccerBall))

    fmt.Println(total)
}
```

The math.Round function will round the soccerBall value from 19.5 to 20, which is then explicitly converted to an int and used in the addition operation. The code in Listing 5-16 produces the following output when compiled and executed:

```
295
```

Parsing from Strings

The Go standard library includes the strconv package, which provides functions for converting string values to the other basic data types. Table 5-8 describes the functions that parse strings into other data types.

Table 5-8. *Functions for Parsing Strings into Other Data Types*

Function	Description
ParseBool(str)	This function parses a string into a bool value. Recognized string values are "true", "false", "TRUE", "FALSE", "True", "False", "T", "F", "0", and "1".
ParseFloat(str, size)	This function parses a string into a floating-point value with the specified size, as described in the "Parsing Floating-Point Numbers" section.
ParseInt(str, base, size)	This function parses a string into an int64 with the specified base and size. Acceptable base values are 2 for binary, 8 for octal, 16 for hex, and 10, as described in the "Parsing Integers" section.
ParseUint(str, base, size)	This function parses a string into an unsigned integer value with the specified base and size.
Atoi(str)	This function parses a string into a base 10 int and is equivalent to calling ParseInt(str, 10, 0), as described in the "Using the Integer Convenience Function" section.

Listing 5-17 shows the use of the ParseBool function to parse strings into bool values.

Listing 5-17. Parsing Strings in the main.go File in the operations Folder

```
package main

import (
```

```
    "fmt"
    "strconv"
)

func main() {

    val1 := "true"
    val2 := "false"
    val3 := "not true"

    bool1, b1err := strconv.ParseBool(val1)
    bool2, b2err := strconv.ParseBool(val2)
    bool3, b3err := strconv.ParseBool(val3)

    fmt.Println("Bool 1", bool1, b1err)
    fmt.Println("Bool 2", bool2, b2err)
    fmt.Println("Bool 3", bool3, b3err)
}
```

As I explain in Chapter 6, Go functions can produce multiple result values. The functions described in Table 5-8 return two result values: the parsed result and an error, as illustrated by Figure 5-2.

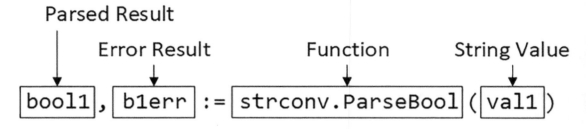

Figure 5-2. *Parsing a string*

You may be used to languages that report problems by throwing an exception, which can be caught and processed using a dedicated keyword, such as catch. Go works by assigning an error to the second result produced by the functions in Table 5-8. If the error result is nil, then the string has been successfully parsed. If the error result is not nil, then parsing has failed. You can see examples of successful and unsuccessful parsing by compiling and executing the code in Listing 5-17, which produces the following output:

```
Bool 1 true <nil>
Bool 2 false <nil>
Bool 3 false strconv.ParseBool: parsing "not true": invalid syntax
```

The first two strings are parsed into the values true and false, and the error result for both function calls is nil. The third string is not on the list of recognized values described in Table 5-8 and cannot be parsed. For this operation, the error result provides details of the problem.

Care must be taken to inspect the error result because the other result will default to the zero value when the string cannot be parsed. If you don't check the error result, you will not be able to differentiate between a false value that has been correctly parsed from a string and the zero value that has been used because parsing failed. The check for an error is typically done using the if/else keywords, as shown in Listing 5-18. I describe the if keyword and related features in Chapter 6.

Listing 5-18. Checking for an Error in the main.go File in the operations Folder

```
package main

import (
    "fmt"
    "strconv"
)

func main() {

    val1 := "0"

    bool1, b1err := strconv.ParseBool(val1)

    if b1err == nil {
        fmt.Println("Parsed value:", bool1)
    } else {
        fmt.Println("Cannot parse", val1)
    }
}
```

The if/else block allows the zero value to be differentiated from a successful processing of a string that parses to the false value. As I explain in Chapter 6, Go if statements can define an initialization statement, and this allows a conversion function to be called and its results to be inspected in a single statement, as shown in Listing 5-19.

Listing 5-19. Checking an Error in a Single Statement in the main.go File in the operations Folder

```
package main

import (
    "fmt"
    "strconv"
)

func main() {

    val1 := "0"

    if bool1, b1err := strconv.ParseBool(val1); b1err == nil {
        fmt.Println("Parsed value:", bool1)
    } else {
        fmt.Println("Cannot parse", val1)
    }
}
```

Listing 5-18 and Listing 5-19 both produce the following output when the project is compiled and executed:

```
Parsed value: false
```

Parsing Integers

The ParseInt and ParseUint functions require the base of the number represented by the string and the size of the data type that will be used to represent the parsed value, as shown in Listing 5-20.

Listing 5-20. Parsing an Integer in the main.go File in the operations Folder

```
package main

import (
    "fmt"
    "strconv"
)

func main() {

    val1 := "100"

    int1, int1err := strconv.ParseInt(val1, 0, 8)

    if int1err == nil {
        fmt.Println("Parsed value:", int1)
    } else {
        fmt.Println("Cannot parse", val1)
    }
}
```

The first argument to the ParseInt function is the string to parse. The second argument is the base for the number, or zero to let the function detect the base from the string's prefix. The final argument is the size of the data type to which the parsed value will be allocated. In this example, I have left the function to detect the base and specified 8 as the size.

Compile and execute the code in Listing 5-20, and you will receive the following output, showing the parsed integer value:

```
Parsed value: 100
```

You might expect that specifying the size will change the type used for the result, but that's not the case, and the function always returns an int64. The size only specifies the data size that the parsed value must be able to fit into. If the string value contains a number value that cannot be represented within the specified size, then the value won't be parsed. In Listing 5-21, I have changed the string value to contain a larger value.

Listing 5-21. Increasing the Value in the main.go File in the operations Folder

```
package main

import (
    "fmt"
    "strconv"
)

func main() {
```

```
val1 := "500"

int1, int1err := strconv.ParseInt(val1, 0, 8)

if int1err == nil {
    fmt.Println("Parsed value:", int1)
} else {
    fmt.Println("Cannot parse", val1, int1err)
}
}
```

The string "500" can be parsed into an integer, but it is too large to represent as an 8-bit value, which is the size specified by the ParseInt argument. When the code is compiled and executed, the output shows the error returned by the function:

```
Cannot parse 500 strconv.ParseInt: parsing "500": value out of range
```

This may seem an indirect approach, but it allows Go to maintain its type rules while ensuring that you can safely perform an explicit conversion on a result if it is successfully parsed, as shown in Listing 5-22.

Listing 5-22. Explicitly Converting a Result in the main.go File in the operations Folder

```
package main

import (
    "fmt"
    "strconv"
)

func main() {

    val1 := "100"

    int1, int1err := strconv.ParseInt(val1, 0, 8)

    if int1err == nil {
        smallInt := int8(int1)
        fmt.Println("Parsed value:", smallInt)
    } else {
        fmt.Println("Cannot parse", val1, int1err)
    }
}
```

Specifying a size of 8 when calling the ParseInt function allows me to perform an explicit conversion to the int8 type without the possibility of overflow. The code in Listing 5-22 produces the following output when compiled and executed:

```
Parsed value: 100
```

Parsing Binary, Octal, and Hexadecimal Integers

The base argument received by the Parse<Type> functions allows nondecimal number strings to be parsed, as shown in Listing 5-23.

Listing 5-23. Parsing a Binary Value in the main.go File in the operations Folder

```
package main

import (
    "fmt"
    "strconv"
)

func main() {

    val1 := "100"

    int1, int1err := strconv.ParseInt(val1, 2, 8)

    if int1err == nil {
        smallInt := int8(int1)
        fmt.Println("Parsed value:", smallInt)
    } else {
        fmt.Println("Cannot parse", val1, int1err)
    }
}
```

The string value "100" can be parsed into the decimal value 100, but it could also represent the binary value 4. Using the second argument to the ParseInt function, I can specify a base of 2, which means the string will be interpreted as a binary value. Compile and execute the code, and you will see a decimal representation of the number parsed from the binary string:

```
Parsed value: 4
```

You can leave the Parse<Type> functions to detect the base for a value using a prefix, as shown in Listing 5-24.

Listing 5-24. Using a Prefix in the main.go File in the operations Folder

```
package main

import (
    "fmt"
    "strconv"
)

func main() {

    val1 := "0b1100100"

    int1, int1err := strconv.ParseInt(val1, 0, 8)
```

```
    if int1err == nil {
        smallInt := int8(int1)
        fmt.Println("Parsed value:", smallInt)
    } else {
        fmt.Println("Cannot parse", val1, int1err)
    }
}
```

The functions described in Table 5-8 can determine the base of the value they are parsing based on its prefix. Table 5-9 describes the set of supported prefixes.

Table 5-9. *The Base Prefixes for Numeric Strings*

Prefix	Description
0b	This prefix denotes a binary value, such as 0b1100100.
0o	This prefix denotes an octal value, such as 0o144.
0x	This prefix denotes a hex value, such as 0x64.

The string in Listing 5-24 has a 0b prefix, which denotes a binary value. When the code is compiled and executed, the following output is produced:

```
Parsed value: 100
```

Using the Integer Convenience Function

For many projects, the most common parsing task is to create int values from strings that contain decimal numbers, as shown in Listing 5-25.

Listing 5-25. Performing a Common Parsing Task in the main.go File in the operations Folder

```
package main

import (
    "fmt"
    "strconv"
)

func main() {

    val1 := "100"

    int1, int1err := strconv.ParseInt(val1, 10, 0)
```

```
    if int1err == nil {
        var intResult int = int(int1)
        fmt.Println("Parsed value:", intResult)
    } else {
        fmt.Println("Cannot parse", val1, int1err)
    }
}
```

This is such a common task that the strconv package provides the Atoi function, which handles the parsing and explicit conversion in a single step, as shown in Listing 5-26.

Listing 5-26. Using the Convenience Function in the main.go File in the operations Folder

```
package main

import (
    "fmt"
    "strconv"
)

func main() {

    val1 := "100"

    int1, int1err := strconv.Atoi(val1)

    if int1err == nil {
        var intResult int = int1
        fmt.Println("Parsed value:", intResult)
    } else {
        fmt.Println("Cannot parse", val1, int1err)
    }
}
```

The Atoi function accepts only the value to be parsed and doesn't support parsing nondecimal values. The type of the result is int, instead of the int64 produced by the ParseInt function. The code in Listings 5-25 and 5-26 produces the following output when compiled and executed:

```
Parsed value: 100
```

Parsing Floating-Point Numbers

The ParseFloat function is used to parse strings containing floating-point numbers, as shown in Listing 5-27.

Listing 5-27. Parsing Floating-Point Values in the main.go File in the operations Folder

```
package main

import (
```

```
        "fmt"
        "strconv"
)

func main() {

    val1 := "48.95"

    float1, float1err := strconv.ParseFloat(val1, 64)

    if float1err == nil {
        fmt.Println("Parsed value:", float1)
    } else {
        fmt.Println("Cannot parse", val1, float1err)
    }
}
```

The first argument to the ParseFloat function is the value to parse. The second argument specifies the size of the result. The result from the ParseFloat function is a float64 value, but if 32 is specified, then the result can be explicitly converted to a float32 value.

The ParseFloat function can parse values expressed with an exponent, as shown in Listing 5-28.

Listing 5-28. Parsing a Value with an Exponent in the main.go File in the operations Folder

```
package main

import (
    "fmt"
    "strconv"
)

func main() {

    val1 := "4.895e+01"

    float1, float1err := strconv.ParseFloat(val1, 64)

    if float1err == nil {
        fmt.Println("Parsed value:", float1)
    } else {
        fmt.Println("Cannot parse", val1, float1err)
    }
}
```

Listings 5-27 and 5-28 both produce the same output when compiled and executed:

```
Parsed value: 48.95
```

Formatting Values as Strings

The Go standard library also provides functionality for converting basic data values into strings, which can be used directly or composed with other strings. The strconv package provides the functions described in Table 5-10.

Table 5-10. *The strconv Functions for Converting Values into Strings*

Function	Description
FormatBool(val)	This function returns the string true or false based on the value of the specified bool.
FormatInt(val, base)	This function returns a string representation of the specified int64 value, expressed in the specified base.
FormatUint(val, base)	This function returns a string representation of the specified uint64 value, expressed in the specified base.
FormatFloat(val, format, precision, size)	This function returns a string representation of the specified float64 value, expressed using the specified format, precision, and size.
Itoa(val)	This function returns a string representation of the specified int value, expressed using base 10.

Formatting Boolean Values

The FormatBool function accepts a bool value and returns a string representation, as shown in Listing 5-29. This is the simplest of the functions described in Table 5-10 because it returns only true and false strings.

Listing 5-29. Formatting a Bool Value in the main.go File in the operations Folder

```
package main

import (
    "fmt"
    "strconv"
)

func main() {

    val1 := true
    val2 := false

    str1 := strconv.FormatBool(val1)
    str2 := strconv.FormatBool(val2)

    fmt.Println("Formatted value 1: " + str1)
    fmt.Println("Formatted value 2: " + str2)
}
```

Notice that I can use the + operator to concatenate the result from the FormatBool function with a literal string so that only a single argument is passed to the fmt.Println function. The code in Listing 5-29 produces the following output when compiled and executed:

```
Formatted value 1: true
Formatted value 2: false
```

Formatting Integer Values

The FormatInt and FormatUint functions format integer values as strings, as demonstrated in Listing 5-30.

Listing 5-30. Formatting an Integer in the main.go File in the operations Folder

```
package main

import (
    "fmt"
    "strconv"
)

func main() {

    val := 275

    base10String := strconv.FormatInt(int64(val), 10)
    base2String := strconv.FormatInt(int64(val), 2)

    fmt.Println("Base 10: " + base10String)
    fmt.Println("Base 2: " + base2String)
}
```

The FormatInt function accepts only int64 values, so I perform an explicit conversion and specify strings that express the value in base 10 (decimal) and base 2 (binary). The code produces the following output when compiled and executed:

```
Base 10: 275
Base 2: 100010011
```

Using the Integer Convenience Function

Integer values are most commonly represented using the int type and are converted to strings using base 10. The strconv package provides the Itoa function, which is a more convenient way to perform this specific conversion, as shown in Listing 5-31.

Listing 5-31. Using the Convenience Function in the main.go File in the operations Folder

```
package main
```

```
import (
    "fmt"
    "strconv"
)

func main() {

    val := 275

    base10String := strconv.Itoa(val)
    base2String := strconv.FormatInt(int64(val), 2)

    fmt.Println("Base 10: " + base10String)
    fmt.Println("Base 2: " + base2String)
}
```

The Itoa function accepts an int value, which is explicitly converted to an int64 and passed to the ParseInt function. The code in Listing 5-31 produces the following output:

```
Base 10: 275
Base 2: 100010011
```

Formatting Floating-Point Values

Expressing floating-point values as strings requires additional configuration options because different formats are available. Listing 5-32 shows a basic formatting operation using the FormatFloat function.

Listing 5-32. Converting a Floating-Point Number in the main.go File in the operations Folder

```
package main

import (
    "fmt"
    "strconv"
)

func main() {

    val := 49.95

    Fstring := strconv.FormatFloat(val, 'f', 2, 64)
    Estring := strconv.FormatFloat(val, 'e', -1, 64)

    fmt.Println("Format F: " + Fstring)
    fmt.Println("Format E: " + Estring)
}
```

The first argument to the FormatFloat function is the value to process. The second argument is a byte value, which specifies the format of the string. The byte is usually expressed as a rune literal value, and

Table 5-11 describes the most commonly used format runes. (As noted in Chapter 4, the byte type is an alias for uint8 and is often expressed using a rune for convenience.)

Table 5-11. *Commonly Used Format Options for Floating-Point String Formatting*

Function	Description
f	The floating-point value will be expressed in the form ±ddd.ddd without an exponent, such as 49.95.
e, E	The floating-point value will be expressed in the form ±ddd.ddd±dd, such as 4.995e+01 or 4.995E+01. The case of the letter denoting the exponent is determined by the case of the rune used as the formatting argument.
g, G	The floating-point value will be expressed using format e/E for large exponents or format f for smaller values.

The third argument to the FormatFloat function specifies the number of digits that will follow the decimal point. The special value -1 can be used to select the smallest number of digits that will create a string that can be parsed back into the same floating-point value without a loss of precision. The final argument determines whether the floating-point value is rounded so that it can be expressed as a float32 or a float64 value, using the value 32 or 64.

These arguments mean that this statement formats the value assigned to the variable named val, using the format option f, with two decimal places, and rounded so that the value can be represented using the float64 type:

```
...
Fstring := strconv.FormatFloat(val, 'f', 2, 64)
...
```

The effect is to format the value into a string that can be used to represent a currency amount. The code in Listing 5-32 produces the following output when compiled and executed:

```
Format F: 49.95
Format E: 4.995e+01
```

Summary

In this chapter, I introduced the Go operators and showed how they can be used to perform arithmetic, comparison, concatenation, and logical operations. I also described the different ways in which one type can be converted to another, using both features integrated into the Go language and functions that are part of the Go standard library. In the next chapter, I describe the Go flow control features.

CHAPTER 6

Flow Control

In this chapter, I describe the Go features for controlling the flow of execution. Go supports keywords that are common in other programming languages, such as if, for, switch, etc., but each has some unusual and innovative features. Table 6-1 puts the Go flow control features in context.

Table 6-1. *Putting Flow Control in Context*

Question	Answer
What is it?	Flow control allows a programmer to selectively execute statements.
Why is it useful?	Without flow control, an application executes a series of code statements in sequence and then exits. Flow control allows this sequence to be altered, deferring the execution of some statements and repeating the execution of others.
How is it used?	Go supports flow control keywords, including if, for, and switch, each of which controls the flow of execution differently.
Are there any pitfalls or limitations?	Go introduces unusual features for each of its flow control keywords that offer additional features, which must be used with care.
Are there any alternatives?	No. Flow control is a fundamental language feature.

Table 6-2 summarizes the chapter.

© Adam Freeman 2022

A. Freeman, *Pro Go*, https://doi.org/10.1007/978-1-4842-7355-5_6

Table 6-2. *Chapter Summary*

Problem	Solution	Listing
Conditionally execute statements	Use an if statement, with optional else if and else clauses and an initialization statement	4–10
Repeatedly execute statements	Use a for loop, with optional initialization and completion statements	11–13
Interrupt a loop	Use the continue or break keyword	14
Enumerate a sequence of values	Use a for loop with the range keyword	15–18
Perform complex comparisons to conditionally execute statements	Use a switch statement, with an optional initialization statement	19–21, 23–26
Force one case statement to flow into the next case statement	Use the fallthrough keyword	22
Specify a location to which execution should jump	Use a label	27

Preparing for This Chapter

To prepare for this chapter, open a new command prompt, navigate to a convenient location, and create a directory named flowcontrol. Navigate to the flowcontrol folder and run the command shown in Listing 6-1 to initialize the project.

■ **Tip** You can download the example project for this chapter—and for all the other chapters in this book—from https://github.com/apress/pro-go. See Chapter 2 for how to get help if you have problems running the examples.

Listing 6-1. Initializing the Project

```
go mod init flowcontrol
```

Add a file named main.go to the flowcontrol folder, with the contents shown in Listing 6-2.

Listing 6-2. The Contents of the main.go File in the flowcontrol Folder

```
package main

import "fmt"

func main() {

    kayakPrice := 275.00
    fmt.Println("Price:", kayakPrice)
}
```

Use the command prompt to run the command shown in Listing 6-3 in the `flowcontrol` folder.

Listing 6-3. Running the Example Project

```
go run .
```

The code in the `main.go` file will be compiled and executed, producing the following output:

```
Price: 275
```

Understanding Flow Control

The flow of execution in a Go application is simple to understand, especially when the application is as simple as the example. The statements defined in the special `main` function, known as the application's *entry point*, are executed in the order in which they are defined. Once these statements have all been executed, the application exits. Figure 6-1 illustrates the basic flow.

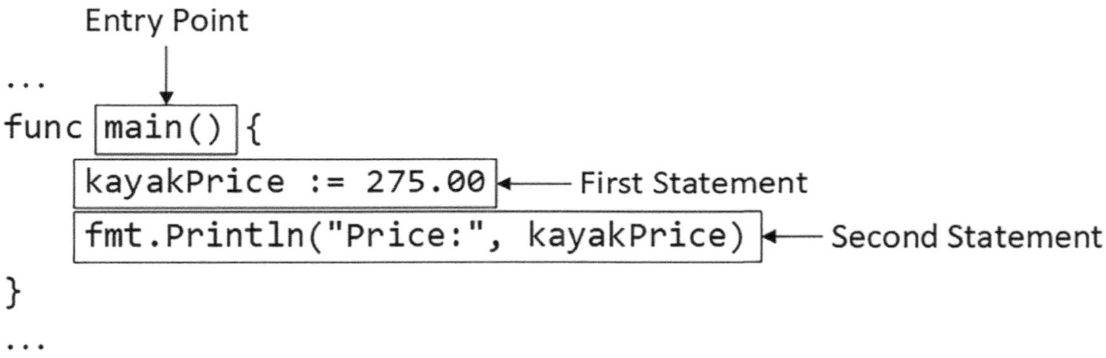

Figure 6-1. *The flow of execution*

After each statement is executed, the flow moves onto the next statement, and the process repeats until there are no statements left to execute.

There are applications where the basic flow of execution is exactly what is required, but, for most applications, the features described in the following sections are used to take control of the flow of execution to selectively execute statements.

Using if Statements

An `if` statement is used to execute a group of statements only when a specified expression produces the `bool` value `true` when it is evaluated, as shown in Listing 6-4.

Listing 6-4. Using an if Statement in the main.go File in the flowcontrol Folder

```
package main
```

```
import "fmt"

func main() {

    kayakPrice := 275.00

    if kayakPrice > 100 {
        fmt.Println("Price is greater than 100")
    }
}
```

The if keyword is followed by the expression and then the group of statements to be executed, surrounded by braces, as illustrated in Figure 6-2.

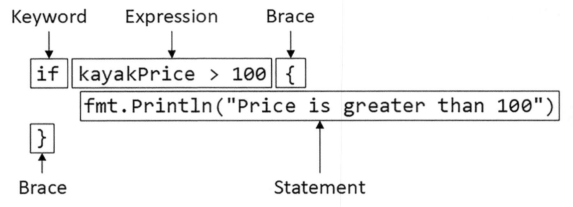

Figure 6-2. *The anatomy of an if statement*

The expression in Listing 6-4 uses the > operator to compare the value of the kayakPrice variable with the literal constant value 100. The expression evaluates to true, which means the statement contained in the braces is executed, producing the following output:

```
Price is greater than 100
```

I tend to enclose the expression in parentheses, as shown in Listing 6-5. Go doesn't require the parentheses, but I use them through habit.

Listing 6-5. Using Parentheses in the main.go File in the flowcontrol Folder

```
package main

import "fmt"

func main() {

    kayakPrice := 275.00
```

```
if (kayakPrice > 100) {
    fmt.Println("Price is greater than 100")
}
}
```

RESTRICTIONS ON FLOW CONTROL STATEMENT SYNTAX

Go is less flexible than other languages when it comes to the syntax for `if` statements and other flow control statements. First, the braces cannot be omitted even when there is only one statement in the code block, meaning this syntax is not allowed:

```
...
if (kayakPrice > 100)
    fmt.Println("Price is greater than 100")
...
```

Second, the opening brace must appear on the same line as the flow control keyword and cannot appear on the following line, meaning this syntax is not allowed either:

```
...
if (kayakPrice > 100)
{
    fmt.Println("Price is greater than 100")
}
...
```

Third, if you want to split a long expression onto multiple lines, you cannot break the line after a value or variable name:

```
...
if (kayakPrice > 100
        && kayakPrice < 500) {
    fmt.Println("Price is greater than 100 and less than 500")
}
...
```

The Go compiler will report an error for all of these statements, and the problem is the way that the build process tries to insert semicolons into the source code. There is no way to change this behavior, and it is the reason that some of the examples in this book are oddly formatted: some of the code statements contain more characters than can be displayed on a single line on the printed page, and I have had to split the statements carefully to avoid this issue.

Using the else Keyword

The else keyword can be used to create additional clauses in an if statement, as shown in Listing 6-6.

Listing 6-6. Using the else Keyword in the main.go File in the flowcontrol Folder

```
package main

import "fmt"

func main() {

    kayakPrice := 275.00

    if (kayakPrice > 500) {
        fmt.Println("Price is greater than 500")
    } else if (kayakPrice < 300) {
        fmt.Println("Price is less than 300")
    }
}
```

When the else keyword is combined with the if keyword, the code statements in the braces are executed only when the expression is true and the expression in the previous clause is false, as illustrated in Figure 6-3.

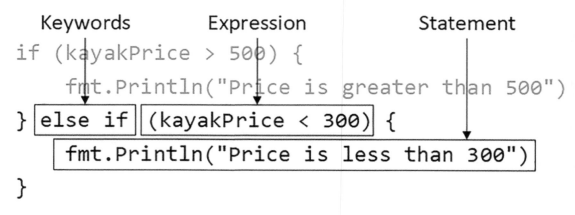

Figure 6-3. *An else/if clause in an if statement*

In Listing 6-6, the expression used in the if clause produces a false result and so execution moves on to the else/if expression, which produces a true result. The code in Listing 6-6 produces the following output when compiled and executed:

```
Price is less than 300
```

The else/if combination can be repeated to create a sequence of clauses, as shown in Listing 6-7, each of which will be executed only when all the earlier expressions have produced false.

Listing 6-7. Defining Multiple else/if Clauses in the main.go File in the flowcontrol Folder

```go
package main

import "fmt"

func main() {

    kayakPrice := 275.00

    if (kayakPrice > 500) {
        fmt.Println("Price is greater than 500")
    } else if (kayakPrice < 100) {
        fmt.Println("Price is less than 100")
    } else if (kayakPrice > 200 && kayakPrice < 300) {
        fmt.Println("Price is between 200 and 300")
    }
}
```

Execution works its way through the if statement, evaluating the expressions until a true value is obtained or until there are no more expressions to evaluate. The code in Listing 6-7 produces the following output when compiled and executed:

```
Price is between 200 and 300
```

The else keyword can also be used to create a fallback clause, whose statements will be executed only if all the if and else/if expressions in the statement produce false results, as shown in Listing 6-8.

Listing 6-8. Creating a Fallback Clause in the main.go File in the flowcontrol Folder

```go
package main

import "fmt"

func main() {

    kayakPrice := 275.00

    if (kayakPrice > 500) {
        fmt.Println("Price is greater than 500")
    } else if (kayakPrice < 100) {
        fmt.Println("Price is less than 100")
    } else {
        fmt.Println("Price not matched by earlier expressions")
    }
}
```

The fallback clause must be defined at the end of the statement and is specified with the else keyword without an expression, as illustrated by Figure 6-4.

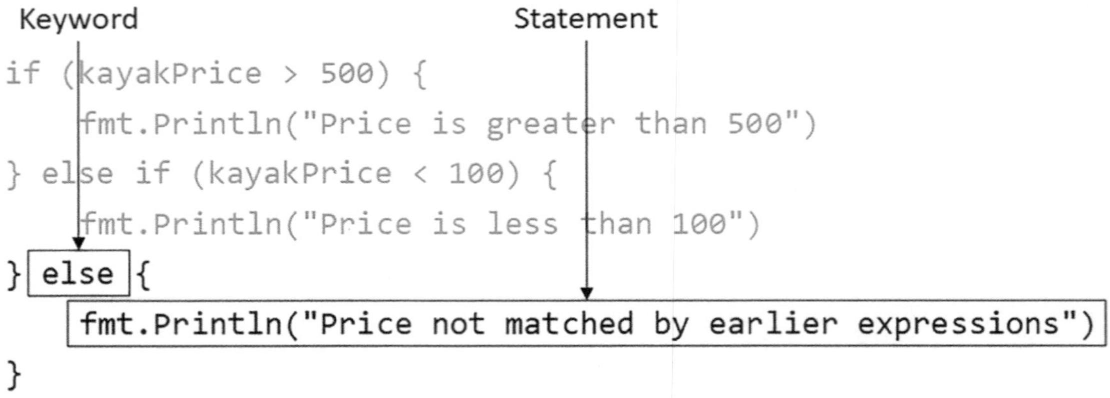

```
       Keyword                              Statement
if (kayakPrice > 500) {
    fmt.Println("Price is greater than 500")
} else if (kayakPrice < 100) {
    fmt.Println("Price is less than 100")
} else {
    fmt.Println("Price not matched by earlier expressions")
}
```

Figure 6-4. *A fallback clause in an if statement*

The code in Listing 6-8 produces the following output when compiled and executed:

```
Price not matched by earlier expressions
```

Understanding if Statement Scope

Each clause in an if statement has its own scope, which means that variables can be accessed only within the clause in which they are defined. It also means you can use the same variable name for different purposes in separate clauses, as shown in Listing 6-9.

Listing 6-9. Relying on Scopes in the main.go File in the flowcontrol Folder

```
package main

import "fmt"

func main() {

    kayakPrice := 275.00

    if (kayakPrice > 500) {
        scopedVar := 500
        fmt.Println("Price is greater than", scopedVar)
    } else if (kayakPrice < 100) {
        scopedVar := "Price is less than 100"
        fmt.Println(scopedVar)
    } else {
        scopedVar := false
        fmt.Println("Matched: ", scopedVar)
    }
}
```

Each clause in the if statement defines a variable named scopedVar, and each has a different type. Each variable is local to its clause, meaning that it cannot be accessed in other clauses or outside the if statement. The code in Listing 6-9 produces the following output when compiled and executed:

```
Matched:  false
```

Using an Initialization Statement with an if Statement

Go allows an if statement to use an initialization statement, which is executed before the if statement's expression is evaluated. The initialization statement is restricted to a Go simple statement, which means—in broad terms—that the statement can define a new variable, assign a new value to an existing variable, or invoke a function.

The most common use for this feature is to initialize a variable that is subsequently used in the expression, as shown in Listing 6-10.

Listing 6-10. Using an Initialization Statement in the main.go File in the flowcontrol Folder

```
package main

import (
    "fmt"
    "strconv"
)

func main() {

    priceString := "275"

    if kayakPrice, err := strconv.Atoi(priceString); err == nil {
        fmt.Println("Price:", kayakPrice)
    } else {
        fmt.Println("Error:", err)
    }
}
```

The if keyword is followed by the initialization statement and then a semicolon and the expression to evaluate, as illustrated by Figure 6-5.

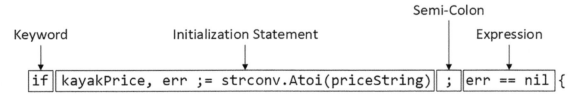

Figure 6-5. *Using an initialization statement*

The initialization statement in Listing 6-10 invokes the strconv.Atoi function, described in Chapter 5, to parse a string into an int value. Two values are returned by the function, which are assigned to variables named kayakPrice and err:

```
...
if kayakPrice, err := strconv.Atoi(priceString); err == nil {
...
```

The scope of variables defined by an initialization statement is the entire if statement, including the expression. The err variable is used in the if statement's expression to determine whether the string was parsed without error:

```
...
if kayakPrice, err := strconv.Atoi(priceString); err == nil {
...
```

The variables can also be used in the if clause and any else/if and else clauses:

```
...
if kayakPrice, err := strconv.Atoi(priceString); err == nil {
    fmt.Println("Price:", kayakPrice)
} else {
    fmt.Println("Error:", err)
}
...
```

The code in Listing 6-10 produces the following output when compiled and executed:

```
Price: 275
```

USING PARENTHESES WITH INITIALIZATION STATEMENTS

As I explained earlier, I tend to use parentheses to enclose the expressions in if statements. This is still possible when using an initialization statement, but you have to ensure that the parentheses are applied only to the expression, like this:

```
...
if kayakPrice, err := strconv.Atoi(priceString); (err == nil) {
...
```

The parentheses cannot be applied to the initialization statement or to enclose both parts of the statement.

Using for Loops

The for keyword is used to create loops that repeatedly execute statements. The most basic for loops will repeat indefinitely unless interrupted by the break keyword, as shown in Listing 6-11. (The return keyword can also be used to terminate a loop.)

Listing 6-11. Using a Basic Loop in the main.go File in the flowcontrol Folder

```
package main

import (
    "fmt"
    //"strconv"
)

func main() {

    counter := 0
    for {
        fmt.Println("Counter:", counter)
        counter++
        if (counter > 3) {
            break
        }
    }
}
```

The for keyword is followed by the statements to repeat, enclosed in braces, as illustrated by Figure 6-6. For most loops, one of the statements will be the break keyword, which terminates the loop.

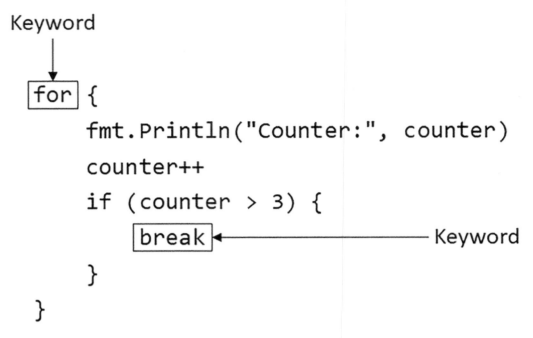

Figure 6-6. *A basic for loop*

The break keyword in Listing 6-11 is contained inside an if statement, which means that the loop isn't terminated until the if statement's expression produces a true value. The code in Listing 6-11 produces the following output when compiled and executed:

```
Counter: 0
Counter: 1
Counter: 2
Counter: 3
```

Incorporating the Condition into the Loop

The loop demonstrated in the previous section represents a common requirement, which is to repeat until a condition is reached. This is such a common requirement that the condition can be incorporated into the loop syntax, as shown in Listing 6-12.

Listing 6-12. Using a Loop Condition in the main.go File in the flowcontrol Folder

```go
package main

import (
    "fmt"
    //"strconv"
)
```

```
func main() {

    counter := 0
    for (counter <= 3) {
        fmt.Println("Counter:", counter)
        counter++
        // if (counter > 3) {
        //     break
        // }
    }
}
```

The condition is specified between the for keyword and the opening brace that encloses the loop's statements, as illustrated by Figure 6-7. Conditions can be enclosed in parentheses, as shown in the example, but this is not a requirement.

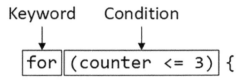

Figure 6-7. *A for loop condition*

The statements enclosed by the braces will be executed repeatedly while the condition evaluates to true. In this example, the condition produces true while the value of the counter variable is less than or equal to 3, and the code produces the following results when compiled and executed:

```
Counter: 0
Counter: 1
Counter: 2
Counter: 3
```

Using Initialization and Completion Statements

Loops can be defined with additional statements that are executed before the first iteration of the loop (known as the *initialization statement*) and after each iteration (the *post statement*), as shown in Listing 6-13.

■ **Tip** As with the if statement, parentheses can be applied to the condition of a for statement but not the initialization or post statements.

Listing 6-13. Using Optional Loop Statements in the main.go File in the flowcontrol Folder

```
package main

import (
    "fmt"
    //"strconv"
)

func main() {

    for counter := 0; counter <= 3; counter++ {
        fmt.Println("Counter:", counter)
        // counter++
    }
}
```

The initialization statement, the condition, and the post statement are separated by semicolons and follow the for keyword, as illustrated by Figure 6-8.

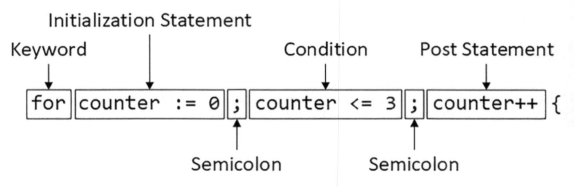

Figure 6-8. *A for loop with initialization and post statements*

The initialization statement is executed, after which the condition is evaluated. If the condition produces a true result, then the statements contained in the braces are executed, followed by the post statement. Then the condition is evaluated again, and the cycle repeats. This means the initialization statement is executed exactly once, and the post statement is executed once each time the condition produces a true result; if the condition produces a false result when it is first evaluated, then the post statement will never be executed. The code in Listing 6-13 produces the following output when compiled and executed:

```
Counter: 0
Counter: 1
Counter: 2
Counter: 3
```

CHAPTER 6 ■ FLOW CONTROL

RE-CREATING DO...WHILE LOOPS

Go doesn't provide a do...while loop, which is a feature provided by other programming languages to define a loop that is executed at least once, after which a condition is evaluated to determine whether subsequent iterations are required. Although awkward, a similar result can be achieved using a for loop, like this:

```
package main

import (
    "fmt"
)

func main() {

    for counter := 0; true; counter++ {
        fmt.Println("Counter:", counter)
        if (counter > 3) {
            break
        }
    }
}
```

The condition for the for loop is true, and subsequent iterations are controlled by the if statement, which uses the break keyword to terminate the loop.

Continuing Loops

The continue keyword can be used to terminate the execution of the for loop's statements for the current value and move to the next iteration, as shown in Listing 6-14.

Listing 6-14. Continuing a Loop in the main.go File in the flowcontrol Folder

```
package main

import (
    "fmt"
    //"strconv"
)

func main() {

    for counter := 0; counter <= 3; counter++ {
        if (counter == 1) {
            continue
        }
        fmt.Println("Counter:", counter)
    }
}
```

The if statement ensures the `continue` keyword is reached only when the value of the counter value is 1. For this value, execution will not reach the statement that calls the `fmt.Println` function, producing the following output when the code is compiled and executed:

```
Counter: 0
Counter: 2
Counter: 3
```

Enumerating Sequences

The `for` keyword can be used with the `range` keyword to create loops that enumerate over sequences, as shown in Listing 6-15.

Listing 6-15. Using the range Keyword in the main.go File in the flowcontrol Folder

```go
package main

import (
    "fmt"
    //"strconv"
)

func main() {

    product := "Kayak"

    for index, character := range product {
        fmt.Println("Index:", index, "Character:", string(character))
    }
}
```

This example enumerates a string, which the `for` loop treats as a sequence of rune values, each of which represents a character. Each iteration of the loop assigns values to two variables, which provide the current index into the sequence and the value at the current index, as illustrated by Figure 6-9.

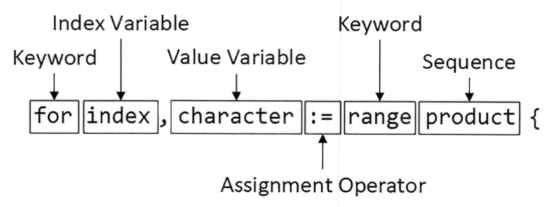

Figure 6-9. *Enumerating a sequence*

The statements contained in the for loop's braces are executed once for each item in the sequence. These statements can read the value of the two variables, providing access to the sequence's elements. For Listing 6-15, this means that the statements in the loop are given access to the individual characters contained in the string, producing the following output when compiled and executed:

```
Index: 0 Character: K
Index: 1 Character: a
Index: 2 Character: y
Index: 3 Character: a
Index: 4 Character: k
```

Receiving Only Indices or Values When Enumerating Sequences

Go will report an error if a variable is defined but not used. You can omit the value variable from the for... range statement if you require only the index values, as shown in Listing 6-16.

Listing 6-16. Receiving Index Values in the main.go File in the flowcontrol Folder

```
package main

import (
    "fmt"
    //"strconv"
)

func main() {

    product := "Kayak"

    for index := range product {
        fmt.Println("Index:", index)
    }
}
```

The for loop in this example will generate a sequence of index values for each character in the product string, producing the following output when compiled and executed:

```
Index: 0
Index: 1
Index: 2
Index: 3
Index: 4
```

The blank identifier can be used when you require only the values in the sequence and not the indices, as shown in Listing 6-17.

Listing 6-17. Receiving Values in the main.go File in the flowcontrol Folder

```
package main

import (
    "fmt"
    //"strconv"
)

func main() {

    product := "Kayak"

    for _, character := range product {
        fmt.Println("Character:", string(character))
    }
}
```

The blank identifier (the _ character) is used for the index variable, and a regular variable is used for values. The code in Listing 6-17 produces the following code when compiled and executed:

```
Character: K
Character: a
Character: y
Character: a
Character: k
```

Enumerating Built-in Data Structures

The range keyword can also be used with the built-in data structures that Go provides—arrays, slices, and maps—all of which are described in Chapter 7, including examples using the for and range keywords. For quick reference, Listing 6-18 shows a for loop that uses the range keyword to enumerate the contents of an array.

Listing 6-18. Enumerating an Array in the main.go File in the flowcontrol Folder

```
package main

import (
    "fmt"
    //"strconv"
)

func main() {

    products := []string { "Kayak", "Lifejacket", "Soccer Ball"}
```

```
for index, element:= range products {
    fmt.Println("Index:", index, "Element:", element)
}
}
```

This example uses the literal syntax for defining arrays, which are fixed-length collections of values. (Go also has built-in variable-length collections, known as *slices*, and key-value maps.) This array contains three string values, and the current index and element are assigned to the two variables each time the for loop is executed, producing the following output when the code is compiled and executed:

```
Index: 0 Element: Kayak
Index: 1 Element: Lifejacket
Index: 2 Element: Soccer Ball
```

Using switch Statements

A switch statement provides an alternative way to control execution flow, based on matching the result of an expression to a specific value, as opposed to evaluating a true or false result, as shown in Listing 6-19. This can be a concise way to perform multiple comparisons, providing a less verbose alternative to a complex if/elseif/else statement.

■ **Note** The switch statement can also be used to differentiate between data types, which is described in Chapter 11.

Listing 6-19. Using a switch Statement in the main.go File in the flowcontrol Folder

```go
package main

import (
    "fmt"
    //"strconv"
)

func main() {

    product := "Kayak"

    for index, character := range product {
        switch (character) {
            case 'K':
                fmt.Println("K at position", index)
            case 'y':
                fmt.Println("y at position", index)
        }
    }
}
```

The switch keyword is followed by a value or expression that produces a result used for the comparison. Comparisons are made against a series of case statements, each of which specifies a value, as illustrated by Figure 6-10.

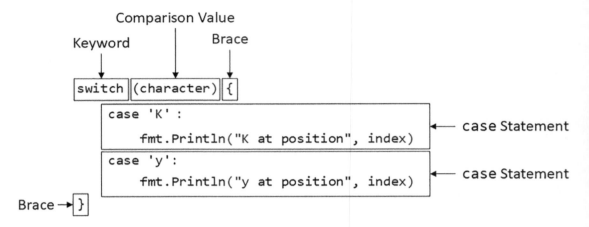

Figure 6-10. *A basic switch statement*

In Listing 6-19, the switch statement is used to inspect each character produced by a for loop applied to a string value, producing a sequence of rune values, with case statements used to match specific characters.

The case keyword is followed by a value, a colon, and one or more statements to execute when the comparison value matches the case statement value, as illustrated in Figure 6-11.

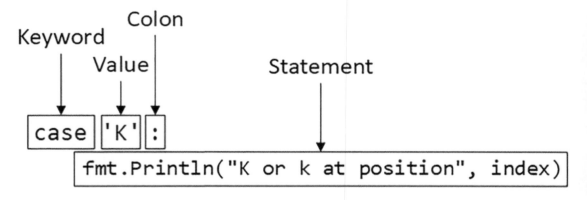

Figure 6-11. *The anatomy of a case statement*

This case statement matches the rune K and, when matched, will execute a statement that calls the fmt. Println function. Compiling and executing the code in Listing 6-19 produces the following output:

```
K at position 0
y at position 2
```

136

Matching Multiple Values

In some languages, switch statements "fall through," which means that once a match is made by a case statement, statements are executed until a break statement is reached, even if that means executing statements from a subsequent case statement. Falling through is often used to allow multiple case statements to execute the same code, but it requires diligent use of the break keyword to stop execution from running on unexpectedly.

Go switch statements do not fall through automatically, but multiple values can be specified with a comma-separated list, as shown in Listing 6-20.

Listing 6-20. Using Multiple Values in the main.go File in the flowcontrol Folder

```
package main

import (
    "fmt"
    //"strconv"
)

func main() {

    product := "Kayak"

    for index, character := range product {
        switch (character) {
            case 'K', 'k':
                fmt.Println("K or k at position", index)
            case 'y':
                fmt.Println("y at position", index)
        }
    }
}
```

The set of values that should be matched by the case statement is expressed as a comma-separated list, as illustrated in Figure 6-12.

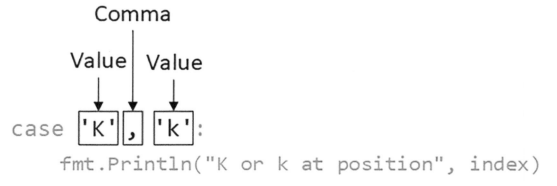

Figure 6-12. Specifying multiple values in a case statement

137

The case statement will match any of the specified values, producing the following output when the code in Listing 6-20 is compiled and executed:

```
K or k at position 0
y at position 2
K or k at position 4
```

Terminate case Statement Execution

Although the break keyword isn't required to terminate every case statement, it can be used to end the execution of statements before the end of the case statement is reached, as shown in Listing 6-21.

Listing 6-21. Using the break Keyword in the main.go File in the flowcontrol Folder

```
package main

import (
    "fmt"
    //"strconv"
)

func main() {

    product := "Kayak"

    for index, character := range product {
        switch (character) {
            case 'K', 'k':
                if (character == 'k') {
                    fmt.Println("Lowercase k at position", index)
                    break
                }
                fmt.Println("Uppercase K at position", index)
            case 'y':
                fmt.Println("y at position", index)
        }
    }
}
```

The if statement checks to see whether the current rune is a k and, if it is, calls the fmt.Println function and then uses the break keyword to halt the execution of the case statement, preventing any subsequent statements from being executed. Listing 6-21 produces the following output when compiled and executed:

```
Uppercase K at position 0
y at position 2
Lowercase k at position 4
```

Forcing Falling Through to the Next case Statement

Go switch statements don't automatically fall through, but this behavior can be enabled using the fallthrough keyword, as shown in Listing 6-22.

Listing 6-22. Falling Through in the main.go File in the flowcontrol Folder

```go
package main

import (
    "fmt"
    //"strconv"
)

func main() {

    product := "Kayak"

    for index, character := range product {
        switch (character) {
            case 'K':
                fmt.Println("Uppercase character")
                fallthrough
            case 'k':
                fmt.Println("k at position", index)
            case 'y':
                fmt.Println("y at position", index)
        }
    }
}
```

The first case statement contains the fallthrough keyword, which means that execution will continue to the statements in the next case statement. The code in Listing 6-22 produces the following output when compiled and executed:

```
Uppercase character
k at position 0
y at position 2
k at position 4
```

Providing a default Clause

The default keyword is used to define a clause that will be executed when none of the case statements matches the switch statement's value, as shown in Listing 6-23.

Listing 6-23. Adding a default Clause in the main.go File in the flowcontrol Folder

```go
package main

import (
    "fmt"
    //"strconv"
)

func main() {

    product := "Kayak"

    for index, character := range product {
        switch (character) {
            case 'K', 'k':
                if (character == 'k') {
                    fmt.Println("Lowercase k at position", index)
                    break
                }
                fmt.Println("Uppercase K at position", index)
            case 'y':
                fmt.Println("y at position", index)
            default:
                fmt.Println("Character", string(character), "at position", index)
        }
    }
}
```

The statements in the default clause will be executed only for values that are not matched by a case statement. In this example, the K, k, and y characters are matched by case statements, so the default clause will be used only for other characters. The code in Listing 6-23 produces the following output:

```
Uppercase K at position 0
Character a at position 1
y at position 2
Character a at position 3
Lowercase k at position 4
```

Using an Initialization Statement

A switch statement can be defined with an initialization statement, which can be a helpful way of preparing the comparison value so that it can be referenced within case statements. Listing 6-24 demonstrates a problem that is common in switch statements where an expression is used to produce the comparison value.

Listing 6-24. Using an Expression in the main.go File in the flowcontrol Folder

```
package main

import (
    "fmt"
    //"strconv"
)

func main() {

    for counter := 0; counter < 20; counter++ {
        switch(counter / 2) {
            case 2, 3, 5, 7:
                fmt.Println("Prime value:", counter / 2)
            default:
                fmt.Println("Non-prime value:", counter / 2)
        }
    }
}
```

The switch statement applies the division operator to the value of the counter variable to produce its comparison value, which means that the same operation must be performed in the case statements to pass the matched value to the fmt.Println function. The duplication can be avoided using an initialization statement, as shown in Listing 6-25.

Listing 6-25. Using an Initialization Statement in the main.go File in the flowcontrol Folder

```
package main

import (
    "fmt"
    //"strconv"
)

func main() {

    for counter := 0; counter < 20; counter++ {
        switch val := counter / 2; val {
            case 2, 3, 5, 7:
                fmt.Println("Prime value:", val)
            default:
                fmt.Println("Non-prime value:", val)
        }
    }
}
```

The initialization statement follows the switch keyword and is separated from the comparison value by a semicolon, as illustrated in Figure 6-13.

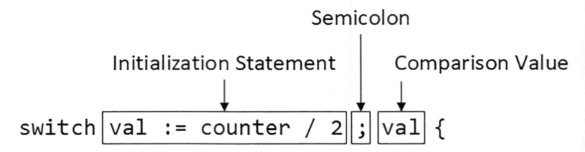

Figure 6-13. *A switch statement initialization statement*

The initialization statement creates a variable named val using the division operator. This means that val can be used as the comparison value and can be accessed within the case statements, avoiding the need to repeat the operation. Listing 6-24 and Listing 6-25 are equivalent, and both produce the following output when compiled and executed:

```
Non-prime value: 0
Non-prime value: 0
Non-prime value: 1
Non-prime value: 1
Prime value: 2
Prime value: 2
Prime value: 3
Prime value: 3
Non-prime value: 4
Non-prime value: 4
Prime value: 5
Prime value: 5
Non-prime value: 6
Non-prime value: 6
Prime value: 7
Prime value: 7
Non-prime value: 8
Non-prime value: 8
Non-prime value: 9
Non-prime value: 9
```

Omitting a Comparison Value

Go offers a different approach for switch statements, which omits the comparison value and uses expressions in the case statements. This reinforces the idea that switch statements are a concise alternative to if statements, as shown in Listing 6-26.

CHAPTER 6 ■ FLOW CONTROL

Listing 6-26. Using Expressions in a switch Statement in the main.go File in the flowcontrol Folder

```
package main

import (
    "fmt"
    //"strconv"
)

func main() {

    for counter := 0; counter < 10; counter++ {
        switch {
            case counter == 0:
                fmt.Println("Zero value")
            case counter < 3:
                fmt.Println(counter, "is < 3")
            case counter >= 3 && counter < 7:
                fmt.Println(counter, "is >= 3 && < 7")
            default:
                fmt.Println(counter, "is >= 7")
        }
    }
}
```

When the comparison value is omitted, each case statement is specified with a condition. When the switch statement is executed, each condition is evaluated until one produces a true result or until the optional default clause is reached. Listing 6-26 produces the following output when the project is compiled and executed:

```
Zero value
1 is < 3
2 is < 3
3 is >= 3 && < 7
4 is >= 3 && < 7
5 is >= 3 && < 7
6 is >= 3 && < 7
7 is >= 7
8 is >= 7
9 is >= 7
```

Using Label Statements

Label statements allow execution to jump to a different point, giving greater flexibility than other flow control features. Listing 6-27 shows the use of a label statement.

143

Listing 6-27. Using a Label Statement in the main.go File in the flowcontrol Folder

```
package main

import (
    "fmt"
    //"strconv"
)

func main() {

    counter := 0
    target: fmt.Println("Counter", counter)
    counter++
    if (counter < 5) {
        goto target
    }
}
```

Labels are defined with a name, followed by a colon and then a regular code statement, as shown in Figure 6-14. The goto keyword is used to jump to a label.

■ **Tip** There are restrictions on when you can jump to a label, such as not being able to jump into a case statement from outside of its enclosing switch statement.

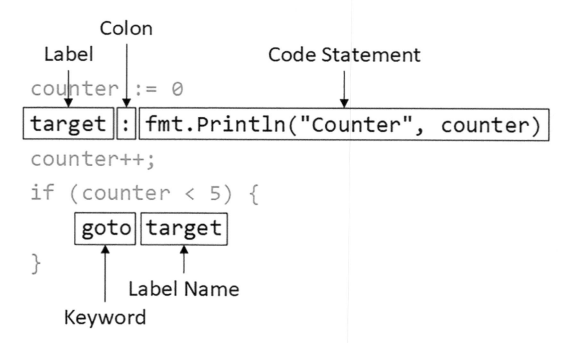

Figure 6-14. Labeling a statement

The name assigned to the label in this example is `target`. When execution reaches the goto keyword, it jumps to the statement with the specified label. The effect is a basic loop that causes the value of the `counter` variable to be incremented while it is less than 5. Listing 6-27 produces the following output when compiled and executed:

```
Counter 0
Counter 1
Counter 2
Counter 3
Counter 4
```

Summary

In this chapter, I described the Go flow control features. I explained how to conditionally execute statements with `if` and `switch` statements and how to repeatedly execute statements with a `for` loop. As this chapter has shown, Go has fewer flow control keywords than other languages, but each has additional features, such as initialization statements and support for the `range` keyword. In the next chapter, I describe the Go collection types: the array, the slice, and the map.

CHAPTER 7

■ ■ ■

Using Arrays, Slices, and Maps

In this chapter, I describe the built-in Go collection types: arrays, slices, and maps. These features allow related values to be grouped and, just as with other features, Go takes a different approach to collections when compared with other languages. I also describe an unusual aspect of Go string values, which can be treated like arrays, but behave in different ways depending on how the elements are used. Table 7-1 puts arrays, slices, and maps in context.

Table 7-1. *Putting Arrays, Slices, and Maps in Context*

Question	Answer
What are they?	The Go collection classes are used to group related values. Arrays store fixed numbers of values, slices store variable numbers of values, and maps store key-value pairs.
Why are they useful?	These collection classes are a convenient way to keep track of related data values.
How are they used?	Each collection type can be used with a literal syntax or using the make function.
Are there any pitfalls or limitations?	Care must be taken to understand the effect operations performed on slices have on the underlying array to avoid unexpected results.
Are there any alternatives?	You do not have to use any of these types, but doing so makes most programming tasks easier.

Table 7-2 summarizes the chapter.

Table 7-2. *Chapter Summary*

Problem	Solution	Listing
Store a fixed number of values	Use an array	4–8
Compare arrays	Use the comparison operators	9
Enumerate an array	Use a for loop with the range keyword	10, 11
Store a variable number of values	Use a slice	12–13, 16, 17, 23
Append an item to a slice	Use the append function	14–15, 18, 20–22

(continued)

© Adam Freeman 2022
A. Freeman, *Pro Go*, https://doi.org/10.1007/978-1-4842-7355-5_7

Table 7-2. (*continued*)

Problem	Solution	Listing
Create a slice from an existing array or select elements from a slice	Use a range	19, 24
Copy elements into a slice	Use the copy function	25, 29
Delete elements from a slice	Use the append function with ranges that omit the elements to remove	30
Enumerate a slice	Use a for loop with the range keyword	31
Sort the elements in a slice	Use the sort package	32
Compare slices	Use the reflect package	33, 34
Obtain a pointer to the array underlying a slice	Perform an explicit conversion to an array type whose length is less than or equal to the number of elements in the slice	35
Store key-value pairs	Use a map	36–40
Remove a key-value pair from a map	Use the delete function	41
Enumerate the contents of a map	Use a for loop with the range keyword	42, 43
Read byte values or characters from a string	Use the string as an array or perform an explicit conversion to the [ ]rune type	44–48
Enumerate the characters in a string	Use a for loop with the range keyword	49
Enumerate the bytes in a string	Perform an explicit conversion to the [ ]byte type and use a for loop with the range keyword	50

Preparing for This Chapter

To prepare for this chapter, open a new command prompt, navigate to a convenient location, and create a directory named collections. Navigate to the collections folder and run the command shown in Listing 7-1 to initialize the project.

Listing 7-1. Initializing the Project

```
go mod init collections
```

Add a file named main.go to the collections folder, with the contents shown in Listing 7-2.

■ **Tip** You can download the example project for this chapter—and for all the other chapters in this book—from https://github.com/apress/pro-go. See Chapter 2 for how to get help if you have problems running the examples.

Listing 7-2. The Contents of the main.go File in the collections Folder

```
package main

import "fmt"

func main() {

    fmt.Println("Hello, Collections")
}
```

Use the command prompt to run the command shown in Listing 7-3 in the collections folder.

Listing 7-3. Running the Example Project

```
go run .
```

The code in the main.go file will be compiled and executed, producing the following output:

```
Hello, Collections
```

Working with Arrays

Go arrays are a fixed length and contain elements of a single type, which are accessed by index, as shown in Listing 7-4.

Listing 7-4. Defining and Using Arrays in the main.go File in the collections Folder

```
package main

import "fmt"

func main() {

    var names [3]string

    names[0] = "Kayak"
    names[1] = "Lifejacket"
    names[2] = "Paddle"

    fmt.Println(names)
}
```

Array types include the size of the array in square brackets, followed by the type of element that the array will contain, known as the *underlying type*, as illustrated in Figure 7-1. The length and element type of an array cannot be changed, and the array length must be specified as a constant. (Slices, described later in this chapter, store a variable number of values.)

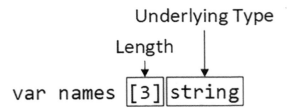

Figure 7-1. Defining an array

The array is created and populated with the zero value for the element type. For this example, the names array will be populated with the empty string (""), which is the zero value for the string type. The elements in an array are accessed using zero-based index notation, as illustrated by Figure 7-2.

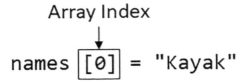

Figure 7-2. Accessing an array element

The final statement in Listing 7-4 passes the array to fmt.Println, which creates a string representation of the array and writes it to the console, producing the following output when the code is compiled and executed:

```
[Kayak Lifejacket Paddle]
```

Using the Array Literal Syntax

Arrays can be defined and populated in a single statement using the literal syntax shown in Listing 7-5.

Listing 7-5. Using the Array Literal Syntax in the main.go File in the collections Folder

```
package main

import "fmt"

func main() {

    names := [3]string { "Kayak", "Lifejacket", "Paddle" }

    fmt.Println(names)
}
```

The array type is followed by curly braces containing the elements that will populate the array, illustrated in Figure 7-3.

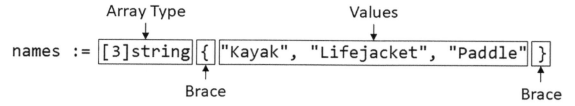

Figure 7-3. *The literal array syntax*

■ **Tip**   The number of elements specified with the literal syntax can be less than the capacity of the array. Any position in the array for which a value is not provided will be assigned the zero value for the array type.

The code in Listing 7-5 produces the following output when compiled and executed:

```
[Kayak Lifejacket Paddle]
```

CREATING MULTIDIMENSIONAL ARRAYS

Go arrays are one-dimensional but can be combined to create multidimensional arrays, like this:

```
...
var coords [3][3]int
...
```

This statement creates an array whose capacity is 3 and whose underlying type is an `int` array also with a capacity of 3, producing a 3×3 array of `int` values. Individual values are specified using two index positions like this:

```
...
coords[1][2] = 10
...
```

The syntax is a little awkward, especially for arrays with more dimensions, but it is functional and maintains consistency with the approach Go takes for arrays.

Understanding Array Types

The type of an array is the combination of its size and underlying type. Here is the statement from Listing 7-5 that defines an array:

```
...
names := [3]string { "Kayak", "Lifejacket", "Paddle" }
...
```

The type of names variable is [3]string, meaning an array whose underlying type is string and whose capacity is 3. Each combination of underlying type and capacity is a distinct type, as Listing 7-6 demonstrates.

Listing 7-6. Working with Array Types in the main.go File in the collections Folder

```
package main

import "fmt"

func main() {

    names := [3]string { "Kayak", "Lifejacket", "Paddle" }

    var otherArray [4]string = names

    fmt.Println(names)
}
```

The underlying types of the two arrays in this example are the same, but the compiler will report an error, even though the capacity of otherArray is sufficient to accommodate the elements from the names array. Here is the error that the compiler produces:

```
.\main.go:9:9: cannot use names (type [3]string) as type [4]string in assignment
```

LETTING THE COMPILER DETERMINE THE ARRAY LENGTH

When using the literal syntax, the compiler can infer the length of the array from the list of elements, like this:

```
...
names := [...]string { "Kayak", "Lifejacket", "Paddle" }
...
```

The explicit length is replaced with three periods (...), which tells the compiler to determine the array length from the literal values. The type of the names variable is still [3]string, and the only difference is that you can add or remove literal values without also having to update the explicitly specified length. I don't use this feature for the examples in this book because I want to make the types used as clear as possible.

Understanding Array Values

As I explained in Chapter 4, Go works with values, rather than references, by default. This behavior extends to arrays, which means that assigning an array to a new variable copies the array and copies the values it contains, as shown in Listing 7-7.

Listing 7-7. Assigning an Array to a New Variable in the main.go File in the collections Folder

```
package main

import "fmt"

func main() {

    names := [3]string { "Kayak", "Lifejacket", "Paddle" }

    otherArray := names

    names[0] = "Canoe"

    fmt.Println("names:", names)
    fmt.Println("otherArray:", otherArray)
}
```

In this example, I assign the names array to a new variable named otherArray and then change the value at index zero of the names array before writing out both arrays. The code produces the following output when compiled and executed, showing that the array and its contents were copied:

```
names: [Canoe Lifejacket Paddle]
otherArray: [Kayak Lifejacket Paddle]
```

A pointer can be used to create a reference to an array, as shown in Listing 7-8.

Listing 7-8. Using a Pointer to an Array in the main.go File in the collections Folder

```
package main

import "fmt"

func main() {

    names := [3]string { "Kayak", "Lifejacket", "Paddle" }

    otherArray := &names

    names[0] = "Canoe"

    fmt.Println("names:", names)
    fmt.Println("otherArray:", *otherArray)
}
```

153

The type of the otherArray variable is *[3]string, denoting a pointer to an array with the capacity to store three string values. An array pointer works just like any other pointer and must be followed to access the array contents. The code in Listing 7-8 produces the following output when compiled and executed:

```
names: [Canoe Lifejacket Paddle]
otherArray: [Canoe Lifejacket Paddle]
```

You can also create arrays that contain pointers, which means the values in the array are not copied when the array is copied. And, as I demonstrated in Chapter 4, you can create pointers to specific positions in the array, which will provide access to the value at that location, even if the contents of the array are changed.

Comparing Arrays

The comparison operators == and != can be applied to arrays, as shown in Listing 7-9.

Listing 7-9. Comparing Arrays in the main.go File in the collections Folder

```
package main

import "fmt"

func main() {

    names := [3]string { "Kayak", "Lifejacket", "Paddle" }
    moreNames := [3]string { "Kayak", "Lifejacket", "Paddle" }

    same := names == moreNames

    fmt.Println("comparison:", same)
}
```

Arrays are equal if they are of the same type and contain equal elements in the same order. The names and moreNames arrays are equal because they are both [3]string arrays and because they contain the same string values. The code in Listing 7-9 produces the following output:

```
comparison: true
```

Enumerating Arrays

Arrays are enumerated using the for and range keywords, as shown in Listing 7-10.

Listing 7-10. Enumerating an Array in the main.go File in the collections Folder

```
package main

import "fmt"

func main() {

    names := [3]string { "Kayak", "Lifejacket", "Paddle" }

    for index, value := range names {
        fmt.Println("Index:", index, "Value:", value)
    }
}
```

I described for loops in detail in Chapter 6, but when used with the range keyword, the for keyword enumerates the contents of an array, producing two values for each element as the array is enumerated, as illustrated by Figure 7-4.

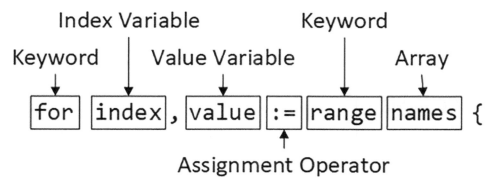

Figure 7-4. *Enumerating an array*

The first value, which is assigned to the index variable in Listing 7-10, is assigned the array location that is being enumerated. The second value, which is assigned to the variable named value in Listing 7-10, is assigned the element at the current location. The listing produces the following output when compiled and executed:

```
Index: 0 Value: Kayak
Index: 1 Value: Lifejacket
Index: 2 Value: Paddle
```

Go doesn't allow variables to be defined and not used. If you don't need both the index and the value, you can use an underscore (the _ character) instead of a variable name, as shown in Listing 7-11.

Listing 7-11. Discarding the Current Index in the main.go File in the collections Folder

```
package main

import "fmt"

func main() {

    names := [3]string { "Kayak", "Lifejacket", "Paddle" }

    for _, value := range names {
        fmt.Println("Value:", value)
    }
}
```

The underscore is known as the *blank identifier* and is used when a feature returns values that are not subsequently used and for which a name should not be assigned. The code in Listing 7-11 discards the current index as the array is enumerated and produces the following output:

```
Value: Kayak
Value: Lifejacket
Value: Paddle
```

Working with Slices

The best way to think of slices is as a variable-length array because they are useful when you don't know how many values you need to store or when the number changes over time. One way to define a slice is to use the built-in make function, as shown in Listing 7-12.

Listing 7-12. Defining a Slice in the main.go File in the collections Folder

```
package main

import "fmt"

func main() {

    names := make([]string, 3)

    names[0] = "Kayak"
    names[1] = "Lifejacket"
    names[2] = "Paddle"

    fmt.Println(names)
}
```

The make function accepts arguments that specify the type and length of the slice, as shown in Figure 7-5.

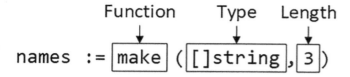

Figure 7-5. *Creating a new slice*

The slice type in this example is [ ]string, which denotes a slice that holds string values. The length is not part of the slice type because the size of slices can vary, as I demonstrate later in this section. Slices can also be created using a literal syntax, as shown in Listing 7-13.

Listing 7-13. Using the Literal Syntax in the main.go File in the collections Folder

```
package main

import "fmt"

func main() {

    names := []string {"Kayak", "Lifejacket", "Paddle"}

    fmt.Println(names)
}
```

The slice literal syntax is similar to the one used for arrays, and the initial length of the slice is inferred from the number of literal values, as illustrated by Figure 7-6.

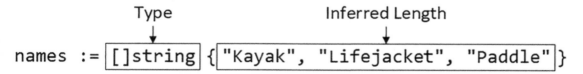

Figure 7-6. *Using the slice literal syntax*

The combination of the slice type and the length is used to create an array, which acts as the data store for the slice. The slice is a data structure that contains three values: a pointer to the array, the length of the slice, and the capacity of the slice. The length of the slice is the number of elements that it can store, and the capacity is the number of elements that can be stored in the array. In this example, the length and the capacity are both 3, as shown in Figure 7-7.

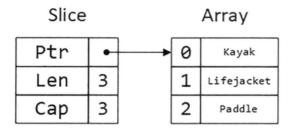

Figure 7-7. *A slice and its backing array*

157

Slices support array-style index notation, which provides access to the elements in the underlying array. Although Figure 7-7 is a more realistic representation of a slice, Figure 7-8 shows the way that the slice is mapped into its array.

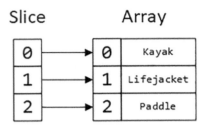

Figure 7-8. *A slice and its backing array*

The mapping between this slice and its array is simple, but slices don't always have such a direct mapping to their array, as later examples demonstrate. The code in Listing 7-12 and Listing 7-13 produces the following output when compiled and executed:

```
[Kayak Lifejacket Paddle]
```

Appending Elements to a Slice

One of the key advantages of slices is that they can be expanded to accommodate additional elements, as shown in Listing 7-14.

Listing 7-14. Appending Elements to a Slice in the main.go File in the collections Folder

```
package main

import "fmt"

func main() {

    names := []string {"Kayak", "Lifejacket", "Paddle"}

    names = append(names, "Hat", "Gloves")

    fmt.Println(names)
}
```

The built-in append function accepts a slice and one or more elements to add to the slice, separated by commas, as illustrated by Figure 7-9.

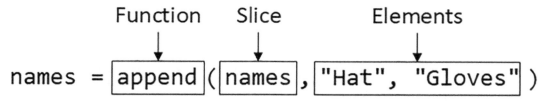

Figure 7-9. *Appending elements to a slice*

The append function creates an array that is large enough to accommodate the new elements, copies the existing array, and adds the new values. The result from the append function is a slice that is mapped onto the new array, as shown by Figure 7-10.

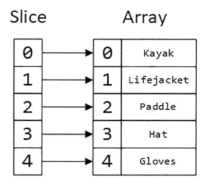

Figure 7-10. *The result of appending elements to a slice*

The code in Listing 7-14 produces the following output when compiled and executed, showing the addition of the two new elements to the slice:

```
[Kayak Lifejacket Paddle Hat Gloves]
```

The original slice—and its backing array—still exists and can be used, as Listing 7-15 demonstrates.

Listing 7-15. Appending Items to a Slice in the main.go File in the collections Folder

```
package main

import "fmt"

func main() {

    names := []string {"Kayak", "Lifejacket", "Paddle"}

    appendedNames := append(names, "Hat", "Gloves")

    names[0] = "Canoe"
```

```
fmt.Println("names:", names)
fmt.Println("appendedNames:", appendedNames)
}
```

In this example, the result from the append function is assigned to a different variable, with the effect that there are two slices, one of which was created from the other. Each slice has a backing array, and the slices are independent. The code in Listing 7-15 produces the following output when compiled and executed, showing that changing a value using one slice does not affect the other slice:

```
names: [Canoe Lifejacket Paddle]
appendedNames: [Kayak Lifejacket Paddle Hat Gloves]
```

Allocating Additional Slice Capacity

Creating and copying arrays can be inefficient. If you expect that you will need to append items to a slice, you can specify additional capacity when using the make function, as shown in Listing 7-16.

Listing 7-16. Allocating Additional Capacity in the main.go File in the collections Folder

```
package main

import "fmt"

func main() {

    names := make([]string, 3, 6)

    names[0] = "Kayak"
    names[1] = "Lifejacket"
    names[2] = "Paddle"

    fmt.Println("len:", len(names))
    fmt.Println("cap:", cap(names))
}
```

As noted earlier, slices have a *length* and a *capacity*. The length of a slice is how many values it can currently contain, while the number of elements that can be stored in the underlying array before the slice must be resized and a new array created. The capacity will always be at least the length but can be larger if additional capacity has been allocated with the make function. The call to the make function in Listing 7-16 creates a slice with a length of 3 and a capacity of 6, as illustrated by Figure 7-11.

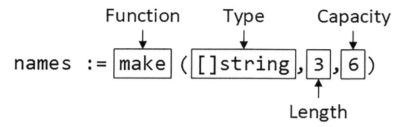

Figure 7-11. *Allocating additional capacity*

■ **Tip** You can also use the len and cap functions on standard fixed-length arrays. Both functions will return the length of the array, such that for an array whose type is [3]string, for example, both functions will return 3. See the "Using the copy Function" section for an example.

The built-in len and cap functions return the length and capacity of a slice. The code in Listing 7-16 produces the following output when compiled and executed:

```
len: 3
cap: 6
```

The effect is that the backing array for the slice has some room to grow, as shown in Figure 7-12.

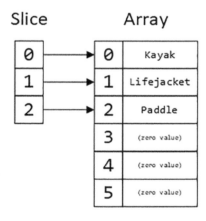

Figure 7-12. *A slice whose backing array has additional capacity*

The underlying array isn't replaced when the append function is called on a slice with enough capacity to accommodate the new elements, as shown in Listing 7-17.

■ **Caution** If you define a slice variable but don't initialize it, then the result is a slice that has a length of zero and a capacity of zero, and this will cause an error when an element is appended to it.

Listing 7-17. Adding Elements to a Slice in the main.go File in the collections Folder

```
package main

import "fmt"

func main() {

    names := make([]string, 3, 6)

    names[0] = "Kayak"
    names[1] = "Lifejacket"
    names[2] = "Paddle"

    appendedNames := append(names, "Hat", "Gloves")

    names[0] = "Canoe"

    fmt.Println("names:",names)
    fmt.Println("appendedNames:", appendedNames)
}
```

The result of the append function is a slice whose length has increased but is still backed by the same underlying array. The original slice still exists and is backed by the same array, with the effect that there are now two views onto a single array, as shown in Figure 7-13.

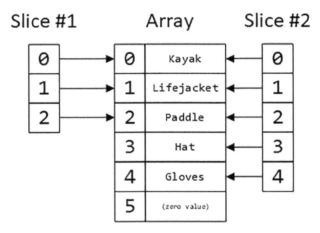

Figure 7-13. *Multiple slices backed by a single array*

Since the slices are backed by the same array, assigning a new value with one slice affects the other slice too, which can be seen in the output from the code in Listing 7-17:

```
names: [Canoe Lifejacket Paddle]
appendedNames: [Canoe Lifejacket Paddle Hat Gloves]
```

Appending One Slice to Another

The append function can be used to append one slice to another, as shown in Listing 7-18.

Listing 7-18. Appending a Slice in the main.go File in the collections Folder

```
package main

import "fmt"

func main() {

    names := make([]string, 3, 6)

    names[0] = "Kayak"
    names[1] = "Lifejacket"
    names[2] = "Paddle"

    moreNames := []string { "Hat Gloves"}

    appendedNames := append(names, moreNames...)

    fmt.Println("appendedNames:", appendedNames)
}
```

The second argument is followed by three periods (. . .), which is required because the built-in append function defines a *variadic parameter*, which I describe in Chapter 8. For this chapter, it is enough to know that you can append the contents of one slice to another slice, just as long as the three periods are used. (If you omit the three periods, the Go compiler will report an error because it thinks you are trying to add the second slice as a single value to the first slice and it knows the types don't match.) The code in Listing 7-18 produces the following output when compiled and executed:

```
appendedNames: [Kayak Lifejacket Paddle Hat Gloves]
```

Creating Slices from Existing Arrays

Slices can be created using existing arrays, which builds on the behavior described in earlier examples and emphasizes the nature of slices as views onto arrays. Listing 7-19 defines an array and uses it to create slices.

Listing 7-19. Creating Slices from an Existing Array in the main.go File in the collections Folder

```
package main

import "fmt"

func main() {

    products := [4]string { "Kayak", "Lifejacket", "Paddle", "Hat"}

    someNames := products[1:3]
    allNames := products[:]
```

163

```
    fmt.Println("someNames:", someNames)
    fmt.Println("allNames", allNames)
}
```

The products variable is assigned a standard, fixed-length array containing string values. The array is used to create slices using a range, which specifies low and high values, as illustrated by Figure 7-14.

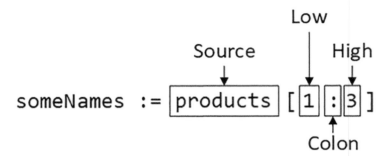

Figure 7-14. *Using a range to create a slice from an existing array*

Ranges are expressed within square brackets, with the low and high values separated by a colon. The first index in the slice is set to be the low value, and the length is the result of the high value minus the low value. This means that the range [1:3] creates a range whose zero index is mapped into index 1 of the array and whose length is 2. As this example shows, slices do not have to be aligned with the start of the backing array.

The start index and count can be omitted from a range to include all the elements from the source, as shown in Figure 7-15. (You can also omit just one of the values, as shown in later examples.)

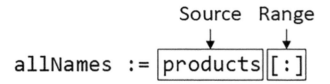

Figure 7-15. *A range that includes all elements*

The code in Listing 7-19 creates two slices, both of which are backed by the same array. The someNames slice has a partial view of the array, while the allNames slice is a view of the entire array, as illustrated by Figure 7-16.

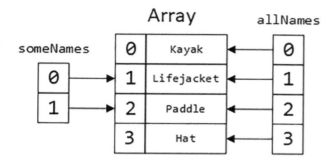

Figure 7-16. *Creating slices from existing arrays*

The code in Listing 7-19 produces the following output when compiled and executed:

```
someNames: [Lifejacket Paddle]
allNames [Kayak Lifejacket Paddle Hat]
```

Appending Elements When Using Existing Arrays for Slices

The relationship between the slice and the existing array can create different results when appending elements.

As the previous example showed, it is possible to offset a slice so that its first index position is not at the start of the array and so that its final index does not point to the final element in the array. In Listing 7-19, index 0 for the someNames slice is mapped into index 1 of the array. Until now, the capacity of slices has been aligned with the length of the underlying array, but this is no longer the case because the effect of the offset is to reduce the amount of the array that can be used by the slice. Listing 7-20 adds statements that write out the length and capacity of the two slices.

Listing 7-20. Displaying Slice Length and Capacity in the main.go File in the collections Folder

```go
package main

import "fmt"

func main() {

    products := [4]string { "Kayak", "Lifejacket", "Paddle", "Hat"}

    someNames := products[1:3]
    allNames := products[:]

    fmt.Println("someNames:", someNames)
    fmt.Println("someNames len:", len(someNames), "cap:", cap(someNames))
    fmt.Println("allNames", allNames)
    fmt.Println("allNames len", len(allNames), "cap:", cap(allNames))
}
```

The code in Listing 7-20 produces the following output when compiled and executed, confirming the effect of the offset slice:

```
someNames: [Lifejacket Paddle]
someNames len: 2 cap: 3
allNames [Kayak Lifejacket Paddle Hat]
allNames len 4 cap: 4
```

Listing 7-21 appends an element to the someNames slice.

Listing 7-21. Appending an Element to a Slice in the main.go File in the collections Folder

```
package main

import "fmt"

func main() {

    products := [4]string { "Kayak", "Lifejacket", "Paddle", "Hat"}

    someNames := products[1:3]
    allNames := products[:]

    someNames = append(someNames, "Gloves")

    fmt.Println("someNames:", someNames)
    fmt.Println("someNames len:", len(someNames), "cap:", cap(someNames))
    fmt.Println("allNames", allNames)
    fmt.Println("allNames len", len(allNames), "cap:", cap(allNames))
}
```

This slice has the capacity to accommodate the new element without resizing, but the array location that will be used to store the element is already included in the allNames slice, which means that the append operation expands the someNames slice and changes one of the values that can be accessed through the allNames slice, as illustrated by Figure 7-17.

MAKING SLICES PREDICTABLE

The way that slices can share an array causes confusion. Some developers expect slices to be independent and get unexpected results when a value is stored in an array used by multiple slices. Other developers write code that expects shared arrays and get unexpected results when a resize separates slices.

Slices can appear unpredictable but only if you treat them inconsistently. My advice is to divide slices into two categories, decide which of them a slice belongs to when it is created, and not change that category.

The first category is as a fixed-length view into a fixed-length array. This is more useful than it sounds because slices can be mapped onto a specific region of an array, which can be selected programmatically. In this category, you can change the elements in the slice but not append new elements, meaning that all slices mapped into that array will use the modified elements.

The second category is as a variable-length data collection. I make sure each slice in this category has its own backing array, which is not shared by any other slice. This approach allows me to freely add new elements to the slice without having to worry about the impact on other slices.

If you get bogged down with slices and don't get the results you expect, then ask yourself which category each of your slices falls into and whether you are treating a slice inconsistently or creating slices from different categories from the same source array.

If you use a slice as a fixed view onto an array, then you can expect multiple slices to give you a consistent view of that array, and any new values you assign will be reflected by all of the slices that map into the modified element.

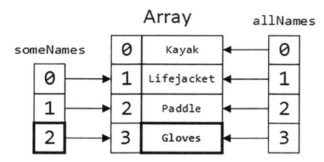

Figure 7-17. *Appending an element to a slice*

This result is confirmed by the output produced when the code in Listing 7-21 is compiled and executed:

```
someNames: [Lifejacket Paddle Gloves]
someNames len: 3 cap: 3
allNames [Kayak Lifejacket Paddle Gloves]
allNames len 4 cap: 4
```

Appending the value Gloves to the someNames slice changes the value returned by allNames[3] because the slices share the same array.

The output also shows that the length and the capacity of the slices are the same, which means there is no longer any room to expand the slice without creating a larger backing array. To confirm this behavior, Listing 7-22 appends another element to the someNames slice.

Listing 7-22. Appending Another Element in the main.go File in the collections Folder

```go
package main

import "fmt"

func main() {

    products := [4]string { "Kayak", "Lifejacket", "Paddle", "Hat"}

    someNames := products[1:3]
    allNames := products[:]

    someNames = append(someNames, "Gloves")
    someNames = append(someNames, "Boots")

    fmt.Println("someNames:", someNames)
    fmt.Println("someNames len:", len(someNames), "cap:", cap(someNames))
    fmt.Println("allNames", allNames)
    fmt.Println("allNames len", len(allNames), "cap:", cap(allNames))
}
```

The first call to the append function expands the someNames slice within the existing backing array. There is no further capacity when the append function is called again, and so a new array is created, the contents are copied, and the two slices are backed by different arrays, as illustrated by Figure 7-18.

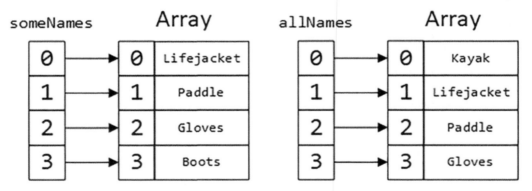

Figure 7-18. *Causing a slice resizing by appending an element*

The resizing process copies only the array elements that are mapped by the slice, which has the effect of realigning the slice and array indices. The code in Listing 7-22 produces the following output when compiled and executed:

```
someNames: [Lifejacket Paddle Gloves Boots]
someNames len: 4 cap: 6
allNames [Kayak Lifejacket Paddle Gloves]
allNames len 4 cap: 4
```

Specifying Capacity When Creating a Slice from an Array

Ranges can include a maximum capacity, which provides some degree of control over when arrays will be duplicated, as shown in Listing 7-23.

Listing 7-23. Specifying a Slice Capacity in the main.go File in the collections Folder

```
package main

import "fmt"

func main() {

    products := [4]string { "Kayak", "Lifejacket", "Paddle", "Hat"}

    someNames := products[1:3:3]
    allNames := products[:]

    someNames = append(someNames, "Gloves")
    //someNames = append(someNames, "Boots")

    fmt.Println("someNames:", someNames)
    fmt.Println("someNames len:", len(someNames), "cap:", cap(someNames))
    fmt.Println("allNames", allNames)
    fmt.Println("allNames len", len(allNames), "cap:", cap(allNames))
}
```

The additional value, known as the *max* value, is specified after the high value, as shown in Figure 7-19, and must be within the bounds of the array that is being sliced.

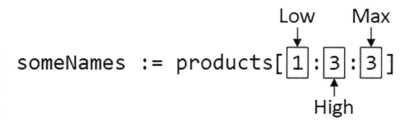

Figure 7-19. *Specifying a capacity in a range*

The max value doesn't specify the maximum capacity directly. Instead, the maximum capacity is determined by subtracting the low value from the max value. In the case of the example, the max value is 3, and the low value is 1, which means that the capacity will be limited to 2. The result is that the append operation causes the slice to be resized and allocated its own array, rather than expanding in the existing array, which can be seen in the output from the code in Listing 7-23:

```
someNames: [Lifejacket Paddle Gloves]
someNames len: 3 cap: 4
allNames [Kayak Lifejacket Paddle Hat]
allNames len 4 cap: 4
```

169

The slice resize means that the Gloves value that is appended to the someNames slice does not become one of the values mapped by the allNames slice.

Creating Slices from Other Slices

Slices can also be created from other slices, although the relationship between slices isn't preserved if they are resized. To demonstrate what this means, Listing 7-24 creates one slice from another.

Listing 7-24. Creating a Slice from a Slice in the main.go File in the collections Folder

```
package main

import "fmt"

func main() {

    products := [4]string { "Kayak", "Lifejacket", "Paddle", "Hat"}

    allNames := products[1:]
    someNames := allNames[1:3]

    allNames = append(allNames, "Gloves")
    allNames[1] = "Canoe"

    fmt.Println("someNames:", someNames)
    fmt.Println("allNames", allNames)
}
```

The range used to create the someNames slice is applied to allNames, which is also a slice:

```
...
someNames := allNames[1:3]
...
```

This range creates a slice that maps onto the second and third elements in the allNames slice. The allNames slice was created with its own range:

```
...
allNames := products[1:]
...
```

The range creates a slice that is mapped onto all but the first element of the source array. The effect of the ranges is combined, which means that the someNames slice will be mapped onto the second and third locations in the array, as shown in Figure 7-20.

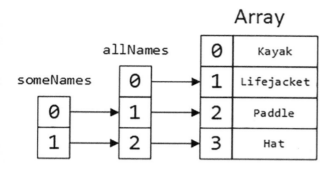

Figure 7-20. *Creating a slice from a slice*

Using one slice to create another is an effective way of carrying over offset start locations, which is what Figure 7-19 shows. But remember that slices are essentially pointers to sections of arrays, which means they can't point at another slice. In reality, the ranges are used to determine the mappings for slices that are backed by the same array, as shown in Figure 7-21.

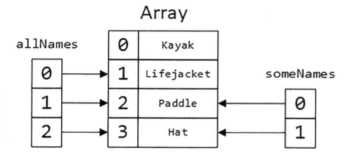

Figure 7-21. *The actual arrangement of slices*

The slices behave consistently with the other examples in this chapter and will be resized if elements are appended when there is no available capacity, at which point they will no longer share a common array.

Using the copy Function

The copy function is used to copy elements between slices. This function can be used to ensure that slices have separate arrays and to create slices that combine elements from different sources.

Using the copy Function to Ensure Slice Array Separation

The copy function can be used to duplicate an existing slice, selecting some or all the elements but ensuring that the new slice is backed by its own array, as shown in Listing 7-25.

Listing 7-25. Duplicating a Slice in the main.go File in the collections Folder

```
package main

import "fmt"

func main() {

    products := [4]string { "Kayak", "Lifejacket", "Paddle", "Hat"}

    allNames := products[1:]
    someNames := make([]string, 2)
    copy(someNames, allNames)

    fmt.Println("someNames:", someNames)
    fmt.Println("allNames", allNames)
}
```

The copy function accepts two arguments, which are the destination slice and the source slice, as illustrated in Figure 7-22.

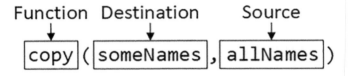

Figure 7-22. *Using the built-in copy function*

The function copies elements to the target slice. The slices don't need to have the same length because the copy function will copy elements only until the end of the destination or source slice is reached. The destination slice is not resized, even when there is capacity available in the existing backing array, which means that you must ensure there is sufficient length to accommodate the number of elements you want to copy.

The effect of the copy statement in Listing 7-25 is that elements are copied from the allNames slice until the length of the someNames slice is exhausted. The listing produces the following output when compiled and executed:

```
someNames: [Lifejacket Paddle]
allNames [Lifejacket Paddle Hat]
```

The length of the someNames slice is 2, which means that two elements are copied from the allNames slice. Even if the someNames slice had additional capacity, no further elements would have been copied because it is the slice length that the copy function relies on.

Understanding the Uninitialized Slice Pitfall

As I explained in the previous section, the copy function doesn't resize the destination slice. A common pitfall is to try to copy elements into a slice that has not been initialized, as shown in Listing 7-26.

Listing 7-26. Copying Elements into an Uninitialized Slice in the main.go File in the collections Folder

```
package main

import "fmt"

func main() {

    products := [4]string { "Kayak", "Lifejacket", "Paddle", "Hat"}

    allNames := products[1:]
    var someNames []string
    copy(someNames, allNames)

    fmt.Println("someNames:", someNames)
    fmt.Println("allNames", allNames)
}
```

I have replaced the statement that initializes the someNames slice with the make function and replaced it with a statement that defines a someNames variable without initializing it. This code compiles and executes without error but produces the following results:

```
someNames: []
allNames [Lifejacket Paddle Hat]
```

No elements have been copied to the destination slice. This happens because uninitialized slices have zero length and zero capacity. The copy function stops copying when the length of the destination length is reached, and since the length is zero, no copying occurs. No error is reported because the copy function worked the way it is supposed to, but this is rarely the intended effect, and this is the likely cause if you encounter an unexpectedly empty slice.

Specifying Ranges When Copying Slices

Fine-grained control over the elements that are copied can be achieved using ranges, as shown in Listing 7-27.

Listing 7-27. Using Ranges when Copying Elements in the main.go File in the collections Folder

```
package main

import "fmt"

func main() {

    products := [4]string { "Kayak", "Lifejacket", "Paddle", "Hat"}

    allNames := products[1:]
    someNames := []string { "Boots", "Canoe"}
    copy(someNames[1:], allNames[2:3])
```

```
    fmt.Println("someNames:", someNames)
    fmt.Println("allNames", allNames)
}
```

The range applied to the destination slice means that the copied elements will start at position 1. The range applied to the source slice means that copying will begin with the element in position 2 and that one element will be copied. The code in Listing 7-27 produces the following output when compiled and executed:

```
someNames: [Boots Hat]
allNames [Lifejacket Paddle Hat]
```

Copying Slices with Different Sizes

The behavior that leads to the problem described in the "Understanding the Uninitialized Slice Pitfall" section allows different sized slices to be copied, just as long as you remember to initialize them. If the destination slice is larger than the source slice, then copying will continue until the last element in the source has been copied, as shown in Listing 7-28.

Listing 7-28. Copying a Smaller Source Slice in the main.go File in the collections Folder

```
package main

import "fmt"

func main() {

    products := []string { "Kayak", "Lifejacket", "Paddle", "Hat"}
    replacementProducts := []string { "Canoe", "Boots"}

    copy(products, replacementProducts)

    fmt.Println("products:", products)
}
```

The source slice contains only two elements, and no range is used. The result is that the copy function starts copying the elements from the replacementProducts slice to the products slice and stops when the end of the replacementProducts slice is reached. The remaining elements in the products slice are unaffected by the copy operation, as the output from the example shows:

```
products: [Canoe Boots Paddle Hat]
```

If the destination slice is smaller than the source slice, then copying continues until all the elements in the destination slice have been replaced, as shown in Listing 7-29.

Listing 7-29. Copying a Larger Source Slice in the main.go File in the collections Folder

```
package main

import "fmt"

func main() {

    products := []string { "Kayak", "Lifejacket", "Paddle", "Hat"}
    replacementProducts := []string { "Canoe", "Boots"}

    copy(products[0:1], replacementProducts)

    fmt.Println("products:", products)
}
```

The range used for the destination creates a slice with length of one, which means that only one element will be copied from the source array, as the output from the example shows:

```
products: [Canoe Lifejacket Paddle Hat]
```

Deleting Slice Elements

There is no built-in function for deleting slice elements, but this operation can be performed using the ranges and the append function, as Listing 7-30 demonstrates.

Listing 7-30. Deleting Slice Elements in the main.go File in the collections Folder

```
package main

import "fmt"

func main() {

    products := [4]string { "Kayak", "Lifejacket", "Paddle", "Hat"}

    deleted := append(products[:2], products[3:]...)
    fmt.Println("Deleted:", deleted)
}
```

To delete a value, the append method is used to combine two ranges that contain all the elements in the slice except the one that is no longer required. Listing 7-30 produces the following output when compiled and executed:

```
Deleted: [Kayak Lifejacket Hat]
```

Enumerating Slices

Slices are enumerated in the same way as arrays, with the for and range keywords, as shown in Listing 7-31.

Listing 7-31. Enumerating a Slice in the main.go File in the collections Folder

```
package main

import "fmt"

func main() {

    products := []string { "Kayak", "Lifejacket", "Paddle", "Hat"}

    for index, value := range products[2:] {
        fmt.Println("Index:", index, "Value:", value)
    }
}
```

I describe the different ways that for loops can be used in Listing 7-31, but when combined with the range keyword, the for keyword can enumerate a slice, producing index and value variables for each element. The code in Listing 7-31 produces the following output:

```
Index: 0 Value: Paddle
Index: 1 Value: Hat
```

Sorting Slices

There is no built-in support for sorting slices, but the standard library includes the sort package, which defines functions for sorting different types of slice. The sort package is described in detail in Chapter 18, but Listing 7-32 demonstrates a simple example to provide some context in this chapter.

Listing 7-32. Sorting a Slice in the main.go File in the collections Folder

```
package main

import (
    "fmt"
    "sort"
)

func main() {

    products := []string { "Kayak", "Lifejacket", "Paddle", "Hat"}

    sort.Strings(products)

    for index, value := range products {
        fmt.Println("Index:", index, "Value:", value)
    }
}
```

The Strings function sorts the values in a [ ]string in place, producing the following results when the example is compiled and executed:

```
Index: 0 Value: Hat
Index: 1 Value: Kayak
Index: 2 Value: Lifejacket
Index: 3 Value: Paddle
```

As Chapter 18 explains, the sort package includes functions for sorting slices containing integers and strings, plus support for sorting custom data types.

Comparing Slices

Go restricts the use of the comparison operator so that slices can be compared only to the nil value. Comparing two slices produces an error, as Listing 7-33 will demonstrate.

Listing 7-33. Comparing Slices in the main.go File in the collections Folder

```
package main

import (
    "fmt"
    //"sort"
)

func main() {

    p1 := []string { "Kayak", "Lifejacket", "Paddle", "Hat"}
    p2 := p1

    fmt.Println("Equal:", p1 == p2)
}
```

When this code is compiled, the following error is produced:

```
.\main.go:13:30: invalid operation: p1 == p2 (slice can only be compared to nil)
```

There is one way to compare slices, however. The standard library includes a package named reflect, which includes a convenience function named DeepEqual. The reflect package is described in Chapters 27–29 and contains advanced features (which is why it takes three chapters to describe the features it provides). The DeepEqual function can be used to compare a wider range of data types than the equality operator, including slices, as shown in Listing 7-34.

Listing 7-34. Comparing Slices with the Convenience Function in the main.go File in the collections Folder

```
package main

import (
    "fmt"
    "reflect"
)

func main() {

    p1 := []string { "Kayak", "Lifejacket", "Paddle", "Hat"}
    p2 := p1

    fmt.Println("Equal:", reflect.DeepEqual(p1, p2))
}
```

The DeepEqual function is convenient, but you should read the chapters that describe the reflect package to understand how it works before using it in your own projects. The listing produces the following output when compiled and executed:

```
Equal: true
```

Getting the Array Underlying a Slice

If you have a slice but you need an array, typically because a function requires one as an argument, then you can perform an explicit conversion on the slice, as shown in Listing 7-35.

Listing 7-35. Obtaining an Array in the main.go File in the collections Folder

```
package main

import (
    "fmt"
    //"reflect"
)

func main() {

    p1 := []string { "Kayak", "Lifejacket", "Paddle", "Hat"}
    arrayPtr := (*[3]string)(p1)
    array := *arrayPtr

    fmt.Println(array)

}
```

I have performed this task in two steps. The first step is to perform an explicit type conversion on the []string slice to a *[3]string. Care must be taken when specifying the array type because an error will occur if the number of elements required by the array exceeds the length of the slice. The length of the array can be smaller than the length of the slice, in which case the array will not contain all of the slice values. In this example, there are four values in the slice, and I specified an array type that can store three values, which means that the array will contain only the first three slice values.

In the second step, I follow the pointer to get the array value, which is then written out. The code in Listing 7-35 produces the following output when compiled and executed:

```
[Kayak Lifejacket Paddle]
```

Working with Maps

Maps are a built-in data structure that associates data values with keys. Unlike arrays, where values are associated with sequential integer locations, maps can use other data types as keys, as shown in Listing 7-36.

Listing 7-36. Using a Map in the main.go File in the collections Folder

```
package main

import "fmt"

func main() {

    products := make(map[string]float64, 10)

    products["Kayak"] = 279
    products["Lifejacket"] = 48.95

    fmt.Println("Map size:", len(products))
    fmt.Println("Price:", products["Kayak"])
    fmt.Println("Price:", products["Hat"])
}
```

Maps are created with the built-in make function, just as for slices. The type for a map is specified using the map keyword, followed by the key type in square brackets, followed by the value type, as illustrated in Figure 7-23. The final argument to the make function specifies the initial capacity of the map. Maps, like slices, are resized automatically, and the size argument can be omitted.

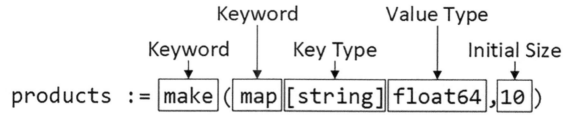

Figure 7-23. *Defining a map*

The statement in Listing 7-36 will store `float64` values, which are indexed with `string` keys. Values are stored in the map using array-style syntax, specifying the key instead of a location, like this:

```
...
products["Kayak"] = 279
...
```

This statement stores the `float64` value using the key Kayak. Values are read from the map using the same syntax:

```
...
fmt.Println("Price:", products["Kayak"])
...
```

If the map contains the specified key, then the value associated with the key is returned. The zero value for the map's value type is returned if the map doesn't contain the key. The number of items stored in the map is obtained using the built-in `len` function, like this:

```
...
fmt.Println("Map size:", len(products))
...
```

The code in Listing 7-36 produces the following output when compiled and executed:

```
Map size: 2
Price: 279
Price: 0
```

Using the Map Literal Syntax

Slices can also be defined using a literal syntax, as shown in Listing 7-37.

Listing 7-37. Using the Map Literal Syntax in the main.go File in the collections Folder

```
package main

import "fmt"

func main() {

    products := map[string]float64 {
        "Kayak" : 279,
        "Lifejacket": 48.95,
    }

    fmt.Println("Map size:", len(products))
    fmt.Println("Price:", products["Kayak"])
    fmt.Println("Price:", products["Hat"])
}
```

The literal syntax specifies the initial contents of the map between braces. Each map entry is specified using the key, a colon, the value, and then a comma, as illustrated by Figure 7-24.

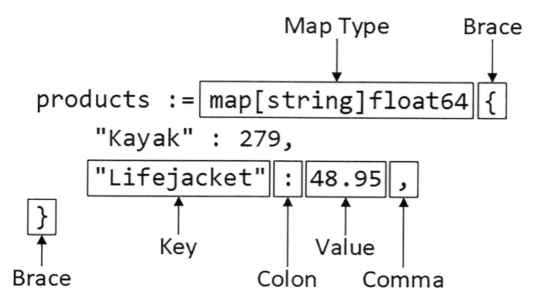

Figure 7-24. *The map literal syntax*

Go is particular about syntax and will produce an error if the map value isn't followed by either a comma or the closing brace. I prefer to use a trailing comma, which allows me to put the closing brace on the next line in the code file.

Keys used in the literal syntax must be unique, and the compiler will report an error if the same name is used for two literal entries. Listing 7-37 produces the following output when compiled and executed:

```
Map size: 2
Price: 279
Price: 0
```

Checking for Items in a Map

As noted earlier, maps return the zero value for the value type when reads are performed for which there is no key. This can make it difficult to differentiate between a stored value that happens to be the zero value and a nonexistent key, as shown in Listing 7-38.

Listing 7-38. Reading Map Values in the main.go File in the collections Folder

```go
package main

import "fmt"

func main() {

    products := map[string]float64 {
        "Kayak" : 279,
        "Lifejacket": 48.95,
        "Hat": 0,
    }

    fmt.Println("Hat:", products["Hat"])
}
```

The problem with this code is that products["Hat"] returns zero, but it isn't known whether this is because zero is the stored value or because there is no value associated with the key Hat. To solve this problem, maps produce two values when reading a value, as shown in Listing 7-39.

Listing 7-39. Determining If a Value Exists in a Map in the main.go File in the collections Folder

```go
package main

import "fmt"

func main() {

    products := map[string]float64 {
        "Kayak" : 279,
        "Lifejacket": 48.95,
        "Hat": 0,
    }

    value, ok := products["Hat"]

    if (ok) {
        fmt.Println("Stored value:", value)
    } else {
        fmt.Println("No stored value")
    }
}
```

This is known as the "comma ok" technique, where values are assigned to two variables when reading a value from a map:

```go
...
value, ok := products["Hat"]
...
```

The first value is either the value associated with the specified key or the zero value if there is no key. The second value is a bool that is true if the map contains the specified key and false otherwise. The second value is conventionally assigned to a variable named ok, which is how the "comma ok" term arises.

This technique can be streamlined using an initialization statement, as shown in Listing 7-40.

Listing 7-40. Using an Initialization Statement in the main.go File in the collections Folder

```
package main

import "fmt"

func main() {

    products := map[string]float64 {
        "Kayak" : 279,
        "Lifejacket": 48.95,
        "Hat": 0,
    }

    if value, ok := products["Hat"]; ok {
        fmt.Println("Stored value:", value)
    } else {
        fmt.Println("No stored value")
    }
}
```

The code in Listings 7-39 and 7-40 produces the following output when compiled and executed, showing that the key Hat was used to store the value 0 in the map:

```
Stored value: 0
```

Removing Items from a Map

Items are removed from the map using the built-in delete function, as shown in Listing 7-41.

Listing 7-41. Deleting from a Map in the main.go File in the collections Folder

```
package main

import "fmt"

func main() {

    products := map[string]float64 {
        "Kayak" : 279,
        "Lifejacket": 48.95,
        "Hat": 0,
    }
```

```
    delete(products, "Hat")

    if value, ok := products["Hat"]; ok {
        fmt.Println("Stored value:", value)
    } else {
        fmt.Println("No stored value")
    }
}
```

The arguments to the delete function are the map and the key to remove. No error will be reported if the specified key is not contained in the map. The code in Listing 7-41 produces the following output when compiled and executed, confirming the Hat key is no longer in the map:

```
No stored value
```

Enumerating the Contents of a Map

Maps are enumerated using the for and range keywords, as shown in Listing 7-42.

Listing 7-42. Enumerating a Map in the main.go File in the collections Folder

```
package main

import "fmt"

func main() {

    products := map[string]float64 {
        "Kayak" : 279,
        "Lifejacket": 48.95,
        "Hat": 0,
    }

    for key, value := range products {
        fmt.Println("Key:", key, "Value:", value)
    }
}
```

When the for and range keywords are used with a map, the two variables are assigned keys and values as the contents of the map are enumerated. The code in Listing 7-42 produces the following output when compiled and executed (although they may appear in a different order, as I explain in the next section):

```
Key: Kayak Value: 279
Key: Lifejacket Value: 48.95
Key: Hat Value: 0
```

Enumerating a Map in Order

You may see the results from Listing 7-42 in a different order because there are no guarantees that the contents of a map will be enumerated in any specific order. If you want to get the values in a map in order, then the best approach is to enumerate the map and create a slice containing the keys, sort the slice, and then enumerate the slice to read the values from the map, as shown in Listing 7-43.

Listing 7-43. Enumerating a Map in Key Order in the main.go File in the collections Folder

```
package main

import (
    "fmt"
    "sort"
)

func main() {

    products := map[string]float64 {
        "Kayak" : 279,
        "Lifejacket": 48.95,
        "Hat": 0,
    }

    keys := make([]string, 0, len(products))
    for key, _ := range products {
        keys = append(keys, key)
    }
    sort.Strings(keys)
    for _, key := range keys {
        fmt.Println("Key:", key, "Value:", products[key])
    }
}
```

Compile and execute the project, and you will see the following output, which displays the values sorted in order of their key:

```
Key: Hat Value: 0
Key: Kayak Value: 279
Key: Lifejacket Value: 48.95
```

Understanding the Dual Nature of Strings

In Chapter 4, I described strings as character sequences. This is true, but there are complications because Go strings have a split personality depending on how you use them.

Go treats strings as arrays of bytes and supports the array index and slice range notation, as shown in Listing 7-44.

Listing 7-44. Indexing and Slicing a String in the main.go File in the collections Folder

```
package main

import (
    "fmt"
    "strconv"
)

func main() {

    var price string = "$48.95"

    var currency byte = price[0]
    var amountString string = price[1:]
    amount, parseErr  := strconv.ParseFloat(amountString, 64)

    fmt.Println("Currency:", currency)
    if (parseErr == nil) {
        fmt.Println("Amount:", amount)
    } else {
        fmt.Println("Parse Error:", parseErr)
    }
}
```

I have used the full variable declaration syntax to emphasize the type of each variable. When the index notation is used, the result is a byte from the specified location in the string:

```
...
var currency byte = price[0]
...
```

This statement selects the byte at position zero and assigns it to a variable named currency. When a string is sliced, the slice is also described using bytes, but the result is a string:

```
...
var amountString string = price[1:]
...
```

The range selects all but the byte in location zero and assigns the shortened string to a variable named amountString. This code produces the following output when compiled and executed with the command shown in Listing 7-44:

```
Currency: 36
Amount: 48.95
```

As I explained in Chapter 4, the byte type is an alias for uint8, which is why the currency value is displayed as a number: Go doesn't have any idea that the numeric value 36 should be expressed as the dollar sign. Figure 7-25 illustrates the string as an array of bytes and shows how they are indexed and sliced.

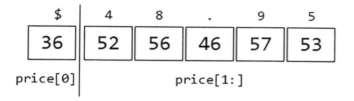

Figure 7-25. *A string as an array of bytes*

Slicing a string produces another string, but an explicit conversion is required to interpret the byte as the character it represents, as shown in Listing 7-45.

Listing 7-45. Converting the Result in the main.go File in the collections Folder

```go
package main

import (
    "fmt"
    "strconv"
)

func main() {

    var price string = "$48.95"

    var currency string = string(price[0])
    var amountString string = price[1:]
    amount, parseErr  := strconv.ParseFloat(amountString, 64)

    fmt.Println("Currency:", currency)
    if (parseErr == nil) {
        fmt.Println("Amount:", amount)
    } else {
        fmt.Println("Parse Error:", parseErr)
    }
}
```

Compile and execute the code, and you will see the following results:

```
Currency: $
Amount: 48.95
```

This looks like it works, but it contains a pitfall, which can be seen if the currency symbol is changed, as shown in Listing 7-46. (If you don't live in a part of the world where the euro currency symbol is on the keyboard, then hold down the Alt key and press 0128 on your numeric keypad.)

Listing 7-46. Changing the Currency Symbol in the main.go File in the collections Folder

```go
package main

import (
    "fmt"
    "strconv"
)

func main() {

    var price string = "€48.95"

    var currency string = string(price[0])
    var amountString string = price[1:]
    amount, parseErr  := strconv.ParseFloat(amountString, 64)

    fmt.Println("Currency:", currency)
    if (parseErr == nil) {
        fmt.Println("Amount:", amount)
    } else {
        fmt.Println("Parse Error:", parseErr)
    }
}
```

Compile and execute the code, and you will see the output similar to the following:

```
Currency: â
Parse Error: strconv.ParseFloat: parsing "\x82\xac48.95": invalid syntax
```

The problem is that the array and range notations select bytes, but not all characters are expressed as just one byte. The new currency symbol is stored using three bytes, as shown in Figure 7-26.

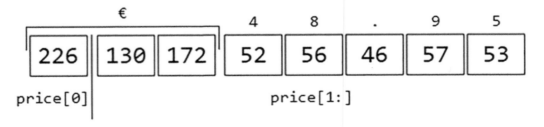

Figure 7-26. *Changing the currency symbol*

The figure shows how taking a single byte value obtains only part of the currency symbol. It also shows that the slice includes two of the three bytes from the symbol, followed by the rest of the string. You can confirm that the change in currency symbol has increased the size of the array using the len function, as shown in Listing 7-47.

Listing 7-47. Obtaining the Length of a String in the main.go File in the collections Folder

```
package main

import (
    "fmt"
    "strconv"
)

func main() {

    var price string = "€48.95"

    var currency string = string(price[0])
    var amountString string = price[1:]
    amount, parseErr  := strconv.ParseFloat(amountString, 64)

    fmt.Println("Length:", len(price))
    fmt.Println("Currency:", currency)
    if (parseErr == nil) {
        fmt.Println("Amount:", amount)
    } else {
        fmt.Println("Parse Error:", parseErr)
    }
}
```

The len function treats the string as the array of bytes, and the code in Listing 7-47 produces the following output when compiled and executed:

```
Length: 8
Currency: â
Parse Error: strconv.ParseFloat: parsing "\x82\xac48.95": invalid syntax
```

The output confirms there are eight bytes in the string, and this is the reason that the indexing and slicing produce odd results.

Converting a String to Runes

The rune type represents a Unicode code point, which is essentially a single character. To avoid slicing strings in the middle of characters, an explicit conversion to a rune slice can be performed, as shown in Listing 7-48.

■ **Tip**   Unicode is incredibly complex, as you would expect from any standard that aims to describe multiple writing systems evolved over thousands of years. I do not describe Unicode in this book, and, for the sake of simplicity, I treat rune values as single characters, which is sufficient for most development projects. I describe Unicode sufficiently enough to explain how Go features work.

Listing 7-48. Converting to Runes in the main.go File in the collections Folder

```
package main

import (
    "fmt"
    "strconv"
)

func main() {

    var price []rune = []rune("€48.95")

    var currency string = string(price[0])
    var amountString string = string(price[1:])
    amount, parseErr  := strconv.ParseFloat(amountString, 64)

    fmt.Println("Length:", len(price))
    fmt.Println("Currency:", currency)
    if (parseErr == nil) {
        fmt.Println("Amount:", amount)
    } else {
        fmt.Println("Parse Error:", parseErr)
    }
}
```

I apply the explicit conversion to the literal string and assign the slice to the price variable. When working with a rune slice, individual bytes are grouped into the characters they represent without reference to the number of bytes each character requires, as illustrated by Figure 7-27.

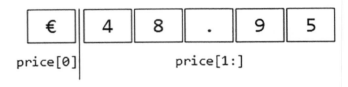

Figure 7-27. A rune slice

As explained in Chapter 4, the rune type is an alias for int32, which means that printing out a rune value will display the numeric value used to represent the character. This means, as with the byte example previously, I have to perform an explicit conversion of a single rune into a string, like this:

```
...
var currency string = string(price[0])
...
```

But, unlike earlier examples, I also have to perform an explicit conversion on the slice I create, like this:

```
...
var amountString string = string(price[1:])
...
```

The result of the slice is []rune; put another way, slicing a rune slice produces another rune slice. The code in Listing 7-48 produces the following output when compiled and executed:

```
Length: 6
Currency: €
Amount: 48.95
```

The len function returns 6 because the array contains characters, rather than bytes. And, of course, the rest of the output is as expected because there are no orphaned bytes to affect the result.

UNDERSTANDING WHY BYTES AND RUNES ARE BOTH USEFUL

The approach Go takes for strings may seem odd, but it has its uses. Bytes are important when you care about storing strings and you need to know how much space to allocate. Characters are important when you are concerned with the contents of strings, such as when inserting a new character into an existing string.

Both facets of strings are important. It is important, however, to understand whether you need to deal with bytes or characters for any given operation.

You might be tempted to work only with bytes, which will work as long as you use only those characters that are represented by a single byte, which typically means ASCII. This may work at first, but it almost always ends badly, specifically when your code processes characters entered by a user with a non-ASCII character set or processes a file containing non-ASCII data. For the small amount of extra work required, it is simpler and safer to accept that Unicode does really exist and rely on Go to deal with translating bytes into characters.

Enumerating Strings

A for loop can be used to enumerate the contents of a string. This feature shows some clever aspects of the way that Go deals with the mapping of bytes to runes. Listing 7-49 enumerates a string.

Listing 7-49. Enumerating a String in the main.go File in the collections Folder

```
package main

import (
    "fmt"
    //"strconv"
)

func main() {

    var price = "€48.95"

    for index, char := range price {
        fmt.Println(index, char, string(char))
    }
}
```

I have used a string that contains the euro currency symbol in this example, which demonstrates that Go treats strings as a sequence of runes when used with a `for` loop. Compile and execute the code in Listing 7-49, and you will receive the following output:

```
0  8364  €
3  52  4
4  56  8
5  46  .
6  57  9
7  53  5
```

The `for` loop treats the string as an array of elements. The values written out are the index of the current element, the numeric value of that element, and the numeric element converted to a `string`.

Notice that the `index` values are not sequential. The `for` loop processes the string as a sequence of characters derived from the underlying sequence of bytes. The index values correspond to the first byte that makes up each character, which was shown in Figure 7-2. The second index value is 3, for example, because the first character in the string is made up of bytes in positions 0, 1, and 2.

If you want to enumerate the underlying bytes without them being converted to characters, then you can perform an explicit conversion to a `byte` slice, as shown in Listing 7-50.

Listing 7-50. Enumerating the Bytes in the String in the main.go File in the collections Folder

```go
package main

import (
    "fmt"
    //"strconv"
)

func main() {

    var price = "€48.95"

    for index, char := range []byte(price) {
        fmt.Println(index, char)
    }
}
```

Compile and execute this code using the command shown in Listing 7-50, and you will see the following output:

```
0  226
1  130
2  172
3  52
4  56
5  46
6  57
7  53
```

The index values are sequential, and the values of individual bytes are displayed without being interpreted as parts of the characters they represent.

Summary

In this chapter, I described the Go collection types. I explained that arrays are fixed-length sequences of values, that slices are variable-length sequences backed by an array, and that maps are collections of key-value pairs. I demonstrated the use of ranges to select elements, explained the relationships between slices and their underlying arrays, and showed you how to perform common tasks, such as removing an element from a slice, for which there are no built-in features. I finished this chapter by explaining the complex nature of strings, which can cause problems for programmers who assume that all characters can be represented using a single byte of data. In the next chapter, I explain the use of functions in Go.

CHAPTER 8

■ ■ ■

Defining and Using Functions

In this chapter, I describe Go functions, which allow code statements to be grouped together and executed when they are needed. Go functions have some unusual characteristics, the most useful of which is the ability to define multiple results. As I explain, this is an elegant solution to a common issue that functions present. Table 8-1 puts functions in context.

Table 8-1. *Putting Functions in Context*

Question	Answer
What are they?	Functions are groups of code statements that are executed only when the function is invoked during the flow of execution.
Why are they useful?	Functions allow features to be defined once and used repeatedly.
How are they used?	Functions are invoked by name and can be provided with data values with which to work using parameters. The outcome of executing the statements in the function can be produced as a function result.
Are there any pitfalls or limitations?	Go functions behave largely as expected, with the addition of useful features such as multiple results and named results.
Are there any alternatives?	No, functions are a core feature of the Go language.

© Adam Freeman 2022
A. Freeman, *Pro Go*, https://doi.org/10.1007/978-1-4842-7355-5_8

Table 8-2 summarizes the chapter.

Table 8-2. *Chapter Summary*

Problem	Solution	Listing
Group statements so they can be executed as needed	Define a function	4
Define a function so the values used by the statements it contains can be changed	Define function parameters	5–8
Allow a function to accept a variable number of arguments	Define a variadic parameter	9–13
Use references to values defined outside of the function	Define parameters that accept pointers	14, 15
Produce output from the statements defined in a function	Define one or more results	16–22
Discard a result produced by a function	Use the blank identifier	23
Schedule a function to be invoked when the currently executed function is complete	Use the defer keyword	24

Preparing for This Chapter

To prepare for this chapter, open a new command prompt, navigate to a convenient location, and create a directory named functions. Navigate to the functions folder and run the command shown in Listing 8-1 to initialize the project.

■ **Tip**   You can download the example project for this chapter—and for all the other chapters in this book—from https://github.com/apress/pro-go. See Chapter 2 for how to get help if you have problems running the examples.

Listing 8-1. Initializing the Project

```
go mod init functions
```

Add a file named main.go to the functions folder, with the contents shown in Listing 8-2.

Listing 8-2. The Contents of the main.go File in the functions Folder

```
package main

import "fmt"

func main() {

    fmt.Println("Hello, Functions")
}
```

Use the command prompt to run the command shown in Listing 8-3 in the functions folder.

Listing 8-3. Running the Example Project

```
go run .
```

The code in the main.go file will be compiled and executed, producing the following output:

```
Hello, Functions
```

Defining a Simple Function

Functions are groups of statements that can be used and reused as a single action. To get started, Listing 8-4 defines a simple function.

Listing 8-4. Defining a Function in the main.go File in the functions Folder

```
package main

import "fmt"

func printPrice() {
    kayakPrice := 275.00
    kayakTax := kayakPrice * 0.2
    fmt.Println("Price:", kayakPrice, "Tax:", kayakTax)
}

func main() {
    fmt.Println("About to call function")
    printPrice()
    fmt.Println("Function complete")
}
```

Functions are defined by the func keyword, followed by the function name, parentheses, and a code block enclosed in braces, as illustrated by Figure 8-1.

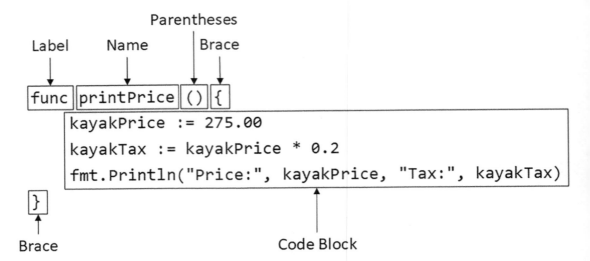

Figure 8-1. *The anatomy of a function*

There are now two functions in the main.go code file. The new function is called printPrice, and it contains statements that define two variables and call the Println function from the fmt package. The main function is the application's entry point, where execution starts and finishes. Go functions must be defined with braces, and the opening brace must be defined on the same line as the func keyword and the function's name. Conventions common in other languages, such as omitting braces or putting the brace on the following line, are not allowed.

■ **Note**   Notice that the printPrice function is defined alongside the existing main function in the main.go file. Go does support defining functions inside other functions, but a different syntax is required, as described in Chapter 9.

The main function invokes the printPrice function, which is done with a statement that specifies the function's name, followed by parentheses, as shown in Figure 8-2.

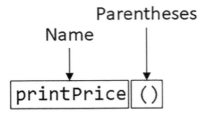

Figure 8-2. *Invoking a function*

When the function is invoked, the statements contained in the function's code block are executed. When all the statements have been invoked, execution continues to the statement after the one that invoked the function. This can be seen in the output produced by the code in Listing 8-4 when it is compiled and executed:

```
About to call function
Price: 275 Tax: 55
Function complete
```

Defining and Using Function Parameters

Parameters allow a function to receive data values when it is called, allowing its behavior to be altered. Listing 8-5 modifies the printPrice function defined in the previous section so that it defines parameters.

Listing 8-5. Defining Function Parameters in the main.go File in the functions Folder

```go
package main

import "fmt"

func printPrice(product string, price float64, taxRate float64) {
    taxAmount := price * taxRate
    fmt.Println(product, "price:", price, "Tax:", taxAmount)
}

func main() {
    printPrice("Kayak", 275, 0.2)
    printPrice("Lifejacket", 48.95, 0.2)
    printPrice("Soccer Ball", 19.50, 0.15)
}
```

Parameters are defined with a name followed by a type. Multiple parameters are separated with commas, as shown in Figure 8-3.

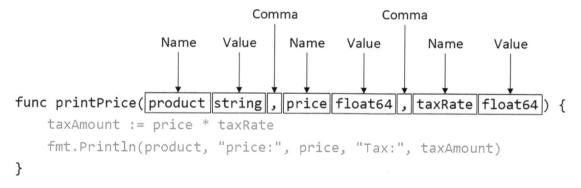

Figure 8-3. *Defining function parameters*

Listing 8-5 adds three parameters to the printPrice function: a string named product, a float64 named price, and a float64 named taxRate. Within the function's code block, the value assigned to the parameter is accessed using its name, as shown in Figure 8-4.

199

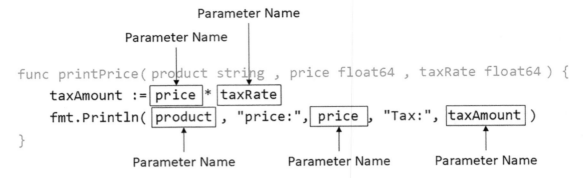

Figure 8-4. Accessing a parameter inside a code block

Values for parameters are supplied as arguments when invoking the function, meaning that different values can be provided each time the function is called. Arguments are provided between the parentheses that follow the function name, separated by commas and in the same order in which the parameters have been defined, as shown in Figure 8-5.

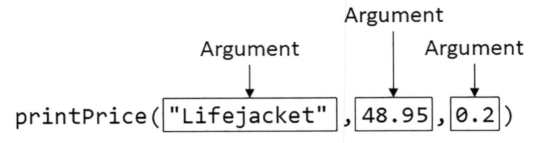

Figure 8-5. Invoking a function with arguments

The values that are used as arguments must match the types of the parameters defined by the function. The code in Listing 8-5 produces the following output when compiled and executed:

```
Kayak price: 275 Tax: 55
Lifejacket price: 48.95 Tax: 9.790000000000001
Soccer Ball price: 19.5 Tax: 2.925
```

The value displayed for the Lifejacket product contains a long fraction value, which would typically be rounded for currency amounts. I explain how to format number values as strings in Chapter 17.

■ **Note** Go does not support optional parameters or default values for parameters.

Omitting Parameter Types

The type can be omitted when adjacent parameters have the same type, as shown in Listing 8-6.

Listing 8-6. Omitting the Parameter Data Type in the main.go File in the functions Folder

```
package main

import "fmt"

func printPrice(product string, price, taxRate float64) {
    taxAmount := price * taxRate
    fmt.Println(product, "price:", price, "Tax:", taxAmount)
}

func main() {
    printPrice("Kayak", 275, 0.2)
    printPrice("Lifejacket", 48.95, 0.2)
    printPrice("Soccer Ball", 19.50, 0.15)
}
```

The price and taxRate parameters are both float64, and since they are adjacent, the data type is applied only to the final parameter of that type. Omitting the parameter data type doesn't change the parameter or its type. The code in Listing 8-6 produces the following output:

```
Kayak price: 275 Tax: 55
Lifejacket price: 48.95 Tax: 9.790000000000001
Soccer Ball price: 19.5 Tax: 2.925
```

Omitting Parameter Names

An underscore (the _ character) can be used for parameters that are defined by a function but not used in the function's code statements, as shown in Listing 8-7.

Listing 8-7. Omitting a Parameter Name in the main.go File in the functions Folder

```
package main

import "fmt"

func printPrice(product string, price, _ float64) {
    taxAmount := price * 0.25
    fmt.Println(product, "price:", price, "Tax:", taxAmount)
}

func main() {
    printPrice("Kayak", 275, 0.2)
    printPrice("Lifejacket", 48.95, 0.2)
    printPrice("Soccer Ball", 19.50, 0.15)
}
```

The underscore is known as the *blank identifier*, and the result is a parameter for which a value must be provided when the function is called but whose value cannot be accessed inside the function's code block. This may seem like an odd feature, but it can be a useful way to indicate that a parameter is not used within a function, which can arise when implementing the methods required by an interface. The code in Listing 8-7 produces the following output when compiled and executed:

```
Kayak price: 275 Tax: 68.75
Lifejacket price: 48.95 Tax: 12.2375
Soccer Ball price: 19.5 Tax: 4.875
```

Functions can also omit names from all their parameters, as shown in Listing 8-8.

Listing 8-8. Omitting All Parameter Names in the main.go File in the functions Folder

```go
package main

import "fmt"

func printPrice(string, float64, float64) {
    // taxAmount := price * 0.25
    fmt.Println("No parameters")
}

func main() {
    printPrice("Kayak", 275, 0.2)
    printPrice("Lifejacket", 48.95, 0.2)
    printPrice("Soccer Ball", 19.50, 0.15)
}
```

Parameters without names cannot be accessed within the function, and this feature is mainly used in conjunction with interfaces, described in Chapter 11, or when defining function types, described in Chapter 9. Listing 8-8 produces the following output when compiled and executed:

```
No parameters
No parameters
No parameters
```

Defining Variadic Parameters

A variadic parameter accepts a variable number of values, which can make functions easier to use. To understand the issue that variadic parameters solve, it can be helpful to consider the alternative, as shown in Listing 8-9.

Listing 8-9. Defining a Function in the main.go File in the functions Folder

```go
package main

import "fmt"

func printSuppliers(product string, suppliers []string ) {
    for _, supplier := range suppliers {
        fmt.Println("Product:", product, "Supplier:", supplier)
    }
}
```

```
func main() {
    printSuppliers("Kayak", []string {"Acme Kayaks", "Bob's Boats", "Crazy Canoes"})
    printSuppliers("Lifejacket", []string {"Sail Safe Co"})
}
```

The second parameter defined by the printSuppliers function accepts a variable number of suppliers using a string slice. This works, but it can be awkward because it requires slices to be constructed even when only a single string is required, like this:

```
...
printSuppliers("Lifejacket", []string {"Sail Safe Co"})
...
```

Variadic parameters allow a function to receive a variable number of arguments more elegantly, as shown in Listing 8-10.

Listing 8-10. Defining a Variadic Parameter in the main.go File in the functions Folder

```
package main

import "fmt"

func printSuppliers(product string, suppliers ...string ) {
    for _, supplier := range suppliers {
        fmt.Println("Product:", product, "Supplier:", supplier)
    }
}

func main() {
    printSuppliers("Kayak", "Acme Kayaks", "Bob's Boats", "Crazy Canoes")
    printSuppliers("Lifejacket", "Sail Safe Co")
}
```

The variadic parameter is defined with an ellipsis (three periods), followed by a type, as shown in Figure 8-6.

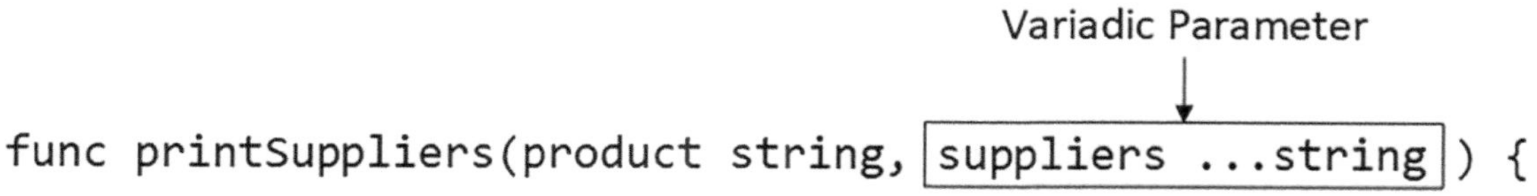

Figure 8-6. A variadic parameter

The variadic parameter must be the last parameter defined by the function, and only a single type can be used, such as the string type in this example. When invoking a function, a variable number of string arguments can be specified without needing to create a slice:

```
...
printSuppliers("Kayak", "Acme Kayaks", "Bob's Boats", "Crazy Canoes")
...
```

The type of a variadic parameter doesn't change, and the values provided are still contained in a slice. For Listing 8-10, this means that the type of the suppliers parameter remains []string. The code in Listings 8-9 and 8-10 produces the following output when compiled and executed:

```
Product: Kayak Supplier: Acme Kayaks
Product: Kayak Supplier: Bob's Boats
Product: Kayak Supplier: Crazy Canoes
Product: Lifejacket Supplier: Sail Safe Co
```

Dealing with No Arguments for a Variadic Parameter

Go allows arguments for variadic parameters to be omitted entirely, which can cause unexpected results, as shown in Listing 8-11.

Listing 8-11. Omitting Arguments in the main.go File in the functions Folder

```
package main

import "fmt"

func printSuppliers(product string, suppliers ...string ) {
    for _, supplier := range suppliers {
        fmt.Println("Product:", product, "Supplier:", supplier)
    }
}

func main() {
    printSuppliers("Kayak", "Acme Kayaks", "Bob's Boats", "Crazy Canoes")
    printSuppliers("Lifejacket", "Sail Safe Co")
    printSuppliers("Soccer Ball")
}
```

The new call to the printSuppliers function does not provide any arguments for the suppliers parameter. When this happens, Go uses nil as the parameter value, which can cause problems with code that assumes there will be at least one value in the slice. Compile and run the code in Listing 8-11; you will receive the following output:

```
Product: Kayak Supplier: Acme Kayaks
Product: Kayak Supplier: Bob's Boats
Product: Kayak Supplier: Crazy Canoes
Product: Lifejacket Supplier: Sail Safe Co
```

There is no output for the Soccer Ball product because nil slices have zero length, so the for loop is never executed. Listing 8-12 corrects this problem by checking for this issue.

Listing 8-12. Checking for Empty Slices in the main.go File in the functions Folder

```
package main

import "fmt"
```

```
func printSuppliers(product string, suppliers ...string ) {
    if (len(suppliers) == 0) {
        fmt.Println("Product:", product, "Supplier: (none)")
    } else {
        for _, supplier := range suppliers {
            fmt.Println("Product:", product, "Supplier:", supplier)
        }
    }
}

func main() {
    printSuppliers("Kayak", "Acme Kayaks", "Bob's Boats", "Crazy Canoes")
    printSuppliers("Lifejacket", "Sail Safe Co")
    printSuppliers("Soccer Ball")
}
```

I have used the built-in len function, described in Chapter 7, to identity empty slices, although I could also have checked for the nil value. Compile and execute the code; you will receive the following output, which caters to the function being called without values for the variadic parameter:

```
Product: Kayak Supplier: Acme Kayaks
Product: Kayak Supplier: Bob's Boats
Product: Kayak Supplier: Crazy Canoes
Product: Lifejacket Supplier: Sail Safe Co
Product: Soccer Ball Supplier: (none)
```

Using Slices as Values for Variadic Parameters

Variadic parameters allow a function to be called without having to create slices, but this isn't helpful when you already have a slice that you want to use. For these situations, following the final argument passed to the function with an ellipsis will allow a slice to be used, as shown in Listing 8-13.

Listing 8-13. Using a Slice as an Argument in the main.go File in the functions Folder

```
package main

import "fmt"

func printSuppliers(product string, suppliers ...string ) {
    if (len(suppliers) == 0) {
        fmt.Println("Product:", product, "Supplier: (none)")
    } else {
        for _, supplier := range suppliers {
            fmt.Println("Product:", product, "Supplier:", supplier)
        }
    }
}
```

```
func main() {

    names := []string {"Acme Kayaks", "Bob's Boats", "Crazy Canoes"}

    printSuppliers("Kayak", names...)
    printSuppliers("Lifejacket", "Sail Safe Co")
    printSuppliers("Soccer Ball")
}
```

This technique avoids the need to unpack a slice into individual values, just so they can be combined back into a slice for the variadic parameter. Compile and execute the code in Listing 8-13, and you will receive the following output:

```
Product: Kayak Supplier: Acme Kayaks
Product: Kayak Supplier: Bob's Boats
Product: Kayak Supplier: Crazy Canoes
Product: Lifejacket Supplier: Sail Safe Co
Product: Soccer Ball Supplier: (none)
```

Using Pointers as Function Parameters

By default, Go copies the values used as arguments so that changes are limited to within the function, as shown in Listing 8-14.

Listing 8-14. Modifying a Parameter Value in the main.go File in the functions Folder

```
package main

import "fmt"

func swapValues(first, second int) {
    fmt.Println("Before swap:", first, second)
    temp := first
    first = second
    second = temp
    fmt.Println("After swap:", first, second)
}

func main() {

    val1, val2 := 10, 20
    fmt.Println("Before calling function", val1, val2)
    swapValues(val1, val2)
    fmt.Println("After calling function", val1, val2)
}
```

The swapValues function receives two int values, writes them out, swaps them, and writes them out again. The values passed to the function are written out before and after the function is called. The output from Listing 8-14 shows that the changes made to the values in the swpValues function do not affect the variables defined in the main function:

```
Before calling function 10 20
Before swap: 10 20
After swap: 20 10
After calling function 10 20
```

Go allows functions to receive pointers, which changes this behavior, as shown in Listing 8-15.

Listing 8-15. Defining a Function with Pointers in the main.go File in the functions Folder

```go
package main

import "fmt"

func swapValues(first, second *int) {
    fmt.Println("Before swap:", *first, *second)
    temp := *first
    *first = *second
    *second = temp
    fmt.Println("After swap:", *first, *second)
}

func main() {

    val1, val2 := 10, 20
    fmt.Println("Before calling function", val1, val2)
    swapValues(&val1, &val2)
    fmt.Println("After calling function", val1, val2)
}
```

The swapValues function still swaps two values but does so using a pointer, which means that the changes are made to the memory locations that are also used by the main function, which can be seen in the output from the code:

```
Before calling function 10 20
Before swap: 10 20
After swap: 20 10
After calling function 20 10
```

There are better ways to perform tasks such as swapping values—including using multiple function results, as described in the next section—but this example demonstrates that functions can work directly with values or indirectly via pointers.

Defining and Using Function Results

Functions define results, which allow functions to provide their callers with the output from operations, as shown in Listing 8-16.

Listing 8-16. Producing a Function Result in the main.go File in the functions Folder

```go
package main
```

```go
import "fmt"

func calcTax(price float64) float64 {
    return price + (price * 0.2)
}

func main() {

    products := map[string]float64 {
        "Kayak" : 275,
        "Lifejacket": 48.95,
    }

    for product, price := range products {
        priceWithTax := calcTax(price)
        fmt.Println("Product: ", product, "Price:", priceWithTax)
    }
}
```

The function declares its result using a data type that follows the parameter, as shown in Figure 8-7.

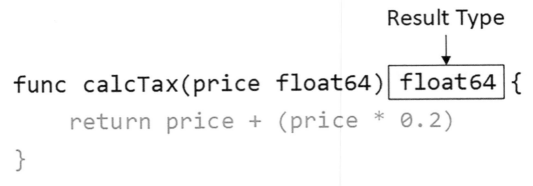

Figure 8-7. *Defining a function result*

The calcTax function produces a float64 result, which is produced by the return statement, as shown in Figure 8-8.

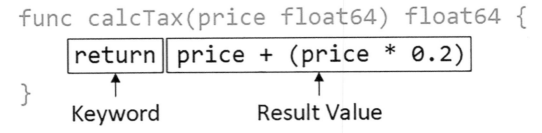

Figure 8-8. *Producing a function*

When the function is called, the result can be assigned to a variable, as shown in Figure 8-9.

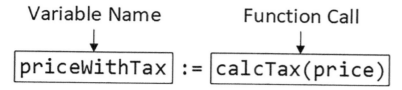

Figure 8-9. *Using a function result*

Function results can be used directly in expressions. Listing 8-17 omits the variable and calls the calcTax function directly to produce an argument for the fmt.PrintLn function.

Listing 8-17. Using a Function Result Directly in the main.go File in the functions Folder

```
package main

import "fmt"

func calcTax(price float64) float64 {
    return price + (price * 0.2)
}

func main() {

    products := map[string]float64 {
        "Kayak" : 275,
        "Lifejacket": 48.95,
    }

    for product, price := range products {
        fmt.Println("Product: ", product, "Price:", calcTax(price))
    }
}
```

Go uses the result produced by the calcTax function without needing to define an intermediate variable. The code in Listings 8-16 and 8-17 produces the following output:

```
Product:  Kayak Price: 330
Product:  Lifejacket Price: 58.74
```

Returning Multiple Function Results

An unusual feature of the Go functions is the ability to produce more than one result, as shown in Listing 8-18.

Listing 8-18. Producing Multiple Results in the main.go File in the functions Folder

```
package main

import "fmt"
```

```
func swapValues(first, second int) (int, int) {
    return second, first
}

func main() {

    val1, val2 := 10, 20
    fmt.Println("Before calling function", val1, val2)
    val1, val2 = swapValues(val1, val2)
    fmt.Println("After calling function", val1, val2)

}
```

The types of the results produced by the function are grouped using parentheses, as shown in Figure 8-10.

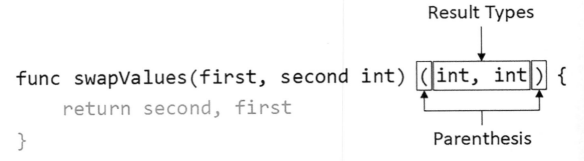

Figure 8-10. *Defining multiple results*

When a function defines multiple results, values for each result are provided with the return keyword, separated by commas, as shown in Figure 8-11.

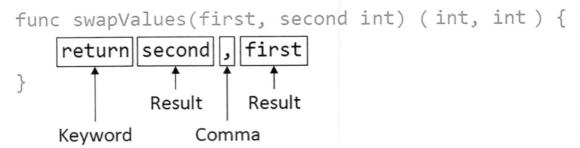

Figure 8-11. *Returning multiple results*

The swapValues function uses the return keyword to produce two int results, which it received through its parameters. These results can be assigned to variables in the statement that calls the function, also separated by commas, as shown in Figure 8-12.

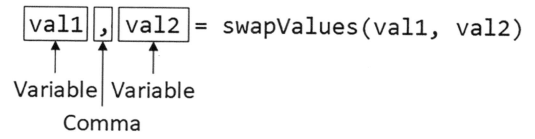

Figure 8-12. *Receiving multiple results*

The code in Listing 8-18 produces the following output when compiled and executed:

```
Before calling function 10 20
After calling function 20 10
```

Using Multiple Results Instead of Multiple Meanings

Multiple function results may seem odd at first, but they can be used to avoid a source of errors that are common in other languages, which is to give different meanings to a single result based on the value that is returned. Listing 8-19 shows the problem caused by imparting additional meanings to a single result.

Listing 8-19. Using a Single Result in the main.go File in the functions Folder

```go
package main

import "fmt"

func calcTax(price float64) float64 {
    if (price > 100) {
        return price * 0.2
    }
    return -1
}

func main() {

    products := map[string]float64 {
        "Kayak" : 275,
        "Lifejacket": 48.95,
    }

    for product, price := range products {
        tax := calcTax(price)
        if (tax != -1) {
            fmt.Println("Product: ", product, "Tax:", tax)
        } else {
            fmt.Println("Product: ", product, "No tax due")
```

```
        }
    }
}
```

The calcTax function uses a float64 result to communicate two outcomes. For values greater than 100, the result will indicate the amount of tax due. For values less than 100, the result will indicate that no tax is due. Compiling and executing the code in Listing 8-19 produces the following result:

```
Product:   Kayak Tax: 55
Product:   Lifejacket No tax due
```

Giving multiple meanings to a single result can become a problem as projects evolve. The tax authority may start giving tax refunds on certain purchases, which makes a value of -1 ambiguous since it could indicate that no tax is due or that a refund of $1 should be issued.

There are many ways to resolve this type of ambiguity, but using multiple function results is an elegant solution, albeit one that can take some time to get used to. In Listing 8-20, I have revised the calcTax function so that it produces multiple results.

Listing 8-20. Using Multiple Results in the main.go File in the functions Folder

```
package main

import "fmt"

func calcTax(price float64) (float64, bool) {
    if (price > 100) {
        return price * 0.2, true
    }
    return 0, false
}

func main() {

    products := map[string]float64 {
        "Kayak" : 275,
        "Lifejacket": 48.95,
    }

    for product, price := range products {
        taxAmount, taxDue := calcTax(price)
        if (taxDue) {
            fmt.Println("Product: ", product, "Tax:", taxAmount)
        } else {
            fmt.Println("Product: ", product, "No tax due")
        }
    }
}
```

The additional result returned by the calcTax method is a bool value that indicates whether tax is due, separating this information from the other result. In Listing 8-20, the two results are obtained in a separate statement, but multiple results are well suited to the if statement's support of an initialization statement, as shown in Listing 8-21. (See Chapter 12 for details of this feature.)

Listing 8-21. Using an Initialization Statement in the main.go File in the functions Folder

```
package main

import "fmt"

func calcTax(price float64) (float64, bool) {
    if (price > 100) {
        return price * 0.2, true
    }
    return 0, false
}

func main() {

    products := map[string]float64 {
        "Kayak" : 275,
        "Lifejacket": 48.95,
    }

    for product, price := range products {
        if taxAmount, taxDue := calcTax(price); taxDue {
            fmt.Println("Product: ", product, "Tax:", taxAmount)
        } else {
            fmt.Println("Product: ", product, "No tax due")
        }

    }
}
```

The two results are obtained by calling the calcTax function in the initialization statement, and the bool result is then used as the statement's expression. The code in Listings 8-20 and 8-21 produces the following output:

```
Product:   Kayak Tax: 55
Product:   Lifejacket No tax due
```

Using Named Results

A function's results can be given names, which can be assigned values during the function's execution. When execution reaches the return keyword, the current values assigned to the results are returned, as shown in Listing 8-22.

Listing 8-22. Using Named Results in the main.go File in the functions Folder

```
package main
```

213

```
import "fmt"

func calcTax(price float64) (float64, bool) {
    if (price > 100) {
        return price * 0.2, true
    }
    return 0, false
}

func calcTotalPrice(products map[string]float64,
        minSpend float64) (total, tax float64)  {
    total = minSpend
    for _, price := range products {
        if taxAmount, due := calcTax(price); due {
            total += taxAmount;
            tax += taxAmount
        } else {
            total += price
        }
    }
    return
}

func main() {

    products := map[string]float64 {
        "Kayak" : 275,
        "Lifejacket": 48.95,
    }

    total1, tax1 := calcTotalPrice(products, 10)
    fmt.Println("Total 1:", total1, "Tax 1:", tax1)
    total2, tax2 := calcTotalPrice(nil, 10)
    fmt.Println("Total 2:", total2, "Tax 2:", tax2)
}
```

Named results are defined as a combination of a name and a result type, as illustrated by Figure 8-13.

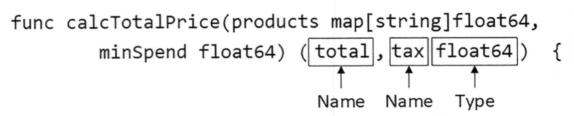

Figure 8-13. *Named results*

The calcTotalPrice function defines results named total and tax. Both are float64 values, which means I can omit the data type from the first name. Within the function, the results can be used as regular variables:

```
...
total = minSpend
for _, price := range products {
    if taxAmount, due := calcTax(price); due {
        total += taxAmount;
        tax += taxAmount
    } else {
        total += price
    }
}
...
```

The return keyword is used on its own, allowing the current values assigned to the named results to be returned. The code in Listing 8-22 produces the following output:

```
Total 1: 113.95 Tax 1: 55
Total 2: 10 Tax 2: 0
```

Using the Blank Identifier to Discard Results

Go requires all declared variables to be used, which can be awkward when a function returns values that you don't require. To avoid compiler errors, the blank identifier (the _ character) can be used to denote results that will not be used, as shown in Listing 8-23.

Listing 8-23. Discarding Function Results in the main.go File in the functions Folder

```
package main

import "fmt"

func calcTotalPrice(products map[string]float64) (count int, total float64)  {
    count = len(products)
    for _, price := range products {
        total += price
    }
    return
}

func main() {

    products := map[string]float64 {
        "Kayak" : 275,
        "Lifejacket": 48.95,
    }

    _, total   := calcTotalPrice(products)
    fmt.Println("Total:", total)
}
```

The calcTotalPrice function returns two results, only one of which is used. The blank identifier is used for the unwanted value, avoiding a compiler error. The code in Listing 8-23 produces the following output:

```
Total: 323.95
```

Using the defer Keyword

The defer keyword is used to schedule a function call that will be performed immediately before the current function returns, as shown in Listing 8-24.

Listing 8-24. Using the defer Keyword in the main.go File in the functions Folder

```
package main

import "fmt"

func calcTotalPrice(products map[string]float64) (count int, total float64) {
    fmt.Println("Function started")
    defer fmt.Println("First defer call")
    count = len(products)
    for _, price := range products {
        total += price
    }
    defer fmt.Println("Second defer call")
    fmt.Println("Function about to return")
    return
}

func main() {

    products := map[string]float64 {
        "Kayak" : 275,
        "Lifejacket": 48.95,
    }

    _, total  := calcTotalPrice(products)
    fmt.Println("Total:", total)
}
```

The defer keyword is used before a function call, as shown in Figure 8-14.

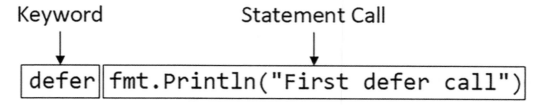

Figure 8-14. *The defer keyword*

The main use for the defer keyword is to call functions that release resources, such as closing open files (described in Chapter 22) or HTTP connections (Chapters 24 and 25). Without the defer keyword, the statement that releases the resource has to appear at the end of a function, which can be many statements after the resource is created and used. The defer keyword lets you group the statements that create, use, and release the resource together.

The defer keyword can be used with any function call, as Listing 8-24 shows, and a single function can use the defer keyword multiple times. Immediately before the function returns, Go will perform the calls scheduled with the defer keyword in the order in which they were defined. The code in Listing 8-24 schedules calls to the fmt.Println function and produces the following output when compiled and executed:

```
Function started
Function about to return
Second defer call
First defer call
Total: 323.95
```

Summary

In this chapter, I described Go functions, explaining how they are defined and used. I demonstrated the different ways in which parameters can be defined and how Go functions can produce results. In the next chapter, I describe the way that functions can be used as types.

CHAPTER 9

■ ■ ■

Using Function Types

In this chapter, I describe the way that Go deals with function types, which is a useful—if sometimes confusing—feature that allows functions to be described consistently and in the same way as other values. Table 9-1 puts function types in context.

Table 9-1. *Putting Function Types in Context*

Question	Answer
What are they?	Functions in Go have a data type, which describes the combination of parameters the function consumes and the results the function produces. This type can be specified explicitly or inferred from a function defined using a literal syntax.
Why are they useful?	Treating functions as data types means that they can be assigned to variables and that one function can be substituted for another, just as long as it has the same combination of parameters and results.
How are they used?	Function types are defined using the func keyword, followed by a signature that describes the parameters and results. No function body is specified.
Are there any pitfalls or limitations?	Advanced uses of function types can become difficult to understand and debug, especially where nested literal functions are defined.
Are there any alternatives?	You do not have to use function types or define functions using the literal syntax, but doing so can reduce code duplication and increase the flexibility of the code you write.

Table 9-2 summarizes the chapter.

Table 9-2. *Chapter Summary*

Problem	Solution	Listing
Describe functions with a specific combination of parameters and results	Use a function type	4–7
Simplify the repeated expression of a function type	Use a function type alias	8
Define a function that is specific to a region of code	Use the literal function syntax	9–12
Access values defined outside of a function	Use a function closure	13–18

© Adam Freeman 2022
A. Freeman, *Pro Go*, https://doi.org/10.1007/978-1-4842-7355-5_9

Preparing for This Chapter

To prepare for this chapter, open a new command prompt, navigate to a convenient location, and create a directory named functionTypes. Navigate to the functionTypes folder and run the command shown in Listing 9-1 to initialize the project.

Listing 9-1. Initializing the Project

```
go mod init functionTypes
```

Add a file named main.go to the functionTypes folder, with the contents shown in Listing 9-2.

> ■ **Tip** You can download the example project for this chapter—and for all the other chapters in this book— from https://github.com/apress/pro-go. See Chapter 2 for how to get help if you have problems running the examples.

Listing 9-2. The Contents of the main.go File in the functionTypes Folder

```go
package main

import "fmt"

func main() {

    fmt.Println("Hello, Function Types")
}
```

Use the command prompt to run the command shown in Listing 9-3 in the functionTypes folder.

Listing 9-3. Running the Example Project

```
go run .
```

The code in the main.go file will be compiled and executed, producing the following output:

```
Hello, Function Types
```

Understanding Function Types

Functions have a data type in Go, which means they can be assigned to variables and used as function parameters, arguments, and results. Listing 9-4 shows a simple use of a function data type.

Listing 9-4. Using a Function Data Type in the main.go File in the functionTypes Folder

```
package main

import "fmt"

func calcWithTax(price float64) float64 {
    return price + (price * 0.2)
}

func calcWithoutTax(price float64) float64 {
    return price
}

func main() {

    products := map[string]float64 {
        "Kayak" : 275,
        "Lifejacket": 48.95,
    }

    for product, price := range products {
        var calcFunc func(float64) float64
        if (price > 100) {
            calcFunc = calcWithTax
        } else {
            calcFunc = calcWithoutTax
        }
        totalPrice := calcFunc(price)
        fmt.Println("Product:", product, "Price:", totalPrice)
    }
}
```

This example contains two functions, each of which defines a float64 parameter and produces a float64 result. The for loop in the main function selects one of these functions and uses it to calculate a total price for a product. The first statement in the loop defines a variable, as shown in Figure 9-1.

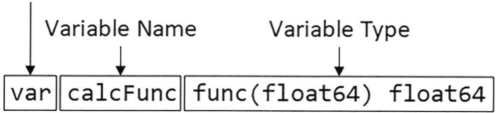

Figure 9-1. *Defining a function type variable*

Function types are specified with the func keyword, followed by the parameter types in parentheses and then the result types. This is known as the *function signature*. If there are multiple results, then the result types are also enclosed in parentheses. The function type in Listing 9-4 describes a function that accepts a float64 argument and produces a float64 result.

The calcFunc variable defined in Listing 9-4 can be assigned any value that matches its type, which means any function that has the right number and type of arguments and results. To assign a specific function to a variable, the function's name is used, as illustrated by Figure 9-2.

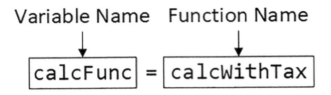

Figure 9-2. *Assigning a function to a variable*

Once a function has been assigned to a variable, it can be invoked as though the variable's name was the function's name. In the example, this means the function assigned to the calcFunc variable can be invoked as shown in Figure 9-3.

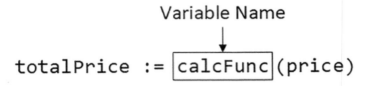

Figure 9-3. *Invoking a function through a variable*

The effect is that whichever function has been assigned to the totalPrice function will be invoked. If the price value is greater than 100, then the calcWithTax function is assigned to the totalPrice variable, and this is the function that will be executed. If price is less than or equal to 100, then the calcWithoutTax function is assigned to the totalPrice variable, and this function will be executed instead. The code in Listing 9-4 produces the following output when compiled and executed (although you may see the results in a different order, as explained in Chapter 7):

```
Product: Kayak Price: 330
Product: Lifejacket Price: 48.95
```

Understanding Function Comparisons and the Zero Type

The Go comparison operators cannot be used to compare functions, but they can be used to determine whether a function has been assigned to a variable, as shown in Listing 9-5.

Listing 9-5. Checking for Assignment in the main.go File in the functionTypes Folder

```
package main

import "fmt"

func calcWithTax(price float64) float64 {
    return price + (price * 0.2)
}

func calcWithoutTax(price float64) float64 {
    return price
}

func main() {

    products := map[string]float64 {
        "Kayak" : 275,
        "Lifejacket": 48.95,
    }

    for product, price := range products {
        var calcFunc func(float64) float64
        fmt.Println("Function assigned:", calcFunc == nil)
        if (price > 100) {
            calcFunc = calcWithTax
        } else {
            calcFunc = calcWithoutTax
        }
        fmt.Println("Function assigned:", calcFunc == nil)
        totalPrice := calcFunc(price)
        fmt.Println("Product:", product, "Price:", totalPrice)
    }
}
```

The zero value for function types is nil, and the new statements in Listing 9-5 use the equality operator to determine whether a function has been assigned to the calcFunc variable. The code in Listing 9-5 produces the following output:

```
Function assigned: true
Function assigned: false
Product: Kayak Price: 330
Function assigned: true
Function assigned: false
Product: Lifejacket Price: 48.95
```

Using Functions as Arguments

Function types can be used in the same way as any other type, including as arguments for other functions, as shown in Listing 9-6.

■ **Note**   Some of the descriptions in the following sections can be hard to follow because the word *function* is required so often. I suggest paying close attention to the code samples, which will help make sense of the text.

Listing 9-6. Using Functions as Arguments in the main.go File in the functionTypes Folder

```go
package main

import "fmt"

func calcWithTax(price float64) float64 {
    return price + (price * 0.2)
}

func calcWithoutTax(price float64) float64 {
    return price
}

func printPrice(product string, price float64, calculator func(float64) float64 ) {
    fmt.Println("Product:", product, "Price:", calculator(price))
}

func main() {

    products := map[string]float64 {
        "Kayak" : 275,
        "Lifejacket": 48.95,
    }

    for product, price := range products {
        if (price > 100) {
            printPrice(product, price, calcWithTax)
        } else {
            printPrice(product, price, calcWithoutTax)
        }
    }
}
```

The printPrice function defines three parameters, the first two of which receive string and float64 values. The third parameter, named calculator, receives a function that receives a float64 value and produces a float64 result, as illustrated by Figure 9-4.

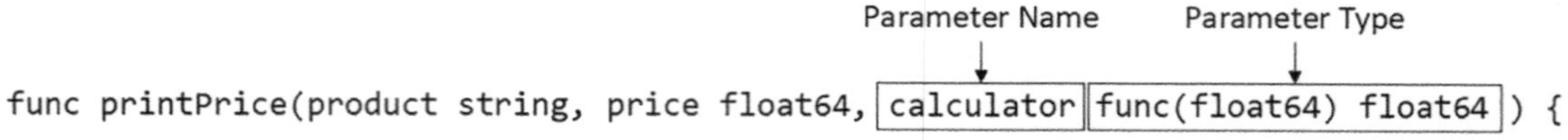

Figure 9-4. *A function parameter*

Within the printPrice function, the calculator parameter is used just like any other function:

```
...
fmt.Println("Product:", product, "Price:", calculator(price))
...
```

What's important is that the printPrice function doesn't know—or care—whether it receives the calcWithTax or calcWithoutTax function through the calculator parameter. All the printPrice function knows is that it will be able to invoke the calculator function with a float64 argument and receive a float64 result because this is the function type of the parameter.

The choice of which function is used is made by the if statement in the main function, and the name is used to pass one function as an argument to another function, like this:

```
...
printPrice(product, price, calcWithTax)
...
```

The code in Listing 9-6 produces the following output when compiled and executed:

```
Product: Kayak Price: 330
Product: Lifejacket Price: 48.95
```

Using Functions as Results

Functions can also be results, meaning that the value returned by a function is another function, as shown in Listing 9-7.

Listing 9-7. Producing a Function Result in the main.go File in the functionTypes Folder

```
package main

import "fmt"

func calcWithTax(price float64) float64 {
    return price + (price * 0.2)
}

func calcWithoutTax(price float64) float64 {
    return price
}

func printPrice(product string, price float64, calculator func(float64) float64 ) {
    fmt.Println("Product:", product, "Price:", calculator(price))
}
```

```
func selectCalculator(price float64) func(float64) float64 {
    if (price > 100) {
        return calcWithTax
    }
    return calcWithoutTax
}

func main() {

    products := map[string]float64 {
        "Kayak" : 275,
        "Lifejacket": 48.95,
    }

    for product, price := range products {
        printPrice(product, price, selectCalculator(price))
    }
}
```

The selectCalculator function receives a float64 value and returns a function, as illustrated by Figure 9-5.

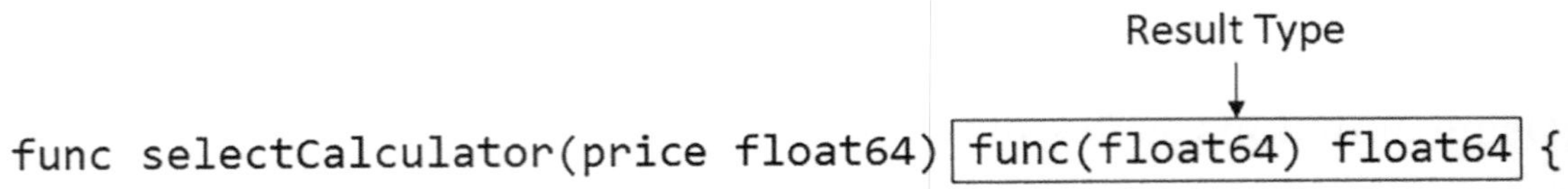

Figure 9-5. *A function type result*

The result produced by selectCalculator is a function that accepts a float64 value and produces a float64 result. Callers to selectCalculator do not know whether they receive the calcWithTax or calcWithoutTax function, only that they will receive a function with the specified signature. The code in Listing 9-7 produces the following output when compiled and executed:

```
Product: Kayak Price: 330
Product: Lifejacket Price: 48.95
```

Creating Function Type Aliases

As the previous examples have shown, using function types can be verbose and repetitive, which produces code that can be hard to read and maintain. Go supports type aliases, which can be used to assign a name to a function signature so that the parameter and result types are not specified every time the function type is used, as shown in Listing 9-8.

Listing 9-8. Using a Type Alias in the main.go File in the functionTypes Folder

```go
package main

import "fmt"

type calcFunc func(float64) float64

func calcWithTax(price float64) float64 {
    return price + (price * 0.2)
}

func calcWithoutTax(price float64) float64 {
    return price
}

func printPrice(product string, price float64, calculator calcFunc) {
    fmt.Println("Product:", product, "Price:", calculator(price))
}

func selectCalculator(price float64) calcFunc {
    if (price > 100) {
        return calcWithTax
    }
    return calcWithoutTax
}

func main() {

    products := map[string]float64 {
        "Kayak" : 275,
        "Lifejacket": 48.95,
    }

    for product, price := range products {
        printPrice(product, price, selectCalculator(price))
    }
}
```

The alias is created with the type keyword, followed by a name for the alias and then by the type, as illustrated by Figure 9-6.

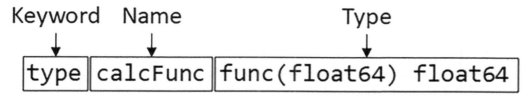

Figure 9-6. *A type alias*

■ **Note**   The type keyword is also used to create custom types, as described in Chapter 10.

The alias in Listing 9-8 assigns the name calcFunc to the function type that accepts a float64 argument and produces a float64 result. The alias name can be used instead of the function type, like this:

```
...
func selectCalculator(price float64) calcFunc {
...
```

You don't have to use aliases for function types, but they can simplify code and make the use of a specific function signature easier to identify. The code in Listing 9-8 produces the following output:

```
Product: Kayak Price: 330
Product: Lifejacket Price: 48.95
```

Using the Literal Function Syntax

The function literal syntax allows functions to be defined so they are specific to a region of code, as shown in Listing 9-9.

Listing 9-9. Using the Literal Syntax in the main.go File in the functionTypes Folder

```
package main

import "fmt"

type calcFunc func(float64) float64

// func calcWithTax(price float64) float64 {
//      return price + (price * 0.2)
// }

// func calcWithoutTax(price float64) float64 {
//      return price
// }

func printPrice(product string, price float64, calculator calcFunc) {
    fmt.Println("Product:", product, "Price:", calculator(price))
}

func selectCalculator(price float64) calcFunc {
    if (price > 100) {
        var withTax calcFunc = func (price float64) float64 {
            return price + (price * 0.2)
        }
        return withTax
    }
```

```
    withoutTax := func (price float64) float64 {
        return price
    }
    return withoutTax
}

func main() {

    products := map[string]float64 {
        "Kayak" : 275,
        "Lifejacket": 48.95,
    }

    for product, price := range products {
        printPrice(product, price, selectCalculator(price))
    }
}
```

The literal syntax omits a name so that the func keyword is followed by the parameters, the result type, and the code block, as shown in Figure 9-7. Because the name is omitted, functions defined this way are called *anonymous functions*.

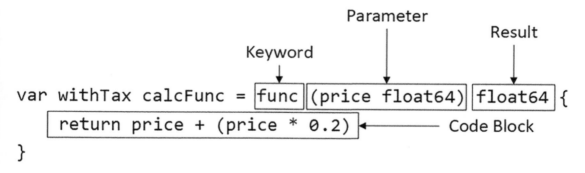

Figure 9-7. *The function literal syntax*

■ **Note**   Go does not support arrow functions, where functions are expressed more concisely using the => operator, without the func keyword and a code block surrounded by braces. In Go, functions must always be defined with the keyword and a body.

The literal syntax creates a function that can be used like any other value, including assigning the function to a variable, which is what I have done in Listing 9-9. The type of a function literal is defined by the function signature, which means that the number and types of the function parameters must match the variable type, like this:

```
...
var withTax calcFunc = func (price float64) float64 {
    return price + (price * 0.2)
}
...
```

This literal function has a signature that matches the calcFunc type alias, with one float64 parameter and one float64 result. Literal functions can also be used with the short variable declaration syntax:

```
...
withoutTax := func (price float64) float64 {
    return price
}
...
```

The Go compiler will determine the variable type using the function signature, which means that the type of the withoutTax variable is func(float64) float64. The code in Listing 9-9 produces the following output when compiled and executed:

```
Product: Kayak Price: 330
Product: Lifejacket Price: 48.95
```

Understanding Function Variable Scope

Functions are treated like any other value, but the function that adds tax can be accessed only through the withTax variable, which, in turn, is accessible only within the if statement's code block, as demonstrated by Listing 9-10.

Listing 9-10. Using a Function Outside of Its Scope in the main.go File in the functionTypes Folder

```
...
func selectCalculator(price float64) calcFunc {
    if (price > 100) {
        var withTax calcFunc = func (price float64) float64 {
            return price + (price * 0.2)
        }
        return withTax
    } else if (price < 10) {
        return withTax
    }
```

```
    withoutTax := func (price float64) float64 {
        return price
    }
    return withoutTax
}
...
```

The statement in the else/if clause tries to access the function assigned to the withTax variable. The variable cannot be accessed because it is in another code block and so the compiler generates the following error:

```
# command-line-arguments
.\main.go:18:16: undefined: withTax
```

Using Functions Values Directly

I assigned the functions to variables in the previous examples because I wanted to demonstrate that Go treats literal functions like any other value. But functions don't have to be assigned to variables and can be used just like any other literal value, as Listing 9-11 shows.

Listing 9-11. Using Functions Directly in the main.go File in the functionTypes Folder

```
package main

import "fmt"

type calcFunc func(float64) float64

func printPrice(product string, price float64, calculator calcFunc) {
    fmt.Println("Product:", product, "Price:", calculator(price))
}

func selectCalculator(price float64) calcFunc {
    if (price > 100) {
        return func (price float64) float64 {
            return price + (price * 0.2)
        }
    }
     return func (price float64) float64 {
        return price
    }
}

func main() {

    products := map[string]float64 {
        "Kayak" : 275,
        "Lifejacket": 48.95,
    }
```

```
    for product, price := range products {
        printPrice(product, price, selectCalculator(price))
    }
}
```

The return keyword is applied directly to the function, without assigning the function to a variable. The code in Listing 9-11 produces the following output:

```
Product: Kayak Price: 330
Product: Lifejacket Price: 48.95
```

Literal functions can also be used as arguments to other functions, as shown in Listing 9-12.

Listing 9-12. Using a Literal Function Argument in the main.go File in the functionTypes Folder

```
package main

import "fmt"

type calcFunc func(float64) float64

func printPrice(product string, price float64, calculator calcFunc) {
    fmt.Println("Product:", product, "Price:", calculator(price))
}

func main() {

    products := map[string]float64 {
        "Kayak" : 275,
        "Lifejacket": 48.95,
    }

    for product, price := range products {
        printPrice(product, price, func (price float64) float64 {
            return price + (price * 0.2)
        })
    }
}
```

The final argument to the printPrice function is expressed using the literal syntax and without assigning the function to a variable. The code in Listing 9-12 produces the following output:

```
Product: Kayak Price: 330
Product: Lifejacket Price: 58.74
```

CHAPTER 9 ■ USING FUNCTION TYPES

Understanding Function Closure

Functions defined using the literal syntax can reference variables from the surrounding code, a feature known as *closure*. This feature can be difficult to understand, so I am going to start with an example that doesn't rely on closure, shown in Listing 9-13, and then explain how it can be improved.

Listing 9-13. Using Multiple Functions in the main.go File in the functionTypes Folder

```
package main

import "fmt"

type calcFunc func(float64) float64

func printPrice(product string, price float64, calculator calcFunc) {
    fmt.Println("Product:", product, "Price:", calculator(price))
}

func main() {

    watersportsProducts := map[string]float64 {
        "Kayak" : 275,
        "Lifejacket": 48.95,
    }

    soccerProducts := map[string] float64 {
        "Soccer Ball": 19.50,
        "Stadium": 79500,
    }

    calc := func(price float64) float64 {
        if (price > 100) {
            return price + (price * 0.2)
        }
        return price;
    }
    for product, price := range watersportsProducts {
        printPrice(product, price, calc)
    }

    calc = func(price float64) float64 {
        if (price > 50) {
            return price + (price * 0.1)
        }
        return price
    }
    for product, price := range soccerProducts {
        printPrice(product, price, calc)
    }
}
```

Two maps contain the names and prices of products in the watersports and soccer categories. The maps are enumerated by for loops, which call the printPrice function for each map element. One of the arguments required by the printPrice function is a calcFunc, which is a function that will calculate the total price, including tax, for a product. Each product category requires a different tax-free threshold and tax rate, as described by Table 9-3.

Table 9-3. *Product Category Thresholds and Tax Rates*

Category	Threshold	Tax Rate
Watersports	100	20%
Soccer	50	10%

■ **Note**   Please do not write to me complaining that my fictional tax rates show a dislike for soccer. I dislike all sports equally, except long-distance running, which I undertake largely because every mile takes me farther away from people who talk about sports.

I use the literal syntax to create functions that apply the thresholds for each category. This works, but there is a high degree of duplication, and if there is a change in the way that prices are calculated, I have to remember to update the calculator function for each category.

What I want is the ability to consolidate the common code required to calculate a price and allow that common code to be configured with the changes for each category. This is easily done using the closure feature, as shown in Listing 9-14.

Listing 9-14. Using Function Closure in the main.go File in the functionTypes Folder

```
package main

import "fmt"

type calcFunc func(float64) float64

func printPrice(product string, price float64, calculator calcFunc) {
    fmt.Println("Product:", product, "Price:", calculator(price))
}

func priceCalcFactory(threshold, rate float64) calcFunc {
    return func(price float64) float64 {
        if (price > threshold) {
            return price + (price * rate)
        }
        return price
    }
}
```

```
func main() {

    watersportsProducts := map[string]float64 {
        "Kayak" : 275,
        "Lifejacket": 48.95,
    }

    soccerProducts := map[string] float64 {
        "Soccer Ball": 19.50,
        "Stadium": 79500,
    }

    waterCalc := priceCalcFactory(100, 0.2);
    soccerCalc := priceCalcFactory(50, 0.1)

    for product, price := range watersportsProducts {
        printPrice(product, price, waterCalc)
    }

    for product, price := range soccerProducts {
        printPrice(product, price, soccerCalc)
    }
}
```

The key addition is the priceCalcFactory function, which I am going to refer to as the *factory function* in this section, to differentiate it from the other parts of the code. The job of the factory function is to create calculator functions for a specific combination of threshold and tax rate. This task is described by the function signature, as shown in Figure 9-8.

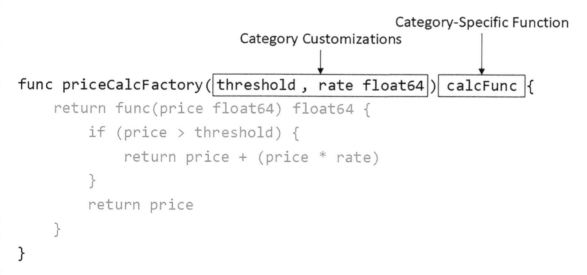

Figure 9-8. *The factory function signature*

CHAPTER 9 ■ USING FUNCTION TYPES

The inputs to the factory function are the threshold and rate for a category, and the output is a function that will calculate prices used for that category. The code in the factory function uses the literal syntax to define a calculator function that contains the common code for performing the calculation, as shown in Figure 9-9.

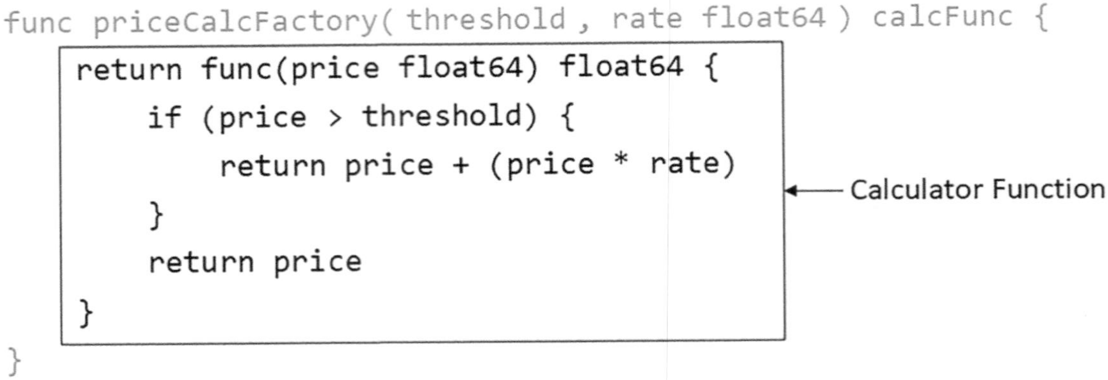

```
func priceCalcFactory( threshold , rate float64 ) calcFunc {
    return func(price float64) float64 {
        if (price > threshold) {
            return price + (price * rate)
        }
        return price
    }
}
```

Calculator Function

Figure 9-9. *The common code*

The closure feature is the link between the factory function and the calculator function. The calculator function relies on two variables to produce a result, like this:

```
...
return func(price float64) float64 {
    if (price > threshold) {
        return price + (price * rate)
    }
    return price
}
...
```

The threshold and rate values are taken from the factory function parameters, like this:

```
...
func priceCalcFactory(threshold, rate float64) calcFunc {
...
```

The closure feature allows a function to access variables—and parameters—in the surrounding code. In this case, the calculator function relies on the parameters of the factory function. When the calculator function is invoked, the parameter values are used to produce a result, as illustrated by Figure 9-10.

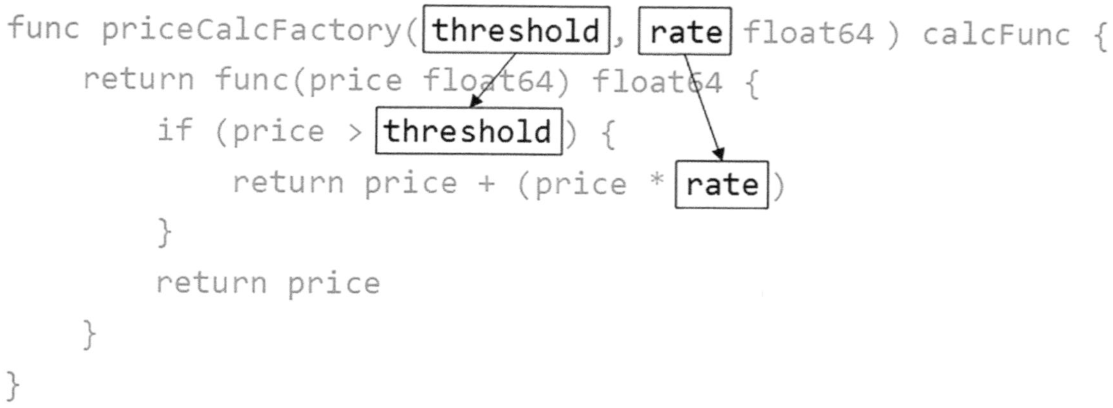

```
func priceCalcFactory( threshold , rate float64 ) calcFunc {
    return func(price float64) float64 {
        if (price > threshold ) {
            return price + (price * rate )
        }
        return price
    }
}
```

Figure 9-10. *Function closure*

A function is said to *close on* the sources of values it requires, such that the calculator function *closes on* the factory function's threshold and rate parameters.

The result is a factory function that creates calculator functions that are customized for a product category's tax threshold and rate. The code required to calculate prices has been consolidated so that changes will be applied to all categories. Listing 9-13 and Listing 9-14 both produce the following output:

```
Product: Kayak Price: 330
Product: Lifejacket Price: 48.95
Product: Soccer Ball Price: 19.5
Product: Stadium Price: 87450
```

Understanding Closure Evaluation

The variables on which a function closes are evaluated each time the function is invoked, which means that changes made outside of a function can affect the results it produces, as shown in Listing 9-15.

Listing 9-15. Modifying a Closed-On Value in the main.go File in the functionTypes Folder

```
package main

import "fmt"

type calcFunc func(float64) float64

func printPrice(product string, price float64, calculator calcFunc) {
    fmt.Println("Product:", product, "Price:", calculator(price))
}

var prizeGiveaway = false
```

```
func priceCalcFactory(threshold, rate float64) calcFunc {
    return func(price float64) float64 {
        if (prizeGiveaway) {
            return 0
        } else if (price > threshold) {
            return price + (price * rate)
        }
        return price
    }
}

func main() {

    watersportsProducts := map[string]float64 {
        "Kayak" : 275,
        "Lifejacket": 48.95,
    }

    soccerProducts := map[string] float64 {
        "Soccer Ball": 19.50,
        "Stadium": 79500,
    }

    prizeGiveaway = false
    waterCalc := priceCalcFactory(100, 0.2);
    prizeGiveaway = true
    soccerCalc := priceCalcFactory(50, 0.1)

    for product, price := range watersportsProducts {
        printPrice(product, price, waterCalc)
    }

    for product, price := range soccerProducts {
        printPrice(product, price, soccerCalc)
    }
}
```

The calculator function closes on the prizeGiveaway variable, which causes the prices to drop to zero. The prizeGiveaway variable is set to false before the function for the watersports category is created and set to true before the function for the soccer category is created.

But, since closures are evaluated when the function is invoked, it is the current value of the prizeGiveaway variable that is used, not the value at the time the function was created. As a consequence, the prices for both categories are dropped to zero, and the code produces the following output:

```
Product: Lifejacket Price: 0
Product: Kayak Price: 0
Product: Soccer Ball Price: 0
Product: Stadium Price: 0
```

Forcing Early Evaluation

Evaluating closures when the function is invoked can be useful, but if you want to use the value that was current when the function was created, then copy the value, as shown in Listing 9-16.

Listing 9-16. Forcing Evaluation in the main.go File in the functionTypes Folder

```
...
func priceCalcFactory(threshold, rate float64) calcFunc {
    fixedPrizeGiveway := prizeGiveaway
    return func(price float64) float64 {
        if (fixedPrizeGiveway) {
            return 0
        } else if (price > threshold) {
            return price + (price * rate)
        }
        return price
    }
}
...
```

The calculator function closes on the fixedPrizeGiveway variable whose value is set when the factory function is invoked. This ensures that the calculator function won't be affected if the prizeGiveaway value is changed. The same effect can also be achieved by adding a parameter to the factory function because function parameters are passed by value by default. Listing 9-17 adds a parameter to the factory function.

Listing 9-17. Adding a Parameter in the main.go File in the functionTypes Folder

```
package main

import "fmt"

type calcFunc func(float64) float64

func printPrice(product string, price float64, calculator calcFunc) {
    fmt.Println("Product:", product, "Price:", calculator(price))
}

var prizeGiveaway = false

func priceCalcFactory(threshold, rate float64, zeroPrices bool) calcFunc {
    return func(price float64) float64 {
        if (zeroPrices) {
            return 0
        } else if (price > threshold) {
            return price + (price * rate)
        }
        return price
    }
}
```

239

```
func main() {

    watersportsProducts := map[string]float64 {
        "Kayak" : 275,
        "Lifejacket": 48.95,
    }

    soccerProducts := map[string] float64 {
        "Soccer Ball": 19.50,
        "Stadium": 79500,
    }

    prizeGiveaway = false
    waterCalc := priceCalcFactory(100, 0.2, prizeGiveaway);
    prizeGiveaway = true
    soccerCalc := priceCalcFactory(50, 0.1, prizeGiveaway)

    for product, price := range watersportsProducts {
        printPrice(product, price, waterCalc)
    }

    for product, price := range soccerProducts {
        printPrice(product, price, soccerCalc)
    }
}
```

In Listing 9-16 and Listing 9-17, the calculator functions are unaffected when the prizeGiveaway variable is changed and the following output is produced:

```
Product: Kayak Price: 330
Product: Lifejacket Price: 48.95
Product: Stadium Price: 0
Product: Soccer Ball Price: 0
```

Closing on a Pointer to Prevent Early Evaluation

Most problems with closure are caused by changes made to variables after a function has been created, which can be addressed using the techniques in the previous section. On occasion, you may find encounter the contrary issue, which is the need to avoid early evaluation to ensure that the current value is used by a function. In these situations, using a pointer will prevent values from being copied, as shown in Listing 9-18.

Listing 9-18. Closing on a Pointer in the main.go File in the functionTypes Folder

```
package main

import "fmt"

type calcFunc func(float64) float64
```

```go
func printPrice(product string, price float64, calculator calcFunc) {
    fmt.Println("Product:", product, "Price:", calculator(price))
}

var prizeGiveaway = false

func priceCalcFactory(threshold, rate float64, zeroPrices *bool) calcFunc {
    return func(price float64) float64 {
        if (*zeroPrices) {
            return 0
        } else if (price > threshold) {
            return price + (price * rate)
        }
        return price
    }
}

func main() {

    watersportsProducts := map[string]float64 {
        "Kayak" : 275,
        "Lifejacket": 48.95,
    }

    soccerProducts := map[string] float64 {
        "Soccer Ball": 19.50,
        "Stadium": 79500,
    }

    prizeGiveaway = false
    waterCalc := priceCalcFactory(100, 0.2, &prizeGiveaway);
    prizeGiveaway = true
    soccerCalc := priceCalcFactory(50, 0.1, &prizeGiveaway)

    for product, price := range watersportsProducts {
        printPrice(product, price, waterCalc)
    }

    for product, price := range soccerProducts {
        printPrice(product, price, soccerCalc)
    }
}
```

In this example, the factory function defines a parameter that receives a pointer to a bool value, on which the calculator function closes. The pointer is followed when the calculator function is invoked, which ensures that the current value is used. The code in Listing 9-18 produces the following output:

```
Product: Kayak Price: 0
Product: Lifejacket Price: 0
Product: Soccer Ball Price: 0
Product: Stadium Price: 0
```

Summary

In this chapter, I described the way that Go treats function types, allowing them to be used like any other data type and allowing functions to be treated like any other value. I explained how function types are described and showed you how they can be used to define parameters and results for other functions. I demonstrated the use of type aliases to avoid repeating complex function types in code, and I explained the use of the function literal syntax and the way that functions closures work. In the next chapter, I explain how you can define custom data types by creating struct types.

CHAPTER 10

■ ■ ■

Defining Structs

In this chapter, I describe structs, which is how custom data types are defined in Go. I show you how to define new struct types, describe how to create values from those types, and explain what happens when values are copied. Table 10-1 puts structs in context.

Table 10-1. *Putting Structs in Context*

Question	Answer
What are they?	Structs are data types, comprised of fields.
Why are they useful?	Structs allow custom data types to be defined.
How are they used?	The type and struct keywords are used to define a type, allowing field names and types to be specified.
Are there any pitfalls or limitations?	Care must be taken to avoid unintentionally duplicating struct values and to ensure that fields that store pointers are initialized before they are used.
Are there any alternatives?	Simple applications can use just the built-in data types, but most applications will need to define custom types, for which structs are the only option.

© Adam Freeman 2022
A. Freeman, *Pro Go*, https://doi.org/10.1007/978-1-4842-7355-5_10

Table 10-2 summarizes the chapter.

Table 10-2. *Chapter Summary*

Problem	Solution	Listing
Define a custom data type	Define a struct type	4, 24
Create a struct value	Use the literal syntax to create a new value and assign values to individual fields	5–7, 15
Define a struct field whose type is another struct	Define an embedded field	8, 9
Compare struct values	Use the comparison operator, ensuring that the values being compared have the same type or types that have the same fields, all of which must be comparable	10, 11
Convert struct types	Perform an explicit conversion, ensuring that the types have the same fields	12
Define a struct without assigning a name	Define an anonymous struct	13–14
Prevent a struct from being duplicated when it is assigned to a variable or used as a function argument	Use a pointer	16–21, 25–29
Create struct values consistently	Define a constructor function	22, 23

Preparing for This Chapter

To prepare for this chapter, open a new command prompt, navigate to a convenient location, and create a directory named structs. Navigate to the structs folder and run the command shown in Listing 10-1 to initialize the project.

■ **Tip** You can download the example project for this chapter—and for all the other chapters in this book—from https://github.com/apress/pro-go. See Chapter 2 for how to get help if you have problems running the examples.

Listing 10-1. Initializing the Project

```
go mod init structs
```

Add a file named main.go to the structs folder, with the contents shown in Listing 10-2.

Listing 10-2. The Contents of the main.go File in the structs Folder

```
package main

import "fmt"

func main() {

    fmt.Println("Hello, Structs")
}
```

Use the command prompt to run the command shown in Listing 10-3 in the structs folder.

Listing 10-3. Running the Example Project

```
go run .
```

The code in the main.go file will be compiled and executed, producing the following output:

```
Hello, Structs
```

Defining and Using a Struct

Custom data types are defined using the Go structs feature, which is demonstrated in Listing 10-4.

Listing 10-4. Creating a Custom Data Type in the main.go File in the structs Folder

```
package main

import "fmt"

func main() {

    type Product struct {
        name, category string
        price float64
    }

    kayak := Product {
        name: "Kayak",
        category: "Watersports",
        price: 275,
    }

    fmt.Println(kayak.name, kayak.category, kayak.price)
    kayak.price = 300
    fmt.Println("Changed price:", kayak.price)
}
```

Custom data types are known as *struct types* in Go and are defined using the type keyword, a name, and the struct keyword. Braces surround a series of fields, each of which is defined with a name and type. Fields of the same type can be declared together, as shown in Figure 10-1, and all fields must have different names.

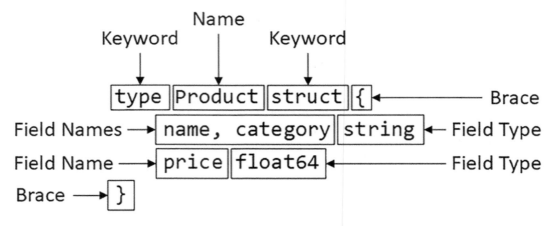

Figure 10-1. Defining a struct type

This struct type is named Product, and it has three fields: the name and category fields hold string values, and the price field holds a float64 value. The name and category fields have the same type and can be defined together.

WHERE ARE THE GO CLASSES?

Go doesn't differentiate between structs and classes, in the way that other languages do. All custom data types are defined as structs, and the decision to pass them by reference or by value is made depending on whether a pointer is used. As I explained in Chapter 4, this achieves the same effect as having separate type categories but with the additional flexibility of allowing the choice to be made every time a value is used. It does, however, require more diligence from the programmer, who must think through the consequences of that choice during coding. Neither approach is better, and the results are essentially the same.

Creating Struct Values

The next step is to create a value using the custom type, which is done using the struct type name, followed by braces containing the values for the struct fields, as shown in Figure 10-2.

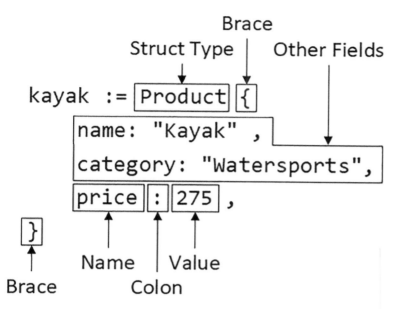

Figure 10-2. *Creating a struct value*

The value created in Listing 10-4 is a Product whose name field is assigned the value Kayak, category field is Watersports, and price field is 275. The struct value is assigned to a variable named kayak.

Go is particular about syntax and will produce an error if the final field's value isn't followed by either a comma or the closing brace. I generally prefer trailing commas, which allows me to put the closing brace on the next line in the code file, just as I did with the map literal syntax in Chapter 7.

■ **Note** Go doesn't allow structs to be used with the const keyword, and the compiler will report an error if you try to define a constant struct. Only the data types described in Chapter 9 can be used to create constants.

Using a Struct Value

The fields of a struct value are accessed through the name given to the variable so that the value of the name field of the struct value assigned to the kayak variable is accessed using kayak.name, as shown in Figure 10-3.

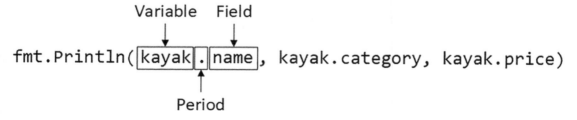

Figure 10-3. *Accessing struct fields*

New values can be assigned to a struct field using the same syntax, as shown in Figure 10-4.

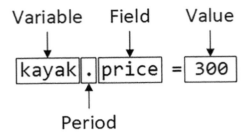

Figure 10-4. Modifying a struct field

This statement assigns the value 300 to the price field of the Product struct value assigned to the kayak variable. The code in Listing 10-4 produces the following output when compiled and executed:

```
Kayak Watersports 275
Changed price: 300
```

UNDERSTANDING STRUCT TAGS

The struct type can be defined with tags, which provide additional information about how a field should be processed. Struct tags are just strings that are interpreted by the code that processes struct values, using the features provided by the reflect package. See Chapter 21 for an example of how struct tags can be used to change the way that structs are encoded in JSON data, and see Chapter 28 for details of how to access struct tags yourself.

Partially Assigning Struct Values

Values do not have to be provided for all fields when creating a struct value, as shown in Listing 10-5.

Listing 10-5. Assigning Some Fields in the main.go File in the structs Folder

```
package main

import "fmt"

func main() {

    type Product struct {
        name, category string
        price float64
    }
```

```
kayak := Product {
    name: "Kayak",
    category: "Watersports",
}

fmt.Println(kayak.name, kayak.category, kayak.price)
kayak.price = 300
fmt.Println("Changed price:", kayak.price)
}
```

No initial value is provided for the price field for the struct assigned to the kayak variable. When no field is provided, the zero value for the field's type is used. For Listing 10-5, the zero type for the price field is 0, because the field type is float64; the code produces the following output when compiled and executed:

```
Kayak Watersports 0
Changed price: 300
```

As the output shows, omitting an initial value doesn't prevent a value from being assigned to a field subsequently.

The zero types are assigned to all fields if you define a struct-typed variable but don't assign a value to it, as shown in Listing 10-6.

Listing 10-6. An Unassigned Variable in the main.go File in the structs Folder

```
package main

import "fmt"

func main() {

    type Product struct {
        name, category string
        price float64
    }

    kayak := Product {
        name: "Kayak",
        category: "Watersports",
    }

    fmt.Println(kayak.name, kayak.category, kayak.price)
    kayak.price = 300
    fmt.Println("Changed price:", kayak.price)

    var lifejacket Product
    fmt.Println("Name is zero value:", lifejacket.name == "")
    fmt.Println("Category is zero value:", lifejacket.category == "")
    fmt.Println("Price is zero value:", lifejacket.price == 0)
}
```

The type of the lifejacket variable is Product, but no values are assigned to its fields. The value of all the lifejacket fields is the zero value for their type, which is confirmed by the output from Listing 10-6:

```
Kayak Watersports 0
Changed price: 300
Name is zero value: true
Category is zero value: true
Price is zero value: true
```

USING THE NEW FUNCTION TO CREATE STRUCT VALUES

You may see code that uses the built-in new function to create struct values, like this:

```
...
var lifejacket = new(Product)
...
```

The result is a pointer to a struct value whose fields are initialized with their type's zero value. This is equivalent to this statement:

```
...
var lifejacket = &Product{}
...
```

These approaches are interchangeable, and choosing between them is a matter of preference.

Using Field Positions to Create Struct Values

Struct values can be defined without using names, as long as the types of the values correspond to the order in which fields are defined by the struct type, as shown in Listing 10-7.

Listing 10-7. Omitting Field Names in the main.go File in the structs Folder

```
package main

import "fmt"

func main() {

    type Product struct {
        name, category string
        price float64
    }
```

```
var kayak = Product { "Kayak", "Watersports", 275.00 }

fmt.Println("Name:", kayak.name)
fmt.Println("Category:", kayak.category)
fmt.Println("Price:", kayak.price)
}
```

The literal syntax used to define the struct value contains just values, which are assigned to the struct fields in the order in which they are specified. The code in Listing 10-7 produces the following output:

```
Name: Kayak
Category: Watersports
Price: 275
```

Defining Embedded Fields

If a field is defined without a name, it is known as an *embedded field*, and it is accessed using the name of its type, as shown in Listing 10-8.

Listing 10-8. Defining Embedded Fields in the main.go File in the structs Folder

```
package main

import "fmt"

func main() {

    type Product struct {
        name, category string
        price float64
    }

    type StockLevel struct {
        Product
        count int
    }

    stockItem := StockLevel {
        Product: Product { "Kayak", "Watersports", 275.00 },
        count: 100,
    }

    fmt.Println("Name:", stockItem.Product.name)
    fmt.Println("Count:", stockItem.count)
}
```

The StockLevel struct type has two fields. The first field is embedded and is defined just using a type, which is the Product struct type, as illustrated by Figure 10-5.

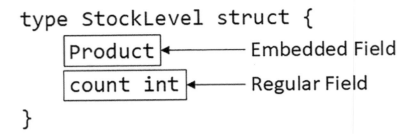

Figure 10-5. *Defining an embedded field*

Embedded fields are accessed using the name of the field type, which is why this feature is most useful for fields whose type is a struct. In this case, the embedded field is defined with the Product type, which means it is assigned and read using Product as the field name, like this:

```
...
stockItem := StockLevel {
    Product: Product { "Kayak", "Watersports", 275.00 },
    count: 100,
}
...
fmt.Println(fmt.Sprint("Name: ", stockItem.Product.name))
...
```

The code in Listing 10-8 produces the following output when it is compiled and executed:

```
Name: Kayak
Count: 100
```

As noted earlier, field names must be unique with the struct type, which means that you can define only one embedded field for a specific type. If you need to define two fields of the same type, then you will need to assign a name to one of them, as shown in Listing 10-9.

Listing 10-9. Defining an Additional Field in the main.go File in the structs Folder

```
package main

import "fmt"

func main() {

    type Product struct {
        name, category string
        price float64
    }

    type StockLevel struct {
        Product
        Alternate Product
        count int
    }
```

```
    stockItem := StockLevel {
        Product: Product { "Kayak", "Watersports", 275.00 },
        Alternate: Product{"Lifejacket", "Watersports", 48.95 },
        count: 100,
    }

    fmt.Println("Name:", stockItem.Product.name)
    fmt.Println("Alt Name:", stockItem.Alternate.name)
}
```

The StockLevel type has two fields whose type is Product, but only one can be an embedded field. For the second field, I have assigned a name through which the field is accessed. The code in Listing 10-9 produces the following output when compiled and executed:

```
Name: Kayak
Alt Name: Lifejacket
```

Comparing Struct Values

Struct values are comparable if all their fields can be compared. Listing 10-10 creates several struct values and applies the comparison operator to determine if they are equal.

Listing 10-10. Comparing Struct Values in the main.go File in the structs Folder

```
package main

import "fmt"

func main() {

    type Product struct {
        name, category string
        price float64
    }

    p1 := Product { name: "Kayak", category: "Watersports", price: 275.00 }
    p2 := Product { name: "Kayak", category: "Watersports", price: 275.00 }
    p3 := Product { name: "Kayak", category: "Boats", price: 275.00 }

    fmt.Println("p1 == p2:", p1 == p2)
    fmt.Println("p1 == p3:", p1 == p3)
}
```

The struct values p1 and p2 are equal because all their fields are equal. The struct values p1 and p3 are not equal because the values assigned to their category fields are different. Compile and execute the project, and you will see the following results:

```
p1 == p2: true
p1 == p3: false
```

Structs cannot be compared if the struct type defines fields with incomparable types, such as slices, as shown in Listing 10-11.

Listing 10-11. Adding an Incomparable Field in the main.go File in the structs Folder

```
package main

import "fmt"

func main() {

    type Product struct {
        name, category string
        price float64
        otherNames []string
    }

    p1 := Product { name: "Kayak", category: "Watersports", price: 275.00 }
    p2 := Product { name: "Kayak", category: "Watersports", price: 275.00 }
    p3 := Product { name: "Kayak", category: "Boats", price: 275.00 }

    fmt.Println("p1 == p2:", p1 == p2)
    fmt.Println("p1 == p3:", p1 == p3)
}
```

As explained in Chapter 7, the Go comparison operator cannot be applied to slices, which means that Product values cannot be compared. When compiled, this code produces the following errors:

```
.\main.go:17:33: invalid operation: p1 == p2 (struct containing []string cannot be compared)
.\main.go:18:33: invalid operation: p1 == p3 (struct containing []string cannot be compared)
```

Converting Between Struct Types

A struct type can be converted into any other struct type that has the same fields, meaning all the fields have the same name and type and are defined in the same order, as demonstrated in Listing 10-12.

Listing 10-12. Converting a Struct Type in the main.go File in the structs Folder

```
package main

import "fmt"

func main() {

    type Product struct {
        name, category string
        price float64
        //otherNames []string
    }
```

```
type Item struct {
    name string
    category string
    price float64
}

prod := Product { name: "Kayak", category: "Watersports", price: 275.00 }
item := Item { name: "Kayak", category: "Watersports", price: 275.00 }

fmt.Println("prod == item:", prod == Product(item))
}
```

Values created from the Product and Item struct types can be compared because they define the same fields in the same order. Compile and execute the project; you will see the following output:

```
prod == item: true
```

Defining Anonymous Struct Types

Anonymous struct types are defined without using a name, as shown in Listing 10-13.

Listing 10-13. Defining an Anonymous Struct Type in the main.go File in the structs Folder

```
package main

import "fmt"

func writeName(val struct {
        name, category string
        price float64}) {
    fmt.Println("Name:", val.name)
}

func main() {

    type Product struct {
        name, category string
        price float64
        //otherNames []string
    }

    type Item struct {
        name string
        category string
        price float64
    }
```

```
    prod := Product { name: "Kayak", category: "Watersports", price: 275.00 }
    item := Item { name: "Stadium", category: "Soccer", price: 75000 }

    writeName(prod)
    writeName(item)
}
```

The writeName function uses an anonymous struct type as its parameter, which means that it can accept any struct type that defines the specified set of fields. Compile and execute the project; you will see the following output:

```
Name: Kayak
Name: Stadium
```

I don't find this feature particularly useful as it is shown in Listing 10-13, but there is a variation that I do use, which is to define an anonymous struct and assign it a value in a single step. This is useful when calling code that inspects the types it receives at runtime using the features provided by the reflect package, which I describe in Chapters 27–29. The reflect package contains advanced features, but it is used by other parts of the standard library, such as the built-in support for encoding JSON data. I explain the JSON features in detail in Chapter 21, but for this chapter, Listing 10-14 demonstrates the use of an anonymous struct to select fields to be included in a JSON string.

Listing 10-14. Assigning a Value to an Anonymous Struct in the main.go File in the structs Folder

```
package main

import (
    "fmt"
    "encoding/json"
    "strings"
)

func main() {

    type Product struct {
        name, category string
        price float64
    }

    prod := Product { name: "Kayak", category: "Watersports", price: 275.00 }

    var builder strings.Builder
    json.NewEncoder(&builder).Encode(struct {
        ProductName string
        ProductPrice float64
    }{
        ProductName: prod.name,
        ProductPrice: prod.price,
    })
    fmt.Println(builder.String())
}
```

Don't worry about the encoding/json and strings packages, which are described in later chapters. This example demonstrates how an anonymous struct can be defined and assigned a value in a single step, which I use in Listing 10-14 to create a struct with ProductName and ProductPrice fields, which I then assign using values from Product fields. Compile and execute the project; you will see the following output:

```
{"ProductName":"Kayak","ProductPrice":275}
```

Creating Arrays, Slices, and Maps Containing Struct Values

The struct type can be omitted when populating arrays, slices, and maps with struct values, as shown in Listing 10-15.

Listing 10-15. Omitting the Struct Type in the main.go File in the structs Folder

```go
package main

import "fmt"

func main() {

    type Product struct {
        name, category string
        price float64
        //otherNames []string
    }

    type StockLevel struct {
        Product
        Alternate Product
        count int
    }

    array := [1]StockLevel {
        {
            Product: Product { "Kayak", "Watersports", 275.00 },
            Alternate: Product{"Lifejacket", "Watersports", 48.95 },
            count: 100,
        },
    }
    fmt.Println("Array:", array[0].Product.name)

    slice := []StockLevel {
        {
            Product: Product { "Kayak", "Watersports", 275.00 },
            Alternate: Product{"Lifejacket", "Watersports", 48.95 },
            count: 100,
        },
    }
```

```
    fmt.Println("Slice:", slice[0].Product.name)

    kvp := map[string]StockLevel {
        "kayak": {
            Product: Product { "Kayak", "Watersports", 275.00 },
            Alternate: Product{"Lifejacket", "Watersports", 48.95 },
            count: 100,
        },
    }
    fmt.Println("Map:", kvp["kayak"].Product.name)
}
```

The code in Listing 10-15 creates an array, a slice, and a map, all of which are populated with a StockLevel value. The compiler can infer the type of the struct value from the containing data structure, allowing the code to be expressed more concisely. Listing 10-15 produces the following output:

```
Array: Kayak
Slice: Kayak
Map: Kayak
```

Understanding Structs and Pointers

Assigning a struct to a new variable or using a struct as a function parameter creates a new value that copies the field values, as demonstrated in Listing 10-16.

Listing 10-16. Copying a Struct Value in the main.go File in the structs Folder

```
package main

import "fmt"

func main() {

    type Product struct {
        name, category string
        price float64
    }

    p1 := Product {
        name: "Kayak",
        category: "Watersports",
        price: 275,
    }

    p2 := p1

    p1.name = "Original Kayak"
```

```
    fmt.Println("P1:", p1.name)
    fmt.Println("P2:", p2.name)
}
```

A struct value is created and assigned to the variable p1 and copied to the variable p2. The name field of the first struct value is changed, and then both name values are written out. The output from Listing 10-16 confirms that assigning a struct value creates a copy:

```
P1: Original Kayak
P2: Kayak
```

Like other data types, references to struct values can be created using pointers, as shown in Listing 10-17.

Listing 10-17. Using a Pointer to a Struct in the main.go File in the structs Folder

```
package main

import "fmt"

func main() {

    type Product struct {
        name, category string
        price float64
    }

    p1 := Product {
        name: "Kayak",
        category: "Watersports",
        price: 275,
    }

    p2 := &p1

    p1.name = "Original Kayak"

    fmt.Println("P1:", p1.name)
    fmt.Println("P2:", (*p2).name)
}
```

I used an ampersand to create a pointer to the p1 variable and assigned the address to p2, whose type becomes *Product, meaning a pointer to a Product value. Notice that I have to use parentheses to follow the pointer to the struct value and then read the value of the name field, as shown in Figure 10-6.

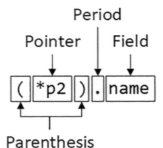

Figure 10-6. *Reading a struct field through a pointer*

The effect is that the change made to the name field is read through both p1 and p2, producing the following output when the code is compiled and executed:

```
P1: Original Kayak
P2: Original Kayak
```

Understanding the Struct Pointer Convenience Syntax

Accessing struct fields through a pointer is awkward, which is an issue because structs are commonly used as function arguments and results, and pointers are required to ensure that structs are not needlessly duplicated and that changes made by functions affect the values received as parameters, as shown in Listing 10-18.

Listing 10-18. Using Struct Pointers in the main.go File in the structs Folder

```go
package main

import "fmt"

type Product struct {
    name, category string
    price float64
}

func calcTax(product *Product) {
    if ((*product).price > 100) {
        (*product).price += (*product).price * 0.2
    }
}
```

```
func main() {

    kayak := Product {
        name: "Kayak",
        category: "Watersports",
        price: 275,
    }

    calcTax(&kayak)

    fmt.Println("Name:", kayak.name, "Category:",
        kayak.category, "Price", kayak.price)
}
```

This code works, but it is hard to read, especially when there are multiple references in the same block of code, such as the body of the calcTax method.

To simplify this type of code, Go will follow pointers to struct fields without needing an asterisk character, as shown in Listing 10-19.

Listing 10-19. Using the Struct Pointer Convenience Syntax in the main.go File in the structs Folder

```
package main

import "fmt"

type Product struct {
    name, category string
    price float64
}

func calcTax(product *Product) {
    if (product.price > 100) {
        product.price += product.price * 0.2
    }
}

func main() {

    kayak := Product {
        name: "Kayak",
        category: "Watersports",
        price: 275,
    }

    calcTax(&kayak)

    fmt.Println("Name:", kayak.name, "Category:",
        kayak.category, "Price", kayak.price)
}
```

The asterisk and the parentheses are not required, allowing a pointer to a struct to be treated as though it were a struct value, as illustrated by Figure 10-7.

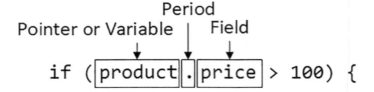

Figure 10-7. *Using a struct or a pointer to a struct*

This feature doesn't change the data type of the function parameter, which is still *Product, and applies only when accessing fields. Listings 10-18 and 10-19 both produce the following output:

```
Name: Kayak Category: Watersports Price 330
```

Understanding Pointers to Values

Earlier examples have used pointers in two steps. The first step is to create a value and assign it to a variable, like this:

```
...
kayak := Product {
    name: "Kayak",
    category: "Watersports",
    price: 275,
}
...
```

The second step is to use the address operator to create a pointer, like this:

```
...
calcTax(&kayak)
...
```

There is no need to assign a struct value to a variable before creating a pointer, and the address operator can be used directly with the literal struct syntax, as shown in Listing 10-20.

Listing 10-20. Creating a Pointer Directly in the main.go File in the structs Folder

```
package main

import "fmt"

type Product struct {
    name, category string
    price float64
}
```

```
func calcTax(product *Product) {
    if (product.price > 100) {
        product.price += product.price * 0.2
    }
}

func main() {

    kayak := &Product {
        name: "Kayak",
        category: "Watersports",
        price: 275,
    }

    calcTax(kayak)

    fmt.Println("Name:", kayak.name, "Category:",
        kayak.category, "Price", kayak.price)
}
```

The address operator is used before the struct type, as shown in Figure 10-8.

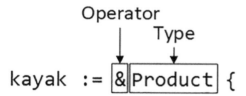

Figure 10-8. *Creating a pointer to a struct value*

The code in Listing 10-20 only uses a pointer to a Product value, which means that there is no benefit in creating a regular variable and then using it to create the pointer. Being able to create pointers directly from values can help make code more concise, as shown in Listing 10-21.

Listing 10-21. Using Pointers Directly in the main.go File in the structs Folder

```
package main

import "fmt"

type Product struct {
    name, category string
    price float64
}

func calcTax(product *Product) *Product {
    if (product.price > 100) {
        product.price += product.price * 0.2
    }
    return product
}
```

```
func main() {

    kayak := calcTax(&Product {
        name: "Kayak",
        category: "Watersports",
        price: 275,
    })

    fmt.Println("Name:", kayak.name, "Category:",
        kayak.category, "Price", kayak.price)
}
```

I altered the calcTax function so that it produces a result, which allows the function to transform a Product value through a pointer. In the main function, I used the address operator with the literal syntax to create a Product value and passed a pointer to it to the calcTax function, assigning the transformed result to a variable whose type is *Pointer. Listings 10-20 and 10-21 both produce the following output:

```
Name: Kayak Category: Watersports Price 330
```

Understanding Struct Constructor Functions

A constructor function is responsible for creating struct values using values received through parameters, as shown in Listing 10-22.

Listing 10-22. Defining a Constructor Function in the main.go File in the structs Folder

```
package main

import "fmt"

type Product struct {
    name, category string
    price float64
}

func newProduct(name, category string, price float64) *Product {
    return &Product{name, category, price}
}

func main() {

    products := [2]*Product {
        newProduct("Kayak", "Watersports", 275),
        newProduct("Hat", "Skiing", 42.50),
    }

    for _, p := range products {
        fmt.Println("Name:", p.name, "Category:",  p.category, "Price", p.price)
    }
}
```

Constructor functions are used to create struct values consistently. Constructor functions are usually named new or New followed by the struct type so that the constructor function for creating Product values is named newProduct. (I explain why the names of constructor functions often start with an uppercase first letter in Chapter 12.)

Constructor functions return struct pointers, and the address operator is used directly with the literal struct syntax, as illustrated by Figure 10-9.

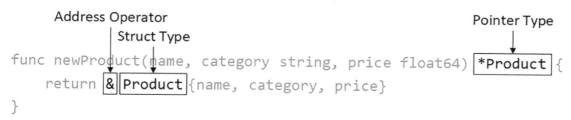

Figure 10-9. *Using pointers in a constructor function*

I like to create values in constructor functions by relying on field positions, as shown in Listing 10-22, although that's just my preference. What's important is that you remember to return a pointer to avoid the struct value being duplicated when the function returns. Listing 10-22 uses an array to store product data, and you can see the use of pointers in the array type:

```
...
products := [2]*Product {
...
```

This type specifies an array that will hold two pointers to Product struct values. The code in Listing 10-22 produces the following output when compiled and executed:

```
Name: Kayak Category: Watersports Price 275
Name: Hat Category: Skiing Price 42.5
```

The benefit of using constructor functions is consistency, ensuring that changes to the construction process are reflected in all the struct values created by the function. As an example, Listing 10-23 modifies the constructor to apply a discount to all products.

Listing 10-23. Modifying a Constructor in the main.go File in the structs Folder

```
...
func newProduct(name, category string, price float64) *Product {
    return &Product{name, category, price - 10}
}
...
```

This is a simple change, but it will be applied to all the Product values created by the newProduct function, meaning that I don't have to find all the points in the code where Product values are created and modify them individually. Unfortunately, Go does not prevent the literal syntax from being used when a constructor function has been defined, which means diligent use of constructor functions is required. The code in Listing 10-23 produces the following output:

```
Name: Kayak Category: Watersports Price 265
Name: Hat Category: Skiing Price 32.5
```

Using Pointer Types for Struct Fields

Pointers can also be used for struct fields, including pointers to other struct types, as shown in Listing 10-24.

Listing 10-24. Using Pointers for Struct Fields in the main.go File in the structs Folder

```
package main

import "fmt"

type Product struct {
    name, category string
    price float64
    *Supplier
}

type Supplier struct {
    name, city string
}

func newProduct(name, category string, price float64, supplier *Supplier) *Product {
    return &Product{name, category, price -10, supplier}
}

func main() {

    acme := &Supplier { "Acme Co", "New York"}

    products := [2]*Product {
        newProduct("Kayak", "Watersports", 275, acme),
        newProduct("Hat", "Skiing", 42.50, acme),
    }

    for _, p := range products {
        fmt.Println("Name:", p.name, "Supplier:",
            p.Supplier.name, p.Supplier.city)
    }
}
```

I have added an embedded field to the Product type that uses the Supplier type and updated the newProduct function so that it accepts a pointer to a Supplier. The fields defined by the Supplier struct are accessed using the field defined by the Product struct, as shown in Figure 10-10.

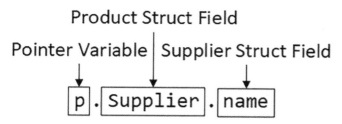

Figure 10-10. *Accessing a nested struct field*

Notice how Go deals with the use of a pointer type for an embedded struct field, allowing me to refer to the field by the name of the struct type, which is Supplier in this example. The code in Listing 10-24 produces the following output:

```
Name: Kayak Supplier: Acme Co New York
Name: Hat Supplier: Acme Co New York
```

Understanding Pointer Field Copying

Care must be taken when copying structs to consider the effect on pointer fields, as shown in Listing 10-25.

Listing 10-25. Copying a Struct in the main.go File in the structs Folder

```
package main

import "fmt"

type Product struct {
    name, category string
    price float64
    *Supplier
}

type Supplier struct {
    name, city string
}

func newProduct(name, category string, price float64, supplier *Supplier) *Product {
    return &Product{name, category, price -10, supplier}
}
```

```
func main() {

    acme := &Supplier { "Acme Co", "New York"}

    p1 := newProduct("Kayak", "Watersports", 275, acme)
    p2 := *p1

    p1.name = "Original Kayak"
    p1.Supplier.name = "BoatCo"

    for _, p := range []Product { *p1, p2 } {
        fmt.Println("Name:", p.name, "Supplier:",
            p.Supplier.name, p.Supplier.city)
    }
}
```

The newProduct function is used to create a pointer to a Product value, which is assigned to a variable named p1. The pointer is followed and assigned to a variable named p2, which has the effect of copying the Product value. The p1.name and p1.Supplier.name fields are changed, and then a for loop is used to write out details of both Product values, producing the following output:

```
Name: Original Kayak Supplier: BoatCo New York
Name: Kayak Supplier: BoatCo New York
```

The output shows that the change to the name field has affected only one of the Product values, while both have been affected by the change to the Supplier.name field. This happens because copying the Product struct has copied the pointer assigned to the Supplier field and not the value it points to, creating the effect shown in Figure 10-11.

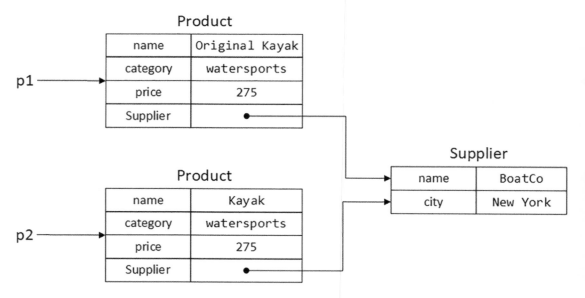

Figure 10-11. *The effect of copying a struct that has a pointer field*

This is often referred to as a *shallow copy,* where pointers are copied but not the values to which they point. Go doesn't have built-in support for performing a *deep copy,* where pointers are followed and their values are duplicated. Instead, manual copying must be performed, as shown in Listing 10-26.

Listing 10-26. Copying a Struct Value in the main.go File in the structs Folder

```
package main

import "fmt"

type Product struct {
    name, category string
    price float64
    *Supplier
}

type Supplier struct {
    name, city string
}

func newProduct(name, category string, price float64, supplier *Supplier) *Product {
    return &Product{name, category, price -10, supplier}
}

func copyProduct(product *Product) Product {
    p := *product
    s := *product.Supplier
    p.Supplier = &s
    return p
}

func main() {

    acme := &Supplier { "Acme Co", "New York"}

    p1 := newProduct("Kayak", "Watersports", 275, acme)
    p2 := copyProduct(p1)

    p1.name = "Original Kayak"
    p1.Supplier.name = "BoatCo"

    for _, p := range []Product { *p1, p2 } {
        fmt.Println("Name:", p.name, "Supplier:",
            p.Supplier.name, p.Supplier.city)
    }
}
```

To ensure the Supplier is duplicated, the copyProduct function assigns it to a separate variable and then creates a pointer to that variable. This is awkward, but the effect is to force a copy of the struct, albeit this is a technique that is specific to a single struct type and must be repeated for each nested struct field. The output from Listing 10-26 shows the effect of the deep copy:

```
Name: Original Kayak Supplier: BoatCo New York
Name: Kayak Supplier: Acme Co New York
```

Understanding Zero Value for Structs and Pointers to Structs

The zero value for a struct type is a struct value whose fields are assigned their zero type. The zero value for a pointer to a struct is nil, as demonstrated in Listing 10-27.

Listing 10-27. Examining Zero Types in the main.go File in the structs Folder

```
package main

import "fmt"

type Product struct {
    name, category string
    price float64
}

func main() {

    var prod Product
    var prodPtr *Product

    fmt.Println("Value:", prod.name, prod.category, prod.price)
    fmt.Println("Pointer:", prodPtr)
}
```

Compile and execute the project, and you will see the zero values represented in the output, with empty strings for the name and category fields, since the empty string is the zero value for the string type:

```
Value: 0
Pointer: <nil>
```

There is a pitfall, which I encounter often, when a struct defines a field with a pointer to another struct type, as shown in Listing 10-28.

Listing 10-28. Adding a Pointer Field in the main.go File in the structs Folder

```
package main

import "fmt"

type Product struct {
    name, category string
    price float64
    *Supplier
}

type Supplier struct {
    name, city string
}

func main() {

    var prod Product
    var prodPtr *Product

    fmt.Println("Value:", prod.name, prod.category, prod.price, prod.Supplier.name)
    fmt.Println("Pointer:", prodPtr)
}
```

The problem here is the attempt to access the name field of the embedded struct. The zero value for the embedded field is nil, which causes the following runtime error:

```
panic: runtime error: invalid memory address or nil pointer dereference
[signal 0xc0000005 code=0x0 addr=0x0 pc=0x5bc592]
goroutine 1 [running]:
main.main()
        C:/structs/main.go:20 +0x92
exit status 2
```

I encounter this error so frequently that I habitually initialize struct pointer fields, as shown in Listing 10-29 and repeated often in later chapters.

Listing 10-29. Initializing a Struct Pointer Field in the main.go File in the structs Folder

```
...
func main() {

    var prod Product = Product{ Supplier: &Supplier{}}
    var prodPtr *Product

    fmt.Println("Value:", prod.name, prod.category, prod.price, prod.Supplier.name)
    fmt.Println("Pointer:", prodPtr)
}
...
```

This avoids the runtime error, which you can see in the output produced by compiling and executing the project:

```
Value:   0
Pointer: <nil>
```

Summary

In this chapter, I describe the Go struct feature, which is used to create custom data types. I explained how to define struct fields, how to create values from struct types, and how to use struct types in collections. I also showed you how to create anonymous structs and how to use pointers to control how values are handled when struct values are copied. In the next chapter, I describe the Go support for methods and interfaces.

CHAPTER 11

Using Methods and Interfaces

In this chapter, I describe the Go support for methods, which can be used to provide features for structs and to create abstraction through interfaces. Table 11-1 puts these features in context.

Table 11-1. *Putting Methods and Interfaces in Context*

Question	Answer
What are they?	Methods are functions that are invoked on a struct and have access to all of the fields defined by the value's type. Interfaces define sets of methods, which can be implemented by struct types.
Why are they useful?	These features allow types to be mixed and used through their common characteristics.
How are they used?	Methods are defined using the func keyword, but with the addition of a receiver. Interfaces are defined using the type and interface keywords.
Are there any pitfalls or limitations?	Careful use of pointers is important when creating methods, and care must be taken when using interfaces to avoid problems with the underlying dynamic types.
Are there any alternatives?	These are optional features, but they make it possible to create complex data types and use them through the common features they provide.

© Adam Freeman 2022
A. Freeman, *Pro Go*, https://doi.org/10.1007/978-1-4842-7355-5_11

Table 11-2 summarizes the chapter.

Table 11-2. *Chapter Summary*

Problem	Solution	Listing
Define a method	Use the function syntax but add a receiver, through which the method will be invoked	4–8, 13–15
Invoke methods on references to struct values	Use a pointer for the method received	9, 10
Define methods on nonstruct types	Use a type alias	11, 12
Describe the common characteristics that will be shared by multiple types	Define an interface	16
Implement an interface	Define all the methods specified by the interface, using the selected struct type as the receiver	17, 18
Use an interface	Invoke the methods on the interface value	19–21
Decide whether copies of struct values will be made when assigned to interface variables	Use a pointer or value when making the assignment or use a pointer type as the receiver when implementing the interface methods	22–25
Compare interface values	Use the comparison operators and ensure the dynamic types are comparable	26, 27
Access an interface value's dynamic type	Use a type assertion	28–31
Define a variable that can be assigned any value	Use the empty interface	32–34

Preparing for This Chapter

To prepare for this chapter, open a new command prompt, navigate to a convenient location, and create a directory named methodsAndInterfaces. Navigate to the methodsAndInterfaces folder and run the command shown in Listing 11-1 to initialize the project.

Listing 11-1. Initializing the Project

```
go mod init methodsandinterfaces
```

Add a file named main.go to the methodsAndInterfaces folder, with the contents shown in Listing 11-2.

■ **Tip** You can download the example project for this chapter—and for all the other chapters in this book—from https://github.com/apress/pro-go. See Chapter 2 for how to get help if you have problems running the examples.

Listing 11-2. The Contents of the main.go File in the methodsAndInterfaces Folder

```
package main

import "fmt"

type Product struct {
    name, category string
    price float64
}

func main() {

    products := []*Product {
        {"Kayak", "Watersports", 275 },
        {"Lifejacket", "Watersports", 48.95 },
        {"Soccer Ball", "Soccer", 19.50},
    }

    for _, p := range products {
        fmt.Println("Name:", p.name, "Category:", p.category, "Price", p.price)
    }
}
```

Use the command prompt to run the command shown in Listing 11-3 in the
methodsAndInterfaces folder.

Listing 11-3. Running the Example Project

```
go run .
```

The code in the main.go file will be compiled and executed, producing the following output:

```
Name: Kayak Category: Watersports Price 275
Name: Lifejacket Category: Watersports Price 48.95
Name: Soccer Ball Category: Soccer Price 19.5
```

Defining and Using Methods

Methods are functions that can be invoked via a value and are a convenient way of expressing functions that
operate on a specific type. The best way to understand how methods work is to start with a regular function,
as shown in Listing 11-4.

Listing 11-4. Defining a Function in the main.go File in the methodsAndInterfaces Folder

```
package main

import "fmt"

type Product struct {
    name, category string
    price float64
}

func printDetails(product *Product) {
    fmt.Println("Name:", product.name, "Category:", product.category,
        "Price", product.price)
}

func main() {

    products := []*Product {
        {"Kayak", "Watersports", 275 },
        {"Lifejacket", "Watersports", 48.95 },
        {"Soccer Ball", "Soccer", 19.50},
    }

    for _, p := range products {
        printDetails(p)
    }
}
```

The printDetails function receives a pointer to a Product, which it uses to write out the value of the name, category, and price fields. The key point for this section is the way that the printDetails function is invoked:

```
...
printDetails(p)
...
```

The function name is followed by arguments enclosed in parentheses. Listing 11-5 implements the same functionality as a method.

Listing 11-5. Defining a Method in the main.go File in the methodsAndInterfaces Folder

```
package main

import "fmt"

type Product struct {
    name, category string
    price float64
}
```

```go
func newProduct(name, category string, price float64) *Product {
    return &Product{ name, category, price }
}

func (product *Product) printDetails() {
    fmt.Println("Name:", product.name, "Category:", product.category,
        "Price", product.price)
}

func main() {

    products := []*Product {
        newProduct("Kayak", "Watersports", 275),
        newProduct("Lifejacket", "Watersports", 48.95),
        newProduct("Soccer Ball", "Soccer", 19.50),
    }

    for _, p := range products {
        p.printDetails()
    }
}
```

Methods are defined as functions, using the same func keyword, but have the addition of a *receiver*, which denotes a special parameter, which is the type on which the method operates, as shown in Figure 11-1.

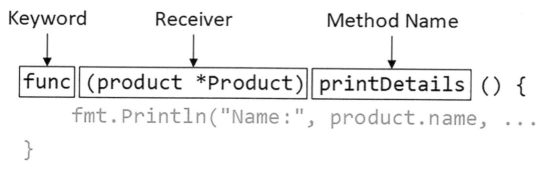

Figure 11-1. *A method*

The type of the receiver for this method is *Product and is given the name product, which can be used within the method just like any normal function parameter. No changes are required to the code block, which can treat the receiver like a regular function parameter:

```go
...
func (product *Product) printDetails() {
    fmt.Println("Name:", product.name, "Category:", product.category,
        "Price", product.price)
}
...
```

What makes methods different from regular functions is the way the method is invoked:

```
...
p.printDetails()
...
```

Methods are invoked through a value whose type matches the receiver. In this case, I use the *Product value generated by the for loop to invoke the printDetails method for each value in a slice, producing the following output:

```
Name: Kayak Category: Watersports Price 275
Name: Lifejacket Category: Watersports Price 48.95
Name: Soccer Ball Category: Soccer Price 19.5
```

Defining Method Parameters and Results

Methods can define parameters and results, just like regular functions, as shown in Listing 11-6, but with the addition of the receiver.

Listing 11-6. A Parameter and a Result in the main.go File in the methodsAndInterfaces Folder

```
package main

import "fmt"

type Product struct {
    name, category string
    price float64
}

func newProduct(name, category string, price float64) *Product {
    return &Product{ name, category, price }
}

func (product *Product) printDetails() {
    fmt.Println("Name:", product.name, "Category:", product.category,
        "Price",  product.calcTax(0.2, 100))
}

func (product *Product) calcTax(rate, threshold float64) float64 {
    if (product.price > threshold) {
        return product.price + (product.price * rate)
    }
    return product.price;
}
```

```
func main() {

    products := []*Product {
        newProduct("Kayak", "Watersports", 275),
        newProduct("Lifejacket", "Watersports", 48.95),
        newProduct("Soccer Ball", "Soccer", 19.50),
    }

    for _, p := range products {
        p.printDetails()
    }
}
```

Method parameters are defined between the parentheses that follow the name, followed by the result type, as illustrated in Figure 11-2.

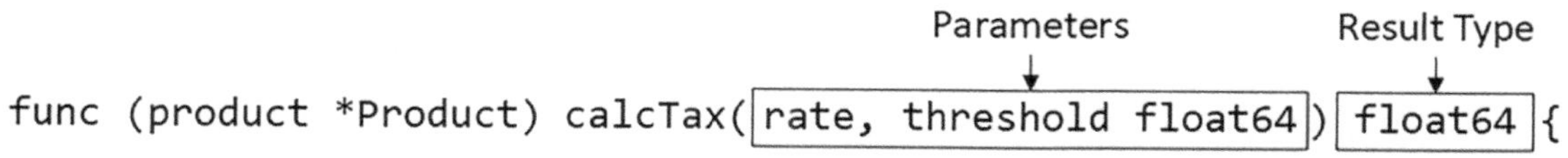

Figure 11-2. A method with parameters and a result

The calcTax method defines rate and threshold parameters and returns a float64 result. Within the method's code block, no special handling is required to differentiate between the receiver and the regular parameters.

When the method is invoked, arguments are provided as they would be for a regular function, like this:

```
...
product.calcTax(0.2, 100)
...
```

In this example, the printDetails method calls the calcTax method, producing the following output:

```
Name: Kayak Category: Watersports Price 330
Name: Lifejacket Category: Watersports Price 48.95
Name: Soccer Ball Category: Soccer Price 19.5
```

Understanding Method Overloading

Go does not support method overloading, where multiple methods can be defined with the same name but different parameters. Instead, each combination of method name and receiver type must be unique, regardless of the other parameters that are defined. In Listing 11-7, I have defined methods that have the same name but different receiver types.

Listing 11-7. Methods with the Same Name in the main.go File in the methodsAndInterfaces Folder

```
package main

import "fmt"

type Product struct {
    name, category string
    price float64
}

type Supplier struct {
    name, city string
}

func newProduct(name, category string, price float64) *Product {
    return &Product{ name, category, price }
}

func (product *Product) printDetails() {
    fmt.Println("Name:", product.name, "Category:", product.category,
        "Price",  product.calcTax(0.2, 100))
}

func (product *Product) calcTax(rate, threshold float64) float64 {
    if (product.price > threshold) {
        return product.price + (product.price * rate)
    }
    return product.price;
}

func (supplier *Supplier) printDetails() {
    fmt.Println("Supplier:", supplier.name, "City:", supplier.city)
}

func main() {

    products := []*Product {
        newProduct("Kayak", "Watersports", 275),
        newProduct("Lifejacket", "Watersports", 48.95),
        newProduct("Soccer Ball", "Soccer", 19.50),
    }

    for _, p := range products {
        p.printDetails()
    }
```

```
    suppliers := []*Supplier {
        { "Acme Co", "New York City"},
        { "BoatCo", "Chicago"},
    }
    for _,s := range suppliers {
        s.printDetails()
    }
}
```

There are printDetails methods for both the *Product and *Supplier types, which is allowed because each presents a unique name and receiver type combination. The code in Listing 11-7 produces the following output:

```
Name: Kayak Category: Watersports Price 330
Name: Lifejacket Category: Watersports Price 48.95
Name: Soccer Ball Category: Soccer Price 19.5
Supplier: Acme Co City: New York City
Supplier: BoatCo City: Chicago
```

The compiler will report an error if I try to define a method that duplicates an existing name/receiver combination, regardless of whether the remaining method parameters are different, as shown in Listing 11-8.

Listing 11-8. Defining Another Method in the main.go File in the methodsAndInterfaces Folder

```
package main

import "fmt"

type Product struct {
    name, category string
    price float64
}

type Supplier struct {
    name, city string
}

// ...other methods omitted for brevity...

func (supplier *Supplier) printDetails() {
    fmt.Println("Supplier:", supplier.name, "City:", supplier.city)
}

func (supplier *Supplier) printDetails(showName bool) {
    if (showName) {
        fmt.Println("Supplier:", supplier.name, "City:", supplier.city)
    } else {
        fmt.Println("Supplier:", supplier.name)
    }
}
```

```
func main() {

    products := []*Product {
        newProduct("Kayak", "Watersports", 275),
        newProduct("Lifejacket", "Watersports", 48.95),
        newProduct("Soccer Ball", "Soccer", 19.50),
    }

    for _, p := range products {
        p.printDetails()
    }

    suppliers := []*Supplier {
        { "Acme Co", "New York City"},
        { "BoatCo", "Chicago"},
    }
    for _,s := range suppliers {
        s.printDetails()
    }
}
```

The new method produces the following compiler error:

```
# command-line-arguments
.\main.go:34:6: method redeclared: Supplier.printDetails
        method(*Supplier) func()
        method(*Supplier) func(bool)
.\main.go:34:27: (*Supplier).printDetails redeclared in this block
        previous declaration at .\main.go:30:6
```

Understanding Pointer and Value Receivers

A method whose receiver is a pointer type can also be invoked through a regular value of the underlying type, meaning that a method whose type is *Product, for example, can be used with a Product value, as shown in Listing 11-9.

Listing 11-9. Invoking a Method in the main.go File in the methodsAndInterfaces Folder

```
package main

import "fmt"

type Product struct {
    name, category string
    price float64
}
```

```go
// type Supplier struct {
//     name, city string
// }

// func newProduct(name, category string, price float64) *Product {
//     return &Product{ name, category, price }
// }

func (product *Product) printDetails() {
    fmt.Println("Name:", product.name, "Category:", product.category,
        "Price",  product.calcTax(0.2, 100))
}

func (product *Product) calcTax(rate, threshold float64) float64 {
    if (product.price > threshold) {
        return product.price + (product.price * rate)
    }
    return product.price;
}

// func (supplier *Supplier) printDetails() {
//     fmt.Println("Supplier:", supplier.name, "City:", supplier.city)
// }

func main() {
    kayak := Product { "Kayak", "Watersports", 275 }
    kayak.printDetails()
}
```

The kayak variable is assigned a Product value but is used with the printDetails method, whose receiver is *Product. Go takes care of the mismatch and invokes the method seamlessly. The opposite process is also true so that a method that receives a value can be invoked using a pointer, as shown in Listing 11-10.

Listing 11-10. Invoking a Method in the main.go File in the methodsAndInterfaces Folder

```go
package main

import "fmt"

type Product struct {
    name, category string
    price float64
}

func (product Product) printDetails() {
    fmt.Println("Name:", product.name, "Category:", product.category,
        "Price",  product.calcTax(0.2, 100))
}
```

```
func (product *Product) calcTax(rate, threshold float64) float64 {
    if (product.price > threshold) {
        return product.price + (product.price * rate)
    }
    return product.price;
}

func main() {
    kayak := &Product { "Kayak", "Watersports", 275 }
    kayak.printDetails()
}
```

This feature means that you can write methods based on how you want them to behave, using pointers to avoid value copying or to allow the receiver to be modified by a method.

■ **Note**   One effect of this feature is that value and pointer types are considered the same when it comes to method overloading, meaning that a method named printDetails whose receiver type is Product will conflict with a printDetails method whose receiver type is *Product.

Listings 11-9 and 11-10 both produce the following output:

```
Name: Kayak Category: Watersports Price 330
```

INVOKING METHODS VIA THE RECEIVER TYPE

An unusual aspect of Go methods is they can be invoked using the receiver type so that a method with this signature:

```
...
func (product Product) printDetails() {
...
```

can be invoked like this:

```
...
Product.printDetails(Product{ "Kayak", "Watersports", 275 })
...
```

The name of the method's receiver type, Product, in this case, is followed by a period and the method name. The argument is the Product value that will be used for the receiver value. The automatic pointer/value mapping feature shown in Listings 11-9 and 11-10 doesn't apply when invoking a method through its receiver type, which means that a method with a pointer signature, like this:

```
...
func (product *Product) printDetails() {
...
```

has to be invoked via the pointer type and passed a pointer argument, like this:

```
...
(*Product).printDetails(&Product{ "Kayak", "Watersports", 275 })
...
```

Do not confuse this feature with static methods provided by languages such as C# or Java. There are no static methods in Go, and invoking a method through its type has the same effect as invoking the method through a value or pointer.

Defining Methods for Type Aliases

Methods can be defined for any type defined in the current package. I explain how to add packages to a project in Chapter 12, but for this chapter, there is a single code file containing a single package, which means that methods can be defined only for types defined in the main.go file.

But this doesn't limit methods to just structs, because the type keyword can be used to create aliases to any type, and methods can be defined for the alias. (I introduced the type keyword in Chapter 9 as a way to simplify dealing with function types.) Listing 11-11 creates an alias and a method.

Listing 11-11. Defining a Method for a Type Alias in the main.go File in the methodsAndInterfaces Folder

```
package main

import "fmt"

type Product struct {
    name, category string
    price float64
}

type ProductList []Product

func (products *ProductList) calcCategoryTotals() map[string]float64 {
    totals := make(map[string]float64)
    for _, p := range *products {
        totals[p.category] = totals[p.category] + p.price
    }
    return totals
}

func main() {

    products := ProductList {
        { "Kayak", "Watersports", 275 },
        { "Lifejacket", "Watersports", 48.95 },
        {"Soccer Ball", "Soccer", 19.50 },
    }
```

```
    for category, total := range products.calcCategoryTotals() {
        fmt.Println("Category: ", category, "Total:", total)
    }
}
```

The type keyword is used to create an alias for the [ ]Product type, with the name ProductList. This type can be used to define methods, either directly for value type receivers or with a pointer, as in this example.

You won't always be able to receive data with the type required to invoke a method defined for an alias, such as when processing the results of a function. In these situations, you can perform a type conversion, as shown in Listing 11-12.

Listing 11-12. Performing a Type Conversion in the main.go File in the methodsAndInterfaces Folder

```
package main

import "fmt"

type Product struct {
    name, category string
    price float64
}

type ProductList []Product

func (products *ProductList) calcCategoryTotals() map[string]float64 {
    totals := make(map[string]float64)
    for _, p := range *products {
        totals[p.category] = totals[p.category] + p.price
    }
    return totals
}

func getProducts() []Product {
    return []Product {
        { "Kayak", "Watersports", 275 },
        { "Lifejacket", "Watersports", 48.95 },
        {"Soccer Ball", "Soccer", 19.50 },
    }
}

func main() {

    products := ProductList(getProducts())

    for category, total := range products.calcCategoryTotals() {
        fmt.Println("Category: ", category, "Total:", total)
    }
}
```

The result from the getProducts function is [ ]Product, which is converted to ProductList with an explicit conversion, allowing the method defined on the alias to be used. The code in Listings 11-11 and Listing 11-12 produces the following output:

```
Category:  Watersports Total: 323.95
Category:  Soccer Total: 19.5
```

Putting Types and Methods in Separate Files

As a project becomes more complex, the amount of code required to define the custom types and their methods quickly becomes too much to manage in a single code file. Go projects can be structured into multiple files, which are combined by the compiler when the project is built.

The examples in the next section are too long to express in a single code listing without filling the rest of the chapter with long sections of code that don't change, so I am going to introduce multiple code files.

This feature is part of the Go support for *packages*, which provides different ways to structure the code files in a project and which I describe in Chapter 12. For this chapter, I am going to use the simplest aspect of packages, which is to use multiple code files in the project folder.

Add a file named product.go to the methodsAndInterfaces folder with the contents shown in Listing 11-13.

Listing 11-13. The Contents of the product.go File in the methodsAndInterfaces Folder

```
package main

type Product struct {
    name, category string
    price float64
}
```

Add a file named service.go to the methodsAndInterfaces folder and use it to define the type shown in Listing 11-14.

Listing 11-14. The Contents of the service.go File in the methodsAndInterfaces Folder

```
package main

type Service struct {
    description string
    durationMonths int
    monthlyFee float64
}
```

Finally, replace the contents of the main.go file with those shown in Listing 11-15.

Listing 11-15. Replacing the Contents of the main.go File in the methodsAndInterfaces Folder

```
package main

import "fmt"

func main() {

    kayak := Product { "Kayak", "Watersports", 275 }
    insurance := Service {"Boat Cover", 12, 89.50 }

    fmt.Println("Product:", kayak.name, "Price:", kayak.price)
    fmt.Println("Service:", insurance.description, "Price:",
        insurance.monthlyFee * float64(insurance.durationMonths))
}
```

This code creates values using the struct types defined in the other files. Compile and execute the project, which will produce the following output:

```
Product: Kayak Price: 275
Service: Boat Cover Price: 1074
```

Defining and Using Interfaces

It is easy to imagine a scenario where the Product and Service types defined in the previous section are used together. A personal accounts package, for example, may need to present the user with a list of expenses, some of which are represented with Product values and others with Service values. Even though these types have a common purpose, the Go type rules prevent them from being used together, such as creating a slice that contains both types of value.

Defining an Interface

This problem is addressed using *interfaces*, which describe a set of methods without specifying the implementation of those methods. If a type implements all the methods defined by the interface, then a value of that type can be used wherever the interface is permitted. The first step is to define an interface, as shown Listing 11-16.

Listing 11-16. Defining an Interface in the main.go File in the methodsAndInterfaces Folder

```
package main

import "fmt"

type Expense interface {
    getName() string
    getCost(annual bool) float64
}
```

```
func main() {

    kayak := Product { "Kayak", "Watersports", 275 }
    insurance := Service {"Boat Cover", 12, 89.50 }

    fmt.Println("Product:", kayak.name, "Price:", kayak.price)
    fmt.Println("Service:", insurance.description, "Price:",
        insurance.monthlyFee * float64(insurance.durationMonths))
}
```

An interface is defined using the type keyword, a name, the interface keyword, and a body consisting of method signatures enclosed in braces, as illustrated by Figure 11-3.

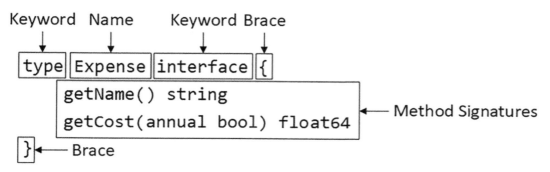

Figure 11-3. *Defining an interface*

This interface has been given the name Expense, and the interface body contains a single method signature. Method signatures consist of a name, parameters, and result types, as shown in Figure 11-4.

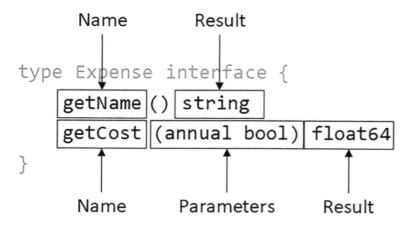

Figure 11-4. *A method signature*

The Expense interface describes two methods. The first method is getName, which accepts no arguments and returns a string. The second method is named getCost, and it accepts a bool argument and produces a float64 result.

Implementing an Interface

To implement an interface, all the methods specified by the interface must be defined for a struct type, as shown in Listing 11-17.

Listing 11-17. Implementing an Interface in the product.go File in the methodsAndInterfaces Folder

```
package main

type Product struct {
    name, category string
    price float64
}

func (p Product) getName() string {
    return p.name
}

func (p Product) getCost(_ bool) float64 {
    return p.price
}
```

Most languages require the use of a keyword to indicate when a type implements an interface, but Go simply requires that all the methods specified by the interface are defined. Go allows different parameter and result names to be used, but the methods must have the same name, parameter types, and result types. Listing 11-18 defines the methods required to implement the interface for the Service type.

Listing 11-18. Implementing an Interface in the service.go File in the methodsAndInterfaces Folder

```
package main

type Service struct {
    description string
    durationMonths int
    monthlyFee float64
}

func (s Service) getName() string {
    return s.description
}

func (s Service) getCost(recur bool) float64 {
    if (recur) {
        return s.monthlyFee * float64(s.durationMonths)
    }
    return s.monthlyFee
}
```

Interfaces describe only methods and not fields. For this reason, interfaces often specify methods that return values stored in struct fields, such as the getName method in Listing 11-17 and Listing 11-18.

Using an Interface

Once you have implemented an interface, you can refer to values through the interface type, as shown in Listing 11-19.

Listing 11-19. Using an Interface in the main.go File in the methodsAndInterfaces Folder

```
package main

import "fmt"

type Expense interface {
    getName() string
    getCost(annual bool) float64
}

func main() {

    expenses := []Expense {
        Product { "Kayak", "Watersports", 275 },
        Service {"Boat Cover", 12, 89.50 },
    }

    for _, expense := range expenses {
        fmt.Println("Expense:", expense.getName(), "Cost:", expense.getCost(true))
    }
}
```

In this example, I have defined an Expense slice and populated it with Product and Service values created using the literal syntax. The slice is used in a for loop, which invokes the getName and getCost methods on each value.

Variables whose type is an interface have two types: the *static type* and the *dynamic type*. The static type is the interface type. The dynamic type is the type of value assigned to the variable that implements the interface, such as Product or Service in this case. The static type never changes—the static type of an Expense variable is always Expense, for example—but the dynamic type can change by assigning a new value of a different type that implements the interface.

The for loop deals only with the static type—Expense—and doesn't know (and doesn't need to know) the dynamic type of those values. The use of the interface has allowed me to group disparate dynamic types together and use the common methods specified by the static interface type. Compile and execute the project; you will receive the following output:

```
Expense: Kayak Cost: 275
Expense: Boat Cover Cost: 1074
```

Using an Interface in a Function

Interface types can be used for variables, function parameters, and function results, as shown in Listing 11-20.

■ **Note**   Methods cannot be defined using interfaces as receivers. The only methods associated with an interface are the ones it specifies.

Listing 11-20. Using an Interface in the main.go File in the methodsAndInterfaces Folder

```
package main

import "fmt"

type Expense interface {
    getName() string
    getCost(annual bool) float64
}

func calcTotal(expenses []Expense) (total float64) {
    for _, item := range expenses {
        total += item.getCost(true)
    }
    return
}

func main() {

    expenses := []Expense {
        Product { "Kayak", "Watersports", 275 },
        Service {"Boat Cover", 12, 89.50 },
     }

    for _, expense := range expenses {
        fmt.Println("Expense:", expense.getName(), "Cost:", expense.getCost(true))
    }
    fmt.Println("Total:", calcTotal(expenses))
}
```

The calcTotal function receives a slice containing Expense values, which are processed using a for loop to produce a float64 total. Compile and execute the project, which will produce the following output:

```
Expense: Kayak Cost: 275
Expense: Boat Cover Cost: 1074
Total: 1349
```

Using an Interface for Struct Fields

Interface types can be used for struct fields, which means that fields can be assigned values of any type that implements the methods defined by the interface, as shown in Listing 11-21.

Listing 11-21. Using an Interface in a Struct Field in the main.go File in the methodsAndInterfaces Folder

```
package main

import "fmt"

type Expense interface {
    getName() string
    getCost(annual bool) float64
}

func calcTotal(expenses []Expense) (total float64) {
    for _, item := range expenses {
        total += item.getCost(true)
    }
    return
}

type Account struct {
    accountNumber int
    expenses []Expense
}

func main() {

    account := Account {
        accountNumber: 12345,
        expenses: []Expense {
            Product { "Kayak", "Watersports", 275 },
            Service {"Boat Cover", 12, 89.50 },
        },
    }

    for _, expense := range account.expenses {
        fmt.Println("Expense:", expense.getName(), "Cost:", expense.getCost(true))
    }
    fmt.Println("Total:", calcTotal(account.expenses))
}
```

The Account struct has an expenses field whose type is a slice of Expense values, which can be used just like any other field. Compile and execute the project, which produces the following output:

```
Expense: Kayak Cost: 275
Expense: Boat Cover Cost: 1074
Total: 1349
```

Understanding the Effect of Pointer Method Receivers

The methods defined by the Product and Service types have value receivers, which means that the methods will be invoked with copies of the Product or Service value. This can be confusing, so Listing 11-22 provides a simple example.

Listing 11-22. Using a Value in the main.go File in the methodsAndInterfaces Folder

```
package main

import "fmt"

type Expense interface {
    getName() string
    getCost(annual bool) float64
}

func main() {

    product := Product { "Kayak", "Watersports", 275 }

    var expense Expense = product

    product.price = 100

    fmt.Println("Product field value:", product.price)
    fmt.Println("Expense method result:", expense.getCost(false))
}
```

This example creates a Product struct value, assigns it to an Expense variable, alters the value of the struct value's price field, and writes out the field value directly and via an interface method. Compile and execute the code; you will receive the following result:

```
Product field value: 100
Expense method result: 275
```

The Product value was copied when it was assigned to the Expense variable, which means that the change to the price field does not affect the result from the getCost method.

A pointer to the struct value can be used when making the assignment to the interface variable, as shown in Listing 11-23.

Listing 11-23. Using a Pointer in the main.go File in the methodsAndInterfaces Folder

```
package main

import "fmt"

type Expense interface {
    getName() string
    getCost(annual bool) float64
}
```

```
func main() {

    product := Product { "Kayak", "Watersports", 275 }

    var expense Expense = &product

    product.price = 100

    fmt.Println("Product field value:", product.price)
    fmt.Println("Expense method result:", expense.getCost(false))
}
```

Using a pointer means that a reference to the Product value is assigned to the Expense variable, but this does not change the interface variable type, which is still Expense. Compile and execute the project, and you will see the effect of the reference in the output, which shows that the change to the price field is reflected in the result from the getCost method:

```
Product field value: 100
Expense method result: 100
```

This is useful because it means you can choose how a value assigned to an interface variable will be used. But it can also be counterintuitive because the variable type is always Expense, regardless of whether it is assigned a Product or *Product value.

You can force the use of references by specifying pointer receivers when implementing the interface methods, as shown in Listing 11-24.

Listing 11-24. Using Pointer Receivers in the product.go File in the methodsAndInterfaces Folder

```
package main

type Product struct {
    name, category string
    price float64
}

func (p *Product) getName() string {
    return p.name
}

func (p *Product) getCost(_ bool) float64 {
    return p.price
}
```

This is a small change, but it means that the Product type no longer implements the Expense interface because the required methods are no longer defined. Instead, it is the *Product type that implements the interface, which means that pointers to Product values can be treated as Expense values but not regular values. Compile and execute the project, and you will receive the same output as for Listing 11-23:

```
Product field value: 100
Expense method result: 100
```

Listing 11-25 assigns a Product value to an Expense variable.

Listing 11-25. Assigning a Value in the main.go File in the methodsAndInterfaces Folder

```
package main

import "fmt"

type Expense interface {
    getName() string
    getCost(annual bool) float64
}

func main() {

    product := Product { "Kayak", "Watersports", 275 }

    var expense Expense = product

    product.price = 100

    fmt.Println("Product field value:", product.price)
    fmt.Println("Expense method result:", expense.getCost(false))
}
```

Compile the project; you will receive the following error, telling you that a pointer receive is required:

```
.\main.go:14:9: cannot use product (type Product) as type Expense in assignment:
        Product does not implement Expense (getCost method has pointer receiver)
```

Comparing Interface Values

Interface values can be compared using the Go comparison operators, as shown in Listing 11-26. Two interface values are equal if they have the same dynamic type and all of their fields are equal.

Listing 11-26. Comparing Interface Values in the main.go File in the methodsAndInterfaces Folder

```
package main

import "fmt"

type Expense interface {
    getName() string
    getCost(annual bool) float64
}

func main() {

    var e1 Expense = &Product { name: "Kayak" }
    var e2 Expense = &Product { name: "Kayak" }
```

```
var e3 Expense = Service { description: "Boat Cover" }
var e4 Expense = Service { description: "Boat Cover" }

fmt.Println("e1 == e2", e1 == e2)
fmt.Println("e3 == e4", e3 == e4)
}
```

Care must be taken when comparing interface values, and inevitably, some knowledge of the dynamic types is required.

The first two Expense values are not equal. That's because the dynamic type for these values is a pointer type, and pointers are equal only if they point to the same memory location. The second two Expense values are equal because they are simple struct values with the same field values. Compile and execute the project to confirm the equality of these values:

```
e1 == e2 false
e3 == e4 true
```

Interface equality checks can also cause runtime errors if the dynamic type is not comparable. Listing 11-27 adds a field to the Service struct.

Listing 11-27. Adding a Field in the service.go File in the methodsAndServices Folder

```
package main

type Service struct {
    description string
    durationMonths int
    monthlyFee float64
    features []string
}

func (s Service) getName() string {
    return s.description
}

func (s Service) getCost(recur bool) float64 {
    if (recur) {
        return s.monthlyFee * float64(s.durationMonths)
    }
    return s.monthlyFee
}
```

As explained in Chapter 7, slices are not comparable. Compile and execute the project, and you will see the effect of the new field:

```
panic: runtime error: comparing uncomparable type main.Service
goroutine 1 [running]:
main.main()
        C:/main.go:20 +0x1c5
exit status 2
```

Performing Type Assertions

Interfaces can be useful, but they can present problems, and it is often useful to be able to access the dynamic type directly, which is known as *type narrowing*, the process of moving from a less precise type to a more precise type.

A *type assertion* is used to access the dynamic type of an interface value, as shown in Listing 11-28.

Listing 11-28. Using a Type Assertion in the main.go File in the methodsAndInterfaces Folder

```
package main

import "fmt"

type Expense interface {
    getName() string
    getCost(annual bool) float64
}

func main() {

    expenses := []Expense {
        Service {"Boat Cover", 12, 89.50, []string{} },
        Service {"Paddle Protect", 12, 8, []string{} },
    }

    for _, expense := range expenses {
        s := expense.(Service)
        fmt.Println("Service:", s.description, "Price:",
            s.monthlyFee * float64(s.durationMonths))
    }
}
```

A type assertion is performed by applying a period after a value, followed by the target type in parentheses, as illustrated by Figure 11-5.

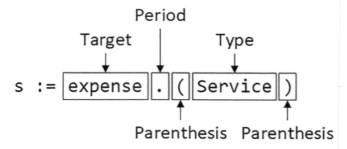

Figure 11-5. *A type assertion*

In Listing 11-28, I used a type assertion to access the dynamic Service value from a slice of Expense interface types. Once I have a Service value to work with, I can use all the fields and methods defined for the Service type, and not just the methods that are defined by the Expense interface.

TYPE ASSERTIONS VS. TYPE CONVERSIONS

Don't confuse type assertions, as shown in Figure 11-6, with the type conversion syntax described in Chapter 5. Type assertions can be applied only to interfaces, and they are used to tell the compiler that an interface value has a specific dynamic type. Type conversions can be applied only to specific types, not interfaces, and only if the structure of those types is compatible, such as converting between struct types that have the same fields.

The code in Listing 11-28 produces the following output when compiled and executed:

```
Service: Boat Cover Price: 1074
Service: Paddle Protect Price: 96
```

Testing Before Performing a Type Assertion

When a type assertion is used, the compiler trusts that the programmer has more knowledge and knows more about the dynamic types in the code than it can infer, such as that an Expense slice contains only Supplier values. To see what happens when this is not the case, Listing 11-29 adds a *Product value to the Expense slice.

Listing 11-29. Mixing Dynamic Types in the main.go File in the methodsAndInterfaces Folder

```
package main

import "fmt"

type Expense interface {
    getName() string
    getCost(annual bool) float64
}

func main() {

    expenses := []Expense {
        Service {"Boat Cover", 12, 89.50, []string{} },
        Service {"Paddle Protect", 12, 8, []string{} },
        &Product { "Kayak", "Watersports", 275 },
    }
```

```
    for _, expense := range expenses {
        s := expense.(Service)
        fmt.Println("Service:", s.description, "Price:",
            s.monthlyFee * float64(s.durationMonths))
    }
}
```

Compile and execute the project; you will see the following error when the code is executed:

```
panic: interface conversion: main.Expense is *main.Product, not main.Service
```

The Go runtime has tried to perform the assertion and failed. To avoid this issue, there is a special form of type assertion that indicates whether an assertion could be performed, as shown in Listing 11-30.

Listing 11-30. Testing an Assertion in the main.go File in the methodsAndInterfaces Folder

```
package main

import "fmt"

type Expense interface {
    getName() string
    getCost(annual bool) float64
}

func main() {

    expenses := []Expense {
        Service {"Boat Cover", 12, 89.50, []string{} },
        Service {"Paddle Protect", 12, 8, []string{} },
        &Product { "Kayak", "Watersports", 275 },
    }

    for _, expense := range expenses {
        if s, ok := expense.(Service); ok {
            fmt.Println("Service:", s.description, "Price:",
                s.monthlyFee * float64(s.durationMonths))
        } else {
            fmt.Println("Expense:", expense.getName(),
                "Cost:", expense.getCost(true))
        }
    }
}
```

Type assertions can produce two results, as shown in Figure 11-6. The first result is assigned the dynamic type, and the second result is a bool that indicates whether the assertion could be performed.

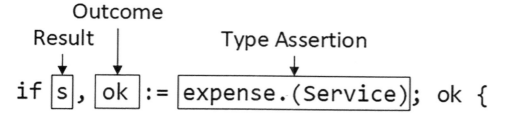

Figure 11-6. *Two results from a type assertion*

The bool value can be used with an `if` statement to execute statements for a specific dynamic type. Compile and execute the project; you will see the following output:

```
Service: Boat Cover Price: 1074
Service: Paddle Protect Price: 96
Expense: Kayak Cost: 275
```

Switching on Dynamic Types

Go `switch` statements can be used to access dynamic types, as shown in Listing 11-31, which can be a more concise way of performing type assertions with `if` statements.

Listing 11-31. Switching on Types in the main.go File in the methodsAndInterfaces Folder

```go
package main

import "fmt"

type Expense interface {
    getName() string
    getCost(annual bool) float64
}

func main() {

    expenses := []Expense {
        Service {"Boat Cover", 12, 89.50, []string{} },
        Service {"Paddle Protect", 12, 8, []string{} },
        &Product { "Kayak", "Watersports", 275 },
    }

    for _, expense := range expenses {
        switch value := expense.(type) {
            case Service:
                fmt.Println("Service:", value.description, "Price:",
                    value.monthlyFee * float64(value.durationMonths))
            case *Product:
```

```
                fmt.Println("Product:", value.name, "Price:", value.price)
            default:
                fmt.Println("Expense:", expense.getName(),
                    "Cost:", expense.getCost(true))
        }
    }
}
```

The switch statement uses a special type assertion that uses the type keyword, as illustrated in Figure 11-7.

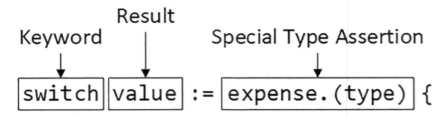

Figure 11-7. *A type switch*

Each case statement specifies a type and a block of code that will be executed when the value evaluated by the switch statement has the specified type. The Go compiler is smart enough to understand the relationship between the values evaluated by the switch statement and will not allow case statements for types that do not match. For example, the compiler will complain if there is a case statement for the Product type because the switch statement is evaluating Expense values and the Product type doesn't have the methods required to implement the interface (because the methods in the product.go file use pointer receivers, shown in Listing 11-24).

Within a case statement, the result can be treated as the specified type, meaning that within the case statement that specifies the Supplier type, for example, all the fields and methods defined by the Supplier type can be used.

A default statement can be used to specify a block of code that will be executed when none of the case statements matches. Compile and execute the project, and you will see the following output:

```
Service: Boat Cover Price: 1074
Service: Paddle Protect Price: 96
Product: Kayak Price: 275
```

Using the Empty Interface

Go allows the user of the empty interface—which means an interface that defines no methods—to represent any type, which can be a useful way to group disparate types that share no common features, as shown in Listing 11-32.

Listing 11-32. Using the Empty Interface in the main.go File in the methodsAndInterfaces Folder

```go
package main

import "fmt"

type Expense interface {
    getName() string
    getCost(annual bool) float64
}

type Person struct {
    name, city string
}

func main() {

    var expense Expense = &Product { "Kayak", "Watersports", 275 }

    data := []interface{} {
        expense,
        Product { "Lifejacket", "Watersports", 48.95 },
        Service {"Boat Cover", 12, 89.50, []string{} },
        Person { "Alice", "London"},
        &Person { "Bob", "New York"},
        "This is a string",
        100,
        true,
    }

    for _, item := range data {
        switch value := item.(type) {
            case Product:
                fmt.Println("Product:", value.name, "Price:", value.price)
            case *Product:
                fmt.Println("Product Pointer:", value.name, "Price:", value.price)
            case Service:
                fmt.Println("Service:", value.description, "Price:",
                    value.monthlyFee * float64(value.durationMonths))
            case Person:
                fmt.Println("Person:", value.name, "City:", value.city)
            case *Person:
                fmt.Println("Person Pointer:", value.name, "City:", value.city)
            case string, bool, int:
                fmt.Println("Built-in type:", value)
            default:
                fmt.Println("Default:", value)

        }
    }
}
```

The empty interface is used in a literal syntax, defined with the interface keyword and empty braces, as illustrated by Figure 11-8.

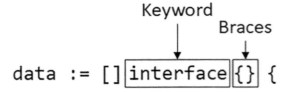

Figure 11-8. *The empty interface*

The empty interface represents all types, including the built-in types and any structs and interfaces that have been defined. In the listing, I define an empty array slice with a mix of Product, *Product, Service, Person, *Person, string, int, and bool values. The slice is processed by a for loop with switch statements that narrow each value to a specific type. Compile and execute the project, which produces the following output:

```
Product Pointer: Kayak Price: 275
Product: Lifejacket Price: 48.95
Service: Boat Cover Price: 1074
Person: Alice City: London
Person Pointer: Bob City: New York
Built-in type: This is a string
Built-in type: 100
Built-in type: true
```

Using the Empty Interface for Function Parameters

The empty interface can be used as the type for a function parameter, allowing a function to be called with any value, as shown in Listing 11-33.

Listing 11-33. Using an Empty Interface Parameter in the main.go File in the methodsAndInterfaces Folder

```
package main

import "fmt"

type Expense interface {
    getName() string
    getCost(annual bool) float64
}

type Person struct {
    name, city string
}
```

```go
func processItem(item interface{}) {
    switch value := item.(type) {
        case Product:
            fmt.Println("Product:", value.name, "Price:", value.price)
        case *Product:
            fmt.Println("Product Pointer:", value.name, "Price:", value.price)
        case Service:
            fmt.Println("Service:", value.description, "Price:",
                value.monthlyFee * float64(value.durationMonths))
        case Person:
            fmt.Println("Person:", value.name, "City:", value.city)
        case *Person:
            fmt.Println("Person Pointer:", value.name, "City:", value.city)
        case string, bool, int:
            fmt.Println("Built-in type:", value)
        default:
            fmt.Println("Default:", value)
    }
}

func main() {

    var expense Expense = &Product { "Kayak", "Watersports", 275 }

    data := []interface{} {
        expense,
        Product { "Lifejacket", "Watersports", 48.95 },
        Service {"Boat Cover", 12, 89.50, []string{} },
        Person { "Alice", "London"},
        &Person { "Bob", "New York"},
        "This is a string",
        100,
        true,
    }

    for _, item := range data {
        processItem(item)
    }
}
```

The empty interface can also be used for variadic parameters, which allows a function to be called with any number of arguments, each of which can be any type, as shown in Listing 11-34.

Listing 11-34. Using a Variadic Parameter in the main.go File in the methodsAndInterfaces Folder

```go
package main

import "fmt"

type Expense interface {
    getName() string
    getCost(annual bool) float64
}
```

```go
type Person struct {
    name, city string
}

func processItems(items ...interface{}) {
    for _, item := range items {
        switch value := item.(type) {
            case Product:
                fmt.Println("Product:", value.name, "Price:", value.price)
            case *Product:
                fmt.Println("Product Pointer:", value.name, "Price:", value.price)
            case Service:
                fmt.Println("Service:", value.description, "Price:",
                    value.monthlyFee * float64(value.durationMonths))
            case Person:
                fmt.Println("Person:", value.name, "City:", value.city)
            case *Person:
                fmt.Println("Person Pointer:", value.name, "City:", value.city)
            case string, bool, int:
                fmt.Println("Built-in type:", value)
            default:
                fmt.Println("Default:", value)
        }
    }
}

func main() {

    var expense Expense = &Product { "Kayak", "Watersports", 275 }

    data := []interface{} {
        expense,
        Product { "Lifejacket", "Watersports", 48.95 },
        Service {"Boat Cover", 12, 89.50, []string{} },
        Person { "Alice", "London"},
        &Person { "Bob", "New York"},
        "This is a string",
        100,
        true,
    }

    processItems(data...)
}
```

Listing 11-33 and Listing 11-34 both produce the following output when the project is compiled and executed:

```
Product Pointer: Kayak Price: 275
Product: Lifejacket Price: 48.95
Service: Boat Cover Price: 1074
Person: Alice City: London
Person Pointer: Bob City: New York
Built-in type: This is a string
Built-in type: 100
Built-in type: true
```

Summary

In this chapter, I described the support Go provides for methods, both in terms of defining them for struct types and of defining sets of method interfaces. I demonstrated how a struct can implement an interface, and this allows mixed types to be used together. In the next chapter, I explain how Go supports structure in projects using packages and modules.

CHAPTER 12

■ ■ ■

Creating and Using Packages

Packages are the Go feature that allows projects to be structured so that related functionality can be grouped together, without the need to put all the code into a single file or folder. In this chapter, I describe how to create and use packages and how to use packages developed by third parties. Table 12-1 puts packages in context.

Table 12-1. *Putting Packages in Context*

Question	Answer
What are they?	Packages allow projects to be structured so that related features can be developed together.
Why are they useful?	Packages are how Go implements access controls so that the implementation of a feature can be hidden from the code that consumes it.
How are they used?	Packages are defined by creating code files in folders and using the package keyword to denote which package they belong to.
Are there any pitfalls or limitations?	There are only so many meaningful names, and conflicts between package names are common, requiring the use of aliases to avoid errors.
Are there any alternatives?	Simple applications can be written without the need for packages.

Table 12-2 summarizes the chapter.

© Adam Freeman 2022
A. Freeman, *Pro Go*, https://doi.org/10.1007/978-1-4842-7355-5_12

Table 12-2. *Chapter Summary*

Problem	Solution	Listing
Define a package	Create a folder and add code files with package statements.	4, 9, 10, 15, 16
Use a package	Add an import statement that specifies the path to the package and its enclosing module.	5
Control access to the features in a package	Export features by using an initial uppercase letter in their names. Lowercase initial letters are unexpected and cannot be used outside the package.	6–8
Deal with package conflicts	Use an alias or a dot import.	11–14
Perform tasks when a package is loaded	Define an initialization function.	17, 18
Execute a package initialization function without importing the features it contains	Use the blank identifier in the import statement.	19, 20
Use an external package	Use the go get command.	21, 22
Remove unused package dependencies	Use the go mod tidy command.	23

Preparing for This Chapter

To prepare for this chapter, open a new command prompt, navigate to a convenient location, and create a directory named packages. Navigate to the packages folder and run the command shown in Listing 12-1 to initialize the project.

■ **Tip** You can download the example project for this chapter—and for all the other chapters in this book—from https://github.com/apress/pro-go. See Chapter 2 for how to get help if you have problems running the examples.

Listing 12-1. Initializing the Project

```
go mod init packages
```

Add a file named main.go to the packages folder, with the contents shown in Listing 12-2.

Listing 12-2. The Contents of the main.go File in the packages Folder

```
package main

import "fmt"
```

```
func main() {
    fmt.Println("Hello, Packages and Modules")
}
```

Use the command prompt to run the command shown in Listing 12-3 in the packages folder.

Listing 12-3. Running the Example Project

```
go run .
```

The code in the main.go file will be compiled and executed, producing the following output:

```
Hello, Packages and Modules
```

Understanding the Module File

The first step for all the example projects in this book has been to create a module file, which was done with the command in Listing 12-1.

The original purpose of a module file was to enable code to be published so that it can be used in other projects and, potentially, by other developers. Module files are still used for this purpose, but Go has started to gain mainstream development, and as this has happened, the percentage of projects that are published has fallen. These days, the most common reason for creating a module file is that it makes it easy to install packages that have been published and has the bonus effect of allowing the use of the command shown in Listing 12-3, rather than having to provide the Go build tools with a list of individual files to compile.

The command in Listing 12-1 created a file named go.mod in the packages folder, with the following content:

```
module packages
go 1.17
```

The module statement specifies the name of the module, which was specified by the command in Listing 12-1. This name is important because it is used to import features from other packages created within the same project and third-party packages, as later examples will demonstrate. The go statement specifies the version of Go that is used, which is 1.17 for this book.

Creating a Custom Package

Packages make it possible to add structure to a project so that related features are grouped together. Create the packages/store folder and add to it a file named product.go, with the contents shown in Listing 12-4.

Listing 12-4. The Contents of the product.go File in the packages/store Folder

```
package store

type Product struct {
    Name, Category string
    price float64
}
```

311

The custom package is defined using the package keyword, and the package I have specified is called store:

```
...
package store
...
```

The name specified by the package statement should match the name of the folder in which the code files are created, which is store in this case.

The Product type has some important differences from similar types defined in earlier chapters, as I explain in the sections that follow.

COMMENTING EXPORTED FEATURES

The Go linter will report an error for any feature that is exported from a package and that has not been described in a comment. Comments should be simple and descriptive, and the convention is to begin the comment with the name of the feature, like this:

```
...
// Product describes an item for sale
type Product struct {
    Name, Category string // Name and type of the product
    price float64
}
...
```

When commenting custom types, exported fields can also be described. Go also supports a comment that describes an entire package, which appears before the package keyword, like this:

```
...
// Package store provides types and methods
// commonly required for online sales
package store
...
```

These comments are processed by the go doc tool, which generates code documentation. I have not added comments to the examples in this book for the sake of brevity, but commenting code is especially important when writing packages that are used by other developers.

Using a Custom Package

Dependencies on custom packages are declared using the import statement, as shown in Listing 12-5.

Listing 12-5. Using a Custom Package in the main.go File in the packages Folder

```go
package main

import (
    "fmt"
    "packages/store"
)

func main() {

    product := store.Product {
        Name: "Kayak",
        Category: "Watersports",
    }

    fmt.Println("Name:", product.Name)
    fmt.Println("Category:", product.Category)
}
```

The import statement specifies the package as a path, comprised of the name of the module created by the command in Listing 12-1 and the name of the package, separated by a forward slash, as illustrated by Figure 12-1.

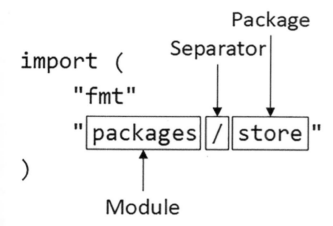

Figure 12-1. Importing a custom package

The exported features provided by the package are accessed using the package name as a prefix, like this:

```go
...
var product *store.Product = &store.Product {
...
```

To specify the Product type, I have to prefix the type with the name of the package, as illustrated by Figure 12-2.

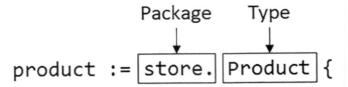

Figure 12-2. *Using the package name*

Build and execute the project, which will produce the following output:

```
Name: Kayak
Category: Watersports
```

Understanding Package Access Control

The Product type defined in Listing 12-4 contains an important difference from the similar types defined in earlier chapters: the Name and Category properties have an initial capital letter.

Go has an unusual approach to access control. Instead of relying on dedicated keywords, like public and private, Go examines the first letter of the names given to the features in a code file, such as types, functions, and methods. If the first letter is lowercase, then the feature can be used only within the package that defines it. Features are exported for use outside of the package by giving them an uppercase first letter.

The name of the struct type in Listing 12-4 is Product, which means the type can be used outside the store package. The names of the Name and Category fields also start with an uppercase letter, which means they are also exported. The price field has a lowercase first letter, which means that it can be accessed only within the store package. Figure 12-3 illustrates these differences.

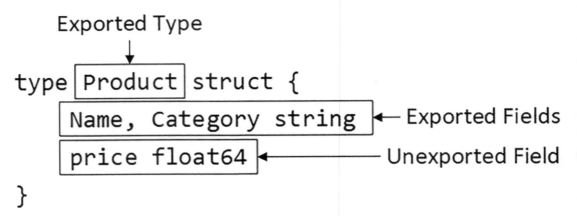

Figure 12-3. *Exported and private features*

The compiler enforces the package export rules, which means that an error will be generated if the price field is accessed outside of the store package, as shown in Listing 12-6.

Listing 12-6. Accessing an Unexported Field in the main.go File in the packages Folder

```
package main
```

```
import (
    "fmt"
    "packages/store"
)

func main() {

    product := store.Product {
        Name: "Kayak",
        Category: "Watersports",
        price: 279,
    }

    fmt.Println("Name:", product.Name)
    fmt.Println("Category:", product.Category)
    fmt.Println("Price:", product.price)
}
```

The first change attempts to set a value for the price field when using the literal syntax to create a Product value. The second change attempts to read the value of the price field.

The access control rules are enforced by the compiler, which reports the following errors when the code is compiled:

```
.\main.go:13:9: cannot refer to unexported field 'price' in struct literal of type
store.Product
.\main.go:18:34: product.price undefined (cannot refer to unexported field or method price)
```

To resolve these errors, I can either export the price field or export methods or functions that provide access to the field value. Listing 12-7 defines a constructor function for creating Product values and methods for getting and setting the price field.

Listing 12-7. Defining Methods in the product.go File in the store Folder

```
package store

type Product struct {
    Name, Category string
    price float64
}

func NewProduct(name, category string, price float64) *Product {
    return &Product{ name, category, price }
}

func (p *Product) Price() float64 {
    return p.price
}

func (p *Product) SetPrice(newPrice float64)  {
    p.price = newPrice
}
```

315

The access control rules do not apply to individual function or method parameters, which means that the NewProduct function has to have an uppercase first character to be exported, but the parameter names can be lowercase.

The methods follow a typical naming convention for exported methods that access a field so that the Price method returns the field value and the SetPrice method assigns a new value. Listing 12-8 updates the code in the main.go file to use the new features.

Listing 12-8. Using Package Features in the main.go File in the packages Folder

```go
package main

import (
    "fmt"
    "packages/store"
)

func main() {

    product := store.NewProduct("Kayak", "Watersports", 279)

    fmt.Println("Name:", product.Name)
    fmt.Println("Category:", product.Category)
    fmt.Println("Price:", product.Price())
}
```

Compile and execute the project using the command in Listing 12-8, and you will receive the following output, demonstrating that code in the main package can read the price field using the Price method:

```
Name: Kayak
Category: Watersports
Price: 279
```

Adding Code Files to Packages

Packages can contain multiple code files, and to simplify development, access control rules and package prefixes do not apply when accessing features defined in the same package. Add a file named tax.go to the store folder with the contents shown in Listing 12-9.

Listing 12-9. The Contents of the tax.go File in the store Folder

```go
package store

const defaultTaxRate float64 = 0.2
const minThreshold = 10

type taxRate struct {
    rate, threshold float64
}
```

```
func newTaxRate(rate, threshold float64) *taxRate {
    if (rate == 0) {
        rate = defaultTaxRate
    }
    if (threshold < minThreshold) {
        threshold = minThreshold
    }
    return &taxRate { rate, threshold }
}

func (taxRate *taxRate) calcTax(product *Product) float64 {
    if (product.price > taxRate.threshold) {
        return product.price + (product.price * taxRate.rate)
    }
    return product.price
}
```

All the features defined in the tax.go file are unexported, which means they can be used only within the store package. Notice that the calcTax method can access the price field of the Product type and that it does so without having to refer to the type as store.Product because it is in the same package:

```
...
func (taxRate *taxRate) calcTax(product *Product) float64 {
    if (product.price > taxRate.threshold) {
        return product.price + (product.price * taxRate.rate)
    }
    return product.price
}
...
```

In Listing 12-10, I have modified the Product.Price method so that it returns the value of the price field plus tax.

Listing 12-10. Calculating Tax in the product.go File in the store Folder

```
package store

var standardTax = newTaxRate(0.25, 20)

type Product struct {
    Name, Category string
    price float64
}

func NewProduct(name, category string, price float64) *Product {
    return &Product{ name, category, price }
}

func (p *Product) Price() float64 {
    return standardTax.calcTax(p)
}
```

```
func (p *Product) SetPrice(newPrice float64)  {
    p.price = newPrice
}
```

The Price method can access the unexported calcTax method, but this method—and the type it applies to—is available for use only within the store package. Compile and execute the code using the command shown in Listing 12-10, and you will receive the following output:

```
Name: Kayak
Category: Watersports
Price: 348.75
```

AVOIDING THE REDEFINITION PITFALL

A common mistake is to reuse names in different files within the same package. This is something that I do often, including when writing the example shown in Listing 12-10. My initial version of the code in the product.go file contained this statement:

```
...
var taxRate = newTaxRate(0.25, 20)
...
```

This causes a compiler error because the tax.go file defines a struct type named taxRate. The compiler doesn't differentiate between names assigned to variables and names assigned to types and reports an error, like this one:

```
store\tax.go:6:6: taxRate redeclared in this block
        previous declaration at store\product.go:3:5
```

You may also see errors in your code editor telling you that taxRate is an invalid type. This is the same problem expressed differently. To avoid these errors, you must ensure that the top-level features defined in a package are given unique names. Names do not have to be unique across packages or inside of functions and methods.

Dealing with Package Name Conflicts

When a package is imported, the combination of the module name and package name ensures that the package is uniquely identified. But only the package name is used when accessing the features provided by the package, which can lead to conflicts. To see how this problem arises, create the packages/fmt folder and add to it a file named formats.go with the code shown in Listing 12-11.

Listing 12-11. The Contents of the formats.go File in the fmt Folder

```
package fmt

import "strconv"
```

```
func ToCurrency(amount float64) string {
    return "$" + strconv.FormatFloat(amount, 'f', 2, 64)
}
```

This file exports a function named ToCurrency that receives a float64 value and produces a formatted dollar amount, using the strconv.FormatFloat function, which I described in Chapter 17.

The fmt package defined in Listing 12-11 has the same name as one of the most widely used standard library packages. This causes a problem when both packages are used, as shown in Listing 12-12.

Listing 12-12. Using Packages with the Same Name in the main.go File in the packages Folder

```
package main

import (
    "fmt"
    "packages/store"
    "packages/fmt"
)

func main() {

    product := store.NewProduct("Kayak", "Watersports", 279)

    fmt.Println("Name:", product.Name)
    fmt.Println("Category:", product.Category)
    fmt.Println("Price:", fmt.ToCurrency(product.Price()))
}
```

Compile the project, and you will receive the following errors:

```
.\main.go:6:5: fmt redeclared as imported package name
        previous declaration at .\main.go:4:5
.\main.go:13:5: undefined: "packages/fmt".Println
.\main.go:14:5: undefined: "packages/fmt".Println
.\main.go:15:5: undefined: "packages/fmt".Println
```

Using a Package Alias

One way to deal with package name conflicts is to use an alias, which allows a package to be accessed using a different name, as shown in Listing 12-13.

Listing 12-13. Using a Package Alias in the main.go File in the packages Folder

```
package main

import (
    "fmt"
    "packages/store"
    currencyFmt "packages/fmt"
)
```

```
func main() {

    product := store.NewProduct("Kayak", "Watersports", 279)

    fmt.Println("Name:", product.Name)
    fmt.Println("Category:", product.Category)
    fmt.Println("Price:", currencyFmt.ToCurrency(product.Price()))
}
```

The alias by which the package will be known is declared before the import path, as shown in Figure 12-4.

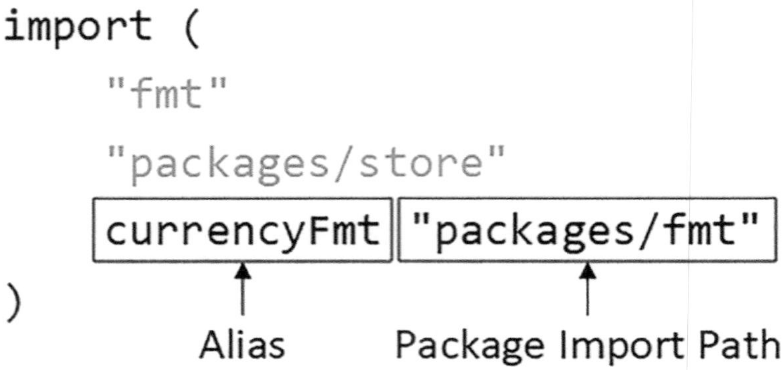

import (

    "fmt"

    "packages/store"

    currencyFmt "packages/fmt"

)

         Alias   Package Import Path

Figure 12-4. *A package alias*

The alias in this example resolves the name conflict so that the features defined by the package imported with the packages/fmt path can be accessed using currencyFmt as the prefix, like this:

```
...
fmt.Println("Price:", currencyFmt.ToCurrency(product.Price()))
...
```

Compile and execute the project, and you will receive the following output, which relies on features defined by the fmt package in the standard library and the custom fmt package that has been aliased:

```
Name: Kayak
Category: Watersports
Price: $348.75
```

Using a Dot Import

There is a special alias, known as the *dot import*, that allows a package's features to be used without using a prefix, as shown in Listing 12-14.

Listing 12-14. Using a Dot Import in the main.go File in the packages Folder

```
package main
```

```
import (
    "fmt"
    "packages/store"
    . "packages/fmt"
)

func main() {

    product := store.NewProduct("Kayak", "Watersports", 279)

    fmt.Println("Name:", product.Name)
    fmt.Println("Category:", product.Category)
    fmt.Println("Price:", ToCurrency(product.Price()))
}
```

A dot import uses a period as the package alias, as illustrated by Figure 12-5.

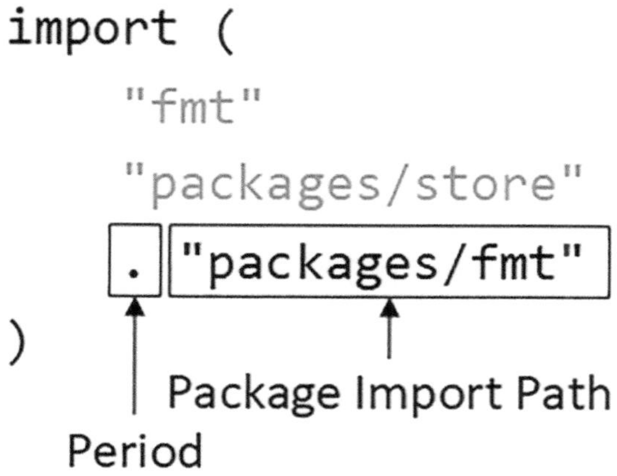

Figure 12-5. *Using a dot import*

The dot import allows me to access the ToCurrency function without using a prefix, like this:

```
...
fmt.Println("Price:", ToCurrency(product.Price()))
...
```

When using a dot import, you must ensure that the names of the features imported from the package are not defined in the importing package. For the example, this means I must ensure that the name ToCurrency is not used by any feature defined in the main package. For this reason, dot imports should be used with caution.

Creating Nested Packages

Packages can be defined within other packages, making it easy to break up complex features into as many units as possible. Create the packages/store/cart folder and add to it a file named cart.go with the contents shown in Listing 12-15.

Listing 12-15. The Contents of the cart.go File in the store/cart Folder

```
package cart

import "packages/store"

type Cart struct {
    CustomerName string
    Products []store.Product
}

func (cart *Cart) GetTotal() (total float64) {
    for _, p := range cart.Products {
        total += p.Price()
    }
    return
}
```

The package statement is used just as with any other package, without the need to include the name of the parent or enclosing package. And dependency on custom packages must include the full package path, as shown in the listing. The code in Listing 12-15 defines a struct type named Cart, which exports CustomerName and Products fields, and a GetTotal method.

When importing a nested package, the package path starts with the module name and lists the sequence of packages, as shown in Listing 12-16.

Listing 12-16. Using a Nested Package in the main.go File in the packages Folder

```
package main

import (
    "fmt"
    "packages/store"
    . "packages/fmt"
    "packages/store/cart"
)

func main() {

    product := store.NewProduct("Kayak", "Watersports", 279)

    cart := cart.Cart {
        CustomerName: "Alice",
        Products: []store.Product{ *product },
    }

    fmt.Println("Name:", cart.CustomerName)
    fmt.Println("Total:",  ToCurrency(cart.GetTotal()))
}
```

The features defined by the nested package are accessed using the package name, just like any other package. In Listing 12-16, this means the type and function exported by the store/cart package are accessed using cart as the prefix. Compile and execute the project, and you will receive the following output:

```
Name: Alice
Total: $348.75
```

Using Package Initialization Functions

Each code file can contain an initialization function that is executed only when all packages have been
loaded and all other initialization—such as defining constants and variables—has been done. The most
common use for initialization functions is to perform calculations that are difficult to perform or that require
duplication to perform, as shown in Listing 12-17.

Listing 12-17. Calculating Maximum Prices in the tax.go File in the store Folder

```
package store

const defaultTaxRate float64 = 0.2
const minThreshold = 10

var categoryMaxPrices = map[string]float64 {
    "Watersports": 250 + (250 * defaultTaxRate),
    "Soccer": 150 + (150 * defaultTaxRate),
    "Chess": 50 + (50 * defaultTaxRate),
}

type taxRate struct {
    rate, threshold float64
}

func newTaxRate(rate, threshold float64) *taxRate {
    if (rate == 0) {
        rate = defaultTaxRate
    }
    if (threshold < minThreshold) {
        threshold = minThreshold
    }
    return &taxRate { rate, threshold }
}

func (taxRate *taxRate) calcTax(product *Product) (price float64) {
    if (product.price > taxRate.threshold) {
        price = product.price + (product.price * taxRate.rate)
    } else {
        price = product.price
    }
    if max, ok := categoryMaxPrices[product.Category]; ok && price > max {
        price = max
    }
    return
}
```

These changes introduce category-specific maximum prices, which are stored in a map. The maximum price for each category is calculated in the same way, which leads to duplication and which results in code that can be difficult to read and maintain.

This is a problem that can easily be resolved with a `for` loop, but Go allows loops only inside of functions, and I need to perform these calculations at the top level of the code file.

The solution is to use an initialization function, which is invoked automatically when the package is loaded and where language features such as `for` loops can be used, as shown in Listing 12-18.

Listing 12-18. Using an Initialization Function in the tax.go File in the store Folder

```go
package store

const defaultTaxRate float64 = 0.2
const minThreshold = 10

var categoryMaxPrices = map[string]float64 {
    "Watersports": 250,
    "Soccer": 150,
    "Chess": 50,
}

func init() {
    for category, price := range categoryMaxPrices {
        categoryMaxPrices[category] = price + (price * defaultTaxRate)
    }
}

type taxRate struct {
    rate, threshold float64
}

func newTaxRate(rate, threshold float64) *taxRate {
    // ...statements omitted for brevity...
}

func (taxRate *taxRate) calcTax(product *Product) (price float64) {
    // ...statements omitted for brevity...
}
```

The initialization function is called `init`, and it is defined without parameters and a result. The `init` function is called automatically and provides an opportunity to prepare the package for use. Listings 12-17 and 12-18 both produce the following output when compiled and executed:

```
Name: Kayak
Price: $300.00
```

The `init` function is not a regular Go function and cannot be invoked directly. And, unlike regular functions, a single file can define multiple `init` functions, all of which will be executed.

AVOIDING THE MULTIPLE INITIALIZATION FUNCTION PITFALL

Each code file can have its own initialization function. When using the standard Go compiler, the initialization functions are executed based on the alphabetic order of the filenames, so the function in the a.go file will be executed before the function in the b.go file, and so on.

But this order is not part of the Go language specification and should not be relied on. Your initialization functions should be self-contained and not rely on other init functions having been invoked previously.

Importing a Package Only for Initialization Effects

Go prevents packages from being imported but not used, which can be a problem if you rely on the effect of an initialization function but don't need to use any of the features the package exports. Create the packages/data folder and add to it a file named data.go with the content shown in Listing 12-19.

Listing 12-19. The Contents of the data.go File in the data Folder

```go
package data

import "fmt"

func init() {
    fmt.Println(("data.go init function invoked"))
}

func GetData() []string {
    return []string {"Kayak", "Lifejacket", "Paddle", "Soccer Ball"}
}
```

The initialization function writes out a message when it is invoked for the purposes of this example. If I need the effect of the initialization function, but I don't need to use the GetData function the package exports, then I can import the package using the blank identifier as an alias for the package name, as shown in Listing 12-20.

Listing 12-20. Importing for Initialization in the main.go File in the packages Folder

```go
package main

import (
    "fmt"
    "packages/store"
    . "packages/fmt"
    "packages/store/cart"
    _ "packages/data"
)

func main() {

    product := store.NewProduct("Kayak", "Watersports", 279)
```

```
    cart := cart.Cart {
        CustomerName: "Alice",
        Products: []store.Product{ *product },
    }

    fmt.Println("Name:", cart.CustomerName)
    fmt.Println("Total:",  ToCurrency(cart.GetTotal()))

}
```

The blank identifier—the underscore character—allows the package to be imported without requiring its exported features to be used. Compile and execute the project, and you will see the message written out by the initialization function defined in Listing 12-19:

```
data.go init function invoked
Name: Alice
Total: $300.00
```

Using External Packages

Projects can be extended using packages developed by third parties. Packages are downloaded and installed using the go get command. Run the command shown in Listing 12-21 in the packages folder to add a package to the example project.

Listing 12-21. Installing a Package

```
go get github.com/fatih/color@v1.10.0
```

The argument to the go get command is the path for the module that contains the package you want to use. The name is followed by the @ character and then the package version number, which is prefixed with the letter v, as shown in Figure 12-6.

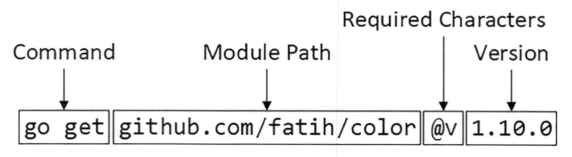

Figure 12-6. *Selecting a package*

The go get command is sophisticated and knows that the path specified in Listing 12-21 is a GitHub URL. The specified version of the module is downloaded, and the packages it contains are compiled and installed so they can be used in the project. (Packages are distributed as source code, which allows them to be compiled for the platform on which you are working.)

FINDING GO PACKAGES

There are two useful resources for finding Go packages. The first is `https://pkg.go.dev`, which provides a search engine. Unfortunately, it can take a while to figure out which keywords are needed to find a specific type of package.

The second resource is `https://github.com/golang/go/wiki/Projects`, which provides a curated list of Go projects, grouped by category. Not all the projects listed at `pkg.go.dev` are on the list, and I tend to use both resources to find packages.

Care must be taken when selecting modules. Many Go modules are written by individual developers to solve a problem and then published for anyone else to use. This creates a rich module ecosystem, but it does mean that maintenance and support can be inconsistent. The `github.com/fatih/color` module I use in this section, for example, has been retired and no longer receives updates. I am happy to continue using it since my use of it in this chapter is simple and the code works well. You must perform the same assessment for the modules you rely on in your projects.

Examine the go.mod file once the go get command has finished, and you will see new configuration statements:

```
module packages
go 1.17
require (
    github.com/fatih/color v1.10.0 // indirect
    github.com/mattn/go-colorable v0.1.8 // indirect
    github.com/mattn/go-isatty v0.0.12 // indirect
    golang.org/x/sys v0.0.0-20200223170610-d5e6a3e2c0ae // indirect
)
```

The require statement notes the dependency on the github.com/fatih/color module and the other modules it needs. The indirect comment at the end of the statements is added automatically because the packages are not used by the code in the project. A file named go.sum is created when the module is obtained and contains checksums used to validate the packages.

■ **Note** You can also use the go.mod file to create dependencies on projects you have created locally, which is the approach I take in Part 3 for the SportsStore example. See Chapter 35 for details.

Once the module is installed, the packages it contains can be used in the project, as shown in Listing 12-22.

Listing 12-22. Using a Third-Party Package in the main.go File in the packages Folder

```
package main

import (
    //"fmt"
    "packages/store"
    . "packages/fmt"
```

```
    "packages/store/cart"
  _ "packages/data"
  "github.com/fatih/color"
)

func main() {

    product := store.NewProduct("Kayak", "Watersports", 279)

    cart := cart.Cart {
        CustomerName: "Alice",
        Products: []store.Product{ *product },
    }

    color.Green("Name: " + cart.CustomerName)
    color.Cyan("Total: " + ToCurrency(cart.GetTotal()))
}
```

External packages are imported and used like custom packages. The import statement specifies the module path, and the last part of that path is used to access the features exported by the package. In this case, the package is named color, and this is the prefix used to access the package features.

The Green and Cyan functions used in Listing 12-22 write colored output, and if you compile and run the project, you will see the output shown in Figure 12-7.

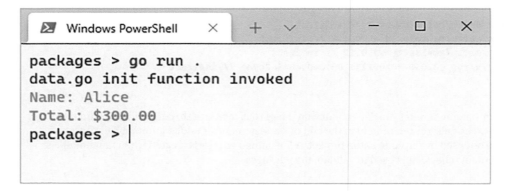

Figure 12-7. *Running the example application*

UNDERSTANDING MINIMAL VERSION SELECTION

The first time you run the go get command in Listing 12-22, you will see a list of the modules that are downloaded, which illustrated that modules have their own dependencies and that these are resolved automatically:

```
go: downloading github.com/fatih/color v1.10.0
go: downloading github.com/mattn/go-isatty v0.0.12
go: downloading github.com/mattn/go-colorable v0.1.8
go: downloading golang.org/x/sys v0.0.0-20200223170610-d5e6a3e2c0ae
```

The downloads are cached, which is why you won't see the messages the next time you use the go get command for the same module.

You may find that your project has dependencies on different versions of a module, especially in complex projects that have a lot of dependencies. In these situations, Go resolves this dependency using the most recent version specified by those dependencies. So, for example, if there are dependencies on version 1.1 and 1.5 of a module, Go will use version 1.5 when building the project. Go will use only the most recent version specified by a dependency, even if there is a more recent version available. If the most recent dependency for a module specifies version 1.5, for example, Go won't use version 1.6, even if it is available.

The effect of this approach is that your project may not be compiled using the module version that you selected with the go get command if a module depends on a later version. Equally, a module may not be compiled with the versions it expects for its dependencies if another module—or the go.mod file—specifies a more recent version.

Managing External Packages

The go get command adds dependencies to the go.mod file, but these are not removed automatically if the external package is no longer required. Listing 12-23 changes the contents of the main.go file to remove the use of the github.com/fatih/color package.

Listing 12-23. Removing a Package in the main.go File in the packages Folder

```
package main

import (
    "fmt"
    "packages/store"
    . "packages/fmt"
    "packages/store/cart"
    _ "packages/data"
    //"github.com/fatih/color"
)

func main() {

    product := store.NewProduct("Kayak", "Watersports", 279)

    cart := cart.Cart {
        CustomerName: "Alice",
        Products: []store.Product{ *product },
    }

    // color.Green("Name: " + cart.CustomerName)
    // color.Cyan("Total: " + ToCurrency(cart.GetTotal()))
    fmt.Println("Name:", cart.CustomerName)
    fmt.Println("Total:", ToCurrency(cart.GetTotal()))
}
```

To update the `go.mod` file to reflect the change, run the command shown in Listing 12-24 in the packages folder.

Listing 12-24. Updating Package Dependencies

```
go mod tidy
```

The command examines the project code, determines that there is no longer a dependency on any of the packages from the require `github.com/fatih/color` module, and removes the `require` statement from the `go.mod` file:

```
module packages
go 1.17
```

Summary

In this chapter, I explained the role packages play in Go development. I showed you how to use packages to add structure to a project and how they can provide access to features developed by third parties. In the next chapter, I describe the Go features for composing types, which allows complex types to be created.

CHAPTER 13

■ ■ ■

Type and Interface Composition

In this chapter, I explain how types are combined to create new features. Go doesn't use inheritance, which you may be familiar with in other languages and instead relies on an approach known as *composition*. This can be difficult to understand, so this chapter describes some features covered in earlier chapters to set a solid foundation on which to explain the composition process. Table 13-1 puts type and interface composition in context.

Table 13-1. *Putting Type and Interface Composition in Context*

Question	Answer
What is it?	Composition is the process by which new types are created by combining structs and interfaces.
Why is it useful?	Composition allows types to be defined based on existing types.
How is it used?	Existing types are embedded in new types.
Are there any pitfalls or limitations?	Composition doesn't work in the same way as inheritance, and care must be taken to achieve the desired outcome.
Are there any alternatives?	Composition is optional, and you can create entirely independent types.

Table 13-2 summarizes the chapter.

Table 13-2. *Chapter Summary*

Problem	Solution	Listing
Compose a struct type	Add an embedded field	7-9, 14–17
Build on an already composed type	Create a chain of embedded types	10–13
Compose an interface type	Add the name of the existing interface to the new interface definition	25–26

© Adam Freeman 2022
A. Freeman, *Pro Go*, https://doi.org/10.1007/978-1-4842-7355-5_13

Preparing for This Chapter

To prepare for this chapter, open a new command prompt, navigate to a convenient location, and create a directory named composition. Run the command shown in Listing 13-1 in the composition folder to create a module file.

■ **Tip** You can download the example project for this chapter—and for all the other chapters in this book—from https://github.com/apress/pro-go. See Chapter 2 for how to get help if you have problems running the examples.

Listing 13-1. Initializing the Module

```
go mod init composition
```

Add a file named main.go to the composition folder, with the contents shown in Listing 13-2.

Listing 13-2. The Contents of the main.go File in the composition Folder

```
package main

import "fmt"

func main() {

    fmt.Println("Hello, Composition")
}
```

Use the command prompt to run the command shown in Listing 13-3 in the composition folder.

Listing 13-3. Running the Example Project

```
go run .
```

The code in the main.go file will be compiled and executed, producing the following output:

```
Hello, Composition
```

Understanding Type Composition

If you are used to languages such as C# or Java, then you will have created a base class and created subclasses to add more specific features. The subclasses inherit functionality from the base class, which prevents code duplication. The result is a set of classes, where the base class defines common functionality that is supplemented by more specific features in individual subclasses, as shown in Figure 13-1.

Figure 13-1. *A set of classes*

Go doesn't support classes or inheritance and focuses on *composition* instead. But, despite the differences, composition can be used to create hierarchies of types, just in a different way.

Defining the Base Type

The starting point is to define a struct type and a method, which I will use to create more specific types in later examples. Create the composition/store folder and add to it a file named product.go with the content shown in Listing 13-4.

Listing 13-4. The Contents of the product.go File in the store Folder

```
package store

type Product struct {
    Name, Category string
    price float64
}

func (p *Product) Price(taxRate float64) float64 {
    return p.price + (p.price * taxRate)
}
```

The Product struct defines Name and Category fields, which are exported, and a price field that is not exported. There is also a method named Price, which accepts a float64 parameter and uses it with the price field to calculate a tax-inclusive price.

Defining a Constructor

Because Go doesn't support classes, it doesn't support class constructors either. As I explained, a common convention is to define a constructor function whose name is New<Type>, such as NewProduct, as shown in Listing 13-5, and that allows values to be provided for all fields, even those that have not been exported. As with other code features, the capitalization of the first letter of the constructor function name determines whether it is exported outside of the package.

Listing 13-5. Defining a Constructor in the product.go File in the store Folder

```
package store

type Product struct {
    Name, Category string
    price float64
}

func NewProduct(name, category string, price float64) *Product {
    return &Product{ name, category, price }
}
```

```
func (p *Product) Price(taxRate float64) float64 {
    return p.price + (p.price * taxRate)
}
```

Constructor functions are only a convention, and their use is not enforced, which means that exported types can be created using the literal syntax, just as long as no values are assigned to the unexported fields. Listing 13-6 shows the use of the constructor function and the literal syntax.

Listing 13-6. Creating Struct Values in the main.go File in the composition Folder

```
package main

import (
    "fmt"
    "composition/store"
)

func main() {

    kayak := store.NewProduct("Kayak", "Watersports", 275)
    lifejacket := &store.Product{ Name: "Lifejacket", Category:  "Watersports"}

    for _, p := range []*store.Product { kayak, lifejacket} {
        fmt.Println("Name:", p.Name, "Category:", p.Category, "Price:", p.Price(0.2))
    }
}
```

Constructors should be used whenever they are defined because they make it easier to manage changes in the way that values are created and because they ensure that fields are properly initialized. In Listing 13-6, using the literal syntax means that no value is assigned to the price field, which affects the output from the Price method. But, since Go doesn't support enforcing the use of constructors, their use requires discipline.

Compile and execute the project, and you will receive the following output:

```
Name: Kayak Category: Watersports Price: 330
Name: Lifejacket Category: Watersports Price: 0
```

Composing Types

Go supports composition, rather than inheritance, which is done by combining struct types. Add a file named boat.go to the store folder with the contents shown in Listing 13-7.

Listing 13-7. The Contents of the boat.go File in the store Folder

```
package store

type Boat struct {
    *Product
    Capacity int
    Motorized bool
}
```

```
func NewBoat(name string, price float64, capacity int, motorized bool) *Boat {
    return &Boat {
        NewProduct(name, "Watersports", price), capacity, motorized,
    }
}
```

The Boat struct type defines an embedded *Product field, as illustrated by Figure 13-2.

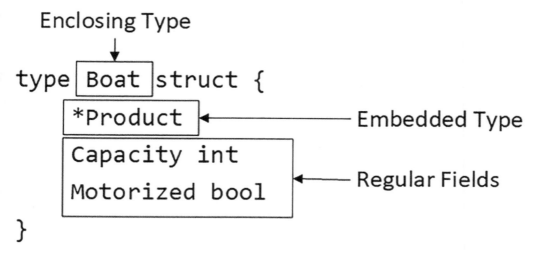

Figure 13-2. *Embedding a type*

A struct can mix regular and embedded field types, but the embedded fields are an important part of the composition feature, as you will see shortly.

The NewBoat function is a constructor that uses its parameters to create a Boat, with its embedded Product value. Listing 13-8 shows the new struct in use.

Listing 13-8. Using the Boat Struct in the main.go File in the composition Folder

```
package main

import (
    "fmt"
    "composition/store"
)

func main() {

    boats := []*store.Boat {
        store.NewBoat("Kayak", 275, 1, false),
        store.NewBoat("Canoe", 400, 3, false),
        store.NewBoat("Tender", 650.25, 2, true),
    }
```

```
for _, b := range boats {
    fmt.Println("Conventional:", b.Product.Name, "Direct:", b.Name)
}
}
```

The new statements create a *Boat slice of Boat, which is populated using the NewBoat constructor function.

Go gives special treatment to struct types that have fields whose type is another struct type, in the way that the Boat type has a *Product field in the example project. You can see this special treatment in the statement in the for loop, which is responsible for writing out details of each Boat.

Go allows the fields of the nested type to be accessed in two ways. The first is the conventional approach of navigating the hierarchy of types to reach the value that is required. The *Product field is embedded, which means that its name its its type. To reach the Name field, I can navigate through the nested type, like this:

```
...
fmt.Println("Conventional:", b.Product.Name, "Direct:", b.Name)
...
```

Go also allows nested field types to be used directly, like this:

```
...
fmt.Println("Conventional:", b.Product.Name, "Direct:", b.Name)
...
```

The Boat type doesn't define a Name field, but it can be treated as though it did because of the direct access feature. This is known as *field promotion*, and Go essentially flattens the types so that the Boat type behaves as though it defines the fields that are provided by the nested Product type, as illustrated by Figure 13-3.

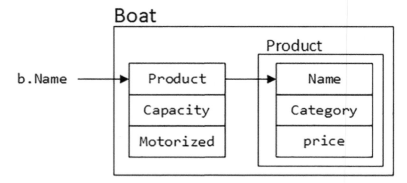

Figure 13-3. *Promoted fields*

Compile and execute the project, and you will see that the values produced by both approaches are the same:

```
Conventional: Kayak Direct: Kayak
Conventional: Canoe Direct: Canoe
Conventional: Tender Direct: Tender
```

Methods are also promoted so that methods defined for the nested type can be invoked from the enclosing type, as shown in Listing 13-9.

Listing 13-9. Calling a Method in the main.go File in the composition Folder

```
package main

import (
    "fmt"
    "composition/store"
)

func main() {

    boats := []*store.Boat {
        store.NewBoat("Kayak", 275, 1, false),
        store.NewBoat("Canoe", 400, 3, false),
        store.NewBoat("Tender", 650.25, 2, true),
    }

    for _, b := range boats {
        fmt.Println("Boat:", b.Name, "Price:", b.Price(0.2))
    }
}
```

If the field type is a value, such as Product, then any methods defined with Product or *Product receivers will be promoted. If the field type is a pointer, such as *Product, then only methods with *Product receivers will be prompted.

There is no Price method defined for the *Boat type, but Go promotes the method defined with a *Product receiver. Compile and execute the project, and you will receive the following output:

```
Boat: Kayak Price: 330
Boat: Canoe Price: 480
Boat: Tender Price: 780.3
```

UNDERSTANDING PROMOTED FIELDS AND THE LITERAL SYNTAX

Go applies its special treatment to promoted fields once a struct value has been created. So, for example, if I use the NewBoat function to create a value like this:

```
...
boat := store.NewBoat("Kayak", 275, 1, false)
...
```

then I can read and assign values to promoted fields, like this:

```
...
boat.Name = "Green Kayak"
...
```

But this feature isn't available when using the literal syntax to create values in the first place, meaning that I can't replace the NewBoat function, like this:

```
...
boat := store.Boat { Name: "Kayak", Category: "Watersports",
    Capacity: 1, Motorized: false }
...
```

The compiler won't allow values to be assigned directly and reports an "unknown field" error when the code is compiled. If you do use the literal syntax, then you must assign a value to the nested field, like this:

```
...
boat := store.Boat { Product: &store.Product{ Name: "Kayak",
    Category: "Watersports"}, Capacity: 1, Motorized: false }
...
```

As I explain in the "Creating a Chain of Nested Types" section, Go makes it easy to use the composition feature to create complex types, which makes the literal syntax increasingly difficult to use and produces code that is error-prone and difficult to maintain. My advice is to use constructor functions and to invoke one constructor from another, as the NewBoat function calls the NewProduct function in Listing 13-7.

Creating a Chain of Nested Types

The composition feature can be used to create complex chains of nested types, whose fields and methods are promoted to the top-level enclosing type. Add a file named rentalboats.go to the store folder with the content shown in Listing 13-10.

Listing 13-10. The Contents of the rentalboats.go File in the store Folder

```
package store

type RentalBoat struct {
    *Boat
    IncludeCrew bool
}

func NewRentalBoat(name string, price float64, capacity int,
        motorized, crewed bool) *RentalBoat {
    return &RentalBoat{NewBoat(name, price, capacity, motorized), crewed}
}
```

The RentalBoat type is composed using the *Boat type, which is, in turn, composed using the *Product type, forming a chain. Go performs promotion so that the fields defined by all three types in the chain can be accessed directly, as shown in Listing 13-11.

Listing 13-11. Accessing Nested Fields Directly in the main.go File in the composition Folder

```
package main

import (
    "fmt"
    "composition/store"
)

func main() {

    rentals := []*store.RentalBoat {
        store.NewRentalBoat("Rubber Ring", 10, 1, false, false),
        store.NewRentalBoat("Yacht", 50000, 5, true, true),
        store.NewRentalBoat("Super Yacht", 100000, 15, true, true),
    }

    for _, r := range rentals {
        fmt.Println("Rental Boat:", r.Name, "Rental Price:", r.Price(0.2))
    }
}
```

Go promotes fields from the nested Boat and Product types so they can be accessed through the top-level RentalBoat type, which allows the Name field to be read in Listing 13-11. Methods are also promoted to the top-level type, which is why I can use the Price method, even though it is defined on the *Product type, which is at the end of the chain. The code in Listing 13-11 produces the following output when compiled and executed:

```
Rental Boat: Rubber Ring Rental Price: 12
Rental Boat: Yacht Rental Price: 60000
Rental Boat: Super Yacht Rental Price: 120000
```

Using Multiple Nested Types in the Same Struct

Types can define multiple struct fields, and Go will promote the fields for all of them. Listing 13-12 defines a new type that describes a boat crew and uses it as the type for a field in another struct.

Listing 13-12. Defining a New Type in the rentalboats.go File in the store Folder

```
package store

type Crew struct {
    Captain, FirstOfficer string
}

type RentalBoat struct {
    *Boat
    IncludeCrew bool
    *Crew
}
```

```
func NewRentalBoat(name string, price float64, capacity int,
    motorized, crewed bool, captain, firstOfficer string) *RentalBoat {
  return &RentalBoat{NewBoat(name, price, capacity, motorized), crewed,
    &Crew{captain, firstOfficer}}
}
```

The RentalBoat type has *Boat and *Crew fields, and Go promotes the fields and methods from both nested types, as shown in Listing 13-13.

Listing 13-13. Using Promoted Fields in the main.go File in the composition Folder

```
package main

import (
    "fmt"
    "composition/store"
)

func main() {

    rentals := []*store.RentalBoat {
        store.NewRentalBoat("Rubber Ring", 10, 1, false, false, "N/A", "N/A"),
        store.NewRentalBoat("Yacht", 50000, 5, true, true, "Bob", "Alice"),
        store.NewRentalBoat("Super Yacht", 100000, 15, true, true,
            "Dora", "Charlie"),
    }

    for _, r := range rentals {
        fmt.Println("Rental Boat:", r.Name, "Rental Price:", r.Price(0.2),
            "Captain:", r.Captain)
    }
}
```

Compile and execute the project, and you will receive the following output, showing the addition of details about the crew:

```
Rental Boat: Rubber Ring Rental Price: 12 Captain: N/A
Rental Boat: Yacht Rental Price: 60000 Captain: Bob
Rental Boat: Super Yacht Rental Price: 120000 Captain: Dora
```

Understanding When Promotion Cannot Be Performed

Go can perform promotion only if there is no field or method defined with the same name on the enclosing type, which can lead to unexpected results. Add a file named specialdeal.go to the store folder with the code shown in Listing 13-14.

Listing 13-14. The Contents of the specialdeal.go File in the store Folder

```
package store

type SpecialDeal struct {
    Name string
    *Product
    price float64
}

func NewSpecialDeal(name string, p *Product, discount float64) *SpecialDeal {
    return &SpecialDeal{ name, p, p.price - discount }
}

func (deal *SpecialDeal ) GetDetails() (string, float64, float64) {
    return deal.Name, deal.price, deal.Price(0)
}
```

The SpecialDeal type defines a *Product embedded field. This combination leads to duplicate fields because both types defined Name and price fields. There is also a constructor function and a GetDetails method, which returns the values of the Name and price fields, as well as the result from the Price method, which is invoked with zero as the argument to make the example easier to follow. Listing 13-15 uses the new type to demonstrate how promotion is handled.

Listing 13-15. Using a New Type in the main.go File in the composition Folder

```
package main

import (
    "fmt"
    "composition/store"
)

func main() {

    product := store.NewProduct("Kayak", "Watersports", 279)

    deal := store.NewSpecialDeal("Weekend Special", product, 50)

    Name, price, Price := deal.GetDetails()

    fmt.Println("Name:", Name)
    fmt.Println("Price field:", price)
    fmt.Println("Price method:", Price)
}
```

This listing creates a *Product, which is then used to create a *SpecialDeal. The GetDetails method is called, and the three results it returns are written out. Compile and run the code, and you will see the following output:

```
Name: Weekend Special
Price field: 229
Price method: 279
```

The first two results are what you might expect: the Name and price fields from the Product type are not promoted because the SpecialDeal type has fields with the same names.

The third result is the one that can cause problems. Go can promote the Price method, but when it is invoked, it uses the price field from the Product and not the SpecialDeal.

It is easy to forget that field and method promotion is just a convenience feature. This statement in Listing 13-14:

```
...
return deal.Name, deal.price, deal.Price(0)
...
```

is a more concise way of expressing this statement:

```
...
return deal.Name, deal.price, deal.Product.Price(0)
...
```

When the method is invoked through its struct field, it is clear that the result from calling the Price method isn't going to use the price field defined by the SpecialDeal type.

If I want to be able to call the Price method and get a result that does rely on the SpecialDeal.price field, then I have to define a new method, as shown in Listing 13-16.

Listing 13-16. Defining a Method in the specialdeal.go File in the store Folder

```
package store

type SpecialDeal struct {
    Name string
    *Product
    price float64
}

func NewSpecialDeal(name string, p *Product, discount float64) *SpecialDeal {
    return &SpecialDeal{ name, p, p.price - discount }
}

func (deal *SpecialDeal ) GetDetails() (string, float64, float64) {
    return deal.Name, deal.price, deal.Price(0)
}

func (deal *SpecialDeal) Price(taxRate float64) float64 {
    return deal.price
}
```

The new Price method stops Go from promoting the Product method and produces the following result when the project is compiled and executed:

```
Name: Weekend Special
Price field: 229
Price method: 229
```

Understanding Promotion Ambiguity

A related issue arises when two embedded fields use the same field or method names, as shown in Listing 13-17.

Listing 13-17. An Ambiguous Method in the main.go File in the composition Folder

```
package main

import (
    "fmt"
    "composition/store"
)

func main() {

    kayak := store.NewProduct("Kayak", "Watersports", 279)

    type OfferBundle struct {
        *store.SpecialDeal
        *store.Product
    }

    bundle := OfferBundle {
        store.NewSpecialDeal("Weekend Special", kayak, 50),
        store.NewProduct("Lifrejacket", "Watersports", 48.95),
    }

    fmt.Println("Price:", bundle.Price(0))
}
```

The OfferBundle type has two embedded fields, both of which have Price methods. Go cannot differentiate between the methods, and the code in Listing 13-17 produces the following error when it is compiled:

```
.\main.go:22:33: ambiguous selector bundle.Price
```

Understanding Composition and Interfaces

Composing types makes it easy to build up specialized functionality without having to duplicate the code required by a more general type so that the Boat type in the project, for example, can build on the functionality provided by the Product type.

343

This can seem similar to writing classes in other languages, but there is an important difference, which is that each composed type is distinct and cannot be used where the types from which it is composed are required, as shown in Listing 13-18.

Listing 13-18. Mixing Types in the main.go File in the composition Folder

```
package main

import (
    "fmt"
    "composition/store"
)

func main() {

    products := map[string]*store.Product {
        "Kayak": store.NewBoat("Kayak", 279, 1, false),
        "Ball": store.NewProduct("Soccer Ball", "Soccer", 19.50),
    }

    for _, p := range products {
        fmt.Println("Name:", p.Name, "Category:", p.Category, "Price:", p.Price(0.2))
    }
}
```

The Go compiler will not allow a Boat to be used as a value in a slice where Product values are required. In a language like C# or Java, this would be allowed because Boat would be a subclass of Product, but this is not how Go deals with types. If you compile the project, you will receive the following error:

```
.\main.go:11:9: cannot use store.NewBoat("Kayak", 279, 1, false) (type *store.Boat) as
type *store.Product in map value
```

Using Composition to Implement Interfaces

As I explained in Chapter 11, Go uses interfaces to describe methods that can be implemented by multiple types.

Go takes promoted methods into account when determining whether a type conforms to an interface, which avoids the need to duplicate methods that are already present through an embedded field. To see how this works, add a file named forsale.go to the store folder, with the contents shown in Listing 13-19.

Listing 13-19. The Contents of the forsale.go File in the store Folder

```
package store

type ItemForSale interface {
    Price(taxRate float64) float64
}
```

The ItemForSale type is an interface that specifies a single method, named Price, with one float64 parameter and one float64 result. Listing 13-20 uses the interface type to create a map, which is populated with items that conform to the interface.

Listing 13-20. Using an Interface in the main.go File in the composition Folder

```
package main

import (
    "fmt"
    "composition/store"
)

func main() {

    products := map[string]store.ItemForSale {
        "Kayak": store.NewBoat("Kayak", 279, 1, false),
        "Ball": store.NewProduct("Soccer Ball", "Soccer", 19.50),
    }

    for key, p := range products {
        fmt.Println("Key:", key, "Price:", p.Price(0.2))
    }
}
```

Changing the map so that it uses the interface allows me to store Product and Boat values. The Product type conforms to the ItemForSale interface directly because there is a Price method that matches the signature specified by the interface and that has a *Product receiver.

There is no Price method that takes a *Boat receiver, but Go takes into account the Price method promoted from the Boat type's embedded field, which it uses to satisfy the interface requirements. Compile and execute the project, and you will receive the following output:

```
Key: Kayak Price: 334.8
Key: Ball Price: 23.4
```

Understanding the Type Switch Limitation

Interfaces can specify only methods, which is why I used the key used to store values in the map in Listing 13-20 when writing the output. In Chapter 11, I explained that switch statements can be used to gain access to underlying types, but this doesn't work as you might expect, as shown in Listing 13-21.

Listing 13-21. Accessing the Underlying Type in the main.go File in the composition Folder

```
package main

import (
    "fmt"
    "composition/store"
)
```

```
func main() {

    products := map[string]store.ItemForSale {
        "Kayak": store.NewBoat("Kayak", 279, 1, false),
        "Ball": store.NewProduct("Soccer Ball", "Soccer", 19.50),
    }

    for key, p := range products {
        switch item := p.(type) {
            case *store.Product, *store.Boat:
                fmt.Println("Name:", item.Name, "Category:", item.Category,
                    "Price:", item.Price(0.2))
            default:
                fmt.Println("Key:", key, "Price:", p.Price(0.2))
        }

    }
}
```

The case statement in Listing 13-21 specifies *Product and *Boat, which causes the compiler to fail with the following error:

```
.\main.go:21:42: item.Name undefined (type store.ItemForSale has no field or method Name)
.\main.go:21:66: item.Category undefined (type store.ItemForSale has no field or method
Category)
```

This issue is that case statements that specify multiple types will match values of all of those types but will not perform type assertion. For Listing 13-21, this means that *Product and *Boat values will be matched by the case statement, but the type of item variable will be ItemForSale, which is why the compiler produces the error. Instead, additional type assertions or single-type case statements must be used, as shown in Listing 13-22.

Listing 13-22. Using Separate case Statements in the main.go File in the composition Folder

```
package main

import (
    "fmt"
    "composition/store"
)

func main() {

    products := map[string]store.ItemForSale {
        "Kayak": store.NewBoat("Kayak", 279, 1, false),
        "Ball": store.NewProduct("Soccer Ball", "Soccer", 19.50),
    }
```

```
    for key, p := range products {
        switch item := p.(type) {
            case *store.Product:
                fmt.Println("Name:", item.Name, "Category:", item.Category,
                    "Price:", item.Price(0.2))
            case *store.Boat:
                fmt.Println("Name:", item.Name, "Category:", item.Category,
                    "Price:", item.Price(0.2))
            default:
                fmt.Println("Key:", key, "Price:", p.Price(0.2))
        }
    }
}
```

A type assertion is performed by the case statement when a single type is specified, albeit it can lead to duplication as each type is processed. The code in Listing 13-22 produces the following output when the project is compiled and executed:

```
Name: Kayak Category: Watersports Price: 334.8
Name: Soccer Ball Category: Soccer Price: 23.4
```

An alternative solution is to define interface methods that provide access to the property values. This can be done by adding methods to an existing interface or by defining a separate interface, as shown in Listing 13-23.

Listing 13-23. Defining an Interface in the product.go File in the store Folder

```
package store

type Product struct {
    Name, Category string
    price float64
}

func NewProduct(name, category string, price float64) *Product {
    return &Product{ name, category, price }
}

func (p *Product) Price(taxRate float64) float64 {
    return p.price + (p.price * taxRate)
}

type Describable interface  {
    GetName() string
    GetCategory() string
}

func (p *Product) GetName() string {
    return p.Name
}
```

```
func (p *Product) GetCategory() string {
    return p.Category
}
```

The Describable interface defines GetName and GetCategory methods, which are implemented for the *Product type. Listing 13-24 revises the switch statement so that interfaces are used instead of fields.

Listing 13-24. Using Interfaces in the main.go File in the composition Folder

```
package main

import (
    "fmt"
    "composition/store"
)

func main() {

    products := map[string]store.ItemForSale {
        "Kayak": store.NewBoat("Kayak", 279, 1, false),
        "Ball": store.NewProduct("Soccer Ball", "Soccer", 19.50),
    }

    for key, p := range products {

        switch item := p.(type) {
            case store.Describable:
                fmt.Println("Name:", item.GetName(), "Category:", item.GetCategory(),
                    "Price:", item.(store.ItemForSale).Price(0.2))
            default:
                fmt.Println("Key:", key, "Price:", p.Price(0.2))
        }
    }
}
```

This works, but it relies on a type assertion to the ItemForSale interface to access the Price method. This is problematic because a type can implement the Describable interface but not the ItemForSale interface, which would cause a runtime error. I could deal with the type assertion by adding a Price method to the Describable interface, but there is an alternative, which I describe in the next section. Compile and execute the project, and you will see the following output:

```
Name: Kayak Category: Watersports Price: 334.8
Name: Soccer Ball Category: Soccer Price: 23.4
```

Composing Interfaces

Go allows interfaces to be composed from other interfaces, as shown in Listing 13-25.

Listing 13-25. Composing an Interface in the product.go File in the store Folder

```go
package store

type Product struct {
    Name, Category string
    price float64
}

func NewProduct(name, category string, price float64) *Product {
    return &Product{ name, category, price }
}

func (p *Product) Price(taxRate float64) float64 {
    return p.price + (p.price * taxRate)
}

type Describable interface  {
    GetName() string
    GetCategory() string
    ItemForSale
}

func (p *Product) GetName() string {
    return p.Name
}

func (p *Product) GetCategory() string {
    return p.Category
}
```

One interface can enclose another, with the effect that types must implement all the methods defined by the enclosing and enclosed interfaces. Interfaces are simpler than structs, and there are no fields or method to promote. The result of composing interfaces is a union of the method defined by the enclosing and enclosed types. In this example, the union means that implementing the Describable interface requires GetName, GetCategory, and Price methods. The GetName and GetCategory methods defined directly by the Describable interface are formed into a union with the Price method defined by the ItemForSale interface.

The change to the Describable interface means that the type assertion I used in the previous section is no longer required, as shown in Listing 13-26.

Listing 13-26. Removing an Assertion in the main.go File in the composition Folder

```go
package main

import (
    "fmt"
    "composition/store"
)
```

```
func main() {

    products := map[string]store.ItemForSale {
        "Kayak": store.NewBoat("Kayak", 279, 1, false),
        "Ball": store.NewProduct("Soccer Ball", "Soccer", 19.50),
    }

    for key, p := range products {

        switch item := p.(type) {
            case store.Describable:
                fmt.Println("Name:", item.GetName(), "Category:", item.GetCategory(),
                    "Price:", item.Price(0.2))
            default:
                fmt.Println("Key:", key, "Price:", p.Price(0.2))
        }
    }
}
```

A value of any type that implements the Describable interface must have a Price method because of the composition performed in Listing 13-25, which means the method can be called without a potentially risky type assertion. Compile and execute the project, and you will receive the following output:

```
Name: Kayak Category: Watersports Price: 334.8
Name: Soccer Ball Category: Soccer Price: 23.4
```

Summary

In this chapter, I describe the way that Go types can be composed to create more complex functionality, providing an alternative to the inheritance-based approach taken by other languages. In the next chapter, I describe goroutines and channels, which are the Go features for managing concurrency.

CHAPTER 14

■ ■ ■

Using Goroutines and Channels

Go has excellent support for writing concurrent applications, using features that are simpler and more intuitive than any other language I have used. In this chapter, I describe the use of *goroutines*, which allow functions to be executed concurrently, and *channels*, through which goroutines can produce results asynchronously. Table 14-1 puts goroutines and channels in context.

Table 14-1. *Putting Goroutines and Channels in Context*

Question	Answer
What are they?	Goroutines are lightweight threads created and managed by the Go runtime. Channels are pipes that carry values of a specific type.
Why are they useful?	Goroutines allow functions to be executed concurrently, without needing to deal with the complications of operating system threads. Channels allow goroutines to produce results asynchronously.
How are they used?	Goroutines are created using the go keyword. Channels are defined as data types.
Are there any pitfalls or limitations?	Care must be taken to manage the direction of channels. Goroutines that share data require additional features, which are described in Chapter 14.
Are there any alternatives?	Goroutines and channels are the built-in Go concurrency features, but some applications can rely on a single thread of execution, which is created by default to execute the main function.

Table 14-2 summarizes the chapter.

Table 14-2. *Chapter Summary*

Problem	Solution	Listing
Execute a function asynchronously	Create a goroutine	7
Produce a result from a function executed asynchronously	Use a channel	10, 15, 16, 22–26
Send and receive values using a channel	Use arrow expressions	11–13
Indicate that no further values will be sent over a channel	Use the close function	17–20
Enumerate the values received from a channel	Use a for loop with the range keyword	21
Send or receive values using multiple channels	Use a select statement	27–32

Preparing for This Chapter

To prepare for this chapter, open a new command prompt, navigate to a convenient location, and create a directory named concurrency. Run the command shown in Listing 14-1 to create a module file.

■ **Tip** You can download the example project for this chapter—and for all the other chapters in this book—from https://github.com/apress/pro-go. See Chapter 2 for how to get help if you have problems running the examples.

Listing 14-1. Initializing the Module

```
go mod init concurrency
```

Add a file named product.go to the concurrency folder with the contents shown in Listing 14-2.

Listing 14-2. The Contents of the product.go File in the concurrency Folder

```
package main

import "strconv"

type Product struct {
    Name, Category string
    Price float64
}

var ProductList = []*Product {
    { "Kayak", "Watersports", 279 },
    { "Lifejacket", "Watersports", 49.95 },
    { "Soccer Ball", "Soccer", 19.50 },
```

```
        { "Corner Flags", "Soccer", 34.95 },
        { "Stadium", "Soccer", 79500 },
        { "Thinking Cap", "Chess", 16 },
        { "Unsteady Chair", "Chess", 75 },
        { "Bling-Bling King", "Chess", 1200 },
}

type ProductGroup []*Product

type ProductData = map[string]ProductGroup

var Products = make(ProductData)

func ToCurrency(val float64) string {
    return "$" + strconv.FormatFloat(val, 'f', 2, 64)
}

func init() {
    for _, p := range ProductList {
        if _, ok := Products[p.Category]; ok {
            Products[p.Category] = append(Products[p.Category], p)
        } else {
            Products[p.Category] = ProductGroup{ p }
        }
    }
}
```

This file defines a custom type named Product, along with type aliases that I use to create a map that organizes products by category. I use the Product type in a slice and a map, and I rely on an init function, described in Chapter 12, to populate the map from the contents of the slice, which is itself populated using the literal syntax. This file also contains a ToCurrency function that formats float64 values into dollar currency strings, which I will use to format the results in this chapter.

Add a file named operations.go to the concurrency folder with the content shown in Listing 14-3.

Listing 14-3. The Contents of the operations.go File in the concurrency Folder

```
package main

import "fmt"

func CalcStoreTotal(data ProductData) {
    var storeTotal float64
    for category, group := range data {
        storeTotal += group.TotalPrice(category)
    }
    fmt.Println("Total:", ToCurrency(storeTotal))
}

func (group ProductGroup) TotalPrice(category string, ) (total float64) {
    for _, p := range group {
        total += p.Price
    }
}
```

```
        fmt.Println(category, "subtotal:", ToCurrency(total))
        return
}
```

This file defines methods that operate on the type aliases created in the product.go file. As I explained in Chapter 11, methods can be defined only on types that are created in the same package, which means that I can't define a method for the []*Product type, for example, but I can create an alias for that type and use the alias as the method receiver.

Add a file named main.go to the concurrency folder, with the contents shown in Listing 14-4.

Listing 14-4. The Contents of the main.go File in the concurrency Folder

```
package main

import "fmt"

func main() {

        fmt.Println("main function started")
        CalcStoreTotal(Products)
        fmt.Println("main function complete")
}
```

Use the command prompt to run the command shown in Listing 14-5 in the concurrency folder.

Listing 14-5. Running the Example Project

```
go run .
```

The code will be compiled and executed, producing the following output:

```
main function started
Watersports subtotal: $328.95
Soccer subtotal: $79554.45
Chess subtotal: $1291.00
Total: $81174.40
main function complete
```

Understanding How Go Executes Code

The key building block for executing a Go program is the *goroutine*, which is a lightweight thread created by the Go runtime. All Go programs use at least one goroutine because this is how Go executes the code in the main function. When compiled Go code is executed, the runtime creates a goroutine that starts executing the statements in the entry point, which is the main function in the main package. Each statement in the main function is executed in the order in which they are defined. The goroutine keeps executing statements until it reaches the end of the main function, at which point the application terminates.

The goroutine executes each statement in the main function *synchronously*, which means that it waits for the statement to complete before moving on to the next statement. The statements in the main function can call other functions, use for loops, create values, and use all the other features described in this book. The main goroutine will work its way through the code, following its path by executing one statement at a time.

For the example application, this means that the map of products is processed sequentially so that each product category is processed in turn, and, within each category, each product is processed, as illustrated by Figure 14-1.

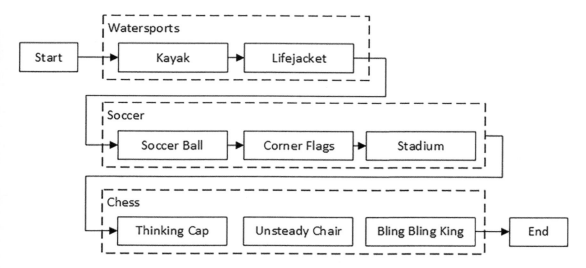

Figure 14-1. *Sequential execution*

Listing 14-6 adds a statement that writes out details of each product as it is processed, which will demonstrate the flow shown in the figure.

Listing 14-6. Adding a Statement in the operations.go File in the concurrency Folder

```
package main

import "fmt"

func CalcStoreTotal(data ProductData) {
    var storeTotal float64
    for category, group := range data {
        storeTotal += group.TotalPrice(category)
    }
    fmt.Println("Total:", ToCurrency(storeTotal))
}

func (group ProductGroup) TotalPrice(category string) (total float64) {
    for _, p := range group {
        fmt.Println(category, "product:", p.Name)
        total += p.Price
    }
    fmt.Println(category, "subtotal:", ToCurrency(total))
    return
}
```

Compile and execute the code, and you will see output similar to the following:

```
main function started
Soccer product: Soccer Ball
Soccer product: Corner Flags
Soccer product: Stadium
Soccer subtotal: $79554.45
Chess product: Thinking Cap
Chess product: Unsteady Chair
Chess product: Bling-Bling King
Chess subtotal: $1291.00
Watersports product: Kayak
Watersports product: Lifejacket
Watersports subtotal: $328.95
Total: $81174.40
main function complete
```

You may see different results based on the order in which keys are retrieved from the map, but what's important is that all the products in a category are processed before execution moves onto the next category.

The advantages of synchronous execution are simplicity and consistency—the behavior of synchronous code is easy to understand and predictable. The disadvantage is that it can be inefficient. Working sequentially through nine data items, as in the example, doesn't present any issues, but most real projects have larger volumes of data or have other tasks to perform, which means that sequential execution takes too long and doesn't produce results fast enough.

Creating Additional Goroutines

Go allows the developer to create additional goroutines, which execute code at the same time as the main goroutine. Go makes it easy to create new goroutines, as shown in Listing 14-7.

Listing 14-7. Creating Go Routines in the operations.go File in the concurrency Folder

```
package main

import "fmt"

func CalcStoreTotal(data ProductData) {
    var storeTotal float64
    for category, group := range data {
        go group.TotalPrice(category)
    }
    fmt.Println("Total:", ToCurrency(storeTotal))
}

func (group ProductGroup) TotalPrice(category string) (total float64) {
    for _, p := range group {
        fmt.Println(category, "product:", p.Name)
        total += p.Price
    }
```

```
    fmt.Println(category, "subtotal:", ToCurrency(total))
    return
}
```

A goroutine is created using the go keyword followed by the function or method that should be executed asynchronously, as shown in Figure 14-2.

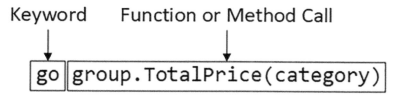

Figure 14-2. *A goroutine*

When the Go runtime encounters the go keyword, it creates a new goroutine and uses it to execute the specified function or method.

This changes the program execution because, at any given moment, there are multiple goroutines, each of which is executing its own set of statements. These statements are executed *concurrently*, which just means they are being executed at the same time.

In the case of the example, a goroutine is created for each call to the TotalPrice method, which means that the categories are processed concurrently, as shown in Figure 14-3.

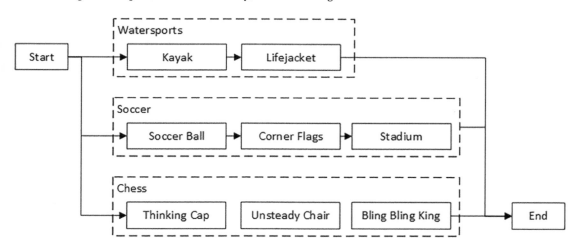

Figure 14-3. *Concurrent function calls*

Go routines make it easy to invoke functions and methods, but the change in Listing 14-7 has introduced a common problem. Compile and execute the project, and you will receive the following results:

```
main function started
Total: $0.00
main function complete
```

You might see slightly different results, which can include one or more category subtotals. But, in most cases, you will see these messages. Before introducing goroutines into the code, the TotalPrice method was invoked like this:

```
...
storeTotal += group.TotalPrice(category)
...
```

This is a synchronous function call. It tells the runtime to execute the statements in the TotalPrice method one by one and assign the result to a variable named storeTotal. Execution won't continue until all the TotalPrice statements have been processed. But Listing 14-7 introduced a goroutine to execute the function, like this:

```
...
go group.TotalPrice(category)
...
```

This statement tells the runtime to execute the statements in the TotalPrice method using a new goroutine. The runtime doesn't wait for the goroutine to execute the method and immediately moves onto the next statement. This is the entire point of goroutines because the TotalPrice method will be invoked asynchronously, meaning that its statements are being evaluated by one goroutine at the same time that the original goroutine is executing the statements in the main function. But, as I explained earlier, the program is terminated when the main goroutine has executed all the statements in the main function.

The result is that the program terminates before the goroutines are created to execute the TotalPrice method complete, which is why there are no subtotals.

I explain how to address this problem as I introduce additional features, but, for the moment, all I need to do is prevent the program from ending long enough for the goroutines to complete, as shown in Listing 14-8.

Listing 14-8. Delaying Program Exit in the main.go File in the concurrency Folder

```
package main

import (
    "fmt"
    "time"
)

func main() {

    fmt.Println("main function started")
    CalcStoreTotal(Products)
    time.Sleep(time.Second * 5)
    fmt.Println("main function complete")
}
```

The time package is part of the standard library and is described in Chapter 19. The time package provides the Sleep function, which pauses the goroutine that executes the statement. The sleep period is specified using a set of numeric constants that represent intervals so that time.Second represents one second and is multiplied by 5 to create a five-second period.

In this case, it will pause the execution of the main goroutine, which will give the goroutines created time to execute the TotalPrice method. When the sleep period has passed, the main goroutine will resume executing statements, reach the end of the function, and cause the program to terminate.

Compile and execute the project, and you will receive the following output:

```
main function started
Watersports product: Kayak
Watersports product: Lifejacket
Watersports subtotal: $328.95
Soccer product: Soccer Ball
Soccer product: Corner Flags
Soccer product: Stadium
Soccer subtotal: $79554.45
Chess product: Thinking Cap
Chess product: Unsteady Chair
Chess product: Bling-Bling King
Chess subtotal: $1291.00
Total: $0.00
main function complete
```

The program no longer exists early, but it is difficult to be sure that the goroutines are working concurrently. This is because the example is so simple that one goroutine can complete in the small amount of time it takes Go to create and start the next one. In Listing 14-9, I have added another pause, which will slow down the execution of the TotalPrice method to help illustrate how the code is executed. (This is something that you should not do in a real project but that is helpful to understand how these features work.)

Listing 14-9. Adding a Sleep Statement in the operations.go File in the concurrency Folder

```go
package main

import (
    "fmt"
    "time"
)

func CalcStoreTotal(data ProductData) {
    var storeTotal float64
    for category, group := range data {
        go group.TotalPrice(category)
    }
    fmt.Println("Total:", ToCurrency(storeTotal))
}

func (group ProductGroup) TotalPrice(category string) (total float64) {
    for _, p := range group {
        fmt.Println(category, "product:", p.Name)
        total += p.Price
        time.Sleep(time.Millisecond * 100)
    }
```

```
    fmt.Println(category, "subtotal:", ToCurrency(total))
    return
}
```

The new statement adds 100 milliseconds to each iteration of the for loop in the TotalPrice method. Compile and execute the code, and you will see output similar to the following:

```
main function started
Total: $0.00
Soccer product: Soccer Ball
Watersports product: Kayak
Chess product: Thinking Cap
Chess product: Unsteady Chair
Watersports product: Lifejacket
Soccer product: Corner Flags
Chess product: Bling-Bling King
Soccer product: Stadium
Watersports subtotal: $328.95
Soccer subtotal: $79554.45
Chess subtotal: $1291.00
main function complete
```

You may see a different ordering of the results, but the key point is that messages for different categories are interleaved, showing that the data is being processed in parallel. (If the change in Listing 14-9 doesn't give you the expected results, then you may have to increase the pause introduced by the time.Sleep function.)

Returning Results from Goroutines

When I created goroutines in Listing 14-7, I changed the way the TotalPrice method was called. Originally, the code looked like this:

```
...
storeTotal += group.TotalPrice(category)
...
```

But when I introduced the Go routine, I changed the statement to this:

```
...
go group.TotalPrice(category)
...
```

I gained asynchronous execution, but I lost the result from the method, which is why the output from Listing 14-9 includes a zero result for the overall total:

```
...
Total: $0.00
...
```

Getting a result from a function that is being executed asynchronously can be complicated because it requires coordination between the goroutine that produces the result and the goroutine that consumes the result.

To address this issue, Go provides *channels*, which are conduits through which data can be sent and received. I am going to introduce a channel into the example in steps, starting in Listing 14-10, which means the example won't compile until the process is complete.

Listing 14-10. Defining a Channel in the operations.go File in the concurrency Folder

```
package main

import (
    "fmt"
    "time"
)

func CalcStoreTotal(data ProductData) {
    var storeTotal float64
    var channel chan float64 = make(chan float64)
    for category, group := range data {
        go group.TotalPrice(category)
    }
    fmt.Println("Total:", ToCurrency(storeTotal))
}

func (group ProductGroup) TotalPrice(category string) (total float64) {
    for _, p := range group {
        fmt.Println(category, "product:", p.Name)
        total += p.Price
        time.Sleep(time.Millisecond * 100)
    }
    fmt.Println(category, "subtotal:", ToCurrency(total))
    return
}
```

Channels are strongly typed, which means that they will carry values of a specified type or interface. The type for a channel is the chan keyword, followed by the type the channel will carry, as shown in Figure 14-4. Channels are created using the built-in make function, specifying the channel type.

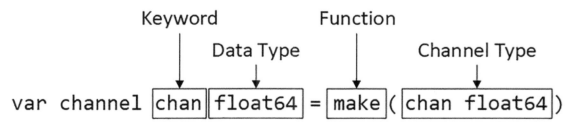

Figure 14-4. *Defining a channel*

I used the full variable declaration syntax in this listing to emphasize the type, which is chan float64, meaning a channel that will carry float64 values.

> ■ **Note** The sync package provides features for managing goroutines that share data, as described in Chapter 30.

Sending a Result Using a Channel

The next step is to update the TotalPrice method so that it sends its result through the channel, as shown in Listing 14-11.

Listing 14-11. Using a Channel to Send a Result in the operations.go File in the concurrency Folder

```
package main

import (
    "fmt"
    "time"
)

func CalcStoreTotal(data ProductData) {
    var storeTotal float64
    var channel chan float64 = make(chan float64)
    for category, group := range data {
        go group.TotalPrice(category)
    }
    fmt.Println("Total:", ToCurrency(storeTotal))
}

func (group ProductGroup) TotalPrice(category string, resultChannel chan float64)  {
    var total float64
    for _, p := range group {
        fmt.Println(category, "product:", p.Name)
        total += p.Price
        time.Sleep(time.Millisecond * 100)
    }
    fmt.Println(category, "subtotal:", ToCurrency(total))
    resultChannel <- total
}
```

The first change is to remove the conventional result and add a chan float64 parameter, whose type matches the channel created in Listing 14-10. I have also defined a variable named total, which was not required previously because the function had a named result.

The other change demonstrates how a result is sent using the channel. The channel is specified, followed by a direction arrow expressed with the < and - characters and then by the value, as shown in Figure 14-5.

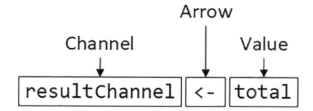

Figure 14-5. *Sending a result*

This statement sends the total value through the resultChannel channel, which makes it available to be received elsewhere in the application. Notice that when a value is sent through a channel, the sender doesn't need to have any insight about how the value will be received and used, just as a regular synchronous function doesn't know how its result will be used.

Receiving a Result Using a Channel

The arrow syntax is used to receive a value from a channel, which will allow the CalcStoreTotal function to receive the data sent by the TotalPrice method, as shown in Listing 14-12.

Listing 14-12. Receiving a Result in the operations.go File in the concurrency Folder

```
package main

import (
    "fmt"
    "time"
)

func CalcStoreTotal(data ProductData) {
    var storeTotal float64
    var channel chan float64 = make(chan float64)
    for category, group := range data {
        go group.TotalPrice(category, channel)
    }
    for i := 0; i < len(data); i++ {
        storeTotal += <- channel
    }
    fmt.Println("Total:", ToCurrency(storeTotal))
}

func (group ProductGroup) TotalPrice(category string, resultChannel chan float64) {
    var total float64
    for _, p := range group {
        fmt.Println(category, "product:", p.Name)
        total += p.Price
        time.Sleep(time.Millisecond * 100)
    }
    fmt.Println(category, "subtotal:", ToCurrency(total))
    resultChannel <- total
}
```

The arrow is placed before the channel to receive a value from it, as shown in Figure 14-6, and the received value can be used as part of any standard Go expression, such as the += operation used in the example.

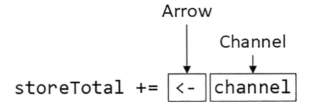

Figure 14-6. Receiving a result

In this example, I know that the number of results that can be received from the channel exactly matches the number of goroutines I created. And, since I created a goroutine for each key in the map, I can use the len function in a for loop to read all the results.

Channels can be safely shared between multiple goroutines, and the effect of the changes made in this section is that the Go routines created to invoke the TotalPrice method all send their results through the channel created by the CalcStoreTotal function, where they are received and processed.

Receiving from a channel is a blocking operation, meaning that execution will not continue until a value has been received, which means I no longer have to prevent the program from terminating, as shown in Listing 14-13.

Listing 14-13. Removing a Sleep Statement in the main.go File in the concurrency Folder

```
package main

import (
    "fmt"
    //"time"
)

func main() {

    fmt.Println("main function started")
    CalcStoreTotal(Products)
    //time.Sleep(time.Second * 5)
    fmt.Println("main function complete")
}
```

The overall effect of these changes is that the program starts and begins executing the statements in the main function. This leads to the CalcStoreTotal function being called, which creates a channel and starts several goroutines. The goroutines execute the statements in the TotalPrice method, which sends its result using the channel.

The main goroutine continues executing the statements in the CalcStoreTotal function, which receives the results through the channel. Those results are used to create an overall total, which is written out. The remaining statements in the main function are executed, and the program terminates.

Compile and execute the project, and you will see the following output:

```
main function started
Watersports product: Kayak
Chess product: Thinking Cap
Soccer product: Soccer Ball
Soccer product: Corner Flags
Watersports product: Lifejacket
Chess product: Unsteady Chair
Chess product: Bling-Bling King
Soccer product: Stadium
Watersports subtotal: $328.95
Chess subtotal: $1291.00
Soccer subtotal: $79554.45
Total: $81174.40
main function complete
```

You may see the messages displayed in a different order, but the key point to note is that the overall total is calculated correctly, like this:

```
...
Total: $81174.40
...
```

The channel is used to coordinate the goroutines, allowing the main goroutine to wait for the individual results produced by the goroutines created in the CalcStoreTotal function. Figure 14-7 shows the relationship between the routines and the channel.

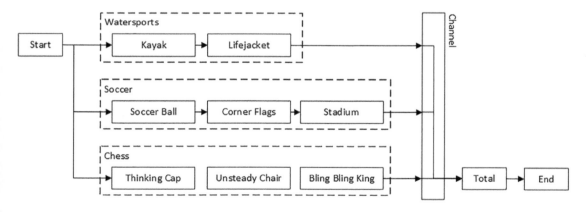

Figure 14-7. *Coordination using a channel*

USING ADAPTERS TO EXECUTE FUNCTIONS ASYNCHRONOUSLY

It isn't always possible to rewrite existing functions or methods to use channels, but it is a simple matter to execute synchronous functions asynchronously in a wrapper, like this:

```
...
calcTax := func(price float64) float64 {
    return price + (price * 0.2)
}
wrapper := func (price float64, c chan float64)  {
    c <- calcTax(price)
}
resultChannel := make(chan float64)
go wrapper(275, resultChannel)
result := <- resultChannel
fmt.Println("Result:", result)
...
```

The wrapper function receives a channel, which it uses to send the value received from executing the calcTax function synchronously. This can be expressed more concisely by defining a function without assigning it to a variable, like this:

```
...
go func (price float64, c chan float64) {
    c <- calcTax(price)
}(275, resultChannel)
...
```

The syntax is a little awkward because the arguments used to invoke the function are expressed immediately following the function definition. But the result is the same, which is that a synchronous function can be executed by a goroutine with the result being sent through a channel.

Working with Channels

The previous section demonstrated the basic use of channels and their use in coordinating goroutines. In the sections that follow I describe different ways of using channels to change how coordination happens, which allows goroutines to be adapted to different situations.

Coordinating Channels

By default, sending and receiving through a channel are blocking operations. This means a goroutine that sends a value will not execute any further statements until another goroutine receives the value from the channel. If a second goroutine sends a value, it will be blocked until the channel is cleared, causing a queue of goroutines waiting for values to be received. This happens in the other direction, too, so that goroutines that receive values will block until another goroutine sends one. Listing 14-14 changes the way that values are sent and received in the example project to highlight this behavior.

Listing 14-14. Sending and Receiving Values in the operations.go File in the concurrency Folder

```
package main

import (
    "fmt"
    "time"
)

func CalcStoreTotal(data ProductData) {
    var storeTotal float64
    var channel chan float64 = make(chan float64)
    for category, group := range data {
        go group.TotalPrice(category, channel)
    }
    time.Sleep(time.Second * 5)
    fmt.Println("-- Starting to receive from channel")
    for i := 0; i < len(data); i++ {
        fmt.Println("-- channel read pending")
        value := <- channel
        fmt.Println("-- channel read complete", value)
        storeTotal += value
        time.Sleep(time.Second)
    }
    fmt.Println("Total:", ToCurrency(storeTotal))
}

func (group ProductGroup) TotalPrice(category string, resultChannel chan float64)  {
    var total float64
    for _, p := range group {
        //fmt.Println(category, "product:", p.Name)
        total += p.Price
        time.Sleep(time.Millisecond * 100)
    }
    fmt.Println(category, "channel sending", ToCurrency(total))
    resultChannel <- total
    fmt.Println(category, "channel send complete")
}
```

The changes introduce a delay after the CalcStoreTotal creates the goroutines and receives the first value from the channel. There is also a delay before and after each value is received.

These delays have the effect of allowing the goroutines to finish their work and send values through the channel before any values are received. Compile and execute the project, and you will see the following output:

```
main function started
Watersports channel sending $328.95
Chess channel sending $1291.00
Soccer channel sending $79554.45
-- Starting to receive from channel
-- channel read pending
Watersports channel send complete
-- channel read complete 328.95
-- channel read pending
-- channel read complete 1291
Chess channel send complete
-- channel read pending
-- channel read complete 79554.45
Soccer channel send complete
Total: $81174.40
main function complete
```

I tend to make sense of concurrent applications by visualizing interactions between people. If Bob has a message for Alice, the default channel behavior requires Alice and Bob to agree on a meeting place, and whoever gets there first will wait for the other to arrive. Bob will only give the message to Alice when they are both present. When Charlie also has a message for Alice, he will form a queue behind Bob. Everyone waits patiently, messages are transferred only when the sender and receiver are both available, and messages are processed sequentially.

You can see this pattern in the output from Listing 14-14. The goroutines are started, process their data, and send their results through the channel:

```
...
Watersports channel sending $328.95
Chess channel sending $1291.00
Soccer channel sending $79554.45
...
```

There is no receiver available and so the goroutines are forced to wait, forming a queue of patient senders until the receiver starts its work. As each value is received, the sending goroutine is unblocked and is able to continue executing the statements in the TotalPrice method.

Using a Buffered Channel

The default channel behavior can lead to bursts of activity as goroutines do their work, followed by a long idle period waiting for messages to be received. This doesn't have an impact on the example application because the goroutines finish once their messages are received, but in a real project goroutines often have repetitive tasks to perform, and waiting for a receiver can cause a performance bottleneck.

An alternative approach is to create a channel with a buffer, which is used to accept values from a sender and store them until a receiver becomes available. This makes sending a message a nonblocking operation, allowing a sender to pass its value to the channel and continue working without having to wait for a receiver. This is similar to Alice having an inbox on her desk. Senders come to Alice's office and put their message into the inbox, leaving it for Alice to read when she is ready. But, if the inbox is full, then they will have to wait until she has processed some of her backlog before sending a new message. Listing 14-15 creates a channel with a buffer.

Listing 14-15. Creating a Buffered Channel in the operations.go File in the concurrency Folder

```
...
func CalcStoreTotal(data ProductData) {
    var storeTotal float64
    var channel chan float64 = make(chan float64, 2)
    for category, group := range data {
        go group.TotalPrice(category, channel)
    }
    time.Sleep(time.Second * 5)
    fmt.Println("-- Starting to receive from channel")
    for i := 0; i < len(data); i++ {
        fmt.Println("-- channel read pending")
        value := <- channel
        fmt.Println("-- channel read complete", value)
        storeTotal += value
        time.Sleep(time.Second)
    }
    fmt.Println("Total:", ToCurrency(storeTotal))
}
...
```

The size of the buffer is specified as an argument to the make function, as illustrated in Figure 14-8.

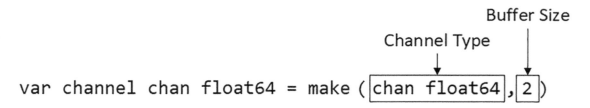

Figure 14-8. A buffered channel

For this example, I have set the size of the buffer to 2, meaning that two senders will be able to send values through the channel without having to wait for them to be received. Any subsequent senders will have to wait until one of the buffered messages is received. You can see this behavior by compiling and executing the project, which produces the following output:

```
main function started
Watersports channel sending $328.95
Watersports channel send complete
Chess channel sending $1291.00
Chess channel send complete
Soccer channel sending $79554.45
-- Starting to receive from channel
-- channel read pending
Soccer channel send complete
-- channel read complete 328.95
-- channel read pending
-- channel read complete 1291
-- channel read pending
-- channel read complete 79554.45
Total: $81174.40
main function complete
```

You can see that the values sent for the Watersports and Chess categories are accepted by the channel, even though there is no receiver ready. The sender for the Soccer channel is made to wait until the time. Sleep call for the receiver expires and values are received from the channel.

In real projects, a larger buffer is used, chosen so that there is sufficient capacity for goroutines to send messages without having to wait. (I usually specify a buffer size of 100, which is generally large enough for most projects but not so large that the amount of memory required is significant.)

Inspecting a Channel Buffer

You can determine the size of a channel's buffer using the built-in cap function and determine how many values are in the buffer using the len function, as shown in Listing 14-16.

Listing 14-16. Inspecting a Channel Buffer in the operations.go File in the concurrency Folder

```
...
func CalcStoreTotal(data ProductData) {
    var storeTotal float64
    var channel chan float64 = make(chan float64, 2)
    for category, group := range data {
        go group.TotalPrice(category, channel)
    }
    time.Sleep(time.Second * 5)

    fmt.Println("-- Starting to receive from channel")
    for i := 0; i < len(data); i++ {
        fmt.Println(len(channel), cap(channel))
        fmt.Println("-- channel read pending",
            len(channel), "items in buffer, size", cap(channel))
        value := <- channel
        fmt.Println("-- channel read complete", value)
        storeTotal += value
        time.Sleep(time.Second)
    }
}
```

```
    fmt.Println("Total:", ToCurrency(storeTotal))
}
...
```

The modified statement uses the len and cap functions to report the number of values in the channel's buffer and the overall size of the buffer. Compile and execute the code, and you will see details of the buffer as values are received:

```
main function started
Watersports channel sending $328.95
Watersports channel send complete
Chess channel sending $1291.00
Chess channel send complete
Soccer channel sending $79554.45
-- Starting to receive from channel
-- channel read pending 2 items in buffer, size 2
Soccer channel send complete
-- channel read complete 328.95
-- channel read pending 2 items in buffer, size 2
-- channel read complete 1291
-- channel read pending 1 items in buffer, size 2
-- channel read complete 79554.45
Total: $81174.40
main function complete
```

Using the len and cap functions can give insight into the channel buffer, but the results should not be used to try to avoid blocking when sending a message. Goroutines are executed in parallel, which means values may be sent to the channel after you check for buffer capacity but before you send a value. See the "Using Select Statements" section for details of how to reliably send and receive without blocking.

Sending and Receiving an Unknown Number of Values

The CalcStoreTotal function uses its knowledge of the data that is being processed to determine how many times it should receive values from the channel. This kind of insight isn't always available, and the number of values that will be sent to a channel is often not known in advance. As a demonstration, add a file named orderdispatch.go to the concurrency folder, with the content shown in Listing 14-17.

Listing 14-17. The Contents of the orderdispatch.go File in the concurrency Folder

```
package main

import (
    "fmt"
    "math/rand"
    "time"
)
```

```
type DispatchNotification struct {
    Customer string
    *Product
    Quantity int
}

var Customers = []string{"Alice", "Bob", "Charlie", "Dora"}

func DispatchOrders(channel chan DispatchNotification) {
    rand.Seed(time.Now().UTC().UnixNano())
    orderCount := rand.Intn(3) + 2
    fmt.Println("Order count:", orderCount)
    for i := 0; i < orderCount; i++ {
        channel <- DispatchNotification{
            Customer: Customers[rand.Intn(len(Customers)-1)],
            Quantity: rand.Intn(10),
            Product:  ProductList[rand.Intn(len(ProductList)-1)],
        }
    }
}
```

The DispatchOrders function creates a random number of DispatchNotification values and sends them through the channel that is received through the channel parameter. I describe the way the math/rand package is used to create random numbers in Chapter 18, but for this chapter, it is enough to know that the details of each dispatch notification are also random so that the customer's name, the product, and the quantity will change, as well as the overall number of values sent through the channel (although at least two will be sent, just so there is some output to see).

There is no way to know in advance how many DispatchNotification values the DispatchOrders function will create, which presents a challenge when writing the code that receives from the channel. Listing 14-18 takes the simplest approach, which is to use a for loop, meaning that the code will keep trying to receive values forever.

Listing 14-18. Receiving Values in a for Loop in the main.go File in the concurrency Folder

```
package main

import (
    "fmt"
    //"time"
)

func main() {

    dispatchChannel := make(chan DispatchNotification, 100)
    go DispatchOrders(dispatchChannel)
    for {
        details := <- dispatchChannel
        fmt.Println("Dispatch to", details.Customer, ":", details.Quantity,
            "x", details.Product.Name)
    }
}
```

The for loop doesn't work because the receiving code will try to get values from the channel after the sender has stopped producing them. The Go runtime will terminate the program if all the goroutines are blocked, which you can see by compiling and executing the project, which will produce the following output:

```
Order count: 4
Dispatch to Charlie : 3 x Lifejacket
Dispatch to Bob : 6 x Soccer Ball
Dispatch to Bob : 7 x Thinking Cap
Dispatch to Charlie : 5 x Stadium
fatal error: all goroutines are asleep - deadlock!
goroutine 1 [chan receive]:
main.main()
        C:/concurrency/main.go:12 +0xa6
exit status 2
```

You will see different output, reflecting the random nature of the DispatchNotification data. What's important is that the goroutine exits after it has sent its values, leaving the main goroutine left bocking as it continues to wait for a value to receive. The Go runtime detects that there are no active goroutines and terminates the application.

Closing a Channel

The solution for this problem is for the sender to indicate when no further values are coming through the channel, which is done by closing the channel, as shown in Listing 14-19.

Listing 14-19. Closing a Channel in the orderdispatch.go File in the concurrency Folder

```
package main

import (
    "fmt"
    "math/rand"
    "time"
)

type DispatchNotification struct {
    Customer string
    *Product
    Quantity int
}

var Customers = []string{"Alice", "Bob", "Charlie", "Dora"}

func DispatchOrders(channel chan DispatchNotification) {
    rand.Seed(time.Now().UTC().UnixNano())
    orderCount := rand.Intn(3) + 2
    fmt.Println("Order count:", orderCount)
    for i := 0; i < orderCount; i++ {
        channel <- DispatchNotification{
```

```
            Customer: Customers[rand.Intn(len(Customers)-1)],
            Quantity: rand.Intn(10),
            Product:  ProductList[rand.Intn(len(ProductList)-1)],
        }
    }
    close(channel)
}
```

The built-in close function accepts a channel as its argument and is used to indicate that there will be no further values sent through the channel. Receivers can check if a channel is closed when requesting a value, as shown in Listing 14-20.

■ **Tip** You need to close channels only when it is helpful to do so to coordinate your goroutines. Go doesn't require channels to be closed to free up resources or perform any kind of housekeeping task.

Listing 14-20. Checking for Closed Channels in the main.go File in the concurrency Folder

```
package main

import (
    "fmt"
    //"time"
)

func main() {

    dispatchChannel := make(chan DispatchNotification, 100)
    go DispatchOrders(dispatchChannel)
    for {
        if details, open := <- dispatchChannel; open {
            fmt.Println("Dispatch to", details.Customer, ":", details.Quantity,
                "x", details.Product.Name)
        } else {
            fmt.Println("Channel has been closed")
            break
        }
    }
}
```

The receive operator can be used to obtain two values. The first value is assigned the value received from the channel, and the second value indicates whether the channel is closed, as illustrated by Figure 14-9.

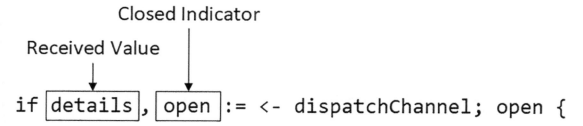

Figure 14-9. Checking for a closed channel

If the channel is open, then the closed indicator will be `false`, and the value received from the channel will be assigned to the other variable. If the channel is closed, the closed indicator will be `true`, and the zero value for the channel type will be assigned to the other variable.

The description is more complex than the code, which is easy to work with because the channel read operation can be used as the initialization statement for an `if` expression, with the closed indicator being used to determine when the channel has been closed. The code in Listing 14-20 defines an `else` clause that is executed when the channel is closed, which prevents further attempts to receive from the channel and allows the program to exit cleanly.

■ **Caution** It is illegal to send values to a channel once it has been closed.

Compile and execute the project, and you will see output similar to the following:

```
Order count: 3
Dispatch to Bob : 2 x Soccer Ball
Dispatch to Alice : 9 x Thinking Cap
Dispatch to Bob : 3 x Soccer Ball
Channel has been closed
```

Enumerating Channel Values

A `for` loop can be used with the `range` keyword to enumerate the values sent through a channel, allowing the values to be received more easily and terminating the loop when the channel is closed, as shown in Listing 14-21.

Listing 14-21. Enumerating Channel Values in the main.go File in the concurrency Folder

```go
package main

import (
    "fmt"
    //"time"
)
```

```
func main() {

    dispatchChannel := make(chan DispatchNotification, 100)

    go DispatchOrders(dispatchChannel)
    for details := range dispatchChannel {
        fmt.Println("Dispatch to", details.Customer, ":", details.Quantity,
            "x", details.Product.Name)
    }
    fmt.Println("Channel has been closed")
}
```

The range expression produces one value per iteration, which is the value received from the channel. The for loop will continue to receive values until the channel is closed. (You can use a for...range loop on a channel that isn't closed, in which case the loop will never exit.) Compile and execute the project, and you will see output similar to the following:

```
Order count: 2
Dispatch to Alice : 9 x Kayak
Dispatch to Charlie : 8 x Corner Flags
Channel has been closed
```

Restricting Channel Direction

By default, channels can be used to send and receive data, but this can be restricted when using channels as arguments, such that only send or receive operations can be performed. I find this feature useful to avoid mistakes where I intended to send a message but performed a receive instead because the syntax for these operations is similar, as shown in Listing 14-22.

Listing 14-22. Mistaking Operations in the orderdispatch.go File in the concurrency Folder

```
package main

import (
    "fmt"
    "math/rand"
    "time"
)

type DispatchNotification struct {
    Customer string
    *Product
    Quantity int
}

var Customers = []string{"Alice", "Bob", "Charlie", "Dora"}
```

```
func DispatchOrders(channel chan DispatchNotification) {
    rand.Seed(time.Now().UTC().UnixNano())
    orderCount := rand.Intn(3) + 2
    fmt.Println("Order count:", orderCount)
    for i := 0; i < orderCount; i++ {
        channel <- DispatchNotification{
            Customer: Customers[rand.Intn(len(Customers)-1)],
            Quantity: rand.Intn(10),
            Product:  ProductList[rand.Intn(len(ProductList)-1)],
        }
        if (i == 1) {
            notification := <- channel
            fmt.Println("Read:", notification.Customer)
        }
    }
    close(channel)
}
```

It is easy to spot this issue in the example code, but I usually make this mistake when an if statement is used to conditionally send additional values through the channel. The result, however, is that the function receives the message it has just sent, removing it from the channel.

Sometimes missing messages will cause the intended receiver's goroutine to block, triggering the deadlock detection described earlier and terminating the program, but often the program will run but produce unexpected results. Compile and execute the code, and you will receive output similar to the following:

```
Order count: 4
Read: Alice
Dispatch to Alice : 4 x Unsteady Chair
Dispatch to Alice : 7 x Unsteady Chair
Dispatch to Bob : 0 x Thinking Cap
Channel has been closed
```

The output reports that four values will be sent through the channel, but only three are received. This problem can be resolved by restricting the direction of the channel, as shown in Listing 14-23.

Listing 14-23. Restricting Channel Direction in the orderdispatch.go File in the concurrency Folder

```
package main

import (
    "fmt"
    "math/rand"
    "time"
)

type DispatchNotification struct {
    Customer string
    *Product
    Quantity int
}
```

```
var Customers = []string{"Alice", "Bob", "Charlie", "Dora"}

func DispatchOrders(channel chan<- DispatchNotification) {
    rand.Seed(time.Now().UTC().UnixNano())
    orderCount := rand.Intn(3) + 2
    fmt.Println("Order count:", orderCount)
    for i := 0; i < orderCount; i++ {
        channel <- DispatchNotification{
            Customer: Customers[rand.Intn(len(Customers))-1)],
            Quantity: rand.Intn(10),
            Product:  ProductList[rand.Intn(len(ProductList))-1)],
        }
        if (i == 1) {
            notification := <- channel
            fmt.Println("Read:", notification.Customer)
        }
    }
    close(channel)
}
```

The direction of the channel is specified alongside the chan keyword, as shown in Figure 14-10.

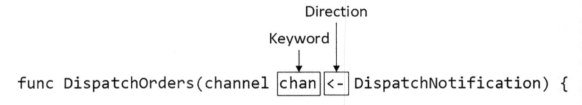

Figure 14-10. *Specifying channel direction*

The location of the arrow specifies the direction of the channel. When the arrow follows the chan keyword, as it does in Listing 14-23, then the channel can be used only to send. The channel can be used to receive only if the arrow precedes the chan keyword (<-chan, for example). Attempting to receive from a send-only (and vice versa) channel is a compile-time error, which you can see if you compile the project:

```
# concurrency
.\orderdispatch.go:29:29: invalid operation: <-channel (receive from send-only type chan<-
DispatchNotification)
```

This makes it easy to see the mistake in the DispatchOrders function, and I can remove the statement that receives from the channel, as shown in Listing 14-24.

Listing 14-24. Correcting a Mistake in the orderdispatch.go File in the concurrency Folder

```
package main

import (
    "fmt"
    "math/rand"
    "time"
)

type DispatchNotification struct {
    Customer string
    *Product
    Quantity int
}

var Customers = []string{"Alice", "Bob", "Charlie", "Dora"}

func DispatchOrders(channel chan<- DispatchNotification) {
    rand.Seed(time.Now().UTC().UnixNano())
    orderCount := rand.Intn(3) + 2
    fmt.Println("Order count:", orderCount)
    for i := 0; i < orderCount; i++ {
        channel <- DispatchNotification{
            Customer: Customers[rand.Intn(len(Customers)-1)],
            Quantity: rand.Intn(10),
            Product:  ProductList[rand.Intn(len(ProductList)-1)],
        }
        // if (i == 1) {
        //     notification := <- channel
        //     fmt.Println("Read:", notification.Customer)
        // }
    }
    close(channel)
}
```

The code will compile without error and produce output similar to that produced by Listing 14-22.

Restricting Channel Argument Direction

The changes in the previous section allow the DispatchOrders function to declare that it needs to only send messages through the channel and not receive them. This is a useful feature, but it doesn't address the situation where you want to provide a unidirectional channel only, rather than allow the function to decide what it receives.

Directional channels are types so that the type of the function parameter in Listing 14-24 is chan<-DispatchNotification, meaning a send-only channel that will carry DispatchNotification values. Go allows bidirectional channels to be assigned to unidirectional channel variables, allowing restrictions to be applied, as shown in Listing 14-25.

Listing 14-25. Creating a Restricted Channel in the main.go File in the concurrency Folder

```go
package main

import (
    "fmt"
    //"time"
)

func receiveDispatches(channel <-chan DispatchNotification) {
    for details := range channel {
        fmt.Println("Dispatch to", details.Customer, ":", details.Quantity,
            "x", details.Product.Name)
    }
    fmt.Println("Channel has been closed")
}

func main() {

    dispatchChannel := make(chan DispatchNotification, 100)

    var sendOnlyChannel chan<- DispatchNotification = dispatchChannel
    var receiveOnlyChannel <-chan DispatchNotification = dispatchChannel

    go DispatchOrders(sendOnlyChannel)
    receiveDispatches(receiveOnlyChannel)
}
```

I use the full variable syntax to define send-only and receive-only channel variables, which are then used as function arguments. This ensures that the recipient of the send-only channel can only send values or close the channel and that the recipient of the receive-only channel can only receive values. These restrictions are applied to the same underlying channel so that the messages sent through sendOnlyChannel will be received through receiveOnlyChannel.

Restrictions on channel direction can also be created through explicit conversion, as shown in Listing 14-26.

Listing 14-26. Using Explicit Conversions for Channels in the main.go File in the concurrency Folder

```go
package main

import (
    "fmt"
    //"time"
)

func receiveDispatches(channel <-chan DispatchNotification) {
    for details := range channel {
        fmt.Println("Dispatch to", details.Customer, ":", details.Quantity,
            "x", details.Product.Name)
    }
    fmt.Println("Channel has been closed")
}
```

```
func main() {
    dispatchChannel := make(chan DispatchNotification, 100)

    // var sendOnlyChannel chan<- DispatchNotification = dispatchChannel
    // var receiveOnlyChannel <-chan DispatchNotification = dispatchChannel

    go DispatchOrders(chan<- DispatchNotification(dispatchChannel))
    receiveDispatches((<-chan DispatchNotification)(dispatchChannel))
}
```

The explicit conversion for the receive-only channel requires parentheses around the channel type to prevent the compiler from interpreting a conversion to the DispatchNotification type. The code in Listings 14-25 and 14-26 produces the same output, which will be similar to the following:

```
Order count: 4
Dispatch to Bob : 0 x Kayak
Dispatch to Alice : 2 x Stadium
Dispatch to Bob : 6 x Stadium
Dispatch to Alice : 3 x Thinking Cap
Channel has been closed
```

Using Select Statements

The select keyword is used to group operations that will send or receive from channels, which allows for complex arrangements of goroutines and channels to be created. There are several uses for select statements, so I will start with the basics and work through the more advanced options. To prepare for the examples in this section, Listing 14-27 increases the number of DispatchNotification values sent by the DispatchOrders function and introduces a delay so they are sent over a longer period.

Listing 14-27. Example Preparation in the orderdispatch.go File in the concurrency Folder

```
package main

import (
    "fmt"
    "math/rand"
    "time"
)

type DispatchNotification struct {
    Customer string
    *Product
    Quantity int
}

var Customers = []string{"Alice", "Bob", "Charlie", "Dora"}
```

```
func DispatchOrders(channel chan<- DispatchNotification) {
    rand.Seed(time.Now().UTC().UnixNano())
    orderCount := rand.Intn(5) + 5
    fmt.Println("Order count:", orderCount)
    for i := 0; i < orderCount; i++ {
        channel <- DispatchNotification{
            Customer: Customers[rand.Intn(len(Customers)-1)],
            Quantity: rand.Intn(10),
            Product:  ProductList[rand.Intn(len(ProductList)-1)],
        }
        // if (i == 1) {
        //     notification := <- channel
        //     fmt.Println("Read:", notification.Customer)
        // }
        time.Sleep(time.Millisecond * 750)
    }
    close(channel)
}
```

Receiving Without Blocking

The simplest use for select statements is to receive from a channel without blocking, ensuring that a goroutine won't have to wait when the channel is empty. Listing 14-28 shows a simple select statement used in this way.

Listing 14-28. Using a select Statement in the main.go File in the concurrency Folder

```
package main

import (
    "fmt"
    "time"
)

// func receiveDispatches(channel <-chan DispatchNotification) {
//     for details := range channel {
//         fmt.Println("Dispatch to", details.Customer, ":", details.Quantity,
//             "x", details.Product.Name)
//     }
//     fmt.Println("Channel has been closed")
// }

func main() {
    dispatchChannel := make(chan DispatchNotification, 100)
    go DispatchOrders(chan<- DispatchNotification(dispatchChannel))
    // receiveDispatches((<-chan DispatchNotification)(dispatchChannel))

    for {
        select {
            case details, ok := <- dispatchChannel:
```

```
                if ok {
                    fmt.Println("Dispatch to", details.Customer, ":",
                        details.Quantity, "x", details.Product.Name)
                } else {
                    fmt.Println("Channel has been closed")
                    goto alldone
                }
            default:
                fmt.Println("-- No message ready to be received")
                time.Sleep(time.Millisecond * 500)
        }
    }
    alldone: fmt.Println("All values received")
}
```

A select statement has a similar structure to a switch statement, except that the case statements are channel operations. When the select statement is executed, each channel operation is evaluated until one that can be performed without blocking is reached. The channel operation is performed, and the statements enclosed in the case statement are executed. If none of the channel operations can be performed, the statements in the default clause are executed. Figure 14-11 illustrates the structure of the select statement.

Figure 14-11. *A select statement*

The select statement evaluates its case statements once, which is why I have also used a for loop in Listing 14-28. The loop continues to execute the select statement, which will receive values from the channel when they become available. If no value is available, then the default clause is executed, which introduces a sleep period.

The case statement channel operation in Listing 14-28 checks to see whether the channel has been closed and, if it has, uses the goto keyword to jump to a labeled statement, which is outside of the for loop.

Compile and execute the project, and you will see output similar to the following, with some differences because the data is generated randomly:

```
-- No message ready to be received
Order count: 5
Dispatch to Bob : 5 x Soccer Ball
-- No message ready to be received
Dispatch to Bob : 0 x Thinking Cap
-- No message ready to be received
Dispatch to Alice : 2 x Corner Flags
-- No message ready to be received
-- No message ready to be received
Dispatch to Bob : 6 x Corner Flags
-- No message ready to be received
Dispatch to Alice : 2 x Corner Flags
-- No message ready to be received
-- No message ready to be received
Channel has been closed
All values received
```

The delays introduced by the time.Sleep method create a small mismatch between the rate at which values are sent through the channel and the rate at which they are received. The result is that the select statement is sometimes executed when the channel is empty. Instead of blocking, which is what would happen with a regular channel operation, the select statement executes the statements in the default clause. Once the channel has been closed, the loop is terminated.

Receiving from Multiple Channels

A select statement can be used to receive without blocking, as the previous example demonstrated, but that feature becomes more useful when there are multiple channels, through which values are sent at different rates. A select statement will allow the receiver to obtain values from whichever channel has them, without blocking on any single channel, as shown in Listing 14-29.

Listing 14-29. Receiving from Multiple Channels in the main.go File in the concurrency Folder

```go
package main

import (
    "fmt"
    "time"
)

func enumerateProducts(channel chan<- *Product) {
    for _, p := range ProductList[:3] {
        channel <- p
        time.Sleep(time.Millisecond * 800)
    }
    close(channel)
}

func main() {
    dispatchChannel := make(chan DispatchNotification, 100)
    go DispatchOrders(chan<- DispatchNotification(dispatchChannel))
```

```
productChannel := make(chan *Product)
go enumerateProducts(productChannel)

openChannels := 2

for  {
    select {
        case details, ok := <- dispatchChannel:
            if ok {
                fmt.Println("Dispatch to", details.Customer, ":",
                    details.Quantity, "x", details.Product.Name)
            } else {
                fmt.Println("Dispatch channel has been closed")
                dispatchChannel = nil
                openChannels--
            }
        case product, ok := <- productChannel:
            if ok {
                fmt.Println("Product:", product.Name)
            } else {
                fmt.Println("Product channel has been closed")
                productChannel = nil
                openChannels--
            }
        default:
            if (openChannels == 0) {
                goto alldone
            }
            fmt.Println("-- No message ready to be received")
            time.Sleep(time.Millisecond * 500)
    }
}
alldone: fmt.Println("All values received")
}
```

In this example, the select statement is used to receive values from two channels, one that carries DispatchNofitication values and one that carries Product values. Each time the select statement is executed, it works its way through the case statements, building up a list of the ones from which a value can be read without blocking. One of the case statements is selected from the list at random and executed. If none of the case statements can be performed, the default clause is executed.

Care must be taken to manage closed channels because they will provide a nil value for every receive operation that occurs after the channel has closed, relying on the closed indicator to show that the channel is closed. Unfortunately, this means that case statements for closed channels will always be chosen by select statements because they are always ready to provide a value without blocking, even though that value isn't useful.

■ **Tip**   If the default clause is omitted, then the select statement will block until one of the channels has a value to be received. This can be useful, but it does not deal with channels that can be closed.

Managing closed channels requires two measures. The first is to prevent the select statement from choosing a channel once it is closed. This can be done by assigning nil to the channel variable, like this:

```
...
dispatchChannel = nil
...
```

A nil channel is never ready and will not be chosen, allowing the select statement to move onto other case statements, whose channels may still be open.

The second measure is to break out of the for loop when all the channels are closed, without which the select statement would endlessly execute the default clause. Listing 14-29 uses an int variable, which is decremented when a channel closes. When the number of open channels reaches zero, a goto statement breaks out of the loop. Compile and execute the project, and you will see output similar to the following, showing how a single receiver gets values from two channels:

```
Order count: 5
Product: Kayak
Dispatch to Alice : 9 x Unsteady Chair
-- No message ready to be received
Dispatch to Bob : 6 x Kayak
-- No message ready to be received
Product: Lifejacket
Dispatch to Charlie : 5 x Thinking Cap
-- No message ready to be received
-- No message ready to be received
Dispatch to Alice : 1 x Stadium
Product: Soccer Ball
-- No message ready to be received
Dispatch to Charlie : 8 x Lifejacket
-- No message ready to be received
Product channel has been closed
-- No message ready to be received
Dispatch channel has been closed
All values received
```

Sending Without Blocking

A select statement can also be used to send to a channel without blocking, as shown in Listing 14-30.

Listing 14-30. Sending Using a select Statement in the main.go File in the concurrency Folder

```
package main

import (
    "fmt"
    "time"
)
```

```
func enumerateProducts(channel chan<- *Product) {
    for _, p := range ProductList {
        select {
            case channel <- p:
                fmt.Println("Sent product:", p.Name)
            default:
                fmt.Println("Discarding product:", p.Name)
                time.Sleep(time.Second)
        }
    }
    close(channel)
}

func main() {
    productChannel := make(chan *Product, 5)
    go enumerateProducts(productChannel)

    time.Sleep(time.Second)

    for p := range productChannel {
        fmt.Println("Received product:", p.Name)
    }
}
```

The channel in Listing 14-30 is created with a small buffer, and values are not received from the channel until after a small delay. This means the enumerateProducts function can send values through the channel without blocking until the buffer is full. The default clause of the select statement discards values that cannot be sent. Compile and execute the code, and you will see output similar to the following:

```
Sent product: Kayak
Sent product: Lifejacket
Sent product: Soccer Ball
Sent product: Corner Flags
Sent product: Stadium
Discarding product: Thinking Cap
Discarding product: Unsteady Chair
Received product: Kayak
Received product: Lifejacket
Received product: Soccer Ball
Received product: Corner Flags
Received product: Stadium
Sent product: Bling-Bling King
Received product: Bling-Bling King
```

The output shows where the select statement determined that the send operation would block and invoked the default clause instead. In Listing 14-30, the case statement contains a statement that writes out a message, but this is not required, and the case statement can specify send operations without additional statements, as shown in Listing 14-31.

Listing 14-31. Omitting Statements in the main.go File in the concurrency Folder

```go
package main

import (
    "fmt"
    "time"
)

func enumerateProducts(channel chan<- *Product) {
    for _, p := range ProductList {
        select {
            case channel <- p:
                //fmt.Println("Sent product:", p.Name)
            default:
                fmt.Println("Discarding product:", p.Name)
                time.Sleep(time.Second)
        }
    }
    close(channel)
}

func main() {
    productChannel := make(chan *Product, 5)
    go enumerateProducts(productChannel)

    time.Sleep(time.Second)

    for p := range productChannel {
        fmt.Println("Received product:", p.Name)
    }
}
```

Sending to Multiple Channels

If there are multiple channels available, a select statement can be used to find a channel for which sending will not block, as shown in Listing 14-32.

■ **Tip** You can combine case statements with send and receive operations in the same select statement. When the select statement is executed, the Go runtime builds a combined list of case statements that can be executed without blocking and picks one at random, which can be either a send or a receive statement.

Listing 14-32. Sending Over Multiple Channels in the main.go File in the concurrency Folder

```
package main

import (
    "fmt"
    "time"
)

func enumerateProducts(channel1, channel2 chan<- *Product) {
    for _, p := range ProductList {
        select {
            case channel1 <- p:
                fmt.Println("Send via channel 1")
            case channel2 <- p:
                fmt.Println("Send via channel 2")
        }
    }
    close(channel1)
    close(channel2)
}

func main() {
    c1 := make(chan *Product, 2)
    c2 := make(chan *Product, 2)
    go enumerateProducts(c1, c2)

    time.Sleep(time.Second)

    for p := range c1 {
        fmt.Println("Channel 1 received product:", p.Name)
    }
    for p := range c2 {
        fmt.Println("Channel 2 received product:", p.Name)
    }
}
```

This example has two channels with small buffers. As with receiving, the select statement builds a list of the channels through which a value can be sent without blocking and then picks one at random from that list. If none of the channels can be used, then the default clause is executed. There is no default clause in this example, which means that the select statement will block until one of the channels can receive a value.

The values from the channel are not received until a second after the goroutine that executes the enumerateProducts function is created, which means that it is only the buffers that determine whether sending to a channel will block. Compile and execute the project, and you will receive the following output:

```
Send via channel 1
Send via channel 1
Send via channel 2
Send via channel 2
Channel 1 received product: Kayak
Channel 1 received product: Lifejacket
Channel 1 received product: Stadium
Send via channel 1
Send via channel 1
Send via channel 1
Send via channel 1
Channel 1 received product: Thinking Cap
Channel 1 received product: Unsteady Chair
Channel 1 received product: Bling-Bling King
Channel 2 received product: Soccer Ball
Channel 2 received product: Corner Flags
```

A common mistake is to assume that a select statement will distribute values evenly across multiple channels. As noted, the select statement selects a case statement that can be used without blocking at random, which means that the distribution of values is unpredictable and can be uneven. You can see this effect by running the example repeatedly, which will show values being sent to channels in a different order.

Summary

In this chapter, I described the use of goroutines, which allow Go functions to be executed concurrently. Goroutines produce results asynchronously using channels, which were also introduced in this chapter. Goroutines and channels make it easy to write concurrent applications without needing to manage individual threads of execution. In the next chapter, I describe the Go support for dealing with errors.

CHAPTER 15

Error Handling

This chapter describes the way that Go deals with errors. I describe the interface that represents errors, show you how to create errors, and explain the different ways they can be handled. I also describe panicking, which is how unrecoverable errors are handled. Table 15-1 puts error handling in context.

Table 15-1. *Putting Error Handling in Context*

Question	Answer
What is it?	Go's error handling allows exceptional conditions and failures to be represented and dealt with.
Why is it useful?	Applications will often encounter unexpected situations, and the error handling features provide a way to respond to those situations when they arise.
How is it used?	The error interface is used to define error conditions, which are typically returned as function results. The panic function is called when an unrecoverable error occurs.
Are there any pitfalls or limitations?	Care must be taken to ensure that errors are communicated to the part of the application that can best decide how serious the situation is.
Are there any alternatives?	You don't have to use the error interface in your code, but it is employed throughout the Go standard library and is difficult to avoid.

Table 15-2 summarizes the chapter.

Table 15-2. *Chapter Summary*

Problem	Solution	Listing
Indicate that an error has occurred	Create a struct that implements the error interface and return it as a function result	7–8, 11, 12
Report an error over a channel	Add an error field to the struct type used for channel messages	9–10
Indicate that an unrecoverable error has occurred	Call the panic function	13, 16
Recover from a panic	Use the defer keyword to register a function that calls the recover function	14, 15, 17–19

© Adam Freeman 2022
A. Freeman, *Pro Go*, https://doi.org/10.1007/978-1-4842-7355-5_15

Preparing for This Chapter

To prepare for this chapter, open a new command prompt, navigate to a convenient location, and create a directory named errorHandling. Run the command shown in Listing 15-1 in the errorHandling folder to create a module file.

■ **Tip** You can download the example project for this chapter—and for all the other chapters in this book—from https://github.com/apress/pro-go. See Chapter 2 for how to get help if you have problems running the examples.

Listing 15-1. Initializing the Module

```
go mod init errorHandling
```

Add a file named product.go to the errorHandling folder with the contents shown in Listing 15-2.

Listing 15-2. The Contents of the product.go File in the errorHandling Folder

```
package main

import "strconv"

type Product struct {
    Name, Category string
    Price float64
}

type ProductSlice []*Product

var Products = ProductSlice {
    { "Kayak", "Watersports", 279 },
    { "Lifejacket", "Watersports", 49.95 },
    { "Soccer Ball", "Soccer", 19.50 },
    { "Corner Flags", "Soccer", 34.95 },
    { "Stadium", "Soccer", 79500 },
    { "Thinking Cap", "Chess", 16 },
    { "Unsteady Chair", "Chess", 75 },
    { "Bling-Bling King", "Chess", 1200 },
}

func ToCurrency(val float64) string {
    return "$" + strconv.FormatFloat(val, 'f', 2, 64)
}
```

This file defines a custom type named Product, an alias for a slice of *Product values, and a slice populated using the literal syntax. I have also defined a function to format float64 values into dollar currency amounts.

Add a file named operations.go to the errorHandling folder with the content shown in Listing 15-3.

Listing 15-3. The Contents of the operations.go File in the errorHandling Folder

```
package main

func (slice ProductSlice) TotalPrice(category string) (total float64) {
    for _, p := range slice {
        if (p.Category == category) {
            total += p.Price
        }
    }
    return
}
```

This file defines a method that receives a ProductSlice and totals the Price field for those Product values with a specified Category value.

Add a file named main.go to the errorHandling folder, with the contents shown in Listing 15-4.

Listing 15-4. The Contents of the main.go File in the errorHandling Folder

```
package main

import "fmt"

func main() {

    categories := []string { "Watersports", "Chess" }

    for _, cat := range categories {
        total := Products.TotalPrice(cat)
        fmt.Println(cat, "Total:", ToCurrency(total))
    }
}
```

Use the command prompt to run the command shown in Listing 15-5 in the errorHandling folder.

Listing 15-5. Running the Example Project

```
go run .
```

The code will be compiled and executed, producing the following output:

```
Watersports Total: $328.95
Chess Total: $1291.00
```

Dealing with Recoverable Errors

Go makes it easy to express exceptional conditions, which allows a function or method to indicate to the calling code that something has gone wrong. As an example, Listing 15-6 adds statements that produce a problematic response from the `TotalPrice` method.

Listing 15-6. Calling a Method in the main.go File in the errorHandling Folder

```
package main

import "fmt"

func main() {

    categories := []string { "Watersports", "Chess", "Running" }

    for _, cat := range categories {
        total := Products.TotalPrice(cat)
        fmt.Println(cat, "Total:", ToCurrency(total))
    }
}
```

Compile and execute the project, and you will receive the following output:

```
Watersports Total: $328.95
Chess Total: $1291.00
Running Total: $0.00
```

The response from the `TotalPrice` method for the `Running` category is ambiguous. A zero result could mean that there are no products in the specified category, or it could mean that there are products but they have a sum value of zero. The code that calls the `TotalPrice` method has no way of knowing what the zero value represents.

In a simple example, it is easy to understand the result from its context: there are no products in the `Running` category. In real projects, this sort of result can be more difficult to understand and respond to.

Go provides a predefined interface named `error` that provides one way to resolve this issue. Here is the definition of the interface:

```
type error interface {
    Error() string
}
```

The interface requires errors to define a method named `Error`, which returns a string.

Generating Errors

Functions and methods can express exceptional or unexpected outcomes by producing `error` responses, as shown in Listing 15-7.

Listing 15-7. Defining an Error in the operations.go File in the errorHandling Folder

```
package main

type CategoryError struct {
    requestedCategory string
}

func (e *CategoryError) Error() string {
    return "Category " + e.requestedCategory + " does not exist"
}

func (slice ProductSlice) TotalPrice(category string) (total float64,
        err *CategoryError) {
    productCount := 0
    for _, p := range slice {
        if (p.Category == category) {
            total += p.Price
            productCount++
        }
    }
    if (productCount == 0) {
        err = &CategoryError{ requestedCategory: category}
    }
    return
}
```

The CategoryError type defines an unexported requestedCategory field, and there is a method that conforms to the error interface. The signature of the TotalPrice method has been updated so that it returns two results: the original float64 value and an error. If the for loop doesn't find any products with the specified category, the err result is assigned a CategoryError value, which indicates that a nonexistent category has been requested. Listing 15-8 updates the calling code to use the error result.

Listing 15-8. Handling an Error in the main.go File in the errorHandling Folder

```
package main

import "fmt"

func main() {

    categories := []string { "Watersports", "Chess", "Running" }

    for _, cat := range categories {
        total, err := Products.TotalPrice(cat)
        if (err == nil) {
            fmt.Println(cat, "Total:", ToCurrency(total))
        } else {
            fmt.Println(cat, "(no such category)")
        }
    }
}
```

The outcome from invoking the TotalPrice method is determined by examining the combination of the two results.

If the error result is nil, then the requested category exists, and the float64 result represents the total of their prices, even if that total is zero. If the error result is not nil, then the requested category does not exist, and the float64 value should be disregarded. Compile and execute the project, and you will see that the error allows the code in Listing 15-8 to identify the nonexistent product category:

```
Watersports Total: $328.95
Chess Total: $1291.00
Running (no such category)
```

IGNORING ERROR RESULTS

I don't recommend ignoring error results because it means you will lose important information—but if you don't need to know when something goes wrong, then you can use the blank identifier instead of a name for the error result, like this:

```
package main

import "fmt"

func main() {
    categories := []string { "Watersports", "Chess", "Running" }
    for _, cat := range categories {
        total, _ := Products.TotalPrice(cat)
        fmt.Println(cat, "Total:", ToCurrency(total))
    }
}
```

This technique prevents the calling code from understanding the complete response from the TotalPrice method and should be used with caution.

Reporting Errors via Channels

If a function is being executed using a goroutine, then the only communication is through the channel, which means that details of any problems must be communicated alongside successful operations. It is important to keep the error handling as simple as possible, and I recommend avoiding trying to use additional channels or creating complex mechanisms for trying to signal error conditions outside of the channel. My preferred approach is to create a custom type that consolidates both outcomes, as shown in Listing 15-9.

Listing 15-9. Defining Types and Functions in the operations.go File in the errorHandling Folder

```go
package main

type CategoryError struct {
    requestedCategory string
}

func (e *CategoryError) Error() string {
    return "Category " + e.requestedCategory + " does not exist"
}

type ChannelMessage struct {
    Category string
    Total float64
    *CategoryError
}

func (slice ProductSlice) TotalPrice(category string) (total float64,
        err *CategoryError) {
    productCount := 0
    for _, p := range slice {
        if (p.Category == category) {
            total += p.Price
            productCount++
        }
    }
    if (productCount == 0) {
        err = &CategoryError{ requestedCategory: category}
    }
    return
}

func (slice ProductSlice) TotalPriceAsync (categories []string,
        channel chan<- ChannelMessage) {
    for _, c := range categories {
        total, err := slice.TotalPrice(c)
        channel <- ChannelMessage{
            Category: c,
            Total: total,
            CategoryError: err,
        }
    }
    close(channel)
}
```

The ChannelMessage type allows me to communicate the pair of results required to accurately reflect the outcome from the TotalPrice method, which is executed asynchronously by the new TotalPriceAsync method. The result is similar to the way that synchronous method results can express errors.

If there is only one sender for a channel, you can close the channel after an error has occurred. But care must be taken to avoid closing the channel if there are multiple senders because they may still be able to generate valid results and will attempt to send them on a closed channel, which will terminate the program with a panic.

Listing 15-10 updates the main function to use the new asynchronous version of the TotalPrice method.

Listing 15-10. Using a New Method in the main.go File in the errorHandling Folder

```
package main

import "fmt"

func main() {

    categories := []string { "Watersports", "Chess", "Running" }

    channel := make(chan ChannelMessage, 10)

    go Products.TotalPriceAsync(categories, channel)
    for message := range channel {
        if message.CategoryError == nil {
            fmt.Println(message.Category, "Total:", ToCurrency(message.Total))
        } else {
            fmt.Println(message.Category, "(no such category)")
        }
    }
}
```

Compile and execute the project, and you will receive output similar to the following:

```
Watersports Total: $328.95
Chess Total: $1291.00
Running (no such category)
```

Using the Error Convenience Functions

It can be awkward to have to define data types for every type of error that an application can encounter. The errors package, which is part of the standard library, provides a New function that returns an error whose content is a string. The drawback of this approach is that it creates simple errors, but it has the advantage of simplicity, as shown in Listing 15-11.

Listing 15-11. Using the Errors Convenience Function in the operations.go File in the errorHandling Folder

```
package main

import "errors"

// type CategoryError struct {
//     requestedCategory string
// }
```

```
// func (e *CategoryError) Error() string {
//     return "Category " + e.requestedCategory + " does not exist"
//}

type ChannelMessage struct {
    Category string
    Total float64
    CategoryError error
}

func (slice ProductSlice) TotalPrice(category string) (total float64,
        err error) {
    productCount := 0
    for _, p := range slice {
        if (p.Category == category) {
            total += p.Price
            productCount++
        }
    }
    if (productCount == 0) {
        err = errors.New("Cannot find category")
    }
    return
}

func (slice ProductSlice) TotalPriceAsync (categories []string,
        channel chan<- ChannelMessage) {
    for _, c := range categories {
        total, err := slice.TotalPrice(c)
        channel <- ChannelMessage{
            Category: c,
            Total: total,
            CategoryError: err,
        }
    }
    close(channel)
}
```

Although I have been able to remove the custom error type in this example, the error that is produced no longer contains details of the category that was requested. This is not a huge issue, since the calling code can reasonably be expected to have this information, but for situations where this is not acceptable, the fmt package can be used to easily create errors with more complex string content.

The fmt package is responsible for formatting strings, which it does with formatting verbs. These verbs are described in detail in Chapter 17, and one of the functions provided by the fmt package is Errorf, which creates error values using a formatted string, as shown in Listing 15-12.

Listing 15-12. Using the Error Formatting Function in the operations.go File in the errorHandling Folder

```go
package main

import "fmt"

type ChannelMessage struct {
    Category string
    Total float64
    CategoryError error
}

func (slice ProductSlice) TotalPrice(category string) (total float64,
        err error) {
    productCount := 0
    for _, p := range slice {
        if (p.Category == category) {
            total += p.Price
            productCount++
        }
    }
    if (productCount == 0) {
        err = fmt.Errorf("Cannot find category: %v", category)
    }
    return
}

func (slice ProductSlice) TotalPriceAsync (categories []string,
        channel chan<- ChannelMessage) {
    for _, c := range categories {
        total, err := slice.TotalPrice(c)
        channel <- ChannelMessage{
            Category: c,
            Total: total,
            CategoryError: err,
        }
    }
    close(channel)
}
```

The %v in the first argument to the Errorf function is an example of a formatting verb, and it is replaced with the next argument, as described in Chapter 17. Listing 15-11 and Listing 15-12 both produce the following output, which is produced independently of the message in the error response:

```
Watersports Total: $328.95
Chess Total: $1291.00
Running (no such category)
```

Dealing with Unrecoverable Errors

Some errors are so serious they should lead to the immediate termination of the application, a process known as *panicking*, as shown in Listing 15-13.

Listing 15-13. Triggering a Panic in the main.go File in the errorHandling Folder

```
package main

import "fmt"

func main() {

    categories := []string { "Watersports", "Chess", "Running" }

    channel := make(chan ChannelMessage, 10)

    go Products.TotalPriceAsync(categories, channel)
    for message := range channel {
        if message.CategoryError == nil {
            fmt.Println(message.Category, "Total:", ToCurrency(message.Total))
        } else {
            panic(message.CategoryError)
            //fmt.Println(message.Category, "(no such category)")
        }
    }
}
```

Instead of printing out a message when a category cannot be found, the main function panics, which is done using the built-in panic function, as shown in Figure 15-1.

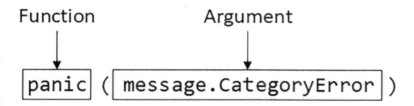

Figure 15-1. *The panic function*

The panic function is invoked with an argument, which can be any value that will help explain the panic. In Listing 15-13, the panic function is invoked with an error, which is a useful way of combining the Go error handling features.

When the panic function is called, the execution of the enclosing function is halted, and any defer functions are performed. (The defer feature is described in Chapter 8.) The panic bubbles up through the call stack, terminating execution of the calling functions and invoking their defer functions. In the example,

401

it is the GetProducts function that panics, which leads to the termination of the CountProducts function and, finally, the main function, at which point the application is terminated. Compile and execute the code, and you will see the following output, which shows the stack trace for the panic:

```
Watersports Total: $328.95
Chess Total: $1291.00
panic: Cannot find category: Running

goroutine 1 [running]:
main.main()
        C:/errorHandling/main.go:16 +0x309
exit status 2
```

The output shows that a panic occurred and that it happened within the main function in the main package, caused by the statement on line 13 of the main.go file. In more complex applications, the stack trace displayed by a panic can help figure out why the panic occurred.

DEFINING PANICKING AND NON-PANICKING FUNCTIONS

There are no definitive rules that dictate when an error is appropriate and when panicking would be more useful. The problem is that the severity of the problem is often best determined by the calling function, which is not where the decision to panic usually occurs. As I explained earlier, using a nonexistent product category could be a serious and nonrecoverable issue in some situations and an expected outcome in others, and these two conditions may well exist in the same project.

A common convention is to offer two versions of the function, one of which returns an error and one of which panics. You can see an example of this arrangement in Chapter 16, where the regexp package defines a Compile function that returns an error and a MustCompile function that panics.

Recovering from Panics

Go provides the built-in function recover, which can be called to stop a panic from working its way up the call stack and terminating the program. The recover function must be called in code that is executed using the defer keyword, as shown in Listing 15-14.

Listing 15-14. Recovering from a Panic in the main.go File in the errorHandling Folder

```
package main

import "fmt"

func main() {

    recoveryFunc := func() {
        if arg := recover(); arg != nil {
            if err, ok := arg.(error); ok {
                fmt.Println("Error:", err.Error())
            } else if str, ok := arg.(string); ok {
```

```
            fmt.Println("Message:", str)
        } else {
            fmt.Println("Panic recovered")
        }
    }
}
defer recoveryFunc()

categories := []string { "Watersports", "Chess", "Running" }

channel := make(chan ChannelMessage, 10)

go Products.TotalPriceAsync(categories, channel)
for message := range channel {
    if message.CategoryError == nil {
        fmt.Println(message.Category, "Total:", ToCurrency(message.Total))
    } else {
        panic(message.CategoryError)
        //fmt.Println(message.Category, "(no such category)")
    }
}
}
```

This example uses the defer keyword to register a function, which will be executed when the main function has completed, even if there has been no panic. Calling the recover function returns a value if there has been a panic, halting the progression of the panic and providing access to the argument used to invoke the panic function, as shown in Figure 15-2.

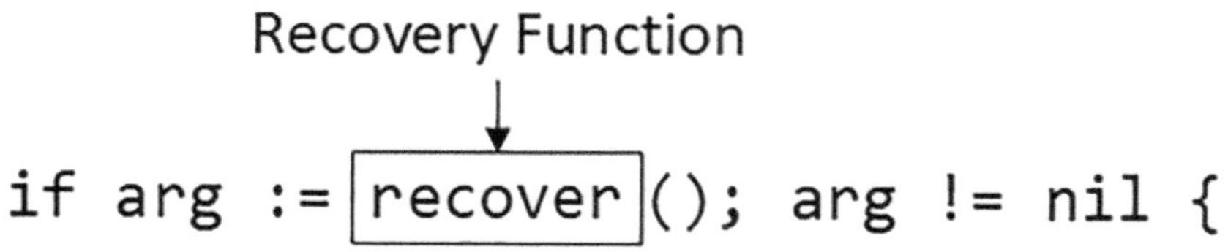

Recovery Function

```
if arg := recover(); arg != nil {
```

Figure 15-2. *Recovering from a panic*

Since any value can be passed to the panic function, the type of the value returned by the recover function is the empty interface (interface{}), which requires a type assertion before it can be used. The recovery function in Listing 15-14 deals with error and string types, which are the two most common types of panic argument.

It can be awkward to define a function and immediately use it with the defer keyword, so panic recovery is usually done using an anonymous function, as shown in Listing 15-15.

Listing 15-15. Using an Anonymous Function in the main.go File in the errorHandling Folder

```go
package main

import "fmt"

func main() {

    defer func() {
        if arg := recover(); arg != nil {
            if err, ok := arg.(error); ok {
                fmt.Println("Error:", err.Error())
            } else if str, ok := arg.(string); ok {
                fmt.Println("Message:", str)
            } else {
                fmt.Println("Panic recovered")
            }
        }
    }()

    categories := []string { "Watersports", "Chess", "Running" }

    channel := make(chan ChannelMessage, 10)

    go Products.TotalPriceAsync(categories, channel)
    for message := range channel {
        if message.CategoryError == nil {
            fmt.Println(message.Category, "Total:", ToCurrency(message.Total))
        } else {
            panic(message.CategoryError)
            //fmt.Println(message.Category, "(no such category)")
        }
    }
}
```

Notice the use of the parentheses following the closing brace anonymous function, which are required to invoke—rather than just define—the anonymous function. Listings 15-14 and 15-15 both produce the same output when compiled and executed:

```
Watersports Total: $328.95
Chess Total: $1291.00
Error: Cannot find category: Running
```

Panicking After a Recovery

You may recover from a panic only to realize that the situation is not recoverable after all. When this happens, you can start a new panic, either providing a new argument or reusing the value received when the recover function was called, as shown in Listing 15-16.

Listing 15-16. Selectively Panicking After a Recovery in the main.go File in the errorHandling Folder

```go
package main

import "fmt"

func main() {

    defer func() {
        if arg := recover(); arg != nil {
            if err, ok := arg.(error); ok {
                fmt.Println("Error:", err.Error())
                panic(err)
            } else if str, ok := arg.(string); ok {
                fmt.Println("Message:", str)
            } else {
                fmt.Println("Panic recovered")
            }
        }
    }()

    categories := []string { "Watersports", "Chess", "Running" }

    channel := make(chan ChannelMessage, 10)

    go Products.TotalPriceAsync(categories, channel)
    for message := range channel {
        if message.CategoryError == nil {
            fmt.Println(message.Category, "Total:", ToCurrency(message.Total))
        } else {
            panic(message.CategoryError)
            //fmt.Println(message.Category, "(no such category)")
        }
    }
}
```

The deferred function recovers the panic, inspects the details of the error, and then panics again. Compile and execute the project, and you will see the effect of the change:

```
Watersports Total: $328.95
Chess Total: $1291.00
Error: Cannot find category: Running
panic: Cannot find category: Running [recovered]
        panic: Cannot find category: Running
goroutine 1 [running]:
main.main.func1()
        C:/errorHandling/main.go:11 +0x1c8
panic({0xad91a0, 0xc000088230})
        C:/Program Files/Go/src/runtime/panic.go:1038 +0x215
main.main()
        C:/errorHandling/main.go:29 +0x333
exit status 2
```

Recovering from Panics in Go Routines

A panic works its way up the stack only to the top of the current goroutine, at which point it causes termination of the application. This restriction means that panics must be recovered within the code that a goroutine executes, as shown in Listing 15-17.

Listing 15-17. Recovering from a Panic in the main.go File in the errorHandling Folder

```
package main

import "fmt"

type CategoryCountMessage struct {
    Category string
    Count int
}

func processCategories(categories [] string, outChan chan <- CategoryCountMessage) {
    defer func() {
        if arg := recover(); arg != nil {
            fmt.Println(arg)
        }
    }()
    channel := make(chan ChannelMessage, 10)
    go Products.TotalPriceAsync(categories, channel)
    for message := range channel {
        if message.CategoryError == nil {
            outChan <- CategoryCountMessage {
                Category: message.Category,
                Count: int(message.Total),
            }
        } else {
            panic(message.CategoryError)
        }
    }
    close(outChan)
}

func main() {

    categories := []string { "Watersports", "Chess", "Running" }

    channel := make(chan CategoryCountMessage)
    go processCategories(categories, channel)

    for message := range channel {
        fmt.Println(message.Category, "Total:", message.Count)
    }
}
```

The `main` function uses a goroutine to invoke the `processCategories` function, which panics if the `TotalPriceAsync` function sends an `error`. The `processCategories` recovers from the panic, but this has an unexpected consequence, which you can see in the output produced by compiling and executing the project:

```
Watersports Total: 328
Chess Total: 1291
Cannot find category: Running
fatal error: all goroutines are asleep - deadlock!
goroutine 1 [chan receive]:
main.main()
        C:/errorHandling/main.go:39 +0x1c5
exit status 2
```

The problem is that recovering from a panic doesn't resume execution of the `processCategories` function, which means that the `close` function is never called on the channel from which the `main` function is receiving messages. The `main` function tries to receive a message that will never be sent and blocks on the channel, triggering the Go runtime's deadlock detection.

The simplest approach is to call the `close` function on the channel during recovery, as shown in Listing 15-18.

Listing 15-18. Ensuring a Channel Is Closed in the main.go File in the errorHandling Folder

```
...
defer func() {
    if arg := recover(); arg != nil {
        fmt.Println(arg)
        close(outChan)
    }
}()
...
```

This prevents deadlock, but it does so without indicating to the `main` function that the `processCategories` function was unable to complete its work, which may have consequences. A better approach is to indicate this outcome through the channel before closing it, as shown in Listing 15-19.

Listing 15-19. Indicating Failure in the main.go File in the errorHandling Folder

```
package main

import "fmt"

type CategoryCountMessage struct {
    Category string
    Count int
    TerminalError interface{}
}
```

```go
func processCategories(categories [] string, outChan chan <- CategoryCountMessage) {
    defer func() {
        if arg := recover(); arg != nil {
            fmt.Println(arg)
            outChan <- CategoryCountMessage{
                TerminalError: arg,
            }
            close(outChan)
        }
    }()
    channel := make(chan ChannelMessage, 10)
    go Products.TotalPriceAsync(categories, channel)
    for message := range channel {
        if message.CategoryError == nil {
            outChan <- CategoryCountMessage {
                Category: message.Category,
                Count: int(message.Total),
            }
        } else {
            panic(message.CategoryError)
        }
    }
    close(outChan)
}

func main() {

    categories := []string { "Watersports", "Chess", "Running" }

    channel := make(chan CategoryCountMessage)
    go processCategories(categories, channel)

    for message := range channel {
        if (message.TerminalError == nil) {
            fmt.Println(message.Category, "Total:", message.Count)
        } else {
            fmt.Println("A terminal error occured")
        }
    }
}
```

The result is that the decision about how to handle the panic is passed from the goroutine to the calling code, which can elect to continue execution or trigger a new panic depending on the problem. Compile and execute the project, and you will receive the following output:

```
Watersports Total: 328
Chess Total: 1291
Cannot find category: Running
A terminal error occured
```

Summary

In this chapter, I described the Go features for handling error conditions. I described the error type and showed you how to create custom errors and how to use the convenience functions to create errors with simple messages. I also explained panics, which is how unrecoverable errors are dealt with. I explained that the decision about whether an error is unrecoverable can be subjective, which is why Go allows panics to be recovered. I explained the recovery process and demonstrated how it can be adapted to work effectively in goroutines. In the next chapter, I begin the process of describing the Go standard library.

## PART II

Using the Go Standard Library

CHAPTER 16

■ ■ ■

String Processing and Regular Expressions

In this chapter, I describe the standard library features for processing string values, which are needed by almost every project and which many languages provide as methods defined on the built-in types. But even though Go defines these features in the standard library, a complete set of functions is available, along with good support for working with regular expressions. Table 16-1 puts these features in context.

Table 16-1. *Putting String Processing and Regular Expressions in Context*

Question	Answer
What are they?	String processing includes a wide range of operations, from trimming whitespace to splitting a string into components. Regular expressions are patterns that allow string matching rules to be concisely defined.
Why are they useful?	These operations are useful when an application needs to process string values. A common example is processing HTTP requests.
How are they used?	These features are contained in the strings and regexp packages, which are part of the standard library.
Are there any pitfalls or limitations?	There are some quirks in the way that some of these operations are performed, but they mostly behave as you would expect.
Are there any alternatives?	The use of these packages is optional, and they do not have to be used. That said, there is little point in creating your own implementations of these features since the standard library is well-written and thoroughly tested.

© Adam Freeman 2022
A. Freeman, *Pro Go*, https://doi.org/10.1007/978-1-4842-7355-5_16

Table 16-2 summarizes the chapter.

Table 16-2. *Chapter Summary*

Problem	Solution	Listing
Compare strings	Use the Contains, EqualFold, or Has* function in the strings package	4
Convert string case	Use the ToLower, ToUpper, Title, or ToTitle function in the strings package	5, 6
Check or change character case	Use the functions provided by the unicode package	7
Find content in strings	Use the functions provided by the strings or regexp package	8, 9, 24–27, 29–32
Split a string	Use the Fields or Split* function in the strings and regexp packages	10–14, 28
Join strings	Use the Join or Repeat function in the strings package	22
Trim characters from a string	Use the Trim* functions in the strings package	15–18
Perform a substitution	Use the Replace* or Map function in the strings package, use a Replacer, or use the Replace* functions in the regexp package	19–21, 33
Efficiently build a string	Use the Builder type in the strings package	23

Preparing for This Chapter

To prepare for this chapter, open a new command prompt, navigate to a convenient location, and create a directory named stringsandregexp. Run the command shown in Listing 16-1 to create a module file.

■ **Tip** You can download the example project for this chapter—and for all the other chapters in this book—from https://github.com/apress/pro-go. See Chapter 2 for how to get help if you have problems running the examples.

Listing 16-1. Initializing the Module

```
go mod init stringsandregexp
```

Add a file named main.go to the stringsandregexp folder, with the contents shown in Listing 16-2.

Listing 16-2. The Contents of the main.go File in the stringsandregexp Folder

```
package main

import (
    "fmt"
)

func main() {

    product := "Kayak"

    fmt.Println("Product:", product)
}
```

Use the command prompt to run the command shown in Listing 16-3 in the stringsandregexp folder.

Listing 16-3. Running the Example Project

```
go run .
```

The code will be compiled and executed, producing the following output:

```
Product: Kayak
```

Processing Strings

The strings package provides a set of functions for processing strings. In the sections that follow, I describe the most useful features of the strings package and demonstrate their use.

Comparing Strings

The strings package provides comparison functions, as described in Table 16-3. These can be used in addition to the equality operators (== and !=).

Table 16-3. The strings Functions for Comparing Strings

Function	Description
Contains(s, substr)	This function returns true if the string s contains substr and false if it does not.
ContainsAny(s, substr)	This function returns true if the string s contains any of the characters contained in the string substr.
ContainsRune(s, rune)	This function returns true if the string s contains a specific rune.
EqualFold(s1, s2)	This function performs a case-insensitive comparison and returns true of strings s1 and s2 are the same.
HasPrefix(s, prefix)	This function returns true if the string s begins with the string prefix.
HasSuffix(s, suffix)	This function returns true if the string ends with the string suffix.

Listing 16-4 demonstrates the use of the functions described in Table 16-3.

Listing 16-4. Comparing Strings in the main.go File in the stringsandregexp Folder

```
package main

import (
    "fmt"
    "strings"
)

func main() {

    product := "Kayak"

    fmt.Println("Contains:", strings.Contains(product, "yak"))
    fmt.Println("ContainsAny:", strings.ContainsAny(product, "abc"))
    fmt.Println("ContainsRune:", strings.ContainsRune(product, 'K'))
    fmt.Println("EqualFold:", strings.EqualFold(product, "KAYAK"))
    fmt.Println("HasPrefix:", strings.HasPrefix(product, "Ka"))
    fmt.Println("HasSuffix:", strings.HasSuffix(product, "yak"))
}
```

The functions in Table 16-3 perform case-sensitive comparisons, with the exception of the EqualFold function. (Folding is the way that Unicode deals with character case, where characters can have different representations for lowercase, uppercase, and title case.) The code in Listing 16-4 produces the following output when executed:

```
Contains: true
ContainsAny: true
ContainsRune: true
HasPrefix: true
HasSuffix: true
EqualFold: true
```

USING THE BYTE-ORIENTED FUNCTIONS

For all the functions in the strings package, which operate on characters, there is a corresponding function in the bytes package that operates on a byte slice, like this:

```
package main

import (
    "fmt"
    "strings"
    "bytes"
)
```

```go
func main() {

    price := "€100"

    fmt.Println("Strings Prefix:", strings.HasPrefix(price, "€"))
    fmt.Println("Bytes Prefix:", bytes.HasPrefix([]byte(price),
        []byte { 226, 130 }))
}
```

This example shows the use of the HasPrefix function provided by both packages. The strings version of the package operates on characters and checks the prefix regardless of how many bytes are used by the characters. This allows me to determine if the price string begins with the euro currency symbol. The bytes version of the function allows me to determine if the price variable begins with a specific sequence of bytes, regardless of how those bytes relate to a character. I use the functions in the strings package throughout this chapter because they are the most widely used. In Chapter 25, I use the bytes.Buffer struct, which is a useful way to store binary data in memory.

Converting String Case

The strings package provides the functions described in Table 16-4 for changing the case of strings.

Table 16-4. *The Case Functions in the strings Package*

Function	Description
ToLower(str)	This function returns a new string containing the characters in the specified string mapped to lowercase.
ToUpper(str)	This function returns a new string containing the characters in the specified string mapped to lowercase.
Title(str)	This function converts the specific string so that the first character of each word is uppercase and the remaining characters are lowercase.
ToTitle(str)	This function returns a new string containing the characters in the specified string mapped to title case.

Care must be taken with the Title and ToTitle functions, which don't work the way you might expect. The Title function returns a string that is suitable for use as a title, but it treats all words the same, as shown in Listing 16-5.

Listing 16-5. Creating a Title in the main.go File in the stringsandregexp Folder

```go
package main

import (
    "fmt"
    "strings"
)
```

```
func main() {

    description := "A boat for sailing"

    fmt.Println("Original:", description)
    fmt.Println("Title:", strings.Title(description))
}
```

Conventionally, title case doesn't capitalize articles, short prepositions, and conjunctions, which means that converting this string:

```
A boat for sailing
```

would conventionally be converted like this:

```
A Boat for Sailing
```

The word *for* is not capitalized, but the other words are. But these rules are complex, open to interpretation, and language-specific, so Go takes a simpler approach, which is to capitalize all words. You can see the effect by compiling and running the code in Listing 16-5, which produces the following output:

```
Original: A boat for sailing
Title: A Boat For Sailing
```

In some languages, there are characters whose appearance changes when they are used in a title. Unicode defines three states for each character—lowercase, uppercase, and title case—and the ToTitle function returns a string containing only title-case characters. This has the same effect as the ToUpper function for English but can produce different results in other languages, which is demonstrated by Listing 16-6.

Listing 16-6. Using Title Case in the main.go File in the stringsandregexp Folder

```
package main

import (
    "fmt"
    "strings"
)

func main() {

    specialChar := "\u01c9"

    fmt.Println("Original:", specialChar, []byte(specialChar))

    upperChar := strings.ToUpper(specialChar)
    fmt.Println("Upper:", upperChar, []byte(upperChar))
```

```
    titleChar := strings.ToTitle(specialChar)
    fmt.Println("Title:", titleChar, []byte(titleChar))
}
```

My limited language skills do not extend to a language that requires a different title case, so I have used a Unicode escape sequence to select a character. (I obtained the character code from the Unicode specification.) When compiled and executed, the code in Listing 16-6 writes out the lowercase, uppercase, and title case versions of the character, along with the bytes that are used to represent it:

```
Original: ǉ [199 137]
Upper: Ǉ [199 135]
Title: ǈ [199 136]
```

You may be able to see the difference in the way the character appears, but even if not, you can see that a different combination of byte values is used for upper and title case.

LOCALIZATION: ALL OR NOTHING

Localizing a product takes time, effort, and resources—and it needs to be done by someone who understands the linguistic, cultural, and monetary conventions of the target country or region. If you don't localize properly, then the result can be worse than not localizing at all.

It is for this reason that I don't describe localization features in detail in this book—or any of my books. Describing features outside of the context in which they will be used feels like setting up readers for a self-inflicted disaster. At least if a product isn't localized, the user knows where they stand and doesn't have to try to figure out whether you just forgot to change the currency code or whether those prices are really in U.S. dollars. (This is an issue that I see all the time living in the United Kingdom.)

You *should* localize your products. Your users *should* be able to do business or perform other operations in a way that makes sense to them. But you *must* take it seriously and allocate the time and effort required to do it properly.

Working with Character Case

The unicode package provides functions that can be used to determine or change the case of individual characters, as described in Table 16-5.

Table 16-5. *Functions in the unicode Package for Character Case*

Function	Description
IsLower(rune)	This function returns true if the specified rune is lowercase.
ToLower(rune)	This function returns the lowercase rune associated with the specified rune.
IsUpper(rune)	This function returns true if the specified rune is uppercase.
ToUpper(rune)	This function returns the upper rune associated with the specified rune.
IsTitle(rune)	This function returns true if the specified rune is title case.
ToTitle(rune)	This function returns the title case rune associated with the specified rune.

Listing 16-7 uses the functions described in Table 16-5 to inspect and change the case of a rune.

Listing 16-7. Using the Rune Case Functions in the main.go File in the stringsandregexp Folder

```
package main

import (
    "fmt"
    //"strings"
    "unicode"
)

func main() {

    product := "Kayak"

    for _, char := range product {
        fmt.Println(string(char), "Upper case:", unicode.IsUpper(char))
    }
}
```

The code in Listing 16-7 enumerates the characters in the product string to determine whether they are uppercase. The code produces the following output when compiled and executed:

```
K Upper case: true
a Upper case: false
y Upper case: false
a Upper case: false
k Upper case: false
```

Inspecting Strings

The functions in Table 16-6 are provided by the strings package for inspecting strings.

Table 16-6. *The strings Functions for Inspecting Strings*

Function	Description
Count(s, sub)	This function returns an int that reports how many times the specified substring is found in the string s.
Index(s, sub) LastIndex(s, sub)	These functions return the index of the first or last occurrence of a specified substring string within the string s, or -1 if there is no occurrence.
IndexAny(s, chars) LastIndexAny(s, chars)	These functions return the first or last occurrence of any character in the specified string within the string s, or -1 if there is no occurrence.
IndexByte(s, b) LastIndexByte(s, b)	These functions return the index of the first or last occurrence of a specified byte within the string s, or -1 if there is no occurrence.
IndexFunc(s, func) LastIndexFunc(s, func)	These functions return the index of the first or last occurrence of the character in the string s for which the specified function returns true, as described in the "Inspecting Strings with Custom Functions" section.

Listing 16-8 demonstrates functions described in Table 16-6, some of which are typically used to slice strings based on their contents.

Listing 16-8. Inspecting Strings in the main.go File in the stringsandregexp Folder

```
package main

import (
    "fmt"
    "strings"
    //"unicode"
)

func main() {

    description := "A boat for one person"

    fmt.Println("Count:", strings.Count(description, "o"))
    fmt.Println("Index:", strings.Index(description, "o"))
    fmt.Println("LastIndex:", strings.LastIndex(description, "o"))
    fmt.Println("IndexAny:", strings.IndexAny(description, "abcd"))
    fmt.Println("LastIndex:", strings.LastIndex(description, "o"))
    fmt.Println("LastIndexAny:", strings.LastIndexAny(description, "abcd"))
}
```

The comparisons performed by these functions are case-sensitive, which means the string used for testing in Listing 16-8 contains person, for example, but not Person. To perform case comparisons, combine the functions described in Table 16-6 with those from Tables 16-4 and 16-5. The code in Listing 16-8 produces the following output when compiled and executed:

```
Count: 4
Index: 3
LastIndex: 19
IndexAny: 2
LastIndex: 19
LastIndexAny: 4
```

Inspecting Strings with Custom Functions

The IndexFunc and LastIndexFunc functions use a custom function to inspect strings, using custom functions, as shown in Listing 16-9.

Listing 16-9. Inspecting Strings with a Custom Function in the main.go File in the stringsandregexp Folder

```
package main

import (
    "fmt"
    "strings"
)
```

```
func main() {

    description := "A boat for one person"

    isLetterB := func (r rune) bool {
        return r == 'B' || r == 'b'
    }

    fmt.Println("IndexFunc:", strings.IndexFunc(description, isLetterB))
}
```

Custom functions receive a rune and return a bool result that indicates if the character meets the desired condition. The IndexFunc function invokes the custom function for each character in the string until a true result is obtained, at which point the index is returned.

The isLetterB variable is assigned a custom function that receives a rune and returns true if the rune is a uppercase or lowercase *B*. The custom function is passed to the strings.IndexFunc function, producing the following output when the code is compiled and executed:

```
IndexFunc: 2
```

Manipulating Strings

The strings package provides useful functions for editing strings, including support for replacing some or all characters or removing whitespace.

Splitting Strings

The first set of functions, described in Table 16-7, is used to split strings. (There is also a useful feature for splitting strings using regular expressions, described in the "Using Regular Expressions" section later in this chapter.)

Table 16-7. *The Functions for Splitting Strings in the strings Package*

Function	Description
Fields(s)	This function splits a string on whitespace characters and returns a slice containing the nonwhitespace sections of the string s.
FieldsFunc(s, func)	This function splits the string s on the characters for which a custom function returns true and returns a slice containing the remaining sections of the string.
Split(s, sub)	This function splits the string s on every occurrence of the specified substring, returning a string slice. If the separator is the empty string, then the slice will contain strings for each character.
SplitN(s, sub, max)	This function is similar to Split, but accepts an additional int argument that specifies the maximum number of substrings to return. The last substring in the result slice will contain the unsplit portion of the source string.
SplitAfter(s, sub)	This function is similar to Split but includes the substring used in the results. See the text after the table for a demonstration.
SplitAfterN(s, sub, max)	This function is similar to SplitAfter, but accepts an additional int argument that specifies the maximum number of substrings to return.

The functions described in Table 16-7 perform the same basic task. The difference between the Split and SplitAfter functions is that the Split function excludes the substring used for splitting from the results, as shown in Listing 16-10.

Listing 16-10. Splitting Strings in the main.go File in the stringsandregexp Folder

```
package main

import (
    "fmt"
    "strings"
)

func main() {

    description := "A boat for one person"

    splits := strings.Split(description, " ")
    for _, x := range splits {
        fmt.Println("Split >>" + x + "<<")
    }

    splitsAfter := strings.SplitAfter(description, " ")
    for _, x := range splitsAfter {
        fmt.Println("SplitAfter >>" + x + "<<")
    }
}
```

To highlight the difference, the code in Listing 16-10 splits the same string using both the Split and SplitAfter functions. The results from both functions are enumerated using for loops, and the messages that the loops write out enclose the results in chevrons without spaces before or after the result. Compile and execute the code, and you will see the following results:

```
Split >>A<<
Split >>boat<<
Split >>for<<
Split >>one<<
Split >>person<<
SplitAfter >>A <<
SplitAfter >>boat <<
SplitAfter >>for <<
SplitAfter >>one <<
SplitAfter >>person<<
```

The strings are split on the space character. As the results show, the space character is not included in the results produced by the Split function but is included in the results from the SplitAfter function.

Restricting the Number of Results

The SplitN and SplitAfterN functions accept an int argument that specifies the maximum number of results that should be included in the results, as shown in Listing 16-11.

Listing 16-11. Restricting the Results in the main.go File in the stringsandregexp Folder

```
package main

import (
    "fmt"
    "strings"
)

func main() {

    description := "A boat for one person"

    splits := strings.SplitN(description, " ", 3)
    for _, x := range splits {
        fmt.Println("Split >>" + x + "<<")
    }

    // splitsAfter := strings.SplitAfter(description, " ")
    // for _, x := range splitsAfter {
    //      fmt.Println("SplitAfter >>" + x + "<<")
    // }
}
```

If the string can be split into more strings than has been specified, then the last element in the result slice will be the unsplit remainder of the string. Listing 16-11 specifies a maximum of three results, which means that the first two elements in the slice will be split as normal, and the third element will be the string remainder. Compile and execute the code, and you will see the following output:

```
Split >>A<<
Split >>boat<<
Split >>for one person<<
```

Splitting on Whitespace Characters

One limitation of the Split, SplitN, SplitAfter, and SplitAfterN functions is they do not deal with repeated sequences of characters, which can be a problem when splitting a string on whitespace characters, as shown in Listing 16-12.

Listing 16-12. Splitting on Whitespace in the main.go File in the stringsandregexp Folder

```go
package main

import (
    "fmt"
    "strings"
)

func main() {

    description := "This  is  double  spaced"

    splits := strings.SplitN(description, " ", 3)
    for _, x := range splits {
        fmt.Println("Split >>" + x + "<<")
    }
}
```

The words in the source string are double-spaced, but the SplitN function splits only on the first space character, which produces odd results. Compile and execute the code, and you will see the following output:

```
Split >>This<<
Split >><<
Split >>is  double  spaced<<
```

The second element in the result slice is a space character. To deal with repeated whitespace characters, the Fields function breaks strings on any whitespace character, as shown in Listing 16-13.

Listing 16-13. Using the Fields Function in the main.go File in the stringsandregexp Folder

```go
package main

import (
    "fmt"
    "strings"
)

func main() {

    description := "This  is  double  spaced"

    splits := strings.Fields(description)
    for _, x := range splits {
        fmt.Println("Field >>" + x + "<<")
    }
}
```

The Fields function doesn't support a limit on the number of results but does deal with the double spaces properly. Compile and execute the project, and you will see the following output:

```
Field >>This<<
Field >>is<<
Field >>double<<
Field >>spaced<<
```

Splitting Using a Custom Function to Split Strings

The FieldsFunc function splits a string by passing each character to a custom function and splitting when that function returns true, as shown in Listing 16-14.

Listing 16-14. Splitting with a Custom Function in the main.go File in the stringsandregexp Folder

```
package main

import (
    "fmt"
    "strings"
)

func main() {

    description := "This  is  double  spaced"

    splitter := func(r rune) bool {
        return r == ' '
    }

    splits := strings.FieldsFunc(description, splitter)
    for _, x := range splits {
        fmt.Println("Field >>" + x + "<<")
    }
}
```

The custom function receives a rune and returns true if that rune should cause the string to split. The FieldsFunc function is smart enough to deal with repeated characters, like the double spaces in Listing 16-14.

■ **Note**   I specified the space character in Listing 16-14 to emphasize that the FieldsFunc function deals with repeated characters. The Fields function has a better approach, which is to split on any character for which the IsSpace function in the unicode package returns true.

Compile and execute the project, and you will see the following output:

```
Field >>This<<
Field >>is<<
Field >>double<<
Field >>spaced<<
```

Trimming Strings

The process of trimming removes leading and trailing characters from a string and is most often used to remove whitespace characters. Table 16-8 describes the functions provided by the strings package for trimming.

Table 16-8. The Functions for Trimming Strings in the strings Package

Function	Description
TrimSpace(s)	This function returns the string s without leading or trailing whitespace characters.
Trim(s, set)	This function returns a string from which any leading or trailing characters contained in the string set are removed from the string s.
TrimLeft(s, set)	This function returns the string s without any leading character contained in the string set. This function matches any of the specified characters—use the TrimPrefix function to remove a complete substring.
TrimRight(s, set)	This function returns the string s without any trailing character contained in the string set. This function matches any of the specified characters—use the TrimSuffix function to remove a complete substring.
TrimPrefix(s, prefix)	This function returns the string s after removing the specified prefix string. This function removes the complete prefix string—use the TrimLeft function to remove characters from a set.
TrimSuffix(s, suffix)	This function returns the string s after removing the specified suffix string. This function removes the complete suffix string—use the TrimRight function to remove characters from a set.
TrimFunc(s, func)	This function returns the string s from which any leading or trailing character for which a custom function returns true are removed.
TrimLeftFunc(s, func)	This function returns the string s from which any leading character for which a custom function returns true are removed.
TrimRightFunc(s, func)	This function returns the string s from which any trailing character for which a custom function returns true are removed.

Trimming Whitespace

The TrimSpace function performs the most common trimming task, which is to remove any leading or trailing whitespace characters. This is especially useful when processing user input, where spaces can be introduced accidentally and will cause confusion if they are not removed, such as when entering usernames, as shown in Listing 16-15.

Listing 16-15. Trimming Whitespace in the main.go File in the stringsandregexp Folder

```
package main

import (
    "fmt"
    "strings"
)

func main() {

    username := " Alice"
    trimmed := strings.TrimSpace(username)
    fmt.Println("Trimmed:", ">>" + trimmed + "<<")
}
```

The user may not realize they have pressed the spacebar when entering a name, and user confusion can be avoided by trimming the entered name before using it. Compile and execute the example project, and you will see the trimmed name displayed:

```
Trimmed: >>Alice<<
```

Trimming Character Sets

The Trim, TrimLeft, and TrimRight functions match any character in a specified string. Listing 16-16 shows the use of the Trim function. The other functions work in the same way but trim only the start or end of the string.

Listing 16-16. Trimming Characters in the main.go File in the stringsandregexp Folder

```
package main

import (
    "fmt"
    "strings"
)

func main() {

    description := "A boat for one person"

    trimmed := strings.Trim(description, "Asno ")

    fmt.Println("Trimmed:", trimmed)
}
```

In Listing 16-16, I specified the letters A, s, n, o, and the space character when calling the Trim function. The function performs a case-sensitive match using any of the characters in the set and will omit any matched characters from the result. Matching stops as soon as a character not in the set is found. The process is performed from the start of the string for the prefix and the end of the string for the suffix. If the string contains none of the characters in the set, then the Trim function will return the string without modification.

For the example, this means that the letter A and the space at the start of the string will be trimmed, and the letters s, o, and n will be trimmed from the end of the string. Compile and execute the project, and the output will show the trimmed string:

```
Trimmed: boat for one per
```

Trimming Substrings

The TrimPrefix and TrimSuffix functions trim substrings rather than characters from a set, as shown in Listing 16-17.

Listing 16-17. Trimming Substrings in the main.go File in the stringsandregexp Folder

```
package main

import (
    "fmt"
    "strings"
)

func main() {

    description := "A boat for one person"

    prefixTrimmed := strings.TrimPrefix(description, "A boat ")
    wrongPrefix := strings.TrimPrefix(description, "A hat ")

    fmt.Println("Trimmed:", prefixTrimmed)
    fmt.Println("Not trimmed:", wrongPrefix)
}
```

The start or end of the target string must exactly match the specified prefix or suffix; otherwise, the result from the trimming function will be the original string. In Listing 16-17, I use the TrimPrefix function twice, but only one of them uses a prefix that matches the start of the string, producing the following results when the code is compiled and executed:

```
Trimmed: for one person
Not trimmed: A boat for one person
```

Trimming with Custom Functions

The TrimFunc, TrimLeftFunc, and TrimRightFunc functions trim strings using custom functions, as shown in Listing 16-18.

Listing 16-18. Trimming with a Custom Function in the main.go File in the stringsandregexp Folder

```
package main

import (
    "fmt"
    "strings"
)

func main() {

    description := "A boat for one person"

    trimmer := func(r rune) bool {
        return r == 'A' || r == 'n'
    }

    trimmed := strings.TrimFunc(description, trimmer)
    fmt.Println("Trimmed:", trimmed)
}
```

The custom function is invoked for the characters at the start and end of the string, and characters will be trimmed until the function returns false. Compile and execute the example, and you will receive the following output, in which the first and last characters have been trimmed from the string:

```
Trimmed:   boat for one perso
```

Altering Strings

The functions described in Table 16-9 are provided by the strings package for altering the content of strings.

Table 16-9. *The Functions for Altering Strings in the strings Package*

Function	Description
Replace (s, old, new, n)	This function alters the string s by replacing occurrences of the string old with the string new. The maximum number of occurrences that will be replaced is specified by the int argument n.
ReplaceAll (s, old, new)	This function alters the string s by replacing all occurrences of the string old with the string new. Unlike the Replace function, there is no limit on the number of occurrences that will be replaced.
Map(func, s)	This function generates a string by invoking the custom function for each character in the string s and concatenating the results. If the function produces a negative value, the current character is dropped without a replacement.

430

The Replace and ReplaceAll functions locate substrings and replace them. The Replace function allows a maximum number of changes to be specified, while the ReplaceAll function will replace all the occurrences of the substring it finds, as shown in Listing 16-19.

Listing 16-19. Replacing Substrings in the main.go file in the stringsandregexp Folder

```
package main

import (
    "fmt"
    "strings"
)

func main() {

    text := "It was a boat. A small boat."

    replace := strings.Replace(text, "boat", "canoe", 1)
    replaceAll := strings.ReplaceAll(text, "boat", "truck")

    fmt.Println("Replace:", replace)
    fmt.Println("Replace All:", replaceAll)
}
```

In Listing 16-19, the Replace function is used to replace a single instance of the word boat, and the ReplaceAll function is used to replace every instance. Compile and execute the code, and you will see the following output:

```
Replace: It was a canoe. A small boat.
Replace All: It was a truck. A small truck.
```

Altering Strings with a Map Function

The Map function alters strings by invoking a function for every character and combining the results to form a new string, as shown in Listing 16-20.

Listing 16-20. Using the Map Function in the main.go File in the stringsandregexp Folder

```
package main

import (
    "fmt"
    "strings"
)

func main() {

    text := "It was a boat. A small boat."
```

```
    mapper := func(r rune) rune {
        if r == 'b' {
            return 'c'
        }
        return r
    }

    mapped := strings.Map(mapper, text)
    fmt.Println("Mapped:", mapped)
}
```

The mapping function in Listing 16-20 replaces the character b with the character c and passes on all the other characters unmodified. Compile and execute the project, and you will see the following results:

```
Mapped: It was a coat. A small coat.
```

Using a String Replacer

The strings package exports a struct type named Replacer that is used to replace strings, providing an alternative to the functions described in Table 16-10. Listing 16-21 demonstrates the use of a Replacer.

Listing 16-21. Using a Replacer in the main.go File in the stringsandregexp Folder

```
package main

import (
    "fmt"
    "strings"
)

func main() {

    text := "It was a boat. A small boat."

    replacer := strings.NewReplacer("boat", "kayak", "small", "huge")

    replaced := replacer.Replace(text)

    fmt.Println("Replaced:", replaced)
}
```

Table 16-10. The Replacer Methods

Name	Description
Replace(s)	This method returns a string for which all the replacements specified with the constructor have been performed on the string s.
WriteString(writer, s)	This method is used to perform the replacements specified with the constructor and write the results to an io.Writer, which is described in Chapter 20.

A constructor function named NewReplacer is used to create a Replacer and accepts pairs of arguments that specify substrings and their replacements. Table 16-10 describes the methods defined for the Replacer type.

The constructor used to create the Replacer in Listing 16-21 specifies that instances of boat should be replaced with kayak and instances of small should be replaced with huge. The Replace method is called to perform the replacements, producing the following output when the code is compiled and executed:

```
Replaced: It was a kayak. A huge kayak.
```

Building and Generating Strings

The strings package provides two functions for generating strings and a struct type whose methods can be used to efficiently build strings gradually. Table 16-11 describes the functions.

Table 16-11. *The strings Functions for Generating Strings*

Function	Description
Join(slice, sep)	This function combines the elements in the specified string slice, with the specified separator string placed between elements.
Repeat(s, count)	This function generates a string by repeating the string s for a specified number of times.

Of these two functions, it is Join that is most useful because it can be used to recombine strings that have been split, as shown in Listing 16-22.

Listing 16-22. Splitting and Joining a String in the main.go File in the stringsandregexp Folder

```go
package main

import (
    "fmt"
    "strings"
)

func main() {

    text := "It was a boat. A small boat."

    elements := strings.Fields(text)
    joined := strings.Join(elements, "--")
    fmt.Println("Joined:", joined)
}
```

This example uses the Fields function to split a string on whitespace characters and joins the elements with two hyphens as the separator. Compile and execute the project, and you will receive the following output:

```
Joined: It--was--a--boat.--A--small--boat.
```

Building Strings

The strings package provides the Builder type, which has not exported fields but does provide a set of methods that can be used to efficiently build strings gradually, as described in Table 16-12.

Table 16-12. *The strings.Builder Methods*

Name	Description
WriteString(s)	This method appends the string s to the string being built.
WriteRune(r)	This method appends the character r to the string being built.
WriteByte(b)	This method appends the byte b to the string being built.
String()	This method returns the string that has been created by the builder.
Reset()	This method resets the string created by the builder.
Len()	This method returns the number of bytes used to store the string created by the builder.
Cap()	This method returns the number of bytes that have been allocated by the builder.
Grow(size)	This method increases the number of bytes used allocated by the builder to store the string that is being built.

The general pattern is to create a Builder; compose a string using the WriteString, WriteRune, and WriteByte functions; and obtain the string that has been built using the String method, as shown in Listing 16-23.

Listing 16-23. Building a String in the main.go File in the stringsandregexp Folder

```
package main

import (
    "fmt"
    "strings"
)

func main() {

    text := "It was a boat. A small boat."

    var builder strings.Builder

    for _, sub := range strings.Fields(text) {
        if (sub == "small") {
            builder.WriteString("very ")
        }
        builder.WriteString(sub)
        builder.WriteRune(' ')
    }

    fmt.Println("String:", builder.String())
}
```

Creating the string using the `Builder` is more efficient than using the concatenation operator on regular `string` values, especially if the `Grow` method is used to allocate storage in advance.

■ **Caution**   Care must be taken to use pointers when passing `Builder` values to and from functions and methods; otherwise, the efficiency gains will be lost when the `Builder` is copied.

Compile and execute the project, and you will receive the following output:

```
String: It was a boat. A very small boat.
```

Using Regular Expressions

The `regexp` package provides support for regular expressions, which allow complex patterns to be found in strings. Table 16-13 describes the basic regular expression functions.

Table 16-13. *The Basic Functions Provided by the regexp Package*

Function	Description
`Match(pattern, b)`	This function returns a `bool` that indicates whether a pattern is matched by the byte slice b.
`MatchString(patten, s)`	This function returns a `bool` that indicates whether a pattern is matched by the string s.
`Compile(pattern)`	This function returns a `RegExp` that can be used to perform repeated pattern matching with the specified pattern, as described in the "Compiling and Reusing Patterns" section.
`MustCompile(pattern)`	This function provides the same feature as `Compile` but panics, as described in Chapter 15, if the specified pattern cannot be compiled.

■ **Note**   The regular expressions used in this section perform basic matches, but the `regexp` package supports an extensive pattern syntax, which is described at `https://pkg.go.dev/regexp/syntax@go1.17.1`.

The `MatchString` method is the simplest way to determine whether a string is matched by a regular expression, as shown in Listing 16-24.

Listing 16-24. Using a Regular Expression in the main.go File in the stringsandregexp Folder

```
package main

import (
    "fmt"
    //"strings"
    "regexp"
)

func main() {

    description := "A boat for one person"

    match, err := regexp.MatchString("[A-z]oat", description)

    if (err == nil) {
        fmt.Println("Match:", match)
    } else {
        fmt.Println("Error:", err)
    }
}
```

The MatchString function accepts a regular expression pattern and the string to search. The results from the MatchString function are a bool value, which is true if there is a match and an error, which will be nil if there have been no issues performing the match. Errors with regular expressions usually arise if the pattern cannot be processed.

The pattern used in Listing 16-24 will match any uppercase or lowercase character A–Z, followed by lowercase oat. The pattern will match the word *boat* in the description string, producing the following output when the code is compiled and executed:

```
Match: true
```

Compiling and Reusing Patterns

The MatchString function is simple and convenient, but the full power of regular expressions is accessed through the Compile function, which compiles a regular expression pattern so that it can be reused, as shown in Listing 16-25.

Listing 16-25. Compiling a Pattern in the main.go File in the stringsandregexp Folder

```
package main

import (
    "fmt"
    "regexp"
)

func main() {

    pattern, compileErr := regexp.Compile("[A-z]oat")
```

```
description := "A boat for one person"
question := "Is that a goat?"
preference := "I like oats"

if (compileErr == nil) {
    fmt.Println("Description:", pattern.MatchString(description))
    fmt.Println("Question:", pattern.MatchString(question))
    fmt.Println("Preference:", pattern.MatchString(preference))
} else {
    fmt.Println("Error:", compileErr)
}
}
```

This is more efficient because the pattern has to be compiled only once. The result of the Compile function is an instance of the RegExp type, which defines the MatchString function. The code in Listing 16-25 produces the following output when compiled and executed:

```
Description: true
Question: true
Preference: false
```

Compiling a pattern also provides access to methods for using regular expression features, the most useful of which are described in Table 16-14. The methods described in this chapter operate on strings, but the RegExp type also provides methods that are used to process byte slices and methods that deal with readers, which are part of the Go support for I/O and which are described in Chapter 20.

Table 16-14. *Useful Basic Regexp Methods*

Function	Description
MatchString(s)	This method returns true if the string s matches the compiled pattern.
FindStringIndex(s)	This method returns an int slice containing the location for the left-most match made by the compiled pattern in the string s. A nil result indicates that no matches were made.
FindAllStringIndex(s, max)	This method returns a slice of int slices that contain the location for all the matches made by the compiled pattern in the string s. A nil result indicates that no matches were made.
FindString(s)	This method returns a string containing the left-most match made by the compiled pattern in the string s. An empty string will be returned if no match is made.
FindAllString(s, max)	This method returns a string slice containing the matches made by the compiled pattern in the string s. The int argument max specifies the maximum number of matches, with -1 specifying no limit. A nil result is returned if there are no matches.
Split(s, max)	This method splits the string s using matches from the compiled pattern as separators and returns a slice containing the split substrings.

The MatchString method is an alternative to the function described in Table 16-3, confirming whether a string is matched by a pattern.

The FindStringIndex and FindAllStringIndex methods provide the index position of matches, which can then be used to extract regions of the string using the array/slice range notation, as shown in Listing 16-26. (The range notation is described in Chapter 7.)

Listing 16-26. Getting Match Indices in the main.go File in the stringsandregexp Folder

```go
package main

import (
    "fmt"
    "regexp"
)

func getSubstring(s string, indices []int) string {
    return string(s[indices[0]:indices[1]])
}

func main() {

    pattern := regexp.MustCompile("K[a-z]{4}|[A-z]oat")

    description := "Kayak. A boat for one person."

    firstIndex := pattern.FindStringIndex(description)
    allIndices := pattern.FindAllStringIndex(description, -1)

    fmt.Println("First index", firstIndex[0], "-", firstIndex[1],
        "=", getSubstring(description, firstIndex))

    for i, idx := range allIndices {
        fmt.Println("Index", i, "=", idx[0], "-",
            idx[1], "=", getSubstring(description, idx))
    }
}
```

The regular expression in Listing 16-26 will make two matches with the description string. The FindStringIndex method returns only the first match, working from left to right. The match is expressed as an int slice, where the first value indicates the start location for the match in the string, and the second number indicates the number of matched characters.

The FindAllStringIndex method returns multiple matches and is called in Listing 16-26 with -1, indicating that all matches should be returned. The matches are returned in a slice of int slices (meaning that each value in the result slice is a slice of int values), each of which describes a single match. In Listing 16-26, the indices are used to extract regions from the string using a function named getSubstring, producing the following results when compiled and executed:

```
First index 0 - 5 = Kayak
Index 0 = 0 - 5 = Kayak
Index 1 = 9 - 13 = boat
```

If you don't need to know the location of the matches, then the FindString and FindAllString methods are more useful because their results are the substrings matched by the regular expression, as shown in Listing 16-27.

Listing 16-27. Getting Match Substrings in the main.go File in the stringsandregexp Folder

```
package main

import (
    "fmt"
    "regexp"
)

// func getSubstring(s string, indices []int) string {
//     return string(s[indices[0]:indices[1]])
// }

func main() {

    pattern := regexp.MustCompile("K[a-z]{4}|[A-z]oat")

    description := "Kayak. A boat for one person."

    firstMatch := pattern.FindString(description)
    allMatches := pattern.FindAllString(description, -1)

    fmt.Println("First match:", firstMatch)

    for i, m := range allMatches {
        fmt.Println("Match", i, "=", m)
    }
}
```

Compile and execute the project, and you will see the following output:

```
First match: Kayak
Match 0 = Kayak
Match 1 = boat
```

Splitting Strings Using a Regular Expression

The Split method splits a string using the matches made by a regular expression, which can provide a more flexible alternative to the splitting functions described earlier in the chapter, as shown in Listing 16-28.

Listing 16-28. Splitting a String in the main.go File in the stringsandregexp Folder

```
package main

import (
    "fmt"
    "regexp"
)

func main() {

    pattern := regexp.MustCompile(" |boat|one")

    description := "Kayak. A boat for one person."

    split := pattern.Split(description, -1)

    for _, s := range split {
        if s != "" {
            fmt.Println("Substring:", s)
        }
    }
}
```

The regular expression in this example matches the space character or the terms boat and one. The description string will be split whenever the expression matches. One oddity of the Split method is that it introduces the empty string into the results around the point where matches have been made, which is why I filter out those values from the result slice in the example. Compile and execute the code, and you will see the following results:

```
Substring: Kayak.
Substring: A
Substring: for
Substring: person.
```

Using Subexpressions

Subexpressions allow parts of a regular expression to be accessed, which can make it easier to extract substrings from within a matched region. Listing 16-29 provides an example of when a subexpression can be useful.

Listing 16-29. Performing a Match in the main.go File in the stringsandregexp Folder

```
package main

import (
    "fmt"
    "regexp"
)
```

```
func main() {

    pattern := regexp.MustCompile("A [A-z]* for [A-z]* person")

    description := "Kayak. A boat for one person."

    str := pattern.FindString(description)
    fmt.Println("Match:", str)
}
```

The pattern in this example matches a specific sentence structure, which allows me to match the part of a string that is of interest. But a lot of the sentence structure is static, and the two variable sections of the pattern contain the content that I want. The FindString method is a blunt instrument in this situation because it matches the entire pattern, including the static regions. Compile and execute the code, and you will receive the following output:

```
Match: A boat for one person
```

I can add subexpressions to identify the regions of content that are important within the pattern, as shown in Listing 16-30.

Listing 16-30. Using Subexpressions in the main.go File in the stringsandregexp Folder

```
package main

import (
    "fmt"
    "regexp"
)

func main() {

    pattern := regexp.MustCompile("A ([A-z]*) for ([A-z]*) person")

    description := "Kayak. A boat for one person."

    subs := pattern.FindStringSubmatch(description)

    for _, s := range subs {
        fmt.Println("Match:", s)
    }
}
```

Subexpressions are denoted with parentheses. In Listing 16-30, I have defined two subexpressions, each of which surrounds a variable section of the pattern. The FindStringSubmatch method performs the same task as FindString, but also includes the substrings matched by the expressions in its result. Compile and execute the code, and you will see the following output:

```
Match: A boat for one person
Match: boat
Match: one
```

441

Table 16-15 describes the RegExp methods for working with subexpressions.

Table 16-15. *The Regexp Methods for Subexpressions*

Name	Description
FindStringSubmatch(s)	This method returns a slice containing the first match made by the pattern and the text for the subexpressions that the pattern defines.
FindAllStringSubmatch(s, max)	This method returns a slice containing all the matches and the text for the subexpressions. The int argument is used to specify the maximum number of matches. A value of -1 specifies all matches.
FindStringSubmatchIndex(s)	This method is equivalent to FindStringSubmatch but returns indices rather than substrings.
FindAllStringSubmatchIndex (s, max)	This method is equivalent to FindAllStringSubmatch but returns indices rather than substrings.
NumSubexp()	This method returns the number of subexpressions.
SubexpIndex(name)	This method returns the index of the subexpression with the specified name or -1 if there is no such subexpression.
SubexpNames()	This method returns the names of the subexpressions, expressed in the order in which they are defined.

Using Named Subexpressions

Subexpressions can be given names, which makes the regular expression harder to understand but makes the results easier to process. Listing 16-31 shows the use of named subexpressions.

Listing 16-31. Using Named Subexpressions in the main.go File in the stringsandregexp Folder

```
package main

import (
    "fmt"
    "regexp"
)

func main() {

    pattern := regexp.MustCompile(
        "A (?P<type>[A-z]*) for (?P<capacity>[A-z]*) person")

    description := "Kayak. A boat for one person."

    subs := pattern.FindStringSubmatch(description)

    for _, name := range []string { "type", "capacity" } {
        fmt.Println(name, "=", subs[pattern.SubexpIndex(name)])
    }
}
```

The syntax for assigning names to subexpressions is awkward: within the parentheses, a question mark, followed by an uppercase *P*, followed by the name within angle brackets. The pattern in Listing 16-31 defines two named subexpressions:

```
...
pattern := regexp.MustCompile("A (?P<type>[A-z]*) for (?P<capacity>[A-z]*) person")
...
```

The subexpressions are given the names type and capacity. The SubexpIndex method returns the position of a named subexpression in the results, which allows me to get the substrings matched by the type and capacity subexpressions. Compile and execute the example, and you will see the following output:

```
type = boat
capacity = one
```

Replacing Substrings Using a Regular Expression

The final set of RegExp methods is used to replace substrings matched by a regular expression, as described in Table 16-16.

Table 16-16. *The Regexp Methods for Replacing Substrings*

Name	Description
ReplaceAllString (s, template)	This method replaces the matched portion of the string s with the specified template, which is expanded before it is included in the result to incorporate subexpressions.
ReplaceAllLiteralString (s, sub)	This method replaces the matched portion of the string s with the specified content, which is included in the result without being expanded for subexpressions.
ReplaceAllStringFunc (s, func)	This method replaces the matched portion of the string s with the result produced by the specified function.

The ReplaceAllString method is used to replace the portion of a string that is matched by the regular expression with a template, which can reference subexpressions, as shown in Listing 16-32.

Listing 16-32. Replacing Content in the main.go File in the stringsandregexp Folder

```
package main

import (
    "fmt"
    "regexp"
)

func main() {

    pattern := regexp.MustCompile(
        "A (?P<type>[A-z]*) for (?P<capacity>[A-z]*) person")
```

```
    description := "Kayak. A boat for one person."

    template := "(type: ${type}, capacity: ${capacity})"
    replaced := pattern.ReplaceAllString(description, template)
    fmt.Println(replaced)
}
```

The result from the ReplaceAllString method is a string with the replaced content. The template can refer to the matches made for subexpressions by name, such as ${type}, or by position, such as ${1}. In the listing, the section of the description string that is matched by the pattern will be replaced with a template containing the matches for the type and capacity subexpressions. Compile and execute the code, and you will see the following output:

```
Kayak. (type: boat, capacity: one).
```

Notice that the template is responsible for only part of the result from the ReplaceAllString method in Listing 16-32. The first part of the description string—the word Kayak, followed by a period and a space, is not matched by the regular expression and is included in the result without being modified.

■ **Tip** Use the ReplaceAllLiteralString method if you want to replace content without the new substring being interpreted for subexpressions.

Replacing Matched Content with a Function

The ReplaceAllStringFunc method replaces the matched section of a string with content generated by a function, as shown in Listing 16-33.

Listing 16-33. Replacing Content with a Function in the main.go File in the stringsandregexp Folder

```
package main

import (
    "fmt"
    "regexp"
)

func main() {

    pattern := regexp.MustCompile(
        "A (?P<type>[A-z]*) for (?P<capacity>[A-z]*) person")

    description := "Kayak. A boat for one person."

    replaced := pattern.ReplaceAllStringFunc(description, func(s string) string {
        return "This is the replacement content"
    })
    fmt.Println(replaced)
}
```

The result from the function isn't processed for subexpression references, which you can see in the output produced when the code is compiled and executed:

```
Kayak. This is the replacement content.
```

Summary

In this chapter, I described the standard library features for processing `string` values and applying regular expressions, which are provided by the `strings`, `unicode`, and `regexp` packages. In the next chapter, I describe related features, which allow strings to be formatted and scanned.

CHAPTER 17

■ ■ ■

Formatting and Scanning Strings

In this chapter, I describe the standard library features for formatting and scanning strings. Formatting is the process of composing a new string from one or more data values, while scanning is the process of parsing values from a string. Table 17-1 puts formatting and scanning strings in context.

Table 17-1. *Putting Formatting and Scanning Strings in Context*

Question	Answer
What are they?	Formatting is the process of composing values into a string. Scanning is the process of parsing a string for the values it contains.
Why are they useful?	Formatting a string is a common requirement and is used to produce strings for everything from logging and debugging to presenting the user with information. Scanning is useful for extracting data from strings, such as from HTTP requests or user input.
How are they used?	Both sets of features are provided through functions defined in the fmt package.
Are there any pitfalls or limitations?	The templates used to format strings can be hard to read, and there is no built-in function that allows a formatted string to be created to which a newline character is appended automatically.
Are there any alternatives?	Larger amounts of text and HTML content can be generated using the template features described in Chapter 23.

Table 17-2 summarizes the chapter.

Table 17-2. *Chapter Summary*

Problem	Solution	Listing
Combine data values to form a string	Use the basic formatting functions provided by the fmt package	5, 6
Specify the structure of a string	Use the fmt functions that use formatting templates and use the formatting verbs	7–9, 11–18
Change the way custom data types are represented	Implement the Stringer interface	10
Parse a string to obtain the data values it contains	Use the scanning functions provided by the fmt package	19–22

© Adam Freeman 2022
A. Freeman, *Pro Go*, https://doi.org/10.1007/978-1-4842-7355-5_17

Preparing for This Chapter

To prepare for this chapter, open a new command prompt, navigate to a convenient location, and create a directory named usingstrings. Run the command shown in Listing 17-1 to create a module file.

■ **Tip** You can download the example project for this chapter—and for all the other chapters in this book—from https://github.com/apress/pro-go. See Chapter 2 for how to get help if you have problems running the examples.

Listing 17-1. Initializing the Module

```
go mod init usingstrings
```

Add a file named product.go to the usingstrings folder with the content shown in Listing 17-2.

Listing 17-2. The Contents of the product.go File in the usingstrings Folder

```go
package main

type Product struct {
    Name, Category string
    Price float64
}

var Kayak = Product {
    Name: "Kayak",
    Category: "Watersports",
    Price: 275,
}

var Products = []Product {
    { "Kayak", "Watersports", 279 },
    { "Lifejacket", "Watersports", 49.95 },
    { "Soccer Ball", "Soccer", 19.50 },
    { "Corner Flags", "Soccer", 34.95 },
    { "Stadium", "Soccer", 79500 },
    { "Thinking Cap", "Chess", 16 },
    { "Unsteady Chair", "Chess", 75 },
    { "Bling-Bling King", "Chess", 1200 },
}
```

Add a file named main.go to the usingstrings folder, with the contents shown in Listing 17-3.

Listing 17-3. The Contents of the main.go File in the usingstrings Folder

```
package main

import "fmt"

func main() {

    fmt.Println("Product:", Kayak.Name, "Price:", Kayak.Price)
}
```

Use the command prompt to run the command shown in Listing 17-4 in the usingstrings folder.

Listing 17-4. Running the Example Project

```
go run .
```

The code will be compiled and executed, producing the following output:

```
Product: Kayak Price: 275
```

Writing Strings

The fmt package provides functions for composing and writing strings. The basic functions are described in Table 17-3. Some of these functions use writers, which are part of the Go support for input/output and which are described in Chapter 20.

Table 17-3. The Basic fmt Functions for Composing and Writing Strings

Name	Description
Print(...vals)	This function accepts a variable number of arguments and writes out their values to the standard out. Spaces are added between values that are not strings.
Println(...vals)	This function accepts a variable number of arguments and writes out their values to the standard out, separated by spaces and followed by a newline character.
Fprint(writer, ...vals)	This function writes out a variable number of arguments to the specified writer, which I describe in Chapter 20. Spaces are added between values that are not strings.
Fprintln(writer, ...vals)	This function writes out a variable number of arguments to the specified writer, which I describe in Chapter 20, followed by a newline character. Spaces are added between all values.

■ **Note**   The Go standard library includes a template package, described in Chapter 23, which can be used to create larger amounts of text and HTML content.

The functions described in Table 17-3 add spaces between the values in the strings they produce, but they do so inconsistently. The Println and Fprintln functions add spaces between all the values, but the Print and Fprint functions only add spaces between values that are not strings. This means that the pairs of functions in Table 17-3 differ in more than just adding a newline character, as shown in Listing 17-5.

Listing 17-5. Writing Strings in the main.go File in the usingstrings Folder

```
package main

import "fmt"

func main() {

    fmt.Println("Product:", Kayak.Name, "Price:", Kayak.Price)
    fmt.Print("Product:", Kayak.Name, "Price:", Kayak.Price, "\n")
}
```

In many programming languages, there would be no difference between the strings produced by the statements in Listing 17-5, because I have added a newline character to the arguments passed to the Print function. But, since the Print function adds spaces only between pairs of nonstring values, the results are different. Compile and execute the code, and you will see the following output:

```
Product: Kayak Price: 275
Product:KayakPrice:275
```

Formatting Strings

I have been using the fmt.Println function to produce output in earlier chapters. I used this function because it is simple, but it doesn't provide control over its output formatting, which means that it is suitable for simple debugging but not for generating complex strings or formatting values for presentation to the user. Other functions in the fmt package that do provide formatting control are shown in Listing 17-6.

Listing 17-6. Formatting a String in the main.go File in the usingstrings Folder

```
package main

import "fmt"

func main() {

    fmt.Printf("Product: %v, Price: $%4.2f", Kayak.Name, Kayak.Price)
}
```

The Printf function accepts a template string and a series of values. The template is scanned for *verbs*, which are denoted by the percentage sign (the % character) followed by a format specifier. There are two verbs in the template in Listing 17-6:

```
...
fmt.Printf("Product: %v, Price: $%4.2f", Kayak.Name, Kayak.Price)
...
```

The first verb is %v, and it specifies the default representation for a type. For a string value, for example, %v simply includes the string in the output. The %4.2f verb specifies the format for a floating-point value, with 4 digits before the decimal point and 2 digits after. The values for the template verbs are taken from the remaining arguments, used in the order they are specified. For the example, this means the %v verb is used to format the Product.Name value, and the %4.2f verb is used to format the Product.Price value. These values are formatted, inserted into the template string, and written out to the console, which you can see by compiling and executing the code:

```
Product: Kayak, Price: $275.00
```

Table 17-4 describes the functions provided by the fmt package, which can format strings. I describe the formatting verbs in the "Understanding the Formatting Verbs" section.

Table 17-4. The fmt Functions for Formatting Strings

Name	Description
Sprintf(t, ...vals)	This function returns a string, which is created by processing the template t. The remaining arguments are used as values for the template verbs.
Printf(t, ...vals)	This function creates a string by processing the template t. The remaining arguments are used as values for the template verbs. The string is written to the standard out.
Fprintf(writer, t, ...vals)	This function creates a string by processing the template t. The remaining arguments are used as values for the template verbs. The string is written to a Writer, which is described in Chapter 20.
Errorf(t, ...values)	This function creates an error by processing the template t. The remaining arguments are used as values for the template verbs. The result is an error value whose Error method returns the formatted string.

In Listing 17-7, I have defined a function that uses Sprintf to format a string result and uses Errorf to create an error.

Listing 17-7. Using Formatted Strings in the main.go File in the usingstrings Folder

```
package main

import "fmt"

func getProductName(index int) (name string, err error) {
    if (len(Products) > index) {
        name = fmt.Sprintf("Name of product: %v", Products[index].Name)
```

451

```
    } else {
        err = fmt.Errorf("Error for index %v", index)
    }
    return
}

func main() {

    name, _ := getProductName(1)
    fmt.Println(name)

    _, err := getProductName(10)
    fmt.Println(err.Error())
}
```

Both of the formatted strings in this example use the %v value, which writes out values in their default form. Compile and execute the project, and you will see one result and one error, as follows:

```
Name of product: Lifejacket
Error for index 10
```

Understanding the Formatting Verbs

The functions described in Table 17-4 support a wide range of formatting verbs in their templates. In the sections that follow, I describe the most useful. I start with those verbs that can be used with any data type and then describe those that are more specific.

Using the General-Purpose Formatting Verbs

The general-purpose verbs can be used to display any value, as described in Table 17-5.

Table 17-5. *The Formatting Verbs for Any Value*

Verb	Description
%v	This verb displays the default format for the value. Modifying the verb with a plus sign (%+v) includes field names when writing out struct values.
%#v	This verb displays a value in a format that could be used to re-create the value in a Go code file.
%T	This verb displays the Go type of a value.

In Listing 17-8, I have defined a custom struct type and used the verbs shown in the table to format a value of that type.

Listing 17-8. Using the General-Purpose Verbs in the main.go File in the usingstrings Folder

```
package main

import "fmt"

func Printfln(template string, values ...interface{}) {
    fmt.Printf(template + "\n", values...)
}

func main() {

    Printfln("Value: %v", Kayak)
    Printfln("Go syntax: %#v", Kayak)
    Printfln("Type: %T", Kayak)
}
```

The Printf function doesn't append a newline character to its output, unlike the Println function, so I defined a Printfln function that appends the newline to the template before calling the Printf function. The statements in the main function define simple string templates with the verbs in Table 17-5. Compile and execute the code, and you will receive the following output:

```
Value: {Kayak Watersports 275}
Go syntax: main.Product{Name:"Kayak", Category:"Watersports", Price:275}
Type: main.Product
```

Controlling Struct Formatting

Go has a default format for all data types that the %v verb relies on. For structs, the default value lists the field values within curly braces. The default verb can be modified with a plus sign to include the field names in the output, as shown in Listing 17-9.

Listing 17-9. Displaying Field Names in the main.go File in the usingstrings Folder

```
package main

import "fmt"

func Printfln(template string, values ...interface{}) {
    fmt.Printf(template + "\n", values...)
}

func main() {

    Printfln("Value: %v", Kayak)
    Printfln("Value with fields: %+v", Kayak)
}
```

Compile and execute the project, and you will see the same Product value formatted with and without field names:

```
Value: {Kayak Watersports 275}
Value with fields: {Name:Kayak Category:Watersports Price:275}
```

The fmt package supports custom struct formatting through an interface named Stringer that is defined as follows:

```
type Stringer interface {
    String() string
}
```

The String method specified by the Stringer interface will be used to obtain a string representation of any type that defines it, as shown in Listing 17-10, allowing custom formatting to be specified.

Listing 17-10. Defining a Custom Struct Format in the product.go File in the usingstrings Folder

```
package main

import "fmt"

type Product struct {
    Name, Category string
    Price float64
}

// ...variables omitted for brevity...

func (p Product) String() string {
    return fmt.Sprintf("Product: %v, Price: $%4.2f", p.Name, p.Price)
}
```

The String method will be invoked automatically when a string representation of a Product value is required. Compile and execute the code, and the output will use the custom format:

```
Value: Product: Kayak, Price: $275.00
Value with fields: Product: Kayak, Price: $275.00
```

Notice that the custom format is also used when the %v verb is modified to display struct fields.

■ **Tip** If you define a GoString method that returns a string, then your type will conform to the GoStringer interface, which allows custom formatting for the %#v verb.

FORMATTING ARRAYS, SLICES, AND MAPS

When arrays and slices are represented as strings, the output is a set of square brackets, within which are the individual elements, like this:

```
...
[Kayak Lifejacket Paddle]
...
```

Notice that no commas are separating the elements. When maps are represented as strings, the key-value pairs are displayed within square brackets, preceded by the map keyword, like this:

```
...
map[1:Kayak 2:Lifejacket 3:Paddle]
...
```

The Stringer interface can be used to change the format used for custom data types contained within an array, slice, or map. No changes can be made to the default formats unless you use a type alias, however, because methods must be defined within the same package as the type they apply to.

Using the Integer Formatting Verbs

Table 17-6 describes the formatting verbs for integer values, regardless of their size.

Table 17-6. *The Formatting Verbs for Integer Values*

Verb	Description
%b	This verb displays an integer value as a binary string.
%d	This verb displays an integer value as a decimal string. This is the default format for integer values, applied when the %v verb is used.
%o, %O	These verbs display an integer value as an octal string. The %O verb adds the 0o prefix.
%x, %X	These verbs display an integer value as a hexadecimal string. The letters A–F are displayed in lowercase by the %x verb and in uppercase by the %X verb.

Listing 17-11 applies the verbs described in Table 17-6 to an integer value.

Listing 17-11. Formatting an Integer Value in the main.go File in the usingstrings Folder

```
package main

import "fmt"

func Printfln(template string, values ...interface{}) {
    fmt.Printf(template + "\n", values...)
}
```

```
func main() {

    number := 250

    Printfln("Binary: %b", number)
    Printfln("Decimal: %d", number)
    Printfln("Octal: %o, %O", number, number)
    Printfln("Hexadecimal: %x, %X", number, number)
}
```

Compile and execute the project, and you will receive the following output:

```
Binary: 11111010
Decimal: 250
Octal: 372, 0o372
Hexadecimal: fa, FA
```

Using the Floating-Point Formatting Verbs

Table 17-7 describes the formatting verbs for floating-point values, which can be applied to both float32 and float64 values.

Table 17-7. *The Formatting Verbs for Floating-Point Values*

Verb	Description
%b	This verb displays a floating-point value with an exponent and without a decimal place.
%e, %E	These verbs display a floating-point value with an exponent and a decimal place. The %e uses a lowercase exponent indicator, while %E uses an uppercase indicator.
%f, %F	These verbs display a floating-point value with a decimal place but no exponent. The %f and %F verbs produce the same output.
%g	This verb adapts to the value it displays. The %e format is used for values with large exponents, and the %f format is used otherwise. This is the default format, applied when the %v verb is used.
%G	This verb adapts to the value it displays. The %E format is used for values with large exponents, and the %f format is used otherwise.
%x, %X	These verbs display a floating-point value in hexadecimal notation, with lowercase (%x) or uppercase (%X) letters.

Listing 17-12 applies the verbs described in Table 17-7 to a floating-point value.

Listing 17-12. Formatting a Floating-Point Value in the main.go File in the usingstrings Folder

```
package main

import "fmt"

func Printfln(template string, values ...interface{}) {
    fmt.Printf(template + "\n", values...)
}

func main() {
    number := 279.00
    Printfln("Decimalless with exponent: %b", number)
    Printfln("Decimal with exponent: %e", number)
    Printfln("Decimal without exponent: %f", number)
    Printfln("Hexadecimal: %x, %X", number, number)
}
```

Compile and execute the project, and you will see the following output:

```
Decimalless with exponent: 4908219906392064p-44
Decimal with exponent: 2.790000e+02
Decimal without exponent: 279.000000
Hexadecimal: 0x1.17p+08, 0X1.17P+08
```

The format for floating-point values can be controlled by modifying the verb to specify width (the number of characters used to express the value) and precision (the number of digits after the decimal place), as shown in Listing 17-13.

Listing 17-13. Controlling Formatting in the main.go File in the usingstrings Folder

```
package main

import "fmt"

func Printfln(template string, values ...interface{}) {
    fmt.Printf(template + "\n", values...)
}

func main() {
    number := 279.00
    Printfln("Decimal without exponent: >>%8.2f<<", number)
}
```

The width is specified after the percent sign, followed by a period, followed by the precision, and then the rest of the verb. In Listing 17-13, the width is 8 characters, and the precision is two characters, which produces the following output when the code is compiled and executed:

```
Decimal without exponent: >>  279.00<<
```

I added chevrons around the formatted value in Listing 17-13 to demonstrate that spaces are used for padding when the specified with is greater than the number of characters required to display the value.

The width can be omitted if you are only interested in precision, as shown in Listing 17-14.

Listing 17-14. Specifying Precision in the main.go File in the usingstrings Folder

```
package main

import "fmt"

func Printfln(template string, values ...interface{}) {
    fmt.Printf(template + "\n", values...)
}

func main() {
    number := 279.00
    Printfln("Decimal without exponent: >>%.2f<<", number)
}
```

The width value is omitted, but the period is still required. The format specified in Listing 17-7 produces the following output when compiled and executed:

```
Decimal without exponent: >>279.00<<
```

The output from the verbs in Table 17-7 can be altered using the modifiers described in Table 17-8.

Table 17-8. *The Formatting Verb Modifiers*

Modifier	Description
+	This modifier (the plus sign) always prints a sign, positive or negative, for numeric values.
0	This modifier uses zeros, rather than spaces, as padding when the width is greater than the number of characters required to display the value.
-	This modifier (the subtracts symbol) adds padding to the right of the number, rather than the left.

Listing 17-15 applies the modifiers to alter the formatting of an integer value.

Listing 17-15. Modifying Formats in the main.go File in the usingstrings Folder

```
package main

import "fmt"

func Printfln(template string, values ...interface{}) {
    fmt.Printf(template + "\n", values...)
}

func main() {
    number := 279.00
```

```
    Printfln("Sign: >>%+.2f<<", number)
    Printfln("Zeros for Padding: >>%010.2f<<", number)
    Printfln("Right Padding: >>%-8.2f<<", number)
}
```

Compile and execute the project, and you will see the effect of the modifiers on the formatted output:

```
Sign: >>+279.00<<
Zeros for Padding: >>0000279.00<<
Right Padding: >>279.00  <<
```

Using the String and Character Formatting Verbs

Table 17-9 describes the formatting verbs for strings and runes.

Table 17-9. *The Formatting Verbs for Strings and Runes*

Verb	Description
%s	This verb displays a string. This is the default format, applied when the %v verb is used.
%c	This verb displays a character. Care must be taken to avoid slicing strings into individual bytes, as explained in the text after the table.
%U	This verb displays a character in the Unicode format so that the output begins with U+ followed by a hexadecimal character code.

Strings are easy to format, but care must be taken when formatting individual characters. As I explained in Chapter 7, some characters are represented using multiple bytes, and you must ensure that you don't try to format only some of the character's bytes. Listing 17-16 demonstrates the use of the verbs described in Table 17-9.

Listing 17-16. Formatting Strings and Characters in the main.go File in the usingstrings Folder

```go
package main

import "fmt"

func Printfln(template string, values ...interface{}) {
    fmt.Printf(template + "\n", values...)
}

func main() {
    name := "Kayak"
    Printfln("String: %s", name)
    Printfln("Character: %c", []rune(name)[0])
    Printfln("Unicode: %U", []rune(name)[0])
}
```

Compile and execute the project, and you will see the following formatted output:

```
String: Kayak
Character: K
Unicode: U+004B
```

Using the Boolean Formatting Verb

Table 17-10 describes the verb that is used to format bool values. This is the default bool format, which means that it will be used by the %v verb.

Table 17-10. *The bool Formatting Verb*

Verb	Description
%t	This verb formats bool values and displays true or false.

Listing 17-17 shows the use of the bool formatting verb.

Listing 17-17. Formatting bool Values in the main.go File in the usingstrings Folder

```
package main

import "fmt"

func Printfln(template string, values ...interface{}) {
    fmt.Printf(template + "\n", values...)
}

func main() {
    name := "Kayak"
    Printfln("Bool: %t", len(name) > 1)
    Printfln("Bool: %t", len(name) > 100)
}
```

Compile and execute the project, and you will see the formatted output:

```
Bool: true
Bool: false
```

Using the Pointer Formatting Verb

The verb described in Table 17-11 is applied to pointers.

Table 17-11. *The Pointer Formatting Verb*

Verb	Description
%p	This verb displays a hexadecimal representation of the pointer's storage location.

Listing 17-18 demonstrates the use of the pointer verb.

Listing 17-18. Formatting a Pointer in the main.go File in the usingstrings Folder

```
package main

import "fmt"

func Printfln(template string, values ...interface{}) {
    fmt.Printf(template + "\n", values...)
}

func main() {
    name := "Kayak"
    Printfln("Pointer: %p", &name)
}
```

Compile and execute the code, and you will see output similar to the following, although you may see a different location:

```
Pointer: 0xc00004a240
```

Scanning Strings

The fmt package provides functions for scanning strings, which is the process of parsing strings that contain values separated by spaces. Table 17-12 describes these functions, some of which are used with features described in later chapters.

Table 17-12. *The fmt Functions for Scanning Strings*

Name	Description
Scan(...vals)	This function reads text from the standard in and stores the space-separated values into specified arguments. Newlines are treated as spaces, and the function reads until it has received values for all of its arguments. The result is the number of values that have been read and an error that describes any problems.
Scanln(...vals)	This function works in the same way as Scan but stops reading when it encounters a newline character.
Scanf(template, ...vals)	This function works in the same way as Scan but uses a template string to select the values from the input it receives.
Fscan(reader, ...vals)	This function reads space-separated values from the specified reader, which is described in Chapter 20. Newlines are treated as spaces, and the function returns the number of values that have been read and an error that describes any problems.

(continued)

461

Table 17-12. (*continued*)

Name	Description
Fscanln(reader, ...vals)	This function works in the same way as Fscan but stops reading when it encounters a newline character.
Fscanf(reader, template, ...vals)	This function works in the same way as Fscan but uses a template to select the values from the input it receives.
Sscan(str, ...vals)	This function scans the specified string for space-separated values, which are assigned to the remaining arguments. The result is the number of values scanned and an error that describes any problems.
Sscanf(str, template, ...vals)	This function works in the same way as Sscan but uses a template to select values from the string.
Sscanln(str, template, ...vals)	This function works in the same way as Sscanf but stops scanning the string as soon as a newline character is encountered.

The decision about which scanning function to use is driven by the source of the string to scan, how newlines are handled, and whether a template should be used. Listing 17-19 shows the basic use of the Scan function, which is a good place to get started.

Listing 17-19. Scanning a String in the main.go File in the usingstrings Folder

```
package main

import "fmt"

func Printfln(template string, values ...interface{}) {
    fmt.Printf(template + "\n", values...)
}

func main() {

    var name string
    var category string
    var price float64

    fmt.Print("Enter text to scan: ")
    n, err := fmt.Scan(&name, &category, &price)

    if (err == nil) {
        Printfln("Scanned %v values", n)
        Printfln("Name: %v, Category: %v, Price: %.2f", name, category, price)
    } else {
        Printfln("Error: %v", err.Error())
    }
}
```

The Scan function reads a string from the standard input and scans it for values separated by spaces. The values parsed from the string are assigned to the parameters in the order in which they are defined. So that the Scan function can assign values, its parameters are pointers.

In Listing 17-19, I define name, category, and price variables and use them as the arguments to the Scan function:

```
...
n, err := fmt.Scan(&name, &category, &price)
...
```

When it is invoked, the Scan function will read a string, extract three space-separated values, and assign them to the variables. Compile and execute the project, and you will be prompted to enter text, like this:

```
...
Enter text to scan:
...
```

Enter Kayak Watersports 279, meaning the word Kayak, followed by a space, followed by the word Watersports, followed by a space, followed by the number 279. Press Enter and the string will be scanned, producing the following output:

```
Scanned 3 values
Name: Kayak, Category: Watersports, Price: 279.00
```

The Scan function has to convert the substrings it receives into Go values and will report an error if the string cannot be processed. Run the code again, but enter Kayak Watersports Zero, and you will receive the following error:

```
Error: strconv.ParseFloat: parsing "": invalid syntax
```

The string Zero cannot be converted into a Go float64 value, which is the type of the Price parameter.

SCANNING INTO A SLICE

If you need to scan a series of values with the same type, the natural approach is to scan into a slice or an array, like this:

```
...
vals := make([]string, 3)
fmt.Print("Enter text to scan: ")
fmt.Scan(vals...)
Println("Name: %v", vals)
...
```

This code won't compile because the string slice can't be properly decomposed for use with the variadic parameter. An additional step is required, as follows:

```
...
vals := make([]string, 3)
ivals := make([]interface{}, 3)
for i := 0; i < len(vals); i++ {
    ivals[i] = &vals[i]
}
```

```
fmt.Print("Enter text to scan: ")
fmt.Scan(ivals...)
Printfln("Name: %v", vals)
...
```

This is an awkward process, but it can be wrapped up in a utility function so that you don't have to create a populate the interface slice each time.

Dealing with Newline Characters

By default, scanning treats newlines in the same way as spaces, acting as separators between values. To see this behavior, execute the project and, when prompted for input, enter Kayak, followed by a space, followed by Watersports, followed the Enter key, 279, and then the Enter key again. This sequence will produce the following output:

```
Scanned 3 values
Name: Kayak, Category: Watersports, Price: 279.00
```

The Scan function doesn't stop looking for values until after it has received the number it expects and the first press of the Enter key is treated as a separator and not the termination of the input. The functions whose name ends with ln in Table 17-12, such as Scanln, change this behavior. Listing 17-20 uses the Scanln function.

Listing 17-20. Using the Scanln Function in the main.go File in the usingstrings Folder

```
package main

import "fmt"

func Printfln(template string, values ...interface{}) {
    fmt.Printf(template + "\n", values...)
}

func main() {

    var name string
    var category string
    var price float64

    fmt.Print("Enter text to scan: ")
    n, err := fmt.Scanln(&name, &category, &price)

    if (err == nil) {
        Printfln("Scanned %v values", n)
        Printfln("Name: %v, Category: %v, Price: %.2f", name, category, price)
    } else {
        Printfln("Error: %v", err.Error())
    }
}
```

Compile and execute the project and repeat the entry sequence. When you first press the Enter key, the newline will terminate the input, leaving the Scanln function with fewer values than it requires, producing the following output:

```
Error: unexpected newline
```

Using a Different String Source

The functions described in Table 17-12 scan strings from three sources: the standard input, a reader (described in Chapter 20), and a value provided as an argument. Providing a string as the argument is the most flexible because it means the string can arise from anywhere. In Listing 17-21, I have replaced the Scanln function with Sscan, which allows me to scan a string variable.

Listing 17-21. Scanning a Variable in the main.go File in the usingstrings Folder

```
package main

import "fmt"

func Printfln(template string, values ...interface{}) {
    fmt.Printf(template + "\n", values...)
}

func main() {

    var name string
    var category string
    var price float64

    source := "Lifejacket Watersports 48.95"
    n, err := fmt.Sscan(source, &name, &category, &price)

    if (err == nil) {
        Printfln("Scanned %v values", n)
        Printfln("Name: %v, Category: %v, Price: %.2f", name, category, price)
    } else {
        Printfln("Error: %v", err.Error())
    }
}
```

The first argument to the Sscan function is the string to scan, but in all other respects, the scanning process is the same. Compile and execute the project, and you will see the following output:

```
Scanned 3 values
Name: Lifejacket, Category: Watersports, Price: 48.95
```

Using a Scanning Template

A template can be used to scan for values in a string that contains characters that are not required, as shown in Listing 17-22.

Listing 17-22. Using a Template in the main.go File in the usingstrings Folder

```
package main

import "fmt"

func Printfln(template string, values ...interface{}) {
    fmt.Printf(template + "\n", values...)
}

func main() {

    var name string
    var category string
    var price float64

    source := "Product Lifejacket Watersports 48.95"
    template := "Product %s %s %f"
    n, err := fmt.Sscanf(source, template, &name, &category, &price)

    if (err == nil) {
        Printfln("Scanned %v values", n)
        Printfln("Name: %v, Category: %v, Price: %.2f", name, category, price)
    } else {
        Printfln("Error: %v", err.Error())
    }
}
```

The template used in Listing 17-22 ignores the term Product, skipping that part of the string and allowing the scanning to begin with the next term. Compile and execute the project, and you will see the following output:

```
Scanned 3 values
Name: Lifejacket, Category: Watersports, Price: 48.95
```

Scanning with a template isn't as flexible as using a regular expression because the scanned string can only contain space-separated values. But using a template can still be useful if you only want some of the values in a string and you don't want to define complex matching rules.

Summary

In this chapter, I described the features in the standard library for formatting and scanning strings, both of which are provided by the fmt package. In the next chapter, I describe the features the standard library provides for math functions and sorting slices.

CHAPTER 18

Math Functions and Data Sorting

In this chapter, I describe two sets of features. First, I describe the support for performing common mathematical tasks, including generating random numbers. Second, I describe the features for sorting the elements in a slice so they are in order. Table 18-1 puts the math and sorting features in context.

Table 18-1. Putting Math Functions and Sorting Data in Context

Question	Answer
What are they?	The math functions allow common calculations to be performed. Random numbers are numbers generated in a sequence that is difficult to predict. Sorting is the process of placing a sequence of values in a predetermined order.
Why are they useful?	These are features that are used throughout development.
How are they used?	These features are provided in the math, math/rand, and sort packages.
Are there any pitfalls or limitations?	Unless initialized with a seed value, the numbers produced by the math/rand package are not random.
Are there any alternatives?	You could implement both sets of features from scratch, although these packages are provided so that this is not required.

Table 18-2 summarizes the chapter.

Table 18-2. Chapter Summary

Problem	Solution	Listing
Perform common calculations	Use the functions defined in the math package	5
Generate random numbers	Use the functions in the math/rand package, taking care to provide a seed value	6–9
Shuffle the elements in a slice	Use the Shuffle function	10
Sort the elements in a slice	Use the functions defined in the sort package	11, 12, 15–20
Locate an element in a sorted slice	Use the Search* functions	13, 14

© Adam Freeman 2022
A. Freeman, *Pro Go*, https://doi.org/10.1007/978-1-4842-7355-5_18

Preparing for This Chapter

To prepare for this chapter, open a new command prompt, navigate to a convenient location, and create a directory named mathandsorting. Run the command shown in Listing 18-1 in the mathandsorting folder to create a module file.

■ **Tip** You can download the example project for this chapter—and for all the other chapters in this book—from https://github.com/apress/pro-go. See Chapter 2 for how to get help if you have problems running the examples.

Listing 18-1. Initializing the Module

```
go mod init mathandsorting
```

Add a file named printer.go to the mathandsorting folder with the content shown in Listing 18-2.

Listing 18-2. The Contents of the printer.go File in the mathandsorting Folder

```
package main

import "fmt"

func Printfln(template string, values ...interface{}) {
    fmt.Printf(template + "\n", values...)
}
```

Add a file named main.go to the mathandsorting folder, with the contents shown in Listing 18-3.

Listing 18-3. The Contents of the main.go File in the mathandsorting Folder

```
package main

func main() {

    Printfln("Hello, Math and Sorting")
}
```

Use the command prompt to run the command shown in Listing 18-4 in the mathandsorting folder.

Listing 18-4. Running the Example Project

```
go run .
```

The code will be compiled and executed, producing the following output:

```
Hello, Math and Sorting
```

Working with Numbers

As I explained in Chapter 4, the Go language supports a set of arithmetic operators that can be applied to numeric values, allowing basic tasks such as addition and multiplication to be performed. For more advanced operations, the Go standard library includes the math package, which provides an extensive set of functions. The functions that are most widely used for a typical project are described in Table 18-3. See the package documentation at https://golang.org/pkg/math for the complete set of functions, including support for more specific areas, such as trigonometry.

Table 18-3. *Useful Functions from the math Package*

Name	Description
Abs(val)	This function returns the absolute value of a float64 value, meaning the distance from zero without considering direction.
Ceil(val)	This function returns the smallest integer that is equal to or greater than the specified float64 value. The result is also a float64 value, even though it represents an integer number.
Copysign(x, y)	This function returns a float64 value, which is the absolute value of x with the sign of y.
Floor(val)	This function returns the largest integer that is smaller or equal to the specified float64 value. The result is also a float64 value, even though it represents an integer number.
Max(x, y)	This function returns whichever of the specified float64 value is the largest.
Min(x, y)	This function returns whichever of the specified float64 value is smallest.
Mod(x, y)	This function returns the remainder of x/y.
Pow(x, y)	This function returns x raised to the exponent y.
Round(val)	This function rounds the specified value to the nearest integer, rounding half values up. The result is a float64 value, even though it represents an integer.
RoundToEven(val)	This function rounds the specified value to the nearest integer, rounding half values to the nearest even number. The result is a float64 value, even though it represents an integer.

These functions all operate on float64 values and produce float64 results, which means you must explicitly convert to and from other types. Listing 18-5 demonstrates the use of the functions described in Table 18-3.

Listing 18-5. Using Functions from the math Package in the main.go File in the mathandsorting Folder

```
package main

import "math"

func main() {

    val1 := 279.00
    val2 := 48.95

    Printfln("Abs: %v", math.Abs(val1))
    Printfln("Ceil: %v", math.Ceil(val2))
    Printfln("Copysign: %v", math.Copysign(val1, -5))
    Printfln("Floor: %v", math.Floor(val2))
    Printfln("Max: %v", math.Max(val1, val2))
    Printfln("Min: %v", math.Min(val1, val2))
    Printfln("Mod: %v", math.Mod(val1, val2))
    Printfln("Pow: %v", math.Pow(val1, 2))
    Printfln("Round: %v", math.Round(val2))
    Printfln("RoundToEven: %v", math.RoundToEven(val2))
}
```

Compile and execute the project, and you will see the following output:

```
Abs: 279
Ceil: 49
Copysign: -279
Floor: 48
Max: 279
Min: 48.95
Mod: 34.249999999999986
Pow: 77841
Round: 49
RoundToEven: 49
```

The math package also provides a set of constants for the limits of the numeric data types, as described in Table 18-4.

Table 18-4. *The Limit Constants*

Name	Description
MaxInt8 MinInt8	These constants represent the largest and smallest values that can be stored using an int8.
MaxInt16 MinInt16	These constants represent the largest and smallest values that can be stored using an int16.
MaxInt32 MinInt32	These constants represent the largest and smallest values that can be stored using an int32.

(Continued)

Table 18-4. (*Continued*)

Name	Description
MaxInt64 MinInt64	These constants represent the largest and smallest values that can be stored using an int64.
MaxUint8	This constant represents the largest value that can be represented using a uint8. The smallest value is zero.
MaxUint16	This constant represents the largest value that can be represented using a uint16. The smallest value is zero.
MaxUint32	This constant represents the largest value that can be represented using a uint32. The smallest value is zero.
MaxUint64	This constant represents the largest value that can be represented using a uint64. The smallest value is zero.
MaxFloat32 MaxFloat64	These constants represent the largest values that can be represented using float32 and float64 values.
SmallestNonzeroFloat32 SmallestNonzeroFloat32	These constants represent the smallest nonzero values that can be represented using float32 and float64 values.

Generating Random Numbers

The math/rand package provides support for generating random numbers. The most useful functions are described in Table 18-5. (Although I use the term *random* in this section, the numbers produced by the math/rand package are pseudorandom, which means they should not be used where randomness is critical, such as for generating cryptographic keys.)

Table 18-5. *Useful math/rand Functions*

Name	Description
Seed(s)	This function sets the seed value using the specified int64 value.
Float32()	This function generates a random float32 value between 0 and 1.
Float64()	This function generates a random float64 value between 0 and 1.
Int()	This function generates a random int value.
Intn(max)	This function generates a random int smaller than a specified value, as described after the table.
UInt32()	This function generates a random uint32 value.
UInt64()	This function generates a random uint64 value.
Shuffle(count, func)	This function is used to randomize the order of elements, as described after the table.

An oddity of the math/rand package is that it returns a sequence of predictable values by default, as shown in Listing 18-6.

Listing 18-6. Generating Predictable Values in the main.go File in the mathandsorting Folder

```
package main

import "math/rand"

func main() {

    for i := 0; i < 5; i++ {
        Printfln("Value %v : %v", i, rand.Int())
    }
}
```

This example calls the Int function and writes out the value. Compile and execute the code, and you will see the following output:

```
Value 0 : 5577006791947779410
Value 1 : 8674665223082153551
Value 2 : 6129484611666145821
Value 3 : 4037200794235010051
Value 4 : 3916589616287113937
```

The code in Listing 18-6 will always produce the same set of numbers, which happens because the initial seed value is always the same. To avoid generating the same sequence of numbers, the Seed function must be called with a value that isn't fixed, as shown in Listing 18-7.

Listing 18-7. Setting a Seed Value in the main.go File in the mathandsorting Folder

```
package main

import (
    "math/rand"
    "time"
)

func main() {
    rand.Seed(time.Now().UnixNano())
    for i := 0; i < 5; i++ {
        Printfln("Value %v : %v", i, rand.Int())
    }
}
```

The convention is to use the current time as the seed value, which is done by invoking the Now function provided by the time package and calling the UnixNano method on the result, which provides an int64 value that can be passed to the Seed function. (I describe the time package in Chapter 19.) Compile and execute the project, and you will see a series of numbers that change each time the program is executed. Here is the output that I received:

```
Value 0 : 8113726196145714527
Value 1 : 3479565125812279859
Value 2 : 8074476402089812953
Value 3 : 3916870404047362448
Value 4 : 8226545715271170755
```

Generating a Random Number Within a Specific Range

The Intn function can be used to generate a number with a specified maximum value, as shown in Listing 18-8.

Listing 18-8. Specifying a Maximum Value in the main.go File in the mathandsorting Folder

```go
package main

import (
    "math/rand"
    "time"
)

func main() {
    rand.Seed(time.Now().UnixNano())
    for i := 0; i < 5; i++ {
        Printfln("Value %v : %v", i, rand.Intn(10))
    }
}
```

The statement specifies that the random numbers should all be less than 10. Compile and execute the code, and you will see output similar to the following but with different random values:

```
Value 0 : 7
Value 1 : 5
Value 2 : 4
Value 3 : 0
Value 4 : 7
```

There is no function to specify a minimum value, but it is easy to shift the values generated by the Intn function into a specific range, as shown in Listing 18-9.

Listing 18-9. Specifying a Lower Bound in the main.go File in the mathandsorting Folder

```go
package main

import (
    "math/rand"
    "time"
)
```

```
func IntRange(min, max int) int {
    return rand.Intn(max - min) + min
}

func main() {

    rand.Seed(time.Now().UnixNano())
    for i := 0; i < 5; i++ {
        Printfln("Value %v : %v", i, IntRange(10, 20))
    }
}
```

The IntRange function returns a random number in a specific range. Compile and execute the project, and you will receive a sequence of numbers between 10 and 19, similar to the following:

```
Value 0 : 10
Value 1 : 19
Value 2 : 11
Value 3 : 10
Value 4 : 17
```

Shuffling Elements

The Shuffle function is used to randomly reorder elements, which it does with the use of a custom function, as shown in Listing 18-10.

Listing 18-10. Shuffling Elements in the main.go File in the mathandsorting Folder

```
package main

import (
    "math/rand"
    "time"
)

var names = []string { "Alice", "Bob", "Charlie", "Dora", "Edith"}

func main() {
    rand.Seed(time.Now().UnixNano())

    rand.Shuffle(len(names), func (first, second int) {
        names[first], names[second] = names[second], names[first]
    })

    for i, name := range names {
        Printfln("Index %v: Name: %v", i, name)
    }
}
```

The arguments to the Shuffle function are the number of elements and a function that will swap two elements, which are identified by index. The function is called to swap elements randomly. In Listing 18-10, the anonymous function switches two elements in the names slice, which means that the use of the Shuffle function has the effect of shuffling the order of the names values. Compile and execute the project, and the output will show the shuffled order of elements in the names slice, similar to the following:

```
Index 0: Name: Edith
Index 1: Name: Dora
Index 2: Name: Charlie
Index 3: Name: Alice
Index 4: Name: Bob
```

Sorting Data

The previous example showed how to shuffle the elements in a slice, but a more common requirement is to arrange elements into a more predictable sequence, which is the responsibility of the functions provided by the sort package. In the sections that follow, I describe the built-in sorting features provided by the package and demonstrate their use.

Sorting Number and String Slices

The functions described in Table 18-6 are used to sort slices containing int, float64, or string values.

Table 18-6. *The Basic Functions for Sorting*

Name	Description
Float64s(slice)	This function sorts a slice of float64 values. The elements are sorted in place.
Float64sAreSorted(slice)	This function returns true if the elements in the specified float64 slice are in order.
Ints(slice)	This function sorts a slice of int values. The elements are sorted in place.
IntsAreSorted(slice)	This function returns true if the elements in the specified int slice are in order.
Strings(slice)	This function sorts a slice of string values. The elements are sorted in place.
StringsAreSorted(slice)	This function returns true if the elements in the specified string slice are in order.

Each of the data types has its own set of functions that sort the data or determine if it is already sorted, as shown in Listing 18-11.

Listing 18-11. Sorting Slices in the main.go File in the mathandsorting Folder

```
package main

import (
    //"math/rand"
    //"time"
    "sort"
)

func main() {

    ints := []int { 9, 4, 2, -1, 10}
    Printfln("Ints: %v", ints)
    sort.Ints(ints)
    Printfln("Ints Sorted: %v", ints)

    floats := []float64 { 279, 48.95, 19.50 }
    Printfln("Floats: %v", floats)
    sort.Float64s(floats)
    Printfln("Floats Sorted: %v", floats)

    strings := []string { "Kayak", "Lifejacket", "Stadium" }
    Printfln("Strings: %v", strings)
    if (!sort.StringsAreSorted(strings)) {
        sort.Strings(strings)
        Printfln("Strings Sorted: %v", strings)
    } else {
        Printfln("Strings Already Sorted: %v", strings)
    }
}
```

This example sorts slices containing int and float64 values. There is also a string slice, which is tested with the StringsAreSorted function to avoid sorting data that is already in order. Compile and execute the project, and you will receive the following output:

```
Ints: [9 4 2 -1 10]
Ints Sorted: [-1 2 4 9 10]
Floats: [279 48.95 19.5]
Floats Sorted: [19.5 48.95 279]
Strings: [Kayak Lifejacket Stadium]
Strings Already Sorted: [Kayak Lifejacket Stadium]
```

Note that the functions in Listing 18-11 sort the elements in place, rather than creating a new slice. If you want to create a new, sorted slice, then you must use the built-in make and copy functions, as shown in Listing 18-12. These functions were introduced in Chapter 7.

Listing 18-12. Creating a Sorted Copy of a Slice in the main.go File in the mathandsorting Folder

```
package main

import (
    "sort"
)

func main() {

    ints := []int { 9, 4, 2, -1, 10}

    sortedInts := make([]int, len(ints))
    copy(sortedInts, ints)
    sort.Ints(sortedInts)
    Printfln("Ints: %v", ints)
    Printfln("Ints Sorted: %v", sortedInts)
}
```

Compile and execute the project, and you will receive the following output:

```
Ints: [9 4 2 -1 10]
Ints Sorted: [-1 2 4 9 10]
```

Searching Sorted Data

The sort package defines the functions described in Table 18-7 for searching sorted data for a specific value.

Table 18-7. The Functions for Searching Sorted Data

Name	Description
SearchInts(slice, val)	This function searches the sorted slice for the specified int value. The result is the index of the specified value or, if the value is not found, the index at which the value can be inserted while maintaining the sorted order.
SearchFloat64s(slice, val)	This function searches the sorted slice for the specified float64 value. The result is the index of the specified value or, if the value is not found, the index at which the value can be inserted while maintaining the sorted order.
SearchStrings(slice, val)	This function searches the sorted slice for the specified string value. The result is the index of the specified value or, if the value is not found, the index at which the value can be inserted while maintaining the sorted order.
Search(count, testFunc)	This function invokes the test function for the specified number of elements. The result is the index for which the function returns true. If there is no match, then the result is the index at which the specified value can be inserted to maintain the sorted order.

477

The functions described in Table 18-7 are slightly awkward. When a value is located, the functions return its position in the slice. But unusually, if the value is not found, then the result is the position it can be inserted while maintaining the sort order, as shown in Listing 18-13.

Listing 18-13. Searching Sorted Data in the main.go File in the mathandsorting Folder

```
package main

import (
    "sort"
)

func main() {

    ints := []int { 9, 4, 2, -1, 10}

    sortedInts := make([]int, len(ints))
    copy(sortedInts, ints)
    sort.Ints(sortedInts)
    Printfln("Ints: %v", ints)
    Printfln("Ints Sorted: %v", sortedInts)

    indexOf4:= sort.SearchInts(sortedInts, 4)
    indexOf3 := sort.SearchInts(sortedInts, 3)
    Printfln("Index of 4: %v", indexOf4)
    Printfln("Index of 3: %v", indexOf3)
}
```

Compile and execute the code, and you will see that searching for a value that is in the slice produces the same result as a search for a nonexistent value:

```
Ints: [9 4 2 -1 10]
Ints Sorted: [-1 2 4 9 10]
Index of 4: 2
Index of 3: 2
```

These functions require an additional test to see if the value at the location returned by these functions is the one that has been searched for, as shown in Listing 18-14.

Listing 18-14. Disambiguating Search Results in the main.go File in the mathandsorting Folder

```
package main

import (
    "sort"
)

func main() {

    ints := []int { 9, 4, 2, -1, 10}
```

```
    sortedInts := make([]int, len(ints))
    copy(sortedInts, ints)
    sort.Ints(sortedInts)
    Printfln("Ints: %v", ints)
    Printfln("Ints Sorted: %v", sortedInts)

    indexOf4:= sort.SearchInts(sortedInts, 4)
    indexOf3 := sort.SearchInts(sortedInts, 3)
    Printfln("Index of 4: %v (present: %v)", indexOf4, sortedInts[indexOf4] == 4)
    Printfln("Index of 3: %v (present: %v)", indexOf3, sortedInts[indexOf3] == 3)
}
```

Compile and execute the project, and you will receive the following results:

```
Ints: [9 4 2 -1 10]
Ints Sorted: [-1 2 4 9 10]
Index of 4: 2 (present: true)
Index of 3: 2 (present: false)
```

Sorting Custom Data Types

To sort custom data types, the sort package defines an interface confusingly named Interface, which specifies the methods described in Table 18-8.

Table 18-8. *The Methods Defined by the sort.Interface Interface*

Name	Description
Len()	This method returns the number of items that will be sorted.
Less(i, j)	This method returns true if the element at index i should appear in the sorted sequence before the element j. If Less(i,j) and Less(j, i) are both false, then the elements are considered equal.
Swap(i, j)	This method swaps the elements at the specified indices.

When a type defines the methods described in Table 18-8, it can be sorted using the functions described in Table 18-9, which are defined by the sort package.

Table 18-9. *The Functions for Sorting Types That Implement Interface*

Name	Description
Sort(data)	This function uses the methods described in Table 18-8 to sort the specified data.
Stable(data)	This function uses the methods described in Table 18-8 to sort the specified data without changing the order of elements of equal value.
IsSorted(data)	This function returns true if the data is in sorted order.
Reverse(data)	This function reverses the order of the data.

The methods defined in Table 18-8 are applied to the collection of data items to be sorted, which means the introduction of a type alias and functions that perform conversions to call the functions defined in Table 18-9. To demonstrate, add a file named productsort.go to the mathandsorting folder, with the code shown in Listing 18-15.

Listing 18-15. The Contents of the productsort.go File in the mathandsorting Folder

```
package main

import "sort"

type Product struct {
    Name string
    Price float64
}

type ProductSlice []Product

func ProductSlices(p []Product) {
    sort.Sort(ProductSlice(p))
}

func ProductSlicesAreSorted(p []Product) {
    sort.IsSorted(ProductSlice(p))
}

func (products ProductSlice) Len() int {
    return len(products)
}

func (products ProductSlice) Less(i, j int) bool {
    return products[i].Price < products[j].Price
}

func (products ProductSlice) Swap(i, j int) {
    products[i], products[j] = products[j], products[i]
}
```

The ProductSlice type is an alias for a Product slice and is the type for which the interface methods have been implemented. In addition to the methods, I have a ProductSlices function, which accepts a Product slice, converts it to the ProductSlice type, and passes it as an argument to the Sort function. There is also a ProductSlicesAreSorted function, which calls the IsSorted function. The names of this function follow the convention established by the sort package of following the alias type name with the letter s. Listing 18-16 uses these functions to sort a slice of Product values.

Listing 18-16. Sorting a Slice in the main.go File in the mathandsorting Folder

```
package main

import (
    //"sort"
)
```

```
func main() {

    products := []Product {
        { "Kayak", 279} ,
        { "Lifejacket", 49.95 },
        { "Soccer Ball",  19.50 },
    }

    ProductSlices(products)

    for _, p := range products {
        Printfln("Name: %v, Price: %.2f", p.Name, p.Price)
    }
}
```

Compile and execute the project, and you will see the output shows the Product values sorted in ascending order of the Price field:

```
Name: Soccer Ball, Price: 19.50
Name: Lifejacket, Price: 49.95
Name: Kayak, Price: 279.00
```

Sorting Using Different Fields

Type composition can be used to support sorting the same struct type using different fields, as shown in Listing 18-17.

Listing 18-17. Sorting Different Fields in the productsort.go File in the mathandsorting Folder

```
package main

import "sort"

type Product struct {
    Name string
    Price float64
}

type ProductSlice []Product

func ProductSlices(p []Product) {
    sort.Sort(ProductSlice(p))
}

func ProductSlicesAreSorted(p []Product) {
    sort.IsSorted(ProductSlice(p))
}
```

```
func (products ProductSlice) Len() int {
    return len(products)
}

func (products ProductSlice) Less(i, j int) bool {
    return products[i].Price < products[j].Price
}

func (products ProductSlice) Swap(i, j int) {
    products[i], products[j] = products[j], products[i]
}

type ProductSliceName struct { ProductSlice }

func ProductSlicesByName(p []Product) {
    sort.Sort(ProductSliceName{ p })
}

func (p ProductSliceName) Less(i, j int) bool {
    return p.ProductSlice[i].Name < p.ProductSlice[j].Name
}
```

A struct type is defined for each struct field for which sorting is required, with an embedded ProductSlice field like this:

```
...
type ProductSliceName struct { ProductSlice }
...
```

The type composition feature means that the methods defined for the ProductSlice type are promoted to the enclosing type. A new Less method is defined for enclosing type, which will be used to sort the data using a different field, like this:

```
...
func (p ProductSliceName) Less(i, j int) bool {
    return p.ProductSlice[i].Name <= p.ProductSlice[j].Name
}
...
```

The final step is to define a function that will perform a conversion from a Product slice to the new type and invoke the Sort function:

```
...
func ProductSlicesByName(p []Product) {
    sort.Sort(ProductSliceName{ p })
}
...
```

The result of the additions in Listing 18-17 is that slices of Product values can be sorted by the values of their Name fields, as shown in Listing 18-18.

Listing 18-18. Sorting by Additional Fields in the main.go File in the mathandsorting Folder

```
package main

import (
    //"sort"
)

func main() {

    products := []Product {
        { "Kayak", 279} ,
        { "Lifejacket", 49.95 },
        { "Soccer Ball",  19.50 },
    }
    ProductSlicesByName(products)

    for _, p := range products {
        Printfln("Name: %v, Price: %.2f", p.Name, p.Price)
    }
}
```

Compile and execute the project, and you will see the Product values sorted by their Name fields, as follows:

```
Name: Kayak, Price: 279.00
Name: Lifejacket, Price: 49.95
Name: Soccer Ball, Price: 19.50
```

Specifying the Comparison Function

An alternative approach is to specify the expression used to compare elements outside of the sort function, as shown in Listing 18-19.

Listing 18-19. Using an External Comparison in the productsort.go File in the mathandsorting Folder

```
package main

import "sort"

type Product struct {
    Name string
    Price float64
}

type ProductSlice []Product

// ...types and functions omitted for brevity...

type ProductComparison func(p1, p2 Product) bool
```

```
type ProductSliceFlex struct {
    ProductSlice
    ProductComparison
}

func (flex ProductSliceFlex) Less(i, j int) bool {
    return flex.ProductComparison(flex.ProductSlice[i], flex.ProductSlice[j])
}

func SortWith(prods []Product, f ProductComparison) {
    sort.Sort(ProductSliceFlex{ prods, f})
}
```

A new type named ProductSliceFlex is created that combines the data and the comparison function, which will allow this approach to fit within the structure of the functions defined by the sort package. A Less method is defined for the ProductSliceFlex type that invokes the comparison function. The final piece of the puzzle is the SortWith function, which combines the data and the function into a ProductSliceFlex value and passes it to the sort.Sort function. Listing 18-20 demonstrates sorting the data by specifying a comparison function.

Listing 18-20. Sorting with a Comparison Function in the main.go File in the mathandsorting Folder

```
package main

import (
    //"sort"
)

func main() {

    products := []Product {
        { "Kayak", 279} ,
        { "Lifejacket", 49.95 },
        { "Soccer Ball",  19.50 },
    }

    SortWith(products, func (p1, p2 Product) bool {
        return p1.Name < p2.Name
    })

    for _, p := range products {
        Printfln("Name: %v, Price: %.2f",  p.Name, p.Price)
    }
}
```

The data is sorted by comparing the Name field, and the code produces the following output when the project is compiled and executed:

```
Name: Kayak, Price: 279.00
Name: Lifejacket, Price: 49.95
Name: Soccer Ball, Price: 19.50
```

Summary

In this chapter, I described the features provided for generating random numbers and shuffling the elements in a slice. I also described the opposing features, which sort the elements in a slice. In the next chapter, I describe the standard library features for times, dates, and durations.

CHAPTER 19

■ ■ ■

Dates, Times, and Durations

In this chapter, I describe the features provided by the time package, which is the part of the standard library responsible for representing moments in time and durations. Table 19-1 puts these features in context.

Table 19-1. *Putting Dates, Times, and Durations in Context*

Question	Answer
What are they?	The features provided by the time package are used to represent specific moments in time and intervals or durations.
Why are they useful?	These features are useful in any application that needs to deal with calendaring or alarm and for the development of any feature that requires delays or notifications in the future.
How are they used?	The time package defines data types for representing dates and individual units of time and functions for manipulating them. There are also features integrated into the Go channel system.
Are there any pitfalls or limitations?	Dates can be complex, and care must be taken to deal with calendar and time zone issues.
Are there any alternatives?	These are optional features, and their use is not required.

Table 19-2 summarizes the chapter.

Table 19-2. *Chapter Summary*

Problem	Solution	Listing
Represent a time, date, or duration	Use the functions and types defined by the time package	5, 13–16
Format dates and times as strings	Use the Format function and a layout	6–7
Parse a date and time from a string	Use the Parse function	8–12
Parse a duration from a string	Use the ParseDuration function	17
Pause execution of a goroutine	Use the Sleep function	18
Deferring execution of a function	Use the AfterFunc function	19
Receive periodic notifications	Use the After function	20–24

© Adam Freeman 2022

A. Freeman, *Pro Go*, https://doi.org/10.1007/978-1-4842-7355-5_19

Preparing for This Chapter

To prepare for this chapter, open a new command prompt, navigate to a convenient location, and create a directory named datesandtimes. Run the command shown in Listing 19-1 in the datesandtimes folder to create a module file.

■ **Tip** You can download the example project for this chapter—and for all the other chapters in this book— from https://github.com/apress/pro-go. See Chapter 2 for how to get help if you have problems running the examples.

Listing 19-1. Initializing the Module

```
go mod init datesandtimes
```

Add a file named printer.go to the datesandtimes folder with the content shown in Listing 19-2.

Listing 19-2. The Contents of the printer.go File in the datesandtimes Folder

```
package main

import "fmt"

func Printfln(template string, values ...interface{}) {
    fmt.Printf(template + "\n", values...)
}
```

Add a file named main.go to the datesandtimes folder, with the contents shown in Listing 19-3.

Listing 19-3. The Contents of the main.go File in the datesandtimes Folder

```
package main

func main() {

    Printfln("Hello, Dates and Times")
}
```

Use the command prompt to run the command shown in Listing 19-4 in the datesandtimes folder.

Listing 19-4. Running the Example Project

```
go run .
```

The code will be compiled and executed, producing the following output:

```
Hello, Dates and Times
```

Working with Dates and Times

The time package provides features for measuring durations and expressing dates and times. In the sections that follow, I describe the most useful of these features.

Representing Dates and Times

The time package provides the Time type, which is used to represent a specific moment in time. The functions described in Table 19-3 are used to create Time values.

Table 19-3. The Functions in the time Package for Creating Time Values

Name	Description
Now()	This function creates a Time representing the current moment in time.
Date(y, m, d, h, min, sec, nsec, loc)	This function creates a Time representing a specified moment in time, which is expressed by the year, month, day, hour, minute, second, nanosecond, and Location arguments. (The Location type is described in the "Parsing Time Values from Strings" section.)
Unix(sec, nsec)	This function creates a Time value from the number of seconds and nanoseconds since January 1, 1970, UTC, commonly known as Unix time.

The components of a Time are accessed through the methods described in Table 19-4.

Table 19-4. The Methods for Accessing Time Components

Name	Description
Date()	This method returns the year, month, and day components. The year and day are expressed as int values and the month as a Month value.
Clock()	This method returns the hour, minutes, and seconds components of the Time.
Year()	This method returns the year component, expressed as an int.
YearDay()	This method returns the day of the year, expressed as an int between 1 and 366 (to accommodate leap years).
Month()	This method returns the month component, expressed using the Month type.
Day()	This method returns the day of the month, expressed as an int.
Weekday()	This method returns the day of the week, expressed as a Weekday.
Hour()	This method returns the hour of the day, expressed as an int between 0 and 23.
Minute()	This method returns the number of minutes elapsed into the hour of the day, expressed as an int between 0 and 59.
Second()	This method returns the number of seconds elapsed into the minute of the hour, expressed as an int between 0 and 59.
Nanosecond()	This method returns the number of nanoseconds elapsed into the second of the minute, expressed as an int between 0 and 999,999,999.

Two types are defined to help describe the components of a Time value, as described in Table 19-5.

Table 19-5. *The Types Used to Describe Time Components*

Name	Description
Month	This type represents a month, and the time package defines constant values for the English-language month names: January, February, etc. The Month type defines a String method that uses these names when formatting strings.
Weekday	This type represents a day of the week, and the time package defines constant values for the English-language weekday names: Sunday, Monday, etc. The Weekday type defines a String method that uses these names when formatting strings.

Using the types and methods described in Tables 19-3 to 19-5, Listing 19-5 demonstrates how to create Time values and access their components.

Listing 19-5. Creating Time Values in the main.go File in the datesandtimes Folder

```
package main

import "time"

func PrintTime(label string, t *time.Time) {
    Printfln("%s: Day: %v: Month: %v Year: %v",
        label, t.Day(), t.Month(), t.Year())
}

func main() {
    current := time.Now()
    specific := time.Date(1995, time.June, 9, 0, 0, 0, 0, time.Local)
    unix := time.Unix(1433228090, 0)

    PrintTime("Current", &current)
    PrintTime("Specific", &specific)
    PrintTime("UNIX", &unix)
}
```

The statements in the main function create three different Time values using the functions described in Table 19-3. The constant value June is used to create one of the Time values, illustrating the use of one of the types described in Table 19-5. The Time values are passed to the PrintTime function, which uses the methods in Table 19-4 to access the day, month, and year components to write out a message describing each Time. Compile and execute the project, and you will see output similar to the following, with a different time returned by the Now function:

```
Current: Day: 2: Month: June Year: 2021
Specific: Day: 9: Month: June Year: 1995
UNIX: Day: 2: Month: June Year: 2015
```

The final argument to the Date function is a Location, which specifies the location whose time zone will be used for the Time value. In Listing 19-5, I used the Local constant defined by the time package, which provides a Location for the system's time zone. I explain how to create Location values that are not determined by the system's configuration in the "Parsing Time Values from Strings" section, later in this chapter.

Formatting Times as Strings

The Format method is used to create formatted strings from Time values. The format of the string is specified by providing a layout string, which shows how which components of the Time are required and the order and precision with which they should be expressed. Table 19-6 describes the Format method for quick reference.

Table 19-6. *The Time Method for Creating Formatted Strings*

Name	Description
Format(layout)	This method returns a formatted string, which is created using the specified layout.

The layout string uses a reference time, which is 15:04:05 (meaning five seconds after four minutes past 3 p.m.) on Monday, January 2nd, 2006, in the MST time zone, which is 7 hours behind Greenwich mean time (GMT). Listing 19-6 demonstrates the use of the reference time to create formatted strings.

Listing 19-6. Formatting Time Values as the main.go File in the datesandtimes Folder

```
package main

import (
    "time"
    "fmt"
)

func PrintTime(label string, t *time.Time) {
    layout := "Day: 02 Month: Jan Year: 2006"
    fmt.Println(label, t.Format(layout))
}

func main() {
    current := time.Now()
    specific := time.Date(1995, time.June, 9, 0, 0, 0, 0, time.Local)
    unix := time.Unix(1433228090, 0)

    PrintTime("Current", &current)
    PrintTime("Specific", &specific)
    PrintTime("UNIX", &unix)
}
```

The layout can mix date components with fixed strings, and, in the example, I have used a layout to re-create the format used in earlier examples, specified using the reference date. Compile and execute the project, and you will see the following output:

```
Current Day: 03 Month: Jun Year: 2021
Specific Day: 09 Month: Jun Year: 1995
UNIX Day: 02 Month: Jun Year: 2015
```

The time package defines a set of constants for common time and date formats, shown in Table 19-7.

Table 19-7. *The Layout Constants Defined by the time Package*

Name	Reference Date Format
ANSIC	Mon Jan _2 15:04:05 2006
UnixDate	Mon Jan _2 15:04:05 MST 2006
RubyDate	Mon Jan 02 15:04:05 -0700 2006
RFC822	02 Jan 06 15:04 MST
RFC822Z	02 Jan 06 15:04 -0700
RFC850	Monday, 02-Jan-06 15:04:05 MST
RFC1123	Mon, 02 Jan 2006 15:04:05 MST
RFC1123Z	Mon, 02 Jan 2006 15:04:05 -0700
RFC3339	2006-01-02T15:04:05Z07:00
RFC3339Nano	2006-01-02T15:04:05.999999999Z07:00
Kitchen	3:04PM
Stamp	Jan _2 15:04:05
StampMilli	Jan _2 15:04:05.000
StampMicro	Jan _2 15:04:05.000000
StampNano	Jan _2 15:04:05.000000000

These constants can be used instead of a custom layout, as shown in Listing 19-7.

Listing 19-7. Using a Predefined Layout in the main.go File in the datesandtimes Folder

```
package main

import (
    "time"
    "fmt"
)

func PrintTime(label string, t *time.Time) {
    //layout := "Day: 02 Month: Jan Year: 2006"
    fmt.Println(label, t.Format(time.RFC822Z))
}

func main() {
    current := time.Now()
    specific := time.Date(1995, time.June, 9, 0, 0, 0, 0, time.Local)
    unix := time.Unix(1433228090, 0)
```

```
    PrintTime("Current", &current)
    PrintTime("Specific", &specific)
    PrintTime("UNIX", &unix)
}
```

The custom layout has been replaced with the RFC822Z layout, which produces the following output when the project is compiled and executed:

```
Current 03 Jun 21 08:04 +0100
Specific 09 Jun 95 00:00 +0100
UNIX 02 Jun 15 07:54 +0100
```

Parsing Time Values from Strings

The time package provides support for creating Time values from strings, as described in Table 19-8.

Table 19-8. *The time Package Functions for Parsing Strings into Time Values*

Name	Description
Parse(layout, str)	This function parses a string using the specified layout to create a Time value. An error is returned to indicate problems parsing the string.
ParseInLocation(layout, str, location)	This function parses a string, using the specified layout and using the Location if no time zone is included in the string. An error is returned to indicate problems parsing the string.

The functions described in Table 19-8 use a reference time, which is used to specify the format of the string to be parsed. The reference time is 15:04:05 (meaning five seconds after four minutes past 3 p.m.) on Monday, January 2nd, 2006, in the MST time zone, which is seven hours behind GMT.

The components of the reference date are arranged to specify the layout of the date string that is to be parsed, as shown in Listing 19-8.

Listing 19-8. Parsing a Date String in the main.go File in the datesandtimes Folder

```
package main

import (
    "time"
    "fmt"
)

func PrintTime(label string, t *time.Time) {
    //layout := "Day: 02 Month: Jan Year: 2006"
    fmt.Println(label, t.Format(time.RFC822Z))
}

func main() {
    layout := "2006-Jan-02"
    dates := []string {
```

```
            "1995-Jun-09",
            "2015-Jun-02",
    }

    for _, d := range dates {
        time, err := time.Parse(layout, d)
        if (err == nil) {
            PrintTime("Parsed", &time)
        } else {
            Printfln("Error: %s", err.Error())
        }
    }
}
```

The layout used in this example includes a four-digit year, a three-letter month, and a two-digit day, all separated with hyphens. The layout is passed to the Parse function along with the string to parse, and the function returns a time value and error that will detail any parsing problems. Compile and execute the project, and you will receive the following output, although you may see a different time zone offset (which I return to shortly):

```
Parsed 09 Jun 95 00:00 +0000
Parsed 02 Jun 15 00:00 +0000
```

Using Predefined Date Layouts

The layout constants described in Table 19-7 can be used to parse dates, as shown in Listing 19-9.

Listing 19-9. Using a Predefined Layout in the main.go File in the datesandtimes Folder

```
package main

import (
    "time"
    "fmt"
)

func PrintTime(label string, t *time.Time) {
    //layout := "Day: 02 Month: Jan Year: 2006"
    fmt.Println(label, t.Format(time.RFC822Z))
}

func main() {
    //layout := "2006-Jan-02"
    dates := []string {
        "09 Jun 95 00:00 GMT",
        "02 Jun 15 00:00 GMT",
    }

    for _, d := range dates {
        time, err := time.Parse(time.RFC822, d)
```

```
        if (err == nil) {
            PrintTime("Parsed", &time)
        } else {
            Printfln("Error: %s", err.Error())
        }
    }
}
```

This example uses the RFC822 constant to parse the date strings and produces the following output, although you may see a different time zone offset:

```
Parsed 09 Jun 95 01:00 +0100
Parsed 02 Jun 15 01:00 +0100
```

Specifying a Parsing Location

The Parse function assumes that dates and times expressed without a time zone are defined in Coordinated Universal Time (UTC). The ParseInLocation method can be used to specify a location that is used when no time zone is specified, as shown in Listing 19-10.

Listing 19-10. Specifying a Location in the main.go File in the datesandtimes Folder

```
package main

import (
    "time"
    "fmt"
)

func PrintTime(label string, t *time.Time) {
    //layout := "Day: 02 Month: Jan Year: 2006"
    fmt.Println(label, t.Format(time.RFC822Z))
}

func main() {
    layout := "02 Jan 06 15:04"
    date := "09 Jun 95 19:30"

    london, lonerr := time.LoadLocation("Europe/London")
    newyork, nycerr := time.LoadLocation("America/New_York")

    if (lonerr == nil && nycerr == nil) {
        nolocation, _ := time.Parse(layout, date)
        londonTime, _ := time.ParseInLocation(layout, date, london)
        newyorkTime, _ := time.ParseInLocation(layout, date, newyork)

        PrintTime("No location:", &nolocation)
        PrintTime("London:", &londonTime)
        PrintTime("New York:", &newyorkTime)
```

```
    } else {
        fmt.Println(lonerr.Error(), nycerr.Error())
    }
}
```

The ParseInLocation accepts a time.Location argument that specifies a location whose time zone will be used when one isn't included in the parsed string. Location values can be created using the functions described in Table 19-9.

Table 19-9. *The Functions for Creating Locations*

Name	Description
LoadLocation(name)	This function returns a *Location for the specified name and an error that indicates any problems.
LoadLocationFromTZData(name, data)	This function returns a *Location from a byte slice that contains a formatted time zone database.
FixedZone(name, offset)	This function returns a *Location that always uses the specified name and offset from UTC.

When a place is passed to the LoadLocation function, the Location that is returned contains details of the time zones used at that location. The place names are defined in the IANA time zone database, https://www.iana.org/time-zones, and are listed by https://en.wikipedia.org/wiki/List_of_tz_database_time_zones. The example in Listing 19-10 specified Europe/London and America/New_York, which produced Location values for London and New York. Compile and execute the code, and you will see the following output:

```
No location: 09 Jun 95 19:30 +0000
London: 09 Jun 95 19:30 +0100
New York: 09 Jun 95 19:30 -0400
```

The three dates show how the string is parsed using different time zones. When the Parse method is used, the time zone is assumed to be UTC, which has zero offset (the +0000 component of the output). When the London location is used, the time is assumed to be one hour ahead of UTC because the date in the parsed string falls within the daylight savings period used in the United Kingdom. Similarly, when the New York location is used, the offset is four hours behind UTC.

EMBEDDING THE TIME ZONE DATABASE

The time zone database used to create Location values is installed alongside the Go tools, which means it may not be available when a compiled application is deployed. The time/tzdata package contains an embedded version of the database that is loaded by a package initialization function (as described in Chapter 12). To ensure that time zone data will always be available, declare a dependency on the package like this:

```
...
import (
    "fmt"
    "time"
```

```
    _ "time/tzdata"
)
...
```

There are no exported features in the package and so the blank identifier must be used to declare a
dependency without generating a compiler error.

Using the Local Location

If the place name used to create a Location is Local, then the time zone setting of the machine running the
application is used, as shown in Listing 19-11.

Listing 19-11. Using the Local Time Zone in the main.go File in the datesandtimes Folder

```
package main

import (
    "time"
    "fmt"
)

func PrintTime(label string, t *time.Time) {
    //layout := "Day: 02 Month: Jan Year: 2006"
    fmt.Println(label, t.Format(time.RFC822Z))
}

func main() {

    layout := "02 Jan 06 15:04"
    date := "09 Jun 95 19:30"

    london, lonerr := time.LoadLocation("Europe/London")
    newyork, nycerr := time.LoadLocation("America/New_York")
    local, _ := time.LoadLocation("Local")

    if (lonerr == nil && nycerr == nil) {
        nolocation, _ := time.Parse(layout, date)
        londonTime, _ := time.ParseInLocation(layout, date, london)
        newyorkTime, _ := time.ParseInLocation(layout, date, newyork)
        localTime, _ := time.ParseInLocation(layout, date, local)

        PrintTime("No location:", &nolocation)
        PrintTime("London:", &londonTime)
        PrintTime("New York:", &newyorkTime)
        PrintTime("Local:", &localTime)
    } else {
        fmt.Println(lonerr.Error(), nycerr.Error())
    }
}
```

The output produced by this example will differ based on your location. I live in the United Kingdom, which means that my local time zone is one hour ahead of UTC during daylight savings, which produces the following output:

```
No location: 09 Jun 95 19:30 +0000
London: 09 Jun 95 19:30 +0100
New York: 09 Jun 95 19:30 -0400
Local: 09 Jun 95 19:30 +0100
```

Specifying Time Zones Directly

Using place names is the most reliable way to ensure that dates are parsed correctly because daylight savings is automatically applied. The FixedZone function can be used to create Location that has a fixed time zone, as shown in Listing 19-12.

Listing 19-12. Specifying Time Zones in the main.go File in the datesandtimes Folder

```go
package main

import (
    "time"
    "fmt"
)

func PrintTime(label string, t *time.Time) {
    //layout := "Day: 02 Month: Jan Year: 2006"
    fmt.Println(label, t.Format(time.RFC822Z))
}

func main() {

    layout := "02 Jan 06 15:04"
    date := "09 Jun 95 19:30"

    london := time.FixedZone("BST", 1 * 60 * 60)
    newyork := time.FixedZone("EDT", -4 * 60 * 60)
    local := time.FixedZone("Local", 0)

    //if (lonerr == nil && nycerr == nil) {
        nolocation, _ := time.Parse(layout, date)
        londonTime, _ := time.ParseInLocation(layout, date, london)
        newyorkTime, _ := time.ParseInLocation(layout, date, newyork)
        localTime, _ := time.ParseInLocation(layout, date, local)

        PrintTime("No location:", &nolocation)
        PrintTime("London:", &londonTime)
        PrintTime("New York:", &newyorkTime)
        PrintTime("Local:", &localTime)
```

```
//  } else {
//      fmt.Println(lonerr.Error(), nycerr.Error())
//  }
}
```

The arguments to the FixedZone function are a name and the number of seconds offset from UTC. This example creates three fixed time zones, one of which is an hour ahead of UTC, one of which is four hours behind, and one of which has no offset. Compile and execute the project, and you will see the following output:

```
No location: 09 Jun 95 19:30 +0000
London: 09 Jun 95 19:30 +0100
New York: 09 Jun 95 19:30 -0400
Local: 09 Jun 95 19:30 +0000
```

Manipulating Time Values

The time package defines methods for working with Time values, as described in Table 19-10. Some of these methods rely on the Duration type, which I describe in the next section.

Table 19-10. *The Methods for Working with Time Values*

Name	Description
Add(duration)	This method adds the specified Duration to the Time and returns the result.
Sub(time)	This method returns a Duration that expresses the difference between the Time on which the method has been called and the Time provided as the argument.
AddDate(y, m, d)	This method adds the specified number of years, months, and days to the Time and returns the result.
After(time)	This method returns true if the Time on which the method has been called occurs after the Time provided as the argument.
Before(time)	This method returns true if the Time on which the method has been called occurs before the Time provided as the argument.
Equal(time)	This method returns true if the Time on which the method has been called is equal to the Time provided as the argument.
IsZero()	This method returns true if the Time on which the method has been called represents the zero-time instant, which is January 1, year 1, 00:00:00 UTC.
In(loc)	This method returns the Time value, expressed in the specified Location.
Location()	This method returns the Location that is associated with the Time, effectively allowing a time to be expressed in a different time zone.
Round(duration)	This method rounds the Time to the nearest interval represented by a Duration value.
Truncate(duration)	This method rounds the Time down to the nearest interval represented by a Duration value.

Listing 19-13 parses a Time from a string and uses some of the methods described in the table.

Listing 19-13. Working with a Time Value in the main.go File in the datesandtimes Folder

```
package main

import (
    "time"
    "fmt"
)

func main() {
    t, err := time.Parse(time.RFC822, "09 Jun 95 04:59 BST")
    if (err == nil) {
        Printfln("After: %v", t.After(time.Now()))
        Printfln("Round: %v", t.Round(time.Hour))
        Printfln("Truncate: %v", t.Truncate(time.Hour))
    } else {
        fmt.Println(err.Error())
    }
}
```

Compile and execute the project, and you will receive the following output, allowing for variations in the date format:

```
After: false
Round: 1995-06-09 05:00:00 +0100 BST
Truncate: 1995-06-09 04:00:00 +0100 BST
```

Time values can be compared using the Equal function, which takes into account time zone differences, as shown in Listing 19-14.

Listing 19-14. Comparing Time Values in the main.go File in the datesandtimes Folder

```
package main

import (
    //"fmt"
    "time"
)

func main() {
    t1, _ := time.Parse(time.RFC822Z, "09 Jun 95 04:59 +0100")
    t2, _ := time.Parse(time.RFC822Z, "08 Jun 95 23:59 -0400")

    Printfln("Equal Method: %v", t1.Equal(t2))
    Printfln("Equality Operator: %v", t1 == t2)
}
```

The Time values in this example express the same moment in different time zones. The Equal function takes the effect of the time zones into account, which doesn't happen when the standard equality operator is used. Compile and execute the project, and you will receive the following output:

```
Equal Method: true
Equality Operator: false
```

Representing Durations

The Duration type is an alias to the int64 type and is used to represent a specific number of milliseconds. Custom Duration values are composed from constant Duration values defined in the time package, described in Table 19-11.

Table 19-11. *The Duration Constants in the time Package*

Name	Description
Hour	This constant represents 1 hour.
Minute	This constant represents 1 minute.
Second	This constant represents 1 second.
Millisecond	This constant represents 1 millisecond.
Microsecond	This constant represents 1 microsecond.
Nanosecond	This constant represents 1 nanosecond.

Once a Duration has been created, it can be inspected using the methods described in Table 19-12.

Table 19-12. *The Duration Methods*

Name	Description
Hours()	This method returns a float64 that represents the Duration in hours.
Minutes()	This method returns a float64 that represents the Duration in minutes.
Seconds()	This method returns a float64 that represents the Duration in seconds.
Milliseconds()	This method returns an int64 that represents the Duration in milliseconds.
Microseconds()	This method returns an int64 that represents the Duration in microseconds.
Nanoseconds()	This method returns an int64 that represents the Duration in nanoseconds.
Round(duration)	This method returns a Duration, which is rounded to the nearest multiple of the specified Duration.
Truncate(duration)	This method returns a Duration, which is rounded down to the nearest multiple of the specified Duration.

Listing 19-15 demonstrates how the constants can be used to create a Duration and uses some of the methods in Table 19-12.

Listing 19-15. Creating and Inspecting a Duration in the main.go File in the datesandtimes Folder

```
package main

import (
    //"fmt"
    "time"
)

func main() {

    var d time.Duration = time.Hour + (30 * time.Minute)

    Printfln("Hours: %v", d.Hours())
    Printfln("Mins: %v", d.Minutes())
    Printfln("Seconds: %v", d.Seconds())
    Printfln("Millseconds: %v", d.Milliseconds())

    rounded := d.Round(time.Hour)
    Printfln("Rounded Hours: %v", rounded.Hours())
    Printfln("Rounded Mins: %v", rounded.Minutes())

    trunc := d.Truncate(time.Hour)
    Printfln("Truncated  Hours: %v", trunc.Hours())
    Printfln("Rounded Mins: %v", trunc.Minutes())
}
```

The Duration is set to 90 minutes, and then the Hours, Minutes, Seconds, and Milliseconds methods are used to produce output. The Round and Truncate methods are used to create new Duration values, which are written out as hours and minutes. Compile and execute the project, and you will receive the following output:

```
Hours: 1.5
Mins: 90
Seconds: 5400
Millseconds: 5400000
Rounded Hours: 2
Rounded Mins: 120
Truncated  Hours: 1
Rounded Mins: 60
```

Note that the methods in Table 19-12 return the entire duration expressed in a specific unit, such as hours or minutes. This is different from the methods with similar names defined by the Time type, which return just one part of the date/time.

Creating Durations Relative to a Time

The time package defines two functions that can be used to create Duration values that represent the amount of time between a specific Time and the current Time, as described in Table 19-13.

Table 19-13. *The time Functions for Creating Duration Values relative to a Time*

Name	Description
Since(time)	This function returns a Duration expressing the elapsed time since the specified Time value.
Until(time)	This function returns a Duration expressing the elapsed time until the specified Time value.

Listing 19-16 demonstrates the use of these functions.

Listing 19-16. Creating Durations Relative to Times in the main.go File in the datesandtimes Folder

```
package main

import (
    //"fmt"
    "time"
)

func main() {
    toYears := func(d time.Duration) int {
        return int( d.Hours() / (24 * 365))
    }

    future := time.Date(2051, 0, 0, 0, 0, 0, 0, time.Local)
    past := time.Date(1965, 0, 0, 0, 0, 0, 0, time.Local)

    Printfln("Future: %v", toYears(time.Until(future)))
    Printfln("Past: %v", toYears(time.Since(past)))
}
```

The example uses the Until and Since methods to work out how many years until 2051 and how many years have passed since 1965. The code in Listing 19-16 produces the following output when compiled, although you may see different results depending on when you run the example:

```
Future: 29
Past: 56
```

Creating Durations from Strings

The time.ParseDuration function parses strings to create Duration values. For quick reference, Table 19-14 describes this function.

Table 19-14. The Function for Parsing Strings into Duration Values

Name	Description
ParseDuration(str)	This function returns a Duration and an error, indicating if there were problems parsing the specified string.

The format of the strings supported by the ParseDuration function is a sequence of number values followed by the unit indicators described in Table 19-15.

Table 19-15. The Duration String Unit Indicators

Unit	Description
h	This unit denotes hours.
m	This unit denotes minutes.
s	This unit denotes seconds.
ms	This unit denotes milliseconds.
us or µs	These units denotes microseconds.
ns	This unit denotes nanoseconds.

No spaces are allowed between values, which can be specified as integer or floating-point amounts. Listing 19-17 demonstrates creating a Duration from a string.

Listing 19-17. Parsing a String in the main.go File in the datesandtimes Folder

```
package main

import (
    "fmt"
    "time"
)

func main() {
    d, err := time.ParseDuration("1h30m")
    if (err == nil) {
        Printfln("Hours: %v", d.Hours())
        Printfln("Mins: %v", d.Minutes())
        Printfln("Seconds: %v", d.Seconds())
        Printfln("Millseconds: %v", d.Milliseconds())
    } else {
        fmt.Println(err.Error())
    }
}
```

The string specifies 1 hour and 30 minutes. Compile and execute the project, and the following output will be produced:

```
Hours: 1.5
Mins: 90
Seconds: 5400
Millseconds: 5400000
```

Using the Time Features for Goroutines and Channels

The time package provides a small set of functions that are useful for working with goroutines and channels, as described in Table 19-16.

Table 19-16. *The time Package Functions*

Name	Description
Sleep(duration)	This function pauses the current goroutine for at least the specified duration.
AfterFunc(duration, func)	This function executes the specified function in its own goroutine after the specified duration. The result is a *Timer, whose Stop method can be used to cancel the execution of the function before the duration elapses.
After(duration)	This function returns a channel that blocks for the specified duration and then yields a Time value. See the "Receiving Timed Notifications" section for details.
Tick(duration)	This function returns a channel that periodically sends a Time value, where the period is specified as a duration.

Although these functions are all defined in the same package, they have different uses, as demonstrated in the sections that follow.

Putting a Goroutine to Sleep

The Sleep function pauses execution of the current goroutine for a specified duration, as shown in Listing 19-18.

Listing 19-18. Pausing a Goroutine in the main.go File in the datesandtimes Folder

```go
package main

import (
    //"fmt"
    "time"
)

func writeToChannel(channel chan <- string) {
    names := []string { "Alice", "Bob", "Charlie", "Dora" }
```

```
    for _, name := range names {
        channel <- name
        time.Sleep(time.Second * 1)
    }
    close(channel)
}

func main() {

    nameChannel := make (chan string)

    go writeToChannel(nameChannel)

    for name := range nameChannel {
        Printfln("Read name: %v", name)
    }
}
```

The duration specified by the Sleep function is the minimum amount of time for which the goroutine will be paused, and you should not rely on exact periods of time, especially for smaller durations. Bear in mind that the Sleep function pauses the goroutine in which it is called, which means that it will also pause the main goroutine, which can give the appearance of locking up the application. (If this happens, the clue that you have called the Sleep function accidentally is that the automatic deadlock detection won't panic.) Compile and execute the project, and you will see the following output, which is produced with a small delay between names:

```
Read name: Alice
Read name: Bob
Read name: Charlie
Read name: Dora
```

Deferring Execution of a Function

The AfterFunc function is used to defer the execution of a function for a specified period, as shown in Listing 19-19.

Listing 19-19. Deferring a Function in the main.go File in the datesandtimes Folder

```
package main

import (
    //"fmt"
    "time"
)

func writeToChannel(channel chan <- string) {
    names := []string { "Alice", "Bob", "Charlie", "Dora" }
    for _, name := range names {
        channel <- name
```

```
        //time.Sleep(time.Second * 1)
    }
    close(channel)
}

func main() {

    nameChannel := make (chan string)

    time.AfterFunc(time.Second * 5, func () {
        writeToChannel(nameChannel)
    })

    for name := range nameChannel {
        Printfln("Read name: %v", name)
    }
}
```

The first AfterFunc argument is the delay period, which is five seconds in this example. The second argument is the function that will be executed. In this example, I want to execute the writeToChannel function, but AfterFunc only accepts functions without parameters or results, and so I have to use a simple wrapper. Compile and execute the project, and you will see the following results, which are written out after a five-second delay:

```
Read name: Alice
Read name: Bob
Read name: Charlie
Read name: Dora
```

Receiving Timed Notifications

The After function waits for a specified duration and then sends a Time value to a channel, which is a useful way of using a channel to receive a notification at a given future time, as shown in Listing 19-20.

Listing 19-20. Receiving a Future Notification in the main.go File in the datesandtimes Folder

```
package main

import (
    //"fmt"
    "time"
)

func writeToChannel(channel chan <- string) {

    Printfln("Waiting for initial duration...")
    _ = <- time.After(time.Second * 2)
    Printfln("Initial duration elapsed.")
```

```
    names := []string { "Alice", "Bob", "Charlie", "Dora" }
    for _, name := range names {
        channel <- name
        time.Sleep(time.Second * 1)
    }
    close(channel)
}

func main() {

    nameChannel := make (chan string)

    go writeToChannel(nameChannel)

    for name := range nameChannel {
        Printfln("Read name: %v", name)
    }
}
```

The result from the After function is a channel that carries Time values. The channel blocks for the specified duration, when a Time value is sent, indicating the duration has passed. In this example, the value sent over the channel acts as a signal and is not used directly, which is why it is assigned to the blank identifier, like this:

```
...
_ = <- time.After(time.Second * 2)
...
```

This use of the After function introduces an initial delay in the writeToChannel function. Compile and execute the project, and you will see the following output:

```
Waiting for initial duration...
Initial duration elapsed.
Read name: Alice
Read name: Bob
Read name: Charlie
Read name: Dora
```

The effect in this example is the same as using the Sleep function, but the difference is that the After function returns a channel that doesn't block until a value is read, which means that a direction can be specified, additional work can be performed, and then a channel read can be performed, with the result that the channel will block only for the remaining part of the duration.

Using Notifications as Timeouts in Select Statements

The After function can be used with select statements to provide a timeout, as shown in Listing 19-21.

Listing 19-21. Using a Timeout in a Select Statement in the main.go File in the datesandtimes Folder

```
package main

import (
    //"fmt"
    "time"
)

func writeToChannel(channel chan <- string) {

    Printfln("Waiting for initial duration...")
    _ = <- time.After(time.Second * 2)
    Printfln("Initial duration elapsed.")

    names := []string { "Alice", "Bob", "Charlie", "Dora" }
    for _, name := range names {
        channel <- name
        time.Sleep(time.Second * 3)
    }
    close(channel)
}

func main() {

    nameChannel := make (chan string)

    go writeToChannel(nameChannel)

    channelOpen := true
    for channelOpen {
        Printfln("Starting channel read")
        select {
            case name, ok := <- nameChannel:
                if (!ok) {
                    channelOpen = false
                    break
                } else {
                    Printfln("Read name: %v", name)
                }
            case <- time.After(time.Second * 2):
                Printfln("Timeout")
        }
    }
}
```

The select statement will block until one of the channels is ready or until the timer expires. This works because the select statement will block until one of its channels is ready and because the After function creates a channel that blocks for a specified period. Compile and execute the project, and you will see the following output:

```
Waiting for initial duration...
Initial duration elapsed.
Timeout
Read name: Alice
Timeout
Read name: Bob
Timeout
Read name: Charlie
Timeout
Read name: Dora
Timeout
```

Stopping and Resetting Timers

The After function is useful when you are sure that you will always need the timed notification. If you need the option to cancel the notification, then the function described in Table 19-17 can be used instead.

Table 19-17. *The time Function for Creating a Timer*

Name	Description
NewTimer(duration)	This function returns a *Timer with the specified period.

The result of the NewTimer function is a pointer to a Timer struct, which defines the methods described in Table 19-18.

Table 19-18. *The Methods Defined by the Timer Struct*

Name	Description
C	This field returns the channel over which the Time will send its Time value.
Stop()	This method stops the timer. The result is a bool that will be true if the timer has been stopped and false if the timer had already sent its message.
Reset(duration)	This method stops a timer and resets it so that its interval is the specified Duration.

Listing 19-22 uses the NewTimer function to create a Timer that is reset before the specified duration elapses.

■ **Caution** Be careful when stopping a timer. The timer's channel is not closed, which means that reads from the channel will continue to block even after the timer has stopped.

Listing 19-22. Resetting a Timer in the main.go File in the datesandtimes Folder

```
package main

import (
    //"fmt"
    "time"
)

func writeToChannel(channel chan <- string) {

    timer := time.NewTimer(time.Minute * 10)

    go func () {
        time.Sleep(time.Second * 2)
        Printfln("Resetting timer")
        timer.Reset(time.Second)
    }()

    Printfln("Waiting for initial duration...")
    <- timer.C
    Printfln("Initial duration elapsed.")

    names := []string { "Alice", "Bob", "Charlie", "Dora" }
    for _, name := range names {
        channel <- name
        //time.Sleep(time.Second * 3)
    }
    close(channel)
}

func main() {

    nameChannel := make (chan string)

    go writeToChannel(nameChannel)

    for name := range nameChannel {
        Printfln("Read name: %v", name)
    }
}
```

The Timer in this example is created with a duration of ten minutes. A goroutine sleeps for two seconds and then resets the timer so its duration is two seconds. Compile and execute the project, and you will see the following output:

```
Waiting for initial duration...
Resetting timer
Initial duration elapsed.
Read name: Alice
```

```
Read name: Bob
Read name: Charlie
Read name: Dora
```

Receiving Recurring Notifications

The Tick function returns a channel over which Time values are sent at a specified interval, as demonstrated in Listing 19-23.

Listing 19-23. Receiving Recurring Notifications in the main.go File in the datesandtimes Folder

```
package main

import (
    //"fmt"
    "time"
)

func writeToChannel(nameChannel chan <- string) {

    names := []string { "Alice", "Bob", "Charlie", "Dora" }

    tickChannel := time.Tick(time.Second)
    index := 0

    for {
        <- tickChannel
        nameChannel <- names[index]
        index++
        if (index == len(names)) {
            index = 0
        }
    }
}

func main() {

    nameChannel := make (chan string)

    go writeToChannel(nameChannel)

    for name := range nameChannel {
        Printfln("Read name: %v", name)
    }
}
```

As before, the utility of the channel created by the Tick function isn't the Time values sent over it, but the periodicity at which they are sent. In this example, the Tick function is used to create a channel over which values will be sent every second. The channel blocks when there is no value to read, which allows channels created with the Tick function t control the rate at which the writeToChannel function generates values. Compile and execute the project and you will see the following output, which repeats until the program is terminated:

```
Read name: Alice
Read name: Bob
Read name: Charlie
Read name: Dora
Read name: Alice
Read name: Bob
...
```

The Tick function is useful when an indefinite sequence of signals is required. If a fixed series of values is required, then the function described in Table 19-19 can be used instead.

Table 19-19. *The time Function for Creating a Ticker*

Name	Description
NewTicker(duration)	This function returns a *Ticker with the specified period.

The result of the NewTicker function is a pointer to a Ticker struct, which defines the field and methods described in Table 19-20.

Table 19-20. *The Field and Methods Defined by the Ticker Struct*

Name	Description
C	This field returns the channel over which the Ticker will send its Time values.
Stop()	This method stops the ticker (but does not close the channel returned by the C field).
Reset(duration)	This method stops a ticker and resets it so that its interval is the specified Duration.

Listing 19-24 uses the NewTicker function to create a Ticker that is stopped once it is no longer required.

Listing 19-24. Creating a Ticker in the main.go File in the datesandtimes Folder

```
package main

import (
    //"fmt"
    "time"
)

func writeToChannel(nameChannel chan <- string) {

    names := []string { "Alice", "Bob", "Charlie", "Dora" }

    ticker := time.NewTicker(time.Second / 10)
    index := 0
```

```go
    for {
        <- ticker.C
        nameChannel <- names[index]
        index++
        if (index == len(names)) {
            ticker.Stop()
            close(nameChannel)
            break
        }
    }
}

func main() {

    nameChannel := make (chan string)

    go writeToChannel(nameChannel)

    for name := range nameChannel {
        Printfln("Read name: %v", name)
    }
}
```

This approach is useful when an application needs to create multiple tickers without leaving those that are no longer required sending messages. Compile and execute the project, and you will see the following output:

```
Read name: Alice
Read name: Bob
Read name: Charlie
Read name: Dora
```

Summary

In this chapter, I described the Go standard library features for working with times, dates, and durations, including the integrated support for channels and goroutines. In the next chapter, I introduce readers and writers, which are the Go mechanism for reading and writing data.

CHAPTER 20

Reading and Writing Data

In this chapter, I describe two of the most important interfaces defined by the standard library: the Reader and Writer interfaces. These interfaces are used wherever data is read or written, which means that any source or destination for data can be treated in much the same way so that writing data to a file, for example, is just the same as writing data to a network connection. Table 20-1 puts the features described in this chapter in context.

Table 20-1. *Putting Readers and Writers in Context*

Question	Answer
What are they?	These interfaces define the basic methods required to read and write data.
Why are they useful?	This approach means that just about any data source can be used in the same way, while still allowing specialized features to be defined using the composition features described in Chapter 13.
How is it used?	The io package defines these interfaces, but the implementations are available from a range of other packages, some of which are described in detail in later chapters.
Are there any pitfalls or limitations?	These interfaces don't entirely hide the detail of sources or destinations for data and additional methods are often required, provided by interfaces that build on Reader and Writer.
Are there any alternatives?	The use of these interfaces is optional, but they are hard to avoid because they are used throughout the standard library.

© Adam Freeman 2022
A. Freeman, *Pro Go*, https://doi.org/10.1007/978-1-4842-7355-5_20

Table 20-2 summarizes the chapter.

Table 20-2. *Chapter Summary*

Problem	Solution	Listing
Read data	Use an implementation of the Reader interface	6
Write data	Use an implementation of the Writer interface	7
Simplify the process of reading and writing data	Use the utility functions	8
Combine readers or writers	Use the specialized implementations	9–16
Buffer reads and writes	Use the features provided by the bufio package	17–23
Scan and format data with readers and writers	Use the functions in the fmt package that accept Reader or Writer arguments	24–27

Preparing for This Chapter

To prepare for this chapter, open a new command prompt, navigate to a convenient location, and create a directory named readersandwriters. Run the command shown in Listing 20-1 to create a module file.

■ **Tip**   You can download the example project for this chapter—and for all the other chapters in this book— from https://github.com/apress/pro-go. See Chapter 2 for how to get help if you have problems running the examples.

Listing 20-1. Initializing the Module

```
go mod init readersandwriters
```

Add a file named printer.go to the readersandwriters folder with the content shown in Listing 20-2.

Listing 20-2. The Contents of the printer.go File in the readersandwriters Folder

```
package main

import "fmt"

func Printfln(template string, values ...interface{}) {
    fmt.Printf(template + "\n", values...)
}
```

Add a file named product.go to the readersandwriters folder with the content shown in Listing 20-3.

Listing 20-3. The Contents of the product.go File in the readersandwriters Folder

```
package main

type Product struct {
    Name, Category string
    Price float64
}

var Kayak = Product {
    Name: "Kayak",
    Category: "Watersports",
    Price: 279,
}

var Products = []Product {
    { "Kayak", "Watersports", 279 },
    { "Lifejacket", "Watersports", 49.95 },
    { "Soccer Ball", "Soccer", 19.50 },
    { "Corner Flags", "Soccer", 34.95 },
    { "Stadium", "Soccer", 79500 },
    { "Thinking Cap", "Chess", 16 },
    { "Unsteady Chair", "Chess", 75 },
    { "Bling-Bling King", "Chess", 1200 },
}
```

Add a file named main.go to the readersandwriters folder, with the contents shown in Listing 20-4.

Listing 20-4. The Contents of the main.go File in the readersandwriters Folder

```
package main

func main() {

    Printfln("Product: %v, Price : %v", Kayak.Name, Kayak.Price)
}
```

Use the command prompt to run the command shown in Listing 20-5 in the readersandwriters folder.

Listing 20-5. Running the Example Project

```
go run .
```

The code will be compiled and executed, producing the following output:

```
Product: Kayak Price: 275
```

Understanding Readers and Writers

The Reader and Writer interfaces are defined by the io package and provide abstract ways to read and write data, without being tied to where the data is coming from or going to. In the sections that follow, I describe these interfaces and demonstrate their use.

Understanding Readers

The Reader interface defines a single method, which is described in Table 20-3.

Table 20-3. *The Reader Interface*

Name	Description
Read(byteSlice)	This method reads data into the specified [ ]byte. The method returns the number of bytes that were read, expressed as an int, and an error.

The Reader interface doesn't include any detail about where data comes from or how it is obtained—it just defines the Read method. The details are left to the types that implement the interface, and there are reader implementations in the standard library for different data sources. One of the simplest readers uses a string as its data source and is demonstrated in Listing 20-6.

Listing 20-6. Using a Reader in the main.go File in the readersandwriters Folder

```
package main

import (
    "io"
    "strings"
)

func processData(reader io.Reader) {
    b := make([]byte, 2)
    for {
        count, err := reader.Read(b);
        if (count > 0) {
            Printfln("Read %v bytes: %v", count, string(b[0:count]))
        }
        if err == io.EOF {
            break
        }
    }
}

func main() {
    r := strings.NewReader("Kayak")
    processData(r)
}
```

Each type of Reader is created differently, as I demonstrate later in this chapter and later chapters. To create a reader based on a string, the strings package provides a NewReader constructor function, which accepts a string as its argument:

```
...
r := strings.NewReader("Kayak")
...
```

To emphasize the use of the interface, I use the result from the NewReader function as an argument to a function that accepts an io.Reader. Within the function, I use the Read method to read bytes of data. I specify the maximum number of bytes that I want to receive by setting the size of the byte slice that is passed to the Read function. The results from the Read function indicate how many bytes of data have been read and whether there has been an error.

The io package defines a special error named EOF, which is used to signal when the Reader reaches the end of the data. If the error result from the Read function is equal to the EOF error, then I break out of the for loop that has been reading data from the Reader:

```
...
if err == io.EOF {
    break
}
...
```

The effect is that the for loop calls the Read function to get a maximum of two bytes at a time and writes them out. When the end of the string is reached, the Read function returns the EOF error, which leads to the termination of the for loop. Compile and execute the code, and you will receive the following output:

```
Read 2 bytes: Ka
Read 2 bytes: ya
Read 1 bytes: k
```

Understanding Writers

The Writer interface defines the method described in Table 20-4.

Table 20-4. *The Writer Interface*

Name	Description
Write(byteSlice)	This method writes the data from the specified byte slice. The method returns the number of bytes that were written and an error. The error will be non-nil if the number of bytes written is less than the length of the slice.

The Writer interface doesn't include any details of how the written data is stored, transmitted, or processed, all of which is left to the types that implement the interface. In Listing 20-7, I have created a Writer that creates a string with the data it receives.

Listing 20-7. Using a Writer in the main.go File in the readersandwriters Folder

```
package main

import (
    "io"
    "strings"
)

func processData(reader io.Reader, writer io.Writer) {
    b := make([]byte, 2)
    for {
        count, err := reader.Read(b);
        if (count > 0) {
            writer.Write(b[0:count])
            Printfln("Read %v bytes: %v", count, string(b[0:count]))
        }
        if err == io.EOF {
            break
        }
    }
}

func main() {
    r := strings.NewReader("Kayak")
    var builder strings.Builder
    processData(r, &builder)
    Printfln("String builder contents: %s", builder.String())
}
```

The strings.Builder struct that I described in Chapter 16 implements the io.Writer interface, which means that I can write bytes to a Builder and then call its String method to create a string from those bytes.

Writers will return an error if they are unable to write all the data in the slice. In Listing 20-7, I check the error result and break out of the for loop if an error is returned. However, since the Writer in this example is building an in-memory string, there is little chance of an error occurring.

Notice that I use the address operator to pass a pointer to the Builder to the processData function, like this:

```
...
processData(r, &builder)
...
```

As a general rule, the Reader and Writer methods are implemented for pointers so that passing a Reader or Writer to a function doesn't create a copy. I didn't have to use the address operator for the Reader in Listing 20-7 because the result from the strings.NewReader function is a pointer.

Compile and execute the project, and you will receive the following output, showing that the bytes were read from one string and used to create another:

```
Read 2 bytes: Ka
Read 2 bytes: ya
Read 1 bytes: k
String builder contents: Kayak
```

Using the Utility Functions for Readers and Writers

The io package contains a set of functions that provide additional ways to read and write data, as described in Table 20-5.

Table 20-5. *Functions in the io Package for Readng and Writing Data*

Name	Description
Copy(w, r)	This function copies data from a Reader to a Writer until EOF is returned or another error is encountered. The results are the number of bytes copies and an error used to describe any problems.
CopyBuffer (w, r, buffer)	This function performs the same task as Copy but reads the data into the specified buffer before it is passed to the Writer.
CopyN (w, r, count)	This function copies count bytes from the Reader to the Writer. The results are the number of bytes copies and an error used to describe any problems.
ReadAll(r)	This function reads data from the specified Reader until EOF is reached. The results are a byte slice containing the read data and an error, which is used to describe any problems.
ReadAtLeast (r, byteSlice, min)	This function reads at least the specified number of bytes from the reader, placing them into the byte slice. An error is reported if fewer bytes than specified are read.
ReadFull (r, byteSlice)	This function fills the specified byte slice with data. The result is the number of bytes read and an error. An error will be reported if EOF was encountered before enough bytes to fill the slice were read.
WriteString(w, str)	This function writes the specified string to a writer.

The functions in Table 20-5 use the Read and Write methods defined by the Reader and Writer interfaces, but do so in more convenient ways, avoiding the need to define a for loop whenever you need to process data. In Listing 20-8, I have used the Copy function to copy the bytes in the example string from the Reader and to the Writer.

Listing 20-8. Copying Data in the main.go File in the readersandwriters Folder

```
package main

import (
    "io"
    "strings"
)

func processData(reader io.Reader, writer io.Writer) {
    count, err := io.Copy(writer, reader)
    if (err == nil) {
        Printfln("Read %v bytes", count)
    } else {
        Printfln("Error: %v", err.Error())
    }
}
```

```
func main() {
    r := strings.NewReader("Kayak")
    var builder strings.Builder
    processData(r, &builder)
    Printfln("String builder contents: %s", builder.String())
}
```

Using the Copy function achieves the same result as the previous example but more concisely. Compile and execute the code, and you will receive the following output:

```
Read 5 bytes
String builder contents: Kayak
```

Using the Specialized Readers and Writers

In addition to the basic Reader and Writer interfaces, the io package provides some specialized implementations that are described in Table 20-6 and demonstrated in the sections that follow.

Table 20-6. *The io Package Functions for Specialized Readers and Writers*

Name	Description
Pipe()	This function returns a PipeReader and a PipeWriter, which can be used to connect functions that require a Reader and a Writer, as described in the "Using Pipes" section.
MultiReader (...readers)	This function defines a variadic parameter that allows an arbitrary number of Reader values to be specified. The result is a Reader that passes on the content from each of its parameters in the sequence they are defined, as described in the "Concatenating Multiple Readers" section.
MultiWriter (...writers)	This function defines a variadic parameter that allows an arbitrary number of Writer values to be specified. The result is a Writer that sends the same data to all the specified writers, as described in the "Combining Multiple Writers" section.
LimitReader (r, limit)	This function creates a Reader that will EOF after the specified number of bytes, as described in the "Limiting Read Data" section.

Using Pipes

Pipes are used to connect code that consumes data through a Reader and code that produces code through a Writer. Add a file named data.go to the readersandwriters folder with the content shown in Listing 20-9.

Listing 20-9. The Contents of the data.go File in the readersandwriters Folder

```
package main

import "io"

func GenerateData(writer io.Writer) {
    data := []byte("Kayak, Lifejacket")
    writeSize := 4
```

```
    for i := 0; i < len(data); i += writeSize {
        end := i + writeSize;
        if (end > len(data)) {
            end = len(data)
        }
        count, err := writer.Write(data[i: end])
        Printfln("Wrote %v byte(s): %v", count, string(data[i: end]))
        if (err != nil)  {
            Printfln("Error: %v", err.Error())
        }
    }
}

func ConsumeData(reader io.Reader) {
    data := make([]byte, 0, 10)
    slice := make([]byte, 2)
    for {
        count, err := reader.Read(slice)
        if (count > 0) {
            Printfln("Read data: %v", string(slice[0:count]))
            data = append(data, slice[0:count]...)
        }
        if (err == io.EOF) {
            break
        }
    }
    Printfln("Read data: %v", string(data))
}
```

The GenerateData function defines a Writer parameter, which it uses to write bytes from a string. The ConsumeData function defines a Reader parameter, which it uses to read bytes of data, which are then used to create a string.

Real projects don't need to read bytes from one string just to create another, but doing so provides a good demonstration of how pipes work, as shown in Listing 20-10.

Listing 20-10. Using Pipes in the main.go File in the readersandwriters Folder

```
package main

import (
    "io"
    //"strings"
)

// func processData(reader io.Reader, writer io.Writer) {
//     count, err := io.Copy(writer, reader)
//     if (err == nil) {
//         Printfln("Read %v bytes", count)
//     } else {
//         Printfln("Error: %v", err.Error())
//     }
// }
```

```
func main() {
    pipeReader, pipeWriter := io.Pipe()
    go func() {
        GenerateData(pipeWriter)
        pipeWriter.Close()
    }()
    ConsumeData(pipeReader)
}
```

The io.Pipe function returns a PipeReader and a PipeWriter. The PipeReader and PipeWriter structs implement the Closer interface, which defines the method shown in Table 20-7.

Table 20-7. *The Closer Method*

Name	Description
Close()	This method closes the reader or writer. The details are implementation specific, but, in general, any subsequent reads from a closed Reader will return zero bytes and the EOF error, while any subsequent writes to a closed Writer will return an error.

Since the PipeWriter implements the Writer interface, I can use it as the argument to the GenerateData function and then invoke the Close method once the function has completed so that the reader will receive EOF, like this:

```
...
GenerateData(pipeWriter)
pipeWriter.Close()
...
```

Pipes are synchronous, such that the PipeWriter.Write method will block until the data is read from the pipe. This means that the PipeWriter needs to be used in a different goroutine from the reader to prevent the application from deadlocking:

```
...
go func() {
    GenerateData(pipeWriter)
    pipeWriter.Close()
}()
...
```

Notice the parentheses at the end of this statement. These are required when creating a goroutine for an anonymous function, but it is easy to forget them.

The PipeReader struct implements the Reader interface, which means I can use it as the argument to the ConsumeData function. The ConsumeData function is executed in the main goroutine, which means that the application won't exit until the function completes.

The effect is that data is written into the pipe using the PipeWriter and read from the pipe using the PipeReader. When the GenerateData function is complete, the Close method is called on the PipeWriter, which causes the next read by the PipeReader to produce EOF. Compile and execute the project, and you will receive the following output:

```
Read data: Ka
Wrote 4 byte(s): Kaya
Read data: ya
Read data: k,
Wrote 4 byte(s): k, L
Read data:  L
Read data: if
Wrote 4 byte(s): ifej
Read data: ej
Read data: ac
Wrote 4 byte(s): acke
Read data: ke
Wrote 1 byte(s): t
Read data: t
Read data: Kayak, Lifejacket
```

The output highlights the fact that pipes are synchronous. The GenerateData function calls the writer's Write method and then blocks until the data is read. This is why the first message in the output is from the reader: the reader is consuming the data two bytes at a time, which means that two read operations are required before the initial call to the Write method, which is used to send four bytes, completes, and the message from the GenerateData function is displayed.

Improving the Example

In Listing 20-10, I called the Close method on the PipeWriter in the goroutine that executes the GenerateData function. This works, but I prefer to check to see whether a Writer implements the Closer interface in the code that produces the data, as shown in Listing 20-11.

Listing 20-11. Closing a Writer in the data.go File in the readersandwriters Folder

```
...
func GenerateData(writer io.Writer) {
    data := []byte("Kayak, Lifejacket")
    writeSize := 4
    for i := 0; i < len(data); i += writeSize {
        end := i + writeSize;
        if (end > len(data)) {
            end = len(data)
        }
        count, err := writer.Write(data[i: end])
        Printfln("Wrote %v byte(s): %v", count, string(data[i: end]))
        if (err != nil)  {
            Printfln("Error: %v", err.Error())
        }
    }
    if closer, ok := writer.(io.Closer); ok {
        closer.Close()
    }
}
...
```

This approach provides consistent handlers of Writers that define a Close method, which includes some of the most useful types described in later chapters. It also allows me to change the goroutine so that it executes the GenerateData function without the need for an anonymous function, as shown in Listing 20-12.

Listing 20-12. Simplifying the Code in the main.go File in the readersandwriters Folder

```
package main

import (
    "io"
    //"strings"
)

func main() {
    pipeReader, pipeWriter := io.Pipe()
    go GenerateData(pipeWriter)
    ConsumeData(pipeReader)
}
```

This example produces the same output as the code in Listing 20-10.

Concatenating Multiple Readers

The MultiReader function concentrates the input from multiple readers so they can be processed in sequence, as shown in Listing 20-13.

Listing 20-13. Concatenating Readers in the main.go File in the readersandwriters Folder

```
package main

import (
    "io"
    "strings"
)

func main() {

    r1 := strings.NewReader("Kayak")
    r2 := strings.NewReader("Lifejacket")
    r3 := strings.NewReader("Canoe")

    concatReader := io.MultiReader(r1, r2, r3)

    ConsumeData(concatReader)
}
```

The Reader returned by the MultiReader function responds to the Read method with content from one of the underlying Reader values. When the first Reader returns EOF, then content is read from the second Reader. This process continues until the final underlying Reader returns EOF. Compile and execute the code, and you will see the following output:

```
Read data: Ka
Read data: ya
Read data: k
Read data: Li
Read data: fe
Read data: ja
Read data: ck
Read data: et
Read data: Ca
Read data: no
Read data: e
Read data: KayakLifejacketCanoe
```

Combining Multiple Writers

The MultiWriter function combines multiple writers so that data is sent to all of them, as shown in Listing 20-14.

Listing 20-14. Combining Writers in the main.go File in the readersandwriters Folder

```
package main

import (
    "io"
    "strings"
)

func main() {

    var w1 strings.Builder
    var w2 strings.Builder
    var w3 strings.Builder

    combinedWriter := io.MultiWriter(&w1, &w2, &w3)

    GenerateData(combinedWriter)

    Printfln("Writer #1: %v", w1.String())
    Printfln("Writer #2: %v", w2.String())
    Printfln("Writer #3: %v", w3.String())
}
```

The writers in this example are string.Builder values, which were described in Chapter 16 and which implement the Writer interface. The MultiWriter function is used to create a Writer, such that calling the Write method will cause the same data to be written to the three individual writers. Compile and execute the project, and you will see the following output:

```
Wrote 4 byte(s): Kaya
Wrote 4 byte(s): k, L
Wrote 4 byte(s): ifej
```

527

```
Wrote 4 byte(s): acke
Wrote 1 byte(s): t
Writer #1: Kayak, Lifejacket
Writer #2: Kayak, Lifejacket
Writer #3: Kayak, Lifejacket
```

Echoing Reads to a Writer

The TeeReader function returns a Reader that echoes the data that it receives to a Writer, as shown in Listing 20-15.

Listing 20-15. Echoing Data in the main.go File in the readersandwriters Folder

```go
package main

import (
    "io"
    "strings"
)

func main() {

    r1 := strings.NewReader("Kayak")
    r2 := strings.NewReader("Lifejacket")
    r3 := strings.NewReader("Canoe")

    concatReader := io.MultiReader(r1, r2, r3)

    var writer strings.Builder
    teeReader := io.TeeReader(concatReader, &writer);

    ConsumeData(teeReader)
    Printfln("Echo data: %v", writer.String())
}
```

The TeeReader function is used to create a Reader that will echo data to a strings.Builder, which was described in Chapter 16 and which implements the Writer interface. Compile and execute the project, and you will see the following output, which includes the echoed data:

```
Read data: Ka
Read data: ya
Read data: k
Read data: Li
Read data: fe
Read data: ja
Read data: ck
Read data: et
Read data: Ca
Read data: no
```

```
Read data: e
Read data: KayakLifejacketCanoe
Echo data: KayakLifejacketCanoe
```

Limiting Read Data

The LimitReader function is used to restrict the amount of data that can be obtained from a Reader, as shown in Listing 20-16.

Listing 20-16. Limiting Data in the main.go File in the readersandwriters Folder

```
package main

import (
    "io"
    "strings"
)

func main() {

    r1 := strings.NewReader("Kayak")
    r2 := strings.NewReader("Lifejacket")
    r3 := strings.NewReader("Canoe")

    concatReader := io.MultiReader(r1, r2, r3)

    limited := io.LimitReader(concatReader, 5)
    ConsumeData(limited)
}
```

The first argument to the LimitReader function is the Reader that will provide the data. The second argument is the maximum number of bytes that can be read. The Reader returned by the LimitReader function will send EOF when the limit is reached—unless the underlying reader sends EOF first. In Listing 20-16, I set the limit to 5 bytes, which produces the following output when the project is compiled and executed:

```
Read data: Ka
Read data: ya
Read data: k
Read data: Kayak
```

Buffering Data

The bufio package provides support for adding buffers to readers and writers. To see how data is processed without a buffer, add a file named custom.go to the readersandwriters folder with the content shown in Listing 20-17.

Listing 20-17. The Contents of the custom.go File in the readersandwriters Folder

```
package main

import "io"

type CustomReader struct {
    reader io.Reader
    readCount int
}

func NewCustomReader(reader io.Reader) *CustomReader {
    return &CustomReader { reader, 0 }
}

func (cr *CustomReader) Read(slice []byte) (count int, err error) {
    count, err = cr.reader.Read(slice)
    cr.readCount++
    Printfln("Custom Reader: %v bytes", count)
    if (err == io.EOF) {
        Printfln("Total Reads: %v", cr.readCount)
    }
    return
}
```

The code in Listing 20-17 defined a struct type named CustomReader that acts as a wrapper around a Reader. The implementation of the Read method generates output that reports how much data is read and how many read operations are performed overall. Listing 20-18 uses the new type as a wrapper around a string-based Reader.

Listing 20-18. Using a Reader Wrapper in the main.go File in the readersandwriters Folder

```
package main

import (
    "io"
    "strings"
)

func main() {

    text := "It was a boat. A small boat."

    var reader io.Reader = NewCustomReader(strings.NewReader(text))
    var writer strings.Builder
    slice := make([]byte, 5)

    for {
        count, err := reader.Read(slice)
        if (count > 0) {
            writer.Write(slice[0:count])
        }
```

```
        if (err != nil) {
            break
        }
    }

    Printfln("Read data: %v", writer.String())
}
```

The NewCustomreader function is used to create a CustomReader that reads from a string and uses a for loop to consume the data using a byte slice. Compile and execute the project, and you will see how the data is read:

```
Custom Reader: 5 bytes
Custom Reader: 5 bytes
Custom Reader: 5 bytes
Custom Reader: 5 bytes
Custom Reader: 5 bytes
Custom Reader: 3 bytes
Custom Reader: 0 bytes
Total Reads: 7
Read data: It was a boat. A small boat.
```

It is the size of the byte slice passed to the Read function that determines how data is consumed. In this case, the size of the slice is five, which means that a maximum of five bytes is read for each call to the Read function. There are two reads that did not obtain 5 bytes of data. The penultimate read produced three bytes because the source data isn't neatly divisible by five and there were three bytes of data left over. The final read returned zero bytes but received the EOF error, indicating that the end of the data had been reached.

In total, reading 28 bytes required 7 reads. (I chose the source data so that all of the characters in the string require a single byte, but you may see a different number of reads if you change the example to introduce characters that require multiple bytes.)

Reading small amounts of data can be problematic when there is a large amount of overhead associated with each operation. This isn't an issue when reading a string stored in memory, but reading data from other data sources, such as files, can be more expensive, and it can be preferable to make a smaller number of larger reads. This is done by introducing a buffer into which a large amount of data is read to service several smaller requests for data. Table 20-8 describes the functions provided by the bufio package that create buffered readers.

Table 20-8. *The bufio Functions for Creating Buffered Readers*

Name	Description
NewReader(r)	This function returns a buffered Reader with the default buffer size (which is 4,096 bytes at the time of writing).
NewReaderSize(r, size)	This function returns a buffered Reader with the specified buffer size.

The results produced by the NewReader and NewReaderSize implement the Reader interface but introduce a buffer, which can reduce the number of read operations made to the underlying data source. Listing 20-19 demonstrates the introduction of a buffer into the example.

Listing 20-19. Using a Buffer in the main.go File in the readersandwriters Folder

```go
package main

import (
    "io"
    "strings"
    "bufio"
)

func main() {

    text := "It was a boat. A small boat."

    var reader io.Reader = NewCustomReader(strings.NewReader(text))
    var writer strings.Builder
    slice := make([]byte, 5)

    reader = bufio.NewReader(reader)

    for {
        count, err := reader.Read(slice)
        if (count > 0) {
            writer.Write(slice[0:count])
        }
        if (err != nil) {
            break
        }
    }

    Printfln("Read data: %v", writer.String())
}
```

I used the NewReader function, which creates a Reader with the default buffer size. The buffered Reader fills its buffer and uses the data it contains to respond to calls to the Read method. Compile and execute the project to see the effect of introducing a buffer:

```
Custom Reader: 28 bytes
Custom Reader: 0 bytes
Total Reads: 2
Read data: It was a boat. A small boat.
```

The default buffer size is 4,096 bytes, which means that the buffered reader was able to read all the data in a single read operation, plus an additional read to produce the EOF result. Introducing the buffer reduces the overhead associated with the read operations, albeit at the cost of the memory used to buffer the data.

Using the Additional Buffered Reader Methods

The NewReader and NewReaderSize functions return bufio.Reader values, which implement the io.
Reader interface and which can be used as drop-in wrappers for other types of Reader methods, seamlessly
introducing a read buffer.

The bufio.Reader struct defines additional methods that make direct use of the buffer, as described in
Table 20-9.

Table 20-9. *The Methods Defined by the Buffered Reader*

Name	Description
Buffered()	This method returns an int that indicates the number of bytes that can be read from the buffer.
Discard(count)	This method discards the specified number of bytes.
Peek(count)	This method returns the specified number of bytes without removing them from the buffer, meaning they will be returned by subsequent calls to the Read method.
Reset(reader)	This method discards the data in the buffer and performs subsequent reads from the specified Reader.
Size()	This method returns the size of the buffer, expressed int.

Listing 20-20 shows the use of the Size and Buffered methods to report the size of the buffer and how
much data it contains.

Listing 20-20. Working with the Buffer in the main.go File in the readersandwriters Folder

```
package main

import (
    "io"
    "strings"
    "bufio"
)

func main() {

    text := "It was a boat. A small boat."

    var reader io.Reader = NewCustomReader(strings.NewReader(text))
    var writer strings.Builder
    slice := make([]byte, 5)

    buffered := bufio.NewReader(reader)

    for {
        count, err := buffered.Read(slice)
        if (count > 0) {
            Printfln("Buffer size: %v, buffered: %v",
                buffered.Size(), buffered.Buffered())
            writer.Write(slice[0:count])
        }
```

```
        if (err != nil) {
            break
        }
    }

    Printfln("Read data: %v", writer.String())
}
```

Compile and execute the project, and you will see that each read operation consumes some of the buffered data:

```
Custom Reader: 28 bytes
Buffer size: 4096, buffered: 23
Buffer size: 4096, buffered: 18
Buffer size: 4096, buffered: 13
Buffer size: 4096, buffered: 8
Buffer size: 4096, buffered: 3
Buffer size: 4096, buffered: 0
Custom Reader: 0 bytes
Total Reads: 2
Read data: It was a boat. A small boat.
```

Performing Buffered Writes

The bufio package also provides support for creating writers that use a buffer, using the functions described in Table 20-10.

Table 20-10. *The bufio Functions for Creating Buffered Writers*

Name	Description
NewWriter(w)	This function returns a buffered Writer with the default buffer size (which is 4,096 bytes at the time of writing).
NewWriterSize(w, size)	This function returns a buffered Writer with the specified buffer size.

The results produced by the functions described in Table 20-10 implement the Writer interface, which means they can be used to seamlessly introduce a buffer for writes. The specific data type returned by these functions is bufio.Writer, which defines the methods described in Table 20-11 for managing the buffer and its contents.

Table 20-11. *The Methods Defined by the bufio.Writer Struct*

Name	Description
Available()	This method returns the number of available bytes in the buffer.
Buffered()	This method returns the number of bytes that have been written to the buffer.
Flush()	This method writes the contents of the buffer to the underlying Writer.
Reset(writer)	This method discards the data in the buffer and performs subsequent writes to the specified Writer.
Size()	This method returns the capacity of the buffer in bytes.

Listing 20-21 defines a custom Writer that reports on its operations and that will show the effect of the buffer. This is the counterpart to the Reader created in the previous section.

Listing 20-21. Defining a Custom Writer in the custom.go File in the readersandwriters Folder

```
package main

import "io"

// ...reader type and functions omitted for brevity...

type CustomWriter struct {
    writer io.Writer
    writeCount int
}

func NewCustomWriter(writer io.Writer) * CustomWriter {
    return &CustomWriter{ writer, 0}
}

func (cw *CustomWriter) Write(slice []byte) (count int, err error) {
    count, err = cw.writer.Write(slice)
    cw.writeCount++
    Printfln("Custom Writer: %v bytes", count)
    return
}

func (cw *CustomWriter) Close() (err error) {
    if closer, ok := cw.writer.(io.Closer); ok {
        closer.Close()
    }
    Printfln("Total Writes: %v", cw.writeCount)
    return
}
```

The NewCustomWriter constructor wraps a Writer with a CustomWriter struct, which reports on its write operations. Listing 20-22 demonstrates the way write operations are performed without buffering.

Listing 20-22. Performing Unbuffered Writes in the main.go File in the readersandwriters Folder

```
package main

import (
    //"io"
    "strings"
    //"bufio"
)

func main() {

    text := "It was a boat. A small boat."

    var builder strings.Builder
    var writer = NewCustomWriter(&builder)
    for i := 0; true; {
        end := i + 5
        if (end >= len(text)) {
            writer.Write([]byte(text[i:]))
            break
        }
        writer.Write([]byte(text[i:end]))
        i = end
    }
    Printfln("Written data: %v", builder.String())
}
```

The example writes five bytes at a time to the Writer, which is backed by a Builder from the strings package. Compile and execute the project, and you can see the effect of each call to the Write method:

```
Custom Writer: 5 bytes
Custom Writer: 5 bytes
Custom Writer: 5 bytes
Custom Writer: 5 bytes
Custom Writer: 5 bytes
Custom Writer: 3 bytes
Written data: It was a boat. A small boat.
```

The buffered Writer keeps data in a buffer and passes it on to the underlying Writer only when the buffer is full or when the Flush method is called. Listing 20-23 introduces a buffer into the example.

Listing 20-23. Using a Buffered Writer in the main.go File in the readersandwriters Folder

```
package main

import (
    //"io"
    "strings"
    "bufio"
)
```

536

```
func main() {

    text := "It was a boat. A small boat."

    var builder strings.Builder
    var writer = bufio.NewWriterSize(NewCustomWriter(&builder), 20)
    for i := 0; true; {
        end := i + 5
        if (end >= len(text)) {
            writer.Write([]byte(text[i:]))
            writer.Flush()
            break
        }
        writer.Write([]byte(text[i:end]))
        i = end
    }
    Printfln("Written data: %v", builder.String())
}
```

The transition to a buffered Writer isn't entirely seamless because it is important to call the Flush method to ensure that all the data is written out. The buffer I selected in Listing 20-23 is 20 bytes, which is much smaller than the default buffer—and too small to have an effect in real projects—but it is ideal for showing how the introduction of a buffer reduces the number of write operations in the example. Compile and execute the project, and you will see the following output:

```
Custom Writer: 20 bytes
Custom Writer: 8 bytes
Written data: It was a boat. A small boat.
```

Formatting and Scanning with Readers and Writers

In Chapter 17, I described the formatting and scanning features provided by the fmt package and demonstrated their use with strings. As I noted in that chapter, the fmt package provides support for applying these features to Readers and Writers, as described in the following sections. I also describe how features from the strings package can be used with Writers.

Scanning Values from a Reader

The fmt package provides functions for scanning values from a Reader and converting them into different types, as shown in Listing 20-24. (Using a function to scan values is not a requirement, and I have done so only to emphasize that the scanning process works on any Reader.)

Listing 20-24. Scanning from a Reader in the main.go File in the readersandwriters Folder

```
package main

import (
    "io"
    "strings"
    //"bufio"
    "fmt"
)

func scanFromReader(reader io.Reader, template string,
        vals ...interface{}) (int, error) {
    return fmt.Fscanf(reader, template, vals...)
}

func main() {

    reader := strings.NewReader("Kayak Watersports $279.00")

    var name, category string
    var price float64
    scanTemplate := "%s %s $%f"

    _, err := scanFromReader(reader, scanTemplate, &name, &category, &price)
    if (err != nil) {
        Printfln("Error: %v", err.Error())
    } else {
        Printfln("Name: %v", name)
        Printfln("Category: %v", category)
        Printfln("Price: %.2f", price)
    }
}
```

The scanning process reads bytes from the Reader and uses the scanning template to parse the data that is received. The scanning template in Listing 20-24 contains two strings and a float64 value, and compiling and executing the code produces the following output:

```
Name: Kayak
Category: Watersports
Price: 279.00
```

A useful technique when using a Reader is to scan data gradually using a loop, as shown in Listing 20-25. This approach works well when bytes arrive over time, such as when reading from an HTTP connection (which I describe in Chapter 25).

Listing 20-25. Scanning Gradually in the main.go File in the readersandwriters Folder

```
package main

import (
    "io"
    "strings"
    //"bufio"
    "fmt"
)

func scanFromReader(reader io.Reader, template string,
        vals ...interface{}) (int, error) {
    return fmt.Fscanf(reader, template, vals...)
}

func scanSingle(reader io.Reader, val interface{}) (int, error) {
    return fmt.Fscan(reader, val)
}

func main() {

    reader := strings.NewReader("Kayak Watersports $279.00")

    for {
        var str string
        _, err := scanSingle(reader, &str)
        if (err != nil) {
            if (err != io.EOF) {
                Println("Error: %v", err.Error())
            }
            break
        }
        Println("Value: %v", str)
    }
}
```

The for loop calls the scanSingle function, which uses the Fscan function to read a string from the Reader. Values are read until EOF is returned, at which point the loop is terminated. Compile and execute the project, and you will receive the following output:

```
Value: Kayak
Value: Watersports
Value: $279.00
```

Writing Formatted Strings to a Writer

The fmt package also provides functions for writing formatted strings to a Writer, as shown in Listing 20-26. (Using a function to format strings is not a requirement, and I have done so only to emphasize that formatting works with any Reader.)

Listing 20-26. Writing a Formatted String in the main.go File in the readersandwriters Folder

```go
package main

import (
    "io"
    "strings"
    //"bufio"
    "fmt"
)

// func scanFromReader(reader io.Reader, template string,
//         vals ...interface{}) (int, error) {
//     return fmt.Fscanf(reader, template, vals...)
// }

// func scanSingle(reader io.Reader, val interface{}) (int, error) {
//     return fmt.Fscan(reader, val)
// }

func writeFormatted(writer io.Writer, template string, vals ...interface{}) {
    fmt.Fprintf(writer, template, vals...)
}

func main() {

    var writer strings.Builder
    template := "Name: %s, Category: %s, Price: $%.2f"

    writeFormatted(&writer, template, "Kayak", "Watersports", float64(279))

    fmt.Println(writer.String())
}
```

The writeFormatted function uses the fmt.Fprintf function to write a string formatted with a template to a Writer. Compile and execute the project, and you will see the following output:

```
Name: Kayak, Category: Watersports, Price: $279.00
```

Using a Replacer with a Writer

The strings.Replacer struct can be used to perform replacements on a string and output the modified result to a Writer, as shown in Listing 20-27.

Listing 20-27. Using a Replacer in the main.go File in the readersandwriters Folder

```go
package main

import (
    "io"
```

```
    "strings"
    //"bufio"
    "fmt"
)

func writeReplaced(writer io.Writer, str string, subs ...string) {
    replacer := strings.NewReplacer(subs...)
    replacer.WriteString(writer, str)
}

func main() {

    text := "It was a boat. A small boat."
    subs := []string { "boat", "kayak", "small", "huge" }

    var writer strings.Builder
    writeReplaced(&writer, text, subs...)
    fmt.Println(writer.String())
}
```

The WriteString method performs its substitutions and writes out the modified string. Compile and execute the code, and you will receive the following output:

```
It was a kayak. A huge kayak.
```

Summary

In this chapter, I described the Reader and Writer interfaces, which are used throughout the standard library wherever data is read or written. I describe the methods these interfaces define, explained the use of the specialized implementations that are available, and showed you how buffering, formatting, and scanning is achieved. In the next chapter, I describe the support for processing JSON data, which makes use of the features described in this chapter.

CHAPTER 21

■ ■ ■

Working with JSON Data

In this chapter, I describe the Go standard library support for the JavaScript Object Notation (JSON) format. JSON has become the de facto standard for representing data, largely because it is simple and works across platforms. See http://json.org for a concise description of the data format if you have not encountered JSON before. JSON is often encountered as the data format used in RESTful web services, which I demonstrate in Part 3. Table 21-1 puts the JSON features in context.

Table 21-1. *Putting Working with JSON Data in Context*

Question	Answer
What is it?	JSON data is the de facto standard for exchanging data, especially in HTTP applications.
Why is it useful?	JSON is simple enough to be supported by any language but can represent relatively complex data.
How is it used?	The encoding/json package provides support for encoding and decoding JSON data.
Are there any pitfalls or limitations?	Not all Go data types can be represented in JSON, which requires the developer to be mindful of how Go data types will be expressed.
Are there any alternatives?	There are many other data encodings available, some of which are supported by the Go standard library.

Table 21-2 summarizes the chapter.

Table 21-2. *Chapter Summary*

Problem	Solution	Listing
Encode JSON data	Create an Encoder with a Writer and invoke the Encode method	2–7, 14, 15
Control struct encoding	Use JSON struct tags or implement the Mashaler interface	8–13, 16
Decode JSON data	Create a Decoder with a Reader and invoke the Decode method	17–25
Control struct decoding	Use JSON struct tags or implement the Unmarshaler interface	26–28

© Adam Freeman 2022
A. Freeman, *Pro Go*, https://doi.org/10.1007/978-1-4842-7355-5_21

Preparing for This Chapter

In this chapter, I continue using the readersandwriters project created in Chapter 20. No changes are required to prepare for this chapter. Open a new command prompt, navigate to the readersandwriters folder, and run the command shown in Listing 21-1 to compile and execute the project.

■ **Tip** You can download the example project for this chapter—and for all the other chapters in this book—from https://github.com/apress/pro-go. See Chapter 2 for how to get help if you have problems running the examples.

Listing 21-1. Compiling the Executing the Project

```
go run .
```

The compiled project produces the following output when it is executed:

```
It was a kayak. A huge kayak.
```

Reading and Writing JSON Data

The encoding/json package provides support for encoding and decoding JSON data, as demonstrated in the following sections. For quick reference, Table 21-3 describes the constructor functions that are used to create the structs to encode and decode JSON data and that are described in detail next.

■ **Note** The Go standard library includes packages for other data formats, including XML and CSV. See https://golang.org/pkg/encoding for details.

Table 21-3. The encoding/json Constructor Functions for JSON Data

Name	Description
NewEncoder(writer)	This function returns an Encoder, which can be used to encode JSON data and write it to the specified Writer.
NewDecoder(reader)	This function returns a Decoder, which can be used to read JSON data from the specified Reader and decode it.

The encoding/json package also provides functions for encoding and decoding JSON without using a Reader or Writer, described in Table 21-4.

Table 21-4. The Functions for Creating and Parsing JSON Data

Name	Description
Marshal(value)	This function encodes the specified value as JSON. The results are the JSON content expressed in a byte slice and an error, which indicates any encoding problems.
Unmarshal(byteSlice, val)	This function parses JSON data contained in the specified slice of bytes and assigns the result to the specified value.

Encoding JSON Data

The NewEncoder constructor function is used to create an Encoder, which can be used to write JSON data to a Writer, using the methods described in Table 21-5.

Table 21-5. The Encoder Methods

Name	Description
Encode(val)	This method encodes the specified value as JSON and writes it to the Writer.
SetEscapeHTML(on)	This method accepts a bool argument that, when true, encodes characters that would be dangerous in HTML to be escaped. The default behavior is to escape these characters.
SetIndent(prefix, indent)	This method specifies a prefix and indentation that is applied to the name of each field in the JSON output.

In any language except JavaScript, the data types expressed by JSON don't line up exactly to the native data types. Table 21-6 summarizes how the basic Go data types are represented in JSON.

Table 21-6. Expressing the Basic Go Data Types in JSON

Data Type	Description
bool	Go bool values are expressed as JSON true or false.
string	Go string values are expressed as JSON strings. By default, unsafe HTML characters are escaped.
float32, float64	Go floating-point values are expressed as JSON numbers.
int, int<size>	Go integer values are expressed as JSON numbers.
uint, uint<size>	Go integer values are expressed as JSON numbers.
byte	Go bytes are expressed as JSON numbers.
rune	Go runes are expressed as JSON numbers.
nil	The Go nil value is expressed as the JSON null value.
Pointers	The JSON encoder follows pointers and encodes the value at the pointer's location.

Listing 21-2 demonstrates the process of creating a JSON encoder and encoding some of the basic Go types.

Listing 21-2. Encoding JSON Data in the main.go File in the readersandwriters Folder

```
package main

import (
    //"io"
    "strings"
    "fmt"
    "encoding/json"
)

// func writeReplaced(writer io.Writer, str string, subs ...string) {
//      replacer := strings.NewReplacer(subs...)
//      replacer.WriteString(writer, str)
// }

func main() {

    var b bool = true
    var str string = "Hello"
    var fval float64 = 99.99
    var ival int = 200
    var pointer *int = &ival

    var writer strings.Builder
    encoder := json.NewEncoder(&writer)

    for _, val := range []interface{} {b, str, fval, ival, pointer} {
        encoder.Encode(val)
    }

    fmt.Print(writer.String())
}
```

Listing 21-2 defines a series of variables of different basic types. The NewEncoder constructor is used to create an Encoder, and a for loop is used to encode each value as JSON. The data is written to a Builder, whose String method is called to display the JSON. Compile and execute the project, and you will see the following output:

```
true
"Hello"
99.99
200
200
```

Notice that I used the fmt.Print function to produce the output in Listing 21-2. The JSON Encoder adds a newline character after each value is encoded.

Encoding Arrays and Slices

Go slices and arrays are encoded as JSON arrays, with the exception that byte slices are expressed as base64-encoded strings. Byte arrays, however, are encoded as an array of JSON numbers. Listing 21-3 demonstrates the support for arrays and slices, including bytes.

Listing 21-3. Encoding Slices and Arrays in the main.go File in the readersandwriters Folder

```go
package main

import (
    "strings"
    "fmt"
    "encoding/json"
)

func main() {

    names := []string {"Kayak", "Lifejacket", "Soccer Ball"}
    numbers := [3]int { 10, 20, 30}
    var byteArray [5]byte
    copy(byteArray[0:], []byte(names[0]))
    byteSlice := []byte(names[0])

    var writer strings.Builder
    encoder := json.NewEncoder(&writer)

    encoder.Encode(names)
    encoder.Encode(numbers)
    encoder.Encode(byteArray)
    encoder.Encode(byteSlice)

    fmt.Print(writer.String())
}
```

The Encoder expresses each array in the JSON syntax, except the byte slice. Compile and execute the project, and you will see the following output:

```
["Kayak","Lifejacket","Soccer Ball"]
[10,20,30]
[75,97,121,97,107]
"S2F5YWs="
```

Notice that byte arrays and byte slices are processed differently, even when their contents are the same.

Encoding Maps

Go maps are encoded as JSON objects, with the map keys used as the object keys. The values contained in the map are encoded based on their type. Listing 21-4 encodes a map that contains float64 values.

> ■ **Tip** Maps can also be useful for creating custom JSON representations of Go data, as described in the "Creating Completely Custom JSON Encodings " section.

Listing 21-4. Encoding a Map in the main.go File in the readersandwriters Folder

```
package main

import (
    "strings"
    "fmt"
    "encoding/json"
)

func main() {

    m := map[string]float64 {
        "Kayak": 279,
        "Lifejacket": 49.95,
    }

    var writer strings.Builder
    encoder := json.NewEncoder(&writer)

    encoder.Encode(m)

    fmt.Print(writer.String())
}
```

Compile and execute the project, and you will see the following output, showing how the keys and values in the map are encoded as a JSON object:

```
{"Kayak":279,"Lifejacket":49.95}
```

Encoding Structs

The Encoder expresses struct values as JSON objects, using the exported struct field names as the object's keys and the field values as the object's values, as shown in Listing 21-5. Unexported fields are ignored.

Listing 21-5. Encoding a Struct in the main.go File in the readersandwriters Folder

```
package main

import (
    "strings"
    "fmt"
    "encoding/json"
)
```

548

```
func main() {

    var writer strings.Builder
    encoder := json.NewEncoder(&writer)
    encoder.Encode(Kayak)
    fmt.Print(writer.String())
}
```

This example encodes the Product struct value named Kayak, which was defined in Chapter 20. The Product struct defines exported Name, Category, and Price fields, and these can be seen in the output produced when the project is compiled and executed:

```
{"Name":"Kayak","Category":"Watersports","Price":279}
```

Understanding the Effect of Promotion in JSON in Encoding

When a struct defines an embedded field that is also a struct, the fields of the embedded struct are promoted and encoded as though they are defined by the enclosing type. Add a file named discount.go to the readersandwriters folder with the content shown in Listing 21-6.

Listing 21-6. The Contents of the discount.go File in the readersandwriters Folder

```
package main

type DiscountedProduct struct {
    *Product
    Discount float64
}
```

The DiscountedProduct struct type defines an embedded Product field. Listing 21-7 creates and encodes a DiscountedProduct as JSON.

Listing 21-7. Encoding a Struct with an Embedded Field in the main.go File in the readersandwriters Folder

```
package main

import (
    "strings"
    "fmt"
    "encoding/json"
)

func main() {

    var writer strings.Builder
    encoder := json.NewEncoder(&writer)
    dp := DiscountedProduct {
        Product: &Kayak,
        Discount: 10.50,
    }
```

```
encoder.Encode(&dp)
    fmt.Print(writer.String())
}
```

The Encoder promotes the Product fields in the JSON output, as shown in the output when the project is compiled and executed:

```
{"Name":"Kayak","Category":"Watersports","Price":279,"Discount":10.5}
```

Notice that Listing 21-7 encodes a pointer to the struct value. The Encode function follows the pointer and encodes the value at its location, which means that the code in Listing 21-7 encodes the DiscountedProduct value without creating a copy.

Customizing the JSON Encoding of Structs

How a struct is encoded can be customized using *struct tags*, which are string literals that follow fields. Struct tags are part of the Go support for reflection, which I describe in Chapter 28, but for this chapter it is enough to know that tags follow fields and can be used to alter two aspects of how a field is encoded in JSON, as shown in Listing 21-8.

Listing 21-8. Using a Struct Tag in the discount.go File in the readersandwriters Folder

```
package main

type DiscountedProduct struct {
    *Product `json:"product"`
    Discount float64
}
```

The struct tag follows a specific format, which is shown in Figure 21-1. The term json is followed by a colon, followed by the name that should be used when the field is encoded, enclosed in double quotes. The entire tag is enclosed in backticks.

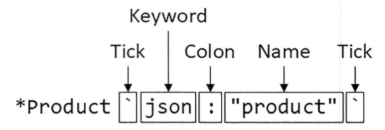

Figure 21-1. *A struct type*

The tag in Listing 21-8 specifies the name product for the embedded field. Compile and execute the project, and you will see the following output, which shows that using the tag has prevented field promotion:

```
{"product":{"Name":"Kayak","Category":"Watersports","Price":279},"Discount":10.5}
```

Omitting a Field

The Encoder skips fields decorated with a tag that specifies a hyphen (the - character) for the name, as shown in Listing 21-9.

Listing 21-9. Omitting a Field in the discount.go File in the readersandwriters Folder

```
package main

type DiscountedProduct struct {
    *Product `json:"product"`
    Discount float64 `json:"-"`
}
```

The new tag tells the Encoder to skip the Discount field when creating the JSON representation of a DIscountedProduct value. Compile and execute the project, and you will see the following output:

```
{"product":{"Name":"Kayak","Category":"Watersports","Price":279}}
```

Omitting Unassigned Fields

By default, the JSON Encoder includes struct fields, even when they have not been assigned a value, as shown in Listing 21-10.

Listing 21-10. An Unassigned Field in the main.go File in the readersandwriters Folder

```
package main

import (
    "strings"
    "fmt"
    "encoding/json"
)

func main() {

    var writer strings.Builder
    encoder := json.NewEncoder(&writer)

    dp := DiscountedProduct {
        Product: &Kayak,
        Discount: 10.50,
    }
    encoder.Encode(&dp)

    dp2 := DiscountedProduct { Discount: 10.50 }
    encoder.Encode(&dp2)

    fmt.Print(writer.String())
}
```

Compile and execute the code, and you can see the default handling for nil fields:

```
{"product":{"Name":"Kayak","Category":"Watersports","Price":279}}
{"product":null}
```

To omit a nil field, the omitempty keyword is added to the tag for the field, as shown in Listing 21-11.

Listing 21-11. Omitting a nil Field in the discount.go File in the readersandwriters Folder

```
package main

type DiscountedProduct struct {
    *Product `json:"product,omitempty"`
    Discount float64 `json:"-"`
}
```

The omitempty keyword is separated from the field name with a comma but without any spaces. Compile and execute the code, and you will see the output without the empty field:

```
{"product":{"Name":"Kayak","Category":"Watersports","Price":279}}
{}
```

To skip a nil field without changing the name or field promotion, specify the omitempty keyword without a name, as shown in Listing 21-12.

Listing 21-12. Omitting a Field in the discount.go File in the readersandwriters Folder

```
package main

type DiscountedProduct struct {
    *Product `json:",omitempty"`
    Discount float64 `json:"-"`
}
```

The Encoder will promote the Product fields if a value has been assigned to the embedded field and omit the field if no value has been assigned. Compile and execute the project, and you will see the following output:

```
{"Name":"Kayak","Category":"Watersports","Price":279}
{}
```

Forcing Fields to be Encoded as Strings

Struct tags can be used to force a field value to be encoded as a string, overriding the normal encoding for the field type, as shown in Listing 21-13.

Listing 21-13. Forcing String Evaluation in the discount.go File in the readersandwriters Folder

```
package main

type DiscountedProduct struct {
    *Product `json:",omitempty"`
    Discount float64 `json:",string"`
}
```

The addition of the string keyword overrides the default encoding and produces a string for the Discount field, which can be seen in the output that is produced when the project is compiled and executed:

```
{"Name":"Kayak","Category":"Watersports","Price":279,"Discount":"10.5"}
{"Discount":"10.5"}
```

Encoding Interfaces

The JSON encoder can be used on values assigned to interface variables, but it is the dynamic type that is encoded. Add a file named interface.go to the readersandwriters folder with the content shown in Listing 21-14.

Listing 21-14. The Contents of the interface.go File in the readersandwriters Folder

```
package main

type Named interface { GetName() string }

type Person struct { PersonName string}
func (p *Person) GetName() string { return p.PersonName}

func (p *DiscountedProduct) GetName() string { return p.Name}
```

This file defines a simple interface and a struct that implements it, as well as defining a method for the DiscountedProduct struct so that it implements the interface, too. Listing 21-15 uses the JSON encoder to encode an interface slice.

Listing 21-15. Encoding an Interface Slice in the main.go File in the readersandwriters Folder

```
package main

import (
    "strings"
    "fmt"
    "encoding/json"
)

func main() {

    var writer strings.Builder
    encoder := json.NewEncoder(&writer)
```

553

```
    dp := DiscountedProduct {
        Product: &Kayak,
        Discount: 10.50,
    }

    namedItems := []Named { &dp, &Person{ PersonName: "Alice"}}
    encoder.Encode(namedItems)

    fmt.Print(writer.String())
}
```

The slice of Named values contains different dynamic types, which can be seen by compiling and executing the project:

```
[{"Name":"Kayak","Category":"Watersports","Price":279,"Discount":"10.5"},
 {"PersonName":"Alice"}]
```

No aspect of the interface is used to adapt the JSON, and all the exported fields of each value in the slice are included in the JSON. This can be a useful feature, but care must be taken when decoding this kind of JSON, because each value can have a different set of fields, as I explain in the "Decoding Arrays" section.

Creating Completely Custom JSON Encodings

The Encoder checks to see whether a struct implements the Marshaler interface, which denotes a type that has a custom encoding and which defines the method described in Table 21-7.

Table 21-7. *The Marshaler Method*

Name	Description
MarshalJSON()	This method is invoked to create a JSON representation of a value and returns a byte slice containing the JSON and an error indicating encoding problems.

Listing 21-16 implements the Marshaler interface for pointers to the DiscountedProduct struct type.

Listing 21-16. Implementing the Marshaler Interface in the discount.go File in the readersandwriters Folder

```
package main

import "encoding/json"

type DiscountedProduct struct {
    *Product `json:",omitempty"`
    Discount float64 `json:",string"`
}

func (dp *DiscountedProduct) MarshalJSON() (jsn []byte, err error) {
    if (dp.Product != nil) {
        m := map[string]interface{} {
            "product": dp.Name,
```

```
        "cost": dp.Price - dp.Discount,
        }
        jsn, err = json.Marshal(m)
    }
    return
}
```

The `MarshalJSON` method can generate JSON in any way that suits the project, but I find the most reliable approach is to use the support for encoding maps. I define a map with `string` keys and use the empty interface for the values. This allows me to build the JSON by adding key-value pairs to the map and then pass the map to the `Marshal` function, described in Table 21-7, which uses the built-in support to encode each of the values contained in the map. Compile and execute the project, and you will see the following output:

```
[{"cost":268.5,"product":"Kayak"},{"PersonName":"Alice"}]
```

Decoding JSON Data

The `NewDecoder` constructor function creates a `Decoder`, which can be used to decode JSON data obtained from a `Reader`, using the methods described in Table 21-8.

Table 21-8. *The Decoder Methods*

Name	Description
Decode(value)	This method reads and decodes data, which is used to create the specified value. The method returns an `error` that indicates problems decoding the data to the required type or EOF.
DisallowUnknownFields()	By default, when decoding a struct type, the Decoder ignores any key in the JSON data for which there is no corresponding struct field. Calling this method causes the Decode to return an error, rather than ignoring the key.
UseNumber()	By default, JSON number values are decoded into `float64` values. Calling this method uses the `Number` type instead, as described in the "Decoding Number Values" section.

Listing 21-17 demonstrates decoding basic data types.

Listing 21-17. Decoding Basic Data Types in the main.go File in the readersandwriters Folder

```
package main

import (
    "strings"
    //"fmt"
    "encoding/json"
    "io"
)
```

```
func main() {

    reader := strings.NewReader(`true "Hello" 99.99 200`)

    vals := []interface{} { }

    decoder := json.NewDecoder(reader)

    for {
        var decodedVal interface{}
        err := decoder.Decode(&decodedVal)
        if (err != nil) {
            if (err != io.EOF) {
                Printfln("Error: %v", err.Error())
            }
            break
        }
        vals = append(vals, decodedVal)
    }

    for _, val := range vals {
        Printfln("Decoded (%T): %v", val, val)
    }
}
```

I create a Reader that will produce data from a string containing a sequence of values, separated by spaces (the JSON specification allows values to be separated by spaces or newline characters).

The first step in decoding the data is to create the Decoder, which accepts a Reader. I want to decode multiple values, so I call the Decode method inside a for loop. The Decoder is able to select the appropriate Go data type for JSON values, and this is achieved by providing a pointer to an empty interface as the argument to the Decode method, like this:

```
...
var decodedVal interface{}
err := decoder.Decode(&decodedVal)
...
```

The Decode method returns an error, which indicates decoding problems but is also used to signal the end of the data using the io.EOF error. A for loop repeatedly decodes values until EOF, and then I use another for loop to write out each decoded type and value using the formatting verbs described in Chapter 17. Compile and execute the project, and you will see the decoded values:

```
Decoded (bool): true
Decoded (string): Hello
Decoded (float64): 99.99
Decoded (float64): 200
```

Decoding Number Values

JSON uses a single data type to represent both floating-point and integer values. The Decoder decodes these numeric values as float64 values, which can be seen in the output from the previous example.

This behavior can be changed by calling the UseNumber method on the Decoder, which causes JSON number values to be decoded into the Number type, defined in the encoding/json package. The Number type defines the methods described in Table 21-9.

Table 21-9. The Methods Defined by the Number Type

Name	Description
Int64()	This method returns the decoded value as a int64 and an error that indicates if the value cannot be converted.
Float64()	This method returns the decoded value as a float64 and an error that indicates if the value cannot be converted.
String()	This method returns the unconverted string from the JSON data.

The methods in Table 21-9 are used in sequence. Not all JSON number values can be expressed as Go int64 values, so this is the method that is typically called first. If attempting to convert to an integer fails, then the Float64 method can be called. If a number cannot be converted to either Go type, then the String method can be used to get the unconverted string from the JSON data. This sequence is shown in Listing 21-18.

Listing 21-18. Decoding Numbers in the main.go File in the readersandwriters Folder

```
package main

import (
    "strings"
    //"fmt"
    "encoding/json"
    "io"
)

func main() {

    reader := strings.NewReader(`true "Hello" 99.99 200`)

    vals := []interface{} { }

    decoder := json.NewDecoder(reader)
    decoder.UseNumber()

    for {
        var decodedVal interface{}
        err := decoder.Decode(&decodedVal)
        if (err != nil) {
            if (err != io.EOF) {
                Printfln("Error: %v", err.Error())
            }
```

```
            break
        }
        vals = append(vals, decodedVal)
    }

    for _, val := range vals {
        if num, ok := val.(json.Number); ok {
            if ival, err := num.Int64(); err == nil {
                Printfln("Decoded Integer: %v", ival)
            } else if fpval, err := num.Float64(); err == nil {
                Printfln("Decoded Floating Point: %v", fpval)
            } else {
                Printfln("Decoded String: %v", num.String())
            }
        } else {
            Printfln("Decoded (%T): %v", val, val)
        }
    }
}
```

Compile and execute the code, and you will see that one of the JSON values has been converted into an int64 value:

```
Decoded (bool): true
Decoded (string): Hello
Decoded Floating Point: 99.99
Decoded Integer: 200
```

Specifying Types for Decoding

The previous examples passed an empty interface variable to the Decode method, like this:

```
...
var decodedVal interface{}
err := decoder.Decode(&decodedVal)
...
```

This lets the Decoder select the Go data type for the JSON value that is decoded. If you know the structure of the JSON data you are decoding, you can direct the Decoder to use specific Go types by using variables of that type to receive a decoded value, as shown in Listing 21-19.

Listing 21-19. Specifying Types for Decoding in the main.go File in the readersandwriters Folder

```
package main

import (
    "strings"
    //"fmt"
    "encoding/json"
```

```
    //"io"
)

func main() {

    reader := strings.NewReader(`true "Hello" 99.99 200`)

    var bval bool
    var sval string
    var fpval float64
    var ival int

    vals := []interface{} { &bval, &sval, &fpval, &ival }

    decoder := json.NewDecoder(reader)

    for i := 0; i < len(vals); i++ {
        err := decoder.Decode(vals[i])
        if err != nil {
            Printfln("Error: %v", err.Error())
            break
        }
    }

    Printfln("Decoded (%T): %v", bval, bval)
    Printfln("Decoded (%T): %v", sval, sval)
    Printfln("Decoded (%T): %v", fpval, fpval)
    Printfln("Decoded (%T): %v", ival, ival)
}
```

Listing 21-19 specifies the data types that should be used for decoding and groups them together in a slice for convenience. The values are decoded into the target types, which can be seen in the output displayed when the project is compiled and executed:

```
Decoded (bool): true
Decoded (string): Hello
Decoded (float64): 99.99
Decoded (int): 200
```

The Decoder will return an error if it can't decode a JSON value into a specified type. This technique should be used only when you are confident that you understand the JSON data that will be decoded.

Decoding Arrays

The Decoder processes arrays automatically, but care must be taken because JSON allows arrays to contain values of different types, which conflicts with the strict type rules enforced by Go. Listing 21-20 demonstrates decoding an array.

Listing 21-20. Decoding an Array in the main.go File in the readersandwriters Folder

```
package main

import (
    "strings"
    //"fmt"
    "encoding/json"
    "io"
)

func main() {

    reader := strings.NewReader(`[10,20,30]["Kayak","Lifejacket",279]`)

    vals := []interface{} { }

    decoder := json.NewDecoder(reader)

    for {
        var decodedVal interface{}
        err := decoder.Decode(&decodedVal)
        if (err != nil) {
            if (err != io.EOF) {
                Printfln("Error: %v", err.Error())
            }
            break
        }
        vals = append(vals, decodedVal)
    }

    for _, val := range vals {
        Printfln("Decoded (%T): %v", val, val)
    }
}
```

The source JSON data contains two arrays, one of which contains only numbers and one of which mixes numbers and strings. The Decoder doesn't try to figure out if a JSON array can be represented using a single Go type and decodes every array into an empty interface slice:

```
Decoded ([]interface {}): [10 20 30]
Decoded ([]interface {}): [Kayak Lifejacket 279]
```

Each value is typed based on the JSON value, but the type of the slice is the empty interface. If you know the structure of the JSON data in advance and you are decoding an array containing a single JSON data type, then you can pass a Go slice of the desired type to the Decode method, as shown in Listing 21-21.

Listing 21-21. Specifying the Decoded Array Type in the main.go File in the readersandwriters Folder

```
package main

import (
    "strings"
    //"fmt"
    "encoding/json"
    //"io"
)

func main() {

    reader := strings.NewReader(`[10,20,30]["Kayak","Lifejacket",279]`)

    ints := []int {}
    mixed := []interface{} {}

    vals := []interface{} { &ints, &mixed}

    decoder := json.NewDecoder(reader)

    for i := 0; i < len(vals); i++ {
        err := decoder.Decode(vals[i])
        if err != nil {
            Printfln("Error: %v", err.Error())
            break
        }
    }

    Printfln("Decoded (%T): %v", ints, ints)
    Printfln("Decoded (%T): %v", mixed, mixed)
}
```

I can specify an int slice to decode the first array in the JSON data because all the values can be represented as Go int values. The second array contains a mix of values, which means that I have to specify the empty interface as the target type. The literal slice syntax is awkward when using the empty interface because two sets of braces are required:

```
...
mixed := []interface{} {}
...
```

The empty interface type includes empty braces (interface{}) and so does specifying an empty slice ({}). Compile and execute the project, and you will see that the first JSON array has been decoded into an int slice:

```
Decoded ([]int): [10 20 30]
Decoded ([]interface {}): [Kayak Lifejacket 279]
```

Decoding Maps

JavaScript objects are expressed as key-value pairs, which makes it easy to decode them into Go maps, as shown in Listing 21-22.

Listing 21-22. Decoding a Map in the main.go File in the readersandwriters Folder

```
package main

import (
    "strings"
    //"fmt"
    "encoding/json"
    //"io"
)

func main() {

    reader := strings.NewReader(`{"Kayak" : 279, "Lifejacket" : 49.95}`)

    m := map[string]interface{} {}

    decoder := json.NewDecoder(reader)

    err := decoder.Decode(&m)
    if err != nil {
        Printfln("Error: %v", err.Error())
    } else {
        Printfln("Map: %T, %v", m, m)
        for k, v := range m {
            Printfln("Key: %v, Value: %v", k, v)
        }
    }
}
```

The safest approach is to define a map with string keys and empty interface values, which ensures that all the key-value pairs in the JSON data can be decoded into the map, as shown in Listing 21-22. Once the JSON is decoded, a for loop is used to enumerate the map content, producing the following output when the project is compiled and executed:

```
Map: map[string]interface {}, map[Kayak:279 Lifejacket:49.95]
Key: Kayak, Value: 279
Key: Lifejacket, Value: 49.95
```

A single JSON object can be used for multiple data types as values, but if you know in advance that you will be decoding a JSON object that has a single value type, then you can be more specific when defining the map into which the data will be decoded, as shown in Listing 21-23.

Listing 21-23. Using a Specific Value Type in the main.go File in the readersandwriters Folder

```
package main

import (
    "strings"
    //"fmt"
    "encoding/json"
    //"io"
)

func main() {

    reader := strings.NewReader(`{"Kayak" : 279, "Lifejacket" : 49.95}`)

    m := map[string]float64 {}

    decoder := json.NewDecoder(reader)

    err := decoder.Decode(&m)
    if err != nil {
        Printfln("Error: %v", err.Error())
    } else {
        Printfln("Map: %T, %v", m, m)
        for k, v := range m {
            Printfln("Key: %v, Value: %v", k, v)
        }
    }
}
```

The values in the JSON object can all be represented using the Go float64 type, so Listing 21-23 changes the map type to map[string]float64. Compile and execute the project, and you will see the change in the map type:

```
Map: map[string]float64, map[Kayak:279 Lifejacket:49.95]
Key: Kayak, Value: 279
Key: Lifejacket, Value: 49.95
```

Decoding Structs

The key-value structure of JSON objects can be decoded into Go struct values, as shown in Listing 21-24, although this requires more knowledge of the JSON data than decoding the data into a map.

DECODING TO INTERFACE TYPES

As I explained earlier in the chapter, the JSON encoder deals with interfaces by encoding the value using the exported fields of the dynamic type. This is because JSON deals with key-value pairs and has no way to express methods. As a consequence, you cannot decode directly to an interface variable from JSON. Instead, you must decode to a struct or map and then assign the value that is created to an interface variable.

Listing 21-24. Decoding to a Struct in the main.go File in the readersandwriters Folder

```
package main

import (
    "strings"
    //"fmt"
    "encoding/json"
    "io"
)

func main() {

    reader := strings.NewReader(`
        {"Name":"Kayak","Category":"Watersports","Price":279}
        {"Name":"Lifejacket","Category":"Watersports" }
        {"name":"Canoe","category":"Watersports", "price": 100, "inStock": true }
    `)

    decoder := json.NewDecoder(reader)

    for {
        var val Product
        err := decoder.Decode(&val)
        if err != nil {
            if err != io.EOF {
                Printfln("Error: %v", err.Error())
            }
            break
        } else {
            Printfln("Name: %v, Category: %v, Price: %v",
                val.Name, val.Category, val.Price)
        }
    }
}
```

The Decoder decodes the JSON object and uses the keys to set the values of the exported struct fields. The capitalization of the fields and JSON keys don't have to match, and the Decoder will ignore any JSON key for which there isn't a struct field and ignore any struct field for which there is no JSON key. The JSON objects in Listings 21-24 contain different capitalization and have more or fewer keys than the Product struct fields. The Decoder processes the data as best as it can, producing the following output when the project is compiled and executed:

```
Name: Kayak, Category: Watersports, Price: 279
Name: Lifejacket, Category: Watersports, Price: 0
Name: Canoe, Category: Watersports, Price: 100
```

Disallowing Unused Keys

By default, the Decoder will ignore JSON keys for which there is no corresponding struct field. This behavior can be changed by calling the DisallowUnknownFields method, as shown in Listing 21-25, which triggers an error when such a key is encountered.

Listing 21-25. Disallowing Unused Keys in the main.go File in the readersandwriters Folder

```
...
decoder := json.NewDecoder(reader)
decoder.DisallowUnknownFields()
...
```

One of the JSON objects defined in Listing 21-25 contains an inStock key, for which there is no corresponding Product field. Normally, this key would be ignored, but since the DisallowUnknownFields method has been called, decoding this object produces an error, which can be seen in the output:

```
Name: Kayak, Category: Watersports, Price: 279
Name: Lifejacket, Category: Watersports, Price: 0
Error: json: unknown field "inStock"
```

Using Struct Tags to Control Decoding

The keys used in a JSON object don't always align with the fields defined by the structs in a Go project. When this happens, struct tags can be used to map between the JSON data and the struct, as shown in Listing 21-26.

Listing 21-26. Using Struct Tags in the discount.go File in the readersandwriters Folder

```
package main

import "encoding/json"

type DiscountedProduct struct {
    *Product `json:",omitempty"`
    Discount float64 `json:"offer,string"`
}

func (dp *DiscountedProduct) MarshalJSON() (jsn []byte, err error) {
    if (dp.Product != nil) {
        m := map[string]interface{} {
            "product": dp.Name,
            "cost": dp.Price - dp.Discount,
        }
```

```
        jsn, err = json.Marshal(m)
    }
    return
}
```

The tag applied to the Discount field tells the Decoder that the value for this field should be obtained from the JSON key named offer and that the value will be parsed from a string, instead of the JSON number that would usually be expected for a Go float64 value. Listing 21-27 decodes a JSON string into a DiscountedProduct struct value.

Listing 21-27. Decoding a Struct with a Tag in the main.go File in the readersandwriters Folder

```go
package main

import (
    "strings"
    //"fmt"
    "encoding/json"
    "io"
)

func main() {

    reader := strings.NewReader(`
        {"Name":"Kayak","Category":"Watersports","Price":279, "Offer": "10"}`)

    decoder := json.NewDecoder(reader)

    for {
        var val DiscountedProduct
        err := decoder.Decode(&val)
        if err != nil {
            if err != io.EOF {
                Printfln("Error: %v", err.Error())
            }
            break
        } else {
            Printfln("Name: %v, Category: %v, Price: %v, Discount: %v",
                val.Name, val.Category, val.Price, val.Discount)
        }
    }
}
```

Compile and execute the project, and you will see how the struct tag has been used to control the decoding of the JSON data:

```
Name: Kayak, Category: Watersports, Price: 279, Discount: 10
```

Creating Completely Custom JSON Decoders

The Decoder checks to see whether a struct implements the Unmarshaler interface, which denotes a type that has a custom encoding, and which defines the method described in Table 21-10.

Table 21-10. *The Unmarshaler Method*

Name	Description
UnmarshalJSON(byteSlice)	This method is invoked to decode JSON data contained in the specified byte slice. The result is an error indicating encoding problems.

Listing 21-28 implements the interface for pointers to the DiscountedProduct struct type.

Listing 21-28. Defining a Custom Decoder in the discount.go File in the readersandwriters Folder

```
package main

import (
    "encoding/json"
    "strconv"
)

type DiscountedProduct struct {
    *Product `json:",omitempty"`
    Discount float64 `json:"offer,string"`
}

func (dp *DiscountedProduct) MarshalJSON() (jsn []byte, err error) {
    if (dp.Product != nil) {
        m := map[string]interface{} {
            "product": dp.Name,
            "cost": dp.Price - dp.Discount,
        }
        jsn, err = json.Marshal(m)
    }
    return
}

func (dp *DiscountedProduct) UnmarshalJSON(data []byte) (err error) {

    mdata := map[string]interface{} {}
    err = json.Unmarshal(data, &mdata)

    if (dp.Product == nil) {
        dp.Product = &Product{}
    }

    if (err == nil) {
        if name, ok := mdata["Name"].(string); ok {
            dp.Name = name
        }
```

```
        if category, ok := mdata["Category"].(string); ok {
            dp.Category = category
        }
        if price, ok := mdata["Price"].(float64); ok {
            dp.Price = price
        }
        if discount, ok := mdata["Offer"].(string); ok {
            fpval, fperr := strconv.ParseFloat(discount, 64)
            if (fperr == nil) {
                dp.Discount = fpval
            }
        }
    }
    return
}
```

This implementation of the UnmarshalJSON method uses the Unmarshal method to decode the JSON data into a map and then checks the type of each value required for the DiscountedProduct struct. Compile and execute the project, and you will see the custom decoding:

```
Name: Kayak, Category: Watersports, Price: 279, Discount: 10
```

Summary

In this chapter, I described the Go support for working with JSON data, which relies on the Reader and Writer interfaces described in Chapter 20. These interfaces are used consistently throughout the standard library, as you will see in the next chapter, where I explain how files can be read and written.

CHAPTER 22

■ ■ ■

Working with Files

In this chapter, I describe the features that the Go standard library provides for working with files and directories. Go runs on multiple platforms, and the standard library takes a platform-neutral approach so that code can be written without needing to understand the file systems used by different operating systems. Table 22-1 puts working with files in context.

Table 22-1. *Putting Working with Files in Context*

Question	Answer
What are they?	These features provide access to the file system so that files can be read and written.
Why are they useful?	Files are used for everything from logging to configuration files.
How are they used?	These features are accessed through the os package, which provides platform-neutral access to the file system.
Are there any pitfalls or limitations?	Some consideration of the underlying file system must be made, especially when dealing with paths.
Are there any alternatives?	Go supports alternative ways of storing data, such as databases, but there are no alternative mechanisms for accessing files.

Table 22-2 summarizes the chapter.

Table 22-2. *Chapter Summary*

Problem	Solution	Listing
Read the contents of a file	Use the ReadFile function	6–8
Control the way that files are read	Obtain a File struct and use the features it provides	9–10
Write the contents of a file	Use the WriteFile function	11
Control the way that files are written	Obtain a File struct and use the features it provides	12, 13
Create new files	Use the Create or CreateTemp function	14
Work with file paths	Use the functions in the path/filepath package or use the common locations for which there are functions in the os package	15
Manage files and directories	Use the functions provided by the os package	16–17, 19, 20
Determine if a file exists	Inspect the error returned by the Stat function	18

© Adam Freeman 2022
A. Freeman, *Pro Go*, https://doi.org/10.1007/978-1-4842-7355-5_22

Preparing for This Chapter

To prepare for this chapter, open a new command prompt, navigate to a convenient location, and create a directory named `files`. Run the command shown in Listing 22-1 to create a module file.

■ **Tip** You can download the example project for this chapter—and for all the other chapters in this book—from `https://github.com/apress/pro-go`. See Chapter 2 for how to get help if you have problems running the examples.

Listing 22-1. Initializing the Module

```
go mod init files
```

Add a file named `printer.go` to the `files` folder with the content shown in Listing 22-2.

Listing 22-2. The Contents of the printer.go File in the files Folder

```
package main

import "fmt"

func Printfln(template string, values ...interface{}) {
    fmt.Printf(template + "\n", values...)
}
```

Add a file named `product.go` to the `files` folder with the content shown in Listing 22-3.

Listing 22-3. The Contents of the product.go File in the files Folder

```
package main

type Product struct {
    Name, Category string
    Price float64
}

var Products = []Product {
    { "Kayak", "Watersports", 279 },
    { "Lifejacket", "Watersports", 49.95 },
    { "Soccer Ball", "Soccer", 19.50 },
    { "Corner Flags", "Soccer", 34.95 },
    { "Stadium", "Soccer", 79500 },
    { "Thinking Cap", "Chess", 16 },
    { "Unsteady Chair", "Chess", 75 },
    { "Bling-Bling King", "Chess", 1200 },
}
```

Add a file named main.go to the files folder, with the contents shown in Listing 22-4.

Listing 22-4. The Contents of the main.go File in the files Folder

```
package main

func main() {
    for _, p := range Products {
        Printfln("Product: %v, Category: %v, Price: $%.2f",
            p.Name, p.Category, p.Price)
    }
}
```

Use the command prompt to run the command shown in Listing 22-5 in the files folder.

Listing 22-5. Running the Example Project

```
go run .
```

The code will be compiled and executed, producing the following output:

```
Product: Kayak, Category: Watersports, Price: $279.00
Product: Lifejacket, Category: Watersports, Price: $49.95
Product: Soccer Ball, Category: Soccer, Price: $19.50
Product: Corner Flags, Category: Soccer, Price: $34.95
Product: Stadium, Category: Soccer, Price: $79500.00
Product: Thinking Cap, Category: Chess, Price: $16.00
Product: Unsteady Chair, Category: Chess, Price: $75.00
Product: Bling-Bling King, Category: Chess, Price: $1200.00
```

Reading Files

The key package when dealing with files is the os package. This package provides access to operating system features—including the file system—in a way that hides most of the implementation details, meaning that the same functions can be used to achieve the same results regardless of the operating system being used.

The neutral approach adopted by the os package leads to some compromises and leans toward UNIX/Linux, rather than, say, Windows. But, even so, the features provided by the os package are solid and reliable and make it possible to write Go code that can be used on different platforms without modification. Table 22-3 describes the functions provided by the os package for reading files.

Table 22-3. The os Package Functions for Reading Files

Name	Description
ReadFile(name)	This function opens the specified file and reads its contents. The results are a byte slice containing the file content and an error indicating problems opening or reading the file.
Open(name)	This function opens the specified file for reading. The result is a File struct and an error that indicates problems opening the file.

To prepare for the examples in this part of the chapter, add a file named `config.json` to the `files` folder with the content shown in Listing 22-6.

Listing 22-6. The Contents of the config.json File in the files Folder

```
{
    "Username": "Alice",
    "AdditionalProducts": [
        {"name": "Hat", "category": "Skiing", "price": 10},
        {"name": "Boots", "category":"Skiing", "price": 220.51 },
        {"name": "Gloves", "category":"Skiing", "price": 40.20 }
    ]
}
```

One of the most common reasons to read a file is to load configuration data. The JSON format is well-suited for configuration files because it is simple to process, has good support in the Go standard library (as demonstrated in Chapter 21), and can represent complex structures.

Using the Read Convenience Function

The `ReadFile` function provides a convenient way to read the complete contents of a file into a byte slice in a single step. Add a file named `readconfig.go` to the `files` folder with the contents shown in Listing 22-7.

Listing 22-7. The Contents of the readconfig.go File in the files Folder

```
package main

import "os"

func LoadConfig() (err error) {
    data, err := os.ReadFile("config.json")
    if (err == nil) {
        Printfln(string(data))
    }
    return
}

func init() {
    err := LoadConfig()
    if (err != nil) {
        Printfln("Error Loading Config: %v", err.Error())
    }
}
```

The `LoadConfig` function uses the `ReadFile` function to read the contents of the `config.json` file. The file will be read from the current working directory when the application is executed, which means that I can open the file just with its name.

The contents of the file are returned as a byte slice, which is converted to a `string` and written out. The `LoadConfig` function is invoked by an initialization function, which ensures the configuration file is read. Compile and execute the code, and you will see the contents of the `config.json` file in the output produced by the application:

```
{
    "Username": "Alice",
    "AdditionalProducts": [
        {"name": "Hat", "category": "Skiing", "price": 10},
        {"name": "Boots", "category":"Skiing", "price": 220.51 },
        {"name": "Gloves", "category":"Skiing", "price": 40.20 }
    ]
}
Product: Kayak, Category: Watersports, Price: $279.00
Product: Lifejacket, Category: Watersports, Price: $49.95
Product: Soccer Ball, Category: Soccer, Price: $19.50
Product: Corner Flags, Category: Soccer, Price: $34.95
Product: Stadium, Category: Soccer, Price: $79500.00
Product: Thinking Cap, Category: Chess, Price: $16.00
Product: Unsteady Chair, Category: Chess, Price: $75.00
Product: Bling-Bling King, Category: Chess, Price: $1200.00
```

Decoding the JSON Data

For the example configuration file, receiving the contents of the file as a string is not ideal, and a more useful approach would be to parse the contents as JSON, which can be easily done by wrapping up the byte data so that it can be accessed through a Reader, as shown in Listing 22-8.

Listing 22-8. Decoding JSON Data in the readconfig.go File in the files Folder

```
package main

import (
    "os"
    "encoding/json"
    "strings"
)

type ConfigData struct {
    UserName string
    AdditionalProducts []Product
}

var Config ConfigData

func LoadConfig() (err error) {
    data, err := os.ReadFile("config.json")
    if (err == nil) {
        decoder := json.NewDecoder(strings.NewReader(string(data)))
        err = decoder.Decode(&Config)
    }
    return
}
```

573

```
func init() {
    err := LoadConfig()
    if (err != nil) {
        Printfln("Error Loading Config: %v", err.Error())
    } else {
        Printfln("Username: %v", Config.UserName)
        Products = append(Products, Config.AdditionalProducts...)
    }
}
```

I could have decoded the JSON data in the config.json file into a map, but I took a more structured approach in Listing 22-8 and defined a struct type whose fields match the structure of the configuration data, which I find makes it easier to use configuration data in real projects. Once the configuration data has been decoded, I write out the value of the UserName field and append the Product values to the slice defined in the product.go file. Compile and execute the project, and you will see the following output:

```
Username: Alice
Product: Kayak, Category: Watersports, Price: $279.00
Product: Lifejacket, Category: Watersports, Price: $49.95
Product: Soccer Ball, Category: Soccer, Price: $19.50
Product: Corner Flags, Category: Soccer, Price: $34.95
Product: Stadium, Category: Soccer, Price: $79500.00
Product: Thinking Cap, Category: Chess, Price: $16.00
Product: Unsteady Chair, Category: Chess, Price: $75.00
Product: Bling-Bling King, Category: Chess, Price: $1200.00
Product: Hat, Category: Skiing, Price: $10.00
Product: Boots, Category: Skiing, Price: $220.51
Product: Gloves, Category: Skiing, Price: $40.20
```

Using the File Struct to Read a File

The Open function opens a file for reading and returns a File value, which represents the open file, and an error, which is used to indicate problems opening the file. The File struct implements the Reader interface, which makes it simple to read and process the example JSON data, without reading the entire file into a byte slice, as shown in Listing 22-9.

USING THE STANDARD INPUT, OUTPUT, AND ERROR

The os package defines three *File variables, named Stdin, Stdout, and Stderr, that provide access to the standard input, standard output, and standard error.

Listing 22-9. Reading the Configuration File in the readconfig.go File in the files Folder

```
package main

import (
    "os"
    "encoding/json"
    //"strings"
)

type ConfigData struct {
    UserName string
    AdditionalProducts []Product
}

var Config ConfigData

func LoadConfig() (err error) {
    file, err := os.Open("config.json")
    if (err == nil) {
        defer file.Close()
        decoder := json.NewDecoder(file)
        err = decoder.Decode(&Config)
    }
    return
}

func init() {
    err := LoadConfig()
    if (err != nil) {
        Printfln("Error Loading Config: %v", err.Error())
    } else {
        Printfln("Username: %v", Config.UserName)
        Products = append(Products, Config.AdditionalProducts...)
    }
}
```

The File struct also implements the Closer interface, described in Chapter 21, which defines a Close method. The defer keyword can be used to call the Close method when the enclosing function completes, like this:

```
...
defer file.Close()
...
```

You can simply call the Close method at the end of the function if you prefer, but using the defer keyword ensures that the file is closed even when a function returns early. The result is the same as the previous example, which you can see by compiling and executing the project.

Username: Alice
Product: Kayak, Category: Watersports, Price: $279.00
Product: Lifejacket, Category: Watersports, Price: $49.95
Product: Soccer Ball, Category: Soccer, Price: $19.50
Product: Corner Flags, Category: Soccer, Price: $34.95
Product: Stadium, Category: Soccer, Price: $79500.00
Product: Thinking Cap, Category: Chess, Price: $16.00
Product: Unsteady Chair, Category: Chess, Price: $75.00
Product: Bling-Bling King, Category: Chess, Price: $1200.00
Product: Hat, Category: Skiing, Price: $10.00
Product: Boots, Category: Skiing, Price: $220.51
Product: Gloves, Category: Skiing, Price: $40.20

Reading from a Specific Location

The File struct defines methods beyond those required by the Reader interface that allows reads to be performed at a specific location in the file, as described in Table 22-4.

Table 22-4. *Methods Defined by the File Struct for Reading at a Specific Location*

Name	Description
ReadAt(slice, offset)	This method is defined by the ReaderAt interface and performs a read into the specific slice at the specified position offset in the file.
Seek(offset, how)	This method is defined by the Seeker interface and moves the offset into the file for the next read. The offset is determined by the combination of the two arguments: the first argument specifies the number of bytes to offset, and the second argument determines how the offset is applied—a value of 0 means the offset is relative to the start of the file, a value of 1 means the offset is relative to the current read position, and a value of 2 means the offset is relative to the end of the file.

Listing 22-10 demonstrates the use of the methods in Table 22-4 to read specific sections of data from a file, which are then composed into a JSON string and decoded.

Listing 22-10. Reading from Specific Locations in the readconfig.go File in the files Folder

```
package main

import (
    "os"
    "encoding/json"
    //"strings"
)

type ConfigData struct {
    UserName string
    AdditionalProducts []Product
}
```

```
var Config ConfigData

func LoadConfig() (err error) {
    file, err := os.Open("config.json")
    if (err == nil) {
        defer file.Close()

        nameSlice := make([]byte, 5)
        file.ReadAt(nameSlice, 20)
        Config.UserName = string(nameSlice)

        file.Seek(55, 0)
        decoder := json.NewDecoder(file)
        err = decoder.Decode(&Config.AdditionalProducts)
    }
    return
}

func init() {
    err := LoadConfig()
    if (err != nil) {
        Printfln("Error Loading Config: %v", err.Error())
    } else {
        Printfln("Username: %v", Config.UserName)
        Products = append(Products, Config.AdditionalProducts...)
    }
}
```

Reading from specific locations requires knowledge of the file structure. In this example, I know the location of the data I want to read, which allows me to use the ReadAt method to read the username value and the Seek method to jump to the start of the product data. Compile and execute the project, and you will see the following output:

```
Username: Alice
Product: Kayak, Category: Watersports, Price: $279.00
Product: Lifejacket, Category: Watersports, Price: $49.95
Product: Soccer Ball, Category: Soccer, Price: $19.50
Product: Corner Flags, Category: Soccer, Price: $34.95
Product: Stadium, Category: Soccer, Price: $79500.00
Product: Thinking Cap, Category: Chess, Price: $16.00
Product: Unsteady Chair, Category: Chess, Price: $75.00
Product: Bling-Bling King, Category: Chess, Price: $1200.00
Product: Hat, Category: Skiing, Price: $10.00
Product: Boots, Category: Skiing, Price: $220.51
Product: Gloves, Category: Skiing, Price: $40.20
```

If you receive an error from this example, then the likely cause is that the locations specified in Listing 22-10 do not correspond to the structure of your JSON file. As a first step, especially on Linux, make sure you have saved the file with both CR and LR characters, which you can do in Visual Studio Code by clicking the LR indicator at the bottom of the window.

Writing to Files

The os package also includes functions for writing files, as described in Table 22-5. These functions are more complex to use than their read-related counterparts because more configuration options are required.

Table 22-5. *The os Package Function for Writing Files*

Name	Description
WriteFile(name, slice, modePerms)	This function creates a file with the specified name, mode, and permissions and writes the content of the specified byte slice. If the file already exists, its contents will be replaced with the byte slice. The result is an error that reports any problems creating the file or writing the data.
OpenFile(name, flag, modePerms)	The function opens the file with the specified name, using the flags to control how the file is opened. If a new file is created, then the specified mode and permissions are applied. The result is a File value that provides access to the file contents and an error that indicates problems opening the file.

Using the Write Convenience Function

The WriteFile function provides a convenient way to write an entire file in a single step and will create the file if it does not exist. Listing 22-11 demonstrates the use of the WriteFile function.

Listing 22-11. Writing a File in the main.go File in the files Folder

```
package main

import (
    "fmt"
    "time"
    "os"
)

func main() {

    total := 0.0
    for _, p := range Products {
        total += p.Price
    }

    dataStr := fmt.Sprintf("Time: %v, Total: $%.2f\n",
        time.Now().Format("Mon 15:04:05"), total)

    err := os.WriteFile("output.txt", []byte(dataStr), 0666)
    if (err == nil) {
        fmt.Println("Output file created")
    } else {
        Printfln("Error: %v", err.Error())
    }
}
```

The first two arguments to the WriteFile function are the name of the file and a byte slice containing the data to write. The third argument combines two settings for the file: the file mode and the file permissions, as shown in Figure 22-1.

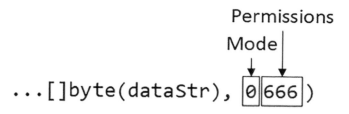

Figure 22-1. *The file mode and file permissions*

The file mode is used to specify special characteristics for the file, but a value of zero is used for regular files, as in the example. You can find a list of the file mode values and their settings at https://golang.org/pkg/io/fs/#FileMode, but they are not required in most projects, and I do not describe them in this book.

The file permissions are more widely used and follow the UNIX style of file permission, which consists of three digits that set the access for the file's owner, group, and other users. Each digit is the sum of the permissions that should be granted, where read has a value of 4, write has a value of 2, and execute has a value of 1. These values are added together so that permission to read and write the file is set by adding the values 4 and 2 to produce a permission of 6. In Listing 22-11, I want to create a file that can be read and written by all users, so I use the value 6 for all three settings, producing a permission of 666.

The WriteFile function creates the file if it does not already exist, which you can see by compiling and executing the project, which produces the following output:

```
Username: Alice
Output file created
```

Examine the contents of the files folder, and you will see that a file named output.txt has been created, with contents similar to the following, although you will see a different timestamp:

```
Time: Sun 07:05:06, Total: $81445.11
```

If the specified file already exists, the WriteFile method replaces its contents, which you can see by executing the compiled program again. Once execution has been completed, the original contents will be replaced with a new timestamp:

```
Time: Sun 07:08:21, Total: $81445.11
```

Using the File Struct to Write to a File

The OpenFile function opens a file and returns a File value. Unlike the Open function, the OpenFile function accepts one or more flags that specify how the file should be opened. The flags are defined as constants in the os package, as described in Table 22-6. Care must be taken with these flags, not all of which are supported by every operating system.

Table 22-6. *The File Opening Flags*

Name	Description
O_RDONLY	This flag opens the file read-only so that it can be read from but not written to.
O_WRONLY	This flag opens the file write-only so that it can be written to but not read from.
O_RDWR	This flag opens the file read-write so that it can be written to and read from.
O_APPEND	This flag will append writes to the end of the file.
O_CREATE	This flag will create the file if it doesn't exist.
O_EXCL	This flag is used in conjunction with O_CREATE to ensure that a new file is created. If the file already exists, this flag will trigger an error.
O_SYNC	This flag enables synchronous writes, such that data is written to the storage device before the write function/method returns.
O_TRUNC	This flag truncates the existing content in the file.

Flags are combined with the bitwise OR operator, as shown in Listing 22-12.

Listing 22-12. Writing to a File in the main.go File in the files Folder

```go
package main

import (
    "fmt"
    "time"
    "os"
)

func main() {

    total := 0.0
    for _, p := range Products {
        total += p.Price
    }

    dataStr := fmt.Sprintf("Time: %v, Total: $%.2f\n",
        time.Now().Format("Mon 15:04:05"), total)

    file, err := os.OpenFile("output.txt",
        os.O_WRONLY | os.O_CREATE | os.O_APPEND, 0666)
    if (err == nil) {
        defer file.Close()
        file.WriteString(dataStr)
    } else {
        Printfln("Error: %v", err.Error())
    }
}
```

I combined the O_WRONLY flag to open the file for writing, the O_CREATE file to create if it doesn't already exist, and the O_APPEND flag to append any written data to the end of the file.

The File struct defines the methods described in Table 22-7 to write data to a file once it has been opened.

Table 22-7. *The File Methods for Writing Data*

Name	Description
Seek(offset, how)	This method sets the location for subsequent operations.
Write(slice)	This method writes the contents of the specified byte slice to the file. The results are the number of bytes written and an error that indicates problems writing the data.
WriteAt(slice, offset)	This method writes the data in the slice at the specified location and is the counterpart to the ReadAt method.
WriteString(str)	This method writes a string to the file. This is a convenience method that converts the string to a byte slice, invokes the Write method, and returns the results it receives.

In Listing 22-12, I used the WriteString convenience method to write a string to the file. Compile and execute the project, and you will see an additional message at the end of the output.txt file once the program has been completed:

```
Time: Sun 07:08:21, Total: $81445.11
Time: Sun 07:49:14, Total: $81445.11
```

Writing JSON Data to a File

The File struct implements the Writer interface, which allows a file to be used with the functions for formatting and processing strings described in earlier chapters. It also means that the JSON features described in Chapter 21 can be used to write JSON data to a file, as shown in Listing 22-13.

Listing 22-13. Writing JSON Data to a File in the main.go File in the files Folder

```
package main

import (
    // "fmt"
    // "time"
    "os"
    "encoding/json"
)

func main() {

    cheapProducts := []Product {}
    for _, p := range Products {
```

```
        if (p.Price < 100) {
            cheapProducts = append(cheapProducts, p)
        }
    }

    file, err := os.OpenFile("cheap.json", os.O_WRONLY | os.O_CREATE, 0666)
    if (err == nil) {
        defer file.Close()
        encoder := json.NewEncoder(file)
        encoder.Encode(cheapProducts)
    } else {
        Printfln("Error: %v", err.Error())
    }
}
```

This example selects the Product values with a Price value of less than 100, places them into a slice, and uses a JSON Encoder to write that slice to a file named cheap.json. Compile and execute the project, and once execution is complete, you will see a file named cheap.json in the files folder with the following content, which I have formatted for fit on the page:

```
[{"Name":"Lifejacket","Category":"Watersports","Price":49.95},
 {"Name":"Soccer Ball","Category":"Soccer","Price":19.5},
 {"Name":"Corner Flags","Category":"Soccer","Price":34.95},
 {"Name":"Thinking Cap","Category":"Chess","Price":16},
 {"Name":"Unsteady Chair","Category":"Chess","Price":75},
 {"Name":"Hat","Category":"Skiing","Price":10},
 {"Name":"Gloves","Category":"Skiing","Price":40.2}]
```

Using the Convenience Functions to Create New Files

Although it is possible to use the OpenFile function to create new files, as demonstrated in the previous section, the os package also provides some useful convenience functions, as described in Table 22-8.

Table 22-8. *The os Package Functions for Creating Files*

Name	Description
Create(name)	This function is equivalent to calling OpenFile with the O_RDWR, O_CREATE, and O_TRUNC flags. The results are the File, which can be used for reading and writing, and an error that is used to indicate problems creating the file. Note that this combination of flags means that if a file exists with the specified name, it will be opened, and its contents will be deleted.
CreateTemp(dirName, fileName)	This function creates a new file in the directory with the specified name. If the name is the empty string, then the system temporary directory is used, obtained using the TempDir function (described in Table 22-9). The file is created with a name that contains a random sequence of characters, as demonstrated in the text after the table. The file is opened with the O_RDWR, O_CREATE, and O_EXCL flags. The file isn't removed when it is closed.

The CreateTemp function can be useful, but it is important to understand that the purpose of this function is to generate a random filename and that in all other respects, the file that is created is just a regular file. The file that is created isn't removed automatically and will remain on the storage device after the application has been executed.

Listing 22-14 demonstrates the use of the CreateTemp function and shows how the location of the randomized component of the name can be controlled.

Listing 22-14. Creating a Temporary File in the main.go File in the files Folder

```
package main

import (
    // "fmt"
    // "time"
    "os"
    "encoding/json"
)

func main() {

    cheapProducts := []Product {}
    for _, p := range Products {
        if (p.Price < 100) {
            cheapProducts = append(cheapProducts, p)
        }
    }

    file, err := os.CreateTemp(".", "tempfile-*.json")
    if (err == nil) {
        defer file.Close()
        encoder := json.NewEncoder(file)
        encoder.Encode(cheapProducts)
    } else {
        Printfln("Error: %v", err.Error())
    }
}
```

The location of the temporary file is specified with a period, meaning the current working directory. As noted in Table 22-8, if the empty string is used, then the file will be created in the default temporary directory, which is obtained using the TempDir function described in Table 22-9. The name of the file can include an asterisk (the * character), and if this is present, the random part of the filename will replace it. If the filename does not contain an asterisk, then the random part of the filename will be added to the end of the name.

Compile and execute the project, and once execution is complete, you will see a new file in the files folder. The file in my project is named tempfile-1732419518.json, but your filename will be different, and you will see a new file and a unique name each time the program is executed.

Working with File Paths

The examples so far in this chapter have used files that are in the current working directory, which is typically the location from which the compiled executable is started. If you want to read and write files in other locations, then you must specify file paths. The issue is that not all of the operating systems that Go supports express file paths in the same way. For example, the path to a file named mydata.json in my home directory on a Linux system might be expressed like this:

```
/home/adam/mydata.json
```

I typically deploy my projects to Linux, but I prefer to develop on Windows, where the path to the same in my home directory is expressed like this:

```
C:\Users\adam\mydata.json
```

Windows is more flexible than you might expect, and the low-level APIs that are invoked by Go functions, such as OpenFile, are agnostic about file separators and will accept both backslashes and forward slashes. That means I can express the path to the file as c:/users/adam/mydata.json or even /users/adam/mydata.json when writing Go code, and Windows will still open the file correctly. But the file separator is only one of the differences between platforms. Volumes are handled differently, and there are different default locations for storing files. So, for example, I might be able to read my hypothetical data file using /home/adam.mydata.json or /users/mydata.json, but the correct choice will depend on which operating system I am using. And as Go is ported to more platforms, there will be a wider range of possible locations. To solve this issue, the os package provides a set of functions that return the paths of common locations, as described in Table 22-9.

Table 22-9. *The Common Location Functions Defined by the os Package*

Name	Description
Getwd()	This function returns the current working directory, expressed as a string, and an error that indicates problems obtaining the value.
UserHomeDir()	This function returns the user's home directory and an error that indicates problems obtaining the path.
UserCacheDir()	This function returns the default directory for user-specific cached data and an error that indicates problems obtaining the path.
UserConfigDir()	This function returns the default directory for user-specific configuration data and an error that indicates problems obtaining the path.
TempDir()	This function returns the default directory for temporary files and an error that indicates problems obtaining the path.

Once you have obtained a path, you can treat it like a string and simply append additional segments to it or, to avoid mistakes, use the functions provided by the path/filepath package for manipulating paths, the most useful of which are described in Table 22-10.

584

Table 22-10. *The path/filepath Functions for Paths*

Name	Description
Abs(path)	This function returns an absolute path, which is useful if you have a relative path, such as a filename.
IsAbs(path)	This function returns true if the specified path is absolute.
Base(path)	This function returns the last element from the path.
Clean(path)	This function tidies up path strings by removing duplicate separators and relative references.
Dir(path)	This function returns all but the last element of the path.
EvalSymlinks(path)	This function evaluates a symbolic link and returns the resulting path.
Ext(path)	This function returns the file extension from the specified path, which is assumed to be the suffix following the final period in the path string.
FromSlash(path)	This function replaces each forward slash with the platform's file separator character.
ToSlash(path)	This function replaces the platform's file separator with forward slashes.
Join(...elements)	This function combines multiple elements using the platform's file separator.
Match(pattern, path)	This function returns true if the path is matched by the specified pattern.
Split(path)	This function returns the components on either side of the final path separator in the specified path.
SplitList(path)	This function splits a path into its components, which are returned as a string slice.
VolumeName(path)	This function returns the volume component of the specified path or the empty string if the path does not contain a volume.

Listing 22-15 demonstrates the process of starting with a path returned by one of the convenience functions described in Table 22-10 and manipulating it with the functions in Table 22-9.

Listing 22-15. Working with a Path in the main.go File in the files Folder

```
package main

import (
    // "fmt"
    // "time"
    "os"
    //"encoding/json"
    "path/filepath"
)

func main() {
    path, err := os.UserHomeDir()
    if (err == nil) {
        path = filepath.Join(path, "MyApp", "MyTempFile.json")
    }
```

```
    Printfln("Full path: %v", path)
    Printfln("Volume name: %v", filepath.VolumeName(path))
    Printfln("Dir component: %v", filepath.Dir(path))
    Printfln("File component: %v", filepath.Base(path))
    Printfln("File extension: %v", filepath.Ext(path))
}
```

This example starts with the path returned by the UserHomeDir function, uses the Join function to add additional segments, and then writes out different parts of the path. The results you receive will depend on your username and your platform. Here is the output I received on my Windows machine:

```
Username: Alice
Full path: C:\Users\adam\MyApp\MyTempFile.json
Volume name: C:
Dir component: C:\Users\adam\MyApp
File component: MyTempFile.json
File extension: .json
```

Here is the output I received on my Ubuntu test machine:

```
Username: Alice
Full path: /home/adam/MyApp/MyTempFile.json
Volume name:
Dir component: /home/adam/MyApp
File component: MyTempFile.json
File extension: .json
```

Managing Files and Directories

The functions described in the previous section process paths, but these are just strings. When I added segments to a path in Listing 22-15, the result was just another string, and there was no corresponding change on the file system. To make such changes, the os package provides the functions described in Table 22-11.

Table 22-11. *The os Package Functions for Managing Files and Directories*

Name	Description
Chdir(dir)	This function changes the current working directory to the specified directory. The result is an error that indicates problems making the change.
Mkdir(name, modePerms)	This function creates a directory with the specified name and mode/permissions. The result is an error that is nil if the directory is created or that describes a problem if one arises.
MkdirAll(name, modePerms)	This function performs the same task as Mkdir but creates any parent directories in the specified path.

(*continued*)

Table 22-11. (*continued*)

Name	Description
MkdirTemp(parentDir, name)	This function is similar to CreateTemp but creates a directory rather than a file. A random string is added to the end of the specified name or in place of an asterisk, and the new directory is created within the specified parent. The results are the name of the directory and an error indicating problems.
Remove(name)	This function removes the specified file or directory. The result is an error that describes any problems that arise.
RemoveAll(name)	This function removes the specified file or directory. If the name specifies a directory, then any children it contains are also removed. The result is an error that describes any problems that arise.
Rename(old, new)	This function renames the specified file or folder. The result is an error that describes any problems that arise.
Symlink(old, new)	This function creates a symbolic link to the specified file. The result is an error that describes any problems that arise.

Listing 22-16 uses the MkdirAll function to ensure that the directories required for a file path are created so that no error occurs when attempting to create the file.

Listing 22-16. Creating Directories in the main.go File in the files Folder

```
package main

import (
    // "fmt"
    // "time"
    "os"
    "encoding/json"
    "path/filepath"
)

func main() {
    path, err := os.UserHomeDir()
    if (err == nil) {
        path = filepath.Join(path, "MyApp", "MyTempFile.json")
    }

    Printfln("Full path: %v", path)

    err = os.MkdirAll(filepath.Dir(path), 0766)
    if (err == nil) {
        file, err := os.OpenFile(path, os.O_CREATE | os.O_WRONLY, 0666)
        if (err == nil) {
            defer file.Close()
            encoder := json.NewEncoder(file)
            encoder.Encode(Products)
        }
```

```
    }
    if (err != nil) {
        Printfln("Error %v", err.Error())
    }
}
```

To make sure that the directories in my path exist, I use the filepath.Dir function and pass the result to the os.MkdirAll function. I can then create the file using the OpenFile function and specifying the O_CREATE flag. I use the File as a Writer for a JSON Encoder and write the contents of the Product slice, defined in Listing 22-3, to the new file. The deferred Close statement closes the file. Compile and execute the project, and you will see a directory named MyApp has been created in your home folder, containing a JSON file named MyTempFile.json. The file will contain the following JSON data, which I have formatted to fit on the page:

```
[{"Name":"Lifejacket","Category":"Watersports","Price":49.95},
 {"Name":"Soccer Ball","Category":"Soccer","Price":19.5},
 {"Name":"Corner Flags","Category":"Soccer","Price":34.95},
 {"Name":"Thinking Cap","Category":"Chess","Price":16},
 {"Name":"Unsteady Chair","Category":"Chess","Price":75},
 {"Name":"Hat","Category":"Skiing","Price":10},
 {"Name":"Gloves","Category":"Skiing","Price":40.2}]
```

Exploring the File System

If you know the location of the files you require, you can simply create paths using the functions described in the previous section and use them to open files. If your project relies on processing the files created by another process, then you will need to explore the file system. The os package provides the function described in Table 22-12.

Table 22-12. *The os Package Function for Listing Directories*

Name	Description
ReadDir(name)	This function reads the specified directory and returns a DirEntry slice, each of which describes an item in the directory.

The result of the ReadDir function is a slice of values that implement the DirEntry interface, which defines the methods described in Table 22-13.

Table 22-13. *The Methods Defined by the DirEntry Interface*

Name	Description
Name()	This method returns the name of the file or directory described by the DirEntry value.
IsDir()	This method returns true if the DirEntry value represents a directory.
Type()	This method returns a FileMode value, which is an alias to uint32, which describes the file more and the permissions of the file or directory represented by the DirEntry value.
Info()	This method returns a FileInfo value that provides additional details about the file or directory represented by the DirEntry value.

The FileInfo interface, which is the result of the Info method, is used to get details about a file or directory. The most useful methods defined by the FileInfo interface are described in Table 22-14.

Table 22-14. *Useful Methods Defined by the FileInfo Interface*

Name	Description
Name()	This method returns a string containing the name of the file or directory.
Size()	This method returns the size of the file, expressed as an int64 value.
Mode()	This method returns the file mode and permission settings for the file or directory.
ModTime()	This method returns the last modified time of the file or directory.

You can also get a FileInfo value about a single file using the function described in Table 22-15.

Table 22-15. *The os Package Function for Inspecting a File*

Name	Description
Stat(path)	This function accepts a path string. It returns a FileInfo value that describes the file and an error, which indicates problems inspecting the file.

Listing 22-17 uses the ReadDir function to enumerate the contents of the project folder.

Listing 22-17. Enumerating Files in the main.go File in the files Folder

```
package main

import (
    // "fmt"
    // "time"
    "os"
    //"encoding/json"
    //"path/filepath"
)

func main() {
    path, err := os.Getwd()
    if (err == nil) {
        dirEntries, err := os.ReadDir(path)
        if (err == nil) {
            for _, dentry := range dirEntries {
                Printfln("Entry name: %v, IsDir: %v", dentry.Name(), dentry.IsDir())
            }
        }
    }
    if (err != nil) {
        Printfln("Error %v", err.Error())
    }
}
```

A for loop is used to enumerate the DirEntry values returned by the ReadDir function, and the results from the Name and IsDir functions are written out. Compile and execute the project, and you will see output similar to the following, allowing for differences in the filename created with the CreateTemp function:

```
Username: Alice
Entry name: cheap.json, IsDir: false
Entry name: config.go, IsDir: false
Entry name: config.json, IsDir: false
Entry name: go.mod, IsDir: false
Entry name: main.go, IsDir: false
Entry name: output.txt, IsDir: false
Entry name: product.go, IsDir: false
Entry name: tempfile-1732419518.json, IsDir: false
```

Determining Whether a File Exists

The os package defines a function named IsNotExist, accepts an error, and returns true if it denotes that the error indicates that a file does not exist, as shown in Listing 22-18.

Listing 22-18. Checking Whether a File Exists in the main.go File in the files Folder

```
package main

import (
    // "fmt"
    // "time"
    "os"
    // "encoding/json"
    // "path/filepath"
)

func main() {

    targetFiles := []string { "no_such_file.txt", "config.json" }
    for _, name := range targetFiles {
        info, err := os.Stat(name)
        if os.IsNotExist(err) {
            Printfln("File does not exist: %v", name)
        } else if err != nil  {
            Printfln("Other error: %v", err.Error())
        } else {
            Printfln("File %v, Size: %v", info.Name(), info.Size())
        }
    }
}
```

The error returned by the Stat function is passed to the IsNotExist function, allowing nonexistent files to be identified. Compile and execute the project, and you will receive the following output:

```
Username: Alice
File does not exist: no_such_file.txt
File config.json, Size: 262
```

Locating Files Using a Pattern

The path/filepath package defines the Glob function, which returns all the names in a directory that match a specified pattern. The function is described in Table 22-16 for quick reference.

Table 22-16. *The path/filepath Function for Locating Files with a Pattern*

Name	Description
Match(pattern, name)	This function matches a single path against a pattern. The results are a bool, which indicates if there is a match, and an error, which indicates problems with the pattern or with performing the match.
Glob(pathPatten)	This function finds all the files that match the specified pattern. The results are a string slice containing the matched paths and an error that indicates problems with performing the search.

The patterns used by the functions in Table 22-16 use the syntax described in Table 22-17.

Table 22-17. *The Search Pattern Syntax for the path/filepath Functions*

Term	Description
*	This term matches any sequence of characters, excluding the path separator.
?	This term matches any single character, excluding the path separator.
[a-Z]	This term matches any character in the specified range.

Listing 22-19 uses the Glob function to get the paths of the JSON files in the current working directory.

Listing 22-19. Locating Files in the main.go File in the files Folder

```go
package main

import (
    // "fmt"
    // "time"
    "os"
    // "encoding/json"
    "path/filepath"
)

func main() {

    path, err := os.Getwd()
    if (err == nil) {
        matches, err := filepath.Glob(filepath.Join(path, "*.json"))
```

591

```
        if (err == nil) {
            for _, m := range matches {
                Printfln("Match: %v", m)
            }
        }
    }
}

    if (err != nil) {
        Printfln("Error %v", err.Error())
    }
}
```

I create the search pattern using the Getwd and Join functions and write out the paths that are turned by the Glob function. Compile and execute the project, and you will see the following output, albeit reflecting the location of your project folder:

```
Username: Alice
Match: C:\files\cheap.json
Match: C:\files\config.json
Match: C:\files\tempfile-1732419518.json
```

Processing All Files in a Directory

An alternative to using patterns is to enumerate all the files in a specific location, which can be done using the function described in Table 22-18, which is defined in the path/filepath package.

Table 22-18. *The Function Provided by the path/filepath Package*

Name	Description
WalkDir(directory, func)	This function calls the specified function for each file and directory in the specified directory.

The callback function invoked by WalkDir receives a string that contains the path, a DirEntry value that provides details about the file or directory, and an error that indicates problems accessing that file or directory. The result of the callback function is an error that prevents the WalkDir function from entering the current directory by returning the special SkipDir value. Listing 22-20 demonstrates the use of the WalkDir function.

Listing 22-20. Walking a Directory in the main.go File in the files Folder

```
package main

import (
    // "fmt"
    // "time"
    "os"
    //"encoding/json"
    "path/filepath"
)
```

```
func callback(path string, dir os.DirEntry, dirErr error) (err error) {
    info, _ := dir.Info()
    Printfln("Path %v, Size: %v", path, info.Size())
    return
}

func main() {

    path, err := os.Getwd()
    if (err == nil) {
        err = filepath.WalkDir(path, callback)
    } else {
        Printfln("Error %v", err.Error())
    }
}
```

This example uses the WalkDir function to enumerate the contents of the current working directory and writes out the path and size of each file that is found. Compile and execute the project, and you will see output similar to the following:

```
Username: Alice
Path C:\files, Size: 4096
Path C:\files\cheap.json, Size: 384
Path C:\files\config.json, Size: 262
Path C:\files\go.mod, Size: 28
Path C:\files\main.go, Size: 467
Path C:\files\output.txt, Size: 74
Path C:\files\product.go, Size: 679
Path C:\files\readconfig.go, Size: 870
Path C:\files\tempfile-1732419518.json, Size: 384
```

Summary

In this chapter, I describe the standard library support for working with files. I describe the convenience features for reading and writing files, explained the use of the File struct, and demonstrated how to explore and manage the file system. In the next chapter, I explain how to create and use HTML and text templates.

CHAPTER 23

■ ■ ■

Using HTML and Text Templates

In this chapter, I describe standard library packages that are used to produce HTML and text content from templates. These template packages are useful when generating large amounts of content and have extensive support for generating dynamic content. Table 23-1 puts the HTML and text templates in context.

Table 23-1. *Putting HTML and Text Templates in Context*

Question	Answer
What are they?	These templates allow HTML and text content to be generated dynamically from Go data values.
Why are they useful?	Templates are useful when large amounts of content are required, such that defining the content as strings would be unmanageable.
How are they used?	The templates are HTML or text files, which are annotated with instructions for the template processing engine. When a template is rendered, the instructions are processed to generate HTML or text content.
Are there any pitfalls or limitations?	The template syntax is counterintuitive and is not checked by the Go compiler. This means that care must be taken to use the correct syntax, which can be a frustrating process.
Are there any alternatives?	Templates are optional, and smaller amounts of content can be produced using strings.

Table 23-2 summarizes the chapter.

Table 23-2. *Chapter Summary*

Problem	Solution	Listing
Generate an HTML document	Define an HTML template with actions that incorporate data values into the output. Load and execute the templates, providing data for the actions.	6–10
Enumerate loaded templates	Enumerate the results of the Templates method.	11
Locate a specific template	Use the Lookup method.	12
Produce dynamic content	Use a template action.	13, 21

(continued)

© Adam Freeman 2022
A. Freeman, *Pro Go*, https://doi.org/10.1007/978-1-4842-7355-5_23

Table 23-2. *(continued)*

Problem	Solution	Listing
Format a data value	Use the formatting functions.	14–16
Suppress whitespace	Add hyphens to the template.	17–19
Process a slice	Use the slice functions.	22
Conditionally execute template content	Use the conditional actions and functions.	23-24
Create a nested template	Use the define and template actions.	25–27
Define a default template	Use the block and template actions.	28–30
Create functions for use in a template	Define template functions.	31–32, 35, 36
Disable encoding for function results	Return one of the type aliases defined by the html/ template package.	33, 34
Store data values for later use in a template	Define template variables.	37–40
Generate a text document	Use the text/template package.	41, 42

Preparing for This Chapter

To prepare for this chapter, open a new command prompt, navigate to a convenient location, and create a directory named htmltext. Run the command shown in Listing 23-1 to create a module file.

■ **Tip**   You can download the example project for this chapter—and for all the other chapters in this book—from https://github.com/apress/pro-go. See Chapter 2 for how to get help if you have problems running the examples.

Listing 23-1. Initializing the Module

```
go mod init htmltext
```

Add a file named printer.go to the htmltext folder with the content shown in Listing 23-2.

Listing 23-2. The Contents of the printer.go File in the htmltext Folder

```
package main

import "fmt"

func Printfln(template string, values ...interface{}) {
    fmt.Printf(template + "\n", values...)
}
```

Add a file named product.go to the htmltext folder with the content shown in Listing 23-3.

Listing 23-3. The Contents of the product.go File in the htmltext Folder

```
package main

type Product struct {
    Name, Category string
    Price float64
}

var Kayak = Product {
    Name: "Kayak",
    Category: "Watersports",
    Price: 279,
}

var Products = []Product {
    { "Kayak", "Watersports", 279 },
    { "Lifejacket", "Watersports", 49.95 },
    { "Soccer Ball", "Soccer", 19.50 },
    { "Corner Flags", "Soccer", 34.95 },
    { "Stadium", "Soccer", 79500 },
    { "Thinking Cap", "Chess", 16 },
    { "Unsteady Chair", "Chess", 75 },
    { "Bling-Bling King", "Chess", 1200 },
}

func (p *Product) AddTax() float64 {
    return p.Price * 1.2
}

func (p * Product) ApplyDiscount(amount float64) float64 {
    return p.Price - amount
}
```

Add a file named main.go to the htmltext folder, with the contents shown in Listing 23-4.

Listing 23-4. The Contents of the main.go File in the usingstrings Folder

```
package main

func main() {
    for _, p := range Products {
        Printfln("Product: %v, Category: %v, Price: $%.2f",
            p.Name, p.Category, p.Price)
    }
}
```

Use the command prompt to run the command shown in Listing 23-5 in the htmltext folder.

Listing 23-5. Running the Example Project

```
go run .
```

The code will be compiled and executed, producing the following output:

```
Product: Kayak, Category: Watersports, Price: $279.00
Product: Lifejacket, Category: Watersports, Price: $49.95
Product: Soccer Ball, Category: Soccer, Price: $19.50
Product: Corner Flags, Category: Soccer, Price: $34.95
Product: Stadium, Category: Soccer, Price: $79500.00
Product: Thinking Cap, Category: Chess, Price: $16.00
Product: Unsteady Chair, Category: Chess, Price: $75.00
Product: Bling-Bling King, Category: Chess, Price: $1200.00
```

Creating HTML Templates

The html/template package provides support for creating templates that are processed using a data structure to generate dynamic HTML output. Create the htmltext/templates folder and add to it a file named template.html with the content shown in Listing 23-6.

■ **Note** The examples in this chapter produce fragments of HTML. See Part 3 for examples that produce complete HTML documents.

Listing 23-6. The Contents of the template.html File in the templates Folder

```
<h1>Template Value: {{ . }}</h1>
```

Templates contain static content mixed with expressions that are enclosed in double curly braces, known as *actions*. The template in Listing 23-6 uses the simplest action, which is a period (the . character) and which prints out the data used to execute the template, which I explain in the next section.

A project can contain multiple templates files. Add a file named extras.html to the templates folder, with the content shown in Listing 23-7.

Listing 23-7. The Contents of the extras.html File in the templates Folder

```
<h1>Extras Template Value: {{ . }}</h1>
```

The new template uses the same action as the previous example but has different static content to make it clear which template has been executed in the next section. Once I have described the basic techniques for using templates, I'll introduce more complex template actions.

Loading and Executing Templates

Using templates is a two-step process. First, the templates files are loaded and processed to create Template values. Table 23-3 describes the functions used for loading template files.

Table 23-3. *The html/template Functions for Loading Template Files*

Name	Description
ParseFiles(...files)	This function loads one or more files, which are specified by name. The result is a Template that can be used to generate content and an error that reports problems loading the templates.
ParseGlob(pattern)	This function loads one or more files, which are selected with a pattern. The result is a Template that can be used to generate content and an error that reports problems loading the templates.

If you name your template files consistently, then you can use the ParseGlob function to load them with a simple pattern. If you want specific files—or the files are not named consistently—then you can specify individual files using the ParseFiles function.

Once the templates files are loaded, the Template value returned by the functions in Table 23-3 is used to select a template and execute it to produce content, using the methods described in Table 23-4.

Table 23-4. *The Template Methods for Selecting and Executing Templates*

Name	Description
Templates()	This function returns a slice containing pointers to the Template values that have been loaded.
Lookup(name)	This function returns a *Template for the specified loaded template.
Name()	This method returns the name of the Template.
Execute(writer, data)	This function executes the Template, using the specified data and writes the output to the specified Writer.
ExecuteTemplate(writer, templateName, data)	This function executes the template with the specified name and data and writes the output to the specified Writer.

In Listing 23-8, I load and execute a template.

Listing 23-8. Loading and Executing a Template in the main.go File in the htmltext Folder

```
package main

import (
    "html/template"
    "os"
)

func main() {
    t, err := template.ParseFiles("templates/template.html")
    if (err == nil) {
        t.Execute(os.Stdout, &Kayak)
```

```
    } else {
        Println("Error: %v", err.Error())
    }
}
```

I used the ParseFiles function to load a single template. The result from the ParseFiles function is a Template, on which I called the Execute method, specifying the standard output as the Writer and a Product as the data for the template to process.

The content of the template.html file is processed, and the action it contains is performed, inserting the data argument passed to the Execute method in the output sent to the Writer. Compile and execute the project, and you will see the following output:

```
<h1>Template Value: {Kayak Watersports 279}</h1>
```

The template output includes a string representation of the Product struct. I describe more useful ways to generate content from struct values later in this chapter.

Loading Multiple Templates

There are two approaches to working with multiple templates. The first is to create a separate Template value for each of them and execute them separately, as shown in Listing 23-9.

Listing 23-9. Using Separate Templates in the main.go File in the htmltext Folder

```
package main

import (
    "html/template"
    "os"
)

func main() {
    t1, err1 := template.ParseFiles("templates/template.html")
    t2, err2 := template.ParseFiles("templates/extras.html")
    if (err1 == nil && err2 == nil) {
        t1.Execute(os.Stdout, &Kayak)
        os.Stdout.WriteString("\n")
        t2.Execute(os.Stdout, &Kayak)
    } else {
        Println("Error: %v %v", err1.Error(), err2.Error())
    }
}
```

Notice that I wrote a newline character in between executing the templates. The output from a template is exactly what is contained in the file. Neither of the files in the templates directory contains a newline character, so I had to add one to the output to separate the content produced by the templates. Compile and execute the project, and you will receive the following output:

```
<h1>Template Value: {Kayak Watersports 279}</h1>
<h1>Extras Template Value: {Kayak Watersports 279}</h1>
```

Using separate `Template` values is the simplest approach, but the alternative is to load multiple files into a single `Template` value and then specify the name of the template you want to execute, as shown in Listing 23-10.

Listing 23-10. Using a Combined Template in the main.go File in the htmltext Folder

```
package main

import (
    "html/template"
    "os"
)

func main() {
    allTemplates, err1 := template.ParseFiles("templates/template.html",
        "templates/extras.html")
    if (err1 == nil) {
        allTemplates.ExecuteTemplate(os.Stdout, "template.html", &Kayak)
        os.Stdout.WriteString("\n")
        allTemplates.ExecuteTemplate(os.Stdout, "extras.html", &Kayak)
    } else {
        Printfln("Error: %v %v", err1.Error())
    }
}
```

When multiple files are loaded with the `ParseFiles`, the result is a `Template` value on which the `ExecuteTemplate` method can be called to execute a specified template. The filename is used as the template name, which means that the templates in this example are named `template.html` and `extras.html`.

■ **Note** You can call the `Execute` method on the `Template` returned by the `ParseFiles` or `ParseGlob` function, and the first template that was loaded will be selected and used to produce the output. Take care when using the `ParseGlob` function because the first template loaded—and therefore the template that will be executed—may not be the file you expect.

You don't have to use file extensions for your template files, but I have done so to differentiate the templates created in this section from the text templates created later in this chapter. Compile and execute the project, and you will see the following output:

```
<h1>Template Value: {Kayak Watersports 279}</h1>
<h1>Extras Template Value: {Kayak Watersports 279}</h1>
```

Loading multiple templates allows content to be defined in several files so that one template can rely on content generated from another, which I demonstrate in the "Defining Template Blocks" section later in this chapter.

Enumerating Loaded Templates

It can be useful to enumerate the templates that have been loaded, especially when using the ParseGlob function, to make sure that all the expected files have been discovered. Listing 23-11 uses the Templates method to get a list of templates and the Name method to get the name of each one.

Listing 23-11. Enumerating Loaded Templates in the main.go File in the htmltext Folder

```
package main

import (
    "html/template"
    //"os"
)

func main() {
    allTemplates, err := template.ParseGlob("templates/*.html")
    if (err == nil) {
        for _, t := range allTemplates.Templates() {
            Printfln("Template name: %v", t.Name())
        }
    } else {
        Printfln("Error: %v %v", err.Error())
    }
}
```

The pattern passed to the ParseGlob function selects all files with the html file extension in the templates folder. Compile and execute the project, and you will see a list of the templates that have been loaded:

```
Template name: extras.html
Template name: template.html
```

Looking Up a Specific Template

An alternative to specifying a name is to use the Lookup method to select a template, which is useful when you want to pass a template as an argument to a function, as shown in Listing 23-12.

Listing 23-12. Looking Up a Template in the main.go File in the htmltext Folder

```
package main

import (
    "html/template"
    "os"
)

func Exec(t *template.Template) error {
    return t.Execute(os.Stdout, &Kayak)
}
```

```
func main() {
    allTemplates, err := template.ParseGlob("templates/*.html")
    if (err == nil) {
        selectedTemplated := allTemplates.Lookup("template.html")
        err = Exec(selectedTemplated)
    }
    if (err != nil) {
        Printfln("Error: %v %v", err.Error())
    }
}
```

This example uses the Lookup method to get the template loaded from the template.txt file and uses it as an argument to the Exec function, which executes the template using the standard out. Compile and execute the project, and you will see the following output:

```
<h1>Template Value: {Kayak Watersports 279}</h1>
```

Understanding Template Actions

Go templates support a wide range of actions, which can be used to generate content from the data that is passed to the Execute or ExecuteTemplate method. For quick reference, Table 23-5 summarizes the template actions, the most useful of which are demonstrated in the sections that follow.

Table 23-5. *The Template Actions*

Action	Description
{{ value }} {{ expr }}	This action inserts a data value or the result of an expression into the template. A period is used to refer to the data value passed to the Execute or ExecuteTemplate function. See the "Inserting Data Values" section for details.
{{ value.fieldname }}	This action inserts the value of a struct field. See the "Inserting Data Values" section for details.
{{ value.method arg }}	This action invokes a method and inserts the result into the template output. Parentheses are not used, and arguments are separated by spaces. See the "Inserting Data Values" section for details.
{{ func arg }}	This action invokes a function and inserts the result into the output. There are built-in functions for common tasks, such as formatting data values, and custom functions can be defined, as described in the "Defining Template Functions" section.
{{ expr | value.method }} {{ expr | func	Expressions can be chained together using a vertical bar so that the result of the first expression is used as the last argument in the second expression.
{{ range value }} ... {{ end }}	This action iterates through the specified slice and adds the content between the range and end keyword for each element. The actions within the nested content are executed, with the current element accessible through the period. See the "Using Slices in Templates" section for details.

(continued)

Table 23-5. *(continued)*

Action	Description
{{ range value }} ... {{ else }} ... {{ end }}	This action is similar to the range/end combination but defines a section of nested content that is used if the slice contains no elements.
{{ if expr }} ... {{ end }}	This action evaluates an expression and executes the nested template content if the result is true, as demonstrated in the "Conditionally Executing Template Content" section. This action can be used with optional else and else if clauses.
{{ with expr }} ... {{ end }}	This action evaluates an expression and executes the nested template content if the result isn't nil or the empty string. This action can be used with optional clauses.
{{ define "name" }} ... {{ end }}	This action defines a template with the specified name
{{ template "name" expr }}	This action executes the template with the specified name and data and inserts the result in the output.
{{ block "name" expr }} ... {{ end }}	This action defines a template with the specified name and invokes it with the specified data. This is typically used to define a template that can be replaced by one loaded from another file, as demonstrated in the "Defining Template Blocks" section.

Inserting Data Values

The simplest task in a template is to insert a value into the output generated by the template, which is done by creating an action that contains an expression that produces the value you want to insert. Table 23-6 describes the basic template expressions, the most useful of which are demonstrated in the sections that follow.

Table 23-6. *The Template Expressions for Inserting Values into Templates*

Expression	Description
.	This expression inserts the value passed to the Execute or ExecuteTemplate method into the template output.
.Field	This expression inserts the value of the specified field into the template output.
.Method	This expression calls the specified method without arguments and inserts the result into the template output.
.Method arg	This expression calls the specified method with the specified argument and inserts the result into the template output.
call .Field arg	This expression invokes a struct function field, using the specified arguments, which are separated by spaces. The result from the function is inserted into the template output.

I used just the period in the previous section, which has the effect of inserting a string representation of the data value used to execute the template. Templates in most real projects include values for specific fields or the results from invoking methods, as shown in Listing 23-13.

Listing 23-13. Inserting Data Values in the template.html File in the templates Folder

```
<h1>Template Value: {{ . }}</h1>
<h1>Name: {{ .Name }}</h1>
<h1>Category: {{ .Category }}</h1>
<h1>Price: {{ .Price }}</h1>
<h1>Tax: {{ .AddTax }}</h1>
<h1>Discount Price: {{ .ApplyDiscount 10 }}</h1>
```

The new actions contain expressions that write out the value of the Name, Category, and Price fields, as well as the results from invoking the AddTax and ApplyDiscount methods. The syntax for accessing the fields is broadly similar to Go code, but the way that methods and functions are invoked is sufficiently different that it is easy to make mistakes. Unlike Go code, methods are not invoked with parentheses, and arguments are simply specified after the name, separated by spaces. It is the responsibility of the developer to ensure that arguments are of a type that can be used by the method or function. Compile and execute the project, and you will see the following output:

```
<h1>Template Value: {Kayak Watersports 279}</h1>
<h1>Name: Kayak</h1>
<h1>Category: Watersports</h1>
<h1>Price: 279</h1>
<h1>Tax: 334.8</h1>
<h1>Discount Price: 269</h1>
```

UNDERSTANDING CONTEXTUAL ESCAPING

Values are automatically escaped to make them safe for inclusion in HTML, CSS, and JavaScript code, with the appropriate escaping rules applied based on context. For example, a string value such as "It was a <big> boat" used as the text content of an HTML element would be inserted into the template as "It was a <big> boat" but as "It was a \u003cbig\u003e boat" when used as a string literal value in JavaScript code. Full details of how values are escaped can be found at https://golang.org/pkg/html/template.

Formatting Data Values

Templates support built-in functions for common tasks, including formatting data values that are inserted into the output, as described in Table 23-7. Additional built-in functions are described in later sections.

Table 23-7. *The Built-in Templates Functions for Formatting Data*

Name	Description
print	This is an alias to the fmt.Sprint function.
printf	This is an alias to the fmt.Sprintf function.
println	This is an alias to the fmt.Sprintln function.
html	This function encodes a value for safe inclusion in an HTML document.
js	This function encodes a value for safe inclusion in a JavaScript document.
urlquery	This function encodes a value for use in a URL query string.

These functions are called by specifying their name, followed by a list of space-separated arguments. In Listing 23-14, I have used the printf function to format some of the data fields included in the template output.

Listing 23-14. Using a Formatting Function in the template.html File in the templates Folder

```
<h1>Template Value: {{ . }}</h1>
<h1>Name: {{ .Name }}</h1>
<h1>Category: {{ .Category }}</h1>
<h1>Price: {{ printf "$%.2f" .Price }}</h1>
<h1>Tax: {{ printf "$%.2f" .AddTax }}</h1>
<h1>Discount Price: {{ .ApplyDiscount 10 }}</h1>
```

Using the printf function allows me to format two of the data values as dollar amounts, producing the following output when the project is compiled and executed:

```
<h1>Extras Template Value: {Kayak Watersports 279}</h1>
<h1>Name: Kayak</h1>
<h1>Category: Watersports</h1>
<h1>Price: $279.00</h1>
<h1>Tax: $334.80</h1>
<h1>Discount Price: 269</h1>
```

Chaining and Parenthesizing Template Expressions

Chaining expressions creates a pipeline for values, which allows the output from one method or function to be used as the input for another. Listing 23-15 creates a pipeline by chaining the result from the ApplyDiscount method so that it can be used as an argument to the printf function.

Listing 23-15. Chaining Expressions in the template.html File in the templates Folder

```
<h1>Template Value: {{ . }}</h1>
<h1>Name: {{ .Name }}</h1>
<h1>Category: {{ .Category }}</h1>
<h1>Price: {{ printf "$%.2f" .Price }}</h1>
<h1>Tax: {{ printf "$%.2f" .AddTax }}</h1>
<h1>Discount Price: {{ .ApplyDiscount 10 | printf "$%.2f" }}</h1>
```

Expressions are chained using a vertical bar (the | character), with the effect that the result of one expression is used as the final argument to the next expression. In Listing 23-15, the result from calling the ApplyDiscount method is used as the final argument to invoke the built-in printf function. Compile and execute the project, and you will see the formatted value in the output produced by the template:

```
<h1>Extras Template Value: {Kayak Watersports 279}</h1>
<h1>Name: Kayak</h1>
<h1>Category: Watersports</h1>
<h1>Price: $279.00</h1>
<h1>Tax: $334.80</h1>
<h1>Discount Price: $269.00</h1>
```

Chaining can be used only for the last argument provided to a function. An alternative approach—and one that can be used to set other function arguments—is to use parentheses, as shown in Listing 23-16.

Listing 23-16. Using Parentheses in the template.html File in the templates Folder

```
<h1>Template Value: {{ . }}</h1>
<h1>Name: {{ .Name }}</h1>
<h1>Category: {{ .Category }}</h1>
<h1>Price: {{ printf "$%.2f" .Price }}</h1>
<h1>Tax: {{ printf "$%.2f" .AddTax }}</h1>
<h1>Discount Price: {{ printf "$%.2f" (.ApplyDiscount 10) }}</h1>
```

The ApplyDiscount method is invoked, and the result is used as an argument to the printf function. The template in Listing 23-16 produces the same output as Listing 23-15.

Trimming Whitespace

By default, the contents of the template are rendered exactly as they are defined in the file, including any whitespace between actions. HTML isn't sensitive to the whitespace between elements, but whitespace can still cause problems for text content and attribute values, especially when you want to structure the content of a template to make it easy to read, as shown in Listing 23-17.

Listing 23-17. Structuring Template Content in the template.html File in the templates Folder

```
<h1>
    Name: {{ .Name }}, Category: {{ .Category }}, Price,
        {{ printf "$%.2f" .Price }}
</h1>
```

I have added newlines and indentation to fit the content on the printed page and separate the element content from its tags. The whitespace is included in the output when the project is compiled and executed:

```
<h1>
    Name: Kayak, Category: Watersports, Price,
        $279.00
</h1>
```

The minus sign can be used to trim whitespace, applied immediately after or before the braces that open or close an action. In Listing 23-18, I used this feature to trim the whitespace introduced in Listing 23-17.

Listing 23-18. Trimming Whitespace in the template.html File in the templates Folder

```
<h1>
    Name: {{ .Name }}, Category: {{ .Category }}, Price,
        {{- printf "$%.2f" .Price -}}
</h1>
```

The minus sign must be separated from the rest of the action's expression with a space. The effect is to remove all of the whitespace to before or after the action, which you can see by compiling and executing the project, which produces the following output:

```
<h1>
    Name: Kayak, Category: Watersports, Price,$279.00</h1>
```

The whitespace around the final action has been removed, but there is still a newline character after the opening h1 tag because the whitespace trimming applies only to actions. If this whitespace cannot be removed from the template, then an action that inserts an empty string into the output can be used just to trim the whitespace, as shown in Listing 23-19.

Listing 23-19. Trimming Additional Whitespace in the template.html File in the templates Folder

```
<h1>
    {{- "" -}} Name: {{ .Name }}, Category: {{ .Category }}, Price,
        {{- printf "$%.2f" .Price -}}
</h1>
```

The new action doesn't introduce any new output and only acts to trim the surrounding whitespace, which can be seen by compiling and executing the project:

```
<h1>Name: Kayak, Category: Watersports, Price,$279.00</h1>
```

Even with this feature, it can be hard to control whitespace while writing templates that are easy to understand, as you will see in later examples. If specific document structure is important, then you have to accept templates that are more difficult to read and maintain. If readability and maintainability are the priority, then you have to accept extra whitespace in the output produced by the template.

Using Slices in Templates

Template actions can be used to generate content for slices, as demonstrated in Listing 23-20, which replaces the entire template.

Listing 23-20. Processing a Slice in the template.html File in the templates Folder

```
{{ range . -}}
    <h1>Name: {{ .Name }}, Category: {{ .Category }}, Price,
        {{- printf "$%.2f" .Price }}</h1>
{{ end }}
```

The range expression iterates through the specified data, and I used the period in Listing 23-20 to select the data value used to execute the template, which I will configure shortly. The template content between the range expression and the end expression will be repeated for each value in the slice, with the current value assigned to the period, so that it can be used in nested actions. The effect in Listing 23-20 is that the Name, Category, and Price fields are inserted into the output for each value in the slice that is enumerated by the range expression.

■ **Note** The range keyword can also be used to enumerate maps, as described in the "Defining Template Variables" section, later in this chapter.

Listing 23-21 updates the code that executes the template to use a slice instead of a single Product value.

Listing 23-21. Using a Slice to Execute the Template in the main.go File in the htmltext Folder

```
package main

import (
    "html/template"
    "os"
)

func Exec(t *template.Template) error {
    return t.Execute(os.Stdout, Products)
}

func main() {
    allTemplates, err := template.ParseGlob("templates/*.html")
    if (err == nil) {
        selectedTemplated := allTemplates.Lookup("template.html")
        err = Exec(selectedTemplated)
    }
    if (err != nil) {
        Printfln("Error: %v %v", err.Error())
    }
}
```

Compile and execute the code, and you will see the following output:

```
<h1>Name: Kayak, Category: Watersports, Price,$279.00</h1>
<h1>Name: Lifejacket, Category: Watersports, Price,$49.95</h1>
<h1>Name: Soccer Ball, Category: Soccer, Price,$19.50</h1>
<h1>Name: Corner Flags, Category: Soccer, Price,$34.95</h1>
<h1>Name: Stadium, Category: Soccer, Price,$79500.00</h1>
<h1>Name: Thinking Cap, Category: Chess, Price,$16.00</h1>
<h1>Name: Unsteady Chair, Category: Chess, Price,$75.00</h1>
<h1>Name: Bling-Bling King, Category: Chess, Price,$1200.00</h1>
```

Notice that I applied the minus sign to the action that contains the range expression in Listing 23-20. I wanted the template content within the range and end actions to be visually distinct by putting it on a new line and add indentation, but this would have led to extra line breaks and spacing in the output. Putting the minus sign at the end of the range expression trims all the leading whitespace from the nested content. I didn't add a minus sign to the end action, which has the effect of preserving the trailing newline characters so that the output for each element in the slice appears on a separate line.

Using the Built-in Slice Functions

Go text templates support the built-in functions described in Table 23-8 for working with slices.

Table 23-8. *The Built-in Template Functions for Slices*

Name	Description
slice	This function creates a new slice. Its arguments are the original slice, the start index, and the end index.
index	This function returns the element at the specified index.
len	This function returns the length of the specified slice.

Listing 23-22 uses the built-in functions to report the size of a slice, get the element at a specific index, and create a new slice.

Listing 23-22. Using the Built-in Functions in the template.html File in the templates Folder

```
<h1>There are {{ len . }} products in the source data.</h1>
<h1>First product: {{ index . 0 }}</h1>
{{ range slice . 3 5 -}}
    <h1>Name: {{ .Name }}, Category: {{ .Category }}, Price,
        {{- printf "$%.2f" .Price }}</h1>
{{ end }}
```

Compile and execute the project, and you will see the following output:

```
<h1>There are 8 products in the source data.</h1>
<h1>First product: {Kayak Watersports 279}</h1>
<h1>Name: Corner Flags, Category: Soccer, Price,$34.95</h1>
<h1>Name: Stadium, Category: Soccer, Price,$79500.00</h1>
```

Conditionally Executing Template Content

Actions can be used to conditionally insert content into the output based on the evaluation of their expressions, as shown in Listing 23-23.

Listing 23-23. Using a Conditional Action in the template.html File in the templates Folder

```
<h1>There are {{ len . }} products in the source data.</h1>
<h1>First product: {{ index . 0 }}</h1>
{{ range . -}}
    {{ if lt .Price 100.00 -}}
        <h1>Name: {{ .Name }}, Category: {{ .Category }}, Price,
            {{- printf "$%.2f" .Price }}</h1>
    {{ end -}}
{{ end }}
```

The if keyword is followed by an expression that determines whether the nested template content is executed. To help write the expressions for these actions, templates support the functions described in Table 23-9.

Table 23-9. *The Template Conditional Functions*

Function	Description
eq arg1 arg2	This function returns true if arg1 == arg2.
ne arg1 arg2	This function returns true if arg1 != arg2.
lt arg1 arg2	This function returns true if arg1 < arg2.
le arg1 arg2	This function returns true if arg1 <= arg2.
gt arg1 arg2	This function returns true if arg1 > arg2.
ge arg1 arg2	This function returns true if arg1 >= arg2.
and arg1 arg2	This function returns true if both arg1 and arg2 are true.
not arg1	This function returns true if arg1 is false, and false if it is true.

The syntax for these functions is consistent with the rest of the template features, which is awkward until you become used to it. In Listing 23-23, I used this expression:

```
...
{{ if lt .Price 100.00 -}}
...
```

The if keyword indicates a conditional action, the lt function performs a less-than comparison, and the remaining arguments specify the Price field of the current value in the range expression and a literal value of 100.00. The comparison functions described in Table 23-9 do not have a sophisticated approach to dealing with data types, which means that I have to specify the literal value as 100.00 so that it is handled as a float64 and cannot rely on the way that Go deals with untyped constants.

The range action enumerates the values in the Product slice and executes the nested if action. The if action will execute its nested content only if the value of the Price field for the current element is less than 100. Compile and execute the project, and you will see the following output:

```
<h1>There are 8 products in the source data.</h1>
<h1>First product: {Kayak Watersports 279}</h1>
<h1>Name: Lifejacket, Category: Watersports, Price,$49.95</h1>
    <h1>Name: Soccer Ball, Category: Soccer, Price,$19.50</h1>
    <h1>Name: Corner Flags, Category: Soccer, Price,$34.95</h1>
    <h1>Name: Thinking Cap, Category: Chess, Price,$16.00</h1>
    <h1>Name: Unsteady Chair, Category: Chess, Price,$75.00</h1>
```

Despite the use of the minus sign to trim whitespace, the output is oddly formatted because of the way I chose to structure the template. As noted earlier, there is a trade-off between structuring templates to be easy to read and manage the whitespace in the output. I have focused on making the templates easy to understand in this chapter, with the result that the output from the examples is awkwardly formatted.

Using the Optional Conditional Actions

The if action can be used with optional else and else if keywords, as shown in Listing 23-24, allowing fallback content, which will be executed when the if expression is false or executed only when a second expression is true.

Listing 23-24. Using the Optional Keywords in the template.html File in the templates Folder

```
<h1>There are {{ len . }} products in the source data.</h1>
<h1>First product: {{ index . 0 }}</h1>
{{ range . -}}
    {{ if lt .Price 100.00 -}}
        <h1>Name: {{ .Name }}, Category: {{ .Category }}, Price,
            {{- printf "$%.2f" .Price }}</h1>
    {{ else if gt .Price 1500.00 -}}
        <h1>Expensive Product {{ .Name }} ({{ printf "$%.2f" .Price}})</h1>
    {{ else -}}
        <h1>Midrange Product: {{ .Name }} ({{ printf "$%.2f" .Price}})</h1>
    {{ end -}}
{{ end }}
```

Compile and execute the project, and you will see that the if, else if, and else actions produce the following output:

```
<h1>There are 8 products in the source data.</h1>
<h1>First product: {Kayak Watersports 279}</h1>
<h1>Midrange Product: Kayak ($279.00)</h1>
    <h1>Name: Lifejacket, Category: Watersports, Price,$49.95</h1>
    <h1>Name: Soccer Ball, Category: Soccer, Price,$19.50</h1>
    <h1>Name: Corner Flags, Category: Soccer, Price,$34.95</h1>
    <h1>Expensive Product Stadium ($79500.00)</h1>
```

612

```
<h1>Name: Thinking Cap, Category: Chess, Price,$16.00</h1>
<h1>Name: Unsteady Chair, Category: Chess, Price,$75.00</h1>
<h1>Midrange Product: Bling-Bling King ($1200.00)</h1>
```

Creating Named Nested Templates

The define action is used to create a nested template that can be executed by name, which allows content to be defined once and used repeatedly with the template action, as shown in Listing 23-25.

Listing 23-25. Defining and Using a Nested Template in the template.html File templates Folder

```
{{ define "currency" }}{{ printf "$%.2f" . }}{{ end }}

{{ define "basicProduct" -}}
    Name: {{ .Name }}, Category: {{ .Category }}, Price,
        {{- template "currency" .Price }}
{{- end }}

{{ define "expensiveProduct" -}}
    Expensive Product {{ .Name }} ({{ template "currency" .Price }})
{{- end }}

<h1>There are {{ len . }} products in the source data.</h1>
<h1>First product: {{ index . 0 }}</h1>
{{ range . -}}
    {{ if lt .Price 100.00 -}}
        <h1>{{ template "basicProduct" . }}</h1>
    {{ else if gt .Price 1500.00 -}}
        <h1>{{ template "expensiveProduct" . }}</h1>
    {{ else -}}
        <h1>Midrange Product: {{ .Name }} ({{ printf "$%.2f" .Price}})</h1>
    {{ end -}}
{{ end }}
```

The define keyword is followed by the template name in quotes, and the template is terminated by the end keyword. The template keyword is used to execute a named template, specifying the template name and a data value:

```
...
{{- template "currency" .Price }}
...
```

This action executes the template named currency and uses the value of the Price field as the data value, which is accessed within the named template using the period:

```
...
{{ define "currency" }}{{ printf "$%.2f" . }}{{ end }}
...
```

A named template can invoke other named templates, as Listing 23-25 demonstrates, with the basicProduct and expensiveProduct templates executing the currency template.

Nested named templates can exacerbate whitespace issues because the whitespace around the templates, which I added in Listing 23-25 for clarity, is included in the output from the main template. One way to resolve this is to define the named templates in a separate file, but the issue can also be addressed by using only named templates, even for the main part of the output, as shown in Listing 23-26.

Listing 23-26. Adding a Named Template in the template.html File in the templates Folder

```
{{ define "currency" }}{{ printf "$%.2f" . }}{{ end }}

{{ define "basicProduct" -}}
    Name: {{ .Name }}, Category: {{ .Category }}, Price,
        {{- template "currency" .Price }}
{{- end }}

{{ define "expensiveProduct" -}}
    Expensive Product {{ .Name }} ({{ template "currency" .Price }})
{{- end }}

{{ define "mainTemplate" -}}
    <h1>There are {{ len . }} products in the source data.</h1>
    <h1>First product: {{ index . 0 }}</h1>
    {{ range . -}}
        {{ if lt .Price 100.00 -}}
            <h1>{{ template "basicProduct" . }}</h1>
        {{ else if gt .Price 1500.00 -}}
            <h1>{{ template "expensiveProduct" . }}</h1>
        {{ else -}}
            <h1>Midrange Product: {{ .Name }} ({{ printf "$%.2f" .Price}})</h1>
        {{ end -}}
    {{ end }}
{{- end}}
```

Using the define and end keywords for the main template content excludes the whitespace used to separate the other named templates. In Listing 23-27, I complete the change by using the name when selecting the template to execute.

Listing 23-27. Selecting a Named Template in the main.go File in the htmltext Folder

```
package main

import (
    "html/template"
    "os"
)

func Exec(t *template.Template) error {
    return t.Execute(os.Stdout, Products)
}
```

```
func main() {
    allTemplates, err := template.ParseGlob("templates/*.html")
    if (err == nil) {
        selectedTemplated := allTemplates.Lookup("mainTemplate")
        err = Exec(selectedTemplated)
    }
    if (err != nil) {
        Printfln("Error: %v %v", err.Error())
    }
}
```

Any of the named templates can be executed directly, but I have selected the mainTemplate, which produces the following output when the project is compiled and executed:

```
<h1>There are 8 products in the source data.</h1>
    <h1>First product: {Kayak Watersports 279}</h1>
    <h1>Midrange Product: Kayak ($279.00)</h1>
        <h1>Name: Lifejacket, Category: Watersports, Price,$49.95</h1>
        <h1>Name: Soccer Ball, Category: Soccer, Price,$19.50</h1>
        <h1>Name: Corner Flags, Category: Soccer, Price,$34.95</h1>
        <h1>Expensive Product Stadium ($79500.00)</h1>
        <h1>Name: Thinking Cap, Category: Chess, Price,$16.00</h1>
        <h1>Name: Unsteady Chair, Category: Chess, Price,$75.00</h1>
        <h1>Midrange Product: Bling-Bling King ($1200.00)</h1>
```

Defining Template Blocks

Template blocks are used to define a template with default content that can be overridden in another template file, which requires multiple templates to be loaded and executed together. This is often used to common content, such as a layout, as shown in Listing 23-28.

Listing 23-28. Defining a Block in the template.html File in the templates Folder

```
{{ define "mainTemplate" -}}
    <h1>This is the layout header</h1>
    {{ block "body" . }}
        <h2>There are {{ len . }} products in the source data.</h2>
    {{ end }}
    <h1>This is the layout footer</h1>
{{ end }}
```

The block action is used to assign a name to a template, but, unlike the define action, the template will be included in the output without needing to use a template action, which you can see by compiling and executing the project (I have formatted the output to remove the whitespace):

```
<h1>This is the layout header</h1>
    <h2>There are 8 products in the source data.</h2>
<h1>This is the layout footer</h1>
```

When used alone, the output from the template file includes the content in the block. But this content can be redefined by another template file. Add a file named list.html to the templates folder with the content shown in Listing 23-29.

Listing 23-29. The Contents of the list.html File in the templates Folder

```
{{ define "body" }}
    {{ range . }}
        <h2>Product: {{ .Name }} ({{ printf "$%.2f" .Price}})</h2>
    {{ end -}}
{{ end }}
```

To use this feature, the template files must be loaded in order, as shown in Listing 23-30.

Listing 23-30. Loading Templates in the main.go File in the htmltext Folder

```
package main

import (
    "html/template"
    "os"
)

func Exec(t *template.Template) error {
    return t.Execute(os.Stdout, Products)
}

func main() {

    allTemplates, err := template.ParseFiles("templates/template.html",
        "templates/list.html")
    if (err == nil) {
        selectedTemplated := allTemplates.Lookup("mainTemplate")
        err = Exec(selectedTemplated)
    }
    if (err != nil) {
        Printfln("Error: %v %v", err.Error())
    }
}
```

The templates must be loaded so that the file that contains the block action is loaded before the file that contains the define action that redefines the template. When the templates are loaded, the template defined in the list.html file redefines the template named body so that the content in the list.html file replaces the content in the template.html file. Compile and execute the project, and you will see the following output, which I have formatted to remove whitespace:

```
<h1>This is the layout header</h1>
    <h2>Product: Kayak ($279.00)</h2>
    <h2>Product: Lifejacket ($49.95)</h2>
    <h2>Product: Soccer Ball ($19.50)</h2>
    <h2>Product: Corner Flags ($34.95)</h2>
```

```
    <h2>Product: Stadium ($79500.00)</h2>
    <h2>Product: Thinking Cap ($16.00)</h2>
    <h2>Product: Unsteady Chair ($75.00)</h2>
    <h2>Product: Bling-Bling King ($1200.00)</h2>
<h1>This is the layout footer</h1>
```

Defining Template Functions

The built-in template functions described in earlier sections can be supplemented by custom functions that are specific to a Template, meaning they are defined and set up in code. Listing 23-31 demonstrates the process of setting up a custom function.

Listing 23-31. Defining a Custom Function in the main.go File in the htmltext Folder

```
package main

import (
    "html/template"
    "os"
)

func GetCategories(products []Product) (categories []string) {
    catMap := map[string]string {}
    for _, p := range products {
        if (catMap[p.Category] == "") {
            catMap[p.Category] = p.Category
            categories = append(categories, p.Category)
        }
    }
    return
}

func Exec(t *template.Template) error {
    return t.Execute(os.Stdout, Products)
}

func main() {
    allTemplates := template.New("allTemplates")
    allTemplates.Funcs(map[string]interface{} {
        "getCats": GetCategories,
    })
    allTemplates, err := allTemplates.ParseGlob("templates/*.html")

    if (err == nil) {
        selectedTemplated := allTemplates.Lookup("mainTemplate")
        err = Exec(selectedTemplated)
    }
    if (err != nil) {
        Printfln("Error: %v %v", err.Error())
    }
}
```

The GetCategories function receives a Product slice and returns the set of unique Category values. To set up the GetCategories function so that it can be used by a Template, the Funcs method is called, passing a map of names to functions, like this:

```
...
allTemplates.Funcs(map[string]interface{} {
    "getCats": GetCategories,
})
...
```

The map in Listing 23-31 specifies that the GetCategories function will be invoked using the name getCats. The Funcs method must be called before template files are parsed, which means creating a Template using the New function, which then allows the custom functions to be registered before the ParseFiles or ParseGlob method is called:

```
...
allTemplates := template.New("allTemplates")
allTemplates.Funcs(map[string]interface{} {
    "getCats": GetCategories,
})
allTemplates, err := allTemplates.ParseGlob("templates/*.html")
...
```

Within the templates, the custom functions can be called using the same syntax as the built-in functions, as shown in Listing 23-32.

Listing 23-32. Using a Custom Function in the template.html File in the templates Folder

```
{{ define "mainTemplate" -}}
    <h1>There are {{ len . }} products in the source data.</h1>
    {{ range getCats . -}}
        <h1>Category: {{ . }}</h1>
    {{ end }}
{{- end }}
```

The range keyword is used to enumerate the categories returned by the custom function, which are included in the template output. Compile and execute the project, and you will see the following output, which I have formatted to remove whitespace:

```
<h1>There are 8 products in the source data.</h1>
<h1>Category: Watersports</h1>
<h1>Category: Soccer</h1>
<h1>Category: Chess</h1>
```

Disabling Function Result Encoding

The results produced by functions are encoded for safe inclusion in an HTML document, which can present a problem for functions that generate HTML, JavaScript, or CSS fragments, as shown in Listing 23-33.

Listing 23-33. Creating an HTML Fragment in the main.go File in the htmltext Folder

```
...
func GetCategories(products []Product) (categories []string) {
    catMap := map[string]string {}
    for _, p := range products {
        if (catMap[p.Category] == "") {
            catMap[p.Category] = p.Category
            categories = append(categories, "<b>p.Category</b>")
        }
    }
    return
}
...
```

The GetCategories function has been modified so that it generates a slice containing HTML strings. The template engine encodes these values, which is shown in the output from compiling and executing the project:

```
<h1>There are 8 products in the source data.</h1>
<h1>Category: &lt;b&gt;p.Category&lt;/b&gt;</h1>
<h1>Category: &lt;b&gt;p.Category&lt;/b&gt;</h1>
<h1>Category: &lt;b&gt;p.Category&lt;/b&gt;</h1>
```

This is good practice, but it causes problems when functions are used to generate content that should be included in the template without encoding. For these situations, the html/template package defines a set of string type aliases that are used to denote that the result from a function requires special handling, as described in Table 23-10.

Table 23-10. *The Types Aliases Used to Denote Content Types*

Name	Description
CSS	This type denotes CSS content.
HTML	This type denotes a fragment of HTML.
HTMLAttr	This type denotes a value that will be used as the value for an HTML attribute.
JS	This type denotes a fragment of JavaScript code.
JSStr	This type denotes a value that is intended to appear between quotes in a JavaScript expression.
Srcset	This type denotes a value that can be used in the srcset attribute of an img element.
URL	This type denotes a URL.

To prevent the usual content handling, the function that produces the content uses one of the types shown in Table 23-10, as shown in Listing 23-34.

Listing 23-34. Returning HTML Content in the main.go File in the htmltext Folder

```
...
func GetCategories(products []Product) (categories []template.HTML) {
    catMap := map[string]string {}
    for _, p := range products {
        if (catMap[p.Category] == "") {
            catMap[p.Category] = p.Category
            categories = append(categories, "<b>p.Category</b>")
        }
    }
    return
}
...
```

This change tells the template system that the results from the GetCategories function are HTML, which produces the following output when the project is compiled and executed:

```
<h1>There are 8 products in the source data.</h1>
<h1>Category: <b>p.Category</b></h1>
<h1>Category: <b>p.Category</b></h1>
<h1>Category: <b>p.Category</b></h1>
```

Providing Access to Standard Library Functions

Template functions can also be used to provide access to the features provided by the standard library, as shown in Listing 23-35.

Listing 23-35. Adding a Function Mapping in the main.go File in the htmltext Folder

```
package main

import (
    "html/template"
    "os"
    "strings"
)

func GetCategories(products []Product) (categories []string) {
    catMap := map[string]string {}
    for _, p := range products {
        if (catMap[p.Category] == "") {
            catMap[p.Category] = p.Category
            categories = append(categories, p.Category)
        }
    }
    return
}
```

```
func Exec(t *template.Template) error {
    return t.Execute(os.Stdout, Products)
}

func main() {
    allTemplates := template.New("allTemplates")
    allTemplates.Funcs(map[string]interface{} {
        "getCats": GetCategories,
        "lower": strings.ToLower,
    })
    allTemplates, err := allTemplates.ParseGlob("templates/*.html")

    if (err == nil) {
        selectedTemplated := allTemplates.Lookup("mainTemplate")
        err = Exec(selectedTemplated)
    }
    if (err != nil) {
        Printfln("Error: %v %v", err.Error())
    }
}
```

The new mapping provides access to the ToLower function, which transforms strings to lowercase, as described in Chapter 16. The function can be accessed within the template using the name lower, as shown in Listing 23-36.

Listing 23-36. Using a Template Function in the template.html File in the templates Folder

```
{{ define "mainTemplate" -}}
    <h1>There are {{ len . }} products in the source data.</h1>
    {{ range getCats .  -}}
        <h1>Category: {{ lower . }}</h1>
    {{ end }}
{{- end }}
```

Compile and execute the project, and you will see the following output:

```
<h1>There are 8 products in the source data.</h1>
<h1>Category: watersports</h1>
<h1>Category: soccer</h1>
<h1>Category: chess</h1>
```

Defining Template Variables

Actions can define variables in their expressions, which can be accessed within embedded template content, as shown in Listing 23-37. This feature is useful when you need to produce a value to assess in the expression and need the same value in the nested content.

Listing 23-37. Defining and Using a Template Variable in the template.html File in the templates Folder

```
{{ define "mainTemplate" -}}
    {{ $length := len . }}
    <h1>There are {{ $length }} products in the source data.</h1>
    {{ range getCats .  -}}
        <h1>Category: {{ lower . }}</h1>
    {{ end }}
{{- end }}
```

Template variable names are prefixed with the $ character and are created with the short variable declaration syntax. The first action creates a variable named length, which is used in the following action. Compile and execute the project, and you will see the following output:

```
<h1>There are 8 products in the source data.</h1>
    <h1>Category: watersports</h1>
    <h1>Category: soccer</h1>
    <h1>Category: chess</h1>
```

Listing 23-38 shows a more complex example of defining and using template variable.

Listing 23-38. Defining and Using a Template Variable in the template.html File in the templates Folder

```
{{ define "mainTemplate" -}}
    <h1>There are {{ len . }} products in the source data.</h1>
    {{- range getCats .  -}}
        {{ if ne ($char := slice (lower .) 0 1) "s"  }}
            <h1>{{$char}}: {{.}}</h1>
        {{- end }}
    {{- end }}
{{- end }}
```

In this example, the if action uses the slice and lower functions to get the first character of the current category and assigns it to a variable named $char before using the character for an if expression. The $char variable is accessed in the nested template content, which avoids having to duplicate the use of the slice and lower functions. Compile and execute the project, and you will see the following output:

```
<h1>There are 8 products in the source data.</h1>
        <h1>w: Watersports</h1>
        <h1>c: Chess</h1>
```

Using Template Variables in Range Actions

Variables can also be used with the range action, which allows maps to be used in templates. In Listing 23-39, I have updated the Go code that executes the template to pass a map to the Execute method.

Listing 23-39. Using a Map in the main.go File in the htmltext Folder

```
...
func Exec(t *template.Template) error {
    productMap := map[string]Product {}
    for _, p := range Products {
        productMap[p.Name] = p
    }
    return t.Execute(os.Stdout, &productMap)
}
...
```

Listing 23-40 updates the template to enumerate the contents of the map using template variables.

Listing 23-40. Enumerating a Map in the template.html File in the templates Folder

```
{{ define "mainTemplate" -}}
    {{ range $key, $value := . -}}
        <h1>{{ $key }}: {{ printf "$%.2f" $value.Price }}</h1>
    {{ end }}
{{- end }}
```

The syntax is awkward, with the range keyword, the variables, and the assignment operator appearing in an unusual order, but the effect is that the keys and values in the map can be used in the template. Compile and execute the project, and you will see the following output:

```
<h1>Bling-Bling King: $1200.00</h1>
    <h1>Corner Flags: $34.95</h1>
    <h1>Kayak: $279.00</h1>
    <h1>Lifejacket: $49.95</h1>
    <h1>Soccer Ball: $19.50</h1>
    <h1>Stadium: $79500.00</h1>
    <h1>Thinking Cap: $16.00</h1>
    <h1>Unsteady Chair: $75.00</h1>
```

Creating Text Templates

The html/template package builds on the features provided by the text/template package, which can be used directly to execute text templates. HTML is, of course, text, and the difference is that the text/template package doesn't automatically escape content. In all other respects, using a text template is the same as using an HTML template. Add a file named template.txt to the templates folder with the content shown in Listing 23-41.

Listing 23-41. The Contents of the template.txt File in the templates Folder

```
{{ define "mainTemplate" -}}
    {{ range $key, $value := . -}}
        {{ $key }}: {{ printf "$%.2f" $value.Price }}
    {{ end }}
{{- end }}
```

This template is similar to the one in Listing 23-40, except that it doesn't contain an h1 element. The template actions, expressions, variables, and whitespace trimming are all the same. And, as Listing 23-42 shows, even the names of the functions used to load and execute templates are the same, just accessed through a different package.

Listing 23-42. Loading and Executing a Text Template in the main.go File in the htmltext Folder

```
package main

import (
    "text/template"
    "os"
    "strings"
)

func GetCategories(products []Product) (categories []string) {
    catMap := map[string]string {}
    for _, p := range products {
        if (catMap[p.Category] == "") {
            catMap[p.Category] = p.Category
            categories = append(categories, p.Category)
        }
    }
    return
}

func Exec(t *template.Template) error {
    productMap := map[string]Product {}
    for _, p := range Products {
        productMap[p.Name] = p
    }
    return t.Execute(os.Stdout, &productMap)
}

func main() {
    allTemplates := template.New("allTemplates")
    allTemplates.Funcs(map[string]interface{} {
        "getCats": GetCategories,
        "lower": strings.ToLower,
    })
    allTemplates, err := allTemplates.ParseGlob("templates/*.txt")

    if (err == nil) {
        selectedTemplated := allTemplates.Lookup("mainTemplate")
        err = Exec(selectedTemplated)
    }
    if (err != nil) {
        Printfln("Error: %v %v", err.Error())
    }
}
```

Aside from changing the package `import` statement and selecting files with the `txt` extension, the process of loading and executing the text template is the same. Compile and execute the project, and you will see the following output:

```
Bling-Bling King: $1200.00
    Corner Flags: $34.95
    Kayak: $279.00
    Lifejacket: $49.95
    Soccer Ball: $19.50
    Stadium: $79500.00
    Thinking Cap: $16.00
    Unsteady Chair: $75.00
```

Summary

In this chapter, I described the standard library for creating HTML and text templates. The templates can contain a wide range of actions, which are used to include content in the output. The syntax for templates can be awkward—and care must be taken to express the content exactly as the template engine requires—but the template engine is flexible and extensible and, as I demonstrate in Part 3, can easily be modified to alter its behavior.

CHAPTER 24

Creating HTTP Servers

In this chapter, I describe the standard library support for creating HTTP servers and processing HTTP and HTTPS requests. I show you how to create a server and explain the different ways in which requests can be handled, including form requests. Table 24-1 puts HTTP servers in context.

Table 24-1. *Putting HTTP Servers in Context*

Question	Answer
What are they?	The features described in this chapter make it easy for Go applications to create HTTP servers.
Why are they useful?	HTTP is one of the most widely used protocols and is useful for both user-facing applications and web services.
How is it used?	The features of the net/http package are used to create a server and handle requests.
Are there any pitfalls or limitations?	These features are well-designed and easy to use.
Are there any alternatives?	The standard library includes support for other network protocols and also for opening and using lower-level network connections. See https://pkg.go.dev/net@go1.17.1 for details of the net package and its subpackages, such as net/smtp, for example, which implements the SMTP protocol.

Table 24-2 summarizes the chapter.

© Adam Freeman 2022
A. Freeman, *Pro Go*, https://doi.org/10.1007/978-1-4842-7355-5_24

Table 24-2. *Chapter Summary*

Problem	Solution	Listing
Create an HTTP or HTTPS server	Use the `ListenAndServe` or `ListenAndServeTLS` functions	6, 7, 11
Inspect an HTTP request	Use the features of the `Request` struct	8
Produce a response	Use the `ResponseWriter` interface or the convenience functions	9
Handle requests to specific URLs	Use the integrated router	10, 12
Serve static content	Use the `FileServer` and `StripPrefix` function	13–17
Use a template to produce a response or produce a JSON response	Write the content to the `ResponseWriter`	18–20
Handle form data	Use the Request methods	21–25
Set or read cookies	Use the `Cookie`, `Cookies`, and `SetCookie` methods	26

Preparing for This Chapter

To prepare for this chapter, open a new command prompt, navigate to a convenient location, and create a directory named `httpserver`. Run the command shown in Listing 24-1 to create a module file.

■ **Tip**   You can download the example project for this chapter—and for all the other chapters in this book—from `https://github.com/apress/pro-go`. See Chapter 2 for how to get help if you have problems running the examples.

Listing 24-1. Initializing the Module

```
go mod init httpserver
```

Add a file named `printer.go` to the `httpserver` folder with the content shown in Listing 24-2.

Listing 24-2. The Contents of the printer.go File in the httpserver Folder

```
package main

import "fmt"

func Printfln(template string, values ...interface{}) {
    fmt.Printf(template + "\n", values...)
}
```

Add a file named `product.go` to the `httpserver` folder with the content shown in Listing 24-3.

Listing 24-3. The Contents of the product.go File in the httpserver Folder

```
package main

type Product struct {
    Name, Category string
    Price float64
}

var Products = []Product {
    { "Kayak", "Watersports", 279 },
    { "Lifejacket", "Watersports", 49.95 },
    { "Soccer Ball", "Soccer", 19.50 },
    { "Corner Flags", "Soccer", 34.95 },
    { "Stadium", "Soccer", 79500 },
    { "Thinking Cap", "Chess", 16 },
    { "Unsteady Chair", "Chess", 75 },
    { "Bling-Bling King", "Chess", 1200 },
}
```

Add a file named main.go to the httpserver folder with the content shown in Listing 24-4.

Listing 24-4. The Contents of the main.go File in the httpserver Folder

```
package main

func main() {
    for _, p := range Products {
        Printfln("Product: %v, Category: %v, Price: $%.2f",
            p.Name, p.Category, p.Price)
    }
}
```

Use the command prompt to run the command shown in Listing 24-5 in the httpserver folder.

Listing 24-5. Running the Example Project

```
go run .
```

The project will be compiled and executed, producing the following output:

```
Product: Kayak, Category: Watersports, Price: $279.00
Product: Lifejacket, Category: Watersports, Price: $49.95
Product: Soccer Ball, Category: Soccer, Price: $19.50
Product: Corner Flags, Category: Soccer, Price: $34.95
Product: Stadium, Category: Soccer, Price: $79500.00
Product: Thinking Cap, Category: Chess, Price: $16.00
Product: Unsteady Chair, Category: Chess, Price: $75.00
Product: Bling-Bling King, Category: Chess, Price: $1200.00
```

Creating a Simple HTTP Server

The net/http package makes it easy to create a simple HTTP server, which can then be extended to add more complex and useful features. Listing 24-6 demonstrates a server that responds to requests with a simple string response.

Listing 24-6. Creating a Simple HTTP Server in the main.go File in the httpserver Folder

```
package main

import (
    "net/http"
    "io"
)

type StringHandler struct {
    message string
}

func (sh StringHandler) ServeHTTP(writer http.ResponseWriter,
        request *http.Request) {
    io.WriteString(writer, sh.message)
}

func main() {
    err := http.ListenAndServe(":5000", StringHandler{ message: "Hello, World"})
    if (err != nil) {
        Printfln("Error: %v", err.Error())
    }
}
```

There are only a few lines of code, but they are enough to create an HTTP server that responds to requests with Hello, World. Compile and execute the project and then use a web browser to request http://localhost:5000, which will produce the result shown in Figure 24-1.

DEALING WITH WINDOWS FIREWALL PERMISSION REQUESTS

Windows users may be prompted by the built-in firewall to allow network access. Unfortunately, the go run command creates an executable in a unique path each time it is run, which means that you will be prompted to grant access every time you make a change and execute the code. To address this issue, create a file named buildandrun.ps1 in the project folder with the following contents:

```
$file = "./httpserver.exe"

&go build -o $file

if ($LASTEXITCODE -eq 0) {
    &$file
}
```

This PowerShell script compiles the project to the same file each time and then executes the result if there are no errors, meaning you will only have to grant firewall access once. The script is executed by running this command in the project folder:

```
./buildandrun.ps1
```

You must use this command every time to build and execute the project to ensure that the compiled output is written to the same location.

Figure 24-1. *A response to an HTTP request*

Although there are few lines of code in Listing 24-6, they take some time to unpack. But it is worth taking the time to understand how the HTTP server was created because it reveals a great deal about the features provided by the net/http package.

Creating the HTTP Listener and Handler

The net/http package provides a set of convenience functions that make it easy to create an HTTP server without needing to specify too many details. Table 24-3 describes the convenience functions for setting up a server.

Table 24-3. *The net/http Convenience Functions*

Name	Description
ListenAndServe(addr, handler)	This function starts listening for HTTP requests on a specified address and passes requests onto the specified handler.
ListenAndServeTLS(addr, cert, key, handler)	This function starts listening for HTTPS requests. The arguments are the address

The ListenAndServe function starts listening for HTTP requests on a specified network address. The ListenAndServeTLS function does the same for HTTP requests, which I demonstrate in the "Supporting HTTPS Requests" section.

The addresses accepted by the functions in Table 24-3 can be used to restrict the HTTP server so that it only accepts requests on a specific interface or to listen for requests on any interface. Listing 24-6 uses the latter approach, which is to specify just the port number:

```
...
err := http.ListenAndServe(":5000", StringHandler{ message: "Hello, World"})
...
```

No name or address is specified, and the port number follows a colon, meaning that this statement creates an HTTP server that listens for requests on port 5000 on all interfaces.

When a request arrives, it is passed onto a handler, which is responsible for producing a response. Handlers must implement the Handler interface, which defines the method described in Table 24-4.

Table 24-4. *The Method Defined by the Handler Interface*

Name	Description
ServeHTTP(writer, request)	This method is invoked to process a HTTP request. The request is described by a Request value, and the response is written using a ResponseWriter, both of which are received as parameters.

I describe the Request and ResponseWriter types in more detail in later sections, but the ResponseWriter interface defines the Write method required by the Writer interface, described in Chapter 20, which means that I can produce a string response by using the WriteString function defined in the io package:

```
...
io.WriteString(writer, sh.message)
...
```

Put these features together and the result is an HTTP server that listens to requests on port 5000, on all interfaces, and which creates responses by writing a string. The details, such as opening the network connection and parsing the HTTP requests, are taken care of behind the scenes.

Inspecting the Request

HTTP requests are represented by the Request struct, defined in the net/http package. Table 24-5 describes the basic fields defined by the Request struct.

Table 24-5. *The Basic Fields Defined by the Request Struct*

Name	Description
Method	This field provides the HTTP method (GET, POST, etc.) as a string. The net/http package defines constants for the HTTP methods, such as MethodGet and MethodPost.
URL	This field returns the requested URL, expressed as a URL value.
Proto	This field returns a string that indicates the version of HTTP used for the request.
Host	This field returns a string containing the requested hos.
Header	This field returns a Header value, which is an alias to map[string][]string and contains the request headers. The map keys are the names of the headers, and the values are string slices containing the header values.
Trailer	This field returns a map[string]string that contains any additional headers that are included in the request after the body.
Body	This filed returns a ReadCloser, which is an interface that combines the Read method of the Reader interface with the Close method of the Closer interface, both of which are described in Chapter 22.

Listing 24-7 adds statements to the request handler function that write out values from the basic Request fields to the standard out.

Listing 24-7. Writing Request Fields in the main.go File in the httpserver Folder

```
package main

import (
    "net/http"
    "io"
)

type StringHandler struct {
    message string
}

func (sh StringHandler) ServeHTTP(writer http.ResponseWriter,
        request *http.Request) {
    Printfln("Method: %v", request.Method)
    Printfln("URL: %v", request.URL)
    Printfln("HTTP Version: %v", request.Proto)
    Printfln("Host: %v", request.Host)
    for name, val := range  request.Header {
        Printfln("Header: %v, Value: %v", name, val)
    }
    Printfln("---")
    io.WriteString(writer, sh.message)
}

func main() {
    err := http.ListenAndServe(":5000", StringHandler{ message: "Hello, World"})
```

```
    if (err != nil) {
        Printfln("Error: %v", err.Error())
    }
}
```

Compile and execute the project and request http://localhost:5000. You will see the same response in the browser window as in the previous example, but this time there will also be output at the command prompt. The exact output will depend on your browser, but here is the output that I received using Google Chrome:

```
Method: GET
URL: /
HTTP Version: HTTP/1.1
Host: localhost:5000
Header: Upgrade-Insecure-Requests, Value: [1]
Header: Sec-Fetch-Site, Value: [none]
Header: Sec-Fetch-Mode, Value: [navigate]
Header: Sec-Fetch-User, Value: [?1]
Header: Accept-Encoding, Value: [gzip, deflate, br]
Header: Connection, Value: [keep-alive]
Header: Cache-Control, Value: [max-age=0]
Header: User-Agent, Value: [Mozilla/5.0 (Windows NT 10.0; Win64; x64)
    AppleWebKit/537.36 (KHTML, like Gecko) Chrome/91.0.4472.124 Safari/537.36]
Header: Accept, Value: [text/html,application/xhtml+xml,application/xml;q=0.9,
    image/avif,image/webp,image/apng,*/*;q=0.8,application/signedexchange;
    v=b3;q=0.9]
Header: Sec-Fetch-Dest, Value: [document]
Header: Sec-Ch-Ua, Value: [" Not;A Brand";v="99", "Google Chrome";v="91",
    "Chromium";v="91"]
Header: Accept-Language, Value: [en-GB,en-US;q=0.9,en;q=0.8]
Header: Sec-Ch-Ua-Mobile, Value: [?0]
---
Method: GET
URL: /favicon.ico
HTTP Version: HTTP/1.1
Host: localhost:5000
Header: Sec-Fetch-Site, Value: [same-origin]
Header: Sec-Fetch-Dest, Value: [image]
Header: Referer, Value: [http://localhost:5000/]
Header: Pragma, Value: [no-cache]
Header: Cache-Control, Value: [no-cache]
Header: User-Agent, Value: [Mozilla/5.0 (Windows NT 10.0; Win64; x64)
    AppleWebKit/537.36 (KHTML, like Gecko) Chrome/91.0.4472.124 Safari/537.36]
Header: Accept-Language, Value: [en-GB,en-US;q=0.9,en;q=0.8]
Header: Sec-Ch-Ua, Value: [" Not;A Brand";v="99", "Google Chrome";v="91",
    "Chromium";v="91"]
Header: Sec-Ch-Ua-Mobile, Value: [?0]
Header: Sec-Fetch-Mode, Value: [no-cors]
Header: Accept-Encoding, Value: [gzip, deflate, br]
Header: Connection, Value: [keep-alive]
```

```
Header: Accept, Value:[image/avif,image/webp,image/apng,image/svg+xml,
    image/*,*/*;q=0.8]
---
```

The browser makes two HTTP requests. The first is for /, which is the path component of the URL that was requested. The second request is for /favicon.ico, which the browser sends to get an icon to display at the top of the window or tab.

<table>
<tr><td>

USING REQUEST CONTEXTS

</td></tr>
</table>

The net/http package defines a Context method for the Request struct, which returns an implementation of the context.Context interface. The Context interface is used to manage the flow of a request through an application and is described in Chapter 30. In Part 3, I use the Context feature in a custom web platform and online store.

Filtering Requests and Generating Responses

The HTTP server responds to all requests in the same way, which isn't ideal. To produce different responses, I need to inspect the URL to figure out what is being requested and use the functions provided by the net/http package to send an appropriate response. The most useful fields and methods defined by the URL struct are described in Table 24-6.

Table 24-6. *Useful Fields and Methods Defined by the URL Struct*

Name	Description
Scheme	This field returns the scheme component of the URL.
Host	This field returns the host component of the URL, which may include the port.
RawQuery	This field returns the query string from the URL. Use the Query method to process the query string into a map.
Path	This field returns the path component of the URL.
Fragment	This field returns the fragment component of the URL, without the # character.
Hostname()	This method returns the hostname component of the URL as a string.
Port()	This method returns the port component of the URL as a string.
Query()	This method returns a map[string][]string (a map with string keys and string slice values), containing the query string fields.
User()	This method returns the user information associated with the request, as described in Chapter 30.
String()	This method returns a string representation of the URL.

The ResponseWriter interface defines the methods that are available when creating a response. As noted earlier, this interface includes the Write method so that it can be used as a Writer, but ResponseWriter also defines the methods described in Table 24-7. Note that you must finish setting headers before using the Write method.

Table 24-7. *The ResponseWriter Methods*

Name	Description
Header()	This method returns a Header, which is an alias to map[string][]string, that can be used to set the response headers.
WriteHeader(code)	This method sets the status code for the response, specified as an int. The net/http package defines constants for most status codes.
Write(data)	This method writes data to the response body and implements the Writer interface.

In Listing 24-8, I have updated my request handler function to produce a 404 Not Found response to requests for icon files.

Listing 24-8. Producing Difference Responses in the main.go File in the httpserver Folder

```
package main

import (
    "net/http"
    "io"
)

type StringHandler struct {
    message string
}

func (sh StringHandler) ServeHTTP(writer http.ResponseWriter,
        request *http.Request) {
    if (request.URL.Path == "/favicon.ico") {
        Printfln("Request for icon detected - returning 404")
        writer.WriteHeader(http.StatusNotFound)
        return
    }
    Printfln("Request for %v", request.URL.Path)
    io.WriteString(writer, sh.message)
}

func main() {
    err := http.ListenAndServe(":5000", StringHandler{ message: "Hello, World"})
    if (err != nil) {
        Printfln("Error: %v", err.Error())
    }
}
```

The request handler checks the URL.Path field to detect icon requests and responds by using the WriteHeader to set a response using the StatusNotFound constant (although I could have simply specified the int literal value 404). Compile and execute the project and use a browser to request http://localhost:5000. The browser will receive the response shown in Figure 24-1, and you will see the following output from the Go application at the command prompt:

```
Request for /
Request for icon detected - returning 404
```

You may find that subsequent requests from the browser for http://localhost:5000 do not trigger a second request for the icon file. That's because the browser notes the 404 response and knows that there is no icon file for this URL. Clear the browser's cache and request http://localhost:5000 to return to the original behavior.

Using the Response Convenience Functions

The net/http package provides a set of convenience functions that can be used to create common responses to HTTP requests, as described in Table 24-8.

Table 24-8. *The Response Convenience Functions*

Name	Description
Error(writer, message, code)	This function sets the header to the specified code, sets the Content-Type header to text/plain, and writes the error message to the response. The X-Content-Type-Options header is also set to stop browsers from interpreting the response as anything other than text.
NotFound(writer, request)	This function calls Error and specifies a 404 error code.
Redirect(writer, request, url, code)	This function sends a redirection response to the specified URL and with the specified status code.
ServeFile(writer, request, fileName)	This function sends a response containing the contents of the specified file. The Content-Type header is set based on the file name but can be overridden by explicitly setting the header before calling the function. See the "Creating a Static HTTP Server" section for an example that serves files.

In Listing 24-9, I have used the NotFound function to implement a simple URL handling scheme.

Listing 24-9. Using the Convenience Functions in the main.go File in the httpserver Folder

```
package main

import (
    "net/http"
    "io"
)

type StringHandler struct {
    message string
}

func (sh StringHandler) ServeHTTP(writer http.ResponseWriter,
        request *http.Request) {
```

```
        Printfln("Request for %v", request.URL.Path)
        switch request.URL.Path {
            case "/favicon.ico":
                http.NotFound(writer, request)
            case "/message":
                io.WriteString(writer, sh.message)
            default:
                http.Redirect(writer, request, "/message", http.StatusTemporaryRedirect)
        }
}

func main() {
    err := http.ListenAndServe(":5000", StringHandler{ message: "Hello, World"})
    if (err != nil) {
        Printfln("Error: %v", err.Error())
    }
}
```

Listing 24-9 uses a `switch` statement to decide how to respond to a request. Compile and execute the project and use a browser to request `http://localhost:5000/message`, which will produce the response previously shown in Figure 24-1. If the browser requests the icon file, then the server will return a 404 response. For all other requests, the browser is sent a redirection to `/message`.

Using the Convenience Routing Handler

The process of inspecting the URL and selecting a response can produce complex code that is difficult to read and maintain. To simplify the process, the net/http package provides a Handler implementation that allows matching the URL to be separated from producing a request, as shown in Listing 24-10.

Listing 24-10. Using the Convenience Routing Handler in the main.go File in the httpserver Folder

```
package main

import (
    "net/http"
    "io"
)

type StringHandler struct {
    message string
}

func (sh StringHandler) ServeHTTP(writer http.ResponseWriter,
        request *http.Request) {
    Printfln("Request for %v", request.URL.Path)
    io.WriteString(writer, sh.message)
}

func main() {
    http.Handle("/message", StringHandler{ "Hello, World"})
    http.Handle("/favicon.ico", http.NotFoundHandler())
```

```
http.Handle("/", http.RedirectHandler("/message", http.StatusTemporaryRedirect))

err := http.ListenAndServe(":5000", nil)
if (err != nil) {
    Printfln("Error: %v", err.Error())
}
}
```

The key to this feature is using nil for the argument to the ListenAndServe function, like this:

```
...
err := http.ListenAndServe(":5000", nil)
...
```

This enables the default handler, which routes requests to handlers based on the rules set up with the functions described in Table 24-9.

Table 24-9. The net/http Functions for Creating Routing Rules

Name	Description
Handle(pattern, handler)	This function creates a rule that invokes the specified ServeHTTP method of the specified Hander for requests that match the pattern.
HandleFunc(pattern, handlerFunc)	This function creates a rule that invokes the specified function for requests that match the pattern. The function is invoked with ResponseWriter and Request arguments.

To help set up the routing rules, the net/http package provides the functions described in Table 24-10, which create Handler implementations, some of which wrap around the response functions described in Table 24-7.

Table 24-10. The net/http Functions for Creating Request Handlers

Name	Description
FileServer(root)	This function creates a Handler that produces responses using the ServeFile function. See the "Creating a Static HTTP Server" section for an example that serves files.
NotFoundHandler()	This function creates a Handler that produces responses using the NotFound function.
RedirectHandler(url, code)	This function creates a Handler that produces responses using the Redirect function.
StripPrefix(prefix, handler)	This function creates a Handler that removes the specified prefix from the request URL and passes on the request to the specified Handler. See the "Creating a Static HTTP Server" section for details.
TimeoutHandler(handler, duration, message)	This function passes on the request to the specified Handler but generates an error response if the response hasn't been produced within the specified duration.

The patterns used to match requests are expressed as paths, such a /favicon.ico, or as trees, which have a trailing slash, such as /files/. The longest patterns are matched first, and the root path ("/") matches any request and acts as a fallback route.

In Listing 24-10, I used the Handle function to set up three routes:

```
...
http.Handle("/message", StringHandler{ "Hello, World"})
http.Handle("/favicon.ico", http.NotFoundHandler())
http.Handle("/", http.RedirectHandler("/message", http.StatusTemporaryRedirect))
...
```

The effect is that requests for /message are routed to the StringHandler, requests for /favicon.ico are handled with a 404 Not Found response, and all other requests produce a redirect to /message. This is the same configuration as in the previous section, but the mapping between the URLs and the request handlers is separate from the code that produces the responses.

Supporting HTTPS Requests

The net/http package provides integrated support for HTTPS. To prepare for HTTPS, you will need to add two files to the httpserver folder: a certificate file and a private key file.

GETTING CERTIFICATES FOR HTTPS

A good way to get started with HTTPS is with a self-signed certificate, which can be used for development and testing. If you don't already have a self-signed certificate, then you can create one online using sites such as https://getacert.com or https://www.selfsignedcertificate. com, both of which will let you create a self-signed certificate easily and without charge.

Two files are required to use HTTPS, regardless of whether your certificate is self-signed or not. The first is the certificate file, which usually has a cer or cert file extension. The second is the private key file, which usually has a key file extension.

When you are ready to deploy your application, then you can use a real certificate. I recommend https://letsencrypt.org, which offers free certificates and which is (relatively) easy to use. I am unable to help readers obtain and use certificates because doing so requires control of the domain for which the certificate is issued and access to the private key, which should remain secret. If you are having problems following the example, then I recommend using a self-signed certificate.

The ListenAndServeTLS function is used to enable HTTPS, where the additional arguments specify the certificate and private key files, which are named certificate.cer and certificate.key in my project, as shown in Listing 24-11.

Listing 24-11. Enabling HTTPS in the main.go File in the httpserver Folder

```
package main

import (
    "net/http"
    "io"
)

type StringHandler struct {
    message string
}
```

```
func (sh StringHandler) ServeHTTP(writer http.ResponseWriter,
        request *http.Request) {
    Printfln("Request for %v", request.URL.Path)
    io.WriteString(writer, sh.message)
}

func main() {
    http.Handle("/message", StringHandler{ "Hello, World"})
    http.Handle("/favicon.ico", http.NotFoundHandler())
    http.Handle("/", http.RedirectHandler("/message", http.StatusTemporaryRedirect))

    go func () {
        err := http.ListenAndServeTLS(":5500", "certificate.cer",
            "certificate.key", nil)
        if (err != nil) {
            Printfln("HTTPS Error: %v", err.Error())
        }
    }()

    err := http.ListenAndServe(":5000", nil)
    if (err != nil) {
        Printfln("Error: %v", err.Error())
    }
}
```

The ListenAndServeTLS and ListenAndServe functions block, so I have used a goroutine to support both HTTP and HTTPS requests, with HTTP handled on port 5000 and HTTPS on port 5500.

The ListenAndServeTLS and ListenAndServe functions have been invoked with nil as the handler, which means that both HTTP and HTTPS requests will be handled using the same set of routes. Compile and execute the project and use a browser to request http://localhost:5000 and https://localhost:5500. The requests will be processed in the same way, as shown in Figure 24-2. If you are using a self-signed certificate, then your browser will warn you that the certificate is invalid, and you will have to accept the security risk before the browser will display the content.

Figure 24-2. *Supporting HTTPS requests*

641

Redirecting HTTP Requests to HTTPS

A common requirement when creating web servers is to redirect HTTP requests to the HTTPS port. This can be done by creating a custom handler, as shown in Listing 24-12.

Listing 24-12. Redirecting to HTTPS in the main.go File in the httpserver Folder

```go
package main

import (
    "net/http"
    "io"
    "strings"
)

type StringHandler struct {
    message string
}

func (sh StringHandler) ServeHTTP(writer http.ResponseWriter,
        request *http.Request) {
    Printfln("Request for %v", request.URL.Path)
    io.WriteString(writer, sh.message)
}

func HTTPSRedirect(writer http.ResponseWriter,
        request *http.Request) {
    host := strings.Split(request.Host, ":")[0]
    target := "https://" + host + ":5500" + request.URL.Path
    if len(request.URL.RawQuery) > 0 {
        target += "?" + request.URL.RawQuery
    }
    http.Redirect(writer, request, target, http.StatusTemporaryRedirect)
}

func main() {
    http.Handle("/message", StringHandler{ "Hello, World"})
    http.Handle("/favicon.ico", http.NotFoundHandler())
    http.Handle("/", http.RedirectHandler("/message", http.StatusTemporaryRedirect))

    go func () {
        err := http.ListenAndServeTLS(":5500", "certificate.cer",
            "certificate.key", nil)
        if (err != nil) {
            Printfln("HTTPS Error: %v", err.Error())
        }
    }()

    err := http.ListenAndServe(":5000", http.HandlerFunc(HTTPSRedirect))
    if (err != nil) {
        Printfln("Error: %v", err.Error())
    }
}
```

The handler for HTTP in Listing 24-12 redirects the client to the HTTPS URL. Compile and execute the project and request http://localhost:5000. The response will redirect the browser to the HTTPS service, producing the output shown in Figure 24-3.

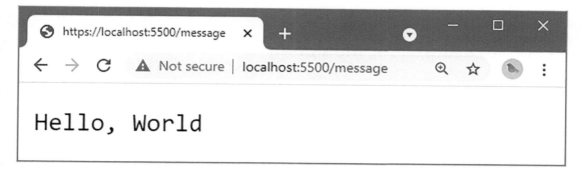

Figure 24-3. *Using HTTPS*

Creating a Static HTTP Server

The net/http package includes built-in support for responding to requests with the contents of files. To prepare for the static HTTP server, create the httpserver/static folder and add to it a file named index. html with the content shown in Listing 24-13.

■ **Note** The class attributes in the HTML files and templates in this chapter all apply styled defined by the Bootstrap CSS package, which is added to the project in Listing 24-15. See https://getbootstrap.com for details of what each class does and the other features provided by the Bootstrap package.

Listing 24-13. The Contents of the index.html File in the static Folder

```
<!DOCTYPE html>
<html>
<head>
    <title>Pro Go</title>
    <meta name="viewport" content="width=device-width" />
    <link href="bootstrap.min.css" rel="stylesheet" />
</head>
<body>
    <div class="m-1 p-2 bg-primary text-white h2">
        Hello, World
    </div>
</body>
</html>
```

Next, add a file named store.html to the httpserver/static folder, with the content shown in Listing 24-14.

Listing 24-14. The Contents of the store.html File in the static Folder

```html
<!DOCTYPE html>
<html>
<head>
    <title>Pro Go</title>
    <meta name="viewport" content="width=device-width" />
    <link href="bootstrap.min.css" rel="stylesheet" />
</head>
<body>
    <div class="m-1 p-2 bg-primary text-white h2 text-center">
        Products
    </div>
    <table class="table table-sm table-bordered table-striped">
        <thead>
            <tr><th>Name</th><th>Category</th><th>Price</th></tr>
        </thead>
        <tbody>
            <tr><td>Kayak</td><td>Watersports</td><td>$279.00</td></tr>
            <tr><td>Lifejacket</td><td>Watersports</td><td>$49.95</td></tr>
        </tbody>
    </table>
</body>
</html>
```

The HTML files depend on the Bootstrap CSS package to style the HTML content. Run the command shown in Listing 24-15 in the httpserver folder to download the Bootstrap CSS file into the static folder. (You may have to install the curl command.)

Listing 24-15. Downloading the CSS File

```
curl https://cdn.jsdelivr.net/npm/bootstrap@5.0.2/dist/css/bootstrap.min.css --output
static/bootstrap.min.css
```

If you are using Windows, you can download the CSS file using the PowerShell command shown in Listing 24-16.

Listing 24-16. Downloading the CSS File (Windows)

```
Invoke-WebRequest -OutFile static/bootstrap.min.css -Uri https://cdn.jsdelivr.net/npm/
bootstrap@5.0.2/dist/css/bootstrap.min.css
```

Creating the Static File Route

Now that there are HTML and CSS files to work with, it is time to define the route that will make them available to request using HTTP, as shown in Listing 24-17.

Listing 24-17. Defining a Route in the main.go File in the httpserver Folder

```
...
func main() {
    http.Handle("/message", StringHandler{ "Hello, World"})
    http.Handle("/favicon.ico", http.NotFoundHandler())
    http.Handle("/", http.RedirectHandler("/message", http.StatusTemporaryRedirect))

    fsHandler := http.FileServer(http.Dir("./static"))
    http.Handle("/files/", http.StripPrefix("/files", fsHandler))

    go func () {
        err := http.ListenAndServeTLS(":5500", "certificate.cer",
            "certificate.key", nil)
        if (err != nil) {
            Println("HTTPS Error: %v", err.Error())
        }
    }()

    err := http.ListenAndServe(":5000", http.HandlerFunc(HTTPSRedirect))
    if (err != nil) {
        Println("Error: %v", err.Error())
    }
}
...
```

The FileServer function creates a handler that will serve files, and the directory is specified using the Dir function. (It is possible to serve files directly, but caution is required because it is easy to allow requests to select files outside of the target folder. The safest option is to use the Dir function as shown in this example.)

I am going to serve the content in the static folder with URL paths that start with files so that a request for /files/store.html, for example, will be handled using the static/store.html file. To do this, I have used the StripPrefix function, which creates a handler that removes a path prefix and passes the request onto another handler to service. Combining these handlers, as I have done in Listing 24-17, means that I can safely expose the contents of the static folder using the files prefix.

Note that I have specified the route with a trailing slash, like this:

```
...
http.Handle("/files/", http.StripPrefix("/files", fsHandler))
...
```

As noted earlier, the built-in router supports paths and trees, and routing for a directory requires a tree, which is specified with the trailing slash. Compile and execute the project and use the browser to request https://localhost:5500/files/store.html, and you will receive the response shown in Figure 24-4.

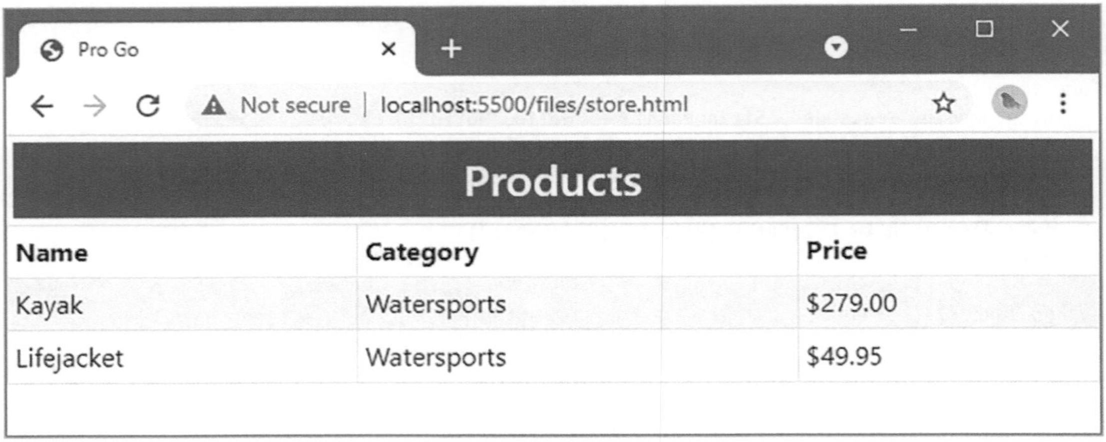

Figure 24-4. Serving static content

The support for serving files has some useful features. First, the Content-Type header of the response is set automatically based on the file extension. Second, requests that don't specify a file are handled using index.html, which you can see by requesting https://localhost:5500/files, which produces the response shown in Figure 24-5. Finally, if a request does specify a file but the file doesn't exist, then a 404 response is sent automatically, also shown in Figure 24-5.

Figure 24-5. Fallback responses

Using Templates to Generate Responses

There is no built-in support for using templates as responses for HTTP requests, but it is a simple process to set up a handler that uses the features provided by the html/template package, which I described in Chapter 23. To get started, create the httpserver/templates folder, and add to it a file named products.html with the content shown in Listing 24-18.

Listing 24-18. The Contents of the products.html File in the templates Folder

```
<!DOCTYPE html>
<html>
<head>
    <meta name="viewport" content="width=device-width" />
    <title>Pro Go</title>
    <link rel="stylesheet" href="/files/bootstrap.min.css" >
```

```
</head>
<body>
    <h3 class="bg-primary text-white text-center p-2 m-2">Products</h3>
    <div class="p-2">
        <table class="table table-sm table-striped table-bordered">
            <thead>
                <tr>
                    <th>Index</th><th>Name</th><th>Category</th>
                    <th class="text-end">Price</th>
                </tr>
            </thead>
            <tbody>
                {{ range $index, $product := .Data }}
                    <tr>
                        <td>{{ $index }}</td>
                        <td>{{ $product.Name }}</td>
                        <td>{{ $product.Category }}</td>
                        <td class="text-end">
                            {{ printf "$%.2f" $product.Price }}
                        </td>
                    </tr>
                {{ end }}
            </tbody>
        </table>
    </div>
</body>
</html>
```

Next, add a file named dynamic.go to the httpserver folder with the content shown in Listing 24-19.

Listing 24-19. The Contents of the dynamic.go File in the httpserver Folder

```go
package main

import (
    "html/template"
    "net/http"
    "strconv"
)

type Context struct {
    Request *http.Request
    Data []Product
}

var htmlTemplates *template.Template

func HandleTemplateRequest(writer http.ResponseWriter, request *http.Request) {
    path := request.URL.Path
    if (path == "") {
        path = "products.html"
    }
```

```
    t := htmlTemplates.Lookup(path)
    if (t == nil) {
        http.NotFound(writer, request)
    } else {
        err := t.Execute(writer, Context{  request, Products})
        if (err != nil) {
            http.Error(writer, err.Error(), http.StatusInternalServerError)
        }
    }
}

func init() {
    var err error
    htmlTemplates = template.New("all")
    htmlTemplates.Funcs(map[string]interface{} {
        "intVal": strconv.Atoi,
    })
    htmlTemplates, err = htmlTemplates.ParseGlob("templates/*.html")
    if (err == nil) {
        http.Handle("/templates/", http.StripPrefix("/templates/",
            http.HandlerFunc(HandleTemplateRequest)))
    } else {
        panic(err)
    }
}
```

The initialization function loads all the templates with the html extension in the templates folder and sets up a route so that requests that start with /templates/ are processed by the HandleTemplateRequest function. This function looks up the template, falling back to the products.html file if no file path is specified, executes the template, and writes the response. Compile and execute the project and use a browser to request https://localhost:5500/templates, which will produce the response shown in Figure 24-6.

■ **Note**   One limitation of the approach I have shown here is the data passed to the template is hard-wired into the HandleTemplateRequest function. I demonstrate a more flexible approach in Part 3.

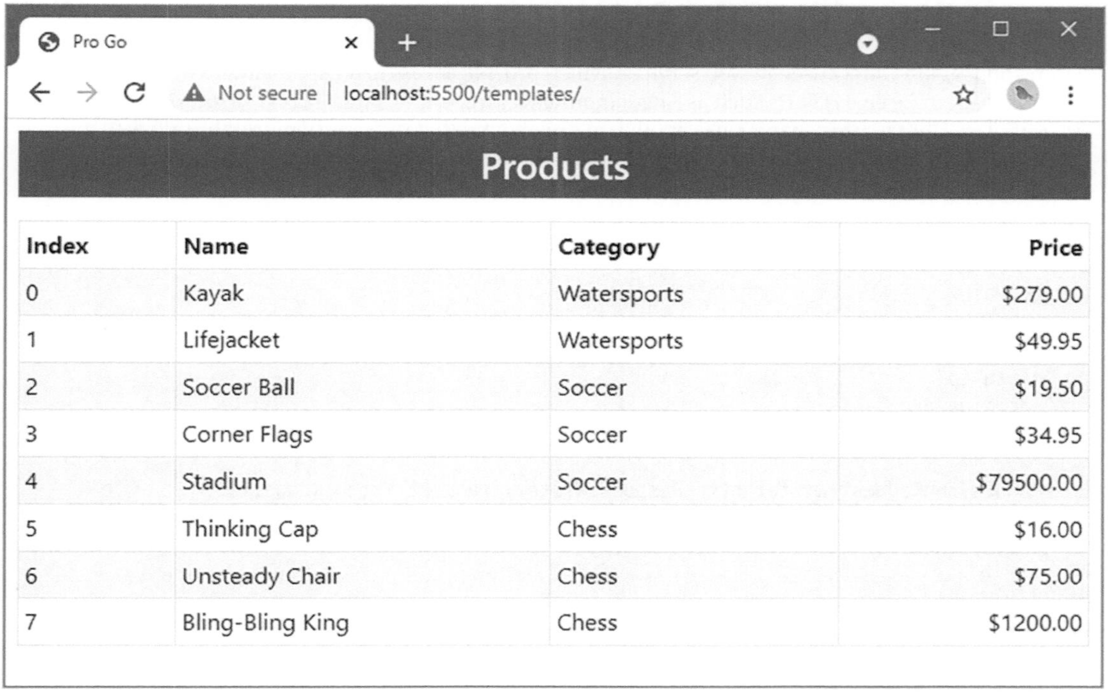

Figure 24-6. *Using an HTML template to generate a response*

UNDERSTANDING CONTENT TYPE SNIFFING

Notice that I didn't have to set the Content-Type header when using a template to generate a response. When serving files, the Content-Type header is set based on the file extension, but that's not possible in this situation because I am writing content directly to the ResponseWriter.

When a response doesn't have a Content-Type header, the first 512 bytes of content written to the ResponseWriter are passed to the DetectContentType function, which implements the MIME Sniffing algorithm defined by https://mimesniff.spec.whatwg.org. The sniffing process can't detect every content type, but it does well with standard web types, such as HTML, CSS, and JavaScript. The DetectContentType function returns a MIME type, which is used as the value for the Content-Type header. In the example, the sniffing algorithm detects that the content is HTML and sets the header to text/html. The content sniffing process can be disabled by explicitly setting the Content-Type header.

Responding with JSON Data

JSON responses are widely used in web services, which provide access to an application's data for clients that don't want to receive HTML, such as Angular or React JavaScript clients. I create a more complex web service in Part 3, but for this chapter, it is enough to understand that the same features that allowed me to serve static and dynamic HTML content can be used to generate JSON responses as well. Add a file named json.go to the httpserver folder with the content shown in Listing 24-20.

Listing 24-20. The Contents of the json.go File in the httpserver Folder

```go
package main

import (
    "net/http"
    "encoding/json"
)

func HandleJsonRequest(writer http.ResponseWriter, request *http.Request) {
    writer.Header().Set("Content-Type", "application/json")
    json.NewEncoder(writer).Encode(Products)
}

func init() {
    http.HandleFunc("/json", HandleJsonRequest)
}
```

The initialization function creates a route, which means that requests for /json will be processed by the HandleJsonRequest function. This function uses the JSON features described in Chapter 21 to encode the slice of Product values created in Listing 24-3. Notice that I have explicitly set the Content-Type header in Listing 24-20:

```
...
writer.Header().Set("Content-Type", "application/json")
...
```

The sniffing feature described earlier in the chapter can't be relied on to identify JSON content and will result in responses with the text/plain content type. Many web service clients will treat responses as JSON regardless of the Content-Type header, but it isn't a good idea to rely on this behavior. Compile and execute the project and use a browser to request https://localhost:5500/json. The browser will display the following JSON content:

```
[{"Name":"Kayak","Category":"Watersports","Price":279},
 {"Name":"Lifejacket","Category":"Watersports","Price":49.95},
 {"Name":"Soccer Ball","Category":"Soccer","Price":19.5},
 {"Name":"Corner Flags","Category":"Soccer","Price":34.95},
 {"Name":"Stadium","Category":"Soccer","Price":79500},
 {"Name":"Thinking Cap","Category":"Chess","Price":16},
 {"Name":"Unsteady Chair","Category":"Chess","Price":75},
 {"Name":"Bling-Bling King","Category":"Chess","Price":1200}]
```

Handling Form Data

The net/http package provides support for easily receiving and processing form data. Add a file named edit.html to the templates folder, with the content shown in Listing 24-21.

Listing 24-21. The Contents of the edit.html File in the templates Folder

```html
<!DOCTYPE html>
<html>
<head>
    <meta name="viewport" content="width=device-width" />
    <title>Pro Go</title>
    <link rel="stylesheet" href="/files/bootstrap.min.css" >
</head>
<body>
    {{ $index := intVal (index (index .Request.URL.Query "index") 0) }}
    {{ if lt $index (len .Data)}}
        {{ with index .Data $index}}
            <h3 class="bg-primary text-white text-center p-2 m-2">Product</h3>
            <form method="POST" action="/forms/edit" class="m-2">
                <div class="form-group">
                    <label>Index</label>
                    <input name="index" value="{{$index}}"
                        class="form-control" disabled />
                    <input name="index" value="{{$index}}" type="hidden" />
                </div>
                <div class="form-group">
                    <label>Name</label>
                    <input name="name" value="{{.Name}}" class="form-control"/>
                </div>
                <div class="form-group">
                    <label>Category</label>
                    <input name="category" value="{{.Category}}"
                        class="form-control"/>
                </div>
                <div class="form-group">
                    <label>Price</label>
                    <input name="price" value="{{.Price}}" class="form-control"/>
                </div>
                <div class="mt-2">
                    <button type="submit" class="btn btn-primary">Save</button>
                    <a href="/templates/" class="btn btn-secondary">Cancel</a>
                </div>
            </form>
        {{ end }}
    {{ else }}
        <h3 class="bg-danger text-white text-center p-2">
            No Product At Specified Index
        </h3>
    {{end }}
</body>
</html>
```

651

This template makes use of template variables, expressions, and functions to get the query string from the request and select the first index value, which is converted to an int and used to retrieve a Product value from the data provided to the template:

```
...
{{ $index := intVal (index (index .Request.URL.Query "index") 0) }}
{{ if lt $index (len .Data)}}
    {{ with index .Data $index}}
...
```

These expressions are more complex than I generally like to see in a template, and I show you an approach that I find more robust in Part 3. For this chapter, however, it allows me to generate an HTML form that presents input elements for the fields defined by the Product struct, which submits its data to the URL specified by the action attribute, as follows:

```
...
<form method="POST" action="/forms/edit" class="m-2">
...
```

Reading Form Data from Requests

Now that I have added a form to the project, I can write the code that receives the data it contains. The Request struct defines the fields and methods described in Table 24-11 for working with form data.

Table 24-11. *The Request Form Data Fields and Methods*

Name	Description
Form	This field returns a map[string][]string containing the parsed form data and the query string parameters. The ParseForm method must be called before this field is read.
PostForm	This field is similar to Form but excludes the query string parameters so that only data from the request body is contained in the map. The ParseForm method must be called before this field is read.
MultipartForm	This field returns a multipart form represented using the Form struct defined in the mime/multipart package. The ParseMultipartForm method must be called before this field is read.
FormValue(key)	This method returns the first value for the specified form key and returns the empty string if there is no value. The source of data for this method is the Form field, and calling the FormValue method automatically calls ParseForm or ParseMultipartForm to parse the form.
PostFormValue(key)	This method returns the first value for the specified form key and returns the empty string if there is no value. The source of data for this method is the PostForm field, and calling the PostFormValue method automatically calls ParseForm or ParseMultipartForm to parse the form.
FormFile(key)	This method provides access to the first file with the specified key in the form. The results are a File and FileHeader, both of which are defined in the mime/multipart package, and an error. Calling this function causes the ParseForm or ParseMultipartForm functions to be invoked to parse the form.
ParseForm()	This method parses a form and populates the Form and PostForm fields. The result is an error that describes any parsing problems.
ParseMultipart Form(max)	This method parses a MIME multipart form and populates the MultipartForm field. The argument specifies the maximum number of bytes to allocate to the form data, and the result is an error that describes any problems processing the form.

The FormValue and PostFormValue methods are the most convenient way to access form data if you know the structure of the form being processed. Add a file named forms.go to the httpserver folder with the content shown in Listing 24-22.

Listing 24-22. The Contents of the forms.go File in the httpserver Folder

```go
package main

import (
    "net/http"
    "strconv"
)

func ProcessFormData(writer http.ResponseWriter, request *http.Request) {
    if (request.Method == http.MethodPost) {
        index, _ := strconv.Atoi(request.PostFormValue("index"))
        p := Product {}
```

```
        p.Name = request.PostFormValue("name")
        p.Category = request.PostFormValue("category")
        p.Price, _ = strconv.ParseFloat(request.PostFormValue("price"), 64)
        Products[index] = p
    }
    http.Redirect(writer, request, "/templates", http.StatusTemporaryRedirect)
}

func init() {
    http.HandleFunc("/forms/edit", ProcessFormData)
}
```

The init function sets up a new route so that the ProcessFormData function handles requests whose path is /forms/edit. Within the ProcessFormData function, the request method is checked, and the form data in the request is used to create a Product struct and replace the existing data value. In a real project, validating the data submitted in the form is essential, but for this chapter I trust that the form contains valid data.

Compile and execute the project and use a browser to request https://localhost:5500/templates/ edit.html?index=2, which selects the Product value at index 2 in the slice defined in Listing 24-3. Change the value of the Category field to Soccer/Football and click the Save button. The data in the form will be applied, and the browser will be redirected, as shown in Figure 24-7.

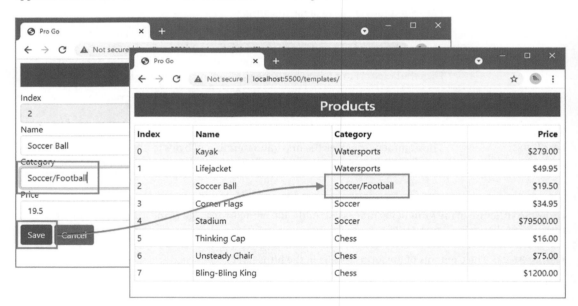

Figure 24-7. *Processing form data*

Reading Multipart Forms

Forms encoded as `multipart/form-data` to allow binary data, such as files, to be safely sent to the server. To create a form that allows the server to receive a file, create a file named `upload.html` in the `static` folder with the content shown in Listing 24-23.

Listing 24-23. The Contents of the upload.html File in the static Folder

```html
<!DOCTYPE html>
<html>
<head>
    <title>Pro Go</title>
    <meta name="viewport" content="width=device-width" />
    <link href="bootstrap.min.css" rel="stylesheet" />
</head>
<body>
    <div class="m-1 p-2 bg-primary text-white h2 text-center">
        Upload File
    </div>
    <form method="POST" action="/forms/upload" class="p-2"
            enctype="multipart/form-data">
        <div class="form-group">
            <label class="form-label">Name</label>
            <input class="form-control" type="text" name="name">
        </div>
        <div class="form-group">
            <label class="form-label">City</label>
            <input class="form-control" type="text" name="city">
        </div>
        <div class="form-group">
            <label class="form-label">Choose Files</label>
            <input class="form-control" type="file" name="files" multiple>
        </div>
        <button type="submit" class="btn btn-primary mt-2">Upload</button>
    </form>
</body>
</html>
```

The enctype attribute on the `form` element creates a multipart form, and the `input` element whose type is `file` creates a form control that allows the user to select a file. The `multiple` attribute tells the browser to allow the user to select multiple files, which I'll come back to shortly. Add a file named `upload.go` in the `httpserver` folder with the code in Listing 24-24 to receive and process the form data.

Listing 24-24. The Contents of the upload.go File in the httpserver Folder

```go
package main

import (
    "net/http"
    "io"
    "fmt"
)
```

```
func HandleMultipartForm(writer http.ResponseWriter, request *http.Request) {
    fmt.Fprintf(writer, "Name: %v, City: %v\n", request.FormValue("name"),
        request.FormValue("city"))
    fmt.Fprintln(writer, "------")
    file, header, err := request.FormFile("files")
    if (err == nil) {
        defer file.Close()
        fmt.Fprintf(writer, "Name: %v, Size: %v\n", header.Filename, header.Size)
        for k, v := range header.Header {
            fmt.Fprintf(writer, "Key: %v, Value: %v\n", k, v)
        }
        fmt.Fprintln(writer, "------")
        io.Copy(writer, file)
    } else {
        http.Error(writer, err.Error(), http.StatusInternalServerError)
    }
}

func init() {
    http.HandleFunc("/forms/upload", HandleMultipartForm)
}
```

The FormValue and PostFormValue methods can be used to access string values in the form, but the file must be accessed using the FormFile method, like this:

```
...
file, header, err := request.FormFile("files")
...
```

The first result from the FormFile method is a File, defined in the mime/multipart package, which is an interface that combines the Reader, Closer, Seeker, and ReaderAt interfaces that are described in Chapters 20 and 22. The effect is that the contents of the uploaded file can be processed as a Reader, with support for seeking or reading from a specific location. In this example, I copy the contents of the uploaded file to the ResponseWriter.

The second result from the FormFile method is a FileHeader, also defined in the mime/multipart package. This struct defines the fields and method described in Table 24-12.

Table 24-12. *The FileHeader Fields and Method*

Name	Description
Name	This field returns a string containing the name of the file.
Size	This field returns an int64 containing the size of the file.
Header	This field returns a map[string][]string, which contains the headers for the MIME part that contains the file.
Open()	This method returns a File that can be used to read the content associated with the header, as demonstrated in the next section.

Compile and execute the project and use a browser to request https://localhost:5500/files/upload.html. Enter your name and city, click the Choose Files button, and select a single file (I explain how to deal with multiple files in the next section). You can select any file on your system, but a text file is the best choice for simplicity. Click the Upload button, and the form will be posted. The response will contain the name and city values and the header and content for the file, as shown in Figure 24-8.

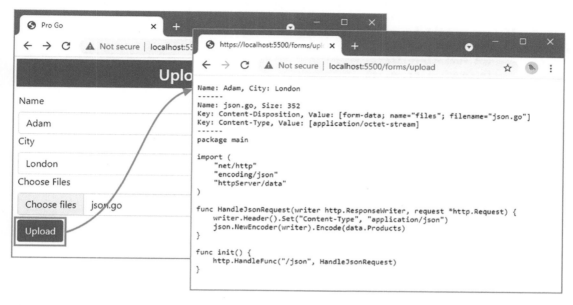

Figure 24-8. *Processing a multipart form containing a file*

Receiving Multiple Files in the Form

The FormFile method returns only the first file with the specified name, which means that it can't be used when the user is allowed to select multiple files for a single form element, which is the case with the example form.

The Request.MultipartForm field provides complete access to the data in a multipart form, as shown in Listing 24-25.

Listing 24-25. Processing Multiple Files in the upload.go File in the httpserver Folder

```go
package main

import (
    "net/http"
    "io"
    "fmt"
)

func HandleMultipartForm(writer http.ResponseWriter, request *http.Request) {
    request.ParseMultipartForm(10000000)
    fmt.Fprintf(writer, "Name: %v, City: %v\n",
        request.MultipartForm.Value["name"][0],
        request.MultipartForm.Value["city"][0])
```

```
    fmt.Fprintln(writer, "------")

    for _, header := range request.MultipartForm.File["files"] {
        fmt.Fprintf(writer, "Name: %v, Size: %v\n", header.Filename, header.Size)
        file, err := header.Open()
        if (err == nil) {
            defer file.Close()
            fmt.Fprintln(writer, "------")
            io.Copy(writer, file)
        } else {
            http.Error(writer, err.Error(), http.StatusInternalServerError)
            return
        }
    }
}

func init() {
    http.HandleFunc("/forms/upload", HandleMultipartForm)
}
```

You must ensure that the ParseMultipartForm method is called before using the MultipartForm field. The MultipartForm field returns a Form struct, which is defined in the mime/multipart package, and which defines the fields described in Table 24-13.

Table 24-13. The Form Fields

Name	Description
Value	This field returns a map[string][]string that contains the form values.
File	This field returns a map[string][]*FileHeader that contains the files.

In Listing 24-25, I use the Value field to get the Name and City values from the form. I use the File field to get all the files in the form with the name files, which are represented by FileHeader values, described in Table 24-13. Compile and execute the project, use a browser to request https://localhost:5500/files/upload.html, and fill out the form. This time, when clicking the Choose Files button, select two or more files. Submit the form, and you will see the contents of all the files you selected, as shown in Figure 24-9. Text files are preferable for this example.

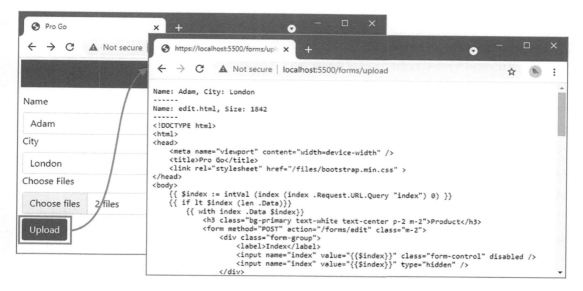

Figure 24-9. *Processing multiple files*

Reading and Setting Cookies

The net/http package defines the SetCookie function, which adds a Set-Cookie header to the response sent to the client. For quick reference, Table 24-14 describes the SetCookie function.

Table 24-14. *The net/http Function for Setting Cookies*

Name	Description
SetCookie(writer, cookie	This function adds a Set-Cookie header to the specified ResponseWriter. The cookie is described using a pointer to a Cookie struct, which is described next.

Cookies are described using the Cookie struct, which is defined in the net/http package and defines the fields described in Table 24-15. A basic cookie can be created with just the Name and Value fields.

■ **Note** Cookies can be complex, and care must be taken to configure them correctly. The detail of how cookies work is beyond the scope of this book, but there is a good description available at https://developer.mozilla.org/en-US/docs/Web/HTTP/Cookies and a detailed breakdown of the cookie fields at https://developer.mozilla.org/en-US/docs/Web/HTTP/Headers/Set-Cookie.

Table 24-15. *The Fields Defined by the Cookie Struct*

Name	Description
Name	This field represents the name of the cookie, expressed as a string.
Value	This field represents the cookie value, expressed as a string.
Path	This optional field specifies the cookie path.
Domain	This optional field specifies the host/domain to which the cookie will be set.
Expires	This field specifies the cookie expiry, expressed as a time.Time value.
MaxAge	This field specifies the number of seconds until the cookie expires, expressed as an int.
Secure	When this bool field is true, the client will only send the cookie over HTTPS connections.
HttpOnly	When this bool field is true, the client will prevent JavaScript code from accessing the cookie.
SameSite	This field specifies the cross-origin policy for the cookie using the SameSite constants, which defines SameSiteDefaultMode, SameSiteLaxMode, SameSiteStrictMode, and SameSiteNoneMode.

The Cookie struct is also used to get the set of cookies that a client sends, which is done using the Request methods described in Table 24-16.

Table 24-16. *The Request Methods for Cookies*

Name	Description
Cookie(name)	This method returns a pointer to the Cookie value with the specified name and an error that indicates when there is no matching cookie.
Cookies()	This method returns a slice of Cookie pointers.

Add a file named cookies.go to the httpserver folder with the code shown in Listing 24-26.

Listing 24-26. The Contents of the cookies.go File in the httpserver Folder

```go
package main

import (
    "net/http"
    "fmt"
    "strconv"
)

func GetAndSetCookie(writer http.ResponseWriter, request *http.Request) {

    counterVal := 1
    counterCookie, err := request.Cookie("counter")
    if (err == nil) {
        counterVal, _ = strconv.Atoi(counterCookie.Value)
        counterVal++
    }
```

```
    http.SetCookie(writer, &http.Cookie{
        Name: "counter", Value: strconv.Itoa(counterVal),
    })

    if (len(request.Cookies()) > 0) {
        for _, c := range request.Cookies() {
            fmt.Fprintf(writer, "Cookie Name: %v, Value: %v", c.Name, c.Value)
        }
    } else {
        fmt.Fprintln(writer, "Request contains no cookies")
    }
}

func init() {
    http.HandleFunc("/cookies", GetAndSetCookie)
}
```

This example sets up a /cookies route, for which the GetAndSetCookie function sets a cookie named counter with an initial value of zero. When a request contains the cookie, the cookie value is read, parsed to an int, and incremented so that it can be used to set a new cookie value. The function also enumerates the cookies in the request and writes the Name and Value fields to the response.

Compile and execute the project and use a browser to request https://localhost:5500/cookies. The client will not have a cookie to send initially, but each time you repeat the request subsequently, the cookie value will be read and incremented, as shown in Figure 24-10.

Figure 24-10. *Reading and setting cookies*

Summary

In this chapter, I described the standard library features for creating HTTP servers and handling HTTP requests. In the next chapter, I describe the complementary features for creating and sending HTTP requests.

## CHAPTER 25

Creating HTTP Clients

In this chapter, I describe the standard library features for making HTTP requests, allowing applications to make use of web servers. Table 25-1 puts HTTP requests in context.

Table 25-1. *Putting HTTP Clients in Context*

Question	Answer
What are they?	HTTP requests are used to retrieve data from HTTP servers, such as those created in Chapter 24.
Why are they useful?	HTTP is one of the most widely used protocols and is commonly used to provide access to content that can be presented to the user as well as data that is consumed programmatically.
How is it used?	The features of the net/http package are used to create and send requests and process responses.
Are there any pitfalls or limitations?	These features are well-designed and easy to use, although some features require a specific sequence to use.
Are there any alternatives?	The standard library includes support for other network protocols and also for opening and using lower-level network connections. See the https://pkg.go.dev/net@go1.17.1 for details of the net package and its subpackages, such as net/smtp, for example, which implements the SMTP protocol.

Table 25-2 summarizes the chapter.

Table 25-2. *Chapter Summary*

Problem	Solution	Listing
Send HTTP requests	Use the convenience methods for specific HTTP methods	8–12
Configure HTTP requests	Use the fields and methods defined by the Client struct	13
Create a preconfigured request	Use the NewRequest convenience functions	14
Use cookies in a request	Use a cookie jar	15–18
Configure how redirections are processed	Use the CheckRedirect field to register a function that is invoked to deal with a redirection	19–21
Send multipart forms	Use the mime/multipart package	22, 23

Preparing for This Chapter

To prepare for this chapter, open a new command prompt, navigate to a convenient location, and create a directory named httpclient. Run the command shown in Listing 25-1 to create a module file.

Tip   You can download the example project for this chapter—and for all the other chapters in this book—from https://github.com/apress/pro-go. See Chapter 2 for how to get help if you have problems running the examples.

Listing 25-1. Initializing the Module

```
go mod init httpclient
```

Add a file named printer.go to the httpclient folder with the content shown in Listing 25-2.

Listing 25-2. The Contents of the printer.go File in the httpclient Folder

```
package main

import "fmt"

func Printfln(template string, values ...interface{}) {
    fmt.Printf(template + "\n", values...)
}
```

Add a file named product.go to the httpclient folder with the content shown in Listing 25-3.

Listing 25-3. The Contents of the product.go File in the httpclient Folder

```
package main

type Product struct {
    Name, Category string
    Price float64
}

var Products = []Product {
    { "Kayak", "Watersports", 279 },
    { "Lifejacket", "Watersports", 49.95 },
    { "Soccer Ball", "Soccer", 19.50 },
    { "Corner Flags", "Soccer", 34.95 },
    { "Stadium", "Soccer", 79500 },
    { "Thinking Cap", "Chess", 16 },
    { "Unsteady Chair", "Chess", 75 },
    { "Bling-Bling King", "Chess", 1200 },
}
```

Add a file named index.html to the httpclient folder with the content shown in Listing 25-4.

Listing 25-4. The Contents of the index.html File in the httpclient Folder

```
<!DOCTYPE html>
<html>
<head>
    <title>Pro Go</title>
    <meta name="viewport" content="width=device-width" />
</head>
<body>
    <h1>Hello, World</div>
</body>
</html>
```

Add a file named server.go to the httpclient folder with the content shown in Listing 25-5.

Listing 25-5. The Contents of the server.go File in the httpclient Folder

```go
package main

import (
    "encoding/json"
    "fmt"
    "io"
    "net/http"
    "os"
)

func init() {

    http.HandleFunc("/html",
        func (writer http.ResponseWriter, request *http.Request) {
            http.ServeFile(writer, request, "./index.html")
        })
    http.HandleFunc("/json",
        func (writer http.ResponseWriter, request *http.Request) {
            writer.Header().Set("Content-Type", "application/json")
            json.NewEncoder(writer).Encode(Products)
        })
    http.HandleFunc("/echo",
        func (writer http.ResponseWriter, request *http.Request) {
            writer.Header().Set("Content-Type", "text/plain")
            fmt.Fprintf(writer, "Method: %v\n", request.Method)
            for header, vals := range request.Header {
                fmt.Fprintf(writer, "Header: %v: %v\n", header, vals)
            }
            fmt.Fprintln(writer, "----")
            data, err := io.ReadAll(request.Body)
```

665

```
            if (err == nil) {
                if len(data) == 0 {
                    fmt.Fprintln(writer, "No body")
                } else {
                    writer.Write(data)
                }
            } else {
                fmt.Fprintf(os.Stdout,"Error reading body: %v\n", err.Error())
            }
        })
}
```

The initialization function in this code file creates routes that generate HTML and JSON responses. There is also a route that echoes details of the request in the response.

Add a file named main.go to the httpclient folder, with the contents shown in Listing 25-6.

Listing 25-6. The Contents of the main.go File in the httpclient Folder

```
package main

import (
    "net/http"
)

func main() {
    Printfln("Starting HTTP Server")
    http.ListenAndServe(":5000", nil)
}
```

Use the command prompt to run the command shown in Listing 25-7 in the usingstrings folder.

Listing 25-7. Running the Example Project

```
go run .
```

DEALING WITH WINDOWS FIREWALL PERMISSION REQUESTS

As noted in Chapter 24, the Windows firewall will prompt for network access each time the code is compiled. To address this issue, create a file named buildandrun.ps1 in the project folder with the following contents:

```
$file = "./httpclient.exe"

&go build -o $file

if ($LASTEXITCODE -eq 0) {
    &$file
}
```

This PowerShell script compiles the project to the same file each time and then executes the result if there are no errors, meaning you will have to grant firewall access only once. The script is executed by running this command in the project folder:

```
./buildandrun.ps1
```

You must use this command every time to build and execute the project to ensure that the compiled output is written to the same location.

The code in httpclient folder will be compiled and executed. Use a web browser to request http://localhost:5000/html and http://localhost:5000/json, which produce the responses shown in Figure 25-1.

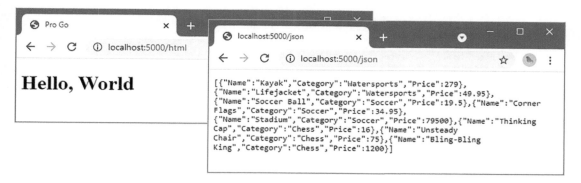

Figure 25-1. *Running the example application*

To see the echo result, request http://localhost:5000/echo, which produces output similar to Figure 25-2, although you may see different details based on your operating system and browser.

Method: GET
Header: Connection: [keep-alive]
Header: Cache-Control: [max-age=0]
Header: User-Agent: [Mozilla/5.0 (Windows NT 10.0; Win64; x64) AppleWebKit/537.36 (KHTML, like Gecko) Chrome/91.0.4472.124 Safari/537.36]
Header: Sec-Fetch-Site: [none]
Header: Sec-Fetch-User: [?1]
Header: Accept: [text/html,application/xhtml+xml,application/xml;q=0.9,image/avif,image/webp,image/apng,*/*;q=0.8,application/signed-exchange;v=b3;q=0.9]
Header: Accept-Language: [en-GB,en-US;q=0.9,en;q=0.8]
Header: Cookie: [counter=2]
Header: Sec-Ch-Ua: [" Not;A Brand";v="99", "Google Chrome";v="91", "Chromium";v="91"]
Header: Sec-Ch-Ua-Mobile: [?0]
Header: Upgrade-Insecure-Requests: [1]
Header: Sec-Fetch-Mode: [navigate]
Header: Sec-Fetch-Dest: [document]
Header: Accept-Encoding: [gzip, deflate, br]

No body

Figure 25-2. *Echoing details of the request in the response*

Sending Simple HTTP Requests

The net/http package provides a set of convenience functions that make basic HTTP requests. The functions are named after the HTTP method of the request they created, as described in Table 25-3.

Table 25-3. *The Convenience Methods for HTTP Requests*

Name	Description
Get(url)	This function sends a GET request to the specified HTTP or HTTPS URL. The results are a Response and an error that reports problems with the request.
Head(url)	This function sends a HEAD request to the specified HTTP or HTTPS URL. A HEAD request returns the headers that would be returned for a GET request. The results are a Response and an error that reports problems with the request.
Post(url, contentType, reader)	This function sends a POST request to the specified HTTP or HTTPS URL, with the specified Content-Type header value. The content for the form is provided by the specified Reader. The results are a Response and an error that reports problems with the request.
PostForm(url, data)	This function sends a POST request to the specified HTTP or HTTPS URL, with the Content-Type header set to application/x-www-form-urlencoded. The content for the form is provided by a map[string][]string. The results are a Response and an error that reports problems with the request.

Listing 25-8 uses the Get method to send a GET request to the server. The server is started in a goroutine to prevent it from blocking and allow the HTTP request to be sent within the same application. This is the pattern that I will use throughout this chapter because it avoids the need to separate client and server projects. I use the time.Sleep function, described in Chapter 19, to ensure that the goroutine has time to start the server. You may need to increase the delay for your system.

Listing 25-8. Sending a GET Request in the main.go File in the httpclient Folder

```
package main

import (
    "net/http"
    "os"
    "time"
)

func main() {
    go http.ListenAndServe(":5000", nil)
    time.Sleep(time.Second)

    response, err := http.Get("http://localhost:5000/html")
    if (err == nil) {
        response.Write(os.Stdout)
    } else {
        Printfln("Error: %v", err.Error())
    }
}
```

The argument to the Get function is a string that contains the URL to request. The results are a Response value and an error that reports any problems sending the request.

Note   The error values returned by the functions in Table 25-3 report problems creating and sending the request but are not used when the server returns an HTTP error status code.

The Response struct describes the response sent by the HTTP server and defines the fields and methods shown in Table 25-4.

Table 25-4. *The Fields and Methods Defined by the Response Struct*

Name	Description
StatusCode	This field returns the response status code, expressed as an int.
Status	This field returns a string containing the status description.
Proto	This field returns a string containing the response HTTP protocol.
Header	This field returns a map[string][]string that contains the response headers.
Body	This field returns a ReadCloser, which is a Reader that defines a Close method and which provides access to the response body.
Trailer	This field returns a map[string][]string that contains the response trailers.
ContentLength	This field returns the value of the Content-Length header, parsed into an int64 value.
TransferEncoding	This field returns the set of Transfer-Encoding header values.
Close	This bool field returns true if the response contains a Connection header set to close, which indicates that the HTTP connection should be closed.
Uncompressed	This field returns true if the server sent a compressed response that was decompressed by the net/http package.
Request	This field returns the Request that was used to obtain the response. The Request struct is described in Chapter 24.
TLS	This field provides details of the HTTPS connection.
Cookies()	This method returns a []*Cookie, which contains the Set-Cookie headers in the response. The Cookie struct is described in Chapter 24.
Location()	This method returns the URL from the response Location header and an error that indicates when the response does not contain this header.
Write(writer)	This method writes a summary of the response to the specified Writer.

I used the Write method in Listing 25-8, which writes out a summary of the response. Compile and execute the project, and you will see the following output, albeit with different header values:

```
HTTP/1.1 200 OK
Content-Length: 182
Accept-Ranges: bytes
Content-Type: text/html; charset=utf-8
Date: Sat, 25 Sep 2021 08:23:21 GMT
Last-Modified: Sat, 25 Sep 2021 06:51:09 GMT
<!DOCTYPE html>
<html>
<head>
    <title>Pro Go</title>
    <meta name="viewport" content="width=device-width" />
</head>
```

```
<body>
    <h1>Hello, World</div>
</body>
</html>
```

The Write method is convenient when you just want to see the response, but most projects will check the status code to ensure the request was successful and then read the response body, as shown in Listing 25-9.

Listing 25-9. Reading the Response Body in the main.go File in the httpclient Folder

```
package main

import (
    "net/http"
    "os"
    "time"
    "io"
)

func main() {
    go http.ListenAndServe(":5000", nil)
    time.Sleep(time.Second)

    response, err := http.Get("http://localhost:5000/html")
    if (err == nil && response.StatusCode == http.StatusOK) {
        data, err := io.ReadAll(response.Body)
        if (err == nil) {
            defer response.Body.Close()
            os.Stdout.Write(data)
        }
    } else {
        Printfln("Error: %v, Status Code: %v", err.Error(), response.StatusCode)
    }
}
```

I used the ReadAll function defined in the io package to read the response Body into a byte slice, which I write to the standard output. Compile and execute the project, and you will see the following output, which shows the body of the response sent by the HTTP server:

```
<!DOCTYPE html>
<html>
<head>
    <title>Pro Go</title>
    <meta name="viewport" content="width=device-width" />
</head>
<body>
    <h1>Hello, World</div>
</body>
</html>
```

When responses contain data, such as JSON, they can be parsed into Go values, as shown in Listing 25-10.

Listing 25-10. Reading and Parsing Data in the main.go File in the httpclient Folder

```
package main

import (
    "net/http"
    //"os"
    "time"
    //"io"
    "encoding/json"
)

func main() {
    go http.ListenAndServe(":5000", nil)
    time.Sleep(time.Second)

    response, err := http.Get("http://localhost:5000/json")
    if (err == nil && response.StatusCode == http.StatusOK) {
        defer response.Body.Close()
        data := []Product {}
        err = json.NewDecoder(response.Body).Decode(&data)
        if (err == nil) {
            for _, p := range data {
                Printfln("Name: %v, Price: $%.2f", p.Name, p.Price)
            }
        } else {
            Printfln("Decode error: %v", err.Error())
        }
    } else {
        Printfln("Error: %v, Status Code: %v", err.Error(), response.StatusCode)
    }
}
```

The JSON data is decoded using the encoding/json package, which is described in Chapter 21. The data is decoded into a Product slice, which is enumerated using a for loop, producing the following output when the project is compiled and executed:

```
Name: Kayak, Price: $279.00
Name: Lifejacket, Price: $49.95
Name: Soccer Ball, Price: $19.50
Name: Corner Flags, Price: $34.95
Name: Stadium, Price: $79500.00
Name: Thinking Cap, Price: $16.00
Name: Unsteady Chair, Price: $75.00
Name: Bling-Bling King, Price: $1200.00
```

Sending POST Requests

The Post and PostForm functions are used to send POST requests. The PostForm function encodes a map of values as form data, as shown in Listing 25-11.

Listing 25-11. Sending a Form in the main.go File in the httpclient Folder

```go
package main

import (
    "net/http"
    "os"
    "time"
    "io"
    //"encoding/json"
)

func main() {
    go http.ListenAndServe(":5000", nil)
    time.Sleep(time.Second)

    formData := map[string][]string {
        "name":   { "Kayak "},
        "category": { "Watersports"},
        "price":   { "279"},
    }

    response, err := http.PostForm("http://localhost:5000/echo", formData)

    if (err == nil && response.StatusCode == http.StatusOK) {
        io.Copy(os.Stdout, response.Body)
        defer response.Body.Close()
    } else {
        Printfln("Error: %v, Status Code: %v", err.Error(), response.StatusCode)
    }
}
```

HTML forms support multiple values for each key, which is why the values in the map are slices of strings. In Listing 25-11, I send only one value for each key in the form, but I still have to enclose that value in braces to create a slice. The PostForm function encodes the map and adds the data to the request body and sets the Content-Type header to application/x-www-form-urlencoded. The form is sent to the /echo URL, which simply sends back the request received by the server in the response. Compile and execute the project, and you will see the following output:

```
Method: POST
Header: User-Agent: [Go-http-client/1.1]
Header: Content-Length: [42]
Header: Content-Type: [application/x-www-form-urlencoded]
Header: Accept-Encoding: [gzip]
----
category=Watersports&name=Kayak+&price=279
```

673

Posting a Form Using a Reader

The Post function sends a POST request to the server and creates the request body by reading content from a Reader, as shown in Listing 25-12. Unlike the PostForm function, the data doesn't have to be encoded as a form.

Listing 25-12. Posting from a Reader in the main.go File in the httpclient Folder

```
package main

import (
    "net/http"
    "os"
    "time"
    "io"
    "encoding/json"
    "strings"
)

func main() {
    go http.ListenAndServe(":5000", nil)
    time.Sleep(time.Second)

    var builder strings.Builder
    err := json.NewEncoder(&builder).Encode(Products[0])
    if (err == nil) {
        response, err := http.Post("http://localhost:5000/echo",
            "application/json",
            strings.NewReader(builder.String()))
        if (err == nil && response.StatusCode == http.StatusOK) {
            io.Copy(os.Stdout, response.Body)
            defer response.Body.Close()
        } else {
            Printfln("Error: %v", err.Error())
        }
    } else {
        Printfln("Error: %v", err.Error())
    }
}
```

This example encodes the first element in the slice of Product values defined in Listing 25-12 as JSON, preparing the data so it can be processed as a Reader. The arguments to the Post function are the URL to which the request is sent, the value for the Content-Type header, and the Reader. Compile and execute the project, and you will see the echoed request data:

```
Method: POST
Header: User-Agent: [Go-http-client/1.1]
Header: Content-Length: [54]
Header: Content-Type: [application/json]
Header: Accept-Encoding: [gzip]
----
{"Name":"Kayak","Category":"Watersports","Price":279}
```

UNDERSTANDING THE CONTENT-LENGTH HEADER

If you examine the requests sent by Listing 25-11 and Listing 25-12, you will see they include a Content-Length header. This header is set automatically but is included in requests only when it is possible to determine how much data will be included in the body in advance. This is done by inspecting the Reader to determine the dynamic type. When the data is stored in memory using the strings. Reader, bytes.Reader, or bytes.Buffer type, the built-in len function is used to determine the amount of data, and the result is used to set the Content-Length header.

For all other types, the Content-Type head is not set, and *chunked encoding* is used instead, which means that the body is written in blocks of data whose size is declared as part of the request body. This approach allows requests to be sent without needing to read all the data from the Reader just to work out how many bytes there are. Chunked encoding is described at https://developer.mozilla. org/en-US/docs/Web/HTTP/Headers/Transfer-Encoding.

Configuring HTTP Client Requests

The Client struct is used when control is required over an HTTP request and defines the fields and methods described in Table 25-5.

Table 25-5. *The Client Fields and Methods*

Name	Description
Transport	This field is used to select the transport that will be used to send the HTTP request. The net/http package provides a default transport.
CheckRedirect	This field is used to specify a custom policy for dealing with repeated redirections, as described in the "Managing Redirections" section.
Jar	This field returns a CookieJar, which is used to manage cookies, as described in the "Working with Cookies" section.
Timeout	This field is used to set a timeout for the request, specified as a time. Duration.
Do(request)	This method sends the specified Request, returning a Response and an error that indicates problems sending the request.
CloseIdleConnections()	This method closes any idle HTTP requests that are currently open and unused.
Get(url)	This method is called by the Get function described in Table 25-3.
Head(url)	This method is called by the Head function described in Table 25-3.
Post(url, contentType, reader)	This method is called by the Post function described in Table 25-3.
PostForm(url, data)	This method is called by the PostForm function described in Table 25-3.

The net/http package defines the DefaultClient variable, which provides a default Client that can be used to use the fields and methods described in Table 25-5, and it is this variable that is used when the functions described in Table 25-3 are used.

The Request struct that describes the HTTP request is the same one that I used in Chapter 24 for HTTP servers. Table 25-6 describes the Request fields and methods that are most useful for client requests.

Table 25-6. *Useful Request Fields and Methods*

Name	Description
Method	This string field specifies the HTTP method that will be used for the request. The net/http package defines constants for HTTP methods, such as MethodGet and MethodPost.
URL	This URL field specifies the URL to which the request will be sent. The URL struct is defined in Chapter 24.
Header	This field is used to specify the headers for the request. The headers are specified in a map[string][]string, and the field will be nil when a Request value is created using the literal struct syntax.
ContentLength	This field is used to set the Content-Length header using an int64 value.
TransferEncoding	This field is used to set the Transfer-Encoding header using a slice of strings.
Body	This ReadCloser field specifies the source for the request body. If you have a Reader that doesn't define a Close method, then the io.NopCloser function can be used to create a ReadCloser whose Close method does nothing.

The simplest way to create a URL value is to use the Parse function provided by the net/url package, which parses a string, and which is described in Table 25-7 for quick reference.

Table 25-7. *The Function for Parsing URL Values*

Name	Description
Parse(string)	This method parses a string into a URL. The results are the URL value and an error that indicates problems parsing the string.

Listing 25-13 combines the features described in the tables to create a simple HTTP POST request.

Listing 25-13. Sending a Request in the main.go File in the httpclient Folder

```go
package main

import (
    "net/http"
    "os"
    "time"
    "io"
    "encoding/json"
    "strings"
    "net/url"
)
```

```
func main() {
    go http.ListenAndServe(":5000", nil)
    time.Sleep(time.Second)

    var builder strings.Builder
    err := json.NewEncoder(&builder).Encode(Products[0])
    if (err == nil) {
        reqURL, err := url.Parse("http://localhost:5000/echo")
        if (err == nil) {
            req := http.Request {
                Method: http.MethodPost,
                URL: reqURL,
                Header: map[string][]string {
                    "Content-Type": { "application.json" },
                },
                Body: io.NopCloser(strings.NewReader(builder.String())),
            }
            response, err := http.DefaultClient.Do(&req)
            if (err == nil && response.StatusCode == http.StatusOK) {
                io.Copy(os.Stdout, response.Body)
                defer response.Body.Close()
            } else {
                Printfln("Request Error: %v", err.Error())
            }
        } else {
            Printfln("Parse Error: %v", err.Error())
        }
    } else {
        Printfln("Encoder Error: %v", err.Error())
    }
}
```

This listing creates a new request using the literal syntax and then sets the Method, URL, and Body fields. The method is set so that a POST request is sent, the URL is created using the Parse function, and the Body field is set using the io.NopCloser function, which accepts a Reader and returns a ReadCloser, which is the type required by the Request struct. The Header field is assigned a map that defines the Content-Type header. A pointer to the Request is passed to the Do method of the Client assigned to the DefaultClient variable, which sends the request.

This example uses the /echo URL set up at the start of the chapter, which echoes the request received by the server in the response. Compile and execute the project, and you will see the following output:

```
Method: POST
Header: Content-Type: [application.json]
Header: Accept-Encoding: [gzip]
Header: User-Agent: [Go-http-client/1.1]
----
{"Name":"Kayak","Category":"Watersports","Price":279}
```

Using the Convenience Functions to Create a Request

The previous example demonstrated that the struct literal syntax can be used to create Request values, but the net/http package also provides convenience functions that streamline the process, as described in Table 25-8.

Table 25-8. *The net/http Convenience Functions for Creating Requests*

Name	Description
NewRequest(method, url, reader)	This function creates a new Reader, configured with the specified method, URL, and body. The function also returns an error that indicates problems creating the value, including parsing the URL, which is expressed as a string.
NewRequestWithContext(context, method, url, reader)	This function creates a new Reader that will be sent in the specified context. Contexts are described in Chapter 30.

Listing 25-14 uses the NewRequest function instead of the literal syntax to create a Request.

Listing 25-14. Using the Convenience Function in the main.go File in the httpclient Folder

```
package main

import (
    "net/http"
    "os"
    "time"
    "io"
    "encoding/json"
    "strings"
    //"net/url"
)

func main() {
    go http.ListenAndServe(":5000", nil)
    time.Sleep(time.Second)

    var builder strings.Builder
    err := json.NewEncoder(&builder).Encode(Products[0])
    if (err == nil) {
        req, err := http.NewRequest(http.MethodPost, "http://localhost:5000/echo",
        io.NopCloser(strings.NewReader(builder.String())))
        if (err == nil) {
            req.Header["Content-Type"] = []string{ "application/json" }
            response, err := http.DefaultClient.Do(req)
            if (err == nil && response.StatusCode == http.StatusOK) {
                io.Copy(os.Stdout, response.Body)
                defer response.Body.Close()
            } else {
                Printfln("Request Error: %v", err.Error())
            }
```

```
        } else {
            Printfln("Request Init Error: %v", err.Error())
        }
    } else {
        Printfln("Encoder Error: %v", err.Error())
    }
}
```

The outcome is the same—a Request that can be passed to the Client.Do method, but I don't need to explicitly parse the URL. The NewRequest function initializes the Header field, so I can add the Content-Type header without needing to create the map first. Compile and execute the project, and you will see the details of the request sent to the server:

```
Method: POST
Header: User-Agent: [Go-http-client/1.1]
Header: Content-Type: [application/json]
Header: Accept-Encoding: [gzip]
----
{"Name":"Kayak","Category":"Watersports","Price":279}
```

Working with Cookies

The Client keeps track of the cookies it receives from the server and automatically includes them in subsequent requests. To prepare, add a file named server_cookie.go to the httpclient folder with the content shown in Listing 25-15.

Listing 25-15. The Contents of the server_cookie.go File in the httpclient Folder

```go
package main

import (
    "net/http"
    "strconv"
    "fmt"
)

func init() {
    http.HandleFunc("/cookie",
    func (writer http.ResponseWriter, request *http.Request) {
        counterVal := 1
        counterCookie, err := request.Cookie("counter")
        if (err == nil) {
            counterVal, _ = strconv.Atoi(counterCookie.Value)
            counterVal++
        }
        http.SetCookie(writer, &http.Cookie{
            Name: "counter", Value: strconv.Itoa(counterVal),
        })
```

```
        if (len(request.Cookies()) > 0) {
            for _, c := range request.Cookies() {
                fmt.Fprintf(writer, "Cookie Name: %v, Value: %v\n",
                    c.Name, c.Value)
            }
        } else {
            fmt.Fprintln(writer, "Request contains no cookies")
        }
    })


}
```

The new route sets and reads a cookie named counter, using code from one of the examples in Chapter 24. Listing 25-16 updates the client request to use the new URL.

Listing 25-16. Changing URL in the main.go File in the httpclient Folder

```
package main

import (
    "net/http"
    "os"
    "time"
    "io"
    // "encoding/json"
    // "strings"
    //"net/url"
    "net/http/cookiejar"
)

func main() {
    go http.ListenAndServe(":5000", nil)
    time.Sleep(time.Second)

    jar, err := cookiejar.New(nil)
    if (err == nil) {
        http.DefaultClient.Jar = jar
    }

    for i := 0; i < 3; i++ {
        req, err := http.NewRequest(http.MethodGet,
            "http://localhost:5000/cookie", nil)
        if (err == nil) {
            response, err := http.DefaultClient.Do(req)
            if (err == nil && response.StatusCode == http.StatusOK) {
                io.Copy(os.Stdout, response.Body)
                defer response.Body.Close()
            } else {
                Printfln("Request Error: %v", err.Error())
            }
```

```
        } else {
            Printfln("Request Init Error: %v", err.Error())
        }
    }
}
```

By default, cookies are ignored by Client values, which is a sensible policy because the cookies set in one response will affect subsequent requests, which can cause unexpected results. To opt into tracking cookies, the Jar field is assigned an implementation of the net/http/CookieJar interface, which defines the methods described in Table 25-9.

Table 25-9. *The Methods Defined by the CookieJar Interface*

Name	Description
SetCookies(url, cookies)	This method stores a *Cookie slice for the specified URL.
Cookes(url)	This method returns a *Cookie slice containing the cookies that should be included in a request for the specified URL.

The net/http/cookiejar package contains an implementation of the CookieJar interface that stores cookies in memory. Cookie jars are created with a constructor function, as described in Table 25-10.

Table 25-10. *The Cookie Jar Constructor Function in the net/http/cookiejar Package*

Name	Description
New(options)	This function creates a new CookieJar, configured with an Options struct, described next. The function also returns an error that reports problems creating the jar.

The New function accepts a net/http/cookiejar/Options struct, which is used to configure the cookie jar. There is only one Options field, PublicSuffixList, which is used to specify an implementation of the interface with the same name, which provides support for preventing cookies from being set too widely, which can cause privacy violations. The standard library doesn't contain an implementation of the PublicSuffixList interface, but there is an implementation available at https://pkg.go.dev/golang.org/x/net/publicsuffix.

In Listing 25-16, I invoked the New function with nil, which means that no implementation of the PublicSuffixList is used, and then assigned the CookieJar to the Jar field of the Client assigned to the DefaultClient variable. Compile and execute the project, and you will see the following output:

```
Request contains no cookies
Cookie Name: counter, Value: 1
Cookie Name: counter, Value: 2
```

Three HTTP requests are sent by the code in Listing 25-16. The first request doesn't contain a cookie, but the server includes one in the response. This cookie is included in the second and third requests, which allows the server to read and increment the value it contains.

Notice that I did not have to manage the cookies in Listing 25-16. Setting up the cookie jar is all that is required, and the Client tracks the cookies automatically.

Creating Separate Clients and Cookie Jars

A consequence of using the DefaultClient is that all requests share the same cookies, which can be useful, especially since the cookie jar will ensure that each request only includes the cookies that are required for each URL.

If you don't want to share cookies, then you can create a Client with its own cookie jar, as shown in Listing 25-17.

Listing 25-17. Creating Separate Clients in the main.go File in the httpclient Folder

```
package main

import (
    "net/http"
    "os"
    "time"
    "io"
    //"encoding/json"
    //"strings"
    //"net/url"
    "net/http/cookiejar"
    "fmt"
)

func main() {
    go http.ListenAndServe(":5000", nil)
    time.Sleep(time.Second)

    clients := make([]http.Client, 3)
    for index, client := range clients {
        jar, err := cookiejar.New(nil)
        if (err == nil) {
            client.Jar = jar
        }

        for i := 0; i < 3; i++ {
            req, err := http.NewRequest(http.MethodGet,
                "http://localhost:5000/cookie", nil)
            if (err == nil) {
                response, err := client.Do(req)
                if (err == nil && response.StatusCode == http.StatusOK) {
                    fmt.Fprintf(os.Stdout, "Client %v: ", index)
                    io.Copy(os.Stdout, response.Body)
                    defer response.Body.Close()
                } else {
                    Println("Request Error: %v", err.Error())
                }
            } else {
                Println("Request Init Error: %v", err.Error())
            }
        }
    }
}
```

This example creates three separate `Client` values, each of which has its own `CookieJar`. Each `Client` makes three requests, and the code produces the following output when the project is compiled and executed:

```
Client 0: Request contains no cookies
Client 0: Cookie Name: counter, Value: 1
Client 0: Cookie Name: counter, Value: 2
Client 1: Request contains no cookies
Client 1: Cookie Name: counter, Value: 1
Client 1: Cookie Name: counter, Value: 2
Client 2: Request contains no cookies
Client 2: Cookie Name: counter, Value: 1
Client 2: Cookie Name: counter, Value: 2
```

If multiple `Client` values are required but cookies should be shared, then a single `CookieJar` can be used, as shown in Listing 25-18.

Listing 25-18. Sharing a CookieJar in the main.go File in the httpclient Folder

```go
package main

import (
    "net/http"
    "os"
    "io"
    "time"
    //"encoding/json"
    //"strings"
    //"net/url"
    "net/http/cookiejar"
    "fmt"
)

func main() {
    go http.ListenAndServe(":5000", nil)
    time.Sleep(time.Second)

    jar, err := cookiejar.New(nil)

    clients := make([]http.Client, 3)
    for index, client := range clients {
        //jar, err := cookiejar.New(nil)
        if (err == nil) {
            client.Jar = jar
        }
```

```
    for i := 0; i < 3; i++ {
        req, err := http.NewRequest(http.MethodGet,
            "http://localhost:5000/cookie", nil)
        if (err == nil) {
            response, err := client.Do(req)
            if (err == nil && response.StatusCode == http.StatusOK) {
                fmt.Fprintf(os.Stdout, "Client %v: ", index)
                io.Copy(os.Stdout, response.Body)
                defer response.Body.Close()
            } else {
                Printfln("Request Error: %v", err.Error())
            }
        } else {
            Printfln("Request Init Error: %v", err.Error())
        }
    }
}
}
```

The cookies received by one Client are used in subsequent requests, as shown in the output produced when the project is compiled and executed:

```
Client 0: Request contains no cookies
Client 0: Cookie Name: counter, Value: 1
Client 0: Cookie Name: counter, Value: 2
Client 1: Cookie Name: counter, Value: 3
Client 1: Cookie Name: counter, Value: 4
Client 1: Cookie Name: counter, Value: 5
Client 2: Cookie Name: counter, Value: 6
Client 2: Cookie Name: counter, Value: 7
Client 2: Cookie Name: counter, Value: 8
```

Managing Redirections

By default, a Client will stop following redirections after ten requests, but this can be changed by specifying a custom policy. Add a file named server_redirects.go to the httpclient folder with the content shown in Listing 25-19.

Listing 25-19. The Contents of the server_redirects.go File in the httpclient Folder

```
package main

import "net/http"

func init() {
```

```
    http.HandleFunc("/redirect1",
        func (writer http.ResponseWriter, request *http.Request) {
            http.Redirect(writer, request, "/redirect2",
                http.StatusTemporaryRedirect)
        })
    http.HandleFunc("/redirect2",
        func (writer http.ResponseWriter, request *http.Request) {
            http.Redirect(writer, request, "/redirect1",
                http.StatusTemporaryRedirect)
        })
}
```

The redirections will continue until the client stops following them. Listing 25-20 creates a request that is sent to the URL handled by the first route defined in Listing 25-19.

Listing 25-20. Sending a Request in the main.go File in the httpclient Folder

```
package main

import (
    "net/http"
    "os"
    "io"
    "time"
    //"encoding/json"
    //"strings"
    //"net/url"
    //"net/http/cookiejar"
    //"fmt"
)

func main() {
    go http.ListenAndServe(":5000", nil)
    time.Sleep(time.Second)

    req, err := http.NewRequest(http.MethodGet,
        "http://localhost:5000/redirect1", nil)
    if (err == nil) {
        var response *http.Response
        response, err = http.DefaultClient.Do(req)
        if (err == nil) {
            io.Copy(os.Stdout, response.Body)
        } else {
            Printfln("Request Error: %v", err.Error())
        }
    } else {
        Printfln("Error: %v", err.Error())
    }
}
```

Compile and execute the project, and you will see an error that stops the Client following redirections after ten requests:

```
Request Error: Get "/redirect1": stopped after 10 redirects
```

A custom policy is defined by assigning a function to the Client.CheckRedirect field, as shown in Listing 25-21.

Listing 25-21. Defining a Custom Redirection Policy in the main.go File in the httpclient Folder

```
package main

import (
    "net/http"
    "os"
    "io"
    "time"
    //"encoding/json"
    //"strings"
    "net/url"
    //"net/http/cookiejar"
    //"fmt"
)

func main() {
    go http.ListenAndServe(":5000", nil)
    time.Sleep(time.Second)

    http.DefaultClient.CheckRedirect = func(req *http.Request,
        previous []*http.Request) error {
        if len(previous) == 3 {
            url, _ := url.Parse("http://localhost:5000/html")
            req.URL =   url
        }
        return nil
    }

    req, err := http.NewRequest(http.MethodGet,
        "http://localhost:5000/redirect1", nil)
    if (err == nil) {
        var response *http.Response
        response, err = http.DefaultClient.Do(req)
        if (err == nil) {
            io.Copy(os.Stdout, response.Body)
        } else {
            Printfln("Request Error: %v", err.Error())
        }
    } else {
        Printfln("Error: %v", err.Error())
    }
}
```

The arguments to the function are a pointer to the Request that is about to be executed, and a *Request slice containing the requests that have led to the redirection. This means that the slice will contain at least one value because the CheckRedirect is called only when the server returns a redirection response.

The CheckRedirect function can block the request by returning an error, which is then returned as the result from the Do method. Or the CheckRedirect function can alter the request that is about to be made, which is what happens in Listing 25-21. When a request has led to three redirections, the custom policy alters the URL field so the Request is for the /html URL set up earlier in the chapter and that produces an HTML result.

The outcome is that a request for the /redirect1 URL will lead to a short cycle of redirections between /redirect2 and /redirect1 before the policy alters the URL, producing the following output:

```
<!DOCTYPE html>
<html>
<head>
    <title>Pro Go</title>
    <meta name="viewport" content="width=device-width" />
</head>
<body>
    <h1>Hello, World</div>
</body>
</html>
```

Creating Multipart Forms

The mime/multipart package can be used to create a request body encoded as multipart/form-data, which allows a form to safely contain binary data, such as the contents of a file. Add a file named server_forms.go to the httpclient folder with the content shown in Listing 25-22.

Listing 25-22. The Contents of the server_forms.go File in the httpclient Folder

```
package main

import (
    "net/http"
    "fmt"
    "io"
)

func init() {

    http.HandleFunc("/form",
        func (writer http.ResponseWriter, request *http.Request) {
            err := request.ParseMultipartForm(10000000)
            if (err == nil) {
                for name, vals := range request.MultipartForm.Value {
                    fmt.Fprintf(writer, "Field %v: %v\n", name, vals)
                }
                for name, files := range request.MultipartForm.File {
                    for _, file := range files {
```

```
                        fmt.Fprintf(writer, "File %v: %v\n", name, file.Filename)
                        if f, err := file.Open(); err == nil {
                            defer f.Close()
                            io.Copy(writer, f)
                        }
                    }
                }
            } else {
                fmt.Fprintf(writer, "Cannot parse form %v", err.Error())
            }
        })
}
```

The new handler function uses the features described in Chapter 24 to parse the multipart form and echo the fields and files it contains.

To create the form at the client-side, the multipart.Writer struct is used, which is a wrapper around an io.Writer and which is created with the constructor function described in Table 25-11.

Table 25-11. *The multipart.Writer Constructor Function*

Name	Description
NewWriter(writer)	This function creates a new multipart.Writer that writes form data to the specified io.Writer.

Once you have a multipart.Writer to work with, form content can be created using the methods described in Table 25-12.

Table 25-12. *The multipart.Writer Methods*

Name	Description
CreateFormField(fieldname)	This method creates a new form field with the specified name. The results are an io.Writer that is used to write the field data and an error that reports problems creating the field.
CreateFormFile(fieldname, filename)	This method creates a new file field with the specified field name and file name. The results are an io.Writer that is used to write the field data and an error that reports problems creating the field.
FormDataContentType()	This method returns a string that is used to set the Content-Type request header and includes the string that denotes the boundaries between the parts of the form.
Close()	This function finalizes the form and writes the terminating boundary that denotes the end of the form data.

There are additional methods defines that provide fine-grained control over how the form is constructed, but the methods in Table 25-12 are the most useful for most projects. Listing 25-23 uses these methods to create a multipart form that is sent to the server.

Listing 25-23. Creating and Sending a Multipart Form in the main.go File in the httpclient Folder

```go
package main

import (
    "net/http"
    "os"
    "io"
    "time"
    //"encoding/json"
    //"strings"
    //"net/url"
    //"net/http/cookiejar"
    //"fmt"
    "mime/multipart"
    "bytes"
)

func main() {
    go http.ListenAndServe(":5000", nil)
    time.Sleep(time.Second)

    var buffer bytes.Buffer
    formWriter := multipart.NewWriter(&buffer)
    fieldWriter, err := formWriter.CreateFormField("name")
    if (err == nil) {
        io.WriteString(fieldWriter, "Alice")
    }
    fieldWriter, err = formWriter.CreateFormField("city")
    if (err == nil) {
        io.WriteString(fieldWriter, "New York")
    }
    fileWriter, err := formWriter.CreateFormFile("codeFile", "printer.go")
    if (err == nil) {
        fileData, err := os.ReadFile("./printer.go")
        if (err == nil) {
            fileWriter.Write(fileData)
        }
    }

    formWriter.Close()

    req, err := http.NewRequest(http.MethodPost,
        "http://localhost:5000/form", &buffer)

    req.Header["Content-Type"] = []string{ formWriter.FormDataContentType()}
```

```
    if (err == nil) {
        var response *http.Response
        response, err = http.DefaultClient.Do(req)
        if (err == nil) {
            io.Copy(os.Stdout, response.Body)
        } else {
            Printfln("Request Error: %v", err.Error())
        }
    } else {
        Printfln("Error: %v", err.Error())
    }
}
```

A specific sequence is required to create a form. First, call the NewWriter function to get a multipart.Writer:

```
...
var buffer bytes.Buffer
formWriter := multipart.NewWriter(&buffer)
...
```

A Reader is required to use the form data as the body for an HTTP request, but a Writer is required to create the form. This is an ideal situation for a bytes.Buffer struct, which provides an in-memory implementation of both the Reader and Writer interfaces.

One the multipart.Writer has been created, the CreateFormField and CreateFormFile methods are used to add fields and files to the form:

```
...
fieldWriter, err := formWriter.CreateFormField("name")
...
fileWriter, err := formWriter.CreateFormFile("codeFile", "printer.go")
...
```

Both of these methods return a Writer that is used to write content to the form. Once the fields and files have been added, the next step is to set the Content-Type header, using the result from the FormDataContentType method:

```
...
req.Header["Content-Type"] = []string{ formWriter.FormDataContentType()}
...
```

The result from the method includes the string used to denote the boundaries between the parts in the form. The final step—and one that is easy to forget—is to call the Close method on the multipart.Writer, which adds a final boundary string to the form.

Caution Don't use the defer keyword on the call to the Close method; otherwise, the final boundary string won't be added to the form until after the request will be sent, producing a form that not all servers will process. It is important to call the Close method before sending the request.

690

Compile and execute the project, and you will see the contents of the multipart form echoed in the response from the server:

```
Field city: [New York]
Field name: [Alice]
File codeFile: printer.go
package main
import "fmt"
func Printfln(template string, values ...interface{}) {
    fmt.Printf(template + "\n", values...)
}
```

Summary

In this chapter, I describe the standard library features for sending HTTP requests, explaining how to use different HTTP verbs, how to send forms, and how to deal with issues such as cookies. In the next chapter, I show you how the Go standard library provides support for working with databases.

CHAPTER 26

■ ■ ■

Working with Databases

In this chapter, I describe the Go standard library for working with SQL databases. These features provide an abstract representation of the capabilities offered by a database and rely on driver packages to deal with the implementation of a specific database.

There are drivers for a wide range of databases, and a list can be found at https://github.com/golang/go/wiki/sqldrivers. Database drivers are distributed as Go packages, and most databases have multiple driver packages. Some driver packages rely on cgo, which allows Go code to use C libraries, and others are written in pure Go.

I use the SQLite database in this chapter (and also in Part 3 where I use a more complex database). SQLite is an excellent embedded database that supports a wide range of platforms, is freely available, and doesn't require a server component to be installed and configured. Table 26-1 puts the standard library database features in context.

Table 26-1. *Putting Working with Databases in Context*

Question	Answer
What is it?	The database/sql package provides features for working with SQL databases.
Why is it useful?	Relational databases remain the most effective way of storing large amounts of structured data and are used in most large projects.
How is it used?	Driver packages provide support for specific databases, while the database/sql package provides a set of types that allow databases to be used consistently.
Are there any pitfalls or limitations?	These features do not automatically populate struct fields from result rows.
Are there any alternatives?	There are third-party packages that build on these features to simplify or enhance their use.

COMPLAINING ABOUT DATABASES

You may be tempted to contact me to complain about the choice of database in this book. You certainly won't be alone, because database selection is one of the topics about which I receive the most emails. Complaints generally suggest that I have chosen the "wrong" database, which generally means "not the database used by the email sender."

Before contacting me, please consider two points. First, this is not a book about databases and the zero-configuration approach taken by SQLite means that most readers will be able to follow the examples

A. Freeman, *Pro Go*, https://doi.org/10.1007/978-1-4842-7355-5_26

without having to diagnose setup and configuration issues. Second, SQLite is an outstanding database that many projects overlook because it doesn't have a traditional server component, even though many projects don't need or benefit from having a separate database server.

I apologize if you are a dedicated Oracle/DB2/MySQL/MariaDB user and wanted to be able to cut and paste the connection code into your project. But this approach lets me focus on Go, and you will find the code samples you need for your choice of database in the documentation for the driver you select.

Table 26-2 summarizes the chapter.

Table 26-2. *Chapter Summary*

Problem	Solution	Listing
Add support to a project for a specific type of database	Use the go get command to add a database driver package	8
Open and close a database	Use the Open function and the Close method	9, 10
Query the database	Use the Query method and process the Rows result using the Scan method	11–16, 22, 23
Query the database for a single row	Use the QueryRow method and process the Row result	17
Execute queries or statements that do not produce row results	Use the Exec method and process the Result it produces	18
Process a statement so that it can be reused	Create a prepared statement	19, 20
Perform multiple queries as a single unit of work	Use a transaction	21

Preparing for This Chapter

To prepare for this chapter, open a new command prompt, navigate to a convenient location, and create a directory named data. Run the command shown in Listing 26-1 in the data folder to create a module file.

■ **Tip** You can download the example project for this chapter—and for all the other chapters in this book—from https://github.com/apress/pro-go. See Chapter 2 for how to get help if you have problems running the examples.

Listing 26-1. Initializing the Module

```
go mod init data
```

Add a file named printer.go to the data folder with the content shown in Listing 26-2.

Listing 26-2. The Contents of the printer.go File in the data Folder

```go
package main

import "fmt"

func Printfln(template string, values ...interface{}) {
    fmt.Printf(template + "\n", values...)
}
```

Add a file named main.go to the data folder with the content shown in Listing 26-3.

Listing 26-3. The Contents of the main.go File in the data Folder

```go
package main

func main() {
    Printfln("Hello, Data")
}
```

Run the command shown in Listing 26-4 in the data folder to compile and run the project.

Listing 26-4. Compiling and Executing the Project

```
go run .
```

This command will produce the following output:

```
Hello, Data
```

Preparing the Database

The SQLite database manager used in this chapter will be installed later, but to get started, a tools package is required to create the database from a SQL file. (In Part 3, I demonstrate the process of creating the database from within the application.)

To define the SQL file that will create the database, add a file named products.sql to the data folder with the content shown in Listing 26-5.

Listing 26-5. The Contents of the products.sql File in the data Folder

```sql
DROP TABLE IF EXISTS Categories;
DROP TABLE IF EXISTS Products;

CREATE TABLE IF NOT EXISTS Categories (
    Id INTEGER NOT NULL PRIMARY KEY,
    Name TEXT
);

CREATE TABLE IF NOT EXISTS Products (
    Id INTEGER NOT NULL PRIMARY KEY,
    Name TEXT,
```

```
    Category INTEGER,
    Price decimal(8, 2),
    CONSTRAINT CatRef FOREIGN KEY(Category) REFERENCES Categories (Id)
);

INSERT INTO Categories (Id, Name) VALUES
    (1, "Watersports"),
    (2, "Soccer");

INSERT INTO Products (Id, Name, Category, Price) VALUES
    (1, "Kayak", 1, 279),
    (2, "Lifejacket", 1, 48.95),
    (3, "Soccer Ball", 2, 19.50),
    (4, "Corner Flags", 2, 34.95);
```

Go to https://www.sqlite.org/download.html, look for the precompiled binaries section for your operating system, and download the tools package. I can't include links in this chapter because the URLs include the package version number, which will have changed by the time you read this chapter.

Unpack the zip archive and copy the sqlite3 or sqlite3.exe file into the data folder. Run the command shown in Listing 26-6 in the data folder to create the database.

■ **Note**   The precompiled binaries for Linux are 32-bit, which can require some additional packages to be installed for 64-bit only operating systems.

Listing 26-6. Creating the Database

```
./sqlite3 products.db ".read products.sql"
```

To confirm that the database has been created and populated with data, run the command shown in Listing 26-7 in the data folder.

Listing 26-7. Testing the Database

```
./sqlite3 products.db "select * from PRODUCTS"
```

If the database has been created correctly, you will see the following output:

```
1|Kayak|1|279
2|Lifejacket|1|48.95
3|Soccer Ball|2|19.5
4|Corner Flags|2|34.95
```

If you need to reset the database while following the examples in this chapter, then you can delete the products.db file and run the command in Listing 26-6 again.

Installing a Database Driver

The Go standard library includes features for working with databases simply and consistently but relies on database driver packages to implement those features for each specific database engine or server. As noted, I use SQLite in this chapter, for which there is a good pure Go driver available. Run the command shown in Listing 26-8 in the data folder to install the driver package.

Listing 26-8. Installing the SQL Driver Package

```
go get modernc.org/sqlite
```

Most database servers are set up separately so that the database driver opens a connection to a separate process. SQLite is an embedded database and is included in the driver package, which means no additional configuration is required.

Opening a Database

The standard library provides the database/sql package for working with databases. The functions described in Table 26-3 are used to open a database so that it can be used within an application.

Table 26-3. *The database/sql Functions for Opening a Database*

Name	Description
Drivers()	This function returns a slice of strings, each of which contains the name of a database driver.
Open(driver, connectionStr)	This function opens a database using the specified driver and connection string. The results are a pointer to a DB struct, which is used to interact with the database and an error that indicates problems opening the database.

Add a file named database.go to the data folder with the code shown in Listing 26-9.

Listing 26-9. The Contents of the database.go file in the data Folder

```go
package main

import (
    "database/sql"
    _ "modernc.org/sqlite"
)

func listDrivers() {
    for _, driver := range sql.Drivers() {
        Printfln("Driver: %v", driver)
    }
}

func openDatabase() (db *sql.DB, err error) {
    db, err = sql.Open("sqlite", "products.db")
    if (err == nil) {
```

```
        Printfln("Opened database")
    }
    return
}
```

The blank identifier is used to import the database driver package, which loads the driver and allows it to register as a provider of the SQL API:

```
...
_ "modernc.org/sqlite"
...
```

The package is imported only for initialization and isn't used directly, although you may find drivers that require some initial configuration. The database is used through the database/sql package, as the functions defined in Listing 26-9 show. The listDrivers function writes out the available drivers, although there is only one in this example project. The openDatabase function uses the Open function described in Table 26-3 to open a database:

```
...
db, err = sql.Open("sqlite", "products.db")
...
```

The arguments to the Open function are the name of the driver to use and a connection string for the database, which will be specific to the database engine in use. SQLite opens databases using the name of the database file.

The results from the Open function are a pointer to a sql.DB struct and an error that reports any issues opening the database. The DB struct provides access to the database without exposing details of the database engine or its connections.

I describe the features that the DB struct provides in the sections that follow. To get started, however, I am going to use just one method, which is shown in Listing 26-10.

Listing 26-10. Using the DB Struct in the main.go File in the data Folder

```
package main

func main() {

    listDrivers()
    db, err := openDatabase()
    if (err == nil) {
        db.Close()
    } else {
        panic(err)
    }
}
```

The main method calls the listDrivers function to print out the names of the loaded drivers and then calls the openDatabase function to open the database. Nothing is done with the database yet, but Close method is called. This method, described in Table 26-4, closes the database and prevents further operations from being performed.

Table 26-4. *The DB Method for Closing the Database*

Name	Description
Close()	This function closes the database and prevents further operations from being performed.

Although it is a good idea to call the Close method, you only need to do so when you have completely finished with the database. A single DB can be used to make repeated queries to the same database, and connections to the database will be managed automatically behind the scenes. There is no need to call the Open method to get a new DB for each query and then use Close to close it once the query is complete.

Compile and execute the project, and you will see the following output, which shows the name of the database driver and confirms that the database has been opened:

```
Driver: sqlite
Opened database
```

Executing Statements and Queries

The DB struct is used to execute SQL statements, using the methods described in Table 26-5, which are demonstrated in the sections that follow.

Table 26-5. *The DB Methods for Executing SQL Statements*

Name	Description
Query(query, ...args)	This method executes the specified query, using the optional placeholder arguments. The results are a Rows struct, which contains the query results, and an error that indicates problems executing the query.
QueryRow(query, ...args)	This method executes the specified query, using the optional placeholder arguments. The result is a Row struct, which represents the first row from the query results. See the "Executing Queries for Single Rows" section.
Exec(query, ...args)	This method executes statements or queries that do not return rows of data. The method returns a Result, which describes the response from the database, and an error that signals problems with execution. See the "Executing Other Queries" section.

USING CONTEXTS WITH DATABASES

In Chapter 30, I describe the context package and the Context interface it defines, which is used to manage requests as they are processed by a server. All the important methods defined in the database/sql package also have versions that accept a Context argument, which is useful if you want to take advantage of features like request handling timeouts. I have not listed these methods in this chapter, but I make extensive use of the Context interface—including using the database/sql methods that accept them as arguments—in Part 3, where I use Go and its standard library to create a web application platform and an online store.

Querying for Multiple Rows

The Query method executes a query that retrieves one or more rows from the database. The Query method returns a Rows struct, which contains the query results and an error that indicates problems. The row data is accessed through the methods described in Table 26-6.

Table 26-6. *The Rows Struct Methods*

Name	Description
Next()	This method advances to the next result row. The result is a bool, which is true when there is data to read and false when the end of the data has been reached, at which point the Close method is automatically called.
NextResultSet()	This method advances to the next result set when there are multiple result sets in the same database response. The method returns true if there is another set of rows to process.
Scan(... targets)	This method assigns the SQL values from the current row to the specified variables. The values are assigned via pointers and the method returns an error that indicates when the values cannot be scanned. See the "Understanding the Scan Method" section for details.
Close()	This method prevents further enumeration of the results and is used when not all of the data is required. There is no need to call this method if the Next method is used to advance until it returns false.

Listing 26-11 demonstrates a simple query, which shows how the Rows struct is used.

Listing 26-11. Querying the Database in the main.go File in the data Folder

```go
package main

import "database/sql"

func queryDatabase(db *sql.DB) {
    rows, err := db.Query("SELECT * from Products")
    if (err == nil) {
        for (rows.Next()) {
            var id, category int
            var name string
            var price float64
            rows.Scan(&id, &name, &category, &price)
            Printfln("Row: %v %v %v %v", id, name, category, price)
        }
    } else {
        Printfln("Error: %v", err)
    }
}

func main() {

    //listDrivers()
    db, err := openDatabase()
```

```
    if (err == nil) {
        queryDatabase(db)
        db.Close()
    } else {
        panic(err)
    }
}
```

The queryDatabase function performs a simple SELECT query on the Products table with the Query method, which produces a Rows result and an error. If the error is nil, a for loop is used to move through the result rows by calling the Next method, which returns true if there is a row to process and returns false when the end of the data has been reached.

The Scan method is used to extract values from a result row and assign them to Go variables, like this:

```
...
rows.Scan(&id, &name, &category, &price)
...
```

Pointers to variables are passed to the Scan method in the same order in which columns are read from the database. Care must be taken to ensure that the Go variables can represent the SQL result they will be assigned. Compile and execute the project, and you will see the following results:

```
Opened database
Row: 1 Kayak 1 279
Row: 2 Lifejacket 1 48.95
Row: 3 Soccer Ball 2 19.5
Row: 4 Corner Flags 2 34.95
```

Understanding the Scan Method

The Scan method is sensitive to the number, order, and types of the parameters it receives. If the number of parameters doesn't match the number of columns in the results or the parameters are unable to store the result values, then an error will be returned, as shown in Listing 26-12.

Listing 26-12. A Mismatched Scan in the main.go File in the data Folder

```
...
func queryDatabase(db *sql.DB) {
    rows, err := db.Query("SELECT * from Products")
    if (err == nil) {
        for (rows.Next()) {
            var id, category int
            var name int
            var price float64
            scanErr := rows.Scan(&id, &name, &category, &price)
            if (scanErr == nil) {
                Println("Row: %v %v %v %v", id, name, category, price)
            } else {
                Println("Scan error: %v", scanErr)
                break
```

```
            }
        }
    } else {
        Printfln("Error: %v", err)
    }
}
...
```

The call to the Scan method in Listing 26-12 provides an int for a value that is stored in the database as the SQL TEXT type. Compile and execute the project, and you will see that the Scan method returns an error:

```
Scan error: sql: Scan error on column index 1, name "Name": converting driver.Value type
string ("Kayak") to a int: invalid syntax
```

The Scan method won't just skip the column that causes the problem, and no values will be scanned if there is a problem.

Understanding the How SQL Values Can Be Scanned

The most common issue with the Scan method is a mismatch between a SQL data type and the Go variable into which it is being scanned. The Scan method does offer some flexibility when mapping SQL values to Go values. Here is a loose summary of the most important rules:

- SQL Strings, Numeric, and Boolean values can be mapped to their Go counterparts, although care must be taken with numeric types to prevent overflow.

- SQL Numeric and Boolean types can be scanned into Go strings.

- SQL strings can be scanned into Go numeric types, but only if the string can be parsed using the normal Go features (described in Chapter 5) and only if there is no overflow.

- SQL time values can be scanned into Go strings or *time.Time values.

- Any SQL value can be scanned into a pointer to the empty interface (*interface{}), which allows you to convert the value into another type.

These are the most useful mappings, but see the Go documentation for the Scan method for full details. In general, I prefer to select types conservatively, and I will often scan into Go strings and then parse the value myself to manage the conversion process. Listing 26-13 scans all the result values into strings.

Listing 26-13. Scanning Into Strings in the main.go File in the data Folder

```
package main

import "database/sql"

func queryDatabase(db *sql.DB) {
    rows, err := db.Query("SELECT * from Products")
    if (err == nil) {
        for (rows.Next()) {
            var id, category string
            var name string
            var price string
```

```
            scanErr := rows.Scan(&id, &name, &category, &price)
            if (scanErr == nil) {
                Printfln("Row: %v %v %v %v", id, name, category, price)
            } else {
                Printfln("Scan error: %v", scanErr)
                break
            }

        }
    } else {
        Printfln("Error: %v", err)
    }
}

func main() {

    //listDrivers()
    db, err := openDatabase()
    if (err == nil) {
        queryDatabase(db)
        db.Close()
    } else {
        panic(err)
    }
}
```

This approach ensures that you get the SQL results into the Go application, although it does require additional work to parse the values to make use of them. Compile and execute the project, and you will see the following output:

```
Row: 1 Kayak 1 279
Row: 2 Lifejacket 1 48.95
Row: 3 Soccer Ball 2 19.5
Row: 4 Corner Flags 2 34.95
```

Scanning Values into a Struct

The Scan method works only on individual fields, which means there is no support for automatically populating the fields of a struct. Instead, you must provide pointers to the individual fields for which the results contain values, as shown in Listing 26-14.

■ **Note** At the end of this chapter, I demonstrate the use of the Go reflect package to scan rows into structs dynamically. See the "Using Reflection to Scan Data into a Struct" section for details.

Listing 26-14. Scanning to a Struct in the main.go File in the data Folder

```
package main

import "database/sql"

type Product struct {
    Id int
    Name string
    Category int
    Price float64
}

func queryDatabase(db *sql.DB) []Product {
    products := []Product {}
    rows, err := db.Query("SELECT * from Products")
    if (err == nil) {
        for (rows.Next()) {
            p := Product{}
            scanErr := rows.Scan(&p.Id, &p.Name, &p.Category, &p.Price)
            if (scanErr == nil) {
                products = append(products, p)
            } else {
                Printfln("Scan error: %v", scanErr)
                break
            }
        }
    } else {
        Printfln("Error: %v", err)
    }
    return products
}

func main() {
    db, err := openDatabase()
    if (err == nil) {
        products := queryDatabase(db)
        for i, p := range products {
            Printfln("#%v: %v", i, p)
        }
        db.Close()
    } else {
        panic(err)
    }
}
```

This example scans the same result data but does so to create a Product slice. Compile and execute the project, and you will receive the following output:

```
Opened database
#0: {1 Kayak 1 279}
#1: {2 Lifejacket 1 48.95}
#2: {3 Soccer Ball 2 19.5}
#3: {4 Corner Flags 2 34.95}
```

This approach can be verbose—and duplicative if you have lots of result types to parse—but it has the advantage of being simple and predictable, and it can be easily adapted to reflect the complexity of the results. As an example, Listing 26-15 changes the query sent to the database so that it includes data from the Categories table.

Listing 26-15. Scanning More Complex Results in the main.go File in the data Folder

```go
package main

import "database/sql"

type Category struct {
    Id int
    Name string
}

type Product struct {
    Id int
    Name string
    Category
    Price float64
}

func queryDatabase(db *sql.DB) []Product {
    products := []Product {}
    rows, err := db.Query(`
        SELECT Products.Id, Products.Name, Products.Price,
                Categories.Id as Cat_Id, Categories.Name as CatName
                FROM Products, Categories
        WHERE Products.Category = Categories.Id`)
    if (err == nil) {
        for (rows.Next()) {
            p := Product{}
            scanErr := rows.Scan(&p.Id, &p.Name, &p.Price,
                &p.Category.Id, &p.Category.Name)
            if (scanErr == nil) {
                products = append(products, p)
            } else {
                Printfln("Scan error: %v", scanErr)
                break
            }
        }
    } else {
        Printfln("Error: %v", err)
    }
```

```
        return products
}

func main() {
    db, err := openDatabase()
    if (err == nil) {
        products := queryDatabase(db)
        for i, p := range products {
            Printfln("#%v: %v", i, p)
        }
        db.Close()
    } else {
        panic(err)
    }
}
```

The results from the SQL query in this example include data from the Categories table, which is scanned into a nested struct field. Compile and execute the project, and you will see the following output, which includes the data from two tables:

```
Opened database
#0: {1 Kayak {1 Watersports} 279}
#1: {2 Lifejacket {1 Watersports} 48.95}
#2: {3 Soccer Ball {2 Soccer} 19.5}
#3: {4 Corner Flags {2 Soccer} 34.95}
```

Executing Statements with Placeholders

The optional arguments to the Query method are values for placeholders in the query string, which allows a single string to be used for different queries, as shown in Listing 26-16.

Listing 26-16. Using Query Placeholders in the main.go File in the data Folder

```
package main

import "database/sql"

type Category struct {
    Id int
    Name string
}

type Product struct {
    Id int
    Name string
    Category
    Price float64
}

func queryDatabase(db *sql.DB, categoryName string) []Product {
    products := []Product {}
```

```
    rows, err := db.Query(`
        SELECT Products.Id, Products.Name, Products.Price,
                Categories.Id as Cat_Id, Categories.Name as CatName
                FROM Products, Categories
        WHERE Products.Category = Categories.Id
            AND Categories.Name = ?`, categoryName)
    if (err == nil) {
        for (rows.Next()) {
            p := Product{}
            scanErr := rows.Scan(&p.Id, &p.Name, &p.Price,
                &p.Category.Id, &p.Category.Name)
            if (scanErr == nil) {
                products = append(products, p)
            } else {
                Printfln("Scan error: %v", scanErr)
                break
            }
        }
    } else {
        Printfln("Error: %v", err)
    }
    return products
}

func main() {
    db, err := openDatabase()
    if (err == nil) {
        for _, cat := range []string { "Soccer", "Watersports"} {
            Printfln("--- %v Results ---", cat)
            products := queryDatabase(db, cat)
            for i, p := range products {
                Printfln("#%v: %v %v %v", i, p.Name, p.Category.Name, p.Price)
            }
        }
        db.Close()
    } else {
        panic(err)
    }
}
```

The SQL query string in this example contains a question mark (the ? character) that denotes a placeholder. This avoids the need to build up strings for each query and ensures that values are escaped properly. Compile and execute the project, and you will see the following output, showing how the queryDatabase function calls the Query method with different values for the placeholder:

```
Opened database
--- Soccer Results ---
#0: Soccer Ball Soccer 19.5
#1: Corner Flags Soccer 34.95
--- Watersports Results ---
#0: Kayak Watersports 279
#1: Lifejacket Watersports 48.95
```

Executing Queries for Single Rows

The QueryRow method executes a query that is expected to return a single row, which avoids the need to enumerate results, as shown in Listing 26-17.

Listing 26-17. Querying for a Single Row in the main.go File in the data Folder

```
package main

import "database/sql"

type Category struct {
    Id int
    Name string
}

type Product struct {
    Id int
    Name string
    Category
    Price float64
}

func queryDatabase(db *sql.DB, id int) (p Product) {
    row := db.QueryRow(`
        SELECT Products.Id, Products.Name, Products.Price,
                Categories.Id as Cat_Id, Categories.Name as CatName
                FROM Products, Categories
        WHERE Products.Category = Categories.Id
            AND Products.Id = ?`, id)
    if (row.Err() == nil) {
        scanErr := row.Scan(&p.Id, &p.Name, &p.Price,
                &p.Category.Id, &p.Category.Name)
        if (scanErr != nil) {
            Printfln("Scan error: %v", scanErr)
        }
    } else {
        Printfln("Row error: %v", row.Err().Error())
    }
    return
}

func main() {
    db, err := openDatabase()
    if (err == nil) {
        for _, id := range []int { 1, 3, 10 } {
            p := queryDatabase(db, id)
            Printfln("Product: %v", p)
        }
        db.Close()
    } else {
```

```
        panic(err)
    }
}
```

The QueryRow method returns a Row struct, which represents a single row result and defines the methods described in Table 26-7.

Table 26-7. *The Methods Defined by the Row Struct*

Name	Description
Scan(... targets)	This method assigns the SQL values from the current row to the specified variables. The values are assigned via pointers, and the method returns an error that indicates when the values cannot be scanned or if there are no rows in the result. If there are multiple rows in the response, all but the first row will be discarded.
Err()	This method returns an error that indicates problems executing the query.

The Row is the only result of the QueryRow method, and its Err method returns errors executing the query. The Scan method will scan only the first row of the results and will return an error if there are no rows in the results. Compile and execute the project, and you will see the following results, which includes the error produced by the Scan method when there are no rows in the results:

```
Opened database
Product: {1 Kayak {1 Watersports} 279}
Product: {3 Soccer Ball {2 Soccer} 19.5}
Scan error: sql: no rows in result set
Product: {0 {0 } 0}
```

Executing Other Queries

The Exec method is used for executing statements that don't produce rows. The result from the Exec method is a Result value, which defines the methods described in Table 26-8, and an error that indicates problems executing the statement.

Table 26-8. *The Result Methods*

Name	Description
RowsAffected()	This method returns the number of rows that were affected by the statement, expressed as an int64. This method also returns an error, which is used when there are problems parsing the response or when the database doesn't support this feature.
LastInsertId()	This method returns an int64 that represents the value generated by the database when executing the statement, which is typically an autogenerated key. This method also returns an error, which is used when the value returned by the database cannot be parsed into a Go int.

Listing 26-18 demonstrates the use of the Exec method to insert a new row into the Products table.

Listing 26-18. Inserting a Row in the main.go File in the data Folder

```go
package main

import "database/sql"

type Category struct {
    Id int
    Name string
}

type Product struct {
    Id int
    Name string
    Category
    Price float64
}

func queryDatabase(db *sql.DB, id int) (p Product) {
    row := db.QueryRow(`
        SELECT Products.Id, Products.Name, Products.Price,
                Categories.Id as Cat_Id, Categories.Name as CatName
                FROM Products, Categories
        WHERE Products.Category = Categories.Id
            AND Products.Id = ?`, id)
    if (row.Err() == nil) {
        scanErr := row.Scan(&p.Id, &p.Name, &p.Price,
                &p.Category.Id, &p.Category.Name)
        if (scanErr != nil) {
            Printfln("Scan error: %v", scanErr)
        }
    } else {
        Printfln("Row error: %v", row.Err().Error())
    }
    return
}

func insertRow(db *sql.DB, p *Product) (id int64) {
    res, err := db.Exec(`
        INSERT INTO Products (Name, Category, Price)
        VALUES (?, ?, ?)`, p.Name, p.Category.Id, p.Price)
    if (err == nil) {
        id, err = res.LastInsertId()
        if (err != nil) {
            Printfln("Result error: %v", err.Error())
        }
    } else {
        Printfln("Exec error: %v", err.Error())
    }
    return
}
```

```
func main() {
    db, err := openDatabase()
    if (err == nil) {
        newProduct := Product { Name: "Stadium", Category:
            Category{ Id: 2}, Price: 79500 }
        newID := insertRow(db, &newProduct)
        p := queryDatabase(db, int(newID))
        Printfln("New Product: %v", p)
        db.Close()
    } else {
        panic(err)
    }
}
```

The Exec method supports placeholders, and the statement in Listing 26-18 inserts a new row into the Products table using fields from a Product struct. The Result.LastInsertId method is called to get the key value assigned to the new row by the database, which is then used to query for the newly added row. Compile and execute the project, and you will see the following output:

```
Opened database
New Product: {5 Stadium {2 Soccer} 79500}
```

You will see different results if you execute the project repeatedly since each new row will be assigned a new primary key value.

Using Prepared Statements

The DB struct provides support for creating prepared statements, which can then be used to execute the prepared SQL. Table 26-9 describes the DB method for creating prepared statements.

Table 26-9. *The DB Method for Creating Prepared Statements*

Name	Description
Prepare(query)	This method creates a prepared statement for the specified query. The results are a Stmt struct and an error that indicates problems preparing the statement.

Prepared statements are represented by the Stmt struct, which defines the methods described in Table 26-10.

■ **Note** An oddity of the database/sql package is that many of the methods described in Table 26-5 also create prepared statements that are discarded after a single query.

Table 26-10. *The Methods Defined by the Stmt Struct*

Name	Description
Query(... vals)	This method executes the prepared statement, with the optional placeholder values. The results are a Rows struct and an error. This method is equivalent to the DB.Query method.
QueryRow(... vals)	This method executes the prepared statement, with the optional placeholder values. The results are a Row struct and an error. This method is equivalent to the DB.QueryRow method.
Exec(...vals)	This method executes the prepared statement, with the optional placeholder values. The results are a Result and an error. This method is equivalent to the DB.Exec method.
Close()	This method closes the statement. Statements cannot be executed after they are closed.

Listing 26-19 demonstrates the creation of prepared statements.

Listing 26-19. Using Prepared Statements in the database.go File in the data Folder

```
package main

import (
    "database/sql"
    _ "modernc.org/sqlite"
)

func listDrivers() {
    for _, driver := range sql.Drivers() {
        Printfln("Driver: %v", driver)
    }
}

var insertNewCategory *sql.Stmt
var changeProductCategory *sql.Stmt

func openDatabase() (db *sql.DB, err error) {
    db, err = sql.Open("sqlite", "products.db")
    if (err == nil) {
        Printfln("Opened database")
        insertNewCategory, _ = db.Prepare("INSERT INTO Categories (Name) VALUES (?)")
        changeProductCategory, _ =
            db.Prepare("UPDATE Products SET Category = ? WHERE Id = ?")
    }
    return
}
```

Prepared statements are created after the database has been opened and are valid only until the DB.Close method is called. Listing 26-20 uses the prepared statements to add a new category to the database and assign a product to it.

Listing 26-20. Using Prepared Statements in the main.go File in the data Folder

```
package main

import "database/sql"

type Category struct {
    Id int
    Name string
}

type Product struct {
    Id int
    Name string
    Category
    Price float64
}

func queryDatabase(db *sql.DB, id int) (p Product) {
    row := db.QueryRow(`
        SELECT Products.Id, Products.Name, Products.Price,
                Categories.Id as Cat_Id, Categories.Name as CatName
                FROM Products, Categories
        WHERE Products.Category = Categories.Id
            AND Products.Id = ?`, id)
    if (row.Err() == nil) {
        scanErr := row.Scan(&p.Id, &p.Name, &p.Price,
                &p.Category.Id, &p.Category.Name)
        if (scanErr != nil) {
            Printfln("Scan error: %v", scanErr)
        }
    } else {
        Printfln("Row error: %v", row.Err().Error())
    }
    return
}

func insertAndUseCategory(name string, productIDs ...int) {
    result, err := insertNewCategory.Exec(name)
    if (err == nil) {
        newID, _ := result.LastInsertId()
        for _, id := range productIDs {
            changeProductCategory.Exec(int(newID), id)
        }
    } else {
        Printfln("Prepared statement error: %v", err)
    }
}

func main() {
    db, err := openDatabase()
    if (err == nil) {
        insertAndUseCategory("Misc Products", 2)
```

```
        p := queryDatabase(db, 2)
        Println("Product: %v", p)
        db.Close()
    } else {
        panic(err)
    }
}
```

The insertAndUseCategory function uses the prepared statements. Compile and execute the project, and you will see the following output, which reflects the addition of a Misc Products category:

```
Opened database
Product: {2 Lifejacket {3 Misc Products} 48.95}
```

Using Transactions

Transactions allow multiple statements to be executed so that they are all applied to the database or none of them are. The DB struct defines the method described in Table 26-11 for creating a new transaction.

Table 26-11. *The DB Method for Creating a Transaction*

Name	Description
Begin()	This method starts a new transaction. The results are a pointer to a Tx value and an error that indicates problems creating the transaction.

Transactions are represented by the Tx struct, which defines the methods described in Table 26-12.

Table 26-12. *The Methods Defined by the Tx Struct*

Name	Description
Query(query, ...args)	This method is equivalent to the DB.Query method described in Table 26-5, but the query is executed within the scope of the transaction.
QueryRow(query, ...args)	This method is equivalent to the DB.QueryRow method described in Table 26-5, but the query is executed within the scope of the transaction.
Exec(query, ...args)	This method is equivalent to the DB.Exec method described in Table 26-5, but the query/statement is executed within the scope of the transaction.
Prepare(query)	This method is equivalent to the DB.Query method described in Table 26-9, but the prepared statement it creates is executed within the scope of the transaction.
Stmt(statement)	This method accepts a prepared statement created outside of the scope of the transaction and returns one that is executed within the scope of the transaction.

(continued)

Table 26-12. (*continued*)

Name	Description
Commit()	This method commits the pending changes to the database, returning an error that indicates problems applying the changes.
Rollback()	This method aborts the transactions so that the pending changes are discarded. This method returns an error that indicates problems aborting the transaction.

The insertAndUseCategory function defined in the previous section is a good—albeit simple—candidate for a transaction since there are two linked operations. Listing 26-21 introduces a transaction, which is rolled back if there are no products that match the specified IDs.

Listing 26-21. Using a Transaction in the main.go File in the data Folder

```
package main

import "database/sql"

// ...statements omitted for brevity...

func insertAndUseCategory(db *sql.DB, name string, productIDs ...int) (err error) {
    tx, err := db.Begin()
    updatedFailed := false
    if (err == nil) {
        catResult, err := tx.Stmt(insertNewCategory).Exec(name)
        if (err == nil) {
            newID, _ := catResult.LastInsertId()
            preparedStatement := tx.Stmt(changeProductCategory)
            for _, id := range productIDs {
                changeResult, err := preparedStatement.Exec(newID, id)
                if (err == nil) {
                    changes, _ := changeResult.RowsAffected()
                    if (changes == 0) {
                        updatedFailed = true
                        break
                    }
                }
            }
        }
    }
    if (err != nil || updatedFailed) {
        Printfln("Aborting transaction %v", err)
        tx.Rollback()
    } else {
        tx.Commit()
    }
    return
}

func main() {
    db, err := openDatabase()
    if (err == nil) {
```

```
        insertAndUseCategory(db, "Category_1", 2)
        p := queryDatabase(db, 2)
        Printfln("Product: %v", p)
        insertAndUseCategory(db, "Category_2", 100)
        db.Close()
    } else {
        panic(err)
    }
}
```

The first call to the insertAndUseCategory will succeed, and the changes are applied to the database. The second call to the insertAndUseCategory will fail, which means that the transaction is terminated and the category that is created by the first statement is not applied to the database. Compile and execute the project, and you will see the following output:

```
Opened database
Product: {2 Lifejacket {4 Category_1} 48.95}
Aborting transaction <nil>
```

You may see slightly different results, especially if you run this example again, because the newly created category database row will be assigned a unique ID that is included in the output.

Using Reflection to Scan Data into a Struct

Reflection is a feature that allows types and values to be inspected and used at runtime. Reflection is an advanced and complex feature and is described in detail in Chapters 27–29. I am not going to describe reflection in this chapter, but there are methods defined by the Rows struct that are useful when using reflection to process a database response, as described in Table 26-13. You may want to return to this example after reading the reflection chapters.

Table 26-13. *The Rows Methods Used with Reflection*

Name	Description
Columns()	This method returns a slice of strings containing the names of the result columns and an error, which is used when the results have been closed.
ColumnTypes()	This method returns a *ColumnType slice, which describes the data types of the result columns. This method also returns an error, which is used when the results have been closed.

```
UNDERSTANDING THE DRAWBACKS OF REFLECTION
```

Reflection is an advanced feature, which can be deduced by the three chapters it takes me to describe how it is used. This example is just to show what is possible with the information provided by the database/sql package. For simplicity, this example has fixed expectations about the way that result rows are structured.

Specifying individual fields, as demonstrated in Listing 26-14, is the simplest and most robust approach to scanning into structs. If you are determined to scan into structs dynamically, then consider one of the well-tested third-party packages available, such as SQLX (https://github.com/jmoiron/sqlx).

These methods describe the structure of the rows returned from the database. The Columns method returns a string slice containing the names of the result columns. The ColumnTypes method returns a slice of pointers to the ColumnType struct, which defines the methods described in Table 26-14.

Table 26-14. *The ColumnType Methods*

Name	Description
Name()	This method returns the name of the column as it is specified in the results, expressed as a string.
DatabaseTypeName()	This method returns the name of the column type in the database, expressed as a string.
Nullable()	This method returns two bool results. The first result is true if the database type can be null. The second result is true if the driver supports nullable values.
DecimalSize()	This method returns details about the size of decimal values. The results are an int64 that specifies precision, an int64 that specifies scale, and a bool that is true for decimal types and false for other types.
Length()	This method returns the length for database types that can have variable lengths. The results are an int64 that specifies the length and a bool that is true for types that define a length and false for other types.
ScanType()	This method returns a reflect.Type that indicates the Go type that will be used when scanning this column with the Rows.Scan method. See Chapters 27–29 for details of using the reflect package.

Listing 26-22 uses the Columns method to match column names in result data to struct fields and uses the ColumnType.ScanType method to ensure that the result types can be safely assigned to the matched struct field.

■ **Caution** As noted, this example relies on features described in later chapters. You should read Chapters 27–29 and return to this example once you understand how Go reflection works.

Listing 26-22. Scanning Structs with Reflection in the database.go File in the data Folder

```go
package main

import (
    "database/sql"
    _ "modernc.org/sqlite"
    "reflect"
    "strings"
)

func listDrivers() {
    for _, driver := range sql.Drivers() {
        Printfln("Driver: %v", driver)
    }
}

var insertNewCategory *sql.Stmt
var changeProductCategory *sql.Stmt

func openDatabase() (db *sql.DB, err error) {
    db, err = sql.Open("sqlite", "products.db")
    if (err == nil) {
        Printfln("Opened database")
        insertNewCategory, _ = db.Prepare("INSERT INTO Categories (Name) VALUES (?)")
        changeProductCategory, _ =
            db.Prepare("UPDATE Products SET Category = ? WHERE Id = ?")
    }
    return
}

func scanIntoStruct(rows *sql.Rows, target interface{}) (results interface{},
        err error) {
    targetVal := reflect.ValueOf(target)
    if (targetVal.Kind() == reflect.Ptr) {
        targetVal = targetVal.Elem()
    }
    if (targetVal.Kind() != reflect.Struct) {
        return
    }
    colNames, _ := rows.Columns()
    colTypes, _ := rows.ColumnTypes()
    references := []interface{} {}
    fieldVal := reflect.Value{}
    var placeholder interface{}

    for i, colName := range colNames {
        colNameParts := strings.Split(colName, ".")
        fieldVal = targetVal.FieldByName(colNameParts[0])
        if (fieldVal.IsValid() && fieldVal.Kind() == reflect.Struct &&
            len(colNameParts) > 1 ) {
            var namePart string
```

```
            for _, namePart = range colNameParts[1:] {
                compFunction := matchColName(namePart)
                fieldVal = fieldVal.FieldByNameFunc(compFunction)
            }
        }

        if (!fieldVal.IsValid() ||
                !colTypes[i].ScanType().ConvertibleTo(fieldVal.Type())) {
            references = append(references, &placeholder)
        } else if (fieldVal.Kind() != reflect.Ptr && fieldVal.CanAddr()) {
            fieldVal = fieldVal.Addr()
            references = append(references, fieldVal.Interface())
        }
    }

    resultSlice := reflect.MakeSlice(reflect.SliceOf(targetVal.Type()), 0, 10)
    for rows.Next() {
        err = rows.Scan(references...)
        if (err == nil) {
            resultSlice = reflect.Append(resultSlice, targetVal)
        } else {
            break
        }
    }
    results = resultSlice.Interface()
    return
}

func matchColName(colName string) func(string) bool {
    return func(fieldName string) bool {
        return strings.EqualFold(colName, fieldName)
    }
}
```

The scanIntoStruct function accepts a Rows value and a target into which values will be scanned. The Go reflection features are used to find a field in the struct with the same name, matched regardless of case. For nested struct fields, the column name must correspond to the field name separated by periods so that the Category.Name field, for example, will be scanned from a result column named category.name.

A slice of pointers is created for the Scan method to work with and the scanned struct values are added to a slice, which is used to produce the method results. If no struct field matches a results column, then a dummy value is used, since the Scan method expects a complete set of pointers for scanning data. Listing 26-23 uses the new function to scan the results of a query.

Listing 26-23. Scanning Query Results in the main.go File in the data Folder

```go
package main

import "database/sql"

type Category struct {
    Id int
    Name string
}

type Product struct {
    Id int
    Name string
    Category
    Price float64
}

func queryDatabase(db *sql.DB) (products []Product, err error) {
    rows, err := db.Query(`SELECT Products.Id, Products.Name, Products.Price,
            Categories.Id as "Category.Id", Categories.Name as "Category.Name"
            FROM Products, Categories
            WHERE Products.Category = Categories.Id`)
    if (err != nil) {
        return
    } else {
        results, err := scanIntoStruct(rows, &Product{})
        if err == nil {
            products = (results).([]Product)
        } else {
            Printfln("Scanning error: %v", err)
        }
    }
    return
}

func main() {
    db, err := openDatabase()
    if (err == nil) {
        products, _ := queryDatabase(db)
        for _, p := range products {
            Printfln("Product: %v", p)
        }
        db.Close()
    } else {
        panic(err)
    }
}
```

The database is queried, specifying column names that will be matched to the fields defined by the Product and Category structs. As I explain in Chapter 27, results produced by reflection require an assertion to narrow their type.

The effect of this example is that scanning is done dynamically based on matching result columns to struct field names and types. Compile and execute the project, and you will see the following output:

```
Opened database
Product: {1 Kayak {1 Watersports} 279}
Product: {2 Lifejacket {4 Category_1} 48.95}
Product: {3 Soccer Ball {2 Soccer} 19.5}
Product: {4 Corner Flags {2 Soccer} 34.95}
Product: {5 Stadium {2 Soccer} 79500}
```

Summary

In this chapter, I described the Go standard library support for working with SQL databases, which are simple but well-thought-out and easy to use. In the next chapter, I start the process of describing the Go reflection features, which allow types to be determined and used at runtime.

CHAPTER 27

Using Reflection

In this chapter, I describe the Go support for reflection, which allows an application to work with types that are not known when the project is compiled, which is useful for creating APIs that will be used by other projects, for example. You can see extensive use of reflection in Part 3, where I create a custom web application framework. In this situation, the code in the application framework doesn't know anything about the data types that will be defined by the applications it is used to run and has to use reflection to get information about those types and to work with values created from them.

Reflection should be used with caution. Because the data types that are being used are unknown, the usual safeguards applied by the compiler cannot be used, and it is the responsibility of the programmer to inspect and use types safely. Reflection code tends to be verbose and difficult to read, and it is easy to make faulty assumptions when writing reflection code that don't manifest as errors until it is used with real data types, which often happens once the code is in the hands of over developers. Mistakes in reflection code typically cause panics.

Code that uses reflection is slower than regular Go code, although this won't be an issue in most projects. Unless you have particularly demanding performance requirements, you will find that all Go code runs at an acceptable speed, regardless of whether it uses reflection or not. There are some Go programming tasks that can be performed only with reflection, and reflection is used throughout the standard library.

That doesn't mean you should rush to use reflection—because it is hard to use and easy to get wrong—but there are times when it cannot be avoided and, once you understand how it works, careful application of the Go reflection features can produce code that is flexible and adaptable, as you will see in Part 3. Table 27-1 puts reflection in context.

Table 27-1. *Putting Reflection in Context*

Question	Answer
What is it?	Reflection allows types and values to be inspected at runtime, even if those types were not defined at compile time.
Why is it useful?	Reflection is useful when writing code that relies on types that will be defined in the future, such as when writing an API that will be used in other projects.
How is it used?	The reflect package provides features that allow types and values to be reflected, such that they can be used without explicit knowledge of the data types in use.
Are there any pitfalls or limitations?	Reflection is complex and requires close attention to detail. It is easy to make assumptions about data types that don't present problems until the code is used in other projects.
Are there any alternatives?	Reflection is required only when types are not known when the project is compiled. The standard Go language features should be used when the types are known in advance.

© Adam Freeman 2022
A. Freeman, *Pro Go*, https://doi.org/10.1007/978-1-4842-7355-5_27

Table 27-2 summarizes the chapter.

Table 27-2. *Chapter Summary*

Problem	Solution	Listing
Obtain reflected types and values	Use the TypeOf and ValueOf functions	8
Inspect a reflected type	Use the methods defined by the Type interface	9
Inspect a reflected value	Use the methods defined by the Value struct	10
Identify a reflected type	Check its kind and, optionally, its element type	11, 12
Get an underlying type	Use the Interface method	13
Setting a reflected value	Use the Set* methods	14–16
Compare reflected values	Use the Comparable method and the Go comparison operator, or use the DeepEqual function	17–19
Convert a reflected value to a different type	Use the ConvertibleTo and Convert methods	20, 21
Create a new reflected value	Use the New type for basic types and one of the Make* methods for other types	22

Preparing for This Chapter

To prepare for this chapter, open a new command prompt, navigate to a convenient location, and create a directory named reflection. Run the command shown in Listing 27-1 in the reflection folder to create a module file.

■ **Tip** You can download the example project for this chapter—and for all the other chapters in this book—from https://github.com/apress/pro-go. See Chapter 2 for how to get help if you have problems running the examples.

Listing 27-1. Initializing the Module

```
go mod init reflection
```

Add a file named printer.go to the reflection folder with the content shown in Listing 27-2.

Listing 27-2. The Contents of the printer.go File in the reflection Folder

```go
package main

import "fmt"

func Printfln(template string, values ...interface{}) {
    fmt.Printf(template + "\n", values...)
}
```

Add a file named types.go to the reflection folder with the content shown in Listing 27-3.

Listing 27-3. The Contents of the types.go File in the reflection Folder

```go
package main

type Product struct {
    Name, Category string
    Price float64
}

type Customer struct {
    Name, City string
}
```

Add a file named main.go to the reflection folder, with the contents shown in Listing 27-4.

Listing 27-4. The Contents of the main.go File in the reflection Folder

```go
package main

func printDetails(values ...Product) {
    for _, elem := range values {
        Printfln("Product: Name: %v, Category: %v, Price: %v",
            elem.Name, elem.Category, elem.Price)
    }
}

func main() {

    product := Product {
        Name: "Kayak", Category: "Watersports", Price: 279,
    }
    printDetails(product)
}
```

Use the command prompt to run the command shown in Listing 27-5 in the usingstrings folder.

Listing 27-5. Running the Example Project

```
go run .
```

The code in the project will be compiled and executed, producing the following results:

```
Product: Name: Kayak, Category: Watersports, Price: 279
```

Understanding the Need for Reflection

The Go type system is rigorously enforced, which means you can't use a value of one type when a different type is inspected. Listing 27-6 creates a Customer value and passes it to the printDetails function, which defines a variadic Product parameter.

Listing 27-6. Mixing Types in the main.go File in the reflection Folder

```
package main

func printDetails(values ...Product) {
    for _, elem := range values {
        Printfln("Product: Name: %v, Category: %v, Price: %v",
            elem.Name, elem.Category, elem.Price)
    }
}

func main() {

    product := Product {
        Name: "Kayak", Category: "Watersports", Price: 279,
    }
    customer := Customer { Name: "Alice", City: "New York" }
    printDetails(product, customer)
}
```

This code won't compile because it violates Go's type rules. You will see the following error when you compile the project:

```
.\main.go:16:17: cannot use customer (type Customer) as type Product in argument to
printDetails
```

In Chapter 11, I introduced interfaces, which allow common characteristics to be defined through methods, which can be invoked regardless of the type that implements the interface. Chapter 11 also introduced the empty interface, which can be used to accept any type, as shown in Listing 27-7.

Listing 27-7. Using the Empty Interface in the main.go File in the reflection Folder

```
package main

func printDetails(values ...interface{}) {
    for _, elem := range values {
        switch val := elem.(type) {
            case Product:
                Printfln("Product: Name: %v, Category: %v, Price: %v",
                    val.Name, val.Category, val.Price)
            case Customer:
                Printfln("Customer: Name: %v, City: %v", val.Name, val.City)
        }

    }
}

func main() {

    product := Product {
        Name: "Kayak", Category: "Watersports", Price: 279,
    }
    customer := Customer { Name: "Alice", City: "New York" }
    printDetails(product, customer)
}
```

The empty interface allows the printDetails function to receive any type but doesn't allow access to specific features because the interface defines no methods. A type assertion is required to narrow the empty interface to a specific type, which then allows each value to be processed. Compile and execute the code, and you will receive the following output:

```
Product: Name: Kayak, Category: Watersports, Price: 279
Customer: Name: Alice, City: New York
```

The limitation of this approach is that the printDetails function can only process types that are known in advance. Each time I add a type to the project, I have to extend the printDetails function to handle that type.

Many projects will deal with a small enough set of types that this won't be an issue or will be able to define interfaces with methods that provides access to common functionality. Reflection solves this issue for those projects for which this isn't the case, either because there are a large number of types to deal with or because interfaces and methods can't be written.

Using Reflection

The reflect package provides the Go reflection features, and the key functions are called TypeOf and ValueOf, both of which are described in Table 27-3 for quick reference.

727

Table 27-3. *The Key Reflection Functions*

Name	Description
TypeOf(val)	This function returns a value that implements the Type interface, which describes the type of the specified value.
ValueOf(val)	This function returns a Value struct, which allows the specified value to be inspected and manipulated.

There is a lot of detail behind the TypeOf and ValueOf functions and their results, and it is easy to lose sight of why reflection can be useful. Before getting into the detail, Listing 27-8 revises the printDetails function to use the reflect package so that it can handle any type, showing the basic pattern required to apply reflection.

Listing 27-8. Using Reflection in the main.go File in the reflection Folder

```
package main

import (
    "reflect"
    "strings"
    "fmt"
)

func printDetails(values ...interface{}) {
    for _, elem := range values {
        fieldDetails := []string {}
        elemType := reflect.TypeOf(elem)
        elemValue := reflect.ValueOf(elem)
        if elemType.Kind() == reflect.Struct {
            for i := 0; i < elemType.NumField(); i++ {
                fieldName := elemType.Field(i).Name
                fieldVal := elemValue.Field(i)
                fieldDetails = append(fieldDetails,
                    fmt.Sprintf("%v: %v", fieldName, fieldVal ))
            }
            Printfln("%v: %v", elemType.Name(), strings.Join(fieldDetails, ", "))
        } else {
            Printfln("%v: %v", elemType.Name(), elemValue)
        }
    }
}

type Payment struct {
    Currency string
    Amount float64
}
```

```
func main() {

    product := Product {
        Name: "Kayak", Category: "Watersports", Price: 279,
    }
    customer := Customer { Name: "Alice", City: "New York" }
    payment := Payment { Currency: "USD", Amount: 100.50 }
    printDetails(product, customer, payment, 10, true)
}
```

Code that uses reflection can be verbose, but the basic pattern becomes easy to follow once you become familiar with the basics. The key point to remember is that there are two aspects of reflection that work together: the reflected type and the reflected value.

The *reflected type* gives you access to details of a Go type without knowing in advance what it is. You can explore the reflected type, exploring its details and characteristics through the methods defined by the Type interface.

The *reflected value* lets you work with the specific value with which you have been provided. You can't just read a struct field or call a method, for example, as you would in normal code when you don't know what type you are dealing with.

The use of the reflected type and reflected value leads to the code verbosity. If you know you are dealing with a Product struct, for example, you can just read the Name field and get a string result. If you don't know what type is being used, then you must use the reflected type to establish whether you are dealing with a struct and whether it has a Name field. Once you have determined there is such as field, you use the reflected value to read that field and get its value.

Reflection can be confusing, so I am going to walk through the statements in Listing 27-8 and briefly describe the effect each of them has, which will provide some context for the detailed description of the reflect package that follows.

The printDetails function defines a variadic parameter using the empty interface, which is enumerated using the range keyword:

```
...
func printDetails(values ...interface{}) {
    for _, elem := range values {
...
```

As noted, the empty interface allows a function to accept any data type but doesn't allow access to any specific type features. The reflect package is used to get the reflected type and reflected value of each received value:

```
...
elemType := reflect.TypeOf(elem)
elemValue := reflect.ValueOf(elem)
...
```

The TypeOf function returns the reflected type, which is described by the Type interface. The ValueOf function returns the reflected value, which is represented by the Value interface.

The next step is to determine what kind of type is being processed, which is done by calling the Type.Kind method:

```
...
if elemType.Kind() == reflect.Struct {
...
```

The reflect package defines constants that identify the different kinds of type in Go, which I describe in Table 27-5. In this statement, an if statement is used to determine if the reflected type is a struct. If it is a struct, then a for loop is used with the NumField method, which returns the number of fields the struct defines:

```
...
for i := 0; i < elemType.NumField(); i++ {
...
```

Within the for loop, the name and value of the field are obtained:

```
...
fieldName := elemType.Field(i).Name
fieldVal := elemValue.Field(i)
...
```

Calling the Field method on a reflected type returns a StructField, which describes a single field, including a Name field. Calling the Field method on the reflected value returns a Value struct, which represents the value of the field.

The name and value of the field are added to a slice of strings, which forms part of the output. The fmt package is used to create a string representation of the field value:

```
...
fieldDetails = append(fieldDetails, fmt.Sprintf("%v: %v", fieldName, fieldVal ))
...
```

Once all of the struct fields are processed, a string is written out containing the name of the reflected type, which is obtained using the Name method, and the details are obtained for each field:

```
...
Printfln("%v: %v", elemType.Name(), strings.Join(fieldDetails, ", "))
...
```

If the reflected type is not a struct, then a simpler message is written out, containing the reflected type name and the value, whose formatting is handled by the fmt package:

```
...
Printfln("%v: %v", elemType.Name(), elemValue)
...
```

The new code allows the printDetails function to receive any data type, including the newly defined Payment struct, and built-in types such as int and bool values. Compile and execute the project, and you will see the following output:

```
Product: Name: Kayak, Category: Watersports, Price: 279
Customer: Name: Alice, City: New York
Payment: Currency: USD, Amount: 100.5
int: 10
bool: true
```

Using the Basic Type Features

The Type interface provides basic details about a type through the methods described in Table 27-4. There are specialized methods for working with specific kinds of types, such as arrays, which are described in later sections, but these are the methods that provide the essential details for all types.

Table 27-4. Basic Methods Defined by the Type Interface

Name	Description
Name()	This method returns the name of the type.
PkgPath()	This method returns the package path for the type. The empty string is returned for built-in types, such as int and bool.
Kind()	This method returns the kind of type, using a value that matches one of the constant values defined by the reflect package, as described in Table 27-5.
String()	This method returns a string representation of the type name, including the package name.
Comparable()	This method returns true if values of this type can be compared using the standard comparison operator, as described in the "Comparing Values" section.
AssignableTo(type)	This method returns true if values of this type can be assigned to variables or fields of the specified reflected type.

The reflect package defines a type named Kind, which is an alias for uint, and which is used for a series of constants that describe different kinds of type, as described in Table 27-5.

Table 27-5. *The Kind Constants*

Name	Description
Bool	This value denotes a bool.
Int, Int8, Int16, Int32, Int64	These values denote the different sizes of integer types.
Uint, Uint8, Uint16, Uint32, Uint64	These values denote the different sizes of unsigned integer types.
Float32, Float64	These values denote the different sizes of floating-point types.
String	This value denotes a string.
Struct	This value denotes a struct.
Array	This value denotes an array.
Slice	This value denotes a slice.
Map	This value denotes a map.
Chan	This value denotes a channel.
Func	This value defines a function.
Interface	This value denotes an interface.
Ptr	This value denotes a pointer
Uintptr	This value denotes an unsafe pointer, which is not described in this book.

Listing 27-9 simplifies the example to display the details from the reflected type of each of the values received by the printDetails function.

Listing 27-9. Printing Type Details in the main.go File in the reflection Folder

```
package main

import (
    "reflect"
    // "strings"
    // "fmt"
)

func getTypePath(t reflect.Type) (path string) {
    path = t.PkgPath()
    if (path == "") {
        path = "(built-in)"
    }
    return
}

func printDetails(values ...interface{}) {
    for _, elem := range values {
```

```
        elemType := reflect.TypeOf(elem)
        Println("Name: %v, PkgPath: %v, Kind: %v",
            elemType.Name(), getTypePath(elemType), elemType.Kind())
    }
}

type Payment struct {
    Currency string
    Amount float64
}

func main() {

    product := Product {
        Name: "Kayak", Category: "Watersports", Price: 279,
    }
    customer := Customer { Name: "Alice", City: "New York" }
    payment := Payment { Currency: "USD", Amount: 100.50 }
    printDetails(product, customer, payment, 10, true)
}
```

I have added a function that replaces empty package names so that built-in types are more obviously described. Compile and execute the project, and you will see the following output:

```
Name: Product, PkgPath: main, Kind: struct
Name: Customer, PkgPath: main, Kind: struct
Name: Payment, PkgPath: main, Kind: struct
Name: int, PkgPath: (built-in), Kind: int
Name: bool, PkgPath: (built-in), Kind: bool
```

Many of the reflection features that are specific to a single kind of type, such as arrays, for example, will cause a panic if they are called on other types, which makes the Kind method especially important when using reflection.

Using the Basic Value Features

For each group of reflected type features, there are corresponding features for reflected values. The Value struct defines the methods described in Table 27-6, which provide access to basic reflection features, including accessing the underlying value.

Table 27-6. *Basic Methods Defined by the Value Struct*

Name	Description
Kind()	This method returns the kind of the value's type, using one of the values from Table 27-5.
Type()	This method returns the Type for the Value.
IsNil()	This method returns true if the value is nil. This method will panic if the underlying value isn't a function, an interface, a pointer, a slice, or a channel.
IsZero()	This method returns true if the underlying value is the zero value for its type.
Bool()	This method returns the underlying bool value. The method panics if the underlying value's Kind is not Bool.
Bytes()	This method returns the underlying [ ]byte value. The method panics if the underlying value is not a byte slice. I demonstrate how to determine the type of a slice in the "Identifying Byte Slices" section.
Int()	This method returns the underlying value as an int64. The method panics if the underlying value's Kind is not Int, Int8, Int16, Int32, or Int64.
Uint()	This method returns the underlying value as an uint64. The method panics if the underlying value's Kind is not Uint, Uint8, Uint16, Uint32, or Uint64.
Float()	This method returns the underlying value as an float64. The method panics if the underlying value's Kind is not Float32, or Float64.
String()	This method returns the underlying value as a string if the value's Kind is String. For other Kind values, this method returns the string <T Value> where T is the underlying type, such as <int Value>.
Elem()	This method returns the Value to which a pointer refers. This method can also be used with interfaces, as described in Chapter 29. This method panics if the underlying value's Kind is not Ptr.
IsValid()	This method returns false if the Value is the zero value, created as Value{} rather than obtained using ValueOf, for example. This method doesn't relate to reflected values that are the zero value of their reflected type. If this method returns false, then all other Value methods will panic.

When using the methods that return the underlying value, it is important to check the Kind result to avoid panics. Listing 27-10 demonstrates some of the methods described in the table.

Listing 27-10. Using the Basic Value Methods in the main.go File in the reflection Folder

```
package main

import (
    "reflect"
    // "strings"
    // "fmt"
)
```

```
func printDetails(values ...interface{}) {
    for _, elem := range values {
        elemValue := reflect.ValueOf(elem)
        switch elemValue.Kind() {
            case reflect.Bool:
                var val bool = elemValue.Bool()
                Printfln("Bool: %v", val)
            case reflect.Int:
                var val int64 = elemValue.Int()
                Printfln("Int: %v", val)
            case reflect.Float32, reflect.Float64:
                var val float64 = elemValue.Float()
                Printfln("Float: %v", val)
            case reflect.String:
                var val string = elemValue.String()
                Printfln("String: %v", val)
            case reflect.Ptr:
                var val reflect.Value = elemValue.Elem()
                if (val.Kind() == reflect.Int) {
                    Printfln("Pointer to Int: %v", val.Int())
                }
            default:
                Printfln("Other: %v", elemValue.String())
        }
    }
}

func main() {

    product := Product {
        Name: "Kayak", Category: "Watersports", Price: 279,
    }
    number := 100
    printDetails(true, 10, 23.30, "Alice", &number, product)
}
```

This example uses a switch statement with the result from the Kind method to determine the type of the value and calls the appropriate method to get the underlying value. Compile and execute the project, and you will see the following output:

```
Bool: true
Int: 10
Float: 23.3
String: Alice
Pointer to Int: 100
Other: <main.Product Value>
```

The String method behaves differently from the other methods and doesn't panic when called on a value that isn't a string. Instead, the method returns a string like this:

```
...
Other: <main.Product Value>
...
```

This isn't the typical use of the String method that is seen elsewhere in the Go standard library, where this method typically returns a string representation of a value. When using reflection, you can either use the techniques described in later sections or rely on the format package, which uses those same techniques, to create string representations of values for you.

Identifying Types

Notice that two steps are required when dealing with pointers in Listing 27-10. The first step uses the Kind method to identify the Ptr value, and the second step uses the Elem method to get the Value that represents the data the pointer refers to:

```
...
case reflect.Ptr:
    var val reflect.Value = elemValue.Elem()
    if (val.Kind() == reflect.Int) {
        Printfln("Pointer to Int: %v", val.Int())
    }
}
...
```

The first step tells me that I am dealing with a pointer, and the second step tells me that it is pointing to an int value. This process can be simplified by performing a comparison of the reflected types. If two values have the same Go data type, then the comparison operator will return true when applied to the results from the reflect.TypeOf function, as shown in Listing 27-11.

Listing 27-11. Comparing Types in the main.go File in the reflection Folder

```
package main

import (
    "reflect"
    // "strings"
    // "fmt"
)

var intPtrType = reflect.TypeOf((*int)(nil))

func printDetails(values ...interface{}) {
    for _, elem := range values {
        elemValue := reflect.ValueOf(elem)
        elemType := reflect.TypeOf(elem)
        if (elemType == intPtrType) {
            Printfln("Pointer to Int: %v", elemValue.Elem().Int())
        } else {
```

```
        switch elemValue.Kind() {
            case reflect.Bool:
                var val bool = elemValue.Bool()
                Printfln("Bool: %v", val)
            case reflect.Int:
                var val int64 = elemValue.Int()
                Printfln("Int: %v", val)
            case reflect.Float32, reflect.Float64:
                var val float64 = elemValue.Float()
                Printfln("Float: %v", val)
            case reflect.String:
                var val string = elemValue.String()
                Printfln("String: %v", val)
            // case reflect.Ptr:
            //     var val reflect.Value = elemValue.Elem()
            //     if (val.Kind() == reflect.Int) {
            //         Printfln("Pointer to Int: %v", val.Int())
            //     }
            default:
                Printfln("Other: %v", elemValue.String())
        }
    }
  }
 }
}

func main() {

    product := Product {
        Name: "Kayak", Category: "Watersports", Price: 279,
    }
    number := 100
    printDetails(true, 10, 23.30, "Alice", &number, product)
}
```

This technique starts with a nil value and converts it to a pointer to an int value, which is then passed to the TypeOf function to get a Type that can be used in comparisons:

```
...
var intPtrType = reflect.TypeOf((*int)(nil))
...
```

The parentheses required to perform this operation makes it difficult to read, but this approach avoids the need to define a variable just to get its Type. The Type can be used with the normal Go comparison operator:

```
...
if (elemType == intPtrType) {
    Printfln("Pointer to Int: %v", elemValue.Elem().Int())
} else {
...
```

Comparing types like this can be simpler than checking the Kind value of both the pointer type and the value it points to. Compile and execute the code, and you will see the following output:

```
Bool: true
Int: 10
Float: 23.3
String: Alice
Pointer to Int: 100
Other: <main.Product Value>
```

Identifying Byte Slices

Using the comparison operator is also a good way of using the Bytes method safety. The Bytes method will panic if it is called on any type other than a slice of bytes, but the Kind method only indicates slices and not their contents. Listing 27-12 defines a type variable for byte slices and uses it with the comparison operator to determine when it is safe to call the Bytes method.

Listing 27-12. Identifying Byte Slices in the main.go File in the reflection Folder

```go
package main

import (
    "reflect"
    // "strings"
    // "fmt"
)

var intPtrType = reflect.TypeOf((*int)(nil))
var byteSliceType = reflect.TypeOf([]byte(nil))

func printDetails(values ...interface{}) {
    for _, elem := range values {
        elemValue := reflect.ValueOf(elem)
        elemType := reflect.TypeOf(elem)
        if (elemType == intPtrType) {
            Printfln("Pointer to Int: %v", elemValue.Elem().Int())
        } else if (elemType == byteSliceType) {
            Printfln("Byte slice: %v", elemValue.Bytes())
        } else {
            switch elemValue.Kind() {
                case reflect.Bool:
                    var val bool = elemValue.Bool()
                    Printfln("Bool: %v", val)
                case reflect.Int:
                    var val int64 = elemValue.Int()
                    Printfln("Int: %v", val)
                case reflect.Float32, reflect.Float64:
                    var val float64 = elemValue.Float()
                    Printfln("Float: %v", val)
```

```
                case reflect.String:
                    var val string = elemValue.String()
                    Printfln("String: %v", val)
                default:
                    Printfln("Other: %v", elemValue.String())
            }
        }
    }
}

func main() {

    product := Product {
        Name: "Kayak", Category: "Watersports", Price: 279,
    }
    number := 100
    slice := []byte("Alice")
    printDetails(true, 10, 23.30, "Alice", &number, product, slice)
}
```

Compile and execute the project, and you will see the following output, which includes the detection of the byte slice:

```
Bool: true
Int: 10
Float: 23.3
String: Alice
Pointer to Int: 100
Other: <main.Product Value>
Byte slice: [65 108 105 99 101]
```

Obtaining Underlying Values

The Value struct defines the methods described in Table 27-7 for obtaining an underlying value.

Table 27-7. *The Value Method for Obtaining an Underlying Value*

Name	Description
Interface()	This method returns the underlying value using the empty interface. This method will panic if it is used on unexported struct fields.
CanInterface()	This method returns true if the Interface method can be used without panicking.

The Interface method allows you to break out of reflection, obtaining a value that can be used by normal Go code, as shown in Listing 27-13.

Listing 27-13. Obtaining an Underlying Value in the main.go File in the reflection Folder

```
package main

import (
    "reflect"
    // "strings"
    // "fmt"
)

func selectValue(data interface{}, index int) (result interface{}) {
    dataVal := reflect.ValueOf(data)
    if (dataVal.Kind() == reflect.Slice) {
        result = dataVal.Index(index).Interface()
    }
    return
}

func main() {

    names := []string {"Alice", "Bob", "Charlie"}
    val := selectValue(names, 1).(string)
    Printfln("Selected: %v", val)
}
```

The selectValue function selects a value from a slice without knowing the slice's element type. The value is retrieved from the slice using the Index method, which is described in Chapter 28. For this chapter, what's important is that the Index method returns a Value, which is only useful for code that uses reflection. The Interface method is used to get a value that can be used as the function result:

```
...
result = dataVal.Index(index).Interface()
...
```

One drawback of using reflection is the way that function and method results have to be handled. If the type of the result isn't fixed, then the caller of the function or method has to take responsibility for converting the result into a specific type, which is what this statement does in Listing 27-13:

```
...
val := selectValue(names, 1).(string)
...
```

The result from the selectValue function will have the same type as the slice elements, but there is no way to express this in Go, which is why the function uses the empty interface as the result and also why the Interface method returns the empty interface.

The problem this creates is that the calling code requires insight into how the function works to process the result. When the behavior of the function changes, this change must be reflected in all of the code that calls the function, which requires a level of diligence that is often hard to maintain.

This isn't ideal—and it is one reason why reflection should be used with caution. Compile and execute the project, and you will see the following output:

```
Selected: Bob
```

Setting a Value Using Reflection

The Value struct defines methods that allow values to be set using reflection, as described in Table 27-8.

Table 27-8. *The Value Methods for Setting Values*

Name	Description
CanSet()	This method returns true if the value can be set and false otherwise.
SetBool(val)	This method sets the underlying value to the specified bool.
SetBytes(slice)	This method sets the underlying value to the specified byte slice.
SetFloat(val)	This method sets the underlying value to the specified float64.
SetInt(val)	This method sets the underlying value to the specified int64.
SetUint(val)	This method sets the underlying value to the specified uint64.
SetString(val)	This method sets the underlying value to the specified string.
Set(val)	This method sets the underlying value to the underlying value of the specified Value.

The Set methods in Table 27-8 will panic if the result from the CanSet method is false or if they are used to set a value that is not of the expected type. Listing 27-14 demonstrates the problem that the CanSet method addresses.

Listing 27-14. Creating Unsettable Values in the main.go File in the reflection Folder

```go
package main

import (
    "reflect"
    "strings"
    // "fmt"
)

func incrementOrUpper(values ...interface{}) {
    for _, elem := range values {
        elemValue := reflect.ValueOf(elem)
        if (elemValue.CanSet()) {
            switch (elemValue.Kind()) {
                case reflect.Int:
                    elemValue.SetInt(elemValue.Int() + 1)
                case reflect.String:
                    elemValue.SetString(strings.ToUpper( elemValue.String()))
            }
```

```
            Printfln("Modified Value: %v", elemValue)
        } else {
            Printfln("Cannot set %v: %v", elemValue.Kind(), elemValue)
        }
    }
}

func main() {

    name := "Alice"
    price := 279
    city := "London"

    incrementOrUpper(name, price, city)
    for _, val := range []interface{} { name, price, city } {
        Printfln("Value: %v", val)
    }
}
```

The incrementOrUpper function increments int values and converts string values to upper case. Compile and execute the code, and you will receive the following output, showing that none of the values received by the incrementOrUpper function can be set:

```
Cannot set string: Alice
Cannot set int: 279
Cannot set string: London
Value: Alice
Value: 279
Value: London
```

The CanSet method causes confusion, but remember that values are copied when used as arguments to functions and methods. When the values are passed to the incrementOrUpper, they are copied:

```
...
incrementOrUpper(name, price, city)
...
```

This prevents the values from being altered because the values are copied for use within the function. Listing 27-15 solves the issue by using pointers.

Listing 27-15. Setting Values in the main.go File in the reflection Folder

```
package main

import (
    "reflect"
    "strings"
    // "fmt"
)
```

```
func incrementOrUpper(values ...interface{}) {
    for _, elem := range values {
        elemValue := reflect.ValueOf(elem)
        if (elemValue.Kind() == reflect.Ptr) {
            elemValue = elemValue.Elem()
        }
        if (elemValue.CanSet()) {
            switch (elemValue.Kind()) {
                case reflect.Int:
                    elemValue.SetInt(elemValue.Int() + 1)
                case reflect.String:
                    elemValue.SetString(strings.ToUpper( elemValue.String()))
            }
            Printfln("Modified Value: %v", elemValue)
        } else {
            Printfln("Cannot set %v: %v", elemValue.Kind(), elemValue)
        }
    }
}

func main() {

    name := "Alice"
    price := 279
    city := "London"

    incrementOrUpper(&name, &price, &city)
    for _, val := range []interface{} { name, price, city }  {
        Printfln("Value: %v", val)
    }
}
```

So, just like regular code, reflection can alter a value only if the original storage can be accessed. In Listing 27-15, pointers are used to invoke the incrementOrUpper function, and this requires a change to the reflection code to detect pointers and, when one is found, use the Elem method to follow the pointer to its value. Compile and execute the project, and you will see the following output:

```
Modified Value: ALICE
Modified Value: 280
Modified Value: LONDON
Value: ALICE
Value: 280
Value: LONDON
```

Setting One Value Using Another

The Set method allows one Value to be set using another, which can be a convenient way of modifying a value with one that has been received by reflection, as shown in Listing 27-16.

Listing 27-16. Setting One Value with Another in the main.go File in the reflection Folder

```go
package main

import (
    "reflect"
    //"strings"
    // "fmt"
)

func setAll(src interface{}, targets ...interface{}) {
    srcVal := reflect.ValueOf(src)
    for _, target := range  targets {
        targetVal := reflect.ValueOf(target)
        if (targetVal.Kind() == reflect.Ptr &&
                targetVal.Elem().Type() == srcVal.Type() &&
                targetVal.Elem().CanSet()) {
            targetVal.Elem().Set(srcVal)
        }
    }
}

func main() {

    name := "Alice"
    price := 279
    city := "London"

    setAll("New String", &name, &price, &city)
    setAll(10, &name, &price, &city)
    for _, val := range []interface{} { name, price, city }  {
        Printfln("Value: %v", val)
    }
}
```

The setAll function uses a for loop to process its variadic parameter and looks for values that are pointers to values with the same type as the src parameter. When a matching pointer is found, the value it refers to is changed with the Set method. Most of the code in the setAll function is responsible for checking that the values are compatible and can be set, but the result is that using a string as the first argument sets all the subsequent string arguments and using an int sets all of the subsequent int values. Compile and execute the code, and you will receive the following output:

```
Value: New String
Value: 10
Value: New String
```

Comparing Values

Not all data types can be compared using the Go comparison operator, which makes it easy to trigger a panic in reflection code, as shown in Listing 27-17.

Listing 27-17. Comparing Value in the main.go File in the reflection Folder

```go
package main

import (
    "reflect"
    //"strings"
    // "fmt"
)

func contains(slice interface{}, target interface{}) (found bool) {
    sliceVal := reflect.ValueOf(slice)
    if (sliceVal.Kind() == reflect.Slice) {
        for i := 0; i < sliceVal.Len(); i++ {
            if sliceVal.Index(i).Interface() == target {
                found = true
            }
        }
    }
    return
}

func main() {

    // name := "Alice"
    // price := 279
    city := "London"

    citiesSlice := []string { "Paris", "Rome", "London"}
    Printfln("Found #1: %v", contains(citiesSlice, city))

    sliceOfSlices := [][]string {
        citiesSlice,  { "First", "Second", "Third"}}
    Printfln("Found #2: %v", contains(sliceOfSlices, citiesSlice))
}
```

The contains function accepts a slice and returns true if it contains a specified value. The slice is enumerated using the Len and Index methods, which are described in Chapter 28, but the statement that is important for this section is this one:

```go
...
if sliceVal.Index(i).Interface() == target {
...
```

This statement applies the comparison operator to the value at a specific index in the slice and the target value. But, since the contains function accepts any types, the application will panic if the function receives types that cannot be compared. Compile and execute the project, and you will see the following output:

```
Found #1: true
panic: runtime error: comparing uncomparable type []string
goroutine 1 [running]:
main.contains(0x243640, 0xc000114078, 0x243f00, 0xc000153f60, 0xc000153f40)
        C:/reflection/main.go:13 +0x1a5
main.main()
        C:/reflection/main.go:33 +0x2e5
exit status 2
```

The main function makes two calls to the contains function in Listing 27-17. The first call works because the slice contains string values, which can be used with the comparison operator. The second call fails, because the slice contains other slices, to which the comparison operator cannot be applied. To help avoid this issue, the Type interface defines the method described in Table 27-9.

Table 27-9. *The Type Method for Determining Whether Types Can Be Compared*

Name	Description
Comparable()	This method returns true if the reflected type can be used with the Go comparison operator and false otherwise.

Listing 27-18 shows the use of the Comparable method to avoid performing comparisons that would cause a panic.

Listing 27-18. Safely Comparing Values in the main.go File in the reflection Folder

```
...
func contains(slice interface{}, target interface{}) (found bool) {
    sliceVal := reflect.ValueOf(slice)
    targetType := reflect.TypeOf(target)
    if (sliceVal.Kind() == reflect.Slice &&
            sliceVal.Type().Elem().Comparable() &&
            targetType.Comparable()) {
        for i := 0; i < sliceVal.Len(); i++ {
            if sliceVal.Index(i).Interface() == target {
                found = true
            }
        }
    }
    return
}
...
```

These changes ensure that the comparison operator is applied only to values whose types are comparable. Compile and execute the project, and you will see the following output:

```
Found #1: true
Found #2: false
```

Using the Comparison Convenience Function

The reflect package defines a function that provides an alternative to the standard Go comparison operator, as described in Table 27-10.

Table 27-10. *The reflect Package Function for Comparing Values*

Name	Description
DeepEqual(val, val)	This function compares any two values and returns true if they are the same.

The DeepEqual function doesn't panic and perform additional comparisons that are not possible with the == operator. All the comparison rules for this function are listed at https://pkg.go.dev/reflect@go1.17.1#DeepEqual, but in general, the DeepEqual function performs a comparison by recursively inspecting all of a value's fields or elements. One of the most useful aspects of this type of comparison is that slices are equal if all of their values are equal, which addresses one of the most commonly encountered limitations of the standard comparison operator, as shown in Listing 27-19.

Listing 27-19. Performing a Comparison in the main.go File in the reflection Folder

```go
package main

import (
    "reflect"
    //"strings"
    // "fmt"
)

func contains(slice interface{}, target interface{}) (found bool) {
    sliceVal := reflect.ValueOf(slice)
    if (sliceVal.Kind() == reflect.Slice) {
        for i := 0; i < sliceVal.Len(); i++ {
            if reflect.DeepEqual(sliceVal.Index(i).Interface(), target) {
                found = true
            }
        }
    }
    return
}
```

```
func main() {

    // name := "Alice"
    // price := 279
    city := "London"

    citiesSlice := []string { "Paris", "Rome", "London"}
    Printfln("Found #1: %v", contains(citiesSlice, city))

    sliceOfSlices := [][]string {
        citiesSlice,  { "First", "Second", "Third"}}

    Printfln("Found #2: %v", contains(sliceOfSlices, citiesSlice))
}
```

This simplification of the contains function doesn't have to check to see if types are comparable and produces the following output when the project is compiled and executed:

```
Found #1: true
Found #2: true
```

This example can compare slices so that both calls to the contains function produce true results.

Converting Values

As explained in Part 3, Go provides support type conversions, allowing values that are defined as one type to be represented using a different type. The Type interface defines the method described in Table 27-11 for determining whether a reflected type can be converted.

Table 27-11. *The Type Method for Assessing Type Conversion*

Name	Description
ConvertibleTo(type)	This method returns true if the Type on which the method is called can be converted to the specified Type.

The method defined by the Type interface allows types to be checked for convertibility. Table 27-12 describes the method defined by the Value struct that performs the conversion.

Table 27-12. *The Value Method for Converting Types*

Name	Description
Convert(type)	This method performs a type conversion and returns a Value with the new type and the original value.

Listing 27-20 demonstrates a simple type conversion performed using reflection.

Listing 27-20. Performing a Type Conversion in the main.go File in the reflection Folder

```go
package main

import (
    "reflect"
    //"strings"
    // "fmt"
)

func convert(src, target interface{}) (result interface{}, assigned bool) {
    srcVal := reflect.ValueOf(src)
    targetVal := reflect.ValueOf(target)
    if (srcVal.Type().ConvertibleTo(targetVal.Type())) {
        result = srcVal.Convert(targetVal.Type()).Interface()
        assigned = true
    } else {
        result = src
    }
    return
}

func main() {

    name := "Alice"
    price := 279
    //city := "London"

    newVal, ok := convert(price, 100.00)
    Printfln("Converted %v: %v, %T", ok, newVal, newVal)
    newVal, ok = convert(name, 100.00)
    Printfln("Converted %v: %v, %T", ok, newVal, newVal)
}
```

The convert function attempts to convert one value to the type of another value, which it does using the ConvertibleTo and Convert methods. The first call to the convert function attempts to convert an int value to a float64, which succeeds, and the second call attempts to convert a string to a float64, which fails. Compile and execute the project, and you will see the following output:

```
Converted true: 279, float64
Converted false: Alice, string
```

Converting Numeric Types

The Value struct defines the methods shown in Table 27-13 for checking whether a value will cause an overflow when expressed in the target type. These methods are useful when converting from one numeric type to another.

Table 27-13. *The Value Methods for Checking Overflows*

Name	Description
OverflowFloat(val)	This method returns true if the specified float64 value would cause an overflow if converted to the type of the Value on which the method is called. This method will panic unless the Value.Kind method returns Float32 or Float64.
OverflowInt(val)	This method returns true if the specified int64 value would cause an overflow if converted to the type of the Value on which the method is called. This method will panic unless the Value.Kind method returns one of the signed integer kinds.
OverflowUint(val)	This method returns true if the specified uint64 value would cause an overflow if converted to the type of the Value on which the method is called. This method will panic unless the Value.Kind method returns one of the unsigned integer kinds.

As explained in Chapter 5, Go numeric values wrap when they overflow. The methods described in Table 27-13 can be used to determine when a conversion would cause an overflow, as shown in Listing 27-21, which may produce an unexpected result.

Listing 27-21. Preventing Overflows in the main.go File in the reflection Folder

```go
package main

import (
    "reflect"
    //"strings"
    // "fmt"
)

func IsInt(v reflect.Value) bool {
    switch v.Kind() {
        case reflect.Int, reflect.Int8, reflect.Int16, reflect.Int32, reflect.Int64:
            return true
    }
    return false
}

func IsFloat(v reflect.Value) bool {
    switch v.Kind() {
    case reflect.Float32, reflect.Float64:
        return true
    }
    return false
}

func convert(src, target interface{}) (result interface{}, assigned bool) {
    srcVal := reflect.ValueOf(src)
    targetVal := reflect.ValueOf(target)
    if (srcVal.Type().ConvertibleTo(targetVal.Type())) {
        if (IsInt(targetVal) && IsInt(srcVal)) &&
                targetVal.OverflowInt(srcVal.Int()) {
```

```
            Printfln("Int overflow")
            return src, false
        } else if (IsFloat(targetVal) && IsFloat(srcVal) &&
                targetVal.OverflowFloat(srcVal.Float())) {
            Printfln("Float overflow")
            return src, false
        }
        result = srcVal.Convert(targetVal.Type()).Interface()
        assigned = true
    } else {
        result = src
    }
    return
}

func main() {

    name := "Alice"
    price := 279
    //city := "London"

    newVal, ok := convert(price, 100.00)
    Printfln("Converted %v: %v, %T", ok, newVal, newVal)
    newVal, ok = convert(name, 100.00)
    Printfln("Converted %v: %v, %T", ok, newVal, newVal)

    newVal, ok = convert(5000, int8(100))
    Printfln("Converted %v: %v, %T", ok, newVal, newVal)
}
```

The new code in Listing 27-21 adds protection against overflows when converting from one integer type to another and from one floating-point value to another. Compile and execute the project, and you will see the following output:

```
Converted true: 279, float64
Converted false: Alice, string
Int overflow
Converted false: 5000, int
```

The final call to the convert function in Listing 27-21 attempts to convert the value 5000 to an int8, which would cause an overflow. The OverflowInt method returns true and so the conversion is not performed.

Creating New Values

The reflect package defines functions for creating new values, which are described in Table 27-14. I demonstrate the functions that are specific to particular data structures, such as slices and maps, in later chapters.

Table 27-14. *The Functions for Creating New Values*

Name	Description
New(type)	This function creates a Value that points to a value of the specified type, initialized to the type's zero value.
Zero(type)	This function creates a Value that represents the zero value of the specified type.
MakeMap(type)	This function creates a new map, as described in Chapter 28.
MakeMapWithSize(type, size)	This function creates a new map with the specified size, as described in Chapter 28.
MakeSlice(type, capacity)	This function creates a new slice, as described in Chapter 28.
MakeFunc(type, args, results)	This function creates a new function with the specified arguments and results, as described in Chapter 29.
MakeChan(type, buffer)	This function creates a new channel with the specified buffer size, as described in Chapter 29.

Care must be taken with the New function because it returns a pointer to a new value of the specified type, which means that it is easy to create a pointer to a pointer. Listing 27-22 uses the New function to create a temporary value in a function that swaps its parameters.

Listing 27-22. Creating a Value in the main.go File in the reflection Folder

```
package main

import (
    "reflect"
    //"strings"
    // "fmt"
)

func swap(first interface{}, second interface{}) {
    firstValue, secondValue := reflect.ValueOf(first), reflect.ValueOf(second)
    if firstValue.Type() == secondValue.Type() &&
            firstValue.Kind() == reflect.Ptr &&
            firstValue.Elem().CanSet() && secondValue.Elem().CanSet() {

        temp :=  reflect.New(firstValue.Elem().Type())
        temp.Elem().Set(firstValue.Elem())
        firstValue.Elem().Set(secondValue.Elem())
        secondValue.Elem().Set(temp.Elem())
    }
}
```

```
func main() {

    name := "Alice"
    price := 279
    city := "London"

    swap(&name, &city)
    for _, val := range []interface{} { name, price, city }  {
        Printfln("Value: %v", val)
    }
}
```

A new value is required to perform the swap, which is created with the New function:

```
...
temp :=  reflect.New(firstValue.Elem().Type())
...
```

The Type passed to the New function is obtained from the Elem result for one of the parameter values, which avoids creating a pointer to a pointer. The Set method is used to set the temporary value and to perform the swap. Compile and execute the project, and you will receive the following output, showing that the values of the name and city variables have been swapped over:

```
Value: London
Value: 279
Value: Alice
```

Summary

In this chapter, I introduced the basic Go reflection features and demonstrated their use. I explained how to obtain reflected types and values, how to determine the kind of type that has been reflected, how to set a reflected value, and how to use the convenience features provided by the reflect package. In the next chapter, I continue describing reflection, showing you how to deal with pointers, slices, maps, and structs.

## CHAPTER 28

Using Reflection, Part 2

In addition to the basic features described in the previous chapter, the reflect package provides additional features that are useful when working with a specific kind of type, such as maps or structs. In the sections that follow, I describe these features and demonstrate their use. Some of the methods and functions described are used with more than one type, and I have listed them several times for quick reference. Table 28-1 summarizes the chapter.

Table 28-1. Chapter Summary

Problem	Solution	Listing
Create or follow a pointer type	Use the PtrTo and Elem methods	3
Create or follow a pointer value	Use the Addr and Elem methods	4
Inspect or create a slice	Use the Type and Value methods for slices	5–8
Create, copy, and append to a slice	Use the reflect functions for slices	9
Inspect or create a map	Use the Type and Value methods for maps	10–14
Inspect or create a struct	Use the reflect functions for structs	15–17, 19–21
Inspect struct tags	Use the methods defined by StructTag	18

Preparing for This Chapter

In this chapter, I continue using the reflection project created in Chapter 27. To prepare for this chapter, add the type shown in Listing 28-1 to the types.go file in the reflection folder.

■ **Tip** You can download the example project for this chapter—and for all the other chapters in this book—from https://github.com/apress/pro-go. See Chapter 2 for how to get help if you have problems running the examples.

© Adam Freeman 2022
A. Freeman, *Pro Go*, https://doi.org/10.1007/978-1-4842-7355-5_28

Listing 28-1. Defining a Type in the types.go File in the reflection Folder

```
package main

type Product struct {
    Name, Category string
    Price float64
}

type Customer struct {
    Name, City string
}

type Purchase struct {
    Customer
    Product
    Total float64
    taxRate float64
}
```

Run the command shown in Listing 28-2 in the reflection folder to compile and execute the project.

Listing 28-2. Compiling and Executing the Project

```
go run .
```

This command will produce the following output:

```
Value: London
Value: 279
Value: Alice
```

Working with Pointers

The reflect package provides the function and method shown in Table 28-2 for working with pointer types.

Table 28-2. *The reflect Package Function and Method for Pointers*

Name	Description
PtrTo(type)	This function returns a Type that is a pointer to the Type received as the argument.
Elem()	This method, which is called on a pointer type, returns the underlying Type. This method panics when used on nonpointer types.

The PtrTo function creates a pointer type, and the Elem method returns the type that is pointed to, as shown in Listing 28-3.

Listing 28-3. Working with Pointer Types in the main.go File in the reflection Folder

```
package main

import (
    "reflect"
    //"strings"
    // "fmt"
)

func createPointerType(t reflect.Type) reflect.Type {
    return reflect.PtrTo(t)
}

func followPointerType(t reflect.Type) reflect.Type {
    if t.Kind() == reflect.Ptr {
        return t.Elem()
    }
    return t
}

func main() {

    name := "Alice"

    t := reflect.TypeOf(name)
    Printfln("Original Type: %v", t)
    pt := createPointerType(t)
    Printfln("Pointer Type: %v", pt)
    Printfln("Follow pointer type: %v", followPointerType(pt))
}
```

The PtrTo function is exported from the reflect package. It can be called on any type, including pointer types, and the result is a type that points to the original type so that the string type produces the *string type, and *string produces **string.

Elem, which is a method defined by the Type interface, can only be used on pointer types, which is why the followPointerType function in Listing 28-3 checks the result of the Kind method before calling the Elem method. Compile and execute the project, and you will see the following output:

```
Original Type: string
Pointer Type: *string
Follow pointer type: string
```

Working with Pointer Values

The Value struct defines the methods shown in Table 28-3 for working with pointer values, as opposed to the types described in the previous section.

Table 28-3. *The Value Methods for Working with Pointer Types*

Name	Description
Addr()	This method returns a Value that is a pointer to the Value on which it is called. This method panics if the CanAddr method returns false.
CanAddr()	This method returns true if the Value can be used with the Addr method.
Elem()	This method follows a pointer and returns its Value. This method panics if it is called on a nonpointer value.

The Elem method is used to follow a pointer to get its underlying value, as shown in Listing 28-4. The other methods are most useful when dealing with struct fields, as described in the "Setting Struct Field Values" section.

Listing 28-4. Following a Pointer in the main.go File in the reflection Folder

```
package main

import (
    "reflect"
    "strings"
    // "fmt"
)

var stringPtrType = reflect.TypeOf((*string)(nil))

func transformString(val interface{}) {
    elemValue := reflect.ValueOf(val)
    if (elemValue.Type() == stringPtrType) {
        upperStr := strings.ToUpper(elemValue.Elem().String())
        if (elemValue.Elem().CanSet()) {
            elemValue.Elem().SetString(upperStr)
        }
    }
}

func main() {

    name := "Alice"

    transformString(&name)
    Printfln("Follow pointer value: %v", name)
}
```

The transformString function identifies *string values and uses the Elem method to get the string value so that it can be passed to the strings.ToUpper function. Compile and execute the project, and you will receive the following output:

```
Follow pointer value: ALICE
```

Working with Array and Slice Types

The Type struct defines methods that can be used to inspect array and slice types, described in Table 28-4.

Table 28-4. *The Type Methods for Arrays and Slices*

Name	Description
Elem()	This method returns the Type for the array or slice elements.
Len()	This method returns the length for an array type. This method will panic if called on other types, including slices.

In addition to these methods, the reflect package provides the functions described in Table 28-5 for creating array and slice types.

■ **Note**   The reflection features for arrays and slices can also be used on string values, although I find it easier to test for strings, use the String method to get the underlying value, and then use the regular standard library functions.

Table 28-5. *The reflect Functions for Creating Array and Slice Types*

Name	Description
ArrayOf(len, type)	This function returns a Type that describes an array with the specified size and element type.
SliceOf(type)	This function returns a Type that describes an array with the specified element type.

Listing 28-5 uses the Elem method to check the type of arrays and slices.

Listing 28-5. Checking Array and Slice Types in the main.go File in the reflection Folder

```go
package main

import (
    "reflect"
    //"strings"
    // "fmt"
)

func checkElemType(val interface{}, arrOrSlice interface{}) bool {
    elemType := reflect.TypeOf(val)
    arrOrSliceType := reflect.TypeOf(arrOrSlice)
    return (arrOrSliceType.Kind() == reflect.Array ||
        arrOrSliceType.Kind() == reflect.Slice) &&
        arrOrSliceType.Elem() == elemType
}

func main() {
```

759

```
    name := "Alice"
    city := "London"
    hobby := "Running"

    slice := []string { name, city, hobby }
    array := [3]string { name, city, hobby}

    Println("Slice (string): %v",  checkElemType("testString", slice))
    Println("Array (string): %v",  checkElemType("testString", array))
    Println("Array (int): %v",  checkElemType(10, array))
}
```

The checkElemType uses the Kind method to identify arrays and slices and uses the Elem method to get the Type for the elements. These are compared to the type of the first parameter to see if the value can be added as an element. Compile and run the project, and you will see the following result:

```
Slice (string): true
Array (string): true
Array (int): false
```

Working with Array and Slice Values

The Value interface defines the methods described in Table 28-6 for working with array and slice values.

Table 28-6. *The Value Methods for Working with Arrays and Slices*

Name	Description
Index(index)	This method returns a Value that represents the element at the specified index.
Len()	This method returns the array or slice's length.
Cap()	This method returns the array or slice's capacity.
SetLen()	This method sets a slice's length. It cannot be used on arrays.
SetCap()	This method sets a slice's capacity. It cannot be used on arrays.
Slice(lo, hi)	This method creates a new slice with the specified low and high values.
Slice3(lo, hi, max)	This method creates a new slice with the specified low, high, and max values.

The Index method returns a Value, which can be used with the Set method, described in Chapter 27, to change a value in a slice or array, as shown in Listing 28-6.

Listing 28-6. Changing a Slice Element in the main.go File in the reflection Folder

```
package main

import (
    "reflect"
    //"strings"
```

```
    // "fmt"
)

func setValue(arrayOrSlice interface{}, index int, replacement interface{}) {
    arrayOrSliceVal := reflect.ValueOf(arrayOrSlice)
    replacementVal := reflect.ValueOf(replacement)
    if (arrayOrSliceVal.Kind() == reflect.Slice) {
        elemVal := arrayOrSliceVal.Index(index)
        if (elemVal.CanSet()) {
            elemVal.Set(replacementVal)
        }
    } else if (arrayOrSliceVal.Kind() == reflect.Ptr &&
        arrayOrSliceVal.Elem().Kind() == reflect.Array &&
        arrayOrSliceVal.Elem().CanSet()) {
            arrayOrSliceVal.Elem().Index(index).Set(replacementVal)
    }
}

func main() {

    name := "Alice"
    city := "London"
    hobby := "Running"

    slice := []string { name, city, hobby }
    array := [3]string { name, city, hobby}

    Printfln("Original slice: %v", slice)
    newCity := "Paris"
    setValue(slice, 1, newCity)
    Printfln("Modified slice: %v", slice)

    Printfln("Original slice: %v", array)
    newCity = "Rome"
    setValue(&array, 1, newCity)
    Printfln("Modified slice: %v", array)
}
```

The setValue function changes the value of an element in a slice or array, but each kind of type has to be handled differently. Slices are the easiest to work with and can be passed as values, like this:

```
...
setValue(slice, 1, newCity)
...
```

As I explained in Chapter 7, slices are references and are not copied when they are used as function arguments. In Listing 28-6, the setValue method uses the Kind method to detect the slice, uses the Index method to get the Value for the element at the specified location, and uses the Set method to change the value of the element. Arrays must be passed as pointers, like this:

```
...
setValue(&array, 1, newCity)
...
```

If you don't use a pointer, then you won't be able to set new values, and the CanSet method will return false. The Kind method is used to detect the pointer, and the Elem method is used to confirm it points to an array:

```
...
} else if (arrayOrSliceVal.Kind() == reflect.Ptr &&
    arrayOrSliceVal.Elem().Kind() == reflect.Array &&
    arrayOrSliceVal.Elem().CanSet()) {
...
```

To set the element value, the pointer is followed with the Elem method to get the reflected Value, the Index method is used to get the Value for the element at the specified index, and the Set method is used to assign the new value:

```
...
arrayOrSliceVal.Elem().Index(index).Set(replacementVal)
...
```

The overall effect is that the setValue function can manipulate slices and arrays without knowing what specific types are used. Compile and execute the project, and you will see the following output:

```
Original slice: [Alice London Running]
Modified slice: [Alice Paris Running]
Original slice: [Alice London Running]
Modified slice: [Alice Rome Running]
```

Enumerating Slices and Arrays

The Len method can be used to set the limit in a for loop to enumerate the elements in an array or slice, as shown in Listing 28-7.

Listing 28-7. Enumerating Arrays and Slices in the main.go File in the reflection Folder

```
package main

import (
    "reflect"
    //"strings"
    // "fmt"
)

func enumerateStrings(arrayOrSlice interface{}) {
    arrayOrSliceVal := reflect.ValueOf(arrayOrSlice)
```

```
    if (arrayOrSliceVal.Kind() == reflect.Array ||
            arrayOrSliceVal.Kind() == reflect.Slice) &&
            arrayOrSliceVal.Type().Elem().Kind() == reflect.String {
        for i := 0; i < arrayOrSliceVal.Len(); i++ {
            Printfln("Element: %v, Value: %v", i, arrayOrSliceVal.Index(i).String())
        }
    }
}

func main() {

    name := "Alice"
    city := "London"
    hobby := "Running"

    slice := []string { name, city, hobby }
    array := [3]string { name, city, hobby}

    enumerateStrings(slice)
    enumerateStrings(array)
}
```

The enumerateStrings function checks the Kind result to make sure that it is dealing with an array or a slice of strings. It is easy to get confused about which Elem method is used in this process because Type and Value both define Kind and Elem methods. The Kind methods perform the same task, but calling the Elem method on a slice or array Value causes a panic, while calling the Elem method on a slice or array Type returns the Type of the elements:

```
...
arrayOrSliceVal.Type().Elem().Kind() == reflect.String {
...
```

Once the function has confirmed that it is dealing with an array or slice of strings, a for loop is used, with the limit set by the result of the Len method:

```
...
for i := 0; i < arrayOrSliceVal.Len(); i++ {
...
```

The Index method is used within the for loop to get the element at the current index, and its value is obtained with the String method:

```
...
Printfln("Element: %v, Value: %v", i, arrayOrSliceVal.Index(i).String())
...
```

Notice that the array does not need to be referenced with a pointer when enumerating its contents. This is a requirement only when making changes. Compile and execute the project, and you will see the following output, which is the enumeration of the slice and array:

```
Element: 0, Value: Alice
Element: 1, Value: London
Element: 2, Value: Running
Element: 0, Value: Alice
Element: 1, Value: London
Element: 2, Value: Running
```

Creating New Slices from Existing Slices

The Slice method is used to create one slice from another, as shown in Listing 28-8.

Listing 28-8. Creating a New Slice in the main.go File in the reflection Folder

```
package main

import (
    "reflect"
    //"strings"
    // "fmt"
)

func findAndSplit(slice interface{}, target interface{}) interface{} {
    sliceVal := reflect.ValueOf(slice)
    targetType := reflect.TypeOf(target)
    if (sliceVal.Kind() == reflect.Slice && sliceVal.Type().Elem() == targetType) {
        for i := 0; i < sliceVal.Len(); i++ {
            if sliceVal.Index(i).Interface() == target {
                return sliceVal.Slice(0, i +1)
            }
        }
    }
    return slice
}

func main() {

    name := "Alice"
    city := "London"
    hobby := "Running"

    slice := []string { name, city, hobby }
    //array := [3]string { name, city, hobby}
    Printfln("Strings: %v", findAndSplit(slice, "London"))

    numbers := []int {1, 3, 4, 5, 7}
    Printfln("Numbers: %v", findAndSplit(numbers, 4))
}
```

The findAndSplit function enumerates the slice, looking for the specified element, which is done using the Interface method, which allows the slice elements to be compared without needing to deal with specific types. Once the target element has been located, the Slice method is used to create and return a new slice. Compile and execute the project, and you will see the following output:

```
Strings: [Alice London]
Numbers: [1 3 4]
```

Creating, Copying, and Appending Elements to Slices

The reflect package defines the functions described in Table 28-7 that allow values to be copied and appended to slices without needing to deal with the underlying types.

Table 28-7. *Functions for Appending Elements to Slices*

Name	Description
MakeSlice(type, len, cap)	This function creates a Value that reflects a new slice, using a Type to denote the element type and with the specified length and capacity.
Append(sliceVal, ...val)	This function appends one or more values to the specified slice, all of which are expressed using the Value interface. The result is the modified slice. The function panics when used on any kind of type other than a slice or if types of the values do not match the slice element type.
AppendSlice(sliceVal, sliceVal)	This function appends one slice to another. The function panics if either Value doesn't represent a slice or if the slice types are not compatible.
Copy(dst, src)	This function copies elements from the slice or array reflected by the src Value to the slice or array reflected by the dst Value. Elements are copied until the destination slice is full or all the source elements have been copied. The source and destination must have the same element type.

These functions accept Type or Value arguments, which can be counterintuitive and require preparation. The MakeSlice function takes a Type argument, which specifies the slice type, and returns a Value, which reflects the new slice. The other functions operator on Value arguments, as shown in Listing 28-9.

Listing 28-9. Creating a New Slice in the main.go File in the reflection Folder

```go
package main

import (
    "reflect"
    //"strings"
    //"fmt"
)

func pickValues(slice interface{}, indices ...int) interface{} {
    sliceVal := reflect.ValueOf(slice)
    if (sliceVal.Kind() == reflect.Slice) {
```

```
            newSlice := reflect.MakeSlice(sliceVal.Type(), 0, 10)
            for _, index := range indices {
                newSlice = reflect.Append(newSlice, sliceVal.Index(index))
            }
            return newSlice
    }
    return nil
}

func main() {

    name := "Alice"
    city := "London"
    hobby := "Running"

    slice := []string { name, city, hobby, "Bob", "Paris", "Soccer" }
    picked := pickValues(slice, 0, 3, 5)
    Printfln("Picked values: %v", picked)
}
```

The pickValues function creates a new slice using the Type reflected from an existing slice and uses the Append function to add values to the new slice. Compile and execute the project, and you will see the following output:

```
Picked values: [Alice Bob Soccer]
```

Working with Map Types

The Type struct defines methods that can be used to inspect map types, described in Table 28-8.

Table 28-8. *The Type Methods for Maps*

Name	Description
Key()	This method returns the Type for the map keys.
Elem()	This method returns the Type for the map values.

In addition to these methods, the reflect package provides the function described in Table 28-9 for creating map types.

Table 28-9. *The reflect Function for Creating Map Types*

Name	Description
MapOf(keyType, valType)	This function returns a new Type that reflects the map type with the specified key and value types, both of which are described using a Type.

Listing 28-10 defines a function that receives a map and reports in its types.

766

■ **Note** Describing reflection for maps is difficult because the term *value* is used to refer to the key-value pairs contained in the map and also the reflected values that are represented by the Value interface. I have tried to be consistent, but you may find that you have to read some parts of this section several times before they make sense.

Listing 28-10. Working with a Map Type in the main.go File in the reflection Folder

```go
package main

import (
    "reflect"
    //"strings"
    //"fmt"
)

func describeMap(m interface{}) {
    mapType := reflect.TypeOf(m)
    if (mapType.Kind() == reflect.Map) {
        Printfln("Key type: %v, Val type: %v", mapType.Key(), mapType.Elem())
    } else {
        Printfln("Not a map")
    }
}

func main() {

    pricesMap := map[string]float64 {
        "Kayak": 279, "Lifejacket": 48.95, "Soccer Ball": 19.50,
    }
    describeMap(pricesMap)
}
```

The Kind method is used to confirm that the describeMap function has received a map and the Key and Elem methods are used to write out the key and value types. Compile and execute the project, and you will see the following output:

```
Key type: string, Val type: float64
```

Working with Map Values

The Value interface defines the methods described in Table 28-10 for working with map values.

Table 28-10. *The Value Methods for Working with Maps*

Name	Description
MapKeys()	This method returns a [ ]Value, containing the map's keys.
MapIndex(key)	This method returns the Value that corresponds to the specified key, which is also expressed as a Value. The zero value is returned if the map does not contain the specified key, which can be detected by calling the IsValid method, which will return false, as described in Chapter 27.
MapRange()	This method returns a *MapIter, which allows the map contents to be iterated, as described after the table.
SetMapIndex(key, val)	This method sets the specified key and value, both of which are expressed using the Value interface.
Len()	This method returns the number of key-value pairs contained in the map.

The reflect package provides two different ways to enumerate the contents of a map. The first is to use the MapKeys method to get a slice containing the reflected key values and obtain each reflected map value using the MapIndex method, as shown in Listing 28-11.

Listing 28-11. Iterating the Contents of a Map in the main.go File in the reflection Folder

```
package main

import (
    "reflect"
    //"strings"
    //"fmt"
)

func printMapContents(m interface{}) {
    mapValue := reflect.ValueOf(m)
    if (mapValue.Kind() == reflect.Map) {
        for _, keyVal := range mapValue.MapKeys() {
            reflectedVal := mapValue.MapIndex(keyVal)
            Printfln("Map Key: %v, Value: %v", keyVal, reflectedVal)
        }
    } else {
        Printfln("Not a map")
    }
}

func main() {

    pricesMap := map[string]float64 {
        "Kayak": 279, "Lifejacket": 48.95, "Soccer Ball": 19.50,
    }
    printMapContents(pricesMap)
}
```

The same effect can be achieved using the MapRange method, which returns a pointer to a MapIter value, which defines the methods described in Table 28-11.

Table 28-11. *The Methods Defined by the MapIter Struct*

Name	Description
Next()	This method advances to the next key-value pair in the map. The result of this method is a bool indicating whether there are further key-value pairs to be read. This method must be called before the Key or Value method.
Key()	This method returns the Value representing the map key at the current position.
Value()	This method returns the Value representing the map value at the current position.

The MapIter struct provides a cursor-based approach to enumerating maps, where the Next method advances through the map contents, and the Key and Value methods provide access to the key and value at the current position. The result of the Next method indicates whether there are remaining values to be read, which makes it convenient to use with a for loop, as shown in Listing 28-12.

Listing 28-12. Using a MapIter in the main.go File in the reflection Folder

```
package main

import (
    "reflect"
    //"strings"
    //"fmt"
)

func printMapContents(m interface{}) {
    mapValue := reflect.ValueOf(m)
    if (mapValue.Kind() == reflect.Map) {
        iter := mapValue.MapRange()
        for iter.Next() {
            Printfln("Map Key: %v, Value: %v", iter.Key(), iter.Value())
        }
    } else {
        Printfln("Not a map")
    }
}

func main() {

    pricesMap := map[string]float64 {
        "Kayak": 279, "Lifejacket": 48.95, "Soccer Ball": 19.50,
    }
    printMapContents(pricesMap)
}
```

It is important to call the Next method before calling the Key and Value methods and to avoid calling those methods when the Next method returns false. Listing 28-11 and Listing 28-12 produce the following output when compiled and executed:

```
Map Key: Kayak, Value: 279
Map Key: Lifejacket, Value: 48.95
Map Key: Soccer Ball, Value: 19.5
```

Setting and Removing Map Values

The SetMapIndex method is used to add, modify, or remove key-value pairs in a map. Listing 28-13 defines functions for modifying a map.

Listing 28-13. Modifying a Map in the main.go File in the reflection Folder

```go
package main

import (
    "reflect"
    //"strings"
    //"fmt"
)

func setMap(m interface{}, key interface{}, val interface{}) {
    mapValue := reflect.ValueOf(m)
    keyValue := reflect.ValueOf(key)
    valValue := reflect.ValueOf(val)
    if (mapValue.Kind() == reflect.Map &&
        mapValue.Type().Key() == keyValue.Type() &&
        mapValue.Type().Elem() == valValue.Type()) {
            mapValue.SetMapIndex(keyValue, valValue)
    } else {
        Printfln("Not a map or mismatched types")
    }
}

func removeFromMap(m interface{}, key interface{}) {
    mapValue := reflect.ValueOf(m)
    keyValue := reflect.ValueOf(key)
    if (mapValue.Kind() == reflect.Map &&
        mapValue.Type().Key() == keyValue.Type()) {
            mapValue.SetMapIndex(keyValue, reflect.Value{})
    }
}

func main() {

    pricesMap := map[string]float64 {
        "Kayak": 279, "Lifejacket": 48.95, "Soccer Ball": 19.50,
    }
    setMap(pricesMap, "Kayak", 100.00)
    setMap(pricesMap, "Hat", 10.00)
    removeFromMap(pricesMap, "Lifejacket")
    for k, v := range pricesMap {
```

```
        Printfln("Key: %v, Value: %v", k, v)
    }
}
```

As noted in Chapter 7, maps are not copied when they are used as arguments and so a pointer isn't required to modify the contents of a map. The setMap function inspects the values it receives to confirm that it has received a map and that the key and value parameters have the expected types before setting the value with the SetMapIndex method.

The SetMapIndex method will remove a key from the map if the value argument is the zero value for the map value type. This is a problem when dealing with the built-in types, such as int and float64, where the zero value is a valid map entry. To prevent the SetMapIndex from setting values to zero, the removeFromMap function creates an instance of the Value struct, like this:

```
...
mapValue.SetMapIndex(keyValue, reflect.Value{})
...
```

This is a handy trick that ensures that the float64 value is removed from the map. Compile and execute the project, and you will see the following output:

```
Key: Kayak, Value: 100
Key: Soccer Ball, Value: 19.5
Key: Hat, Value: 10
```

Creating New Maps

The reflect package defines the functions described in Table 28-12 for creating new maps using reflected types.

Table 28-12. *Functions for Creating Maps*

Name	Description
MakeMap(type)	This function returns a Value that reflects a map created with the specified Type.
MakeMapWithSize(type, size)	This function returns a Value that reflects a map created with the specified Type and size.

When creating a map, the MapOf function described in Table 28-9 can be used to create the Type value, as shown in Listing 28-14.

Listing 28-14. Creating a Map in the main.go File in the reflection Folder

```
package main

import (
    "reflect"
    "strings"
    //"fmt"
)
```

```
func createMap(slice interface{}, op func(interface{}) interface{}) interface{} {
    sliceVal := reflect.ValueOf(slice)
    if (sliceVal.Kind() == reflect.Slice) {
        mapType := reflect.MapOf(sliceVal.Type().Elem(), sliceVal.Type().Elem())
        mapVal := reflect.MakeMap(mapType)
        for i := 0; i < sliceVal.Len(); i++ {
            elemVal := sliceVal.Index(i)
            mapVal.SetMapIndex(elemVal, reflect.ValueOf(op(elemVal.Interface())))
        }
        return mapVal.Interface()
    }
    return nil
}

func main() {

    names := []string { "Alice", "Bob", "Charlie"}
    reverse := func(val interface{}) interface{} {
        if str, ok := val.(string); ok {
            return strings.ToUpper(str)
        }
        return val
    }

    namesMap := createMap(names, reverse).(map[string]string)
    for k, v := range namesMap {
        Printfln("Key: %v, Value:%v", k, v)
    }
}
```

The createMap function accepts a slice of values and a function. The slice is enumerated, and the function is invoked on each element, with the original and transformed values used to populate a map, which is returned as the function result.

The calling code must perform an assertion on the result from the createMap code to narrow the specific map type (map[string]string in this example). The transformation function in this example has to be written to accept and return the empty interface so that it can be used by the createMap function. I explain how to use reflection to improve the handling of functions in Chapter 29. Compile and execute the project, and you will see the following output:

```
Key: Alice, Value:ALICE
Key: Bob, Value:BOB
Key: Charlie, Value:CHARLIE
```

Working with Struct Types

The Type struct defines methods that can be used to inspect struct types, described in Table 28-13.

Table 28-13. *The Type Methods for Structs*

Name	Description
NumField()	This method returns the number of fields defined by the struct type.
Field(index)	This method returns the field at the specified index, represented with a StructField.
FieldByIndex(indices)	This method accepts an int slice, which it uses to locate a nested field, which is represented with a StructField.
FieldByName(name)	This method returns the field with the specified name, which is represented by a StructField. The results are a StructField that represents the field and a bool that indicates if a match was found.
FieldByNameFunc(func)	This method passes the name of each field—included nested fields—to the specified function and returns the first field for which the function returns true. The results are a StructField that represents the field and a bool that indicates if a match was found.

The reflect package represents reflected fields with the StructField struct, which defines the fields described in Table 28-14.

Table 28-14. *The StructField Fields*

Name	Description
Name	This field stores the name of the reflected field.
PkgPath	This field returns the name of the package, which is used to determine whether a field has been exported. For reflected fields that are exported, this field returns the empty string. For reflected fields that have not been exported, this field returns the name of the package, which is the only package in which the field can be used.
Type	This field returns the reflected type of the reflected field, described using a Type.
Tag	This field returns the struct tag associated with the reflected field, as described in the "Inspecting Struct Tags" section.
Index	This field returns an int slice, which denotes the index of the field used by the FieldByIndex method described in Table 28-13.
Anonymous	This field returns true if the reflected field is embedded and false otherwise.

Listing 28-15 uses the methods and fields described in Table 28-13 and Table 28-14 to inspect a struct type.

Listing 28-15. Inspecting a Struct Type in the main.go File in the reflection Folder

```
package main

import (
    "reflect"
    // "strings"
    // "fmt"
)

func inspectStructs(structs ...interface{}) {
    for _, s := range structs {
        structType := reflect.TypeOf(s)
        if (structType.Kind() == reflect.Struct) {
            inspectStructType(structType)
        }
    }
}

func inspectStructType(structType reflect.Type) {
    Printfln("--- Struct Type: %v", structType)
    for i := 0; i < structType.NumField(); i++ {
        field := structType.Field(i)
        Printfln("Field %v: Name: %v, Type: %v, Exported: %v",
            field.Index, field.Name, field.Type, field.PkgPath == "")
    }
    Printfln("--- End Struct Type: %v", structType)
}

func main() {
    inspectStructs( Purchase{} )
}
```

The inspectStructs function defines a variadic parameter through which it receives values. The TypeOf function is used to get the reflected type, and the Kind method is used to confirm that each type is a struct. The reflected Type is passed on to the inspectStructType function, in which the NumField method is used in a for loop, which allows the structs fields to be enumerated using the Field method. Compile and execute the project, and you will see the details of the Purchase struct type:

```
--- Struct Type: main.Purchase
Field [0]: Name: Customer, Type: main.Customer, Exported: true
Field [1]: Name: Product, Type: main.Product, Exported: true
Field [2]: Name: Total, Type: float64, Exported: true
Field [3]: Name: taxRate, Type: float64, Exported: false
--- End Struct Type: main.Purchase
```

Processing Nested Fields

The output from Listing 28-15 includes the StructField.Index field, which is used to identify the position of each field defined by a struct type, like this:

```
...
Field [2]: Name: Total, Type: float64, Exported: true
...
```

The Total field is at index 2. The index of fields is determined by the order in which they are defined in the source code, which means that changing the order of fields will change their index when the struct type is reflected.

Identifying fields becomes more complex when nested struct fields are inspected, as shown in Listing 28-16.

Listing 28-16. Inspecting Nested Struct Fields in the main.go File in the reflection Folder

```
package main

import (
    "reflect"
    // "strings"
    // "fmt"
)

func inspectStructs(structs ...interface{}) {
    for _, s := range structs {
        structType := reflect.TypeOf(s)
        if (structType.Kind() == reflect.Struct) {
            inspectStructType([]int {}, structType)
        }
    }
}

func inspectStructType(baseIndex []int, structType reflect.Type) {
    Printfln("--- Struct Type: %v", structType)
    for i := 0; i < structType.NumField(); i++ {
        fieldIndex := append(baseIndex, i)
        field := structType.Field(i)
        Printfln("Field %v: Name: %v, Type: %v, Exported: %v",
            fieldIndex, field.Name, field.Type, field.PkgPath == "")
        if (field.Type.Kind() == reflect.Struct) {
            field := structType.FieldByIndex(fieldIndex)
            inspectStructType(fieldIndex, field.Type)
        }
    }
    Printfln("--- End Struct Type: %v", structType)
}

func main() {
    inspectStructs( Purchase{} )
}
```

The new code detects struct fields and processes them by recursively calling the inspectStructType function.

■ **Tip** The same approach can be used to inspect fields that are pointers to struct types, with the use of the Type.Elem method to obtain the type to which the pointer refers.

Compile and execute the project, and you will see the following output, to which I have added indentation to make the relationships between the fields more obvious:

```
--- Struct Type: main.Purchase
Field [0]: Name: Customer, Type: main.Customer, Exported: true
  --- Struct Type: main.Customer
  Field [0 0]: Name: Name, Type: string, Exported: true
  Field [0 1]: Name: City, Type: string, Exported: true
  --- End Struct Type: main.Customer
Field [1]: Name: Product, Type: main.Product, Exported: true
  --- Struct Type: main.Product
  Field [1 0]: Name: Name, Type: string, Exported: true
  Field [1 1]: Name: Category, Type: string, Exported: true
  Field [1 2]: Name: Price, Type: float64, Exported: true
  --- End Struct Type: main.Product
Field [2]: Name: Total, Type: float64, Exported: true
Field [3]: Name: taxRate, Type: float64, Exported: false
--- End Struct Type: main.Purchase
```

You can see that the exploration of the Purchase struct type now includes the nested Product and Customer fields and displays the fields defined by those nested types. You will notice that the output identifies each field by its index within the type that defines it and the parent type like this:

```
...
Field [1 2]: Name: Price, Type: float64, Exported: true
...
```

The Price field is at index 2 in its enclosing Product struct, which is at index 1 in the enclosing Purchase struct.

There is an inconsistency in the way that nested struct fields are handled by the reflect package. The FieldByIndex method is used to locate nested fields so that I can request a field directly if I know the sequence of indices so that I can get the Price field directly by passing the FieldByIndex method []int {1, 2}. The problem is that the StructField returned by the FieldByIndex method has an Index field that returns only one element, reflecting only the index within the enclosing struct.

This means that the result from the FieldByIndex method can't easily be used for subsequent calls to the same method, and it is for that reason that I need to keep track of indices using my own int slice and use this as the argument to the FieldByIndex method in Listing 28-16:

```
...
fieldIndex := append(baseIndex, i)
...
field := structType.FieldByIndex(fieldIndex)
...
```

This issue makes it a little awkward to explore a struct type, but it is easy to work around once you know it happens, and most projects won't try to walk the tree of fields in this way.

Locating a Field by Name

The problem described in the previous section doesn't affect the FieldByName method, which performs a search for a field with a specific name and correctly sets the Index field of the StructField it returns, as shown in Listing 28-17.

Listing 28-17. Locating a Struct Field by Name in the main.go File in the reflection Folder

```
package main

import (
    "reflect"
    //"strings"
    //"fmt"
)

func describeField(s interface{}, fieldName string) {
    structType := reflect.TypeOf(s)
    field, found := structType.FieldByName(fieldName)
    if (found) {
        Printfln("Found: %v, Type: %v, Index: %v",
            field.Name, field.Type, field.Index)
        index := field.Index
        for len(index) > 1 {
            index = index[0: len(index) -1]
            field = structType.FieldByIndex(index)
            Printfln("Parent : %v, Type: %v, Index: %v",
                field.Name, field.Type, field.Index)
        }
        Printfln("Top-Level Type: %v" , structType)
    } else {
        Printfln("Field %v not found", fieldName)
    }
}

func main() {
    describeField( Purchase{}, "Price" )
}
```

The describeField function uses the FieldByName method, which locates the first field with the specified name and returns a StructField with a correctly set Index field. A for loop is used to work back up the type hierarchy, examining each parent in turn. Compile and execute the project, and you will see the following result:

```
Found: Price, Type: float64, Index: [1 2]
Parent : Product, Type: main.Product, Index: [1]
Top-Level Type: main.Purchase
```

Note that I have to use the Index value from the StructField returned by the FieldByName method because working up the hierarchy using the FieldByIndex method introduces the problem described in the previous section.

Inspecting Struct Tags

The StructField.Tag field provides details of the struct tag associated with a field. Struct tags can only be inspected using reflection, which limits their use, and most projects will only use tags when defining structs to provide direction to other packages, as demonstrated in Chapter 21 for working with JSON data.

The Tag field returns a StructTag value, which is an alias for string. Struct tags are essentially a string with encoded key-value pairs, and the reason that the StructTag alias type has been created is to allow the methods described in Table 28-15 to be defined.

Table 28-15. *The Methods Defined by the StructTag Type*

Name	Description
Get(key)	This method returns a string containing the value for the specified key or the empty string if no value has been defined.
Lookup(key)	This method returns a string containing the value for the specified key or the empty string if no value has been defined, and a bool that is true if the value was defined and false otherwise.

The methods in Table 28-15 are similar, and the difference is that the Lookup method differentiates between keys for which no value has been defined and keys that have been defined with the empty string as the value. Listing 28-18 defines a struct with tags and demonstrates the use of these methods.

Listing 28-18. Inspecting Struct Tags in the main.go File in the reflection Folder

```
package main

import (
    "reflect"
    //"strings"
    //"fmt"
)

func inspectTags(s interface{}, tagName string) {
    structType := reflect.TypeOf(s)
    for i := 0; i < structType.NumField(); i++ {
        field := structType.Field(i)
        tag := field.Tag
        valGet := tag.Get(tagName)
        valLookup, ok := tag.Lookup(tagName)
        Printfln("Field: %v, Tag %v: %v", field.Name, tagName, valGet)
        Printfln("Field: %v, Tag %v: %v, Set: %v",
            field.Name, tagName, valLookup, ok)
    }
}

type Person struct {
```

```
    Name string `alias:"id"`
    City string `alias:""`
    Country string
}

func main() {
    inspectTags(Person{}, "alias")
}
```

The inspectTags function enumerates the fields defined by a struct type and uses both the Get and Lookup methods to get a specified tag. The function is applied to the Person type, which defines the alias tag on some of its fields. Compile and execute the project, and you will see the following output:

```
Field: Name, Tag alias: id
Field: Name, Tag alias: id, Set: true
Field: City, Tag alias:
Field: City, Tag alias: , Set: true
Field: Country, Tag alias:
Field: Country, Tag alias: , Set: false
```

The additional result returned by the Lookup method makes it possible to differentiate between the City field, which has the alias tag defined as the empty string, and the Country field, which does not have the alias tag at all.

Creating Struct Types

The reflect package provides the function described in Table 28-16 for creating struct types. This is not a feature that is often required because the result is a type that can be used only with reflection.

Table 28-16. *The reflect Function for Creating Struct Types*

Name	Description
StructOf(fields)	This function creates a new struct type, using the specified StructField slice to define the fields. Only exported fields may be specified.

Listing 28-19 creates a struct type and then inspects its tags.

Listing 28-19. Creating a Struct Type in the main.go File in the reflection Folder

```
package main

import (
    "reflect"
    //"strings"
    //"fmt"
)

func inspectTags(s interface{}, tagName string) {
    structType := reflect.TypeOf(s)
```

```
    for i := 0; i < structType.NumField(); i++ {
        field := structType.Field(i)
        tag := field.Tag
        valGet := tag.Get(tagName)
        valLookup, ok := tag.Lookup(tagName)
        Printfln("Field: %v, Tag %v: %v", field.Name, tagName, valGet)
        Printfln("Field: %v, Tag %v: %v, Set: %v",
            field.Name, tagName, valLookup, ok)
    }
}

func main() {

    stringType := reflect.TypeOf("this is a string")

    structType := reflect.StructOf([] reflect.StructField {
        { Name: "Name", Type: stringType, Tag: `alias:"id"` },
        { Name: "City", Type: stringType,Tag: `alias:""`},
        { Name: "Country", Type: stringType },
    })

    inspectTags(reflect.New(structType), "alias")
}
```

This example creates a struct that has the same characteristics as the Person struct in the previous section, with Name, City, and Country fields. The fields are described by creating StructField values, which are just regular Go structs. The New function is used to create a new value from the struct, which is passed to the inspectTags function. Compile and execute the project, and you will receive the following output:

```
Field: typ, Tag alias:
Field: typ, Tag alias: , Set: false
Field: ptr, Tag alias:
Field: ptr, Tag alias: , Set: false
Field: flag, Tag alias:
Field: flag, Tag alias: , Set: false
```

Working with Struct Values

The Value interface defines the methods described in Table 28-17 for working with struct values.

Table 28-17. *The Value Methods for Working with Structs*

Name	Description
NumField()	This method returns the number of fields defined by the struct value's type.
Field(index)	This method returns a Value that reflects the field at the specified index.
FieldByIndex(indices)	This method returns a Value that reflects the nested field at the specified indices.
FieldByName(name)	This method returns a Value that reflects the first field located with the specified name.
FieldByNameFunc(func)	This method passes the name of each field—included nested fields—to the specified function and returns a Value that reflects the first field for which the function returns true, and a bool that indicates if a match was found.

The methods in Table 28-17 correspond to those described in the previous section for working with struct types. Once you understand the composition of a struct type, you can obtain a Value for each of the fields you are interested in and apply the basic reflection features, as shown in Listing 28-20.

Listing 28-20. Reading Struct Field Values in the main.go File in the reflection Folder

```
package main

import (
    "reflect"
    //"strings"
    //"fmt"
)

func getFieldValues(s interface{}) {
    structValue := reflect.ValueOf(s)
    if structValue.Kind() == reflect.Struct {
        for i := 0; i < structValue.NumField(); i++ {
            fieldType := structValue.Type().Field(i)
            fieldVal := structValue.Field(i)
            Printfln("Name: %v, Type: %v, Value: %v",
                fieldType.Name, fieldType.Type, fieldVal)
        }
    } else {
        Printfln("Not a struct")
    }
}

func main() {
    product := Product{ Name: "Kayak", Category: "Watersports", Price: 279 }
    customer := Customer{ Name: "Acme", City: "Chicago" }
    purchase := Purchase { Customer: customer, Product: product, Total: 279,
        taxRate: 10 }

    getFieldValues(purchase)
}
```

The getFieldValues function enumerates the fields defined by a struct and writes out the details of field type and value. Compile and execute the project, and you will see the following output:

```
Name: Customer, Type: main.Customer, Value: {Acme Chicago}
Name: Product, Type: main.Product, Value: {Kayak Watersports 279}
Name: Total, Type: float64, Value: 279
Name: taxRate, Type: float64, Value: 10
```

Setting Struct Field Values

Once you have obtained the Value for a struct field, the field can be changed just like any other reflected value, as shown in Listing 28-21.

Listing 28-21. Setting a Struct Field in the main.go File in the reflection Folder

```go
package main

import (
    "reflect"
    //"strings"
    //"fmt"
)

func setFieldValue(s interface{}, newVals map[string]interface{}) {
    structValue := reflect.ValueOf(s)
    if (structValue.Kind() == reflect.Ptr &&
            structValue.Elem().Kind() == reflect.Struct) {
        for name, newValue := range newVals {
            fieldVal := structValue.Elem().FieldByName(name)
            if (fieldVal.CanSet()) {
                fieldVal.Set(reflect.ValueOf(newValue))
            } else if (fieldVal.CanAddr()) {
                ptr := fieldVal.Addr()
                if (ptr.CanSet()) {
                    ptr.Set(reflect.ValueOf(newValue))
                } else {
                    Printfln("Cannot set field via pointer")
                }
            } else {
                Printfln("Cannot set field")
            }
        }
    } else {
        Printfln("Not a pointer to a struct")
    }
}

func getFieldValues(s interface{}) {
    structValue := reflect.ValueOf(s)
```

```
    if structValue.Kind() == reflect.Struct {
        for i := 0; i < structValue.NumField(); i++ {
            fieldType := structValue.Type().Field(i)
            fieldVal := structValue.Field(i)
            Printfln("Name: %v, Type: %v, Value: %v",
                fieldType.Name, fieldType.Type, fieldVal)
        }
    } else {
        Printfln("Not a struct")
    }
}

func main() {
    product := Product{ Name: "Kayak", Category: "Watersports", Price: 279 }
    customer := Customer{ Name: "Acme", City: "Chicago" }
    purchase := Purchase { Customer: customer, Product: product, Total: 279,
        taxRate: 10 }

    setFieldValue(&purchase, map[string]interface{} {
        "City": "London", "Category": "Boats", "Total": 100.50,
    })

    getFieldValues(purchase)
}
```

As with other data types, reflection can only be used to change values via a pointer to the struct. The Elem method is used to follow the pointer so that the Value that reflects the field can be obtained using one of the methods described in Table 28-17. The CanSet method is used to determine if a field can be set.

An additional step is required for fields that are not nested structs, which is to create a pointer to the field value using the Addr method, like this:

```
...
} else if (fieldVal.CanAddr()) {
    ptr := fieldVal.Addr()
    if (ptr.CanSet()) {
        ptr.Set(reflect.ValueOf(newValue))
...
```

Without this additional step, the value for non-nested fields cannot be changed. The changes in Listing 28-21 alter the values of the City, Category, and Total fields, producing the following output when the project is compiled and executed:

```
Name: Customer, Type: main.Customer, Value: {Acme London}
Name: Product, Type: main.Product, Value: {Kayak Boats 279}
Name: Total, Type: float64, Value: 100.5
Name: taxRate, Type: float64, Value: 10
```

Notice that I use the CanSet method even after I have called the Addr method to create a pointer value in Listing 28-21. Reflection cannot be used to set unexported struct fields, so I need to perform the additional check to avoid causing a panic by attempting to set a field that can never be set. (In fact, there are some workarounds to set unexported fields, but they are nasty, and I don't recommend their use. A web search will give you the details you need if you are determined to set unexported fields.)

Summary

In this chapter, I continued to describe the Go reflection features, explaining how they are used with pointers, arrays, slices, maps, and structs. In the next chapter, I complete my description of this important—but complex—feature.

CHAPTER 29

Using Reflection, Part 3

In this chapter, I complete the description of the Go support for reflection, which I started in Chapter 27 and continued in Chapter 28. In this chapter, I explain how reflection is used for functions, methods, interfaces, and channels. Table 29-1 summarizes the chapter.

Table 29-1. *Chapter Summary*

Problem	Solution	Listing
Inspect and invoke reflected functions	Use the Type and Value methods for functions	5–7
Create new functions	Use the FuncOf and MakeFunc functions	8, 9
Inspect and invoke reflected methods	Use the Type and Value methods for methods	10–12
Inspect reflected interfaces	Use the Type and Value methods for interfaces	13–15
Inspect and use reflected channels	Use the Type and Value methods for channels	16–19

Preparing for This Chapter

In this chapter, I continue using the reflection project from Chapter 28. To prepare for this chapter, add a file named interfaces.go to the reflection project with the content shown in Listing 29-1.

Tip You can download the example project for this chapter—and for all the other chapters in this book—from https://github.com/apress/pro-go. See Chapter 2 for how to get help if you have problems running the examples.

Listing 29-1. The Contents of the interfaces.go File in the reflection Folder

```
package main

import "fmt"

type NamedItem interface {
    GetName() string
    unexportedMethod()
}
```

```go
type CurrencyItem interface {
    GetAmount() string
    currencyName() string
}

func (p *Product) GetName() string {
    return p.Name
}

func (c *Customer) GetName() string {
    return c.Name
}

func (p *Product) GetAmount() string {
    return fmt.Sprintf("$%.2f", p.Price)
}

func (p *Product) currencyName() string {
    return "USD"
}

func (p *Product) unexportedMethod() {}
```

Add a file named functions.go to the reflection folder with the content shown in Listing 29-2.

Listing 29-2. The Contents of the functions.go File in the reflection Folder

```go
package main

func Find(slice []string, vals... string) (matches bool) {
    for _, s1 := range slice {
        for _, s2 := range vals {
            if s1 == s2 {
                matches = true
                return
            }
        }
    }
    return
}
```

Add a file named methods.go to the reflection folder with the content shown in Listing 29-3.

Listing 29-3. The Contents of the methods.go File in the reflection Folder

```go
package main

func (p Purchase) calcTax(taxRate float64) float64 {
    return p.Price * taxRate
}
```

```
func (p Purchase) GetTotal() float64 {
    return p.Price + p.calcTax(.20)
}
```

Run the command shown in Listing 29-4 in the reflection folder to compile and execute the project.

Listing 29-4. Compiling and Executing the Project

```
go run .
```

This command produces the following output:

```
Name: Customer, Type: main.Customer, Value: {Acme London}
Name: Product, Type: main.Product, Value: {Kayak Boats 279}
Name: Total, Type: float64, Value: 100.5
Name: taxRate, Type: float64, Value: 10
```

Working with Function Types

As explained in Chapter 9, functions are types in Go, and as you might expect, functions can be examined and used with reflection The Type struct defines methods that can be used to inspect function types, described in Table 29-2.

Table 29-2. *The Type Methods for Working with Functions*

Name	Description
NumIn()	This method returns the number of parameters defined by the function.
In(index)	This method returns a Type that reflects the parameter at the specified index.
IsVariadic()	This method returns true if the last parameter is variadic.
NumOut()	This method returns the number of results defined by the function.
Out(index)	This method returns a Type that reflects the result at the specified index.

Listing 29-5 uses reflection to describe a function.

Listing 29-5. Reflecting a Function in the main.go File in the reflection Folder

```
package main

import (
    "reflect"
    //"strings"
    //"fmt"
)
```

```
func inspectFuncType(f interface{}) {
    funcType := reflect.TypeOf(f)
    if (funcType.Kind() == reflect.Func) {
        Printfln("Function parameters: %v", funcType.NumIn())
        for i := 0 ; i < funcType.NumIn(); i++ {
            paramType := funcType.In(i)
            if (i < funcType.NumIn() -1) {
                Printfln("Parameter #%v, Type: %v", i, paramType)
            } else {
                Printfln("Parameter #%v, Type: %v, Variadic: %v", i, paramType,
                    funcType.IsVariadic())
            }
        }
        Printfln("Function results: %v", funcType.NumOut())
        for i := 0 ; i < funcType.NumOut(); i++ {
            resultType := funcType.Out(i)
            Printfln("Result #%v, Type: %v", i, resultType)
        }
    }
}

func main() {
    inspectFuncType(Find)
}
```

The inspectFuncType function uses the methods described in Table 29-2 to examine a function type, reporting on its parameters and results. Compile and execute the project, and you will see the following output, which describes the Find function defined in Listing 29-2:

```
Parameter #0, Type: []string
Parameter #1, Type: []string, Variadic: true
Function results: 1
Result #0, Type: bool
```

The output shows that the Find function has two parameters, the last of which is variadic, and one result.

Working with Function Values

The Value interface defines the method described in Table 29-3 for invoking functions.

Table 29-3. *The Value Method for Invoking Functions*

Name	Description
Call(params)	This function invokes the reflected function using the []Value as parameters. The result is a []Value that contains the function results. The values provided as parameters must match those defined by the function.

The Call method invokes a function and returns a slice containing the results. The parameters for the function are specified using a Value slice, and the Call method automatically detects variadic parameters. The results are returned as another Value slice, as shown in Listing 29-6.

Listing 29-6. Invoking a Function in the main.go File in the reflection Folder

```
package main

import (
    "reflect"
    //"strings"
    //"fmt"
)

func invokeFunction(f interface{}, params ...interface{}) {
    paramVals := []reflect.Value {}
    for _, p := range params {
        paramVals = append(paramVals, reflect.ValueOf(p))
    }
    funcVal := reflect.ValueOf(f)
    if (funcVal.Kind() == reflect.Func) {
        results := funcVal.Call(paramVals)
        for i, r := range results {
            Printfln("Result #%v: %v", i, r)
        }
    }
}

func main() {
    names := []string { "Alice", "Bob", "Charlie" }
    invokeFunction(Find, names, "London", "Bob")
}
```

Compile and execute the project, and you will see the following output:

```
Result #0: true
```

Invoking a function this way isn't a common requirement because the calling code could have just invoked the function directly, but this example makes the use of the Call method clear and emphasizes that the parameters and the results are both expressed using Value slices. Listing 29-7 provides a more realistic example.

Listing 29-7. Calling a Function on Slice Elements in the main.go File in the reflection Folder

```
package main

import (
    "reflect"
    "strings"
    //"fmt"
)
```

```
func mapSlice(slice interface{}, mapper interface{}) (mapped []interface{}) {
    sliceVal := reflect.ValueOf(slice)
    mapperVal := reflect.ValueOf(mapper)
    mapped = []interface{} {}
    if sliceVal.Kind() == reflect.Slice && mapperVal.Kind() == reflect.Func &&
            mapperVal.Type().NumIn() == 1 &&
            mapperVal.Type().In(0) == sliceVal.Type().Elem() {
        for i := 0; i < sliceVal.Len(); i++ {
            result := mapperVal.Call([]reflect.Value {sliceVal.Index(i)})
            for _, r := range result {
                mapped = append(mapped, r.Interface())
            }
        }
    }
    return
}

func main() {
    names := []string { "Alice", "Bob", "Charlie" }
    results := mapSlice(names, strings.ToUpper)
    Printfln("Results: %v", results)
}
```

The mapSlice function accepts a slice and a function, passes each slice element to the function, and returns the results. It can be tempting to describe function parameters to specify the number of parameters, like this:

```
...
mapper func(interface{}) interface{}
...
```

The problem with this approach is that it restricts the functions that can be used to those that are defined with parameters and results that are the empty interface. Instead, specify the entire function as a single empty interface value, like this:

```
...
func mapSlice(slice interface{}, mapper interface{}) (mapped []interface{}) {
...
```

This allows any function to be used but requires that the function is inspected to make sure that it can be used as intended:

```
...
if sliceVal.Kind() == reflect.Slice && mapperVal.Kind() == reflect.Func &&
    mapperVal.Type().NumIn() == 1 &&
    mapperVal.Type().In(0) == sliceVal.Type().Elem() {
...
```

These checks ensure that the function defines a single parameter and that the parameter type matches the slice element type. Compile and execute the project, and you will see the following results:

```
Results: [ALICE BOB CHARLIE]
```

Creating and Invoking New Function Types and Values

The `reflect` package defines the functions described in Table 29-4 for creating new function types and values.

Table 29-4. *The reflect Function for Creating New Function Types and Function Values*

Name	Description
FuncOf(params, results, variadic)	This function creates a new Type that reflects a function type with the specified parameters and results. The final argument specifies whether the function type has a variadic parameter. The parameters and results are specified as Type slices.
MakeFunc(type, fn)	This function returns a Value that reflects a new function that is a wrapper around the function fn. The function must accept a Value slice as its only parameter and return a Value slice as its only result.

One use of the `FuncOf` function is to create a type signature and use it to check the signature of a function value, replacing the checks performed in the previous section, as shown in Listing 29-8.

Listing 29-8. Creating a Function Type in the main.go File in the reflection Folder

```
package main

import (
    "reflect"
    "strings"
    //"fmt"
)

func mapSlice(slice interface{}, mapper interface{}) (mapped []interface{}) {
    sliceVal := reflect.ValueOf(slice)
    mapperVal := reflect.ValueOf(mapper)
    mapped = []interface{} {}

    if sliceVal.Kind() == reflect.Slice && mapperVal.Kind() == reflect.Func {
        paramTypes := []reflect.Type { sliceVal.Type().Elem() }
        resultTypes := []reflect.Type {}
        for i := 0; i < mapperVal.Type().NumOut(); i++ {
            resultTypes = append(resultTypes, mapperVal.Type().Out(i))
        }
```

```
        expectedFuncType := reflect.FuncOf(paramTypes,
            resultTypes, mapperVal.Type().IsVariadic())
        if (mapperVal.Type() == expectedFuncType) {
            for i := 0; i < sliceVal.Len(); i++ {
                result := mapperVal.Call([]reflect.Value {sliceVal.Index(i)})
                for _, r := range result {
                    mapped = append(mapped, r.Interface())
                }
            }
        } else {
            Printfln("Function type not as expected")
        }
    }
    return
}

func main() {
    names := []string { "Alice", "Bob", "Charlie" }
    results := mapSlice(names, strings.ToUpper)
    Printfln("Results: %v", results)
}
```

This approach is no less verbose, not least because I want to accept functions that have the same parameter type as the slice element type but with any result type. Getting the slice element type is simple, but I have to do some work to create a Type slice that reflects the results from the mapper function to ensure that I create a type that will be compared correctly. Compile and execute the project, and you will see the following output:

```
Results: [ALICE BOB CHARLIE]
```

The FuncOf function is complemented by the MakeFunc function, which creates new functions using a function type as the template. Listing 29-9 demonstrates the use of the MakeFunc function to create a reusable typed mapping function.

Listing 29-9. Creating a Function in the main.go File in the reflection Folder

```
package main

import (
    "reflect"
    "strings"
    "fmt"
)

func makeMapperFunc(mapper interface{}) interface{} {
    mapVal := reflect.ValueOf(mapper)
    if mapVal.Kind() == reflect.Func && mapVal.Type().NumIn() == 1 &&
            mapVal.Type().NumOut() == 1  {
        inType := reflect.SliceOf( mapVal.Type().In(0))
        inTypeSlice := []reflect.Type { inType }
```

```
        outType := reflect.SliceOf( mapVal.Type().Out(0))
        outTypeSlice := []reflect.Type { outType }
        funcType := reflect.FuncOf(inTypeSlice, outTypeSlice, false)
        funcVal := reflect.MakeFunc(funcType,
                func (params []reflect.Value) (results []reflect.Value) {
            srcSliceVal := params[0]
            resultsSliceVal := reflect.MakeSlice(outType, srcSliceVal.Len(), 10)
            for i := 0; i < srcSliceVal.Len(); i++ {
                r := mapVal.Call([]reflect.Value { srcSliceVal.Index(i)})
                resultsSliceVal.Index(i).Set(r[0])
            }
            results = []reflect.Value { resultsSliceVal }
            return
        })
        return funcVal.Interface()
    }
    Printfln("Unexpected types")
    return nil
}

func main() {

    lowerStringMapper := makeMapperFunc(strings.ToLower).(func([]string)[]string)
    names := []string { "Alice", "Bob", "Charlie" }
    results := lowerStringMapper(names)
    Printfln("Lowercase Results: %v", results)

    incrementFloatMapper := makeMapperFunc(func (val float64) float64 {
        return val + 1
    }).(func([]float64)[]float64)
    prices := []float64 { 279, 48.95, 19.50}
    floatResults := incrementFloatMapper(prices)
    Printfln("Increment Results: %v", floatResults)

    floatToStringMapper := makeMapperFunc(func (val float64) string {
        return fmt.Sprintf("$%.2f", val)
    }).(func([]float64)[]string)
    Printfln("Price Results: %v", floatToStringMapper(prices))
}
```

The makeMapperFunc function demonstrates how flexible reflection can be, but also shows how verbose and dense reflection can be. The best way to understand this function is to focus on the inputs and outputs. The makeMapperFunc accepts a function that transforms one value into another, with a signature like this:

```
...
func mapper(int) string
...
```

This hypothetical function receives an int value and produces a string result. The makeMapperFunc uses the types of this function to produce a function that would be expressed like this in regular Go code:

```
...
func useMapper(slice []int) []string {
    results := []string {}
    for _, val := range slice {
        results = append(results, mapper(val))
    }
    return results
}
...
```

The useMapper function is a wrapper around the mapper function. The mapper and useMapper functions are easy to define in regular Go code, but they are specific to a single set of types. The makeMapperFunc uses reflection so that it can receive any mapping function and generate the appropriate wrapper, which can then be used with the standard Go type safety features.

The first step is to identify the types of the mapping function:

```
...
inType := reflect.SliceOf( mapVal.Type().In(0))
inTypeSlice := []reflect.Type { inType }
outType := reflect.SliceOf( mapVal.Type().Out(0))
outTypeSlice := []reflect.Type { outType }
...
```

These types are then used to create the function type for the wrapper:

```
...
funcType := reflect.FuncOf(inTypeSlice, outTypeSlice, false)
...
```

Once I have the function type, I can use it to create the wrapper function using the MakeFunc function:

```
...
funcVal := reflect.MakeFunc(funcType,
    func (params []reflect.Value) (results []reflect.Value) {
...
```

The MakeFunc function accepts the Type that describes the function and a function that the new function will call. In Listing 29-9, the function enumerates the elements in a slice, calls the mapper function for each of them, and builds up a slice of results.

The result is a function that is type-safe, although it does require a type assertion:

```
...
lowerStringMapper := makeMapperFunc(strings.ToLower).(func([]string)[]string)
...
```

The makeMapperFunc is passed the strings.ToLower function and produces a function that accepts a slice of string and returns a slice of strings. The other calls to the makeMapperFunc create functions that transform float64 values into other float64 values and convert float64 values into currency format strings. Compile and execute the project, and you will see the following output:

```
Lowercase Results: [alice bob charlie]
Increment Results: [280 49.95 20.5]
Price Results: [$279.00 $48.95 $19.50]
```

Working with Methods

The Type struct defines the methods described in Table 29-5 for inspecting the methods defined by a struct.

Table 29-5. *The Type Methods for Working with Methods*

Name	Description
NumMethod()	This method returns the number of exported methods defined for the reflected struct type.
Method(index)	This method returns the reflected method at the specified index, represented with the Method struct.
MethodByName(name)	This method returns the reflected method with the specified name. The results are a Method struct, and a bool that indicates whether a method with the specified name exists.

Note Reflection does not provide support for creating new methods. It can only be used to examine and invoke existing methods.

Methods are represented with the Method struct, which defines the fields described in Table 29-6.

Table 29-6. *The Fields Defined by the Method Struct*

Name	Description
Name	This field returns the name of the method as a string.
PkgPath	This field is used with interfaces, as explained in the "Working with Interfaces" section, and not to methods accessed through a struct type. The field returns a string containing the package path. The empty string is used for exported fields and will contain the struct package name for unexported fields.
Type	This field returns a Type that describes the method function type.
Func	This field returns a Value that reflects the method function value. When invoking the method, the first argument must be the struct on which the method is being called, as demonstrated in the "Invoking Methods" section.
Index	This field returns an int that specifies the method index, for use with the Method method described in Table 29-5.

Note   When examining structs, methods that are promoted from embedded fields are included in the results produced by the methods described in this section.

The Value interface also defines methods for working with reflected methods, as described in Table 29-7.

Table 29-7. *The Value Methods for Working with Methods*

Name	Description
NumMethod()	This method returns the number of exported methods defined for the reflected struct type. It invokes the Type.NumMethod method.
Method(index)	This method returns a Value that reflects the method function at the specified index. The receiver is not provided as the first argument when invoking the function, as demonstrated in the "Invoking Methods" section.
MethodByName(name)	This method returns a Value that reflects the method function with the specified name. The receiver is not provided as the first argument when invoking the function, as demonstrated in the "Invoking Methods" section.

The methods in Table 29-7 are convenience features that provide access to the same underlying features as the methods in Table 29-5, albeit there are differences in how methods are invoked, as described in the next section.

Listing 29-10 defines a function that describes the methods defined by a struct, using the methods provided by the Type struct.

Listing 29-10. Describing Methods in the main.go File in the reflection Folder

```
package main

import (
    "reflect"
    //"strings"
    //"fmt"
)

func inspectMethods(s interface{}) {
    sType := reflect.TypeOf(s)
    if sType.Kind() == reflect.Struct || (sType.Kind() == reflect.Ptr &&
            sType.Elem().Kind() == reflect.Struct) {
        Printfln("Type: %v, Methods: %v", sType, sType.NumMethod())
        for i := 0; i < sType.NumMethod(); i++ {
            method := sType.Method(i)
            Printfln("Method name: %v, Type: %v",
                method.Name, method.Type)
        }
    }
}
```

```
func main() {

    inspectMethods(Purchase{})
    inspectMethods(&Purchase{})
}
```

Go makes it easy to invoke methods, allowing methods defined for a struct to be invoked via a struct pointer and vice versa. When using reflection to inspect types, however, the results are not as consistent, which you can see in the output when the project is compiled and executed:

```
Type: main.Purchase, Methods: 1
Method name: GetTotal, Type: func(main.Purchase) float64
Type: *main.Purchase, Methods: 2
Method name: GetAmount, Type: func(*main.Purchase) string
Method name: GetTotal, Type: func(*main.Purchase) float64
```

When reflection is used on the Purchase type, only the methods defined for Product are listed. But when reflection is used on the *Purchase type, methods defined for Product and *Product are listed. Note that only exported methods are accessible via reflection—unexported methods cannot be inspected or invoked.

Invoking Methods

The Method struct defines the Func field, which returns a Value that can be used to invoke a method, using the same approach described earlier in the chapter, as shown in Listing 29-11.

Listing 29-11. Invoking a Method in the main.go File in the reflection Folder

```
package main

import (
    "reflect"
    //"strings"
    //"fmt"
)

func executeFirstVoidMethod(s interface{}) {
    sVal := reflect.ValueOf(s)
    for i := 0; i < sVal.NumMethod(); i++ {
        method := sVal.Type().Method(i)
        if method.Type.NumIn() == 1 {
            results := method.Func.Call([]reflect.Value{ sVal })
            Printfln("Type: %v, Method: %v, Results: %v",
                sVal.Type(), method.Name, results)
            break
        } else {
            Printfln("Skipping method %v %v", method.Name, method.Type.NumIn())
        }
    }
}
```

```
func main() {
    executeFirstVoidMethod(&Product { Name: "Kayak", Price: 279})
}
```

The executeFirstVoidMethod function enumerates the methods defined by the parameter's type and invokes the first method that defines one parameter. When invoking a method via the Method.Func field, the first argument must be the receiver, which is the struct value on which the method will be invoked:

```
...
results := method.Func.Call([]reflect.Value{ sVal })
...
```

This means that looking for a method that has one parameter selects a method that takes no arguments, which can be seen in the results produced when the project is compiled and executed:

```
Type: *main.Product, Method: GetAmount, Results: [$279.00]
```

The executeFirstVoidMethod has selected the GetAmount method. The receiver isn't specified when the method is invoked via the Value interface, as shown in Listing 29-12.

Listing 29-12. Invoking a Method via a Value in the main.go File in the reflection Folder

```
package main

import (
    "reflect"
    //"strings"
    //"fmt"
)

func executeFirstVoidMethod(s interface{}) {
    sVal := reflect.ValueOf(s)
    for i := 0; i < sVal.NumMethod(); i++ {
        method := sVal.Method(i)
        if method.Type().NumIn() == 0 {
            results := method.Call([]reflect.Value{})
            Printfln("Type: %v, Method: %v, Results: %v",
                sVal.Type(), sVal.Type().Method(i).Name, results)
            break
        } else {
            Printfln("Skipping method %v %v",
                sVal.Type().Method(i).Name, method.Type().NumIn())
        }
    }
}

func main() {
    executeFirstVoidMethod(&Product { Name: "Kayak", Price: 279})
}
```

To find a method that I can invoke without providing additional arguments, I have to look for zero parameters, since the receiver is not explicitly specified. Instead, the receiver is determined from the `Value` on which the `Call` method is invoked:

```
...
results := method.Call([]reflect.Value{})
...
```

This example produces the same output as the code in Listing 29-11.

Working with Interfaces

The `Type` struct defines methods that can be used to inspect interface types, described in Table 29-8. Most of these methods can also be applied to structs, as demonstrated in the previous section, but the behavior is slightly different.

Table 29-8. *The Type Methods for Interfaces*

Name	Description
Implements(type)	This method returns `true` if the reflected `Value` implements the specified interface, which is also represented by a `Value`.
Elem()	This method returns `Value` that reflects the value contained by the interface.
NumMethod()	This method returns the number of exported methods defined for the reflected struct type.
Method(index)	This method returns the reflected method at the specified index, represented with the `Method` struct.
MethodByName(name)	This method returns the reflected method with the specified name. The results are a `Method` struct, and a `bool` that indicates whether a method with the specified name exists.

Care must be taken when using reflection for interfaces because the `reflect` package always starts with a value and will attempt to work with that value's underlying type. The simplest way to solve this problem is to convert a `nil` value, as shown in Listing 29-13.

Listing 29-13. Reflecting an Interface in the main.go File in the reflection Folder

```
package main

import (
    "reflect"
    //"strings"
    //"fmt"
)
```

```
func checkImplementation(check interface{}, targets ...interface{}) {
    checkType := reflect.TypeOf(check)
    if (checkType.Kind() == reflect.Ptr &&
            checkType.Elem().Kind() == reflect.Interface) {
        checkType := checkType.Elem()
        for _, target := range targets {
            targetType := reflect.TypeOf(target)
            Printfln("Type %v implements %v: %v",
                targetType, checkType, targetType.Implements(checkType))
        }
    }
}

func main() {
    currencyItemType := (*CurrencyItem)(nil)
    checkImplementation(currencyItemType, Product{}, &Product{}, &Purchase{})
}
```

To specify the interface that I want to check, I convert nil to a pointer of the interface, like this:

```
...
currencyItemType := (*CurrencyItem)(nil)
...
```

This must be done with a pointer, which is then followed in the checkImplementation function using the Elem method, to get a Type that reflects the interface, which is CurrencyItem in this example:

```
...
if (checkType.Kind() == reflect.Ptr &&
        checkType.Elem().Kind() == reflect.Interface) {
    checkType := checkType.Elem()
...
```

After that, it is easy to check whether a type implements the interface using the Implements method. Compile and execute the project, and you will see the following output:

```
Type main.Product implements main.CurrencyItem: false
Type *main.Product implements main.CurrencyItem: true
Type *main.Purchase implements main.CurrencyItem: true
```

The output shows that the Product struct doesn't implement the interface, but *Product does because *Product is the receiver type used to implement the methods required by CurrencyItem. The *Purchase type also implements the interface because it has nested struct fields that define the required methods.

Getting Underlying Values from Interfaces

Although reflection will typically produce concrete types, there are occasions when the Elem method must be used to move from an interface to the type that implements it, as shown in Listing 29-14.

Listing 29-14. Getting Underlying Interface Values in the main.go File in the reflection Folder

```
package main

import (
    "reflect"
    //"strings"
    //"fmt"
)

type Wrapper struct {
    NamedItem
}

func getUnderlying(item Wrapper, fieldName string) {
    itemVal := reflect.ValueOf(item)
    fieldVal := itemVal.FieldByName(fieldName)
    Printfln("Field Type: %v", fieldVal.Type())
    if (fieldVal.Kind() == reflect.Interface) {
        Printfln("Underlying Type: %v", fieldVal.Elem().Type())
    }
}

func main() {
    getUnderlying(Wrapper{NamedItem: &Product{}}, "NamedItem")
}
```

The Wrapper type defines a nested NamedItem field. The getUnderlying function uses reflection to get the field and writes out the field type and the underlying type obtained with the Elem method. Compile and execute the project, and you will see the following results:

```
Field Type: main.NamedItem
Underlying Type: *main.Product
```

The field type is the NamedItem interface, but the Elem method shows that the underlying value assigned to the NamedItem field is a *Product.

Examining Interface Methods

The NumMethod, Method, and MethodByName methods can be used on interface types, but the results include unexported methods, which isn't the case when examining the struct type directly, as shown in Listing 29-15.

Listing 29-15. Examining Interface Methods in the main.go File in the reflection Folder

```go
package main

import (
    "reflect"
    //"strings"
    //"fmt"
)

type Wrapper struct {
    NamedItem
}

func getUnderlying(item Wrapper, fieldName string) {
    itemVal := reflect.ValueOf(item)
    fieldVal := itemVal.FieldByName(fieldName)
    Printfln("Field Type: %v", fieldVal.Type())
    for i := 0; i < fieldVal.Type().NumMethod(); i++ {
        method := fieldVal.Type().Method(i)
        Printfln("Interface Method: %v, Exported: %v",
            method.Name, method.PkgPath == "")
    }
    Printfln("--------")
    if (fieldVal.Kind() == reflect.Interface) {
        Printfln("Underlying Type: %v", fieldVal.Elem().Type())
        for i := 0; i < fieldVal.Elem().Type().NumMethod(); i++ {
            method := fieldVal.Elem().Type().Method(i)
            Printfln("Underlying Method: %v", method.Name)
        }
    }
}

func main() {
    getUnderlying(Wrapper{NamedItem: &Product{}}, "NamedItem")
}
```

The changes write out details of the methods obtained from the interface and underlying types. Compile and execute the project, and you will see the following output:

```
Field Type: main.NamedItem
Interface Method: GetName, Exported: true
Interface Method: unexportedMethod, Exported: false
--------
Underlying Type: *main.Product
Underlying Method: GetAmount
Underlying Method: GetName
```

The list of methods for the NamedItem interface includes unexportedMethod, which isn't included in the list for *Product. There are additional methods defined for *Product beyond those required by the interface, which is why the GetAmount method appears in the output.

Methods can be invoked via an interface, but you must ensure they are exported before using the Call method. If you attempt to invoke an unexported method, Call will panic.

Working with Channel Types

The Type struct defines methods that can be used to inspect channel types, described in Table 29-9.

Table 29-9. *The Type Methods for Channels*

Name	Description
ChanDir()	This method returns a ChanDir value that describes the channel direction, using one of the values shown in Table 29-10.
Elem()	This method returns a Type that reflects type carried by the channel.

The ChanDir result returned by the ChanDir method indicates the direction of the channel, which can be compared to one of the reflect package constants described in Table 29-10.

Table 29-10. *The ChanDir Values*

Name	Description
RecvDir	This value indicates that the channel can be used to receive data. When expressed as a string, this value returns <-chan.
SendDir	This value indicates that the channel can be used to send data. When expressed as a string, this value returns chan<-.
BothDir	This value indicates that the channel can be used to send and receive data. When expressed as a string, this value returns chan.

Listing 29-16 demonstrates the use of the methods in Table 29-9 to inspect a channel type.

Listing 29-16. Inspecting a Channel Type in the main.go File in the reflection Folder

```
package main

import (
    "reflect"
    //"strings"
    //"fmt"
)
```

```
func inspectChannel(channel interface{}) {
    channelType := reflect.TypeOf(channel)
    if (channelType.Kind() == reflect.Chan) {
        Printfln("Type %v, Direction: %v",
            channelType.Elem(), channelType.ChanDir())
    }
}

func main() {
    var c chan<- string
    inspectChannel(c)
}
```

The channel examined in this example is send-only and produces the following output when the project is compiled and executed:

```
Type string, Direction: chan<-
```

Working with Channel Values

The Value interface defines the methods described in Table 29-11 for working with channels.

Table 29-11. *The Value Method for Channels*

Name	Description
Send(val)	This method sends the value reflected by the Value argument on the channel. This method blocks until the value is sent.
Recv()	This method receives a value from the channel, which is returned as a Value for reflection. This method also returns a bool, which indicates if a value was received and will be false if the channel has closed. This method blocks until a value is received or the channel has been closed.
TrySend(val)	This method sends the specified value but will not block. The bool result indicates whether the value was sent.
TryRecv()	This method attempts to receive a value from the channel but will not block. The results are a Value reflecting the received value, and a bool indicating whether a value has been received.
Close()	This method closes the channel.

Listing 29-17 defines a function that receives a channel and a slice containing values that will be sent over the channel.

Listing 29-17. Using a Channel in the main.go File in the reflection Folder

```
package main

import (
    "reflect"
    //"strings"
    //"fmt"
)

func sendOverChannel(channel interface{}, data interface{}) {
    channelVal := reflect.ValueOf(channel)
    dataVal := reflect.ValueOf(data)
    if (channelVal.Kind() == reflect.Chan &&
            dataVal.Kind() == reflect.Slice &&
            channelVal.Type().Elem() == dataVal.Type().Elem()) {
        for i := 0; i < dataVal.Len(); i++ {
            val := dataVal.Index(i)
            channelVal.Send(val)
        }
        channelVal.Close()
    } else {
        Printfln("Unexpected types: %v, %v", channelVal.Type(), dataVal.Type())
    }
}

func main() {

    values := []string { "Alice", "Bob", "Charlie", "Dora"}
    channel := make(chan string)

    go sendOverChannel(channel, values)
    for {
        if val, open := <- channel; open {
            Printfln("Received value: %v", val)
        } else {
            break
        }
    }
}
```

The sendOverChannel checks the types it receives, enumerates the values in the slice, and sends each of them over the channel. Once all the values have been sent, the channel is closed. Compile and execute the project, and you will see the following output:

```
Received value: Alice
Received value: Bob
Received value: Charlie
Received value: Dora
```

805

Creating New Channel Types and Values

The reflect package defines the functions described in Table 29-12 for creating new channel types and values.

Table 29-12. *The reflect Package Functions for Creating Channel Types and Values*

Name	Description
ChanOf(dir, type)	This function returns a Type that reflects a channel with the specified direction and data type, which are expressed using a ChanDir and a Value.
MakeChan(type, buffer)	This function returns a Value that reflects a new channel, created using the specified Type and int buffer size.

Listing 29-18 defines a function that accepts a slice and uses it to create a channel, which is then used to send the elements in the slice.

Listing 29-18. Creating a Channel in the main.go File in the reflection Folder

```
package main

import (
    "reflect"
    //"strings"
    //"fmt"
)

func createChannelAndSend(data interface{}) interface{} {
    dataVal := reflect.ValueOf(data)
    channelType := reflect.ChanOf(reflect.BothDir, dataVal.Type().Elem())
    channel := reflect.MakeChan(channelType, 1)
    go func() {
        for i := 0; i < dataVal.Len(); i++ {
            channel.Send(dataVal.Index(i))
        }
        channel.Close()
    }()
    return channel.Interface()
}

func main() {

    values := []string { "Alice", "Bob", "Charlie", "Dora"}
    channel := createChannelAndSend(values).(chan string)
```

```
for {
    if val, open := <- channel; open {
        Printfln("Received value: %v", val)
    } else {
        break
    }
}
}
```

The createChannelAndSend function uses the element type of the slice to create a channel type, which is then used to create a channel. A goroutine is used to send the elements in the slice to the channel, and the channel is returned as the function result. Compile and execute the project, and you will see the following output:

```
Received value: Alice
Received value: Bob
Received value: Charlie
Received value: Dora
```

Selecting from Multiple Channels

The channel select feature described in Chapter 14 can be used within reflection code using the Select function defined by the reflect package, which is described in Table 29-13 for quick reference.

Table 29-13. *The reflect Package Function for Selecting Channels*

Name	Description
Select(cases)	This function accepts a SelectCase slice, where each element describes a set of send or receive operations. The results are the int index of the SelectCase that was executed, the Value that was received (if the selected case was a read operation), and a bool that indicates whether a value was read or if the channel was blocked or closed.

The SelectCase struct is used to represent a single case statement, using the fields described in Table 29-14.

Table 29-14. *The SelectCase struct Fields*

Name	Description
Chan	This field is assigned the Value that reflects the channel.
Dir	This field is assigned a SelectDir value, which specifies the type of channel operation for this case.
Send	This field is assigned the Value that reflects the value that will be sent over the channel for send operations.

The SelectDir type is an alias for int, and the reflect package defines the constants described in Table 29-15 for specifying the type of select case.

Table 29-15. *The SelectDir Constants*

Name	Description
SelectSend	This constant denotes an operation to send a value over a channel.
SelectRecv	This constant denotes an operation to receive a value from the channel.
SelectDefault	This constant denotes the default clause for the select.

Defining select statements using reflection is verbose, but the results can be flexible and accept a wider range of types than regular Go code. Listing 29-19 uses the Select function to read values from multiple channels.

Listing 29-19. Using the Select Function in the main.go File in the reflection Folder

```
package main

import (
    "reflect"
    //"strings"
    //"fmt"
)

func createChannelAndSend(data interface{}) interface{} {
    dataVal := reflect.ValueOf(data)
    channelType := reflect.ChanOf(reflect.BothDir, dataVal.Type().Elem())
    channel := reflect.MakeChan(channelType, 1)
    go func() {
        for i := 0; i < dataVal.Len(); i++ {
            channel.Send(dataVal.Index(i))
        }
        channel.Close()
    }()
    return channel.Interface()
}

func readChannels(channels ...interface{}) {
    channelsVal := reflect.ValueOf(channels)
    cases := []reflect.SelectCase {}
    for i := 0; i < channelsVal.Len(); i++ {
        cases = append(cases, reflect.SelectCase{
            Chan: channelsVal.Index(i).Elem(),
            Dir: reflect.SelectRecv,
        })
    }
}
```

```
    for {
        caseIndex, val, ok := reflect.Select(cases)
        if (ok) {
            Printfln("Value read: %v, Type: %v", val, val.Type())
        } else {
            if len(cases) == 1 {
                Printfln("All channels closed.")
                return
            }
            cases = append(cases[:caseIndex], cases[caseIndex+1:]... )
        }
    }
}

func main() {

    values := []string { "Alice", "Bob", "Charlie", "Dora"}
    channel := createChannelAndSend(values).(chan string)

    cities := []string { "London", "Rome", "Paris"}
    cityChannel := createChannelAndSend(cities).(chan string)

    prices := []float64 { 279, 48.95, 19.50}
    priceChannel := createChannelAndSend(prices).(chan float64)

    readChannels(channel, cityChannel, priceChannel)
}
```

This example creates three channels using the createChannelAndSend function and passes them to the readChannels function, which uses the Select function to read values until all of the channels are closed. To ensure that reads are only performed on open channels, the SelecCase values are removed from the slice passed to the Select function when the channel they represent closes. Compile and execute the project, and you will see the following output:

```
Value read: London, Type: string
Value read: Alice, Type: string
Value read: Rome, Type: string
Value read: Bob, Type: string
Value read: Paris, Type: string
Value read: Charlie, Type: string
Value read: 279, Type: float64
Value read: Dora, Type: string
Value read: 48.95, Type: float64
Value read: 19.5, Type: float64
All channels closed.
```

You may see the values displayed in a different order because goroutines are used to send values through the channels.

Summary

In this chapter, I described the reflection features for working with functions, methods, interfaces, and channels, completing the description of the Go reflection features started in Chapter 27 and continued in Chapter 28. In the next chapter, I describe the standard library features for coordinating goroutines.

CHAPTER 30

■ ■ ■

Coordinating Goroutines

In this chapter, I describe the Go standard library packages with features that are used to coordinate goroutines. Table 30-1 puts the features described in this chapter in context.

Table 30-1. *Putting Features for Coordinating Goroutines in Context*

Question	Answer
What are they?	These features are useful when an application uses multiple goroutines.
Why are they useful?	The use of goroutines can be complex when they share data or when a goroutine is used to handle a request across multiple API components in a server.
How are they used?	The sync package provides types and functions for managing goroutines, including ensuring exclusive access to data. The context package provides features that are used to support a server processing a request, which is typically done using a goroutine.
Are there any pitfalls or limitations?	These are advanced features and should be used with caution.
Are there any alternatives?	Not all applications require these features, especially if they use goroutines that do not share data.

Table 30-2 summarizes the chapter.

Table 30-2. *Chapter Summary*

Problem	Solution	Listing
Wait for one or more goroutines to finish	Use a wait group	5, 6
Prevent multiple goroutines from accessing data at the same time	Use mutual exclusion	7–10
Wait for an event to occur	Use a condition	11, 12
Ensure a function is executed once	Use a Once struct	13
Provide a context for requests being processed across API boundaries in servers	Use a context	14–17

© Adam Freeman 2022
A. Freeman, *Pro Go*, https://doi.org/10.1007/978-1-4842-7355-5_30

Preparing for This Chapter

To prepare for this chapter, open a new command prompt, navigate to a convenient location, and create a directory named coordination. Run the command shown in Listing 30-1 in the coordination folder to create a module file.

■ **Tip** You can download the example project for this chapter—and for all the other chapters in this book—from https://github.com/apress/pro-go. See Chapter 2 for how to get help if you have problems running the examples.

Listing 30-1. Initializing the Module

```
go mod init coordination
```

Add a file named printer.go to the coordination folder with the content shown in Listing 30-2.

Listing 30-2. The Contents of the printer.go File in the coordination Folder

```
package main

import "fmt"

func Println(template string, values ...interface{}) {
    fmt.Printf(template + "\n", values...)
}
```

Add a file named main.go to the coordination folder with the content shown in Listing 30-3.

Listing 30-3. The Contents of the main.go File in the coordination Folder

```
package main

func doSum(count int, val *int)  {
    for i := 0; i < count; i++ {
        *val++
    }
}

func main() {
    counter := 0
    doSum(5000, &counter)
    Println("Total: %v", counter)
}
```

Run the command shown in Listing 30-4 in the coordination folder to compile and execute the project.

Listing 30-4. Compiling and Executing the Project

```
go run .
```

This command will produce the following output:

```
Total: 5000
```

Using Wait Groups

A common problem is ensuring that the main function doesn't finish before the goroutines it starts are complete, at which point the program terminates. For me, at least, this usually happens when a goroutine is introduced into existing code, as shown in Listing 30-5.

Listing 30-5. Introducing a Goroutine in the main.go File in the coordination Folder

```
package main

func doSum(count int, val *int) {
    for i := 0; i < count; i++ {
        *val++
    }
}

func main() {
    counter := 0
    go doSum(5000, &counter)
    Printfln("Total: %v", counter)
}
```

Goroutines are so simple to create that it is easy to forget the impact they have. In this case, the execution of the main function continues in parallel with the goroutine, which means that the final statement in the main function is executed before the goroutine finishes executing the doSum function, producing the following output when the project is compiled and executed:

```
Total: 0
```

The sync package provides the WaitGroup struct, which can be used to wait for one or more goroutines to finish, using the methods described in Table 30-3.

Table 30-3. *The Methods Defined by the WaitGroup Struct*

Name	Description
Add(num)	This method increases the number of goroutines that the WaitGroup is waiting for by the specified int.
Done()	This method decreases the number of goroutines that the WaitGroup is waiting for by one.
Wait()	This method blocks until the Done method has been called once for the total number of goroutines specified by the calls to the Add method.

The WaitGroup acts as a counter. When the goroutines are created, the Add method is called to specify the number of goroutines that are started, which increments the counter, after which the Wait method is called, which blocks. As each goroutine completes, it calls the Done method, which decrements the counter. When the counter is zero, the Wait method stops blocking, completing the waiting process. Listing 30-6 adds a WaitGroup to the example.

Listing 30-6. Using a WaitGroup in the main.go File in the coordination Folder

```
package main

import (
    "sync"
)

var waitGroup = sync.WaitGroup{}

func doSum(count int, val *int)  {
    for i := 0; i < count; i++ {
        *val++
    }
    waitGroup.Done()
}

func main() {
    counter := 0

    waitGroup.Add(1)
    go doSum(5000, &counter)
    waitGroup.Wait()
    Printfln("Total: %v", counter)
}
```

The WaitGroup will panic if the counter becomes negative, so it is important to call the Add method before starting the goroutine to prevent the Done method from being called early. It is also important to make sure that the total of the values passed to the Add method equals the number of times the Done method is called. If there are too few calls to Done, then the Wait method will block forever, but if the Done method is called too many times, then the WaitGroup will panic. There is only one goroutine in the example, but if you compile and execute the project, you will see that it prevents the main function from completing early and produces the following output:

```
Total: 5000
```

AVOIDING THE COPY PITFALL

It is important not to copy WaitGroup values because it means that goroutines will be calling Done and Wait on different values, which generally means that the application deadlocks. If you want to pass a WaitGroup as a function argument, this means you need to use a pointer, like this:

```go
package main

import (
    "sync"
)

    func doSum(count int, val *int, waitGroup * sync.WaitGroup)  {
    for i := 0; i < count; i++ {
        *val++
    }
    waitGroup.Done()
}
func main() {
    counter := 0

    waitGroup := sync.WaitGroup{}

    waitGroup.Add(1)
    go doSum(5000, &counter, &waitGroup)
    waitGroup.Wait()
    Printfln("Total: %v", counter)
}
```

This applies to all of the structs described in this section. As a rule of thumb, coordination requires that all goroutines use the same struct value.

Using Mutual Exclusion

If multiple goroutines access the same data, then it is possible that two goroutines will access that data at the same time and cause unexpected results. As a simple demonstration, Listing 30-7 increases the number of goroutines the example uses.

Listing 30-7. Using More Goroutines in the main.go File in the coordination Folder

```go
package main

import (
    "sync"
    "time"
)

var waitGroup = sync.WaitGroup{}
```

```
func doSum(count int, val *int)  {
    time.Sleep(time.Second)
    for i := 0; i < count; i++ {
        *val++
    }
    waitGroup.Done()
}

func main() {
    counter := 0

    numRoutines := 3
    waitGroup.Add(numRoutines)
    for i := 0; i < numRoutines; i++ {
        go doSum(5000, &counter)
    }
    waitGroup.Wait()
    Printfln("Total: %v", counter)
}
```

This listing increases the number of goroutines that execute the doSum function, all of which are accessing the same variable at the same time. (The call to the time.Sleep function is to ensure that the goroutines are all running at once, which is helpful to emphasize the problem addressed in this section but not something that you should do in real projects.) Compile and execute the project, and you will see the following output:

```
Total: 12129
```

You may see a different result, and running the project repeatedly can generate a different result each time. You may get the correct result—which is 15,000, since there are three goroutines each performing 5,000 operations—but that happens rarely on my machine. This behavior can differ between operating systems. In my simple testing, I consistently encountered problems on Windows while Linux worked more often.

The problem is that the increment operator isn't atomic, which means that it requires several steps to complete: the counter variable is read, incremented, and written. This is a simplification, but the problem is that these steps are being performed in parallel by goroutines, and they start to overlap, as shown in Figure 30-1.

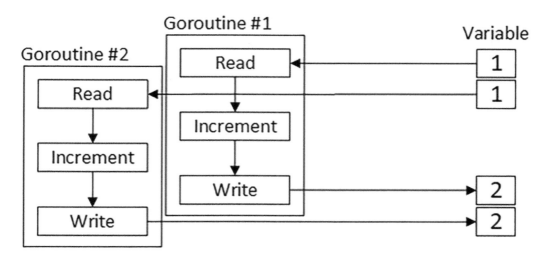

Figure 30-1. *Multiple goroutines accessing the same variable*

The second goroutine reads the value before the first goroutine can update it, which means that both goroutines are trying to increment the same value. The effect is that both goroutines produce the same result and write the same value. This is only one of the potential problems that sharing data between goroutines can cause, but all such problems arise because operations take time to perform, during which other goroutines are also trying to work with the data.

One way to solve this problem is with *mutual exclusion*, which ensures that a goroutine has exclusive access to the data it requires and prevents other goroutines from accessing that data.

Mutual exclusion is like checking out a book from the library. Only one person can check out the book at any given time, and all the other people who would like that book have to wait until the first person has finished, at which point the book can be checked out by someone else.

The sync package provides mutual exclusion with the Mutex struct, which defines the methods described in Table 30-4.

Table 30-4. *The Methods Defined by the Mutex Struct*

Name	Description
Lock()	This method locks the Mutex. If the Mutex is already locked, this method blocks until it is unlocked.
Unlock()	This method unlocks the Mutex.

Listing 30-8 uses a Mutex to resolve the problem with the example.

■ **Note** The standard library includes the sync/atomic package, which defines functions for low-level operations, such as incrementing an integer, in an atomic manner, meaning they are not subject to the kind of problem illustrated by Figure 30-1. I have not described these functions because they are difficult to use correctly and because the Go development team recommends using the features described in this chapter instead.

Listing 30-8. Using a Mutex in the main.go File in the coordination Folder

```go
package main

import (
    "sync"
    "time"
)

var waitGroup = sync.WaitGroup{}
var mutex = sync.Mutex{}

func doSum(count int, val *int)  {
    time.Sleep(time.Second)
    for i := 0; i < count; i++ {
        mutex.Lock()
        *val++
        mutex.Unlock()
    }
    waitGroup.Done()
}

func main() {
    counter := 0

    numRoutines := 3
    waitGroup.Add(numRoutines)
    for i := 0; i < numRoutines; i++ {
        go doSum(5000, &counter)
    }
    waitGroup.Wait()
    Printfln("Total: %v", counter)
}
```

A Mutex is unlocked when it is created, which means that the first goroutine that calls the Lock method won't block and will be able to increment the counter variable. The goroutine is said to have *acquired the lock*. Any other goroutine that calls the Lock method will block until the Unlock method is called, known as *releasing the lock*, at which point another goroutine will be able to acquire the lock and proceed with its access to the counter variable. The result is that only one goroutine at a time can increment the variable, as shown in Figure 30-2.

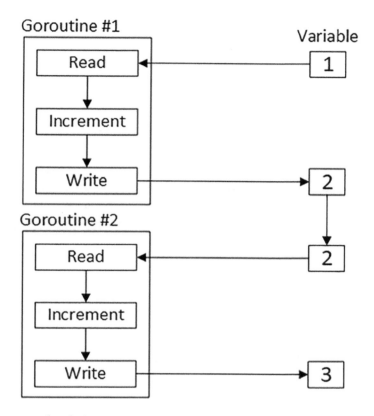

Figure 30-2. *Using mutual exclusion*

Compile and execute the project, and you will see the following output, showing that the goroutines were able to increment the counter variable correctly:

```
Total: 15000
```

Care must be taken when using mutual exclusion, and it is important to think through the impact of how a mutex is used. In Listing 30-8, for example, I locked and unlocked the mutex each time the variable was incremented. Using a mutex has an impact, and an alternative approach is to lock the mutex before executing the for loop, as shown in Listing 30-9.

Listing 30-9. Performing Fewer Mutex Operations in the main.go File in the coordination Folder

```
...
func doSum(count int, val *int)  {
    time.Sleep(time.Second)
    mutex.Lock()
    for i := 0; i < count; i++ {
        *val++
    }
    mutex.Unlock()
```

```
    waitGroup.Done()
}
...
```

This is a more sensible approach for such a simple example, but the situation is usually more complex, and locking larger sections of code can make applications less responsive and reduce overall performance. My advice is to start locking just the statements that access shared data.

AVOIDING THE MUTEX PITFALLS

The best approach to using mutual exclusion is to be careful and be conservative. You must ensure that all code that accesses shared data does so using the same Mutex, and every call to a Lock method must be balanced by a call to the Unlock method. It can be tempting to try to create clever enhancements or optimizations, but doing so can lead to poor performance or application deadlocks.

Using a Read-Write Mutex

A Mutex treats all goroutines as being equal and allows only one goroutine to acquire the lock. The RWMutex struct is more flexible and supports two categories of goroutine: readers and writers. Any number of readers can acquire the lock simultaneously, or a single writer can acquire the lock. The idea is that readers only care about conflicts with writers and can execute concurrently with other readers without difficulty. The RWMutex struct defines the methods described in Table 30-5.

Table 30-5. *The Methods Defined by the RWMutex*

Name	Description
RLock()	This method attempts to acquire the read lock and will block until it is acquired.
RUnlock()	This method releases the read lock.
Lock()	This method attempts to acquire the write lock and will block until it is acquired.
Unlock()	This method releases the write lock.
RLocker()	This method returns a pointer to a Locker for acquiring and releasing the read lock, as described in the "Using Conditions to Coordinate Goroutines" section.

The RWMutex is not as complex as it may appear. Here are the rules the RWMutex follows:

- If the RWMutex is unlocked, then the lock can be acquired by a reader (by calling the RLock method) or a writer (by calling the Lock method).

- If the lock is acquired by a reader, then other readers may also acquire the lock by calling the RLock method, which will not block. The Lock method will block until all of the readers release the lock by calling the RUnlock method.

- If the lock is acquired by a writer, then both the RLock and Lock methods will block to prevent other goroutines from acquiring the lock until the Unlock method is called.

- If the lock is acquired by a reader and a writer calls the Lock method, both the Lock and RLock methods will block until the Unlock method is called. This prevents the

820

mutex from being perpetually locked by readers without giving writers a chance to
acquire the write lock.

Listing 30-10 demonstrates the use of the RWMutex.

Listing 30-10. Using the RWMutex in the main.go File in the coordination Folder

```
package main

import (
    "sync"
    "time"
    "math"
    "math/rand"
)

var waitGroup = sync.WaitGroup{}
var rwmutex = sync.RWMutex{}

var squares = map[int]int {}

func calculateSquares(max, iterations int) {
    for i := 0; i < iterations; i++ {
        val := rand.Intn(max)
        rwmutex.RLock();
        square, ok := squares[val]
        rwmutex.RUnlock()
        if (ok) {
            Printfln("Cached value: %v = %v", val, square)
        } else {
            rwmutex.Lock()
            if _, ok := squares[val]; !ok {
                squares[val] = int(math.Pow(float64(val), 2))
                Printfln("Added value: %v = %v", val, squares[val])
            }
            rwmutex.Unlock()
        }
    }
    waitGroup.Done()
}

func main() {
    rand.Seed(time.Now().UnixNano())
    //counter := 0
    numRoutines := 3
    waitGroup.Add(numRoutines)
    for i := 0; i < numRoutines; i++ {
        go calculateSquares(10, 5)
    }
    waitGroup.Wait()
    Printfln("Cached values: %v", len(squares))
}
```

The calculateSquares function acquires the read lock to check to see if a map contains a randomly chosen key. If the map does contain the key, the associated value is read, and the read lock is released. If the map doesn't contain the key, then the write lock is acquired, a value is added to the map for the key, and then the write lock is released.

The use of the RWMutex means that when one goroutine has the read lock, other routines can also acquire the lock and make reads. Reading data doesn't cause any concurrency issues unless it is being modified at the same time. If a goroutine calls the Lock method, it won't be able to acquire the write lock until the read lock has been released by all the goroutines that acquired it.

Notice that goroutines release the read lock before acquiring the write lock in Listing 30-10. The RWMutex doesn't support upgrading from read lock to the write lock, which you may have encountered in other languages, and you must release the read lock before calling the Lock method to avoid deadlock. There can be a delay between releasing the read lock and acquiring the write lock, during which other goroutines may acquire the write lock and make changes, so it is important to check that the state of the data hasn't changed once the write lock is acquired, like this:

```
...
rwmutex.Lock()
if _, ok := squares[val]; !ok {
    squares[val] = int(math.Pow(float64(val), 2))
...
```

Compile and execute the project, and you will see output similar to the following, although the specific results are determined by the randomly chosen keys:

```
Added value: 6 = 36
Added value: 2 = 4
Added value: 7 = 49
Cached value: 7 = 49
Added value: 8 = 64
Cached value: 6 = 36
Added value: 1 = 1
Cached value: 1 = 1
Added value: 3 = 9
Cached value: 8 = 64
Cached value: 8 = 64
Cached value: 1 = 1
Cached value: 1 = 1
Added value: 5 = 25
Cached values: 7
```

Using Conditions to Coordinate Goroutines

The goroutines in the previous example share the same data but are otherwise independent from one another. When goroutines need coordination, such as waiting for some event to occur, the Cond struct can be used. The sync package provides the function described in Table 30-6 for creating Cond struct values.

Table 30-6. *The sync Function for Creating Cond Values*

Name	Description
NewCond(*locker)	This function creates a Cond using the pointer to the specified Locker.

The argument to the NewCond function is a Locker, which is an interface that defines the methods described in Table 30-7.

Table 30-7. *The Methods Defined by the Locker Interface*

Name	Description
Lock()	This method acquires the lock managed by the Locker.
Unlock()	This method releases the lock managed by the Locker.

The Mutex and RWMutex structs define the method required by the Locker interface. In the case of the RWMutex, the Lock and Unlock methods operate on the write lock, and the RLocker method can be used to get a Locker that operates on the read lock. Table 30-8 describes the field and methods defined by the Cond struct.

Table 30-8. *The Field and Methods Defined by the Cond Struct*

Name	Description
L	This field returns the Locker that was passed to the NewCond function and is used to acquire the lock.
Wait()	This method releases the lock and suspends the goroutine.
Signal()	This method wakes one waiting goroutine.
Broadcast()	This method wakes all waiting goroutines.

Listing 30-11 demonstrates the use of a Cond to notify waiting goroutines of an event.

Listing 30-11. Using a Cond in the main.go File in the coordination Folder

```
package main

import (
    "sync"
    "time"
    "math"
    "math/rand"
)

var waitGroup = sync.WaitGroup{}
var rwmutex = sync.RWMutex{}
var readyCond = sync.NewCond(rwmutex.RLocker())

var squares = map[int]int {}
```

```
func generateSquares(max int) {
    rwmutex.Lock()
    Printfln("Generating data...")
    for val := 0; val < max; val++ {
        squares[val] = int(math.Pow(float64(val), 2))
    }
    rwmutex.Unlock()
    Printfln("Broadcasting condition")
    readyCond.Broadcast()
    waitGroup.Done()
}

func readSquares(id, max, iterations int) {
    readyCond.L.Lock()
    for len(squares) == 0 {
        readyCond.Wait()
    }
    for i := 0; i < iterations; i++ {
        key := rand.Intn(max)
        Printfln("#%v Read value: %v = %v", id, key, squares[key])
        time.Sleep(time.Millisecond * 100)
    }
    readyCond.L.Unlock()
    waitGroup.Done()
}

func main() {
    rand.Seed(time.Now().UnixNano())
    numRoutines := 2
    waitGroup.Add(numRoutines)
    for i := 0; i < numRoutines; i++ {
        go readSquares(i, 10, 5)
    }

    waitGroup.Add(1)
    go generateSquares(10)
    waitGroup.Wait()
    Printfln("Cached values: %v", len(squares))
}
```

This example requires coordination between goroutines that would be difficult to achieve without a Cond. One goroutine is responsible for populating a map with data values, which is then read by other goroutines. The readers require notification that the data generation is complete before they run.

The readers wait by acquiring the Cond lock and calling the Wait method, like this:

```
...
readyCond.L.Lock()
for len(squares) == 0 {
    readyCond.Wait()
}
...
```

Calling the Wait method suspends the goroutine and releases the lock so that it can be acquired. The call to the Wait method is usually performed inside a for loop that checks that the condition for which the goroutine is waiting has happened, just to make sure that the data is in the expected state.

There is no need to acquire the lock again when the Wait method unblocks and a goroutine can either call the Wait method again or access the shared data. When finished with the shared data, the lock must be released:

```
...
readyCond.L.Unlock()
...
```

The goroutine that generates the data acquires the write lock using the RWMutex, modifies the data, releases the write lock, and then calls the Cond.Broadcast method, which wakes up all of the waiting goroutines. Compile and execute the project, and you will see output similar to the following, allowing for the random key values that are chosen:

```
Generating data...
Broadcasting condition
#0 Read value: 4 = 16
#1 Read value: 1 = 1
#1 Read value: 5 = 25
#0 Read value: 6 = 36
#0 Read value: 2 = 4
#1 Read value: 2 = 4
#1 Read value: 6 = 36
#0 Read value: 6 = 36
#0 Read value: 6 = 36
#1 Read value: 8 = 64
Cached values: 10
```

The call to the time.Sleep function in the readSquares function slows down the process of reading the data so that both reader goroutines are processing data at the same time, which you can see in the interleaving of the first number in the output lines. Since these goroutines acquire an RWMutex read lock, both acquire the lock and can read data simultaneously. Listing 30-12 changes the type of lock used by the Cond.

Listing 30-12. Changing Lock Type in the main.go File in the coordination Folder

```
...
var waitGroup = sync.WaitGroup{}
var rwmutex = sync.RWMutex{}
var readyCond = sync.NewCond(&rwmutex)
...
```

This change means that all of the goroutines are using the write lock, which means that only one goroutine will be able to acquire the lock. Compile and execute the project, and you will see that the output is no longer interleaved:

```
Generating data...
Broadcasting condition
```

```
#0 Read value: 5 = 25
#0 Read value: 8 = 64
#0 Read value: 9 = 81
#0 Read value: 0 = 0
#0 Read value: 4 = 16
#1 Read value: 7 = 49
#1 Read value: 8 = 64
#1 Read value: 5 = 25
#1 Read value: 8 = 64
#1 Read value: 5 = 25
Cached values: 10
```

Ensuring a Function Is Executed Once

An alternative approach to the previous example is to ensure that the generateSquares function is executed once, using the sync.Once struct. The Once struct defines one method, described in Table 30-9.

Table 30-9. *The Once Method*

Name	Description
Do(func)	This method executes the specified function, but only if it has not already been executed.

Listing 30-13 demonstrates the use of the Once struct.

Listing 30-13. Executing a Function Once in the main.go File in the coordination Folder

```
package main

import (
    "sync"
    "time"
    "math"
    "math/rand"
)

var waitGroup = sync.WaitGroup{}
//var rwmutex = sync.RWMutex{}
//var readyCond = sync.NewCond(rwmutex.RLocker())
var once = sync.Once{}

var squares = map[int]int {}

func generateSquares(max int) {
    //rwmutex.Lock()
    Printfln("Generating data...")
    for val := 0; val < max; val++ {
        squares[val] = int(math.Pow(float64(val), 2))
    }
```

```
    // rwmutex.Unlock()
    // Printfln("Broadcasting condition")
    // readyCond.Broadcast()
    // waitGroup.Done()
}

func readSquares(id, max, iterations int) {
    once.Do(func () {
        generateSquares(max)
    })
    // readyCond.L.Lock()
    // for len(squares) == 0 {
    //     readyCond.Wait()
    // }
    for i := 0; i < iterations; i++ {
        key := rand.Intn(max)
        Printfln("#%v Read value: %v = %v", id, key, squares[key])
        time.Sleep(time.Millisecond * 100)
    }
    //readyCond.L.Unlock()
    waitGroup.Done()
}

func main() {
    rand.Seed(time.Now().UnixNano())
    numRoutines := 2
    waitGroup.Add(numRoutines)
    for i := 0; i < numRoutines; i++ {
        go readSquares(i, 10, 5)
    }
    // waitGroup.Add(1)
    // go generateSquares(10)
    waitGroup.Wait()
    Printfln("Cached values: %v", len(squares))
}
```

Using the Once struct simplifies the example because the Do method blocks until the function it receives has been executed, after which it returns without executing the function again. Since the only changes to the shared data in this example are made by the generateSquares function, using the Do method to execute this function ensures that the changes are made safely. Not all code fits the Once model so well, but in this example, I can remove the RWMutex and the Cond. Compile and execute the project, and you will see output similar to the following:

```
Generating data...
#1 Read value: 0 = 0
#0 Read value: 0 = 0
#0 Read value: 4 = 16
#1 Read value: 9 = 81
#1 Read value: 2 = 4
#0 Read value: 9 = 81
#0 Read value: 8 = 64
```

```
#1 Read value: 3 = 9
#1 Read value: 7 = 49
#0 Read value: 3 = 9
Cached values: 10
```

Using Contexts

Go makes it easy to create server apps, which receive requests on behalf of clients and process them in their own goroutine. The context package provides the Context interface, which makes it easier to manage requests using the methods described in Table 30-10.

Table 30-10. *The Methods Defined by the Context Interface*

Name	Description
Value(key)	This method returns the value associated with the specified key.
Done()	This method returns a channel that can be used to receive a cancelation notification.
Deadline()	This method returns the time.Time that represents the deadline for the request and a bool value that will be false if no deadline has been specified.
Err()	This method returns an error that indicates why the Done channel received a signal. The context package defines two variables that can be used to compare the error: Canceled indicates that the request was canceled, and DeadlineExeeded indicates that the deadline passed.

The context package provides the functions described in Table 30-11 for creating Context values.

Table 30-11. *The context Package Functions for Creating Context Values*

Name	Description
Background()	This method returns the default Context, from which other contexts are derived.
WithCancel(ctx)	This method returns a context and a cancelation function, as described in the "Canceling a Request" section.
WithDeadline(ctx, time)	This method returns a context with a deadline, which is expressed using a time.Time value, as described in the "Setting a Deadline" section.
WithTimeout(ctx, duration)	This method returns a context with a deadline, which is expressed using a time.Duration value, as described in the "Setting a Deadline" section.
WithValue(ctx, key, val)	This method returns a context containing the specified key-value pair, as described in the "Providing Request Data" section.

To prepare for this section, Listing 30-14 defines a function that simulates request processing.

Listing 30-14. Simulating Request Processing in the main.go File in the coordination Folder

```
package main

import (
    "sync"
    "time"
    // "math"
    // "math/rand"
)

func processRequest(wg *sync.WaitGroup, count int) {
    total := 0
    for i := 0; i < count; i++ {
        Printfln("Processing request: %v", total)
        total++
        time.Sleep(time.Millisecond * 250)
    }
    Printfln("Request processed...%v", total)
    wg.Done()
}

func main() {
    waitGroup := sync.WaitGroup {}
    waitGroup.Add(1)
    Printfln("Request dispatched...")
    go processRequest(&waitGroup, 10)
    waitGroup.Wait()
}
```

The processRequest function simulates processing a request by incrementing a counter, with a call to the time.Sleep function to slow everything down. The main function uses a goroutine to invoke the processRequest function, taking the place of a request arriving from a client. (See Part 3 for an example that processes actual requests. This section is just about how contexts work.) Compile and execute the project, and you will see the following output:

```
Request dispatched...
Processing request: 0
Processing request: 1
Processing request: 2
Processing request: 3
Processing request: 4
Processing request: 5
Processing request: 6
Processing request: 7
Processing request: 8
Processing request: 9
Request processed...10
```

Canceling a Request

The first use for a Context is to notify the code processing the request when the request is canceled, as shown in Listing 30-15.

Listing 30-15. Canceling a Request in the main.go File in the coordination Folder

```
package main

import (
    "sync"
    "time"
    // "math"
    // "math/rand"
    "context"
)

func processRequest(ctx context.Context, wg *sync.WaitGroup, count int) {
    total := 0
    for i := 0; i < count; i++ {
        select {
            case <- ctx.Done():
                Printfln("Stopping processing - request cancelled")
                goto end
            default:
                Printfln("Processing request: %v", total)
                total++
                time.Sleep(time.Millisecond * 250)
        }
    }
    Printfln("Request processed...%v", total)
    end:
    wg.Done()
}

func main() {
    waitGroup := sync.WaitGroup {}
    waitGroup.Add(1)
    Printfln("Request dispatched...")
    ctx, cancel := context.WithCancel(context.Background())
    go processRequest(ctx, &waitGroup, 10)

    time.Sleep(time.Second)
    Printfln("Canceling request")
    cancel()

    waitGroup.Wait()
}
```

The Background function returns the default Context, which doesn't do anything useful but does provide a starting point for deriving new Context values with the other functions described in Table 30-11.

The WithCancel function returns a Context that can be canceled and the function that is invoked to perform the cancelation:

```
...
ctx, cancel := context.WithCancel(context.Background())
go processRequest(ctx, &waitGroup, 10)
...
```

The derived context is passed to the processRequest function. The main function calls the time.Sleep function to give the processRequest function a change to do some work and then invokes the cancelation function:

```
...
time.Sleep(time.Second)
Printfln("Canceling request")
cancel()
...
```

Invoking the cancelation function sends a message to the channel returned by the context's Done method, which is monitored using a select statement:

```
...
case <- ctx.Done():
    Printfln("Stopping processing - request cancelled")
    goto end
default:
    Printfln("Processing request: %v", total)
    total++
    time.Sleep(time.Millisecond * 250)
}
...
```

The Done channel blocks if the request hasn't been canceled, so the default clause will be executed, allowing the request to be processed. The channel is checked after each unit of work, and a goto statement is used to break out of the processing loop so that the WaitGroup can be signaled and the function ends. Compile and execute the project, and you will see that the simulated request processing is terminated early, as follows:

```
Request dispatched...
Processing request: 0
Processing request: 1
Processing request: 2
Processing request: 3
Canceling request
Stopping processing - request cancelled
```

Setting a Deadline

Contexts can be created with a deadline, after which a signal is sent on the Done channel, just as it would be when the request is cancelled. An absolute time can be specified using the WithDeadline function, which accepts a time.Time value, or, as shown in Listing 30-16, the WithTimeout function accepts a time.Duration, which specifies a deadline relative to the current time. The Context.Deadline method can be used to check the deadline during request processing.

Listing 30-16. Specifying a Deadline in the main.go File in the coordination Folder

```
package main

import (
    "sync"
    "time"
    // "math"
    // "math/rand"
    "context"
)

func processRequest(ctx context.Context, wg *sync.WaitGroup, count int) {
    total := 0
    for i := 0; i < count; i++ {
        select {
            case <- ctx.Done():
                if (ctx.Err() == context.Canceled) {
                    Printfln("Stopping processing - request cancelled")
                } else {
                    Printfln("Stopping processing - deadline reached")
                }
                goto end
            default:
                Printfln("Processing request: %v", total)
                total++
                time.Sleep(time.Millisecond * 250)
        }
    }
    Printfln("Request processed...%v", total)
    end:
    wg.Done()
}

func main() {
    waitGroup := sync.WaitGroup {}
    waitGroup.Add(1)
    Printfln("Request dispatched...")
    ctx, _ := context.WithTimeout(context.Background(), time.Second * 2)
    go processRequest(ctx, &waitGroup, 10)
```

```
// time.Sleep(time.Second)
// Printfln("Canceling request")
// cancel()

    waitGroup.Wait()
}
```

The WithDeadline and WithTimeout functions return the derived context and a cancelation function, which allows the request to be canceled before the deadline expires. In this example, the amount of time required by the processRequest function exceeds the deadline, which means that the Done channel will terminate processing. Compile and execute the project, and you will see output similar to the following:

```
Request dispatched...
Processing request: 0
Processing request: 1
Processing request: 2
Processing request: 3
Processing request: 4
Processing request: 5
Processing request: 6
Processing request: 7
Stopping processing - deadline reached
```

Providing Request Data

The WithValue function creates a derived Context with a key-value pair that can be read during request processing, as shown in Listing 30-17.

Listing 30-17. Using Request Data in the main.go File in the coordination Folder

```
package main

import (
    "sync"
    "time"
    // "math"
    // "math/rand"
    "context"
)

const (
    countKey  = iota
    sleepPeriodKey
)
```

```
func processRequest(ctx context.Context, wg *sync.WaitGroup) {
    total := 0
    count := ctx.Value(countKey).(int)
    sleepPeriod := ctx.Value(sleepPeriodKey).(time.Duration)
    for i := 0; i < count; i++ {
        select {
            case <- ctx.Done():
                if (ctx.Err() == context.Canceled) {
                    Printfln("Stopping processing - request cancelled")
                } else {
                    Printfln("Stopping processing - deadline reached")
                }
                goto end
            default:
                Printfln("Processing request: %v", total)
                total++
                time.Sleep(sleepPeriod)
        }
    }
    Printfln("Request processed...%v", total)
    end:
    wg.Done()
}

func main() {
    waitGroup := sync.WaitGroup {}
    waitGroup.Add(1)
    Printfln("Request dispatched...")
    ctx, _ := context.WithTimeout(context.Background(), time.Second * 2)
    ctx = context.WithValue(ctx, countKey, 4)
    ctx = context.WithValue(ctx, sleepPeriodKey, time.Millisecond * 250)
    go processRequest(ctx, &waitGroup)

    // time.Sleep(time.Second)
    // Printfln("Canceling request")
    // cancel()

    waitGroup.Wait()
}
```

The WithValue function accepts only a single key-value pair, but the functions in Table 30-11 can be called repeatedly to create the required combination of features. In Listing 30-17, the WithTimeout function is used to derive a Context with a deadline, and the derived Context is used as the argument to the WithValue function to add two key-value pairs. This data is accessed through the Value method, which means that request processing functions do not have to define parameters for all the data values they require. Compile and execute the project, and you will see the following output:

```
Request dispatched...
Processing request: 0
Processing request: 1
Processing request: 2
Processing request: 3
Request processed...4
```

Summary

In this chapter, I described the standard library features for coordinating goroutines, which included the use of wait groups, which allows one goroutine to wait for others to finish, and mutual exclusion, which stops goroutines modifying the same data at the same time. I also described the Context feature, which allows a request to be handled more consistently by a server. This is a feature that I make repeated use of in Part 3 of this book, in which I create a custom web application framework and an online store that uses it. In the next chapter, I describe the standard library support for unit testing.

CHAPTER 31

■ ■ ■

Unit Testing, Benchmarking, and Logging

In this chapter, I finish describing the most useful standard library packages with unit testing, benchmarking, and logging. The logging features are fine, if a little basic, and there are plenty of third-party packages available for directing log messages to different destinations. The testing and benchmarking features are integrated into the go command, but, as I explain, I am not enthusiastic about either feature. Table 31-1 summarizes the chapter.

Table 31-1. Chapter Summary

Problem	Solution	Listing
Create a unit test	Add a file whose name ends with the _test.go, define a function whose name starts with Test followed by an uppercase letter, and use the features provided by the testing package	4, 6, 7, 10, 11
Run unit tests	Use the go test command	5, 8, 9
Create a benchmark	Define a function whose name starts with Benchmark, followed by an uppercase letter	12, 14, 15
Run a benchmark	Use the go test command with the -bench argument	13
Log data	Use the features provided by the log package	16, 17

Preparing for This Chapter

To prepare for this chapter, open a new command prompt, navigate to a convenient location, and create a directory named tests. Run the command shown in Listing 31-1 in the tests folder to create a module file.

■ **Tip** You can download the example project for this chapter—and for all the other chapters in this book—from https://github.com/apress/pro-go. See Chapter 2 for how to get help if you have problems running the examples.

Listing 31-1. Initializing the Module

```
go mod init tests
```

Add a file named main.go to the tests folder with the content shown in Listing 31-2.

Listing 31-2. The Contents of the main.go File in the tests Folder

```
package main

import (
    "sort"
    "fmt"
)

func sortAndTotal(vals []int) (sorted []int, total int) {
    sorted = make([]int, len(vals))
    copy(sorted, vals)
    sort.Ints(sorted)
    for _, val := range sorted {
        total += val
        total++
    }
    return
}

func main() {
    nums := []int { 100, 20, 1, 7, 84 }
    sorted, total := sortAndTotal(nums)
    fmt.Println("Sorted Data:", sorted)
    fmt.Println("Total:", total)
}
```

The sortAndTotal function contains a deliberate error that will help demonstrate the testing features in the next section. Run the command shown in Listing 31-3 in the tests folder to compile and execute the project.

Listing 31-3. Compiling and Running the Project

```
go run .
```

This command produces the following output:

```
Sorted Data: [1 7 20 84 100]
Total: 217
```

Using Testing

Unit tests are defined in files whose name ends with _test.go. To create a simple test, add a file named simple_test.go to the tests folder with the content shown in Listing 31-4.

Listing 31-4. The Contents of the simple_test.go File in the tests Folder

```
package main

import "testing"

func TestSum(t *testing.T) {
    testValues := []int{ 10, 20, 30 }
    _, sum := sortAndTotal(testValues)
    expected := 60
    if (sum != expected) {
        t.Fatalf("Expected %v, Got %v", expected, sum)
    }
}
```

The Go standard library provides support for writing unit tests through the testing package. Unit tests are expressed as functions whose name starts with Test, followed by a term that begins with an uppercase letter, such as TestSum. (The uppercase letter is important because the test tools will not recognize a function name such as Testsum as a unit test.)

DECIDING WHETHER TO USE THE TEST TOOLS

I like the idea of integrated testing, but I have found that I don't use the Go test features a great deal and, when I do, I don't use them as they are intended.

I like unit testing, but I only write tests when I am trying to sort out code that has complex issues or when I am writing a feature that I know is going to be difficult to get right. It may just be the way that I think about tests or that I am used to the classic arrange/act/assert test tool pattern, but there is something about the Go test tools that I don't like.

I end up using tests so that I can create simple entry points into specific packages to make sure they work properly. But, even then, I just create a single test that I use to create instances of the types in a package, allowing me to access the fields, functions, and methods they define, without having to change my main function. The code in these tests is always a scruffy mess, and I use println statements for the output instead of the methods described in Table 31-2. Once I am happy that the code works, I delete the test file.

I am perfectly willing to admit this is a failing on my part, but I just don't have any enthusiasm for the Go testing tools. That doesn't mean that you won't find them useful, possibly because you are a more diligent tester than I am. But, if you do find the features described in this section don't motivate you to write tests, then know that you are not alone.

Unit test functions receive a pointer to a T struct, which defines methods for managing tests and reporting test outcomes. Go tests don't rely on assertions and are written using regular code statements. All that the test tools care about is whether the test fails, which is reported using the methods described in Table 31-2.

Table 31-2. *T Methods for Reporting Test Outcomes*

Name	Description
Log(...vals)	This method writes the specified values to the test error log.
Logf(template, ...vals)	This method uses the specified template and values to write a message to the test error log.
Fail()	Calling this method marks the test as failed but continues executing the test.
FailNow()	Calling this method marks the test as failed and stops executing the test.
Failed()	This method returns true if the test has failed.
Error(...errs)	Calling this method is equivalent to calling the Log method, followed by the Fail method.
Errorf(template, ...vals)	Calling this method is equivalent to calling the Logf method, followed by the Fail method.
Fatal(...vals)	Calling this method is equivalent to calling the Log method, followed by the FailNow method.
Fatalf(template, ...vals)	Calling this method is equivalent to calling the Logf method, followed by the FailNow method.

The test in Listing 31-4 called the sumAndTotal function with a set of values and compared the result to the expected outcome using a standard Go comparison operator. If the result isn't equal to the expected value, then the Fatalf method is called, which reports the test failure and stops any remaining statements in the unit test from being executed (although there are no remaining statements in this example).

UNDERSTANDING TEST PACKAGE ACCESS

The test file in Listing 31-4 uses the package keyword to specify the main package. Since tests are written in standard Go, this means that tests in this file have access to all of the features defined in the main package, including those that are not exported outside the package.

If you want to write tests that have access only to exported features, then you can use the package statement to specify the main_test package. The _test suffix won't cause compiler issues and allows tests to be written that only have access to the exported features from the package that is being tested.

Running Unit Tests

To discover and run the unit tests in the project, run the command shown in Listing 31-5 in the tests folder.

```
┌──────────────────────────────────────────────────────────────────────┐
│                   WRITING MOCKS FOR UNIT TESTS                          │
└──────────────────────────────────────────────────────────────────────┘
```

The only way to create mock implementations for unit tests is to create interface implementations, which allow custom methods to be defined that produce the results required for a test. If you want to use mocks for your unit tests, then you should write your APIs so they accept interface types.

But even though the use of mocks is restricted to interfaces, it is usually possible to create struct values whose fields are assigned specific values that you can test for. This can sometimes be a little awkward, but most functions and methods can be tested one way or another, even if some persistence is required to figure out the details.

Listing 31-5. Performing Unit Tests

```
go test
```

As noted, there is an error in the code defined in Listing 31-2, which causes the unit test to fail:

```
tests > go test
--- FAIL: TestSum (0.00s)
    simple_test.go:10: Expected 60, Got 63
FAIL
exit status 1
FAIL    tests    0.090s
```

The output from the tests reports the error as well as the overall outcome of the test run. Listing 31-6 fixes the error in the sortAndTotal function.

Listing 31-6. Fixing an Error in the main.go File in the tests Folder

```
...
func sortAndTotal(vals []int) (sorted []int, total int) {
    sorted = make([]int, len(vals))
    copy(sorted, vals)
    sort.Ints(sorted)
    for _, val := range sorted {
        total += val
        //total++
    }
    return
}
...
```

Save the change and run the go test command, and the output will show that the test passes:

```
PASS
ok      tests    0.102s
```

A test file can contain multiple tests, which will be discovered and executed automatically. Listing 31-7 added a second test function to the simple_test.go file.

Listing 31-7. Defining a Test in the simple_test.go File in the tests Folder

```
package main

import (
    "testing"
    "sort"
)

func TestSum(t *testing.T) {
    testValues := []int{ 10, 20, 30 }
    _, sum := sortAndTotal(testValues)
    expected := 60
    if (sum != expected) {
        t.Fatalf("Expected %v, Got %v", expected, sum)
    }
}

func TestSort(t *testing.T) {
    testValues := []int{ 1, 279, 48, 12, 3}
    sorted, _ := sortAndTotal(testValues)
    if (!sort.IntsAreSorted(sorted)) {
        t.Fatalf("Unsorted data %v", sorted)
    }
}
```

The TestSort test verifies that the sortAndTotal function sorts data. Notice that I can rely on the features provided by the Go standard library in unit tests and use the sort.IntsAreSorted function to perform the test. Run the go test command, and you will see the following outcome:

```
ok      tests   0.087s
```

The go test command doesn't report any detail by default, but more information can be generated by running the command shown in Listing 31-8 in the tests folder.

Listing 31-8. Performing Verbose Tests

```
go test -v
```

The -v argument enables verbose mode, which reports on each of the tests:

```
=== RUN   TestSum
--- PASS: TestSum (0.00s)
=== RUN   TestSort
--- PASS: TestSort (0.00s)
PASS
ok      tests   0.164s
```

Running Specific Tests

The go test command can be used to run tests selected by name. Run the command shown in Listing 31-9 in the tests folder.

Listing 31-9. Selecting Tests in the main.go File in the tests Folder

```
go test -v -run "um"
```

The tests are selected with a regular expression, and the command in Listing 31-9 selects tests whose function name contains um (there is no need to include the Test part of the function name). The only test whose name is matched by the expression is TestSum, and the command produces the following output:

```
=== RUN   TestSum
--- PASS: TestSum (0.00s)
PASS
ok      tests   0.123s
```

Managing Test Execution

The T struct also provides a set of methods for managing test execution, as described in Table 31-3.

Table 31-3. The T Methods for Managing Test Execution

Name	Description
Run(name, func)	Calling this method executes the specified function as a subtest. The method blocks while the test is executed in its own goroutine and returns a bool that indicates whether the test succeeded.
SkipNow()	Calling this method stops executing the test and marks it as skipped.
Skip(...args)	This method is equivalent to calling the Log method, followed by the SkipNow method.
Skipf(template, ...args)	This method is equivalent to calling the Logf method, followed by the SkipNow method.
Skipped()	This method returns true if the test has been skipped.

The Run method is used to execute a subtest, which is a convenient way to run a series of related tests from a single function, as shown in Listing 31-10.

Listing 31-10. Running Subtests in the simple_test.go File in the tests Folder

```
package main

import (
    "testing"
    "sort"
```

```
    "fmt"
)

func TestSum(t *testing.T) {
    testValues := []int{ 10, 20, 30 }
    _, sum := sortAndTotal(testValues)
    expected := 60
    if (sum != expected) {
        t.Fatalf("Expected %v, Got %v", expected, sum)
    }
}

func TestSort(t *testing.T) {
    slices := [][]int {
        { 1, 279, 48, 12, 3 },
        { -10, 0, -10 },
        { 1, 2, 3, 4, 5, 6, 7 },
        { 1 },
    }
    for index, data := range slices {
        t.Run(fmt.Sprintf("Sort #%v", index), func(subT *testing.T) {
            sorted, _ := sortAndTotal(data)
            if (!sort.IntsAreSorted(sorted)) {
                subT.Fatalf("Unsorted data %v", sorted)
            }
        })
    }
}
```

The arguments to the Run method are the name of the test and a function that accepts a T struct and performs the test. In Listing 31-10 the Run method is used to test that a set of different int slices are correctly sorted. Use the go test -v command to run the tests with verbose output, and you will see the following output:

```
=== RUN    TestSum
--- PASS: TestSum (0.00s)
=== RUN    TestSort
=== RUN    TestSort/Sort_#0
=== RUN    TestSort/Sort_#1
=== RUN    TestSort/Sort_#2
=== RUN    TestSort/Sort_#3
--- PASS: TestSort (0.00s)
    --- PASS: TestSort/Sort_#0 (0.00s)
    --- PASS: TestSort/Sort_#1 (0.00s)
    --- PASS: TestSort/Sort_#2 (0.00s)
    --- PASS: TestSort/Sort_#3 (0.00s)
PASS
ok      tests    0.112s
```

Skipping Tests

Tests can be skipped using the methods described in Table 31-3, which can be useful when a failure of one test means that there is little point in performing related tests, as shown in Listing 31-11.

Listing 31-11. Skipping Tests in the simple_test.go File in the tests Folder

```
package main

import (
    "testing"
    "sort"
    "fmt"
)

type SumTest struct {
    testValues []int
    expectedResult int
}

func TestSum(t *testing.T) {
    testVals := []SumTest {
        { testValues: []int{10, 20, 30}, expectedResult:  10},
        { testValues: []int{ -10, 0, -10 }, expectedResult:  -20},
        { testValues: []int{ -10, 0, -10 }, expectedResult:  -20},
    }
    for index, testVal := range testVals {
        t.Run(fmt.Sprintf("Sum #%v", index), func(subT *testing.T) {
            if (t.Failed()) {
                subT.SkipNow()
            }
            _, sum := sortAndTotal(testVal.testValues)
            if (sum != testVal.expectedResult) {
                subT.Fatalf("Expected %v, Got %v", testVal.expectedResult, sum)
            }
        })
    }
}

func TestSort(t *testing.T) {
    slices := [][]int {
        { 1, 279, 48, 12, 3 },
        { -10, 0, -10 },
        { 1, 2, 3, 4, 5, 6, 7 },
        { 1 },
    }
    for index, data := range slices {
        t.Run(fmt.Sprintf("Sort #%v", index), func(subT *testing.T) {
            sorted, _ := sortAndTotal(data)
            if (!sort.IntsAreSorted(sorted)) {
                subT.Fatalf("Unsorted data %v", sorted)
            }
```

```
        })
    }
}
```

The TestSum function has been rewritten to run subtests. When using subtests, if any individual test fails, then the overall test also fails. In Listing 31-11, I rely on this behavior by calling the Failed method on the T struct for the overall test and using the SkipNow method to skip subtests once there has been a failure. The expected result defined for the first subtest performed by the TestSum is incorrect and causes the test to fail, which produces the following output when the go test -v command is used:

```
=== RUN    TestSum
=== RUN    TestSum/Sum_#0
    simple_test.go:27: Expected 10, Got 60
=== RUN    TestSum/Sum_#1
=== RUN    TestSum/Sum_#2
--- FAIL: TestSum (0.00s)
    --- FAIL: TestSum/Sum_#0 (0.00s)
    --- SKIP: TestSum/Sum_#1 (0.00s)
    --- SKIP: TestSum/Sum_#2 (0.00s)
=== RUN    TestSort
=== RUN    TestSort/Sort_#0
=== RUN    TestSort/Sort_#1
=== RUN    TestSort/Sort_#2
=== RUN    TestSort/Sort_#3
--- PASS: TestSort (0.00s)
    --- PASS: TestSort/Sort_#0 (0.00s)
    --- PASS: TestSort/Sort_#1 (0.00s)
    --- PASS: TestSort/Sort_#2 (0.00s)
    --- PASS: TestSort/Sort_#3 (0.00s)
FAIL
exit status 1
FAIL    tests    0.138s
```

Benchmarking Code

Functions whose name started with Benchmark, followed by a term that begins with an uppercase letter, such as Sort, are benchmarks, whose execution is timed. Benchmark functions receive a pointer to the testing.B struct, which defines the field described in Table 31-4.

Table 31-4. *The Field Defined by the B Struct*

Name	Description
N	This int field specifies the number of times the benchmark function should execute the code to be measured.

The value of N is used in a for loop within the benchmark function to repeat the code whose performance is being measured. The benchmark tools may call the benchmark function repeatedly, using different values of N, to establish a stable measurement. Add a file named benchmark_test.go to the tests folder with the content shown in Listing 31-12.

DECIDING WHEN TO BENCHMARK

Performance tuning code is like performance tuning a car: it can be fun, it is usually expensive, and, almost every time, it causes more problems than it solves.

The most expensive part of any project is programmer time, both during the initial development and in the maintenance phase. Not only does performance tuning take time that could be spent completing the project, but it often produces code that is harder to understand, which is going to suck up more time in the future as some other developer tries to make sense of your clever optimizations.

I am willing to accept that there are projects that have specific performance requirements, but the chances are that your project isn't one of them. But don't worry because my projects don't have those requirements either. For normal projects, it is cheaper to buy more server or storage capacity than it is to have an expensive developer do a tune-up.

Benchmarking can be educational, and you can learn a lot about a project by understanding how its code is executed. But the time for educational benchmarking is in the brief window between deployment and the arrival of the first defect report, which would otherwise be spent organizing the printer paper by color. Until that moment, my advice is to focus on writing code that is easy to understand and easy to maintain.

Listing 31-12. The Contents of the benchmark_test.go File in the tests Folder

```go
package main

import (
    "testing"
    "math/rand"
    "time"
)

func BenchmarkSort(b *testing.B) {
    rand.Seed(time.Now().UnixNano())
    size := 250
    data := make([]int, size)
    for i := 0; i < b.N; i++ {
        for j := 0; j < size; j++ {
            data[j] = rand.Int()
        }
        sortAndTotal(data)
    }
}
```

The BenchmarkSort function creates a slice with random data and passes it to the sortAndTotal function, which was defined in Listing 31-2. To perform the benchmark, run the command shown in Listing 31-13 in the tests folder.

Listing 31-13. Performing Benchmarks

```
go test -bench . -run notest
```

The period following the -bench argument causes all of the benchmarks that the go test tool discovers to be performed. The period can be replaced with a regular expression to select specific benchmarks. By default, the unit tests are also performed, but since I introduced a deliberate error into the TestSum function in Listing 31-12, I used the -run argument to specify a value that won't match any of the test function names in the project, with the result that only the benchmarks will be performed.

The command in Listing 31-13 finds and executes the BenchmarkSort function and produces output similar to the following, varying to reflect your system:

```
goos: windows
goarch: amd64
pkg: tests
BenchmarkSort-12              23853               42642 ns/op
PASS
ok      tests   1.577s
```

The name of the benchmark function is followed by the number of CPUs or cores, which is 12 on my system, but which won't have an impact on the test results since the code doesn't use goroutines:

```
...
BenchmarkSort-12             23853               42642 ns/op
...
```

The next field reports the value of N that was passed to the benchmark function to generate these results:

```
...
BenchmarkSort-12             23853               42642 ns/op
...
```

On my system, the test tools ran the BenchmarkSort function with an N value of 23853. This number will change from test to test and from system to system. The final value reports on the duration, in nanoseconds, taken to perform each iteration of the benchmark loop:

```
...
BenchmarkSort-12             23853               42642 ns/op
...
```

For this test run, the benchmark took 42,642 nanoseconds to complete.

Removing Setup from the Benchmark

For each iteration of the for loop, the BenchmarkSort function has to generate random data, and the time taken to produce this data is included in the benchmark results. The B struct defines the methods described in Table 31-5, which are used to control the timer used for benchmarking.

Table 31-5. The B Methods for Timing Control

Name	Description
StopTimer()	This method stops the timer.
StartTimer()	This method starts the timer.
ResetTimer()	This method resets the timer.

The ResetTimer method is useful when a benchmark requires some initial setup, and the other methods are useful when there is overhead associated with each benchmarked activity. Listing 31-14 uses these methods to exclude the preparation from the benchmark results.

Listing 31-14. Controlling the Timer in the benchmark_test.go File in the tests Folder

```
package main

import (
    "testing"
    "math/rand"
    "time"
)

func BenchmarkSort(b *testing.B) {
    rand.Seed(time.Now().UnixNano())
    size := 250
    data := make([]int, size)
    b.ResetTimer()
    for i := 0; i < b.N; i++ {
        b.StopTimer()
        for j := 0; j < size; j++ {
            data[j] = rand.Int()
        }
        b.StartTimer()
        sortAndTotal(data)
    }
}
```

The timer is reset after the random seed is set and the slice has been initialized. Within the `for` loop, the `StopTimer` method is used to stop the timer before the slice is populated with random data, and the `StartTimer` method is used to start the timer before the `sortAndTotal` function is called. Run the command shown in Listing 31-14 in the `tests` folder, and the revised benchmark will be performed. On my system, this produced the following results:

```
goos: windows
goarch: amd64
pkg: tests
BenchmarkSort-12              35088              32095 ns/op
PASS
ok      tests   4.133s
```

Excluding the work required to prepare for the benchmark has produced a more accurate assessment of the time taken to execute the `sortAndTotal` function.

Performing Sub-benchmarks

A benchmark function can perform sub-benchmarks, just as a test function can run subtests. For quick reference, Table 31-6 describes the method used to run a sub-benchmark.

Table 31-6. *The B Method for Running Sub-benchmarks*

Name	Description
Run(name, func)	Calling this method executes the specified function as a sub-benchmark. The method blocks while the benchmark is performed.

Listing 31-15 updates the `BenchmarkSort` function so that a series of benchmarks for different array sizes are performed.

Listing 31-15. Performing Sub-Benchmarks in the benchmarks_test.go File in the tests Folder

```
package main

import (
    "testing"
    "math/rand"
    "time"
    "fmt"
)

func BenchmarkSort(b *testing.B) {
    rand.Seed(time.Now().UnixNano())
    sizes := []int { 10, 100, 250 }
    for _, size := range sizes {
        b.Run(fmt.Sprintf("Array Size %v", size), func(subB *testing.B) {
            data := make([]int, size)
```

```
            subB.ResetTimer()
            for i := 0; i < subB.N; i++ {
                subB.StopTimer()
                for j := 0; j < size; j++ {
                    data[j] = rand.Int()
                }
                subB.StartTimer()
                sortAndTotal(data)
            }
        })
    }
}
```

These benchmarks can take some time to complete. Here are the results on my system, produced using the command shown in Listing 31-13:

```
goos: windows
goarch: amd64
pkg: tests
BenchmarkSort/Array_Size_10-12              753120          1984 ns/op
BenchmarkSort/Array_Size_100-12             110248         10953 ns/op
BenchmarkSort/Array_Size_250-12              34369         31717 ns/op
PASS
ok      tests    61.453s
```

Logging Data

The log package provides a simple logging API that creates log entries and sends them to an io.Writer, allowing an application to generate logging data without needing to know where that data will be stored. The most useful functions defined by the log package are described in Table 31-7.

Table 31-7. *Useful log Functions*

Name	Description
Output()	This function returns the Writer to which log messages will be passed. By default, log messages are written to the standard output.
SetOutput(writer)	This function uses the specified Writer for logging.
Flags()	This function returns the flags used to format logging messages.
SetFlags(flags)	This function uses the specified flags to format logging messages.
Prefix()	This function returns the prefix that is applied to logging messages. There is no prefix by default.
SetPrefix(prefix)	This function uses the specified string as a prefix for logging messages.
Output(depth, message)	This function writes the specified message to the Writer returned by the Output function, with the specified call depth, which defaults to 2. The call depth is used to control the selection of the code file and is not typically changed.
Print(...vals)	This function creates a log message by calling fmt.Sprint and passing the result to the Output function.
Printf(template, ...vals)	This function creates a log message by calling fmt.Sprintf and passing the result to the Output function.
Fatal(...vals)	This function creates a log message by calling fmt.Sprint, passes the result to the Output function, and then terminates the application.
Fatalf(template, ...vals)	This function creates a log message by calling fmt.Sprintf, passes the result to the Output function, and then terminates the application.
Panic(...vals)	This function creates a log message by calling fmt.Sprint and then passes the result to the Output function and then the panic function.
Panicf(template, ...vals)	This function creates a log message by calling fmt.Sprintf and passes the result to the Output function and then the panic function.

The format of log messages is controlled with the SetFlags function, for which the log package defines the constants described in Table 31-8.

Table 31-8. *The log Package Constants*

Name	Description
Ldate	Selecting this flag includes the date in the log output.
Ltime	Selecting this flag includes the time in the log output.
Lmicroseconds	Selecting this flag includes microseconds in the time.
Llongfile	Selecting this flag includes the code filename, including directories, and the line number that logged the message.
Lshortfile	Selecting this flag includes the code filename, excluding directories, and the line number that logged the message.
LUTC	Selecting this flag uses UTC for dates and times, instead of the local time zone.
Lmsgprefix	Selecting this flag moves the prefix from its default position, which is at the start of the log message, to just before the string passed to the Output function.
LstdFlags	This constant represents the default format, which is selecting Ldate and Ltime.

Listing 31-16 uses the functions in Table 31-7 to perform simple logging.

Listing 31-16. Logging Messages in the main.go File in the tests Folder

```go
package main

import (
    "sort"
    //"fmt"
    "log"
)

func sortAndTotal(vals []int) (sorted []int, total int) {
    sorted = make([]int, len(vals))
    copy(sorted, vals)
    sort.Ints(sorted)
    for _, val := range sorted {
        total += val
        //total++
    }
    return
}

func main() {
    nums := []int { 100, 20, 1, 7, 84 }
    sorted, total := sortAndTotal(nums)
    log.Print("Sorted Data: ", sorted)
    log.Print("Total: ", total)
}
```

```
func init() {
    log.SetFlags(log.Lshortfile | log.Ltime)
}
```

The initialization function uses the SetFlags function to select the Lshortfile and Ltime flags, which will include the filename and the time in the logging output. Within the main function, log messages are created using the Print function. Compile and execute the project using the go run . command, and you will see output similar to the following:

```
08:51:25 main.go:26: Sorted Data: [1 7 20 84 100]
08:51:25 main.go:27: Total: 212
```

Creating Custom Loggers

The log package can be used to set up different logging options so that different parts of the application can write log messages to different destinations or use different formatting options. The function described in Table 31-9 is used to create a custom logging destination.

Table 31-9. *The log Package Function for Custom Logging*

Name	Description
New(writer, prefix, flags)	This function returns a Logger that will write messages to the specified writer, configured with the specified prefix and flags.

The result from the New function is a Logger, which is a struct that defines methods that correspond to the functions described in Table 31-7. The functions in Table 31-7 simply invoke the method of the same name on a default logger. Listing 31-17 uses the New function to create a Logger.

Listing 31-17. Creating a Custom Logger in the main.go File in the tests Folder

```
package main

import (
    "sort"
    //"fmt"
    "log"
)

func sortAndTotal(vals []int) (sorted []int, total int) {
    var logger = log.New(log.Writer(), "sortAndTotal: ",
        log.Flags() | log.Lmsgprefix)
    logger.Printf("Invoked with %v values", len(vals))
    sorted = make([]int, len(vals))
    copy(sorted, vals)
    sort.Ints(sorted)
    logger.Printf("Sorted data: %v", sorted)
    for _, val := range sorted {
        total += val
```

```
        //total++
    }
    logger.Printf("Total: %v", total)
    return
}

func main() {
    nums := []int { 100, 20, 1, 7, 84 }
    sorted, total := sortAndTotal(nums)
    log.Print("Sorted Data: ", sorted)
    log.Print("Total: ", total)
}

func init() {
    log.SetFlags(log.Lshortfile | log.Ltime)
}
```

The Logger struct is created with a new prefix and the addition of the Lmsgprefix flag, using the Writer obtained from the Output function described in Table 31-7. The result is that log messages are still written to the same destination, but with an additional prefix that denotes messages from the sortAndTotal function. Compile and execute the project, and you will see additional logging messages:

```
09:12:37 main.go:11: sortAndTotal: Invoked with 5 values
09:12:37 main.go:15: sortAndTotal: Sorted data: [1 7 20 84 100]
09:12:37 main.go:20: sortAndTotal: Total: 212
09:12:37 main.go:27: Sorted Data: [1 7 20 84 100]
09:12:37 main.go:28: Total: 212
```

Summary

In this chapter, I finished my description of the most useful standard library packages with unit testing, benchmarking, and logging. As I explained, I find the testing features unappealing, and I have strong reservations about the benchmarking, but both sets of features are well-integrated into the Go tools, which makes them easier to use if your views on these topics don't align with mine. The logging features are less controversial, and I use them in the custom web application platform that I create in Part 3.

PART III

Applying Go

CHAPTER 32

Creating a Web Platform

In this chapter, I begin development on a custom web application platform, which I continue in Chapters 33 and 34. In Chapters 35–38, I use this platform to create an application named SportsStore, which I include in just about all of my books in some form.

The purpose of this part of the book is to show Go being applied to solve the kinds of problems that arise in real development projects. For the web application platform, this means creating features for logging, sessions, HTML templates, authorization, and so on. For the SportsStore application, this means using a product database, keeping track of a user's product selections, validating user input, and checking out of the store.

Bear in mind that the code in these chapters has been written specifically for this book and tested only to the extent that features in subsequent chapters work as they should. There are good third-party packages that provide some or all of the features created in this part of the book, and these are a good place to start for your projects. I recommend the Gorilla Web Toolkit (www.gorillatoolkit.org), which provides some useful packages (and I use one of these packages in Chapter 34).

■ **Caution** These chapters are advanced and complex, and it is important to follow the examples exactly as shown. If you encounter difficulties, then you should start by checking the errata for this book at the GitHub repository for this book (https://github.com/apress/pro-go) where I will list solutions to any problems that arise.

Creating the Project

Open a command prompt, navigate to a convenient location, and create a new directory named platform. Navigate to the platform directory and run the command shown in Listing 32-1.

■ **Tip** You can download the example project for this chapter—and for all the other chapters in this book— from https://github.com/apress/pro-go. See Chapter 2 for how to get help if you have problems running the examples.

© Adam Freeman 2022
A. Freeman, *Pro Go*, https://doi.org/10.1007/978-1-4842-7355-5_32

Listing 32-1. Initializing the Project

```
go mod init platform
```

Add a file named `main.go` to the `platform` folder, with the content shown in Listing 32-2.

Listing 32-2. The Contents of the main.go File in the platform Folder

```
package main

import (
    "fmt"
)

func writeMessage() {
    fmt.Println("Hello, Platform")
}

func main() {
    writeMessage()
}
```

Run the command shown in Listing 32-3 in the `platform` folder.

Listing 32-3. Compiling and Executing the Project

```
go run .
```

The project will be compiled and executed and will produce the following output:

```
Hello, Platform
```

Creating Some Basic Platform Features

To get started, I am going to define some basic services that will provide the foundation for running web applications.

Creating the Logging System

The first server feature to implement is logging. The `log` package in the Go standard library provides a good set of basic features for creating logs but needs some additional features to filter those messages for detail. Create the `platform/logging` folder and add to it a file named `logging.go` with the content shown in Listing 32-4.

Listing 32-4. The Contents of the logging.go File in the logging Folder

```
package logging

type LogLevel int

const (
    Trace LogLevel = iota
    Debug
    Information
    Warning
    Fatal
    None
)

type Logger interface {

    Trace(string)
    Tracef(string, ...interface{})

    Debug(string)
    Debugf(string, ...interface{})

    Info(string)
    Infof(string, ...interface{})

    Warn(string)
    Warnf(string, ...interface{})

    Panic(string)
    Panicf(string, ...interface{})
}
```

This file defines the Logger interface, which specifies methods for logging messages with different levels of severity, which is set using a LogLevel value ranging from Trace to Fatal. There is also a None level that specifies no logging output. For each level of severity, the Logger interface defines one method that accepts a simple string and one method that accepts a template string and placeholder values.

I define interfaces for all the features that the platform provides and use those interfaces to provide default implementations. This will allow the application to replace the default implementation if required and also make it possible to provide applications with features as services, which I describe later in this chapter.

To create the default implementation of the Logger interface, add a file named logger_default.go in the logging folder with the content shown in Listing 32-5.

Listing 32-5. The Contents of the logger_default.go File in the logging Folder

```
package logging

import (
    "log"
    "fmt"
)
```

```go
type DefaultLogger struct {
    minLevel LogLevel
    loggers map[LogLevel]*log.Logger
    triggerPanic bool
}

func (l *DefaultLogger) MinLogLevel() LogLevel {
    return l.minLevel
}

func (l *DefaultLogger) write(level LogLevel, message string) {
    if (l.minLevel <= level) {
        l.loggers[level].Output(2, message)
    }
}

func (l *DefaultLogger) Trace(msg string) {
    l.write(Trace, msg)
}

func (l *DefaultLogger) Tracef(template string, vals ...interface{}) {
    l.write(Trace, fmt.Sprintf(template, vals...))
}

func (l *DefaultLogger) Debug(msg string) {
    l.write(Debug, msg)
}

func (l *DefaultLogger) Debugf(template string, vals ...interface{}) {
    l.write(Debug, fmt.Sprintf(template, vals...))
}

func (l *DefaultLogger) Info(msg string) {
    l.write(Information, msg)
}

func (l *DefaultLogger) Infof(template string, vals ...interface{}) {
    l.write(Information, fmt.Sprintf(template, vals...))
}

func (l *DefaultLogger) Warn(msg string) {
    l.write(Warning, msg)
}

func (l *DefaultLogger) Warnf(template string, vals ...interface{}) {
    l.write(Warning, fmt.Sprintf(template, vals...))
}

func (l *DefaultLogger) Panic(msg string) {
    l.write(Fatal, msg)
    if (l.triggerPanic) {
```

```
        panic(msg)
    }
}

func (l *DefaultLogger) Panicf(template string, vals ...interface{}) {
    formattedMsg := fmt.Sprintf(template, vals...)
    l.write(Fatal, formattedMsg)
    if (l.triggerPanic) {
        panic(formattedMsg)
    }
}
```

The DefaultLogger struct implements the Logger interface using the features provided by the log package in the standard library, described in Chapter 31. Each severity level is assigned a log.Logger, which means that messages can be sent to different destinations or formatted in different ways. Add a file named default_create.go to the logging folder with the code shown in Listing 32-6.

Listing 32-6. The Contents of the default_create.go File in the logging Folder

```
package logging

import (
    "log"
    "os"
)

func NewDefaultLogger(level LogLevel) Logger {
    flags := log.Lmsgprefix | log.Ltime
    return &DefaultLogger {
        minLevel: level,
        loggers: map[LogLevel]*log.Logger {
            Trace: log.New(os.Stdout, "TRACE ",  flags),
            Debug: log.New(os.Stdout, "DEBUG ",  flags),
            Information: log.New(os.Stdout, "INFO ",  flags),
            Warning: log.New(os.Stdout, "WARN ",  flags),
            Fatal: log.New(os.Stdout, "FATAL ",  flags),
        },
        triggerPanic: true,
    }
}
```

The NewDefaultLogger function creates a DefaultLogger with a minimum severity level and log. Loggers that write messages to standard out. As a simple test, Listing 32-7 changes the main function so that it writes out its message using the logging feature.

Listing 32-7. Using the Logging Feature in the main.go File in the platform Folder

```
package main

import (
    //"fmt"
    "platform/logging"
```

863

```go
)

func writeMessage(logger logging.Logger) {
    logger.Info("Hello, Platform")
}

func main() {
    var logger logging.Logger = logging.NewDefaultLogger(logging.Information)
    writeMessage(logger)
}
```

The minimum severity level of the Logger created by the NewDefaultLogger is set to Information, which means that messages with a lower severity level (Trace and Debug) will be discarded. Compile and execute the project, and you will see the following output, albeit with different timestamps:

```
18:28:46 INFO Hello, Platform
```

Creating the Configuration System

The next step is to add the ability to configure the application so that settings don't have to be defined in code files. Create the platform/config folder and add to it a file named config.go with the content shown in Listing 32-8.

Listing 32-8. The Contents of the config.go File in the config Folder

```go
package config

type Configuration interface {

    GetString(name string) (configValue string, found bool)
    GetInt(name string) (configValue int, found bool)
    GetBool(name string) (configValue bool, found bool)
    GetFloat(name string) (configValue float64, found bool)

    GetStringDefault(name, defVal string) (configValue string)
    GetIntDefault(name string, defVal int) (configValue int)
    GetBoolDefault(name string, defVal bool) (configValue bool)
    GetFloatDefault(name string, defVal float64) (configValue float64)

    GetSection(sectionName string) (section Configuration, found bool)
}
```

The Configuration interface defines methods for retrieving configuration settings, with support for obtaining string, int, float64, and bool values. There is also a set of methods that allow a default value to be supplied. The configuration data will allow nested configuration sections, which can be obtained using the GetSection method.

Defining the Configuration File

It helps to understand the implementation of the configuration system if you can see the type of configuration file that I am going to use. Add a file named config.json to the platform folder with the content shown in Listing 32-9.

Listing 32-9. The Contents of the config.json File in the platform Folder

```
{
    "logging" : {
        "level": "debug"
    },
    "main" : {
        "message" : "Hello from the config file"
    }
}
```

This configuration file defines two configuration sections, named logging and main. The logging section contains a single string configuration setting, named level. The main section contains a single string configuration setting named message. I will add configuration settings as I add features to the platform and when I start work on the SportsStore application, but this file shows the basic structure that the configuration file uses. When adding configuration settings, pay close attention to the quote marks and the commas, both of which are required by JSON, but which are easy to omit.

Implementing the Configuration Interface

To create an implementation of the Configuration interface, add a file named config_default.go to the config folder with the content shown in Listing 32-10.

Listing 32-10. The Contents of the config_default.go File in the config Folder

```
package config

import "strings"

type DefaultConfig struct {
    configData map[string]interface{}
}

func (c *DefaultConfig) get(name string) (result interface{}, found bool) {
    data := c.configData
    for _, key := range strings.Split(name, ":") {
        result, found = data[key]
        if newSection, ok := result.(map[string]interface{}); ok && found {
            data = newSection
        } else {
            return
        }
    }
    return
}
```

```
func (c *DefaultConfig) GetSection(name string) (section Configuration, found bool) {
    value, found := c.get(name)
    if (found) {
        if sectionData, ok := value.(map[string]interface{}) ; ok {
            section = &DefaultConfig { configData: sectionData }
        }
    }
    return
}

func (c *DefaultConfig) GetString(name string) (result string, found bool) {
    value, found := c.get(name)
    if (found) { result = value.(string) }
    return
}

func (c *DefaultConfig) GetInt(name string) (result int, found bool) {
    value, found := c.get(name)
    if (found) { result =  int(value.(float64)) }
    return
}

func (c *DefaultConfig) GetBool(name string) (result bool, found bool) {
    value, found := c.get(name)
    if (found) { result = value.(bool) }
    return
}

func (c *DefaultConfig) GetFloat(name string) (result float64, found bool) {
    value, found := c.get(name)
    if (found) { result = value.(float64) }
    return
}
```

The DefaultConfig struct implements the Configuration interface using a map. Nested configuration sections are also expressed as maps. An individual configuration setting can be requested by separating a section name from a setting name, such as logging:level, or a map containing all of the settings can be requested using a section name, such as logging. To define the methods that accept a default value, add a file named config_default_fallback.go to the config folder with the content shown in Listing 32-11.

Listing 32-11. The Contents of the config_default_fallback.go File in the config Folder

```
package config

func (c *DefaultConfig) GetStringDefault(name, val string) (result string) {
    result, ok := c.GetString(name)
    if !ok {
        result = val
    }
    return
}
```

```
func (c *DefaultConfig) GetIntDefault(name string, val int) (result int) {
    result, ok := c.GetInt(name)
    if !ok {
        result = val
    }
    return
}

func (c *DefaultConfig) GetBoolDefault(name string, val bool) (result bool) {
    result, ok := c.GetBool(name)
    if !ok {
        result = val
    }
    return
}

func (c *DefaultConfig) GetFloatDefault(name string, val float64) (result float64) {
    result, ok := c.GetFloat(name)
    if !ok {
        result = val
    }
    return
}
```

To define the function that will load the data from the configuration file, add a file named config_json. go to the config folder with the content shown in Listing 32-12.

Listing 32-12. The Contents of the config_json.go File in the config Folder

```
package config

import (
    "os"
    "strings"
    "encoding/json"
)

func Load(fileName string) (config Configuration,  err error) {
    var data []byte
    data, err = os.ReadFile(fileName)
    if (err == nil) {
        decoder := json.NewDecoder(strings.NewReader(string(data)))
        m := map[string]interface{} {}
        err = decoder.Decode(&m)
        if (err == nil) {
            config = &DefaultConfig{ configData: m }
        }
    }
    return
}
```

The Load function reads the contents of a file, decodes the JSON it contains into a map, and uses the map to create a DefaultConfig value.

Using the Configuration System

To obtain the logging level from the configuration system, make the changes shown in Listing 32-13 to the default_create.go file in the logging folder.

Listing 32-13. Using the Configuration System in the default_create.go File in the logging Folder

```
package logging

import (
    "log"
    "os"
    "strings"
    "platform/config"
)

func NewDefaultLogger(cfg config.Configuration) Logger {

    var level LogLevel = Debug
    if configLevelString, found := cfg.GetString("logging:level"); found {
        level = LogLevelFromString(configLevelString)
    }

    flags := log.Lmsgprefix | log.Ltime
    return &DefaultLogger {
        minLevel: level,
        loggers: map[LogLevel]*log.Logger {
            Trace: log.New(os.Stdout, "TRACE ",  flags),
            Debug: log.New(os.Stdout, "DEBUG ",  flags),
            Information: log.New(os.Stdout, "INFO ",  flags),
            Warning: log.New(os.Stdout, "WARN ",  flags),
            Fatal: log.New(os.Stdout, "FATAL ",  flags),
        },
        triggerPanic: true,
    }
}

func LogLevelFromString(val string) (level LogLevel) {
    switch strings.ToLower(val) {
        case "debug":
            level = Debug
        case "information":
            level = Information
        case "warning":
            level = Warning
        case "fatal":
            level = Fatal
        case "none":
```

```
            level = None
        default:
            level = Debug
    }
    return
}
```

There is no good way to represent iota values in JSON, so I have used a string and defined the LogLevelFromString function to convert the configuration setting to a LogLevel value. Listing 32-14 updates the main function to load and apply the configuration data and to use the configuration system to read the message that it writes out.

Listing 32-14. Reading Configuration Settings in the main.go File in the platform Folder

```
package main

import (
        //"fmt"
        "platform/config"
        "platform/logging"
)

func writeMessage(logger logging.Logger, cfg config.Configuration) {
    section, ok := cfg.GetSection("main")
    if (ok) {
        message, ok := section.GetString("message")
        if (ok) {
            logger.Info(message)
        } else {
            logger.Panic("Cannot find configuration setting")
        }
    } else {
        logger.Panic("Config section not found")
    }
}

func main() {

    var cfg config.Configuration
    var err error
    cfg, err = config.Load("config.json")
    if (err != nil) {
        panic(err)
    }

    var logger logging.Logger = logging.NewDefaultLogger(cfg)
    writeMessage(logger, cfg)
}
```

The configuration is loaded from the config.json file, and the Configuration implementation is passed to the NewDefaultLogger function, which uses it to read the log level setting.

The writeMessage function demonstrates the use of a configuration section, which can be a good way to provide a component with the settings it needs, especially if multiple instances are required with different settings, each of which can be defined in its own section.

The code in Listing 32-14 produces the following output when compiled and executed:

```
18:49:12 INFO Hello from the config file
```

Managing Services with Dependency Injection

To get implementations of the Logger and Configuration interfaces, the code in the main function needs to know how to create instances of structs that implement those interfaces:

```
...
cfg, err = config.Load("config.json")
...
var logger logging.Logger = logging.NewDefaultLogger(cfg)
...
```

This is a workable approach, but it undermines the purpose of defining an interface, it requires care to ensure that instances are created consistently, and it complicates the process of replacing one interface implementation with another.

My preferred approach is to use dependency injection (DI), in which code that depends on an interface can obtain an implementation without needing to select an underlying type or create an instance directly. I am going to start with *service location*, which will provide the foundation for more advanced features later.

During application startup, the interfaces defined by the application will be added to a register, along with a factory function that creates instances of an implementation struct. So, for example, the platform. logger.Logger interface will be registered with a factory function that invokes the NewDefaultLogger function. When an interface is added to the register, it is known as a *service*.

During execution, application components that need the features described by the service go to the registry and request the interface they want. The registry invokes the factory function and returns the struct that is created, which allows the application component to use the interface features without knowing or specifying which implementation struct will be used or how it is created. Don't worry if this doesn't make sense—this can be a difficult topic to understand, and it becomes easier once you see it in action.

Defining Service Lifecycles

Services are registered with lifecycles, which specify when the factory function is invoked to create new struct values. I am going to use three service lifecycles, described in Table 32-1.

Table 32-1. *The Service Lifecycles*

Lifecycle	Description
Transient	For this lifecycle, the factory function is invoked for every service request.
Singleton	For this lifecycle, the factory function is invoked once, and every request receives the same struct instance.
Scoped	For this lifecycle, the factory function is invoked once for the first request within a scope, and every request within that scope receives the same struct instance.

Create the platform/services folder and add to it a file named lifecycles.go with the content shown in Listing 32-15.

Listing 32-15. The Contents of the lifecycles.go File in the services Folder

```
package services

type lifecycle int

const (
    Transient lifecycle = iota
    Singleton
    Scoped
)
```

I am going to implement the Scoped lifecycle using the context package in the standard library, which I described in Chapter 30. A Context will be automatically created for each HTTP request received by the server, which means that all the request handling code that processes that request can share the same set of services so that, for example, a single struct that provides session information can be used throughout processing for a given request.

To make it easier to work with contexts, add a file named context.go to the services folder with the content shown in Listing 32-16.

Listing 32-16. The Contents of the context.go File in the services Folder

```
package services

import (
    "context"
    "reflect"
)

const ServiceKey = "services"

type serviceMap map[reflect.Type]reflect.Value

func NewServiceContext(c context.Context) context.Context {
    if (c.Value(ServiceKey) == nil) {
        return context.WithValue(c, ServiceKey, make(serviceMap))
    } else {
```

```
        return c
    }
}
```

The NewServiceContext function derives a context using the WithValue function, adding a map that stores the services that have been resolved. See Chapter 30 for details of the different ways that contexts can be derived.

Defining the Internal Service Functions

I am going handle service registration by inspecting a factory function and using its result to determine the interface that it handles. This is an example of the type of factory function that will be used when registering a new service:

```
...
func ConfigurationFactory() config.Configuration {
    // TODO create struct that implements Configuration interface
}
...
```

The result type of this function is config.Configuration. Using reflection to inspect the function will allow me to get the result type and determine the interface for which this is a factory.

Some factory functions will depend on other services. Here is another example factory function:

```
...
func Loggerfactory(cfg config.Configuration) logging.Logger {
    // TODO create struct that implements Logger interface
}
...
```

This factory function resolves requests for the Logger interface, but it depends on an implementation of the Configuration interface to do so. This means that the Configuration interface has to be resolved to provide the argument required to resolve the Logger interface. This is an example of *dependency injection*, where the factory function's dependencies—the parameters—are resolved so that the function can be invoked.

■ **Note** Defining factory functions that depend on other services can alter the lifecycles of the nested services. For example, if you define a singleton service that depends on a transient service, then the nested service will be resolved only once when the singleton is first instantiated. This is not an issue in most projects but is something to bear in mind.

Add a file named core.go to the services folder with the content shown in Listing 32-17.

Listing 32-17. The Contents of the core.go File in the services Folder

```
package services

import (
```

```go
        "reflect"
        "context"
        "fmt"
)

type BindingMap struct {
    factoryFunc reflect.Value
    lifecycle
}

var services = make(map[reflect.Type]BindingMap)

func addService(life lifecycle, factoryFunc interface{}) (err error) {
    factoryFuncType := reflect.TypeOf(factoryFunc)
    if factoryFuncType.Kind() == reflect.Func && factoryFuncType.NumOut() == 1 {
        services[factoryFuncType.Out(0)] = BindingMap{
            factoryFunc: reflect.ValueOf(factoryFunc),
            lifecycle: life,
        }
    } else {
        err = fmt.Errorf("Type cannot be used as service: %v", factoryFuncType)

    }
    return
}
var contextReference = (*context.Context)(nil)
var contextReferenceType = reflect.TypeOf(contextReference).Elem()

func resolveServiceFromValue(c context.Context, val reflect.Value) (err error ){
    serviceType := val.Elem().Type()
    if serviceType == contextReferenceType {
        val.Elem().Set(reflect.ValueOf(c))
    } else if binding, found := services[serviceType]; found {
        if (binding.lifecycle == Scoped) {
            resolveScopedService(c, val, binding)
        } else {
            val.Elem().Set(invokeFunction(c, binding.factoryFunc)[0])
        }
    } else {
        err = fmt.Errorf("Cannot find service %v", serviceType)
    }
    return
}

func resolveScopedService(c context.Context, val reflect.Value,
        binding BindingMap) (err error) {
    sMap, ok := c.Value(ServiceKey).(serviceMap)
    if (ok) {
        serviceVal, ok := sMap[val.Type()]
        if (!ok) {
            serviceVal = invokeFunction(c, binding.factoryFunc)[0]
```

```
            sMap[val.Type()] = serviceVal
        }
        val.Elem().Set(serviceVal)
    } else {
        val.Elem().Set(invokeFunction(c, binding.factoryFunc)[0])
    }
    return
}

func resolveFunctionArguments(c context.Context,  f reflect.Value,
        otherArgs ...interface{}) []reflect.Value {
    params := make([]reflect.Value, f.Type().NumIn())
    i := 0
    if (otherArgs != nil) {
        for ; i < len(otherArgs); i++ {
            params[i] = reflect.ValueOf(otherArgs[i])
        }
    }
    for ; i < len(params); i++ {
        pType := f.Type().In(i)
        pVal := reflect.New(pType)
        err := resolveServiceFromValue(c, pVal)
        if err != nil {
            panic(err)
        }
        params[i] = pVal.Elem()
    }
    return params
}

func invokeFunction(c context.Context, f reflect.Value,
        otherArgs ...interface{}) []reflect.Value {
    return f.Call(resolveFunctionArguments(c, f, otherArgs...))
}
```

The BindingMap struct represents the combination of a factory function, expressed as a reflect.Value, and a lifecycle. The addService function is used to register a service, which it does by creating BindingMap and adding to the map assigned to the services variable.

The resolveServiceFromValue function is called to resolve a service, and its arguments are a Context and a Value that is a pointer to a variable whose type is the interface to be resolved (this will make more sense when you see a service resolution in action). To resolve a service, the getServiceFromValue function looks to see if there is a BindingMap in the services map, using the requested type as the key. If there is a BindingMap, then its factory function is invoked, and the value is assigned via the pointer.

The invokeFunction function is responsible for calling the factory function, using the resolveFunctionArguments function to inspect the factory function's parameters and resolve each of them. These functions accept optional additional arguments, which are used when a function should be invoked with a mix of services and regular value parameters (in which case the parameters that require regular values must be defined first).

Special handling is required for scoped services. The resolveScopedService checks to see if the Context contains a value from a previous request to resolve the service. If not, the service is resolved and added to the Context so that it can be reused within the same scope.

874

Defining the Service Registration Functions

None of the functions defined in Listing 32-17 is exported. To create the functions that will be used in the rest of the application to register services, add a file named `registration.go` to the `services` folder with the content shown in Listing 32-18.

Listing 32-18. The Contents of the registration.go File in the services Folder

```
package services

import (
    "reflect"
    "sync"
)

func AddTransient(factoryFunc interface{}) (err error) {
    return addService(Transient, factoryFunc)
}

func AddScoped(factoryFunc interface{}) (err error) {
    return addService(Scoped, factoryFunc)
}

func AddSingleton(factoryFunc interface{}) (err error) {
    factoryFuncVal := reflect.ValueOf(factoryFunc)
    if factoryFuncVal.Kind() == reflect.Func && factoryFuncVal.Type().NumOut() == 1 {
        var results []reflect.Value
        once := sync.Once{}
        wrapper := reflect.MakeFunc(factoryFuncVal.Type(),
            func ([]reflect.Value) []reflect.Value {
                once.Do(func() {
                    results = invokeFunction(nil, factoryFuncVal)
                })
                return results
            })
        err = addService(Singleton, wrapper.Interface())
    }
    return
}
```

The `AddTransient` and `AddScoped` functions simply pass on a factory function to the `addService` function. A little more work is required for the singleton lifecycle, and the `AddSingleton` function creates a wrapper around the factory function that ensures that it is executed only once, for the first request to resolve the service. This ensures that there is only one instance of the implementation struct created and that it won't be created until the first time it is needed.

Defining the Service Resolution Functions

The next set of features includes the functions that allow services to be resolved. Add a file named `resolution.go` to the `services` folder with the content shown in Listing 32-19.

Listing 32-19. The Contents of the resolution.go File in the services Folder

```
package services

import (
    "reflect"
    "errors"
    "context"
)

func GetService(target interface{}) error {
    return GetServiceForContext(context.Background(), target)
}

func GetServiceForContext(c context.Context, target interface{}) (err error) {
    targetValue := reflect.ValueOf(target)
    if targetValue.Kind() == reflect.Ptr &&
            targetValue.Elem().CanSet() {
        err = resolveServiceFromValue(c, targetValue)
    } else {
        err = errors.New("Type cannot be used as target")
    }
    return
}
```

The GetServiceForContext accepts a context and a pointer to a value that can be set using reflection. For convenience, the GetService function resolves a service using the background context.

Registering and Using Services

The basic service features are in place, which means that I can register services and then resolve them. Add a file named services_default.go to the services folder with the content shown in Listing 32-20.

Listing 32-20. The Contents of the services_default.go File in the services Folder

```
package services

import (
    "platform/logging"
    "platform/config"
)

func RegisterDefaultServices() {

    err := AddSingleton(func() (c config.Configuration) {
        c, loadErr :=  config.Load("config.json")
        if (loadErr != nil) {
            panic(loadErr)
        }
        return
    })
```

```
    err = AddSingleton(func(appconfig config.Configuration) logging.Logger {
        return logging.NewDefaultLogger(appconfig)
    })
    if (err != nil) {
        panic(err)
    }
}
```

The RegisterDefaultServices creates Configuration and Logger services. These services are created using the AddSingleton function, which means that a single instance of the structs that implement each interface will be shared by the entire application. Listing 32-21 updates the main function to use services, rather than instantiate structs directly.

Listing 32-21. Resolving Services in the main.go File in the platform Folder

```
package main

import (
    //"fmt"
    "platform/config"
    "platform/logging"
    "platform/services"
)

func writeMessage(logger logging.Logger, cfg config.Configuration) {

    section, ok := cfg.GetSection("main")
    if (ok) {
        message, ok := section.GetString("message")
        if (ok) {
            logger.Info(message)
        } else {
            logger.Panic("Cannot find configuration setting")
        }
    } else {
        logger.Panic("Config section not found")
    }
}

func main() {

    services.RegisterDefaultServices()

    var cfg config.Configuration
    services.GetService(&cfg)

    var logger logging.Logger
    services.GetService(&logger)

    writeMessage(logger, cfg)
}
```

Resolving a service is done by passing a pointer to a variable whose type is an interface. In Listing 32-21, the GetService function is used to obtain implementations of the Repository and Logger interfaces, without needing to know which struct type will be used, the process by which it is created, or the service lifecycles.

Both steps—creating the variable and passing a pointer—are required to resolve a service. Compile and execute the project, and you will see the following output:

```
19:17:06 INFO Hello from the config file
```

Adding Support for Invoking Functions

Once the basic service features are in place, it is easy to create enhancements that make service resolution simpler and easier. To add support for executing functions directly, add a file named functions.go to the services folder with the content shown in Listing 32-22.

Listing 32-22. The Contents of the functions.go File in the services Folder

```go
package services

import (
    "reflect"
    "errors"
    "context"
)

func Call(target interface{}, otherArgs ...interface{}) ([]interface{}, error) {
    return CallForContext(context.Background(), target, otherArgs...)
}

func CallForContext(c context.Context, target interface{}, otherArgs ...interface{})
(results []interface{}, err error) {
    targetValue := reflect.ValueOf(target)
    if (targetValue.Kind() == reflect.Func) {
        resultVals := invokeFunction(c, targetValue, otherArgs...)
        results = make([]interface{}, len(resultVals))
        for i := 0; i < len(resultVals); i++ {
            results[i] = resultVals[i].Interface()
        }
    } else {
        err = errors.New("Only functions can be invoked")
    }
    return
}
```

The CallForContext function receives a function and uses services to produce the values that are used as arguments to invoke the function. The Call function is a convenience for use when a Context isn't available. The implementation of this feature relies on the code used to invoke factory functions in Listing 32-22. Listing 32-23 demonstrates how calling functions directly can simplify the use of services.

Listing 32-23. Calling a Function Directly in the main.go File in the platform Folder

```
package main

import (
    //"fmt"
    "platform/config"
    "platform/logging"
    "platform/services"
)

func writeMessage(logger logging.Logger, cfg config.Configuration) {

    section, ok := cfg.GetSection("main")
    if (ok) {
        message, ok := section.GetString("message")
        if (ok) {
            logger.Info(message)
        } else {
            logger.Panic("Cannot find configuration setting")
        }
    } else {
        logger.Panic("Config section not found")
    }
}

func main() {

    services.RegisterDefaultServices()

    // var cfg config.Configuration
    // services.GetService(&cfg)

    // var logger logging.Logger
    // services.GetService(&logger)

    services.Call(writeMessage)
}
```

The function is passed to Call, which will inspect its parameters and resolve them using services. (Note that parentheses do not follow the function name because that would invoke the function rather than pass it to services.Call.) I no longer have to request services directly and can rely on the services package to take care of the details. Compile and execute the code, and you will see the following output:

```
19:19:08 INFO Hello from the config file
```

Adding Support for Resolving Struct Fields

The final feature I am going to add to the `service` package is the ability to resolve dependencies on struct fields. Add a file named `structs.go` to the `services` folder with the content shown in Listing 32-24.

Listing 32-24. The Contents of the structs.go File in the services Folder

```
package services

import (
    "reflect"
    "errors"
    "context"
)

func Populate(target interface{}) error {
    return PopulateForContext(context.Background(), target)
}

func PopulateForContext(c context.Context, target interface{}) (err error) {
    return PopulateForContextWithExtras(c, target,
        make(map[reflect.Type]reflect.Value))
}

func PopulateForContextWithExtras(c context.Context, target interface{},
        extras map[reflect.Type]reflect.Value) (err error) {
    targetValue := reflect.ValueOf(target)
    if targetValue.Kind() == reflect.Ptr &&
            targetValue.Elem().Kind() == reflect.Struct {
        targetValue = targetValue.Elem()
        for i := 0; i < targetValue.Type().NumField(); i++ {
            fieldVal := targetValue.Field(i)
            if fieldVal.CanSet() {
                if extra, ok := extras[fieldVal.Type()]; ok {
                    fieldVal.Set(extra)
                } else {
                    resolveServiceFromValue(c,  fieldVal.Addr() )
                }
            }
        }

    } else {
        err = errors.New("Type cannot be used as target")
    }
    return
}
```

These functions inspect the fields defined by a struct and attempt to resolve them using the defined services. Any fields whose type is not an interface or for which there is no service are skipped. The `PopulateForContextWithExtras` function allows additional values to be provided for struct fields.

Listing 32-25 defines a struct whose fields declare dependencies on services.

Listing 32-25. Injecting Struct Dependencies in the main.go File in the platform Folder

```
package main

import (
    //"fmt"
    "platform/config"
    "platform/logging"
    "platform/services"
)

func writeMessage(logger logging.Logger, cfg config.Configuration) {

    section, ok := cfg.GetSection("main")
    if (ok) {
        message, ok := section.GetString("message")
        if (ok) {
            logger.Info(message)
        } else {
            logger.Panic("Cannot find configuration setting")
        }
    } else {
        logger.Panic("Config section not found")
    }
}

func main() {

    services.RegisterDefaultServices()

    services.Call(writeMessage)

    val := struct {
        message string
        logging.Logger
    }{
        message: "Hello from the struct",
    }
    services.Populate(&val)
    val.Logger.Debug(val.message)
}
```

The main function defines an anonymous struct and resolves the services it requires by passing a pointer to the Populate function. The result is that the embedded Logger fields is populated using a service. The Populate function skips the message field, but a value is defined when the struct is initialized. Compile and execute the project, and you will see the following output:

```
19:21:43 INFO Hello from the config file
19:21:43 DEBUG Hello from the struct
```

Summary

In this chapter, I started the development of the custom web application platform. I created logging and configuration features, and I added support for services and dependency injection. In the next chapter, I continue development by creating a requesting handling pipeline and a customized template system.

CHAPTER 33

■ ■ ■

Middleware, Templates, and Handlers

In this chapter, I continue development of the web application platform started in Chapter 32, adding support for handling HTTP requests.

■ **Tip** You can download the example project for this chapter—and for all the other chapters in this book—from https://github.com/apress/pro-go. See Chapter 2 for how to get help if you have problems running the examples.

Creating the Request Pipeline

The next step in building the platform is to create a web service that will handle HTTP requests from browsers. To prepare, I am going to create a simple pipeline that will contain middleware components that can inspect and modify requests.

When an HTTP request arrives, it will be passed to each registered middleware component in the pipeline, giving each component the chance to process the request and contribute to the response. Components will also be able to terminate request processing, preventing the request from being forwarded to the remaining components in the pipeline.

Once the request has reached the end of the pipeline, it works its way back along the pipeline so that components have a chance to make further changes or do further work, as shown in Figure 33-1.

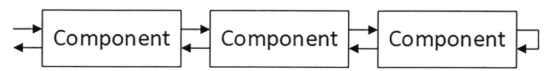

Figure 33-1. *The request processing pipeline*

© Adam Freeman 2022

A. Freeman, *Pro Go*, https://doi.org/10.1007/978-1-4842-7355-5_33

Defining the Middleware Component Interface

Create the platform/pipeline folder and add to it a file named component.go with the content shown in Listing 33-1.

Listing 33-1. The Contents of the component.go File in the pipeline Folder

```
package pipeline

import (
    "net/http"
)

type ComponentContext struct {
    *http.Request
    http.ResponseWriter
    error
}

func (mwc *ComponentContext) Error(err error) {
    mwc.error = err
}

func (mwc *ComponentContext) GetError() error {
    return mwc.error
}

type MiddlewareComponent interface {

    Init()

    ProcessRequest(context *ComponentContext, next func(*ComponentContext))
}
```

As its name suggests, the MiddlewareComponent interface describes the functionality required by a middleware component. The Init method is used to perform any one-off setup, and the other method, named ProcessRequest, is responsible for processing HTTP requests. The parameters defined by the ProcessRequest method are a pointer to a ComponentContext struct and a function that passes the request to the next component in the pipeline.

Everything a component needs to process a request is provided by the ComponentContext struct, through which http.Request and http.ResponseWriter can be accessed. The ComponentContext struct also defines an unexported error field, which is used to indicate a problem processing a request and which is set using the Error method.

Creating the Request Pipeline

To create the pipeline that will process requests, add a file named pipeline.go to the pipeline folder with the content shown in Listing 33-2.

Listing 33-2. The Contents of the pipeline.go File in the pipeline Folder

```go
package pipeline

import (
    "net/http"
)

type RequestPipeline func(*ComponentContext)

var emptyPipeline RequestPipeline = func(*ComponentContext) { /* do nothing */ }

func CreatePipeline(components ...MiddlewareComponent) RequestPipeline {
    f := emptyPipeline
    for i := len(components) -1 ; i >= 0; i-- {
        currentComponent := components[i]
        nextFunc := f
        f = func(context *ComponentContext) {
            if (context.error == nil) {
                currentComponent.ProcessRequest(context, nextFunc)
            }
        }
        currentComponent.Init()
    }
    return f
}

func (pl RequestPipeline) ProcessRequest(req *http.Request,
        resp http.ResponseWriter) error {
    ctx := ComponentContext {
        Request: req,
        ResponseWriter: resp,
    }
    pl(&ctx)
    return ctx.error
}
```

The CreatePipeline function is the most important part of this listing because it accepts a series of components and connects them to produce a function that accepts a pointer to a ComponentContext struct. This function invokes the ProcessRequest method of the first component in the pipeline with a next argument that invokes the ProcessRequest method of the next component. This chain passes on the ComponentContext struct to all the components in turn, unless one of them calls the Error method. Requests are processed using the ProcessRequest method, which creates the ComponentContext value and uses it to start request handling.

Creating Basic Components

The definition of the component interface and pipeline are simple, but they provide a flexible foundation on which components can be written. Applications can define and choose their own components, but there are some basic features that I am going to include as part of the platform.

Creating the Services Middleware Component

Create the platform/pipeline/basic folder and add to it a file named services.go with the content shown in Listing 33-3.

Listing 33-3. The Contents of the services.go File in the pipeline/basic Folder

```
package basic

import (
    "platform/pipeline"
    "platform/services"
)

type ServicesComponent struct {}

func (c *ServicesComponent) Init() {}

func (c *ServicesComponent)  ProcessRequest(ctx *pipeline.ComponentContext,
        next func(*pipeline.ComponentContext))  {
    reqContext := ctx.Request.Context()
    ctx.Request.WithContext(services.NewServiceContext(reqContext))
    next(ctx)
}
```

This middleware component modifies the Context associated with the request so that context-scoped services can be used during request processing. The http.Request.Context method is used to get the standard Context created with the request, which is prepared for services and then updated using the WithContext method.

Once the context has been prepared, the request is passed along the pipeline by invoking the function received through the parameter named next:

```
...
next(ctx)
...
```

This parameter gives middleware components control over request processing and allows it to modify the context data that subsequent components receive. It also allows components to short-circuit request processing by not invoking the next function.

Creating a Logging Middleware Component

Next, add a file named logging.go to the basic folder with the content shown in Listing 33-4.

Listing 33-4. The Contents of the logging.go File in the basic Folder

```
package basic

import (
    "net/http"
    "platform/logging"
```

```
    "platform/pipeline"
    "platform/services"
)

type LoggingResponseWriter struct {
    statusCode int
    http.ResponseWriter
}

func (w *LoggingResponseWriter) WriteHeader(statusCode int) {
    w.statusCode = statusCode
    w.ResponseWriter.WriteHeader(statusCode)
}

func (w *LoggingResponseWriter) Write(b []byte) (int, error) {
    if (w.statusCode == 0) {
        w.statusCode = http.StatusOK
    }
    return w.ResponseWriter.Write(b)
}

type LoggingComponent struct {}

func (lc *LoggingComponent) Init() {}

func (lc *LoggingComponent) ProcessRequest(ctx *pipeline.ComponentContext,
        next func(*pipeline.ComponentContext))  {

    var logger logging.Logger
    err := services.GetServiceForContext(ctx.Request.Context(), &logger)
    if (err != nil) {
        ctx.Error(err)
        return
    }

    loggingWriter := LoggingResponseWriter{ 0, ctx.ResponseWriter}
    ctx.ResponseWriter = &loggingWriter

    logger.Infof("REQ --- %v - %v", ctx.Request.Method, ctx.Request.URL)
    next(ctx)
    logger.Infof("RSP %v %v", loggingWriter.statusCode, ctx.Request.URL )
}
```

This component logs basic details of the request and response using the Logger service created in Chapter 32. The ResponseWriter interface doesn't provide access to the status code sent in a response and so a LoggingResponseWriter is created and passed to the next component in the pipeline.

This component performs actions before and after the next function is invoked, logging a message before passing on the request and logging another message that writes out the status code after the request has been processed.

This component obtains a Logger service when it processes a request. I could obtain a Logger just once, but that works only because I know that the Logger has been registered as a singleton service. Instead, I prefer not to make assumptions about the Logger lifecycle, which means that I won't get unexpected results if the lifecycle is changed in the future.

Creating the Error Handling Component

The request pipeline allows components to terminate processing when an error arises. To define a component that will process the error, add a file named errors.go to the platform/pipeline/basic folder with the content shown in Listing 33-5.

Listing 33-5. The Contents of the errors.go File in the basic Folder

```
package basic

import (
    "fmt"
    "net/http"
    "platform/logging"
    "platform/pipeline"
    "platform/services"
)

type ErrorComponent struct {}

func recoveryFunc (ctx *pipeline.ComponentContext, logger logging.Logger) {
    if arg := recover(); arg != nil {
        logger.Debugf("Error: %v", fmt.Sprint(arg))
        ctx.ResponseWriter.WriteHeader(http.StatusInternalServerError)
    }
}

func (c *ErrorComponent) Init() {}

func (c *ErrorComponent) ProcessRequest(ctx *pipeline.ComponentContext,
        next func(*pipeline.ComponentContext))  {

    var logger logging.Logger
    services.GetServiceForContext(ctx.Context(), &logger)
    defer recoveryFunc(ctx, logger)
    next(ctx)
    if (ctx.GetError() != nil) {
        logger.Debugf("Error: %v", ctx.GetError())
        ctx.ResponseWriter.WriteHeader(http.StatusInternalServerError)
    }
}
```

This component recovers from any panic that occurs when subsequent components process the request and also handles any expected error. In both cases, the error is logged, and the response status code is set to indicate an error.

Creating the Static File Component

Almost all web applications require support for serving static files, even if it is just for CSS stylesheets. The standard library contains built-in support for serving files, which is helpful because it is a task that is fraught with potential problems. But fortunately, it is a simple matter to integrate the standard library features into the request pipeline in the example project. Add a file named files.go to the basic folder with the content shown in Listing 33-6.

Listing 33-6. The Contents of the files.go File in the basic Folder

```
package basic

import (
    "net/http"
    "platform/config"
    "platform/pipeline"
    "platform/services"
    "strings"
)

type StaticFileComponent struct {
    urlPrefix string
    stdLibHandler http.Handler
}

func (sfc *StaticFileComponent) Init() {
    var cfg config.Configuration
    services.GetService(&cfg)
    sfc.urlPrefix = cfg.GetStringDefault("files:urlprefix", "/files/")
    path, ok := cfg.GetString("files:path")
    if (ok) {
        sfc.stdLibHandler = http.StripPrefix(sfc.urlPrefix,
            http.FileServer(http.Dir(path)))
    } else {
        panic ("Cannot load file configuration settings")
    }
}

func (sfc *StaticFileComponent) ProcessRequest(ctx *pipeline.ComponentContext,
    next func(*pipeline.ComponentContext)) {

    if  !strings.EqualFold(ctx.Request.URL.Path, sfc.urlPrefix) &&
            strings.HasPrefix(ctx.Request.URL.Path, sfc.urlPrefix) {
        sfc.stdLibHandler.ServeHTTP(ctx.ResponseWriter, ctx.Request)
    } else {
        next(ctx)
    }
}
```

This handler uses the Init method to read the configuration settings that specify the prefix used for file requests and the directory from which to serve files and uses the handlers provided by the net/http package to serve files.

Creating the Placeholder Response Component

The project doesn't contain any middleware components that generate responses, which would typically be defined as part of the application. For the moment, however, I need a placeholder component that will generate simple responses as I develop other features. Create the platform/placeholder folder and add to it a file named message_middleware.go with the content shown in Listing 33-7.

Listing 33-7. The Contents of the message_middleware.go File in the placeholder Folder

```go
package placeholder

import (
    "io"
    "errors"
    "platform/pipeline"
    "platform/config"
    "platform/services"
)

type SimpleMessageComponent struct {}

func (c *SimpleMessageComponent) Init() {}

func (c *SimpleMessageComponent) ProcessRequest(ctx *pipeline.ComponentContext,
        next func(*pipeline.ComponentContext))  {

    var cfg config.Configuration
    services.GetService(&cfg)
    msg, ok := cfg.GetString("main:message")
    if (ok) {
        io.WriteString(ctx.ResponseWriter, msg)
    } else {
        ctx.Error(errors.New("Cannot find config setting"))
    }
    next(ctx)
}
```

This component produces a simple text response, which is just enough to ensure that the pipeline works as expected. Next, create the platform/placeholder/files folder and add to it a file named hello.json with the content shown in Listing 33-8.

Listing 33-8. The Contents of the hello.json File in the placeholder/files Folder

```json
{
    "message": "Hello from the JSON file"
}
```

To set the location from which static files will be read, add the setting shown in Listing 33-9 to the config.json file in the platform folder.

Listing 33-9. Adding a Configuration Setting in the config.json File in the platform Folder

```
{
    "logging" : {
        "level": "debug"
    },
    "main" : {
        "message" : "Hello from the config file"
    },
    "files": {
        "path": "placeholder/files"
    }
}
```

Creating the HTTP Server

It is time to create the HTTP server and use a pipeline to handle the requests it receives. Create the platform/http folder and add to it a file named server.go with the content shown in Listing 33-10.

Listing 33-10. The Contents of the server.go File in the http Folder

```
package http

import (
    "fmt"
    "sync"
    "net/http"
    "platform/config"
    "platform/logging"
    "platform/pipeline"
)

type pipelineAdaptor struct {
    pipeline.RequestPipeline
}

func (p pipelineAdaptor) ServeHTTP(writer http.ResponseWriter,
    request *http.Request) {
        p.ProcessRequest(request, writer)
}

func Serve(pl pipeline.RequestPipeline, cfg config.Configuration, logger logging.Logger )
*sync.WaitGroup {
    wg := sync.WaitGroup{}

    adaptor := pipelineAdaptor { RequestPipeline: pl }

    enableHttp := cfg.GetBoolDefault("http:enableHttp", true)
    if (enableHttp) {
        httpPort := cfg.GetIntDefault("http:port", 5000)
        logger.Debugf("Starting HTTP server on port %v", httpPort)
```

```
        wg.Add(1)
        go func() {
            err := http.ListenAndServe(fmt.Sprintf(":%v", httpPort), adaptor)
            if (err != nil) {
                panic(err)
            }
        }()
    }
    enableHttps := cfg.GetBoolDefault("http:enableHttps", false)
    if (enableHttps) {
        httpsPort := cfg.GetIntDefault("http:httpsPort", 5500)
        certFile, cfok := cfg.GetString("http:httpsCert")
        keyFile, kfok := cfg.GetString("http:httpsKey")
        if cfok && kfok {
            logger.Debugf("Starting HTTPS server on port %v", httpsPort)
            wg.Add(1)
            go func() {
                err := http.ListenAndServeTLS(fmt.Sprintf(":%v", httpsPort),
                    certFile, keyFile, adaptor)
                if (err != nil) {
                    panic(err)
                }
            }()
        } else {
            panic("HTTPS certificate settings not found")
        }
    }
    return &wg
}
```

The Serve function uses the Configuration service to read the settings for HTTP and HTTPS and uses the features provided by the standard library to receive requests and pass them to the pipeline for processing. (I will enable HTTPS support in Chapter 38 when I prepare for deployment, but until then, I will use the default settings that listen for HTTP requests on port 5000.)

Configuring the Application

The final step is to configure the pipeline required by the application and use it to configure and start the HTTP server. This is a task that will be performed by the application once I start development in Chapter 35. For now, however, add a file named startup.go to the placeholder folder with the content shown in Listing 33-11.

Listing 33-11. The Contents of the startup.go File in the placeholder Folder

```
package placeholder

import (
    "platform/http"
    "platform/pipeline"
    "platform/pipeline/basic"
```

```
        "platform/services"
        "sync"
)

func createPipeline() pipeline.RequestPipeline {
    return pipeline.CreatePipeline(
        &basic.ServicesComponent{},
        &basic.LoggingComponent{},
        &basic.ErrorComponent{},
        &basic.StaticFileComponent{},
        &SimpleMessageComponent{},
    )
}

func Start() {
    results, err := services.Call(http.Serve, createPipeline())
    if (err == nil) {
        (results[0].(*sync.WaitGroup)).Wait()
    } else {
        panic(err)
    }
}
```

The createPipeline function creates a pipeline with the middleware components created previously. The Start function calls createPipeline and uses the result to configure and start the HTTP server. Listing 33-12 uses the main function to complete the setup and start the HTTP server.

Listing 33-12. Completing App Startup in the main.go File in the platform Folder

```
package main

import (
    "platform/services"
    "platform/placeholder"
)

func main() {
    services.RegisterDefaultServices()
    placeholder.Start()
}
```

Compile and execute the project and use a web browser to request http://localhost:5000.

DEALING WITH WINDOWS FIREWALL PERMISSION REQUESTS

As explained in earlier chapters, Windows will prompt for firewall permissions every time the project is compiled with the go run command. A simple Powershell script can be used instead of the go run command to avoid these prompts. Create a file named buildandrun.ps1 with the following content:

```
$file = "./platform.exe"

&go build -o $file

if ($LASTEXITCODE -eq 0) {
    &$file
}
```

To build and execute the project, use the command ./buildandrun.ps1 in the platform folder.

The HTTP request will be received by the server and passed along the pipeline, producing the response shown in Figure 33-2. Request http://localhost:5000/files/hello.json, and you will see the contents of the static file, also shown in Figure 33-2.

Output similar to the following will be written to the standard output, showing the server receiving and processing the request (you may also see requests for /favicon.ico depending on your browser):

```
20:10:12 DEBUG Starting HTTP server on port 5000
20:10:23 INFO REQ --- GET - /
20:10:23 INFO RSP 200 /
20:10:33 INFO REQ --- GET - /files/hello.json
20:10:33 INFO RSP 200 /files/hello.json
```

The server currently responds to all requests that are not for files in the same way, which is why the log shows that the requests for the /favicon.ico file generate 200 OK responses.

Figure 33-2. *Getting a response from the HTTP server*

Streamlining Service Resolution

At present, middleware components have to directly resolve the services they require. But, since the dependency injection system can invoke functions and populate structs, a little additional work will allow components to declare the services on which they depend and obtain them automatically. First, an interface is required that will allow components to indicate they require dependency injection to handle requests, as shown in Listing 33-13.

Listing 33-13. Defining an Interface in the component.go File in the pipeline Folder

```
package pipeline

import (
    "net/http"
)

type ComponentContext struct {
    *http.Request
    http.ResponseWriter
    error
}

func (mwc *ComponentContext) Error(err error) {
    mwc.error = err
}

func (mwc *ComponentContext) GetError() error {
    return mwc.error
}

type MiddlewareComponent interface {

    Init()
    ProcessRequest(context *ComponentContext, next func(*ComponentContext))
}

type ServicesMiddlwareComponent interface {
    Init()
    ImplementsProcessRequestWithServices()
}
```

By implementing a method named ImplementsProcessRequestWithServices, components can indicate they require services. It isn't possible to include the method that requires the services in the interface because each component needs a different method signature for the services it requires. Instead, I am going to detect the ServicesMiddlwareComponent and then use reflection to determine whether the component implements a method named ProcessRequestWithServices, whose first two parameters are the same as the ProcessRequest method defined by the MiddlewareComponent interface. Listing 33-14 adds the new feature to the function that creates the pipeline and also populates the component struct fields with services when the pipeline is prepared.

Listing 33-14. Adding Support for Services in the pipeline.go File in the pipeline Folder

```
package pipeline

import (
    "net/http"
    "platform/services"
    "reflect"
)

type RequestPipeline func(*ComponentContext)

var emptyPipeline RequestPipeline = func(*ComponentContext) { /* do nothing */ }

func CreatePipeline(components ...interface{}) RequestPipeline {
    f := emptyPipeline
    for i := len(components) -1 ; i >= 0; i-- {
        currentComponent := components[i]
        services.Populate(currentComponent)
        nextFunc := f
        if servComp, ok := currentComponent.(ServicesMiddlwareComponent ); ok {
            f = createServiceDependentFunction(currentComponent, nextFunc)
            servComp.Init()
        } else if stdComp, ok := currentComponent.(MiddlewareComponent ); ok {
            f = func(context *ComponentContext) {
                if (context.error == nil) {
                    stdComp.ProcessRequest(context, nextFunc)
                }
            }
            stdComp.Init()
        } else {
            panic("Value is not a middleware component")
        }
    }
    return f
}

func createServiceDependentFunction(component interface{},
        nextFunc RequestPipeline) RequestPipeline {
    method := reflect.ValueOf(component).MethodByName("ProcessRequestWithServices")
    if (method.IsValid()) {
        return  func(context *ComponentContext) {
            if (context.error == nil) {
                _, err := services.CallForContext(context.Request.Context(),
                    method.Interface(), context, nextFunc)
                if (err != nil) {
                    context.Error(err)
                }
            }
        }
```

```
    } else {
        panic("No ProcessRequestWithServices method defined")
    }
}

func (pl RequestPipeline) ProcessRequest(req *http.Request,
        resp http.ResponseWriter) error {
    ctx := ComponentContext {
        Request: req,
        ResponseWriter: resp,
    }
    pl(&ctx)
    return ctx.error
}
```

These changes allow a middleware component to take advantage of dependency injection so that
dependencies on services can be declared as parameters, as shown in Listing 33-15.

Listing 33-15. Using Dependency Injection in the logging.go File in the pipeline/basic Folder

```
package basic

import (
    "net/http"
    "platform/logging"
    "platform/pipeline"
    //"platform/services"
)

type LoggingResponseWriter struct {
    statusCode int
    http.ResponseWriter
}

func (w *LoggingResponseWriter) WriteHeader(statusCode int) {
    w.statusCode = statusCode
    w.ResponseWriter.WriteHeader(statusCode)
}

func (w *LoggingResponseWriter) Write(b []byte) (int, error) {
    if (w.statusCode == 0) {
        w.statusCode = http.StatusOK
    }
    return w.ResponseWriter.Write(b)
}

type LoggingComponent struct {}

func (lc *LoggingComponent) ImplementsProcessRequestWithServices() {}

func (lc *LoggingComponent) Init() {}
```

```
func (lc *LoggingComponent) ProcessRequestWithServices(
    ctx *pipeline.ComponentContext,
    next func(*pipeline.ComponentContext),
    logger logging.Logger)  {

    // var logger logging.Logger
    // err := services.GetServiceForContext(ctx.Request.Context(), &logger)
    // if (err != nil) {
    //     ctx.Error(err)
    //     return
    // }

    loggingWriter := LoggingResponseWriter{ 0, ctx.ResponseWriter}
    ctx.ResponseWriter = &loggingWriter

    logger.Infof("REQ --- %v - %v", ctx.Request.Method, ctx.Request.URL)
    next(ctx)
    logger.Infof("RSP %v %v", loggingWriter.statusCode, ctx.Request.URL )
}
```

Defining the ImplementsProcessRequestWithServices method implements the interface that the pipeline uses as an indication that there will be a ProcessRequestWithServices method that requires dependency injection. Components can also rely on services resolved through their struct fields, as shown in Listing 33-16.

Listing 33-16. Using Dependency Injection in the files.go File in the pipeline/basic Folder

```
package basic

import (
    "net/http"
    "platform/config"
    "platform/pipeline"
    //"platform/services"
    "strings"
)

type StaticFileComponent struct {
    urlPrefix string
    stdLibHandler http.Handler
    Config config.Configuration
}

func (sfc *StaticFileComponent) Init() {
    // var cfg config.Configuration
    // services.GetService(&cfg)
    sfc.urlPrefix = sfc.Config.GetStringDefault("files:urlprefix", "/files/")
    path, ok := sfc.Config.GetString("files:path")
    if (ok) {
        sfc.stdLibHandler = http.StripPrefix(sfc.urlPrefix,
            http.FileServer(http.Dir(path)))
```

```
    } else {
        panic ("Cannot load file configuration settings")
    }
}

func (sfc *StaticFileComponent) ProcessRequest(ctx *pipeline.ComponentContext,
    next func(*pipeline.ComponentContext)) {

    if !strings.EqualFold(ctx.Request.URL.Path, sfc.urlPrefix) &&
            strings.HasPrefix(ctx.Request.URL.Path, sfc.urlPrefix) {
        sfc.stdLibHandler.ServeHTTP(ctx.ResponseWriter, ctx.Request)
    } else {
        next(ctx)
    }
}
```

Compile and execute the project, and use a browser to request http://localhost:5000 and http://localhost:5000/files/hello.json, which will produce the same results as in the previous section. You may see a 304 result when requesting the JSON file since it has not changed since the request in the previous section.

Creating HTML Responses

I described the HTML template processing features in Chapter 23, but they don't work in the way that I think about HTML content. I want to be able to define an HTML template and specify a shared layout that will be used within that template. This is the opposite way to the standard approach taken by the html/template package, but it is easy to customize the default behavior to get the effect I want.

■ **Note**   Because I am reversing the order in which templates are processed, templates cannot use the block features to provide default content for a template that is overridden by another template.

Creating the Layout and Template

The process of adapting a template engine is easier when you know what the structure of the templates will be. Add a file named simple_message.html to the platform/placeholder folder with the content shown in Listing 33-17.

Listing 33-17. The Contents of the simple_message.html File in the placeholder Folder

```
{{ layout "layout.html" }}

<h3>
    Hello from the template
</h3>
```

This template specifies the layout it requires using the layout expression but is otherwise a standard template that uses the features described in Chapter 23. The template contains an h3 element, whose content includes an action that inserts a data value.

To define the layout, add a file named `layout.html` to the `placeholder` folder with the content shown in Listing 33-18.

Listing 33-18. The Contents of the layout.html File in the placeholder Folder

```
<!DOCTYPE html>
<html>
<head>
    <meta name="viewport" content="width=device-width" />
    <title>Pro Go</title>
</head>
<body>
    <h2>Hello from the layout</h2>
    {{ body }}
</body>
</html>
```

The layout contains the elements required to define an HTML document, with the addition of an action that contains a body expression, which will insert the contents of the selected template into the output.

To render content, the template will be selected and executed, which will identify the layout that it requires. The layout will also be rendered and combined with the content from the template to produce a complete HTML response. This is the approach I prefer, partly because it avoids the need to know which layout is required when selecting a template and partly because it is what I am used to in other languages and platforms.

Implementing Template Execution

The built-in template package is excellent and makes it easy to support the model where templates specify their layouts. Create the `platform/templates` folder and add to it a file named `template_executor.go` with the content shown in Listing 33-19.

Listing 33-19. The Contents of the template_executor.go File in the templates Folder

```
package templates

import "io"

type TemplateExecutor interface {

    ExecTemplate(writer io.Writer, name string, data interface{}) (err error)
}
```

The `TemplateProcessor` interface defines a method named `ExecTemplate` that processes a template using the supplied data values and writes the content to a `Writer`. To create an implementation of the interface, add a file named `layout_executor.go` to the `templates` folder with the content shown in Listing 33-20.

Listing 33-20. The Contents of the layout_executor.go File in the templates Folder

```go
package templates

import (
    "io"
    "strings"
    "html/template"
)

type LayoutTemplateProcessor struct {}

func (proc *LayoutTemplateProcessor) ExecTemplate(writer io.Writer,
        name string, data interface{}) (err error) {
    var sb strings.Builder
    layoutName := ""
    localTemplates := getTemplates()
    localTemplates.Funcs(map[string]interface{} {
        "body": insertBodyWrapper(&sb),
        "layout": setLayoutWrapper(&layoutName),
    })
    err = localTemplates.ExecuteTemplate(&sb, name, data)
    if (layoutName != "") {
        localTemplates.ExecuteTemplate(writer, layoutName, data)
    } else {
        io.WriteString(writer, sb.String())
    }
    return
}

var getTemplates func() (t *template.Template)

func insertBodyWrapper(body *strings.Builder) func() template.HTML {
    return func() template.HTML {
        return template.HTML(body.String())
    }
}

func setLayoutWrapper(val *string) func(string) string {
    return func(layout string) string {
        *val = layout
        return ""
    }
}
```

The implementation of the ExecTemplate method executes a template and stores the content in a strings.Builder. To support the layout and body expressions described in the previous section, custom template functions are created, like this:

```
...
localTemplates.Funcs(map[string]interface{} {
    "body": insertBodyWrapper(&sb),
    "layout": setLayoutWrapper(&layoutName),
})
...
```

When the built-in template engine encounters the template expression, it invokes the function created by setLayoutWrapper, which sets the value of a variable, which is then used to execute the specified layout template. During execution of the layout, the body expression invokes the function created by the insertBodyWrapper function, which inserts the content generated by the original template into the output produced from the layout. To prevent the built-in template engine from escaping the HTML characters, the result of this operation is a template.HTML value:

```
...
func insertBodyWrapper(body *strings.Builder) func() template.HTML {
    return func() template.HTML {
        return template.HTML(body.String())
    }
}
...
```

As explained in Chapter 23, the Go template system automatically encodes content to make it safe for inclusion in HTML documents. This is usually a helpful feature, but in this instance, escaping the content from the template as it is inserted into the layout would prevent it from being interpreted as HTML.

The ExecTemplate method obtains the loaded templates by invoking a function named getTemplates, for which a variable is defined in Listing 33-20. To add support for loading the templates and creating the function value that will be assigned to the getTemplates variable, add a file named template_loader.go to the templates folder with the content shown in Listing 33-21.

Listing 33-21. The Contents of the template_loader.go File in the templates Folder

```
package templates

import (
    "html/template"
    "sync"
    "errors"
    "platform/config"
)

var once = sync.Once{}

func LoadTemplates(c config.Configuration) (err error) {
    path, ok := c.GetString("templates:path")
    if !ok {
        return errors.New("Cannot load template config")
    }
```

```
    reload := c.GetBoolDefault("templates:reload", false)
    once.Do(func() {
        doLoad := func() (t *template.Template) {
            t = template.New("htmlTemplates")
            t.Funcs(map[string]interface{} {
                "body": func() string { return "" },
                "layout": func() string { return "" },
            })
            t, err = t.ParseGlob(path)
            return
        }
        if (reload) {
            getTemplates = doLoad
        } else {
            var templates *template.Template
            templates = doLoad()
            getTemplates = func() *template.Template {
                t, _ := templates.Clone()
                return t
            }
        }
    })
    return
}
```

The LoadTemplates function loads the template from a location specified in the configuration file. There is also a configuration setting that enables reloading for every request, which is something that should not be done in a deployed project, but is useful during development because it means that changes to templates can be seen without restarting the application. Listing 33-22 adds the new settings to the configuration file.

Listing 33-22. Adding Settings in the config.json File in the platform Folder

```
{
    "logging" : {
        "level": "debug"
    },
    "main" : {
        "message" : "Hello from the config file"
    },
    "files": {
        "path": "placeholder/files"
    },
    "templates": {
        "path": "placeholder/*.html",
        "reload": true
    }
}
```

The value received through the reload setting determines the function assigned to the getTemplates variable. If reload is true, then calling getTemplates will load the templates from disk; if it is false, then the previously loaded templates will be cloned.

Cloning or reloading the templates is required to ensure that the custom body and layout functions work correctly. The LoadTemplates function defines placeholder functions so that the templates can be parsed when they are loaded.

Creating and Using the Template Service

The custom template engine will be available as a service. Add the statements shown in Listing 33-23 to the services_default.go file in the platform/services folder.

Listing 33-23. Creating the Template Service in the services_default.go File in the services Folder

```
package services

import (
    "platform/logging"
    "platform/config"
    "platform/templates"
)

func RegisterDefaultServices() {

    err := AddSingleton(func() (c config.Configuration) {
        c, loadErr :=  config.Load("config.json")
        if (loadErr != nil) {
            panic(loadErr)
        }
        return
    })

    err = AddSingleton(func(appconfig config.Configuration) logging.Logger {
        return logging.NewDefaultLogger(appconfig)
    })
    if (err != nil) {
        panic(err)
    }

    err = AddSingleton(
        func(c config.Configuration) templates.TemplateExecutor {
            templates.LoadTemplates(c)
            return &templates.LayoutTemplateProcessor{}
        })
    if (err != nil) {
        panic(err)
    }
}
```

To ensure that the template engine works, make the changes shown in Listing 33-24 to the placeholder middleware component created earlier in the chapter so that it returns an HTML response rather than a simple string.

Listing 33-24. Using a Template in the message_middleware.go File in the placeholder Folder

```
package placeholder

import (
    //"io"
    //"errors"
    "platform/pipeline"
    "platform/config"
    //"platform/services"
    "platform/templates"
)

type SimpleMessageComponent struct {
    Message string
    config.Configuration
}

func (lc *SimpleMessageComponent) ImplementsProcessRequestWithServices() {}

func (c *SimpleMessageComponent) Init() {
    c.Message = c.Configuration.GetStringDefault("main:message",
        "Default Message")
}

func (c *SimpleMessageComponent) ProcessRequestWithServices(
    ctx *pipeline.ComponentContext,
    next func(*pipeline.ComponentContext),
    executor templates.TemplateExecutor)  {
    err := executor.ExecTemplate(ctx.ResponseWriter,
        "simple_message.html", c.Message)
    if (err != nil) {
        ctx.Error(err)
    } else {
        next(ctx)
    }
}
```

The component now implements the ProcessRequestWithServices method and receives services through dependency injection. One of the requested services is an implementation of the TemplateExecutor interface, which is used to display the simple_message.html template. Compile and execute the project and use a browser to request http://localhost:5000, and you will see the HTML response shown in Figure 33-3.

Figure 33-3. *Creating an HTML response*

Introducing Request Handlers

The next step is to introduce support for defining the logic that will handle an HTTP request and produce an appropriate response, which will allow me to write code that responds to specific URLs without needing to repeat too much code. To understand how this will work, the best place to start is with an example of a request handler, which will be defined as a type with a set of methods that handle requests. Add a file named name_handler.go to the placeholder folder with the content shown in Listing 33-25.

Listing 33-25. The Contents of the name_handler.go File in the placeholder Folder

```
package placeholder

import (
    "fmt"
    "platform/logging"
)

var names = []string{"Alice", "Bob", "Charlie", "Dora"}

type NameHandler struct {
        logging.Logger
}

func (n NameHandler) GetName(i int) string {
    n.Logger.Debugf("GetName method invoked with argument: %v", i)
    if (i < len(names)) {
        return fmt.Sprintf("Name #%v: %v", i, names[i])
    } else {
        return fmt.Sprintf("Index out of bounds")
    }
}
```

```
func (n NameHandler) GetNames() string {
    n.Logger.Debug("GetNames method invoked")
    return fmt.Sprintf("Names: %v", names)
}

type NewName struct {
    Name string
    InsertAtStart bool
}

func (n NameHandler) PostName(new NewName) string {
    n.Logger.Debugf("PostName method invoked with argument %v", new)
    if (new.InsertAtStart) {
        names = append([] string { new.Name}, names... )
    } else {
        names = append(names, new.Name)
    }
    return fmt.Sprintf("Names: %v", names)
}
```

The NameHandler struct defines three methods: GetName, GetNames, and PostName. When the application starts, the set of registered handlers will be inspected, and the names of the methods they define will be used to create routes that will match HTTP requests.

The first part of each method name specifies the HTTP method that the route will match so that the GetName method, for example, will match GET requests. The rest of the method name will be used as the first segment in the URL path matched by the route, with additional segments added for the parameters of GET requests.

Table 33-1 shows the details of the requests that will be handled by the methods defined in Listing 33-25.

Table 33-1. *The Requests Matched by the Example Handler Methods*

Name	HTTP Method	Example URL
GetName	GET	/name/1
GetNames	GET	/names
PostName	POST	/names

When a request arrives that matches a method's route, the parameter values are obtained from the request URL and the query string and, if present, the request form. If the type of a method parameter is a struct, then its fields will be populated using the same request data.

The services required to handle the requests are declared as fields defined by the handler struct. In Listing 33-25, the NameHandler struct defines a field that declares a dependency on the logging.Logger service. A new instance of the struct will be created, its fields will be populated, and then the method that has been selected to handle the request will be invoked.

Generating URL Routes

The first step is to add support for generating the URL routes from request handler methods. Create the platform/http/handling folder and add to it a file named routes.go with the content shown in Listing 33-26.

Listing 33-26. The Contents of the routes.go File in the http/handling Folder

```
package handling

import (
    "reflect"
    "regexp"
    "strings"
    "net/http"
)

type HandlerEntry struct {
    Prefix string
    Handler interface{}
}

type Route struct {
    httpMethod string
    prefix string
    handlerName string
    actionName string
    expression regexp.Regexp
    handlerMethod reflect.Method
}

var httpMethods = []string { http.MethodGet, http.MethodPost,
    http.MethodDelete, http.MethodPut }

func generateRoutes(entries ...HandlerEntry) []Route {
    routes := make([]Route, 0, 10)
    for _, entry := range entries {
        handlerType := reflect.TypeOf(entry.Handler)
        promotedMethods := getAnonymousFieldMethods(handlerType)

        for i := 0; i < handlerType.NumMethod(); i++ {
            method := handlerType.Method(i)
            methodName := strings.ToUpper(method.Name)
            for _, httpMethod := range httpMethods {
                if strings.Index(methodName, httpMethod) == 0 {
                    if (matchesPromotedMethodName(method, promotedMethods)) {
                        continue
                    }
                    route := Route{
                        httpMethod: httpMethod,
                        prefix: entry.Prefix,
                        handlerName: strings.Split(handlerType.Name(), "Handler")[0],
```

```go
                    actionName: strings.Split(methodName, httpMethod)[1],
                    handlerMethod: method,
                }
                generateRegularExpression(entry.Prefix, &route)
                routes = append(routes, route)
            }
        }
    }
    return routes
}

func matchesPromotedMethodName(method reflect.Method,
        methods []reflect.Method) bool {
    for _, m := range methods {
        if m.Name == method.Name {
            return true
        }
    }
    return false
}

func getAnonymousFieldMethods(target []reflect.Type) reflect.Method {
    methods := []reflect.Method {}
    for i := 0; i < target.NumField(); i++ {
        field := target.Field(i)
        if (field.Anonymous && field.IsExported()) {
            for j := 0; j < field.Type.NumMethod(); j++ {
                method := field.Type.Method(j)
                if (method.IsExported()) {
                    methods = append(methods, method)
                }
            }
        }
    }
    return methods
}

func generateRegularExpression(prefix string, route *Route) {
    if (prefix != "" && !strings.HasSuffix(prefix, "/")) {
        prefix += "/"
    }
    pattern := "(?i)" + "/" + prefix + route.actionName
    if (route.httpMethod == http.MethodGet) {
        for i := 1; i < route.handlerMethod.Type.NumIn(); i++ {
            if route.handlerMethod.Type.In(i).Kind() == reflect.Int {
                pattern += "/([0-9]*)"
            } else {
                pattern += "/([A-z0-9]*)"
            }
        }
    }
```

```
    }
    pattern = "^" + pattern + "[/]?$"
    route.expression = *regexp.MustCompile(pattern)
}
```

Routes will be configured with an optional prefix, which will let me create distinct URLs for different parts of the application, such as when I introduce access control in Chapter 34. The HandlerEntry struct describes the handler and its prefix, and the Route struct defines the processed result for a single route. The generateRoutes function creates Route values for the methods defined by a handler, relying on the generateRegularExpression function to create and compile regular expressions that will be used to match URL paths.

■ **Note** As noted in Chapter 28, methods promoted from anonymous embedded fields are included when using reflection on a struct. The code in Listing 33-26 filters out these promoted methods to prevent generating routes that allow these methods to be targeted with HTTP requests.

Preparing Parameter Values for a Handler Method

When an HTTP request is received and matched by a route, values must be extracted from the request so they can be used as arguments to the handler method. All the values that can be obtained from a request are expressed using the Go string type because HTTP doesn't provide support for including type information in URLs or form data. I could pass on the string values from the request to the handler method, but that just means each handler method will have to go through the process of parsing the string values into the types it requires. Instead, I am going to automatically parse values based on the handler method parameter type, which allows the code to be defined once. Create the http/handling/params folder and add to it a file named parser.go with the content shown in Listing 33-27.

Listing 33-27. The Contents of the parser.go File in the http/handling/params Folder

```
package params

import (
    "reflect"
    "fmt"
    "strconv"
)

func parseValueToType(target reflect.Type, val string) (result reflect.Value,
        err error) {
    switch target.Kind() {
        case reflect.String:
            result = reflect.ValueOf(val)
        case reflect.Int:
            iVal, convErr := strconv.Atoi(val)
            if convErr == nil {
                result = reflect.ValueOf(iVal)
```

```
            } else {
                return reflect.Value{}, convErr
            }
        case reflect.Float64:
            fVal, convErr := strconv.ParseFloat(val, 64)
            if (convErr == nil) {
                result = reflect.ValueOf(fVal)
            } else {
                return reflect.Value{}, convErr
            }
        case reflect.Bool:
            bVal, convErr := strconv.ParseBool(val)
            if (convErr == nil) {
                result = reflect.ValueOf(bVal)
            } else {
                return reflect.Value{}, convErr
            }
        default:
            err = fmt.Errorf("Cannot use type %v as handler method parameter",
                target.Name())
        }
    return
}
```

The parseValueToType function inspects the kind of type that is required and uses the functions defined by the strconv package to parse the value into the expected type. I am going to support four basic types: string, float64, int, and bool. I will also support structs whose fields are those four types. The parseValueToType function returns an error if a parameter is defined with a different type or the value received in the request cannot be parsed.

The next step is to use the parseValueToType function to deal with handler methods that define parameters of the four supported types, such as the GetName method defined in Listing 33-25:

```
...
func (n NameHandler) GetName(i int) string {
...
```

Values for this type of parameter will be obtained from the regular expression generated when the handler was registered. Add a file named simple_params.go to the http/handling/params folder with the content shown in Listing 33-28.

Listing 33-28. The Contents of the simple_params.go File in the http/handling/params Folder

```
package params

import (
    "reflect"
    "errors"
)

func getParametersFromURLValues(funcType reflect.Type,
        urlVals []string) (params []reflect.Value, err error) {
```

```
    if (len(urlVals) == funcType.NumIn() -1) {
        params = make([]reflect.Value, funcType.NumIn() -1)
        for i := 0; i < len(urlVals); i++ {
            params[i], err = parseValueToType(funcType.In(i + 1), urlVals[i])
            if (err != nil) {
                return
            }
        }
    } else {
        err = errors.New("Parameter number mismatch")
    }
    return
}
```

The getParametersFromURLValues function inspects the parameters defined by the handler method and calls the parseValueToType function to try to get a value for each of them. Notice that I skip over the first parameter defined by the method. As explained in Chapter 28, when using reflection, the first parameter is the receiver on which the method is called.

Handler methods that need to access values from the URL query string or form data can do so by defining a parameter whose type is a struct with field names that match the names of the request data values like this method defined in Listing 33-25:

```
...
type NewName struct {
    Name string
    InsertAtStart bool
}

func (n NameHandler) PostName(new NewName) string {
...
```

This parameter indicates that the handler method requires name and insertAtStart values from the request. To populate struct fields from the request, add a file named struct_params.go to the http/handling/params folder with the content shown in Listing 33-29.

Listing 33-29. The Contents of the struct_params.go File in the http/handling/params Folder

```
package params

import (
    "reflect"
    "encoding/json"
    "io"
    "strings"
)

func populateStructFromForm(structVal reflect.Value,
        formVals map[string][]string) (err error) {
    for i := 0; i < structVal.Elem().Type().NumField(); i++ {
        field := structVal.Elem().Type().Field(i)
        for key, vals := range formVals {
```

```
            if strings.EqualFold(key, field.Name) && len(vals) > 0 {
                valField := structVal.Elem().Field(i)
                if (valField.CanSet()) {
                    valToSet, convErr := parseValueToType(valField.Type(), vals[0])
                    if (convErr == nil) {
                        valField.Set(valToSet)
                    } else {
                        err = convErr
                    }
                }
            }
        }
    }
    return
}

func populateStructFromJSON(structVal reflect.Value,
        reader io.ReadCloser) (err error) {
    return json.NewDecoder(reader).Decode(structVal.Interface())
}
```

The populateStructFromForm function will be used for any handler method that requires a struct and sets the struct field values from a map. The populateStructFromJSON function uses a JSON decoder to read the request body and will be used when a request contains a JSON payload. To apply these functions, add a file named processor.go to the http/handling/params folder with the content shown in Listing 33-30.

Listing 33-30. The Contents of the processor.go File in the http/handling/params Folder

```
package params

import (
    "net/http"
    "reflect"
)

func GetParametersFromRequest(request *http.Request, handlerMethod reflect.Method,
        urlVals []string) (params []reflect.Value, err error) {
    handlerMethodType := handlerMethod.Type
    params = make([]reflect.Value, handlerMethodType.NumIn() -1)
    if (handlerMethodType.NumIn() == 1) {
        return []reflect.Value {}, nil
    } else if handlerMethodType.NumIn() == 2 &&
            handlerMethodType.In(1).Kind() == reflect.Struct {
        structVal := reflect.New(handlerMethodType.In(1))
        err = request.ParseForm()
        if err == nil && getContentType(request) == "application/json" {
            err = populateStructFromJSON(structVal, request.Body)
        }
        if err == nil {
            err = populateStructFromForm(structVal, request.Form)
        }
        return []reflect.Value { structVal.Elem() }, err
```

```
    } else {
        return getParametersFromURLValues(handlerMethodType, urlVals)
    }
}

func getContentType(request *http.Request) (contentType string) {
    headerSlice := request.Header["Content-Type"]
    if headerSlice != nil && len(headerSlice) > 0 {
        contentType = headerSlice[0]
    }
    return
}
```

The GetParametersFromRequest is exported for use elsewhere in the project. It receives a request, a reflected handler method, and a slice containing the values matched by the route. The method is inspected to see if a struct parameter is required, and the parameters needed by the method are created using the functions previously.

Matching Requests to Routes

The final step for this chapter is to match incoming HTTP requests to routes and execute a handler method to generate a response. Add a file named request_dispatch.go to the http/handling folder with the content shown in Listing 33-31.

Listing 33-31. The Contents of the request_dispatch.go File in the http/handling Folder

```
package handling

import (
    "platform/http/handling/params"
    "platform/pipeline"
    "platform/services"
    "net/http"
    "reflect"
    "strings"
    "io"
    "fmt"
)

func NewRouter(handlers ...HandlerEntry) *RouterComponent {
    return &RouterComponent{ generateRoutes(handlers...) }
}

type RouterComponent struct {
    routes []Route
}

func (router *RouterComponent) Init() {}

func (router *RouterComponent) ProcessRequest(context *pipeline.ComponentContext,
        next func(*pipeline.ComponentContext)) {
```

914

```
    for _, route := range router.routes {
        if (strings.EqualFold(context.Request.Method, route.httpMethod)) {
            matches := route.expression.FindAllStringSubmatch(context.URL.Path, -1)
            if len(matches) > 0 {
                rawParamVals := []string {}
                if len(matches[0]) > 1 {
                    rawParamVals = matches[0][1:]
                }
                err := router.invokeHandler(route, rawParamVals, context)
                if (err == nil) {
                    next(context)
                } else {
                    context.Error(err)
                }
                return
            }
        }
    }
    context.ResponseWriter.WriteHeader(http.StatusNotFound)
}

func (router *RouterComponent) invokeHandler(route Route, rawParams []string,
        context *pipeline.ComponentContext) error {
    paramVals, err := params.GetParametersFromRequest(context.Request,
        route.handlerMethod, rawParams)
    if (err == nil) {
        structVal := reflect.New(route.handlerMethod.Type.In(0))
        services.PopulateForContext(context.Context(), structVal.Interface())
        paramVals = append([]reflect.Value { structVal.Elem() }, paramVals...)
        result := route.handlerMethod.Func.Call(paramVals)
        io.WriteString(context.ResponseWriter, fmt.Sprint(result[0].Interface()))
    }
    return err
}
```

The NewRouter function is used to create a new middleware component that processes requests using routes, which are generated from a series of HandlerEntry values. The RouterComponent struct implements the MiddlewareComponent interface, and its ProcessRequest method matches routes using the HTTP method and URL path. When a matching route is found, the invokeHandler function is called, which prepares the values for the parameters defined by the handler method, which is then invoked.

This middleware component has been written to assume that it is applied at the end of the pipeline, which means that a 404 - Not Found response is returned if none of the routes matches the request.

The final point to note is that the response produced by the handler method is simply written out as a string, like this:

```
...
io.WriteString(context.ResponseWriter, fmt.Sprint(result[0].Interface()))
...
```

This is a step back from the templates introduced earlier in the chapter, but I address this in Chapter 34. Listing 33-32 changes the placeholder configuration to use the new routing middleware component.

Listing 33-32. Configuring the Application in the startup.go File in the placeholder Folder

```
package placeholder

import (
    "platform/http"
    "platform/pipeline"
    "platform/pipeline/basic"
    "platform/services"
    "sync"
    "platform/http/handling"
)

func createPipeline() pipeline.RequestPipeline {
    return pipeline.CreatePipeline(
        &basic.ServicesComponent{},
        &basic.LoggingComponent{},
        &basic.ErrorComponent{},
        &basic.StaticFileComponent{},
        //&SimpleMessageComponent{},
        handling.NewRouter(
            handling.HandlerEntry{ "",  NameHandler{}},
        ),
    )
}

func Start() {
    results, err := services.Call(http.Serve, createPipeline())
    if (err == nil) {
        (results[0].(*sync.WaitGroup)).Wait()
    } else {
        panic(err)
    }
}
```

Compile and execute the project and use a browser to request http://localhost:5000/names. This URL will be matched by the route for the GetNames method defined by the placeholder request handler and will produce the result shown in Figure 33-4.

Figure 33-4. *Using a request handler to generate a response*

To test support for simple handler method parameters, use the browser to request `http://localhost:5000/name/0` and `http://localhost:5000/name/100`. Note that it is name (singular) and not names (plural) in these URLs, which produce the responses shown in Figure 33-5.

Figure 33-5. *Targeting a request handler method with a simple parameter*

To test sending a POST request, run the command shown in Listing 33-33 from a command prompt.

Listing 33-33. Sending a POST Request with JSON Data

```
curl --header "Content-Type: application/json" --request POST --data '{"name" :
"Edith","insertatstart" : false}' http://localhost:5000/name
```

If you are using Windows, run the command shown in Listing 33-34 in a PowerShell command prompt instead.

Listing 33-34. Sending a POST Request with JSON Data on Windows

```
Invoke-WebRequest http://localhost:5000/name -Method Post -Body `
(@{name="Edith";insertatstart=$false} | ConvertTo-Json) `
-ContentType "application/json"
```

These commands send the same request to the server, the effect of which can be seen by requesting `http://localhost:5000/names`, as shown in Figure 33-6.

Figure 33-6. *The effect of sending a POST request*

Summary

In this chapter, I continued the development of the web application platform by creating a pipeline that uses middleware components to process requests. I added support for templates that can specify their layouts and introduced request handlers, which I will build on in the next chapter.

Actions, Sessions, and Authorization

In this chapter, I complete the development of the custom web application platform started in Chapter 32 and continued in Chapter 33.

Introducing Action Results

At the moment, the platform deals with the responses generated by request handlers by writing them as strings. I don't want to make each handler method deal with the specifics of how to generate a response because most responses will be similar—rendering a template, for the most part—and I don't want to duplicate the same code each time.

Instead, I am going to add support for action results, which are instructions about what kind of response is required, along with any additional information that is required to produce it. When a handler method wants to render a template as its response, it will return an action result that selects the template, and the action will be performed without the handler method needing to understand how it happens. Create the `platform/http/actionresults` folder and add to it a file named `actionresult.go` with the content shown in Listing 34-1.

Listing 34-1. The Contents of the actionresult.go File in the http/actionresults Folder

```
package actionresults

import (
    "context"
    "net/http"
)

type ActionContext struct {
    context.Context
```

```
    http.ResponseWriter
}

type ActionResult interface {

    Execute(*ActionContext) error
}
```

The ActionResult interface defines an Execute method, which will be used to generate a response using the facilities provided by the ActionContext struct, which are a Context (for obtaining services) and a ResponseWriter (for generating a response).

Listing 34-2 updates the code that invokes handler methods so that it executes action results when they are used.

Listing 34-2. Executing Action Results in the request_dispatch.go File in the http/handling Folder

```
package handling

import (
    "platform/http/handling/params"
    "platform/pipeline"
    "platform/services"
    "net/http"
    "reflect"
    "strings"
    "io"
    "fmt"
    "platform/http/actionresults"
)

// ...functions and types omitted for brevity...

func (router *RouterComponent) invokeHandler(route Route, rawParams []string,
        context *pipeline.ComponentContext) error {
    paramVals, err := params.GetParametersFromRequest(context.Request,
        route.handlerMethod, rawParams)
    if (err == nil) {
        structVal := reflect.New(route.handlerMethod.Type.In(0))
        services.PopulateForContext(context.Context(), structVal.Interface())
        paramVals = append([]reflect.Value { structVal.Elem() }, paramVals...)
        result := route.handlerMethod.Func.Call(paramVals)
        if len(result) > 0 {
            if action, ok := result[0].Interface().(actionresults.ActionResult); ok {
                err = services.PopulateForContext(context.Context(), action)
                if (err == nil) {
                    err = action.Execute(&actionresults.ActionContext{
                        context.Context(), context.ResponseWriter   })
                }
            } else {
                io.WriteString(context.ResponseWriter,
                    fmt.Sprint(result[0].Interface()))
            }
```

```
        }
    }
    return err
}
```

The struct that implements the `ActionResult` interface is passed to the `services.PopulateForContext` function so that its fields are populated with services and then the `Execute` method is invoked to produce a result.

Defining Common Action Results

The most common kind of response will be produced using a template, so add a file named `templateresult.go` to the `platform/http/actionresults` folder with the content shown in Listing 34-3.

Listing 34-3. The Contents of the templateresult.go File in the http/actionresults Folder

```
package actionresults

import (
    "platform/templates"
)

func NewTemplateAction(name string, data interface{}) ActionResult {
    return &TemplateActionResult{ templateName:  name, data: data }
}

type TemplateActionResult struct {
    templateName string
    data interface{}
    templates.TemplateExecutor
}

func (action *TemplateActionResult) Execute(ctx *ActionContext) error {
    return action.TemplateExecutor.ExecTemplate(ctx.ResponseWriter,
        action.templateName, action.data)
}
```

The `TemplateActionResult` struct is an action that renders a template when it is executed. Its fields specify the name of the template, the data that will be passed to the template executor, and the template executor service. The `NewTemplateAction` creates a new instance of the `TemplateActionResult` struct.

Another common result is redirection, which is often performed after a POST or PUT request has been processed. To create this type of result, add a file named `redirectresult.go` to the `platform/http/actionresults` folder with the content shown in Listing 34-4.

Listing 34-4. The Contents of the redirectresult.go File in the http/actionresults Folder

```
package actionresults

import "net/http"

func NewRedirectAction(url string) ActionResult {
```

921

```
    return &RedirectActionResult{ url: url}
}

type RedirectActionResult struct {
    url string
}

func (action *RedirectActionResult) Execute(ctx *ActionContext) error {
    ctx.ResponseWriter.Header().Set("Location", action.url)
    ctx.ResponseWriter.WriteHeader(http.StatusSeeOther)
    return nil
}
```

This action result produces a result with the 303 See Other response. This is a redirection that specifies a new URL and ensures that the browser doesn't reuse the HTTP method or URL from the original request.

The next action result to define in this section will allow a handler method to return a JSON result, which will be useful when creating a web service in Chapter 38. Create a file named jsonresult.go in the platform/http/actionresults folder with the content shown in Listing 34-5.

Listing 34-5. The Contents of the jsonresult.go File in the http/actionresults Folder

```
package actionresults

import "encoding/json"

func NewJsonAction(data interface{}) ActionResult {
    return &JsonActionResult{ data: data}
}

type JsonActionResult struct {
    data interface{}
}

func (action *JsonActionResult) Execute(ctx *ActionContext) error {
    ctx.ResponseWriter.Header().Set("Content-Type", "application/json")
    encoder := json.NewEncoder(ctx.ResponseWriter)
    return encoder.Encode(action.data)
}
```

This action result sets the Content-Type header to indicate that the response contains JSON and uses an encoder from the enconding/json package to serialize the data and send it to the client.

The final built-in action will allow a request handler to indicate that an error has occurred and that a normal response cannot be created. Add a file named errorresult.go to the platform/http/actionresults folder with the content shown in Listing 34-6.

Listing 34-6. The Contents of the errorresult.go File in the http/actionresults Folder

```
package actionresults

func NewErrorAction(err error) ActionResult {
        return &ErrorActionResult{err}
}
```

```go
type ErrorActionResult struct {
        error
}

func (action *ErrorActionResult) Execute(*ActionContext) error {
        return action.error
}
```

This action result doesn't generate a response and simply relays an error from the request handler method to the rest of the platform.

Updating the Placeholders to Use Action Results

To ensure that the action results work as expected, Listing 34-7 changes the results from the placeholder handler methods.

Listing 34-7. Using Action Results in the name_handler.go File in the placeholder Folder

```go
package placeholder

import (
    "fmt"
    "platform/logging"
    "platform/http/actionresults"
)

var names = []string{"Alice", "Bob", "Charlie", "Dora"}

type NameHandler struct {
        logging.Logger
}

func (n NameHandler) GetName(i int) actionresults.ActionResult {
    n.Logger.Debugf("GetName method invoked with argument: %v", i)
    var response string
    if (i < len(names)) {
        response = fmt.Sprintf("Name #%v: %v", i, names[i])
    } else {
        response =  fmt.Sprintf("Index out of bounds")
    }
    return actionresults.NewTemplateAction("simple_message.html", response)
}

func (n NameHandler) GetNames() actionresults.ActionResult {
    n.Logger.Debug("GetNames method invoked")
    return actionresults.NewTemplateAction("simple_message.html", names)
}

type NewName struct {
    Name string
    InsertAtStart bool
```

```
}

func (n NameHandler) PostName(new NewName) actionresults.ActionResult {
    n.Logger.Debugf("PostName method invoked with argument %v", new)
    if (new.InsertAtStart) {
        names = append([] string { new.Name}, names... )
    } else {
        names = append(names, new.Name)
    }
    return actionresults.NewRedirectAction("/names")
}

func (n NameHandler) GetJsonData() actionresults.ActionResult {
    return actionresults.NewJsonAction(names)
}
```

These changes mean that the GetName and GetNames methods return template action results, the PostName method returns a redirection that targets the GetNames method, and the new GetJsonData method returns JSON data. The final change is to add an expression to the placeholder template, as shown in Listing 34-8.

Listing 34-8. Updating the Template in the simple_message.html File in the placeholder Folder

```
{{ layout "layout.html" }}

<h3>
    {{ . }}
</h3>
```

Compile and execute the project and use a browser to request http://localhost:5000/names. The response is now an HTML document produced by executing a template, as shown in Figure 34-1. Request http://localhost:5000/jsondata, and the response will be JSON data, also as shown in Figure 34-1.

Figure 34-1. *Using action results to produce responses*

Invoking Request Handlers from Within Templates

In later chapters, I am going to want to include template content from one handler in the output from another handler so that I can display details about a shopping cart, for example, as part of a template that presents a list of products. This is an awkward feature to implement, but it will avoid the need for handlers to provide their templates with data that isn't directly related to their purpose. Listing 34-9 changes the interface used for the template service.

Listing 34-9. Changing the Template Interface in the template_executor.go File in the templates Folder

```
package templates

import "io"

type TemplateExecutor interface {

    ExecTemplate(writer io.Writer, name string, data interface{}) (err error)

    ExecTemplateWithFunc(writer io.Writer, name string,
        data interface{}, handlerFunc InvokeHandlerFunc) (err error)
}

type InvokeHandlerFunc func(handlerName string, methodName string,
    args ...interface{}) interface{}
```

The ExecTemplate method has been revised so that it defines an ExecTemplateWithFunc method that accepts an InvokeHandlerFunc argument, which will be used to invoke a handler method within a template. To support the new feature, Listing 34-10 defines a new placeholder function that will allow templates to be parsed when they contain the keyword that will execute a handler.

Listing 34-10. Adding a Placeholder Function in the template_loader.go File in the templates Folder

```
package templates

import (
    "html/template"
    "sync"
    "errors"
    "platform/config"
)

var once = sync.Once{}

func LoadTemplates(c config.Configuration) (err error) {
    path, ok := c.GetString("templates:path")
    if !ok {
        return errors.New("Cannot load template config")
    }
    reload := c.GetBoolDefault("templates:reload", false)
    once.Do(func() {
        doLoad := func() (t *template.Template) {
            t = template.New("htmlTemplates")
```

925

```
            t.Funcs(map[string]interface{} {
                "body": func() string { return "" },
                "layout": func() string { return "" },
                "handler": func() interface{} { return "" },
            })
            t, err = t.ParseGlob(path)
            return
        }
        if (reload) {
            getTemplates = doLoad
        } else {
            var templates *template.Template
            templates = doLoad()
            getTemplates = func() *template.Template {
                t, _ := templates.Clone()
                return t
            }
        }
    })
    return
}
```

As the listing shows, I am going to use the keyword handler to invoke a handler method from within a template. Listing 34-11 updates the template executor to support the handler keyword.

Listing 34-11. Updating Template Execution in the layout_executor.go File in the templates Folder

```
package templates

import (
    "io"
    "strings"
    "html/template"
)

type LayoutTemplateProcessor struct {}

var emptyFunc = func(handlerName, methodName string,
    args ...interface{}) interface{} { return "" }

func (proc *LayoutTemplateProcessor) ExecTemplate(writer io.Writer,
        name string, data interface{}) (err error) {
    return proc.ExecTemplateWithFunc(writer, name, data, emptyFunc)
}

func (proc *LayoutTemplateProcessor) ExecTemplateWithFunc(writer io.Writer,
        name string, data interface{},
        handlerFunc InvokeHandlerFunc) (err error) {

    var sb strings.Builder
    layoutName := ""
    localTemplates := getTemplates()
```

```
        localTemplates.Funcs(map[string]interface{} {
            "body": insertBodyWrapper(&sb),
            "layout": setLayoutWrapper(&layoutName),
            "handler": handlerFunc,
        })
        err = localTemplates.ExecuteTemplate(&sb, name, data)
        if (layoutName != "") {
            localTemplates.ExecuteTemplate(writer, layoutName, data)
        } else {
            io.WriteString(writer, sb.String())
        }
        return
}

var getTemplates func() (t *template.Template)

func insertBodyWrapper(body *strings.Builder) func() template.HTML {
    return func() template.HTML {
        return template.HTML(body.String())
    }
}

func setLayoutWrapper(val *string) func(string) string {
    return func(layout string) string {
        *val = layout
        return ""
    }
}
```

Listing 34-12 updates the template action result so that it calls the ExecTemplate method with the new argument.

Listing 34-12. Adding an Argument in the templateresult.go File in the http/actionresults Folder

```
package actionresults

import (
    "platform/templates"
)

func NewTemplateAction(name string, data interface{}) ActionResult {
    return &TemplateActionResult{ templateName:  name, data: data }
}

type TemplateActionResult struct {
    templateName string
    data interface{}
    templates.TemplateExecutor
    templates.InvokeHandlerFunc
}

func (action *TemplateActionResult) Execute(ctx *ActionContext) error {
```

```
    return action.TemplateExecutor.ExecTemplateWithFunc(ctx.ResponseWriter,
        action.templateName, action.data, action.InvokeHandlerFunc)
}
```

The Execute method uses the services feature to get an InvokeHandlerFunc value, which is then passed to the template executor.

Updating Request Handling

To complete this feature, I need to create a service for the InvokeHandlerFunc type. Add a file named handler_func.go to the platform/http folder with the content shown in Listing 34-13.

Listing 34-13. The Contents of the handler_func.go File in the http/handling Folder

```
package handling

import (
    "context"
    "fmt"
    "html/template"
    "net/http"
    "platform/http/actionresults"
    "platform/services"
    "platform/templates"
    "reflect"
    "strings"
)

func createInvokehandlerFunc(ctx context.Context,
        routes []Route) templates.InvokeHandlerFunc {
    return func(handlerName, methodName string, args ...interface{}) interface{} {
        var err error
        for _, route := range routes {
            if strings.EqualFold(handlerName, route.handlerName) &&
                    strings.EqualFold(methodName, route.handlerMethod.Name) {
                paramVals := make([]reflect.Value, len(args))
                for i := 0; i < len(args); i++ {
                    paramVals[i] = reflect.ValueOf(args[i])
                }
                structVal := reflect.New(route.handlerMethod.Type.In(0))
                services.PopulateForContext(ctx, structVal.Interface())
                paramVals = append([]reflect.Value { structVal.Elem() },
                    paramVals...)
                result := route.handlerMethod.Func.Call(paramVals)
                if action, ok := result[0].Interface().
                        (*actionresults.TemplateActionResult); ok {
                    invoker := createInvokehandlerFunc(ctx, routes)
                    err = services.PopulateForContextWithExtras(ctx,
                    action,
                    map[reflect.Type]reflect.Value {
                        reflect.TypeOf(invoker): reflect.ValueOf(invoker),
```

928

```
                })
                writer := &stringResponseWriter{ Builder: &strings.Builder{} }
                if err == nil {
                    err = action.Execute(&actionresults.ActionContext{
                        Context: ctx,
                        ResponseWriter: writer,
                    })
                    if err == nil {
                        return (template.HTML)(writer.Builder.String())
                    }
                }
            } else {
                return fmt.Sprint(result[0])
            }
        }
    }
    if err == nil {
        err = fmt.Errorf("No route found for %v %v", handlerName, methodName)
    }
    panic(err)
    }
}

type stringResponseWriter struct {
    *strings.Builder
}
func (sw *stringResponseWriter) Write(data []byte) (int, error) {
    return sw.Builder.Write(data)
}
func (sw *stringResponseWriter) WriteHeader(statusCode int) {}
func (sw *stringResponseWriter) Header() http.Header { return http.Header{}}
```

The createInvokehandlerFunc creates a function that uses a set of routes to find and execute a handler method. The handler's output is a string that can be included in a template.

Listing 34-14 updates the code that executes action results to provide a function that can be used to invoke a handler.

Listing 34-14. Updating Result Execution in the request_dispatch.go File in the http/handling Folder

```
...
func (router *RouterComponent) invokeHandler(route Route, rawParams []string,
        context *pipeline.ComponentContext) error {
    paramVals, err := params.GetParametersFromRequest(context.Request,
        route.handlerMethod, rawParams)
    if (err == nil) {
        structVal := reflect.New(route.handlerMethod.Type.In(0))
        services.PopulateForContext(context.Context(), structVal.Interface())
        paramVals = append([]reflect.Value { structVal.Elem() }, paramVals...)
        result := route.handlerMethod.Func.Call(paramVals)
        if len(result) > 0 {
            if action, ok := result[0].Interface().(actionresults.ActionResult); ok {
                invoker := createInvokehandlerFunc(context.Context(), router.routes)
```

929

```
                err = services.PopulateForContextWithExtras(context.Context(),
                    action,
                    map[reflect.Type]reflect.Value {
                        reflect.TypeOf(invoker): reflect.ValueOf(invoker),
                    })
                if (err == nil) {
                    err = action.Execute(&actionresults.ActionContext{
                        context.Context(), context.ResponseWriter  })
                }
            } else {
                io.WriteString(context.ResponseWriter,
                    fmt.Sprint(result[0].Interface()))
            }
        }
    }
    return err
}
...
```

I could have created a service for the function that invokes handlers, but I want to make sure that an action receives a function that invokes handers using the URL router that is processing the request. As you will see later in this chapter, I am going to use multiple URL routes to handle different kinds of request, and I don't want handlers managed by one router to invoke methods on handlers managed by another router.

Configuring the Application

Some changes are required to make sure that a template can invoke a handler method. First, create a new request handler by adding a file named day_handler.go to the placeholder folder with the content shown in Listing 34-15.

Listing 34-15. The Contents of the day_handler.go File in the placeholder Folder

```
package placeholder

import (
    "platform/logging"
    "time"
    "fmt"
)

type DayHandler struct {
    logging.Logger
}

func (dh DayHandler) GetDay() string {
    return  fmt.Sprintf("Day: %v", time.Now().Day())
}
```

Next, register the new request handler, as shown in Listing 34-16.

Listing 34-16. Registering a New Handler in the startup.go File in the placeholder Folder

```
...
func createPipeline() pipeline.RequestPipeline {
    return pipeline.CreatePipeline(
        &basic.ServicesComponent{},
        &basic.LoggingComponent{},
        &basic.ErrorComponent{},
        &basic.StaticFileComponent{},
        //&SimpleMessageComponent{},
        handling.NewRouter(
            handling.HandlerEntry{ "",   NameHandler{}},
            handling.HandlerEntry{ "",   DayHandler{}},
        ),
    )
}
...
```

Finally, add an expression that invokes the GetDay method defined in Listing 34-15, as shown in Listing 34-17.

Listing 34-17. Adding an Expression in the simple_message.html File in the placeholder Folder

```
{{ layout "layout.html" }}

<h3>
    {{ . }}
</h3>

{{ handler "day" "getday"}}
```

Compile and execute the application and request http://localhost:5000/names; you will see that the result produced by rendering the simple_message.html template contains the result from the GetDay method, as shown in Figure 34-2, albeit with the additional output reflecting the day on which you run the example.

Figure 34-2. Invoking a handler from a template

Generating URLs from Routes

When I wanted to redirect the browser to a new URL in Listing 34-7, I had to specify the URL like this:

```
...
return actionresults.NewRedirectAction("/names")
...
```

This isn't ideal because it means that changing the routing configuration can break this kind of hard-coded URL. A more robust approach is to add support for specifying a handler method and generating a URL based on the routing configuration associated with it. Add a file named url_generation.go to the http/handling folder with the content shown in Listing 34-18.

Listing 34-18. The Contents of the url_generation.go File in the http/handling Folder

```go
package handling

import (
    "fmt"
    "net/http"
    "strings"
    "errors"
    "reflect"
)

type URLGenerator interface {

    GenerateUrl(method interface{}, data ...interface{}) (string, error)

    GenerateURLByName(handlerName, methodName string,
        data ...interface{}) (string, error)

    AddRoutes(routes []Route)
}

type routeUrlGenerator struct {
    routes []Route
}

func (gen *routeUrlGenerator) AddRoutes(routes []Route) {
    if gen.routes == nil {
        gen.routes = routes
    } else {
        gen.routes = append(gen.routes, routes...)
    }
}

func (gen *routeUrlGenerator) GenerateUrl(method interface{},
        data ...interface{}) (string, error) {
    methodVal := reflect.ValueOf(method)
    if methodVal.Kind() == reflect.Func &&
```

```
            methodVal.Type().In(0).Kind() == reflect.Struct {
        for _, route := range gen.routes {
            if route.handlerMethod.Func.Pointer() == methodVal.Pointer() {
                return generateUrl(route, data...)
            }
        }
    }
    return "", errors.New("No matching route")
}

func (gen *routeUrlGenerator) GenerateURLByName(handlerName, methodName string,
        data ...interface{}) (string, error) {
    for _, route := range gen.routes {
        if strings.EqualFold(route.handlerName, handlerName) &&
                strings.EqualFold(route.httpMethod + route.actionName, methodName) {
            return generateUrl(route, data...)
        }
    }
    return "", errors.New("No matching route")
}

func generateUrl(route Route, data ...interface{}) (url string, err error) {
    url = "/" + route.prefix
    if (!strings.HasPrefix(url, "/")) {
        url = "/" + url
    }
    if (!strings.HasSuffix(url, "/")) {
        url += "/"
    }
    url+= strings.ToLower(route.actionName)
    if len(data) > 0 && !strings.EqualFold(route.httpMethod, http.MethodGet) {
        err = errors.New("Only GET handler can have data values")
    } else if strings.EqualFold(route.httpMethod, http.MethodGet) &&
            len(data) != route.handlerMethod.Type.NumIn() -1 {
        err = errors.New("Number of data values doesn't match method params")
    } else {
        for _, val := range data {
            url = fmt.Sprintf("%v/%v", url, val)
        }
    }
    return
}
```

The URLGenerator interface defines methods named GenerateURL and GenerateURLByName. The GenerateURL method receives a handler function and uses it to locate a route, while the GenerateURLByName method locates a handler function using string values. The routeUrlGenerator struct implements the URLGenerator methods using routes to generate URLs.

Creating the URL Generator Service

I want to create a service for the URLGenerator interface, but I want it to be available only when the request pipeline is configured to use the routing features defined in Chapter 33. Listing 34-19 sets up the service when the routing middleware component is instantiated.

Listing 34-19. Creating the Service in the request_dispatch.go File in the http/handling Folder

```
...
func NewRouter(handlers ...HandlerEntry) *RouterComponent {
    routes := generateRoutes(handlers...)

    var urlGen URLGenerator
    services.GetService(&urlGen)
    if urlGen == nil {
        services.AddSingleton(func () URLGenerator {
            return &routeUrlGenerator { routes: routes }
        })
    } else {
        urlGen.AddRoutes(routes)
    }
    return &RouterComponent{ routes: routes }
}
...
```

The new service means that I can generate a URL programmatically, as shown in Listing 34-20.

Listing 34-20. Generating a URL in the name_handler.go File in the placeholder Folder

```
package placeholder

import (
    "fmt"
    "platform/logging"
    "platform/http/actionresults"
    "platform/http/handling"
)

var names = []string{"Alice", "Bob", "Charlie", "Dora"}

type NameHandler struct {
            logging.Logger
    handling.URLGenerator
}

func (n NameHandler) GetName(i int) actionresults.ActionResult {
    n.Logger.Debugf("GetName method invoked with argument: %v", i)
    var response string
    if (i < len(names)) {
        response = fmt.Sprintf("Name #%v: %v", i, names[i])
    } else {
        response =  fmt.Sprintf("Index out of bounds")
```

```
    }
    return actionresults.NewTemplateAction("simple_message.html", response)
}

func (n NameHandler) GetNames() actionresults.ActionResult {
    n.Logger.Debug("GetNames method invoked")
    return actionresults.NewTemplateAction("simple_message.html", names)
}

type NewName struct {
    Name string
    InsertAtStart bool
}

func (n NameHandler) PostName(new NewName) actionresults.ActionResult {
    n.Logger.Debugf("PostName method invoked with argument %v", new)
    if (new.InsertAtStart) {
        names = append([] string { new.Name}, names... )
    } else {
        names = append(names, new.Name)
    }
    return n.redirectOrError(NameHandler.GetNames)
}

func (n NameHandler) GetRedirect() actionresults.ActionResult {
    return n.redirectOrError(NameHandler.GetNames)
}

func (n NameHandler) GetJsonData() actionresults.ActionResult {
    return actionresults.NewJsonAction(names)
}

func (n NameHandler) redirectOrError(handler interface{},
        data ...interface{}) actionresults.ActionResult {
    url, err := n.GenerateUrl(handler)
    if (err == nil) {
        return actionresults.NewRedirectAction(url)
    } else {
        return actionresults.NewErrorAction(err)
    }
}
```

The new service makes it possible to generate URLs dynamically, reflecting the routes that have been defined. It is awkward testing a POST request, so Listing 34-20 adds a new handler method, named GetRedirect, that receives a GET request and performs a redirection to a URL that is created by specifying the GetNames method:

```
...
return n.redirectOrError(NameHandler.GetNames)
...
```

Note that parentheses are not used when selecting the handler method, because it is the method—and not the result produced by invoking it—that is required to generate a URL.

Compile and execute the project and use a browser to request http://localhost:5000/redirect. The browser will be automatically redirected to the URL that targets the GetNames method, as shown in Figure 34-3.

Figure 34-3. *Generating a redirection URL*

Defining Alias Routes

The support for generating URLs simplifies the process of defining routes that match a URL to a handler method, in addition to those routes generated directly from the handler. There is a gap, for example, in the URLs supported by the placeholder routes, which means that requests for the default URL, http://localhost:5000/, produce a 404 - Not Found result. In this section, I am going to add support for defining additional routes that are not derived directly from handler structs and their methods, which will allow gaps like this one to be addressed.

Add a file named alias_route.go to the platform/http/handling folder with the content shown in Listing 34-21.

Listing 34-21. The Contents of the alias_route.go File in the http/handling Folder

```
package handling

import (
    "platform/http/actionresults"
    "platform/services"
    "net/http"
    "reflect"
    "regexp"
    "fmt"
)

func (rc *RouterComponent) AddMethodAlias(srcUrl string,
        method interface{}, data ...interface{}) *RouterComponent {
    var urlgen URLGenerator
    services.GetService(&urlgen)
    url, err := urlgen.GenerateUrl(method, data...)
    if (err == nil) {
```

```
        return rc.AddUrlAlias(srcUrl, url)
    } else {
        panic(err)
    }
}

func (rc *RouterComponent) AddUrlAlias(srcUrl string,
        targetUrl string) *RouterComponent {
    aliasFunc := func(interface{}) actionresults.ActionResult {
        return actionresults.NewRedirectAction(targetUrl)
    }
    alias := Route {
        httpMethod: http.MethodGet,
        handlerName: "Alias",
        actionName: "Redirect",
        expression: *regexp.MustCompile(fmt.Sprintf("^%v[/]?$", srcUrl)),
        handlerMethod: reflect.Method{
            Type: reflect.TypeOf(aliasFunc),
            Func: reflect.ValueOf(aliasFunc),
        },
    }
    rc.routes = append([]Route { alias },  rc.routes... )
    return rc
}
```

This file defines additional methods for the RouterComponent struct. The AddUrlAlias method creates a Route, but does so by creating a reflect.Method that invokes a function that produces a redirection action result. It is easy to forget that the types defined by the reflect package are just regular Go structs and interfaces, but a Method is just a struct, and I can set the Type and Func fields so that my alias function looks like a regular method to the code that executes routes.

The AddMethodAlias method allows a route to be created using a URL and a handler method. The URLGenerator service is used to generate a URL for the handler method, which is passed on to the AddUrlAlias method.

Listing 34-22 adds an alias to the set of placeholder routes so that requests for the default URL are redirected so they will be handled by the GetNames handler method.

Listing 34-22. Defining an Alias Route in the startup.go File in the placeholder Folder

```
package placeholder

import (
    "platform/http"
    "platform/pipeline"
    "platform/pipeline/basic"
    "platform/services"
    "sync"
    "platform/http/handling"
)

func createPipeline() pipeline.RequestPipeline {
    return pipeline.CreatePipeline(
        &basic.ServicesComponent{},
```

```
        &basic.LoggingComponent{},
        &basic.ErrorComponent{},
        &basic.StaticFileComponent{},
        //&SimpleMessageComponent{},
        handling.NewRouter(
            handling.HandlerEntry{ "",  NameHandler{}},
            handling.HandlerEntry{ "",  DayHandler{}},
        ).AddMethodAlias("/", NameHandler.GetNames),
    )
}

func Start() {
    results, err := services.Call(http.Serve, createPipeline())
    if (err == nil) {
        (results[0].(*sync.WaitGroup)).Wait()
    } else {
        panic(err)
    }
}
```

Compile and execute the project and use a browser to request http://localhost:5000. Instead of a 404 response, the browser is redirected, as shown in Figure 34-4.

Figure 34-4. *The effect of an alias route*

Validating Request Data

As soon as an application starts to accept data from users, the need for validation arises. Users will enter just about anything into a form field, sometimes because the instructions are not clear but also because they are working through a process to get to the end as quickly as possible. By defining validation as a service, I can minimize the amount of code that individual handlers have to implement.

Since the service can't know what validation requirements handlers require, I need some way to describe them as part of the data types that handlers process. The simplest approach is to use struct tags, through which some basic validation requirements can be expressed.

Create the platform/validation folder and add to it a file named validator.go with the content shown in Listing 34-23.

Listing 34-23. The Contents of the validator.go File in the validation Folder

```
package validation

type Validator interface {
    Validate(data interface{}) (ok bool, errs []ValidationError)
}

type ValidationError struct {
    FieldName string
    Error error
}

type ValidatorFunc func(fieldName string, value interface{},
    arg string) (bool, error)

func DefaultValidators() map[string]ValidatorFunc {
    return map[string]ValidatorFunc {
        "required": required,
        "min": min,
    }
}
```

The Validator interface will be used to provide validation as a service, with individual validation
checks being performed by ValidatorFunc functions. I am going to define two validators, required and
min, which will ensure that a value is provided for a string value and enforce a minimum value for int and
float64 values and a minimum length for string values. Additional validators can be defined as needed,
but these two will be enough for this project. To define the validator functions, add a file value named
validator_functions.go to the platform/validation folder with the content shown in Listing 34-24.

Listing 34-24. The Contents of the validator_functions.go File in the validation Folder

```
package validation

import (
    "errors"
    "fmt"
    "strconv"
)

func required(fieldName string, value interface{},
        arg string) (valid bool, err error) {
    if str, ok := value.(string); ok {
        valid = str != ""
        err = fmt.Errorf("A value is required")
    } else {
        err = errors.New("The required validator is for strings")
    }
    return
}

func min(fieldName string, value interface{}, arg string) (valid bool, err error) {
```

939

```
    minVal, err := strconv.Atoi(arg)
    if err != nil {
        panic("Invalid arguments for validator: " + arg)
    }
    err = fmt.Errorf("The minimum value is %v", minVal)
    if iVal, iValOk := value.(int); iValOk {
        valid = iVal >= minVal
    } else if fVal, fValOk := value.(float64); fValOk {
        valid = fVal >= float64(minVal)
    } else if strVal, strValOk := value.(string); strValOk {
        err = fmt.Errorf("The minimum length is %v characters", minVal)
        valid = len(strVal) >= minVal
    } else {
        err = errors.New("The min validator is for int, float64, and str values")
    }
    return
}
```

To perform validation, each function receives the name of the struct field that is being validated, the value obtained from the request, and optional arguments that configure the validation process. To create the implementation and the functions that will set up the service, add a file named tag_validator.go to the platform/validation folder with the content shown in Listing 34-25.

Listing 34-25. The Contents of the tag_validator.go File in the validation Folder

```
package validation

import (
    "reflect"
    "strings"
)

func NewDefaultValidator(validators map[string]ValidatorFunc) Validator {
    return &TagValidator{ DefaultValidators() }
}

type TagValidator struct {
    validators map[string]ValidatorFunc
}

func (tv *TagValidator) Validate(data interface{}) (ok bool,
        errs []ValidationError) {
    errs = []ValidationError{}
    dataVal := reflect.ValueOf(data)
    if (dataVal.Kind() == reflect.Ptr) {
        dataVal = dataVal.Elem()
    }
    if (dataVal.Kind() != reflect.Struct) {
        panic("Only structs can be validated")
    }
    for i := 0; i < dataVal.NumField(); i++ {
        fieldType := dataVal.Type().Field(i)
```

```
        validationTag, found := fieldType.Tag.Lookup("validation")
        if found {
            for _, v := range strings.Split(validationTag, ",") {
                var name, arg string = "", ""
                if strings.Contains(v, ":") {
                    nameAndArgs := strings.SplitN(v, ":", 2)
                    name = nameAndArgs[0]
                    arg = nameAndArgs[1]
                } else {
                    name = v
                }
                if validator, ok := tv.validators[name]; ok {
                    valid, err := validator(fieldType.Name,
                        dataVal.Field(i).Interface(), arg )
                    if (!valid) {
                        errs = append(errs, ValidationError{
                            FieldName: fieldType.Name,
                            Error: err,
                        })
                    }
                } else {
                    panic("Unknown validator: " + name)
                }
            }
        }
    }
    ok = len(errs) == 0
    return
}
```

The TagValidator struct implements the Validator interface by looking for a struct tag named validation and parsing it to see what, if any, validation is required for each field of a struct. Each specified validator is used, and errors are collected and returned as the result of the Validate method. The NewDefaultValidation function instantiates the struct and is used to create the validation service, as shown in Listing 34-26.

Listing 34-26. Registering the Validation Service in the services_default.go File in the services Folder

```
package services

import (
    "platform/logging"
    "platform/config"
    "platform/templates"
    "platform/validation"
)

func RegisterDefaultServices() {

    // ...statements omitted for brevity...

    err = AddSingleton(
```

```
        func() validation.Validator {
            return validation.NewDefaultValidator(validation.DefaultValidators())
        })
    if (err != nil) {
        panic(err)
    }
}
```

I have registered the new service as a singleton, using the validators returned by the `DefaultValidators` function.

Performing Data Validation

Some preparation is required to check that data validation works. First, Listing 34-27 creates a new handler method and applies the validation struct tag to the placeholder request handler.

Listing 34-27. Preparing for Validation in the name_handler.go File in the placeholder Folder

```
package placeholder

import (
    "fmt"
    "platform/logging"
    "platform/http/actionresults"
    "platform/http/handling"
    "platform/validation"
)

var names = []string{"Alice", "Bob", "Charlie", "Dora"}

type NameHandler struct {
            logging.Logger
    handling.URLGenerator
    validation.Validator
}

func (n NameHandler) GetName(i int) actionresults.ActionResult {
    n.Logger.Debugf("GetName method invoked with argument: %v", i)
    var response string
    if (i < len(names)) {
        response = fmt.Sprintf("Name #%v: %v", i, names[i])
    } else {
        response =  fmt.Sprintf("Index out of bounds")
    }
    return actionresults.NewTemplateAction("simple_message.html", response)
}

func (n NameHandler) GetNames() actionresults.ActionResult {
    n.Logger.Debug("GetNames method invoked")
    return actionresults.NewTemplateAction("simple_message.html", names)
}
```

```go
type NewName struct {
    Name string `validation:"required,min:3"`
    InsertAtStart bool
}

func (n NameHandler) GetForm() actionresults.ActionResult {
    postUrl, _ := n.URLGenerator.GenerateUrl(NameHandler.PostName)
    return actionresults.NewTemplateAction("name_form.html", postUrl)
}

func (n NameHandler) PostName(new NewName) actionresults.ActionResult {
    n.Logger.Debugf("PostName method invoked with argument %v", new)
    if ok, errs := n.Validator.Validate(&new); !ok {
        return actionresults.NewTemplateAction("validation_errors.html", errs)
    }
    if (new.InsertAtStart) {
        names = append([] string { new.Name}, names... )
    } else {
        names = append(names, new.Name)
    }
    return n.redirectOrError(NameHandler.GetNames)
}

func (n NameHandler) GetRedirect() actionresults.ActionResult {
    return n.redirectOrError(NameHandler.GetNames)
}

func (n NameHandler) GetJsonData() actionresults.ActionResult {
    return actionresults.NewJsonAction(names)
}

func (n NameHandler) redirectOrError(handler interface{},
        data ...interface{}) actionresults.ActionResult {
    url, err := n.GenerateUrl(handler)
    if (err == nil) {
        return actionresults.NewRedirectAction(url)
    } else {
        return actionresults.NewErrorAction(err)
    }
}
```

The validation tag has been added to the Name field, applying the required and min validators, meaning that a value is required with a minimum number of three characters. To make validation easier to test, I have added a handler method named GetForm that renders a template named name_form.html. When the data is received by the PostName method, it is validated using the service, and the validation_errors. html template is used to generate a response if there are validation errors.

Add a file named name_form.html to the placeholder folder with the content shown in Listing 34-28.

Listing 34-28. The Contents of the name_form.html File in the placeholder Folder

```
{{ layout "layout.html" }}

<form method="POST" action="{{ . }}">
    <div style="padding: 5px;">
        <label>Name:</label>
        <input name="name" />
    </div>
    <div style="padding: 5px;">
        <label>Insert At Front:</label>
        <input name="insertatstart" type="checkbox" value="true" />
    </div>
    <div style="padding: 5px;">
        <button type="submit">Submit</button>
    </div>
</form>
```

This template produces a simple HTML form that sends data to the URL received from the handler method. Add a file named `validation_errors.html` to the `placeholder` folder with the content shown in Listing 34-29.

Listing 34-29. The Contents of the validation_errors.html File in the placeholder Folder

```
{{ layout "layout.html" }}

<h3>Validation Errors</h3>

<ul>
    {{ range . }}
        <li>{{.FieldName}}: {{ .Error }}</li>
    {{ end }}
</ul>
```

The slice of validation errors received from the handler method is displayed in a list. Compile and execute the project and use a browser to request `http://localhost:5000/form`. Click the Submit button without entering a value into the Name field, and you will see errors from both the `required` and `min` validators, as shown in Figure 34-5.

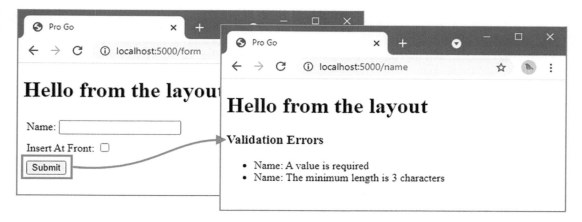

Figure 34-5. Displaying validation errors

If you enter a name with fewer than three characters, then you will see a warning from just the min validator. If you enter a name with three or more characters, then it will be added to the list of names, as shown in Figure 34-6.

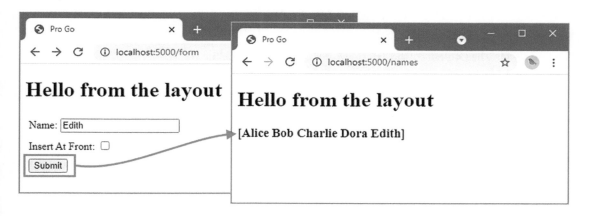

Figure 34-6. Passing data validation

Adding Sessions

Sessions use cookies to identify related HTTP requests, allowing the results of one user action to be reflected in subsequent actions. As much as I recommend writing your own platform to learn about Go and the standard library, this does not extend to security-related features, where well-designed and thoroughly tested code is essential. Cookies and sessions may not seem like they are related to security, but they form the basis by which many applications identify users once their credentials are validated. A carelessly written session feature may allow users to gain access to bypass access controls or access other users' data.

In Chapter 32, I recommended the Gorilla web toolkit as a good place to start as an alternative to writing your own framework. One of the packages provided by the Gorilla toolkit is named `sessions`, and it provides support for creating and managing sessions securely. It is this package that I am going to use to add session support in this chapter. Run the command shown in Listing 34-30 in the `platform` folder to download and install the `sessions` package.

Listing 34-30. Installing a Package

```
go get github.com/gorilla/sessions
```

Delaying Writing Response Data

Using cookies for sessions presents a problem with the pipeline approach I have taken to handling requests. Sessions are obtained before a handler method is executed, modified during execution, and then the session cookie is updated once the handler method has completed. This is an issue because the handler will have written data to the `ResponseWriter`, after which it is not possible to update the cookie in the header. Add a code file named `deferredwriter.go` to the `pipeline` folder with the content shown in Listing 34-31. (This writer is similar to the one that I created for invoking handlers within templates. I prefer to define separate types when intercepting request and response data because the way the intercepted data is used can change over time.)

Listing 34-31. The Contents of the deferredwriter.go File in the pipeline Folder

```
package pipeline

import (
    "net/http"
    "strings"
)

type DeferredResponseWriter struct {
    http.ResponseWriter
    strings.Builder
    statusCode int
}

func (dw *DeferredResponseWriter) Write(data []byte) (int, error) {
    return dw.Builder.Write(data)
}

func (dw *DeferredResponseWriter) FlushData()  {
    if (dw.statusCode == 0) {
        dw.statusCode = http.StatusOK
    }
    dw.ResponseWriter.WriteHeader(dw.statusCode)
    dw.ResponseWriter.Write([]byte(dw.Builder.String()))
}
```

```
func (dw *DeferredResponseWriter) WriteHeader(statusCode int) {
    dw.statusCode = statusCode
}
```

The DeferredResponseWriter is a wrapper around a ResponseWriter that doesn't write the response until the FlushData method is called, until which time the data is kept in memory. Listing 34-32 uses a DeferredResponseWriter when creating the context passed to middleware components.

Listing 34-32. Using the Modified Writer in the pipeline.go File in the pipeline Folder

```
...
func (pl RequestPipeline) ProcessRequest(req *http.Request,
        resp http.ResponseWriter) error {
    deferredWriter := &DeferredResponseWriter{ ResponseWriter:  resp }
    ctx := ComponentContext {
        Request: req,
        ResponseWriter: deferredWriter,
    }
    pl(&ctx)
    if (ctx.error == nil) {
        deferredWriter.FlushData()
    }
    return ctx.error
}
...
```

This change allows response headers to be set as the request makes its return trip along the pipeline.

Creating the Session Interface, Service, and Middleware

I am going to provide access to sessions as a service, and I am going to use an interface so that other parts of the platform don't depend directly on the Gorilla toolkit package, making it easy to use a different session package if required.

Create the platform/sessions folder and add a file named sessions.go with the content shown in Listing 34-33.

Listing 34-33. The Contents of the session.go File in the sessions Folder

```
package sessions

import (
    "context"
    "platform/services"
    gorilla "github.com/gorilla/sessions"
)

const SESSION__CONTEXT_KEY string = "pro_go_session"

func RegisterSessionService() {
    err := services.AddScoped(func(c context.Context) Session {
        val := c.Value(SESSION__CONTEXT_KEY)
```

```
            if s, ok := val.(*gorilla.Session); ok {
                return &SessionAdaptor{ gSession: s}
            } else {
                panic("Cannot get session from context ")
            }
        })
        if (err != nil) {
            panic(err)
        }
    }

    type Session interface {
        GetValue(key string) interface{}
        GetValueDefault(key string, defVal interface{}) interface{}
        SetValue(key string, val interface{})
    }

    type SessionAdaptor struct {
        gSession *gorilla.Session
    }

    func (adaptor *SessionAdaptor) GetValue(key string) interface{} {
        return adaptor.gSession.Values[key]
    }

    func (adaptor *SessionAdaptor) GetValueDefault(key string,
            defVal interface{}) interface{} {
        if val, ok := adaptor.gSession.Values[key]; ok {
            return val
        }
        return defVal
    }

    func (adaptor *SessionAdaptor) SetValue(key string, val interface{}) {
        if val == nil {
            adaptor.gSession.Values[key] = nil
        } else {
            switch typedVal := val.(type) {
                case int, float64, bool, string:
                    adaptor.gSession.Values[key] = typedVal
                default:
                    panic("Sessions only support int, float64, bool, and string values")
            }
        }
    }
```

To avoid a name conflict, I have imported the Gorilla toolkit package using the name gorilla. The Session interface defines methods for getting and setting session values, and this interface is implemented and mapped onto the Gorilla features by the SessionAdaptor struct. The RegisterSessionService function registers a singleton service that obtains a session from the Gorilla package from the current Context and wraps it in a SessionAdaptor.

Any data that is with the session will be saved to a cookie. To avoid problems with structs and slices, the SetValue method will only accept int, float64, bool, and string values, along with support for nil for removing a value from the session.

A middleware component will be responsible for creating a session when a request is passed along the pipeline and for saving the session when it makes the return journey. Add a file named session_middleware.go to the platform/sessions folder with the content shown in Listing 34-34.

■ **Note**   I am using the simplest option for storing sessions, which means that the session data is stored in the response cookie sent to browsers. This limits the range of data types that can be safely stored in a session and is suitable only for sessions that store small amounts of data. There are additional session stores available that store data in a database, which can address these issues. See https://github.com/gorilla/sessions for the list of available storage packages.

Listing 34-34. The Contents of the session_middleware.go File in the sessions Folder

```go
package sessions

import (
    "context"
    "time"
    "platform/config"
    "platform/pipeline"
    gorilla "github.com/gorilla/sessions"
)

type SessionComponent struct {
    store *gorilla.CookieStore
    config.Configuration
}

func (sc *SessionComponent) Init() {
    cookiekey, found := sc.Configuration.GetString("sessions:key")
    if !found {
        panic("Session key not found in configuration")
    }
    if sc.GetBoolDefault("sessions:cyclekey", true) {
        cookiekey += time.Now().String()
    }
    sc.store = gorilla.NewCookieStore([]byte(cookiekey))
}

func (sc *SessionComponent) ProcessRequest(ctx *pipeline.ComponentContext,
        next func(*pipeline.ComponentContext)) {
    session, _ := sc.store.Get(ctx.Request, SESSION_CONTEXT_KEY)
    c := context.WithValue(ctx.Request.Context(), SESSION_CONTEXT_KEY, session)
    ctx.Request = ctx.Request.WithContext(c)
    next(ctx)
    session.Save(ctx.Request, ctx.ResponseWriter)
}
```

CHAPTER 34 ■ ACTIONS, SESSIONS, AND AUTHORIZATION

The Init method creates a cookie store, which is one of the ways that the Gorilla package supports storing sessions. The ProcessRequest method gets a session from the store before passing the request along the pipeline with the next parameter function. The session is saved to the store when the request makes its way back along the pipeline.

If the sessions:cyclekey configuration setting is true, then the name used for the session cookies will include the time when the middleware component is initialized. This is useful during development because it means that sessions are reset each time the application is started.

Creating a Handler That Uses Sessions

To provide a simple check that the session feature works, add a file named counter_handler.go to the placeholder folder with the content shown in Listing 34-35.

Listing 34-35. The Contents of the counter_handler.go File in the placeholder Folder

```
package placeholder

import (
    "fmt"
    "platform/sessions"
)

type CounterHandler struct {
    sessions.Session
}

func (c CounterHandler) GetCounter() string {
    counter := c.Session.GetValueDefault("counter", 0).(int)
    c.Session.SetValue("counter", counter + 1)
    return fmt.Sprintf("Counter: %v", counter)
}
```

The handler declares its dependency on a Session by defining a struct field, which will be populated when the struct is instantiated to handle a request. The GetCounter method gets a value named counter from the session, increments it, and updates the session before using the value as the response.

Configuring the Application

To set up the session service and the request pipeline, make the changes shown in Listing 34-36 to the startup.go file in the placeholder folder.

Listing 34-36. Configuring Sessions in the startup.go File in the placeholder Folder

```
package placeholder

import (
    "platform/http"
    "platform/pipeline"
    "platform/pipeline/basic"
    "platform/services"
```

950

```
    "sync"
    "platform/http/handling"
    "platform/sessions"
)

func createPipeline() pipeline.RequestPipeline {
    return pipeline.CreatePipeline(
        &basic.ServicesComponent{},
        &basic.LoggingComponent{},
        &basic.ErrorComponent{},
        &basic.StaticFileComponent{},
        &sessions.SessionComponent{},
        //&SimpleMessageComponent{},
        handling.NewRouter(
            handling.HandlerEntry{ "",  NameHandler{}},
            handling.HandlerEntry{ "",  DayHandler{}},
            handling.HandlerEntry{ "",  CounterHandler{}},
        ).AddMethodAlias("/", NameHandler.GetNames),
    )
}

func Start() {
    sessions.RegisterSessionService()
    results, err := services.Call(http.Serve, createPipeline())
    if (err == nil) {
        (results[0].(*sync.WaitGroup)).Wait()
    } else {
        panic(err)
    }
}
```

Finally, add the configuration setting shown in Listing 34-37 to the `config.json` file. The Gorilla session package uses a key to protect session data. Ideally, this should be stored outside of the project folder so that it isn't accidentally checked into a public source code repository, but I have included it in the configuration file for simplicity.

Listing 34-37. Defining the Session Key in the config.json File in the platform Folder

```
{
    "logging" : {
        "level": "debug"
    },
    "main" : {
        "message" : "Hello from the config file"
    },
    "files": {
        "path": "placeholder/files"
    },
```

```
    "templates": {
        "path": "placeholder/*.html",
        "reload": true
    },
    "sessions": {
        "key": "MY_SESSION_KEY",
        "cyclekey": true
    }
}
```

Compile and execute the project and use a browser to request `http://localhost:5000/counter`. Each time you reload the browser, the value stored in the session will be incremented, as shown in Figure 34-7.

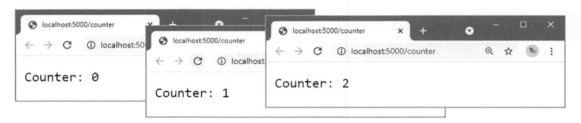

Figure 34-7. *Using sessions*

Adding User Authorization

The final feature required for the platform is support for authorization, with the ability to restrict access to URLs to certain users. In this section, I define the interfaces that describe users and add support for using those interfaces to control access.

It is important not to confuse authorization with authentication and user management. Authorization is the process of enforcing access control, which is the topic of this section.

Authentication is the process of receiving and validating a user's credentials so they can be identified for authorization. User management is the process of managing a user's details, including passwords and other credentials.

I create only a placeholder for authentication in this book and do not address user management at all. In real projects, authentication and user management should be provided by a well-tested service, of which there are many available. These services provide HTTP APIs, which are easily consumed using the Go standard library, whose features for making HTTP requests were described in Chapter 25.

Defining the Basic Authorization Types

Create the `platform/authorization/identity` folder and add a file named `user.go` with the content shown in Listing 34-38.

Listing 34-38. The Contents of the user.go File in the authorization/identity Folder

```
package identity

type User interface {

    GetID() int

    GetDisplayName() string

    InRole(name string) bool

    IsAuthenticated() bool
}
```

The User interface will represent an authenticated user so that requests to restricted resources can be evaluated. To create a default implementation of the User interface, which will be useful for applications with simple authorization requirements, add a file named basic_user.go to the authorization/identity folder with the content shown in Listing 34-39.

Listing 34-39. The Contents of the basic_user.go File in the authorization/identity Folder

```
package identity

import "strings"

var UnauthenticatedUser User = &basicUser{}

func NewBasicUser(id int, name string, roles ...string) User {
    return &basicUser {
        Id: id,
        Name: name,
        Roles: roles,
        Authenticated: true,
    }
}

type basicUser struct {
    Id int
    Name string
    Roles []string
    Authenticated bool
}

func (user *basicUser) GetID() int {
    return user.Id
}

func (user *basicUser) GetDisplayName() string {
    return user.Name
}
```

```
func (user *basicUser) InRole(role string) bool {
    for _, r := range user.Roles {
        if strings.EqualFold(r, role) {
            return true
        }
    }
    return false
}

func (user *basicUser) IsAuthenticated() bool {
    return user.Authenticated
}
```

The NewBasicUser function creates a simple implementation of the User interface, and the UnauthenticatedUser variable will be used to represent a user who has not signed into the application.

Add a file named signin_mgr.go to the platform/authorization/identity folder with the content shown in Listing 34-40.

Listing 34-40. The Contents of the signin_mgr.go File in the authorization/identity Folder

```
package identity

type SignInManager interface {

    SignIn(user User) error
    SignOut(user User) error
}
```

The SignInManager interface will be used to define a service that the application will use to sign a user into and out of the application. The details of how the user is authenticated are left to the application.

Add a file named user_store.go to the platform/authorization/identity folder with the content shown in Listing 34-41.

Listing 34-41. The Contents of the user_store.go File in the authorization/identity Folder

```
package identity

type UserStore interface {

    GetUserByID(id int) (user User, found bool)

    GetUserByName(name string) (user User, found bool)
}
```

The user store provides access to the users who are known to the application, which can be located by ID or name.

Next, I need an interface that will be used to describe an access control requirement. Add a file named auth_condition.go to the platform/authorization/identity folder with the content shown in Listing 34-42.

Listing 34-42. The Contents of the auth_condition.go File in the authorization/identity Folder

```
package identity

type AuthorizationCondition interface {

    Validate(user User) bool
}
```

The AuthorizationCondition interface will be used to assess whether a signed-in user has access to a protected URL and will be used as part of the request handling process.

Implementing the Platform Interfaces

The next step is to implement the interfaces that the platform will provide for authorization. Add a file named sessionsignin.go to the platform/authorization folder with the content shown in Listing 34-43.

Listing 34-43. The Contents of the sessionsignin.go File in the authorization Folder

```
package authorization

import (
    "platform/authorization/identity"
    "platform/services"
    "platform/sessions"
    "context"
)

const USER_SESSION_KEY string = "USER"

func RegisterDefaultSignInService() {
    err := services.AddScoped(func(c context.Context) identity.SignInManager {
        return &SessionSignInMgr{ Context : c}
    })
    if (err != nil) {
        panic(err)
    }
}

type SessionSignInMgr struct {
    context.Context
}

func (mgr *SessionSignInMgr) SignIn(user identity.User) (err error) {
    session, err := mgr.getSession()
    if err == nil {
        session.SetValue(USER_SESSION_KEY, user.GetID())
    }
    return
}
```

```
func (mgr *SessionSignInMgr) SignOut(user identity.User) (err error) {
    session, err := mgr.getSession()
    if err == nil {
        session.SetValue(USER_SESSION_KEY, nil)
    }
    return
}

func (mgr *SessionSignInMgr) getSession() (s sessions.Session, err error) {
    err = services.GetServiceForContext(mgr.Context, &s)
    return
}
```

The SessionSignInMgr struct implements the SignInManager interface by storing the signed-in user's ID in the session and removing it when the user is signed out. Relying on sessions ensures that a user will remain signed in until they sign out or their session expires. The RegisterDefaultSignInService function creates a scoped service for the SignInManager interface, which is resolved using the SessionSignInMgr struct.

To provide a service that presents the signed-in user, add a file named user_service.go to the platform/authorization folder with the content shown in Listing 34-44.

Listing 34-44. The Contents of the user_service.go File in the authorization Folder

```
package authorization

import (
    "platform/services"
    "platform/sessions"
    "platform/authorization/identity"
)

func RegisterDefaultUserService() {
    err := services.AddScoped(func(session sessions.Session,
            store identity.UserStore) identity.User {
        userID, found := session.GetValue(USER_SESSION_KEY).(int)
        if found {
            user, userFound := store.GetUserByID(userID)
            if (userFound) {
                return user
            }
        }
        return identity.UnauthenticatedUser
    })
    if (err != nil) {
        panic(err)
    }
}
```

The RegisterDefaultUserService function creates a scoped service for the User interface, which reads the value stored in the current session and uses it to query the UserStore service.

To create a simple access condition that checks to see if a user is in a role, add a file named role_condition.go to the platform/authorization folder with the content shown in Listing 34-45.

Listing 34-45. The Contents of the role_condition.go File in the authorization Folder

```go
package authorization

import ("platform/authorization/identity")

func NewRoleCondition(roles ...string) identity.AuthorizationCondition {
    return &roleCondition{ allowedRoles: roles}
}

type roleCondition struct {
    allowedRoles []string
}

func (c *roleCondition) Validate(user identity.User) bool {
    for _, allowedRole := range c.allowedRoles {
        if user.InRole(allowedRole) {
            return true
        }
    }
    return false
}
```

The NewRoleCondition function accepts a set of roles, which are used to create a condition that will return true if a user has been assigned to any one of them.

Implementing Access Controls

The next step is to add support for defining an access restriction and applying it to requests. Add a file named auth_middleware.go to the platform/authorization folder with the content shown in Listing 34-46.

Listing 34-46. The Contents of the auth_middleware.go File in the authorization Folder

```go
package authorization

import (
    "net/http"
    "platform/authorization/identity"
    "platform/config"
    "platform/http/handling"
    "platform/pipeline"
    "strings"
    "regexp"
)

func NewAuthComponent(prefix string, condition identity.AuthorizationCondition,
        requestHandlers ...interface{}) *AuthMiddlewareComponent {

    entries := []handling.HandlerEntry {}
    for _, handler := range requestHandlers {
        entries = append(entries, handling.HandlerEntry{prefix, handler})
    }
```

```
    router := handling.NewRouter(entries...)

    return &AuthMiddlewareComponent{
        prefix: "/" + prefix ,
        condition:  condition,
        RequestPipeline: pipeline.CreatePipeline(router),
        fallbacks: map[*regexp.Regexp]string {},
    }
}

type AuthMiddlewareComponent struct {
    prefix string
    condition identity.AuthorizationCondition
    pipeline.RequestPipeline
    config.Configuration
    authFailURL string
    fallbacks map[*regexp.Regexp]string
}

func (c *AuthMiddlewareComponent) Init() {
        c.authFailURL, _ = c.Configuration.GetString("authorization:failUrl")
}

func (*AuthMiddlewareComponent) ImplementsProcessRequestWithServices() {}

func (c *AuthMiddlewareComponent) ProcessRequestWithServices(
        context *pipeline.ComponentContext,
        next func(*pipeline.ComponentContext),
        user identity.User) {

    if strings.HasPrefix(context.Request.URL.Path, c.prefix) {
        for expr, target := range c.fallbacks {
            if expr.MatchString(context.Request.URL.Path) {
                http.Redirect(context.ResponseWriter, context.Request,
                    target, http.StatusSeeOther)
                    return
            }
        }
        if c.condition.Validate(user) {
            c.RequestPipeline.ProcessRequest(context.Request, context.ResponseWriter)
        } else {
            if c.authFailURL != "" {
                http.Redirect(context.ResponseWriter, context.Request,
                    c.authFailURL, http.StatusSeeOther)
            } else if user.IsAuthenticated() {
                context.ResponseWriter.WriteHeader(http.StatusForbidden)
            } else {
                context.ResponseWriter.WriteHeader(http.StatusUnauthorized)
            }
        }
    } else {
```

```
            next(context)
        }
}

func (c *AuthMiddlewareComponent) AddFallback(target string,
        patterns ...string) *AuthMiddlewareComponent {
    for _, p := range patterns {
        c.fallbacks[regexp.MustCompile(p)] = target
    }
    return c
}
```

The AuthMiddlewareComponent struct is a middleware component that creates a branch in the request pipeline, with a URL router whose handlers receive a request only when an authorization condition is met.

Implementing the Application Placeholder Features

Following the pattern established for earlier features, I am going to create basic implementations of the authorization features that an application using the platform will provide. Add a file named placeholder_store.go to the platform/placeholder with the content shown in Listing 34-47.

Listing 34-47. The Contents of the placeholder_store.go File in the placeholder Folder

```
package placeholder

import (
    "platform/services"
    "platform/authorization/identity"
    "strings"
)

func RegisterPlaceholderUserStore() {
    err := services.AddSingleton(func () identity.UserStore {
        return &PlaceholderUserStore{}
    })
    if (err != nil) {
        panic(err)
    }
}

var users = map[int]identity.User {
    1: identity.NewBasicUser(1, "Alice", "Administrator"),
    2: identity.NewBasicUser(2, "Bob"),
}

type PlaceholderUserStore struct {}

func (store *PlaceholderUserStore) GetUserByID(id int) (identity.User, bool) {
    user, found := users[id]
    return user, found
}
```

959

```
func (store *PlaceholderUserStore) GetUserByName(name string) (identity.User, bool) {
    for _, user := range users {
        if strings.EqualFold(user.GetDisplayName(), name) {
            return user, true
        }
    }
    return nil, false
}
```

The PlaceholderUserStore struct implements the UserStore interface with statically defined data for two users, Alice and Bob, and is used by the RegisterPlaceholderUserStore function to create a singleton service.

Creating the Authentication Handler

To allow some simple authentication, add a file named authentication_handler.go to the placeholder folder with the content shown in Listing 34-48.

Listing 34-48. The Contents of the authentication_handler.go File in the placeholder Folder

```
package placeholder

import (
    "platform/http/actionresults"
    "platform/authorization/identity"
    "fmt"
)

type AuthenticationHandler struct {
    identity.User
    identity.SignInManager
    identity.UserStore
}

func (h AuthenticationHandler) GetSignIn() actionresults.ActionResult {
    return actionresults.NewTemplateAction("signin.html",
    fmt.Sprintf("Signed in as: %v", h.User.GetDisplayName()))
}

type Credentials struct {
    Username string
    Password string
}

func (h AuthenticationHandler) PostSignIn(creds Credentials) actionresults.ActionResult {
    if creds.Password == "mysecret" {
        user, ok := h.UserStore.GetUserByName(creds.Username)
        if (ok) {
```

```
        h.SignInManager.SignIn(user)
        return actionresults.NewTemplateAction("signin.html",
            fmt.Sprintf("Signed in as: %v", user.GetDisplayName()))
        }
    }
    return actionresults.NewTemplateAction("signin.html", "Access Denied")
}

func (h AuthenticationHandler) PostSignOut() actionresults.ActionResult {
    h.SignInManager.SignOut(h.User)
    return actionresults.NewTemplateAction("signin.html", "Signed out")
}
```

This request handler has a hardwired password—mysecret—for all users. The GetSignIn method displays a template to collect the user's name and password. The PostSignIn method checks the password and makes sure there is a user in the store with the specified name, before signing the user into the application. The PostSignOut method signs the user out of the application. To create the template used by the handler, add a file named signin.html to the placeholder folder with the content shown in Listing 34-49.

Listing 34-49. The Contents of the signin.html File in the placeholder Folder

```
{{ layout "layout.html" }}

{{ if ne . "" }}
    <h3 style="padding: 10px;">{{. }}</h3>
{{ end }}

<form method="POST" action="/signin">
    <div style="padding: 5px;">
        <label>Username:</label>
        <input name="username" />
    </div>
    <div style="padding: 5px;">
        <label>Password:</label>
        <input name="password" />
    </div>
    <div style="padding: 5px;">
        <button type="submit">Sign In</button>
        <button type="submit" formaction="/signout">Sign Out</button>
    </div>
</form>
```

The template displays a basic HTML form with a message provided by the handler method that renders it.

Configuring the Application

All that remains is to configure the application to create a protected handler and set up the authorization features, as shown in Listing 34-50.

Listing 34-50. Configuring the Application in the startup.go File in the placeholder Folder

```
package placeholder

import (
    "platform/http"
    "platform/pipeline"
    "platform/pipeline/basic"
    "platform/services"
    "sync"
    "platform/http/handling"
    "platform/sessions"
    "platform/authorization"
)

func createPipeline() pipeline.RequestPipeline {
    return pipeline.CreatePipeline(
        &basic.ServicesComponent{},
        &basic.LoggingComponent{},
        &basic.ErrorComponent{},
        &basic.StaticFileComponent{},
        &sessions.SessionComponent{},
        //&SimpleMessageComponent{},
        authorization.NewAuthComponent(
            "protected",
            authorization.NewRoleCondition("Administrator"),
            CounterHandler{},
        ),
        handling.NewRouter(
            handling.HandlerEntry{ "",  NameHandler{}},
            handling.HandlerEntry{ "",  DayHandler{}},
            //handling.HandlerEntry{ "",  CounterHandler{}},
            handling.HandlerEntry{ "", AuthenticationHandler{}},
        ).AddMethodAlias("/", NameHandler.GetNames),
    )
}

func Start() {
    sessions.RegisterSessionService()
    authorization.RegisterDefaultSignInService()
    authorization.RegisterDefaultUserService()
    RegisterPlaceholderUserStore()
    results, err := services.Call(http.Serve, createPipeline())
    if (err == nil) {
        (results[0].(*sync.WaitGroup)).Wait()
    } else {
        panic(err)
    }
}
```

The changes create a branch of the pipeline that has the /protected prefix, which is restricted to users who have been assigned to the Administrator role. The CounterHandler, defined earlier in the chapter, is the only handler on the branch. The AuthenticationHandler is added to the main branch of the pipeline.

Compile and execute the application and use a browser to request http://localhost:5000/protected/counter. This is a protected handler method and, since there is no signed-in user, the result shown in Figure 34-8 will be shown.

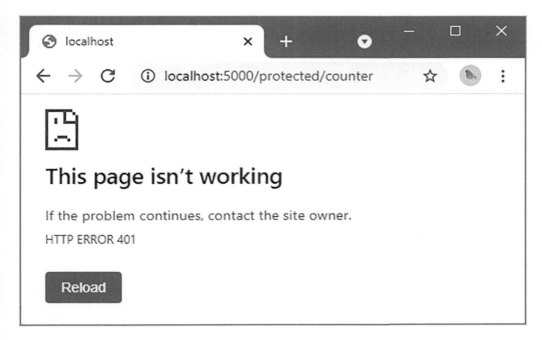

Figure 34-8. *An unauthenticated request*

A 401 response is sent when an unauthenticated user requests a protected resource and is known as the challenge response, which is often used to present the user with a chance to sign in.

Next, request http://localhost:5000/signin, enter bob into the Username field, enter mysecret into the Password field, and click Sign In, as shown in Figure 34-9. Request http://localhost:5000/protected/counter, and you will receive a 403 response, which is sent when a user who has already presented their credentials requests access to a protected resource.

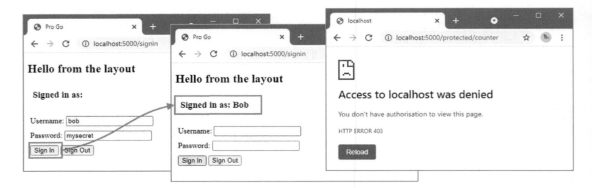

Figure 34-9. *An unauthorized request*

Finally, request `http://localhost:5000/signin`, enter alice into the Username field and mysecret into the Password field, and click Sign In, as shown in Figure 34-10. Request `http://localhost:5000/protected/counter`, and you will receive the response from the handler, also shown in Figure 34-10, since Alice is in the Adminstrator role.

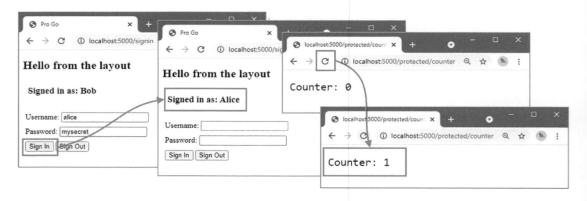

Figure 34-10. *An authorized request*

Summary

In this chapter, I completed the development of my custom web application framework by adding support for action results, data validation, sessions, and authorization. In the next chapter, I begin the process of using the platform to create an online store.

CHAPTER 35

SportsStore: A Real Application

In this chapter, I start the development of an application named SportsStore, which is an online store for sports products. This is an example that I include in many of my books, allowing me to demonstrate how the same set of features is implemented in different languages and frameworks.

Creating the SportsStore Project

I am going to create an application that uses the platform project created in Chapters 32–34 but that is defined in its own project. Open a command prompt and use it to create a folder named sportsstore in the same folder that contains the platform folder. Navigate to the sportsstore folder and run the command shown in Listing 35-1.

■ **Tip** You can download the example project for this chapter—and for all the other chapters in this book—from https://github.com/apress/pro-go. See Chapter 2 for how to get help if you have problems running the examples.

Listing 35-1. Initializing the Project

```
go mod init sportsstore
```

This command creates the go.mod file. To declare a dependency on the platform project, run the commands shown in Listing 35-2 in the sportsstore folder.

Listing 35-2. Creating a Dependency

```
go mod edit -require="platform@v1.0.0"
go mod edit -replace="platform@v1.0.0"="../platform"
go get -d "platform@v1.0.0"
```

Open the go.mod file, and you will see the effect of these commands, as shown in Listing 35-3.

© Adam Freeman 2022
A. Freeman, *Pro Go*, https://doi.org/10.1007/978-1-4842-7355-5_35

Listing 35-3. The Effect of the go Commands in the go.mod File in the sportsstore Folder

```
module sportsstore

go 1.17

require platform v1.0.0

require (
        github.com/gorilla/securecookie v1.1.1 // indirect
        github.com/gorilla/sessions v1.2.1 // indirect
)

replace platform v1.0.0 => ../platform
```

The require directive declares a dependency on the platform module. In real projects, this can be specified as the URL for your version control repository, such as a GitHub URL. This project won't be committed to version control, so I have just used the name platform.

The replace directive provides a local path where the platform module can be found. When the Go tools resolve a dependency on a package in the platform module, they will do so using the platform folder, which is at the same level as the sportsstore folder.

The platform project has dependencies on third-party packages, which must be resolved before they can be used. This was done by the go get command, which produced the require directive, which declares indirect dependencies on the packages used to implement sessions in Chapter 34.

Configuring the Application

Add a file named config.json to the sportsstore folder and use it to define the configuration settings shown in Listing 35-4.

Listing 35-4. The Contents of the config.json File in the sportsstore Folder

```
{
    "logging" : {
        "level": "debug"
    },
    "files": {
        "path": "files"
    },
    "templates": {
        "path": "templates/*.html",
        "reload": true
    },
    "sessions": {
        "key": "MY_SESSION_KEY",
        "cyclekey": true
    }
}
```

Next, add a file named main.go the sportsstore folder, with the content shown in Listing 35-5.

Listing 35-5. The Contents of the main.go File in the sportsstore Folder

```
package main

import (
        "platform/services"
    "platform/logging"
)

func writeMessage(logger logging.Logger) {
    logger.Info("SportsStore")
}

func main() {
    services.RegisterDefaultServices()
    services.Call(writeMessage)
}
```

Compile and execute the project using the command shown in Listing 35-6 in the sportsstore folder.

Listing 35-6. Compiling and Executing the Project

```
go run .
```

The main method sets up the default platform services and invokes the writeMessage, producing the following output:

```
07:55:03 INFO SportsStore
```

Starting the Data Model

Almost all projects have a data model of some sort, and this is where I usually start development. I like to begin with a few simple data types and then start work on making them available to the rest of the project. As I add features to the application, I return to the data model and expand its capabilities.

Create the sportsstore/models folder and add to it a file named product.go with the content shown in Listing 35-7.

Listing 35-7. The Contents of the product.go File in the models Folder

```
package models

type Product struct {
    ID int
    Name string
    Description string
    Price float64
    *Category
}
```

My preference is to define one type in each file, along with any related constructor functions or methods that are associated with that type. To create the data type for the embedded Category field, add a file named category.go in the models folder with the content shown in Listing 35-8.

Listing 35-8. The Contents of the category.go File in the models Folder

```
package models

type Category struct {
    ID int
    CategoryName string
}
```

When defining types for embedded fields, I try to pick field names that will be useful when the field is promoted. In this case, the name of the CategoryName field has been chosen so that it doesn't conflict with the fields defined by the enclosing Product type, even though the name isn't one that I would have chosen for a stand-alone type.

Defining the Repository Interface

I like to use a repository as a way to separate the source of the data in an application from the code that consumes it. Add a file named repository.go the sportsstore/models folder with the content shown in Listing 35-9.

Listing 35-9. The Contents of the repository.go File in the models Folder

```
package models

type Repository interface {

    GetProduct(id int) Product

    GetProducts() []Product

    GetCategories() []Category

    Seed()
}
```

I will create a service for the Repository interface, which will allow me to easily change the source of the data used in the application.

Notice that the GetProduct, GetProducts, and GetCategories methods defined in Listing 35-9 do not return pointers. I prefer to use values to prevent code that uses the data making changes via pointers that affect the data managed by the repository. This approach means that data values will be duplicated but ensures that there are no odd effects caused by accidental changes via a shared reference. Put another way, I don't want the repository to provide access to data without sharing references with the code that uses that data.

Implementing the (Temporary) Repository

I will store the SportsStore data in a relational database, but I prefer to start with a simple memory-based implementation of the repository, which I use until some of the basic application features are done.

There are inevitable changes in approach as a project is developed, and if I start with a database for the repository, then I become reluctant to make changes to the SQL queries I have written. This means I end up adapting the application code to work around the limitations of the SQL, which I know makes no sense, but I also know that I'll do it anyway. You may be more disciplined, but I get the best results by working with a simple memory-based repository and then writing the SQL only when I understand what the final shape of the data will be.

Create the sportsstore/models/repo folder and add to it a file named memory_repo.go with the content shown in Listing 35-10.

Listing 35-10. The Contents of the memory_repo.go in the models/repo Folder

```go
package repo

import (
    "platform/services"
    "sportsstore/models"
)

func RegisterMemoryRepoService() {
    services.AddSingleton(func() models.Repository {
        repo := &MemoryRepo{}
        repo.Seed()
        return repo
    })
}

type MemoryRepo struct {
    products []models.Product
    categories []models.Category
}

func (repo *MemoryRepo) GetProduct(id int) (product models.Product) {
    for _, p := range repo.products {
        if (p.ID == id) {
            product = p
            return
        }
    }
    return
}

func (repo *MemoryRepo) GetProducts() (results []models.Product) {
    return repo.products
}

func (repo *MemoryRepo) GetCategories() (results []models.Category) {
    return repo.categories
}
```

The MemoryRepo struct defines most of the functionality required to implement the Repository interface, storing values in a slice. To implement the Seed method, add a file named memory_repo_seed.go to the repo folder with the content shown in Listing 35-11.

Listing 35-11. The Contents of the memory_repo_seed.go File in the models/repo Folder

```
package repo

import (
    "fmt"
    "math/rand"
    "sportsstore/models"
)

func (repo *MemoryRepo) Seed() {
    repo.categories = make([]models.Category, 3)
    for i := 0; i < 3; i++ {
        catName := fmt.Sprintf("Category_%v", i + 1)
        repo.categories[i]= models.Category{ID: i + 1, CategoryName: catName}
    }

    for i := 0; i < 20; i++ {
        name := fmt.Sprintf("Product_%v", i + 1)
        price := rand.Float64() * float64(rand.Intn(500))
        cat := &repo.categories[rand.Intn(len(repo.categories))]
        repo.products = append(repo.products, models.Product{
            ID: i + 1,
            Name: name, Price: price,
            Description: fmt.Sprintf("%v (%v)", name, cat.CategoryName),
            Category: cat,
        })
    }
}
```

I have defined this method separately to avoid listing the seeding code when I add features to the repository.

Displaying a List of Products

The first step in displaying content is to show a list of products for sale. Create the sportsstore/store folder and add to it a file named product_handler.go with the content shown in Listing 35-12.

Listing 35-12. The Contents of the product_handler.go File in the store Folder

```
package store

import (
    "sportsstore/models"
    "platform/http/actionresults"
)
```

```
type ProductHandler struct {
    Repository models.Repository
}

type ProductTemplateContext struct {
    Products []models.Product
}

func (handler ProductHandler) GetProducts() actionresults.ActionResult {
    return actionresults.NewTemplateAction("product_list.html",
        ProductTemplateContext {
            Products: handler.Repository.GetProducts(),
        })
}
```

The GetProducts method renders a template named product_list.html, passing in a ProductTemplateContext value, which I will use to provide additional information to the template later.

■ **Note** Routes are not generated for methods that are promoted from anonymous embedded struct fields, so as not to accidentally create routes and expose the inner workings of request handlers to HTTP requests. One consequence of this decision is that it also excludes methods defined by a struct that share a name with a promoted method. It is for this reason that I have assigned a name to the Products field defined by the ProductHandler struct. If I had not done so, then the GetProducts method would not have been used to generate a route because it matches the name of a method defined by the models.Repository interface.

Creating the Template and Layout

To define the template, create the sportsstore/templates folder and add to it a file named product_list. html with the content shown in Listing 35-13.

Listing 35-13. The Contents of the product_list.html File in the templates Folder

```
{{ layout "store_layout.html" }}

{{ range .Products }}
    <div>
        {{.ID}}, {{ .Name }}, {{ printf "$%.2f" .Price }}, {{ .CategoryName }}
    </div>
{{ end }}
```

The layout uses a range expression on the Product field of the struct provided by the handler to generate a div element for each Product in the Repository.

To create the layout specified in Listing 35-13, add a file named store_layout.html to the sportsstore/templates folder with the content shown in Listing 35-14.

Listing 35-14. The Contents of the store_layout.html File in the templates Folder

```
<!DOCTYPE html>
<html>
<head>
    <meta name="viewport" content="width=device-width" />
    <title>SportsStore</title>
</head>
<body>
    {{ body }}
</body>
</html>
```

Configuring the Application

To register the services and create the pipeline required by the SportsStore application, replace the contents of the main.go file with those shown in Listing 35-15.

Listing 35-15. Replacing the Contents of the main.go File in the sportsstore Folder

```
package main

import (
    "sync"
    "platform/http"
    "platform/http/handling"
    "platform/services"
    "platform/pipeline"
    "platform/pipeline/basic"
    "sportsstore/store"
    "sportsstore/models/repo"
)

func registerServices() {
    services.RegisterDefaultServices()
    repo.RegisterMemoryRepoService()
}

func createPipeline() pipeline.RequestPipeline {
    return pipeline.CreatePipeline(
        &basic.ServicesComponent{},
        &basic.LoggingComponent{},
        &basic.ErrorComponent{},
        &basic.StaticFileComponent{},
        handling.NewRouter(
            handling.HandlerEntry{ "",  store.ProductHandler{}},
        ).AddMethodAlias("/", store.ProductHandler.GetProducts),
    )
}

func main() {
    registerServices()
```

```
    results, err := services.Call(http.Serve, createPipeline())
    if (err == nil) {
        (results[0].(*sync.WaitGroup)).Wait()
    } else {
        panic(err)
    }
}
```

The default services are registered, along with the memory repository. The pipeline contains the basic components created in Chapter 34, with a router set up with the ProductHandler.

Compile and execute the project and use a browser to request http://localhost:5000, which will produce the response shown in Figure 35-1.

Figure 35-1. *Displaying a list of products*

DEALING WITH WINDOWS FIREWALL PERMISSION REQUESTS

As explained in earlier chapters, Windows will prompt for firewall permissions every time the project is compiled with the go run command, which can be avoided by using a simple PowerShell script. As a reminder, here are the contents of the script, which I save as buildandrun.ps1:

```
$file = "./sportsstore.exe"

&go build -o $file

if ($LASTEXITCODE -eq 0) {
    &$file
}
```

To build and execute the project, use the command ./buildandrun.ps1 in the sportsstore folder.

Adding Pagination

The output in Figure 35-1 shows that all the products in the repository are displayed in a single list. The next step is to add support for pagination so the user is presented with a small number of products and can move between pages. I like to make changes in the repository and then work through until reaching the template that displays the data. Listing 35-16 adds a method to the Repository interface that allows a page of Product values to be requested.

Listing 35-16. Adding a Method in the repository.go File in the models Folder

```
package models

type Repository interface {

    GetProduct(id int) Product

    GetProducts() []Product

    GetProductPage(page, pageSize int) (products []Product, totalAvailable int)

    GetCategories() []Category

    Seed()
}
```

The GetProductPage method returns a Product slice and the total number of items in the repository. Listing 35-17 implements the new method in the memory repository.

Listing 35-17. Implementing a Method in the memory_repo.go File in the models/repo Folder

```
package repo

import (
    "platform/services"
    "sportsstore/models"
    "math"
)

func RegisterMemoryRepoService() {
    services.AddSingleton(func() models.Repository {
        repo := &MemoryRepo{}
        repo.Seed()
        return repo
    })
}

type MemoryRepo struct {
    products []models.Product
    categories []models.Category
}
```

974

```
func (repo *MemoryRepo) GetProduct(id int) (product models.Product) {
    for _, p := range repo.products {
        if (p.ID == id) {
            product = p
            return
        }
    }
    return
}

func (repo *MemoryRepo) GetProducts() (results []models.Product) {
    return repo.products
}

func (repo *MemoryRepo) GetCategories() (results []models.Category) {
    return repo.categories
}

func (repo *MemoryRepo) GetProductPage(page, pageSize int) ([]models.Product, int) {
    return getPage(repo.products, page, pageSize), len(repo.products)
}

func getPage(src []models.Product, page, pageSize int) []models.Product {
    start := (page -1) * pageSize
    if page > 0 && len(src) > start {
        end := (int)(math.Min((float64)(len(src)), (float64)(start + pageSize)))
        return src[start : end]
    }
    return []models.Product{}
}
```

Listing 35-18 updates the request handler so that it selects a page of data and passes it to the template, along with extra struct fields required to support pagination.

Listing 35-18. Updating the Handler Method in the product_handler.go File in the store Folder

```
package store

import (
    "sportsstore/models"
    "platform/http/actionresults"
    "platform/http/handling"
    "math"
)

const pageSize = 4

type ProductHandler struct {
    Repository models.Repository
    URLGenerator handling.URLGenerator
}
```

```go
type ProductTemplateContext struct {
    Products []models.Product
    Page int
    PageCount int
    PageNumbers []int
    PageUrlFunc func(int) string
}

func (handler ProductHandler) GetProducts(page int) actionresults.ActionResult {
    prods, total := handler.Repository.GetProductPage(page, pageSize)
    pageCount := int(math.Ceil(float64(total) / float64(pageSize)))
    return actionresults.NewTemplateAction("product_list.html",
        ProductTemplateContext {
            Products: prods,
            Page: page,
            PageCount: pageCount,
            PageNumbers: handler.generatePageNumbers(pageCount),
            PageUrlFunc: handler.createPageUrlFunction(),
        })
}

func (handler ProductHandler) createPageUrlFunction() func(int) string {
    return func(page int) string {
        url, _ := handler.URLGenerator.GenerateUrl(ProductHandler.GetProducts, page)
        return url
    }
}

func (handler ProductHandler) generatePageNumbers(pageCount int) (pages []int) {
    pages = make([]int, pageCount)
    for i := 0; i < pageCount; i++ {
        pages[i] = i + 1
    }
    return
}
```

There are a lot of new statements in Listing 35-18 because the handler has to provide a lot more information to the template to support pagination. The GetProducts method has been modified to accept a parameter, which is used to obtain a page of data. The additional fields defined for the struct passed to the template include the selected page, a function for generating URLs to navigate to a page, and a slice containing a sequent of numbers (which is required because templates can use ranges but not for loops to generate content). Listing 35-19 updates the template to use the new information.

Listing 35-19. Supporting Pagination in the product_list.html File in the templates Folder

```
{{ layout "store_layout.html" }}
{{ $context := . }}
```

```
{{ range .Products }}
    <div>
        {{.ID}}, {{ .Name }}, {{ printf "$%.2f" .Price }}, {{ .CategoryName }}
    </div>
{{ end }}

{{ range .PageNumbers}}
    {{ if eq $context.Page .}}
        {{ . }}
    {{ else }}
        <a href="{{ call $context.PageUrlFunc . }}">{{ . }}</a>
    {{ end }}
{{ end }}
```

I have defined a $context variable so that I always have easy access to the struct value passed to the template by the handler method. The new range expression enumerates the list of page numbers and displays a navigation link for all of them except the currently selected page. The URL for the link is created by calling the function assigned to the PageUrlFunc field of the context struct.

Next, a change is required to the aliases set up for the routing system so that the default URL and the /products URL both trigger redirections to the first page of products, as shown in Listing 35-20.

Listing 35-20. Updating Aliases in the main.go File in the sportsstore Folder

```
...
func createPipeline() pipeline.RequestPipeline {
    return pipeline.CreatePipeline(
        &basic.ServicesComponent{},
        &basic.LoggingComponent{},
        &basic.ErrorComponent{},
        &basic.StaticFileComponent{},
        handling.NewRouter(
            handling.HandlerEntry{ "", store.ProductHandler{}},
        ).AddMethodAlias("/", store.ProductHandler.GetProducts, 1).
            AddMethodAlias("/products", store.ProductHandler.GetProducts, 1),
    )
}
...
```

Compile and execute the project and use a browser to request http://localhost:5000. You will be presented with products displayed in pages of four, with navigation links that request other pages, as shown in Figure 35-2.

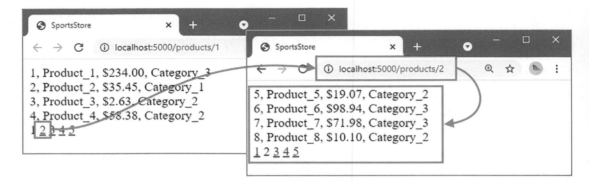

Figure 35-2. *Adding support for pagination*

Styling the Template Content

Before I add any further features to the application, I am going to address the appearance of the products in the list. I am going to use Bootstrap, which is a popular CSS framework and the one I like to use. Bootstrap applies styles using the class attributes of HTML elements and is described in detail at https://getbootstrap.com.

Installing the Bootstrap CSS File

Go doesn't have a good way to install packages outside of the Go ecosystem. To add the CSS file to the project, create the sportsstore/files folder and use a command prompt to run the command shown in Listing 35-21 in the sportsstore folder.

Listing 35-21. Downloading the CSS Stylesheet

```
curl https://cdnjs.cloudflare.com/ajax/libs/bootstrap/5.1.1/css/bootstrap.min.css --output
files/bootstrap.min.css
```

If you are using Windows, then use the PowerShell command shown in Listing 35-22 instead.

Listing 35-22. Downloading the CSS Stylesheet on Windows

```
Invoke-WebRequest -Uri ` "https://cdnjs.cloudflare.com/ajax/libs/bootstrap/5.1.1/css/
bootstrap.min.css" `
-OutFile "files/bootstrap.min.css"
```

Updating the Layout

Add the element shown in Listing 35-23 to the store_layout.html file in the templates folder.

Listing 35-23. Adding Bootstrap in the store_layout.html File in the templates Folder

```
<!DOCTYPE html>
<html>
<head>
    <meta name="viewport" content="width=device-width" />
    <title>SportsStore</title>
    <link href="/files/bootstrap.min.css" rel="stylesheet" />
</head>
<body>
    <div class="bg-dark text-white p-2">
        <span class="navbar-brand ml-2">SPORTS STORE</span>
    </div>
    <div class="row m-1 p-1">
        <div id="sidebar" class="col-3">
            {{ template "left_column" . }}
        </div>
        <div class="col-9">
            {{ template "right_column" . }}
        </div>
    </div>
</body>
</html>
```

The new elements add a link element for the Bootstrap CSS file and use the Bootstrap features to create a header and a two-column layout. The contents of the columns are obtained from templates named left_column and right_column.

Styling the Template Content

The role of the product_list.html template must change to follow the expectations of the layout and define the templates for the left and right columns in the layout, as shown in Listing 35-24.

Listing 35-24. Creating Column Content in the product_list.html File in the templates Folder

```
{{ layout "store_layout.html" }}

{{ define "left_column" }}
    Put something useful here
{{end}}

{{ define "right_column" }}
    {{ $context := . }}
    {{ range $context.Products }}
        <div class="card card-outline-primary m-1 p-1">
            <div class="bg-faded p-1">
                <h4>
```

979

```
                {{ .Name }}
                <span class="badge rounded-pill bg-primary" style="float:right">
                    <small>{{ printf "$%.2f" .Price }}</small>
                </span>
            </h4>
        </div>
        <div class="card-text p-1">{{ .Description }}</div>
    </div>
    {{ end }}
    {{ template "page_buttons.html" $context }}
{{end}}
```

The new structure defines a placeholder for the left column and generates a list of styled products in the right column.

I have defined a separate template for the pagination buttons. Add a file named page_buttons.html to the templates folder with the content shown in Listing 35-25.

Listing 35-25. The Contents of the page_buttons.html File in the templates Folder

```
{{ $context := . }}
<div class="btn-group pull-right m-1">
    {{ range .PageNumbers}}
        {{ if eq $context.Page .}}
        <a class="btn btn-primary">{{ . }}</a>
        {{ else }}
            <a href="{{ call $context.PageUrlFunc . }}"
                class="btn btn-outline-primary">{{ . }}</a>
        {{ end }}
    {{ end }}
</div>
```

Compile and execute the project and request http://localhost:5000. You will see the styled content shown in Figure 35-3.

Figure 35-3. Styling content

Adding Support for Category Filtering

The next step is to replace the placeholder content in the left column with buttons that allow the user to select a category by which to filter the products shown in the list. To start, add the method shown in Listing 35-26 to the Repository interface.

Listing 35-26. Adding a Method in the repository.go File in the models Folder

```
package models

type Repository interface {

    GetProduct(id int) Product

    GetProducts() []Product

    GetProductPage(page, pageSize int) (products []Product, totalAvailable int)

    GetProductPageCategory(categoryId int, page, pageSize int) (products []Product,
        totalAvailable int)

    GetCategories() []Category

    Seed()
}
```

The new method allows a category to be specified when requesting a page. Listing 35-27 implements the new method in the memory repository.

Listing 35-27. Implementing a Method in the memory_repository.go File in the models Folder

```
package repo

import (
    "platform/services"
    "sportsstore/models"
    "math"
)

func RegisterMemoryRepoService() {
    services.AddSingleton(func() models.Repository {
        repo := &MemoryRepo{}
        repo.Seed()
        return repo
    })
}

type MemoryRepo struct {
    products []models.Product
    categories []models.Category
}

func (repo *MemoryRepo) GetProduct(id int) (product models.Product) {
    for _, p := range repo.products {
        if (p.ID == id) {
            product = p
            return
        }
    }
    return
}

func (repo *MemoryRepo) GetProducts() (results []models.Product) {
    return repo.products
}

func (repo *MemoryRepo) GetCategories() (results []models.Category) {
    return repo.categories
}

func (repo *MemoryRepo) GetProductPage(page, pageSize int) ([]models.Product, int) {
    return getPage(repo.products, page, pageSize), len(repo.products)
}

func (repo *MemoryRepo) GetProductPageCategory(category int, page,
        pageSize int) (products []models.Product, totalAvailable int) {
    if category == 0 {
        return repo.GetProductPage(page, pageSize)
```

```
    } else {
        filteredProducts := make([]models.Product, 0, len(repo.products))
        for _, p := range repo.products {
            if p.Category.ID == category {
                filteredProducts = append(filteredProducts, p)
            }
        }
        return getPage(filteredProducts, page, pageSize), len(filteredProducts)
    }
}

func getPage(src []models.Product, page, pageSize int) []models.Product {
    start := (page -1) * pageSize
    if page > 0 && len(src) > start {
        end := (int)(math.Min((float64)(len(src)), (float64)(start + pageSize)))
        return src[start : end]
    }
    return []models.Product{}
}
```

The new method enumerates the product data, filtering for the selected category, and then selects the specified page of data.

Updating the Request Handler

The next step is to modify the request handler method so it will receive a category parameter and use it to obtain filtered data, which is then passed to the template, along with additional context data required to generate navigation buttons that allow a different category to be selected, as shown in Listing 35-28.

Listing 35-28. Adding Support for Category Filtering in the product_handler.go File in the store Folder

```
package store

import (
    "sportsstore/models"
    "platform/http/actionresults"
    "platform/http/handling"
    "math"
)

const pageSize = 4

type ProductHandler struct {
    Repository models.Repository
    URLGenerator handling.URLGenerator
}
```

```
type ProductTemplateContext struct {
    Products []models.Product
    Page int
    PageCount int
    PageNumbers []int
    PageUrlFunc func(int) string
    SelectedCategory int
}

func (handler ProductHandler) GetProducts(category,
        page int) actionresults.ActionResult {
    prods, total := handler.Repository.GetProductPageCategory(category,
        page, pageSize)
    pageCount := int(math.Ceil(float64(total) / float64(pageSize)))
    return actionresults.NewTemplateAction("product_list.html",
        ProductTemplateContext {
            Products: prods,
            Page: page,
            PageCount: pageCount,
            PageNumbers: handler.generatePageNumbers(pageCount),
            PageUrlFunc: handler.createPageUrlFunction(category),
            SelectedCategory: category,
        })
}

func (handler ProductHandler) createPageUrlFunction(category int) func(int) string {
    return func(page int) string {
        url, _ := handler.URLGenerator.GenerateUrl(ProductHandler.GetProducts,
            category, page)
        return url
    }
}

func (handler ProductHandler) generatePageNumbers(pageCount int) (pages []int) {
    pages = make([]int, pageCount)
    for i := 0; i < pageCount; i++ {
        pages[i] = i + 1
    }
    return
}
```

I have also had to update the existing function that generates URLs that select a page and introduce a function that generates URLs for selecting a new category.

Creating the Category Handler

The reason I added support for invoking handlers from templates was so that I could display self-contained content, like category buttons. Add a file named category_handler.go to the sportsstore/store folder with the content shown in Listing 35-29.

Listing 35-29. The Contents of the category_handler.go File in the store Folder

```go
package store

import (
    "sportsstore/models"
    "platform/http/actionresults"
    "platform/http/handling"
)

type CategoryHandler struct {
    Repository models.Repository
    URLGenerator handling.URLGenerator
}

type categoryTemplateContext struct {
    Categories []models.Category
    SelectedCategory int
    CategoryUrlFunc func(int) string
}

func (handler CategoryHandler) GetButtons(selected int) actionresults.ActionResult {
    return actionresults.NewTemplateAction("category_buttons.html",
        categoryTemplateContext {
            Categories: handler.Repository.GetCategories(),
            SelectedCategory: selected,
            CategoryUrlFunc: handler.createCategoryFilterFunction(),
        })
}

func (handler CategoryHandler) createCategoryFilterFunction() func(int) string {
    return func(category int) string {
        url, _ := handler.URLGenerator.GenerateUrl(ProductHandler.GetProducts,
            category, 1)
        return url
    }
}
```

The handler obtains the set of categories for which buttons are required through the repository, which is obtained as a service. The selected category is received through a parameter of the handler method.

To create the template rendered by the GetButtons handler method, add a file named category_buttons.html to the templates folder with the content shown in Listing 35-30.

Listing 35-30. The Contents of the category_buttons.html File in the templates Folder

```html
{{ $context := . }}

<div class="d-grid gap-2">
        <a
    {{ if eq $context.SelectedCategory 0}}
        class="btn btn-primary"
    {{ else }}
```

```
          class="btn btn-outline-primary"
    {{ end }}
          href="{{ call $context.CategoryUrlFunc 0 }}">All</a>
    {{ range $context.Categories }}
          <a
        {{ if eq $context.SelectedCategory .ID}}
              class="btn btn-primary"
        {{ else }}
              class="btn btn-outline-primary"
        {{ end }}
              href="{{ call $context.CategoryUrlFunc .ID }}">{{ .CategoryName }}</a>
    {{ end }}
</div>
```

I generally prefer to put complete elements in the clauses of if/else/end blocks, but, as this template shows, you can use the condition to select just the part of the element that differs, which is the class attribute in this case. Although there is less duplication, I find this more difficult to read, but it does serve to demonstrate that you can use the template system in a way that suits your personal preferences.

Displaying Category Navigation in the Product List Template

Listing 35-31 shows the changes required to the template that lists products to include the category filter features.

Listing 35-31. Displaying Categories in the product_list.html File in the templates Folder

```
{{ layout "store_layout.html" }}

{{ define "left_column" }}
    {{ $context := . }}
    {{ handler "category" "getbuttons" $context.SelectedCategory}}
{{end}}

{{ define "right_column" }}
    {{ $context := . }}
    {{ range $context.Products }}
        <div class="card card-outline-primary m-1 p-1">
            <div class="bg-faded p-1">
                <h4>
                    {{ .Name }}
                    <span class="badge rounded-pill bg-primary" style="float:right">
                        <small>{{ printf "$%.2f" .Price }}</small>
                    </span>
                </h4>
            </div>
            <div class="card-text p-1">{{ .Description }}</div>
        </div>
    {{ end }}
    {{ template "page_buttons.html" $context }}
{{end}}
```

The changes replace the placeholder message with the response from the GetButtons method defined in Listing 35-30.

Registering the Handler and Updating the Aliases

The final change is to update the aliases that map URLs onto the handler method, as shown in Listing 35-32.

Listing 35-32. Updating the Route Aliases in the main.go File in the sportsstore Folder

```
...
func createPipeline() pipeline.RequestPipeline {
    return pipeline.CreatePipeline(
        &basic.ServicesComponent{},
        &basic.LoggingComponent{},
        &basic.ErrorComponent{},
        &basic.StaticFileComponent{},
        handling.NewRouter(
            handling.HandlerEntry{ "",  store.ProductHandler{}},
            handling.HandlerEntry{ "",  store.CategoryHandler{}},
        ).AddMethodAlias("/", store.ProductHandler.GetProducts, 0, 1).
            AddMethodAlias("/products[/]?[A-zo-9]*?",
                store.ProductHandler.GetProducts, 0, 1),
    )
}
...
```

Compile and execute the project and request http://localhost:5000, and you will see the category buttons and be able to select products from a single category, as shown in Figure 35-4.

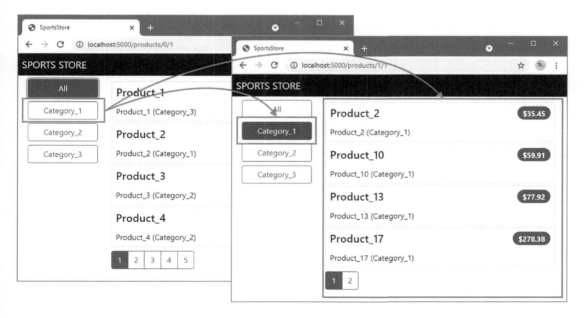

Figure 35-4. Filtering by category

Summary

In this chapter, I started the development of the SportsStore application, using the platform created in Chapters 32–34. I started with a basic data model and repository and created a handler that displays products, with support for pagination and filtering by category. I continue the development of the SportsStore application in the next chapter.

CHAPTER 36

SportsStore: Cart and Database

In this chapter, I continue the development of the SportsStore application, adding support for a shopping cart and introducing a database to replace the temporary repository I created in Chapter 35.

Tip You can download the example project for this chapter—and for all the other chapters in this book—from https://github.com/apress/pro-go. See Chapter 2 for how to get help if you have problems running the examples.

Building the Shopping Cart

The SportsStore application is proceeding nicely, but I cannot sell any products unless I implement a shopping cart, which will allow users to gather their selections together before checking out.

Defining the Cart Model and Repository

To define the cart data type, create the sportsstore/store/cart folder and add to it a file named cart.go with the content shown in Listing 36-1.

Listing 36-1. The Contents of the cart.go File in the store/cart Folder

```
package cart

import "sportsstore/models"

type CartLine struct {
    models.Product
    Quantity int
}

func (cl *CartLine) GetLineTotal() float64 {
    return cl.Price * float64(cl.Quantity)
}

type Cart interface {
```

```
    AddProduct(models.Product)
    GetLines() []*CartLine
    RemoveLineForProduct(id int)
    GetItemCount() int
    GetTotal() float64

    Reset()
}

type BasicCart struct {
    lines []*CartLine
}

func (cart *BasicCart) AddProduct(p models.Product) {
    for _, line := range cart.lines {
        if (line.Product.ID == p.ID) {
            line.Quantity++
            return
        }
    }
    cart.lines = append(cart.lines, &CartLine{
        Product: p, Quantity: 1,
    })
}

func (cart *BasicCart) GetLines() []*CartLine {
    return cart.lines
}

func (cart *BasicCart) RemoveLineForProduct(id int) {
    for index, line := range cart.lines {
        if (line.Product.ID == id) {
            cart.lines = append(cart.lines[0: index], cart.lines[index + 1:]...)
        }
    }
}

func (cart *BasicCart) GetItemCount() (total int) {
    for _, l := range cart.lines {
        total += l.Quantity
    }
    return
}

func (cart *BasicCart) GetTotal() (total float64) {
    for _, line := range cart.lines {
        total += float64(line.Quantity) * line.Product.Price
    }
    return
}
```

```go
func (cart *BasicCart) Reset() {
    cart.lines = []*CartLine{}
}
```

The Cart interface will be provided as a service, and I have defined a BasicCart struct that implements the Cart methods using a slice. To define the service, add a file named cart_service.go to the sportsstore/store/cart folder with the content shown in Listing 36-2.

Listing 36-2. The Contents of the cart_service.go File in the store/cart Folder

```go
package cart

import (
    "platform/services"
    "platform/sessions"
    "sportsstore/models"
    "encoding/json"
    "strings"
)

const CART_KEY string = "cart"

func RegisterCartService() {
    services.AddScoped(func(session sessions.Session) Cart {
        lines := []*CartLine {}
        sessionVal := session.GetValue(CART_KEY)
        if strVal, ok := sessionVal.(string); ok {
            json.NewDecoder(strings.NewReader(strVal)).Decode(&lines)
        }
        return &sessionCart{
            BasicCart: &BasicCart{ lines: lines},
            Session: session,
        }
    })
}

type sessionCart struct {
    *BasicCart
    sessions.Session
}

func (sc *sessionCart) AddProduct(p models.Product) {
    sc.BasicCart.AddProduct(p)
    sc.SaveToSession()
}

func (sc *sessionCart) RemoveLineForProduct(id int) {
    sc.BasicCart.RemoveLineForProduct(id)
    sc.SaveToSession()
}

func (sc *sessionCart) SaveToSession() {
```

```
    builder := strings.Builder{}
    json.NewEncoder(&builder).Encode(sc.lines)
    sc.Session.SetValue(CART_KEY, builder.String())
}

func (sc *sessionCart) Reset() {
    sc.lines = []*CartLine{}
    sc.SaveToSession()
}
```

The sessionCart struct responds to changes by adding a JSON representation of its CartLine values to the session. The RegisterCartService function creates a scoped Cart service that creates a sessionCart and populates its lines from the session JSON data.

Creating the Cart Request Handler

Add a file named cart_handler.go to the sportsstore/store folder with the content shown in Listing 36-3.

Listing 36-3. The Contents of the cart_handler.go File in the store Folder

```
package store

import (
    "platform/http/actionresults"
    "platform/http/handling"
    "sportsstore/models"
    "sportsstore/store/cart"
)

type CartHandler struct {
    models.Repository
    cart.Cart
    handling.URLGenerator
}

type CartTemplateContext struct {
    cart.Cart
    ProductListUrl string
    CartUrl string
    CheckoutUrl string
    RemoveUrl string
}

func (handler CartHandler) GetCart() actionresults.ActionResult {
    return actionresults.NewTemplateAction("cart.html", CartTemplateContext {
        Cart: handler.Cart,
        ProductListUrl: handler.mustGenerateUrl(ProductHandler.GetProducts, 0, 1),
        RemoveUrl: handler.mustGenerateUrl(CartHandler.PostRemoveFromCart),
    })
}
```

```
type CartProductReference struct {
    ID int
}

func (handler CartHandler) PostAddToCart(ref CartProductReference) actionresults.
ActionResult {
    p := handler.Repository.GetProduct(ref.ID)
    handler.Cart.AddProduct(p)
    return actionresults.NewRedirectAction(
        handler.mustGenerateUrl(CartHandler.GetCart))
}

func (handler CartHandler) PostRemoveFromCart(ref CartProductReference) actionresults.
ActionResult {
    handler.Cart.RemoveLineForProduct(ref.ID)
    return actionresults.NewRedirectAction(
        handler.mustGenerateUrl(CartHandler.GetCart))
}

func (handler CartHandler) mustGenerateUrl(method interface{}, data ...interface{}) string {
    url, err := handler.URLGenerator.GenerateUrl(method, data...)
    if (err != nil) {
        panic(err)
    }
    return url
}
```

The GetCart method will render a template that displays the contents of the user's cart. The PostAddToCart method will be called to add a product to the cart, after which the browser is redirected to the GetCart method. To create the template used by the GetCart method, add a file named cart.html to the templates folder with the content shown in Listing 36-4.

Listing 36-4. The Contents of the cart.html File in the templates Folder

```
{{ layout "simple_layout.html" }}
{{ $context := . }}

<div class="p-1">
    <h2>Your cart</h2>
    <table class="table table-bordered table-striped">
        <thead>
            <tr>
                <th>Quantity</th><th>Item</th>
                <th class="text-end">Price</th>
                <th class="text-end">Subtotal</th>
                <th />
            </tr>
        </thead>
        <tbody>
            {{ range $context.Cart.GetLines }}
                <tr>
                    <td class="text-start">{{ .Quantity }}</td>
```

```
                            <td class="text-start">{{ .Name }}</td>
                            <td class="text-end">{{ printf "$%.2f" .Price }}</td>
                            <td class="text-end">
                                {{ printf "$%.2f" .GetLineTotal }}
                            </td>
                            <td>
                                <form method="POST" action="{{ $context.RemoveUrl }}">
                                    <input type="hidden" name="id" value="{{ .ID }}" />
                                    <button class="btn btn-sm btn-danger" type="submit">
                                        Remove
                                    </button>
                                </form>
                            </td>
                        </tr>

                    {{ end }}
                </tbody>
                <tfoot>
                    <tr>
                        <td colspan="3" class="text-end">Total:</td>
                        <td class="text-end">
                            {{ printf "$%.2f" $context.Cart.GetTotal }}
                        </td>
                    </tr>
                </tfoot>
            </table>
            <div class="text-center">
                <a class="btn btn-secondary" href="{{ $context.ProductListUrl }}">
                    Continue shopping
                </a>
            </div>
        </div>
</div>
```

This template produces an HTML table with rows for each of the products the user has selected. There is also a button that returns the user to the list of products so that further selections can be made. To create the layout used for this template, add a file named simple_layout.html to the templates folder with the content shown in Listing 36-5.

Listing 36-5. The Contents of the simple_layout.html File in the templates Folder

```
<!DOCTYPE html>
<html>
<head>
    <meta name="viewport" content="width=device-width" />
    <title>SportsStore</title>
    <link href="/files/bootstrap.min.css" rel="stylesheet" />
</head>
<body>
    <div class="bg-dark text-white p-2">
        <div class="container-fluid">
            <div class="row">
                <div class="col navbar-brand">SPORTS STORE</div>
```

```
            </div>
         </div>
      </div>
      {{ body }}
   </body>
</html>
```

This layout displays the SportsStore header but does not apply the column layout that is used for the product list.

Adding Products to the Cart

Each product will be displayed with an Add To Cart button that will send a request to the `PostAddToCart` method created in Listing 36-3. First, add the elements shown in Listing 36-6, which define the button and the form that it submits.

Listing 36-6. Adding a Form in the product_list.html File in the templates Folder

```
{{ layout "store_layout.html" }}

{{ define "left_column" }}
    {{ $context := . }}
    {{ handler "category" "getbuttons" $context.SelectedCategory}}
{{end}}

{{ define "right_column" }}
    {{ $context := . }}
    {{ range $context.Products }}
        <div class="card card-outline-primary m-1 p-1">
            <div class="bg-faded p-1">
                <h4>
                    {{ .Name }}
                    <span class="badge rounded-pill bg-primary" style="float:right">
                        <small>{{ printf "$%.2f" .Price }}</small>
                    </span>
                </h4>
            </div>
            <div class="card-text p-1">
                <form method="POST" action="{{ $context.AddToCartUrl }}">
                    {{ .Description }}
                    <input type="hidden" name="id" value="{{.ID}}" />
                    <button type="submit"class="btn btn-success btn-sm pull-right"
                        style="float:right">
                            Add To Cart
                    </button>
                </form>
            </div>
        </div>
    {{ end }}
    {{ template "page_buttons.html" $context }}
{{end}}
```

To provide the template with the URL that is used in the form, make the changes shown in Listing 36-7 to its handler.

Listing 36-7. Adding Context Data in the product_handler.go File in the store Folder

```
package store

import (
    "sportsstore/models"
    "platform/http/actionresults"
    "platform/http/handling"
    "math"
)

const pageSize = 4

type ProductHandler struct {
    Repository models.Repository
    URLGenerator handling.URLGenerator
}

type ProductTemplateContext struct {
    Products []models.Product
    Page int
    PageCount int
    PageNumbers []int
    PageUrlFunc func(int) string
    SelectedCategory int
    AddToCartUrl string
}

func (handler ProductHandler) GetProducts(category,
        page int) actionresults.ActionResult {
    prods, total := handler.Repository.GetProductPageCategory(category,
        page, pageSize)
    pageCount := int(math.Ceil(float64(total) / float64(pageSize)))
    return actionresults.NewTemplateAction("product_list.html",
        ProductTemplateContext {
            Products: prods,
            Page: page,
            PageCount: pageCount,
            PageNumbers: handler.generatePageNumbers(pageCount),
            PageUrlFunc: handler.createPageUrlFunction(category),
            SelectedCategory: category,
            AddToCartUrl: mustGenerateUrl(handler.URLGenerator,
                CartHandler.PostAddToCart),
        })
}

func (handler ProductHandler) createPageUrlFunction(category int) func(int) string {
    return func(page int) string {
        url, _ := handler.URLGenerator.GenerateUrl(ProductHandler.GetProducts,
```

```
            category, page)
        return url
    }
}

func (handler ProductHandler) generatePageNumbers(pageCount int) (pages []int) {
    pages = make([]int, pageCount)
    for i := 0; i < pageCount; i++ {
        pages[i] = i + 1
    }
    return
}

func mustGenerateUrl(generator handling.URLGenerator, target interface{}) string {
    url, err := generator.GenerateUrl(target)
    if (err != nil) {
        panic(err)
    }
    return url;
}
```

The changes add a new property to the context struct used to pass data to the template, allowing the handler to provide a URL that can be used in the HTML form.

Configuring the Application

The final step to get the basic cart feature working is to configure the services, middleware, and handler required for sessions and the cart, as shown in Listing 36-8.

Listing 36-8. Configuring the Application for the Cart in the main.go File in the sportsstore Folder

```
package main

import (
    "sync"
    "platform/http"
    "platform/http/handling"
    "platform/services"
    "platform/pipeline"
    "platform/pipeline/basic"
    "sportsstore/store"
    "sportsstore/models/repo"
    "platform/sessions"
    "sportsstore/store/cart"
)

func registerServices() {
    services.RegisterDefaultServices()
    repo.RegisterMemoryRepoService()
    sessions.RegisterSessionService()
    cart.RegisterCartService()
```

```go
}

func createPipeline() pipeline.RequestPipeline {
    return pipeline.CreatePipeline(
        &basic.ServicesComponent{},
        &basic.LoggingComponent{},
        &basic.ErrorComponent{},
        &basic.StaticFileComponent{},
        &sessions.SessionComponent{},
        handling.NewRouter(
            handling.HandlerEntry{ "",  store.ProductHandler{}},
            handling.HandlerEntry{ "",  store.CategoryHandler{}},
            handling.HandlerEntry{ "", store.CartHandler{}},
            ).AddMethodAlias("/", store.ProductHandler.GetProducts, 0, 1).
            AddMethodAlias("/products[/]?[A-z0-9]*?",
                store.ProductHandler.GetProducts, 0, 1),
    )
}

func main() {
    registerServices()
    results, err := services.Call(http.Serve, createPipeline())
    if (err == nil) {
        (results[0].(*sync.WaitGroup)).Wait()
    } else {
        panic(err)
    }
}
```

Compile and execute the project and use a browser to request http://localhost:5000. The products are shown with an Add To Cart button that, when clicked, adds the product to the cart and redirects the browser to display the contents of the cart, as shown in Figure 36-1.

Figure 36-1. *Creating the store cart*

Adding the Cart Summary Widget

Users expect to see a summary of their product selections when they are browsing the list of available products. Add the method shown in Listing 36-9 to the CartHandler request handler.

Listing 36-9. Adding a Method in the cart_handler.go File in the store Folder

```
package store

import (
    "platform/http/actionresults"
    "platform/http/handling"
    "sportsstore/models"
    "sportsstore/store/cart"
)

type CartHandler struct {
    models.Repository
    cart.Cart
    handling.URLGenerator
}

type CartTemplateContext struct {
    cart.Cart
    ProductListUrl string
    CartUrl string
}

func (handler CartHandler) GetCart() actionresults.ActionResult {
```

999

```
    return actionresults.NewTemplateAction("cart.html", CartTemplateContext {
        Cart: handler.Cart,
        ProductListUrl: handler.mustGenerateUrl(ProductHandler.GetProducts, 0, 1),
    })
}

func (handler CartHandler) GetWidget() actionresults.ActionResult {
    return actionresults.NewTemplateAction("cart_widget.html", CartTemplateContext {
        Cart: handler.Cart,
        CartUrl: handler.mustGenerateUrl(CartHandler.GetCart),
    })
}

// ...statements omitted for brevity...
```

To define the template used by the new method, add a file named cart_widget.html to the templates folder with the content shown in Listing 36-10.

Listing 36-10. The Contents of the cart_widget.html File in the templates Folder

```
{{ $context := . }}
{{ $count := $context.Cart.GetItemCount }}
    <small class="navbar-text">
        {{ if gt $count 0 }}
            <b>Your cart:</b>
            {{ $count }} item(s)
            {{ printf "$%.2f" $context.Cart.GetTotal }}
        {{ else }}
            <span class="px-2 text-secondary">(empty cart)</span>
        {{ end }}
    </small>
<a href={{ $context.CartUrl }}
        class="btn btn-sm btn-secondary navbar-btn">
    <i class="fa fa-shopping-cart"></i>
</a>
```

Invoking the Handler and Adding the CSS Icon Stylesheet

Listing 36-10 invokes the GetWidget method to insert the cart widget into the layout. The cart widget template requires a shopping cart icon, which is provided by the excellent Font Awesome package. In Chapter 35, I copied the Bootstrap CSS file so that it can be served using the static file features provided by the web platform, but multiple files are required for the Font Awesome package, so Listing 36-11 adds a link element with a URL for a content distribution network. (This means that you will have to be online to see the icons. See https://fontawesome.com for details of how to download the files, which can be installed in the sportsstore/files folder.)

Listing 36-11. Adding a Stylesheet Link in the store_layout.html File in the templates Folder

```
<!DOCTYPE html>
<html>
<head>
    <meta name="viewport" content="width=device-width" />
    <title>SportsStore</title>
    <link href="/files/bootstrap.min.css" rel="stylesheet" />
    <link rel="stylesheet"
href="https://cdnjs.cloudflare.com/ajax/libs/font-awesome/5.15.4/css/all.min.css" />
</head>
<body>
    <div class="bg-dark text-white p-2">
        <div class="container-fluid">
            <div class="row">
                <div class="col navbar-brand">SPORTS STORE</div>
                <div class="col-6 navbar-text text-end">
                    {{ handler "cart" "getwidget" }}
                </div>
            </div>
        </div>
    </div>
    <div class="row m-1 p-1">
        <div id="sidebar" class="col-3">
            {{ template "left_column" . }}
        </div>
        <div class="col-9">
            {{ template "right_column" . }}
        </div>
    </div>
</body>
</html>
```

Compile and execute the project, and you will see the widget displayed in the page header. The widget will indicate that the cart is empty. Click one of the Add To Cart buttons and then click the Continue Shopping button to see the effect of the product selection reflected, shown in Figure 36-2.

Figure 36-2. *Displaying a cart widget*

Using a Database Repository

Most of the basic features are in place, and it is time to retire the temporary repository I created in Chapter 35 and replace it with one that uses a persistent database. I am going to use SQLite. Use a command prompt to run the command shown in Listing 36-12 in the sportsstore folder to download and install the SQLite driver, which also includes the SQLite runtime.

Listing 36-12. Installing the SQLite Driver and Database Package

```
go get modernc.org/sqlite
```

Creating the Repository Types

Add a file named sql_repo.go to the models/repo folder with the content shown in Listing 36-13, which defines the basic types for the SQL repository.

Listing 36-13. The Contents of the sql_repo.go File in the models/repo Folder

```
package repo

import (
    "database/sql"
    "platform/config"
    "platform/logging"
    "context"
)
```

```
type SqlRepository struct {
    config.Configuration
    logging.Logger
    Commands SqlCommands
    *sql.DB
    context.Context
}

type SqlCommands struct {
    Init,
    Seed,
    GetProduct,
    GetProducts,
    GetCategories,
    GetPage,
    GetPageCount,
    GetCategoryPage,
    GetCategoryPageCount *sql.Stmt
}
```

The SqlRepository struct will be used to implement the Repository interface and will be provided to the rest of the application as a service. This struct defines a *sql.DB field that provides access to the database and a Commands field, which is a collection of *sql.Stmt fields that will be populated with the prepared statements required to implement the features of the Repository interface.

Opening the Database and Loading the SQL Commands

In Chapter 26, I defined SQL commands as Go strings. In real projects, I prefer to define SQL commands in text files with a .sql file extension, which means that my editor can perform syntax checking. This means I need to open a database and then locate and process the SQL files that correspond to the fields defined by the SqlCommands struct defined in Listing 36-13. Add a file named sql_loader.go to the models/repo folder with the content shown in Listing 36-14.

Listing 36-14. The Contents of the sql_loader.go File in the models/repo Folder

```
package repo

import (
    "os"
    "database/sql"
    "reflect"
    "platform/config"
    "platform/logging"
    _ "modernc.org/sqlite"
)

func openDB(config config.Configuration, logger logging.Logger) (db *sql.DB,
        commands *SqlCommands, needInit bool) {
    driver := config.GetStringDefault("sql:driver_name", "sqlite")
    connectionStr, found := config.GetString("sql:connection_str")
    if !found {
```

```
        logger.Panic("Cannot read SQL connection string from config")
        return
    }
    if _, err := os.Stat(connectionStr); os.IsNotExist(err) {
        needInit = true
    }
    var err error
    if db, err = sql.Open(driver, connectionStr); err == nil {
        commands = loadCommands(db, config, logger)
    } else {
        logger.Panic(err.Error())
    }
    return
}

func loadCommands(db *sql.DB, config config.Configuration,
        logger logging.Logger) (commands *SqlCommands)  {
    commands = &SqlCommands {}
    commandVal := reflect.ValueOf(commands).Elem()
    commandType := reflect.TypeOf(commands).Elem()
    for i := 0; i < commandType.NumField(); i++ {
        commandName := commandType.Field(i).Name
        logger.Debugf("Loading SQL command: %v", commandName)
        stmt := prepareCommand(db, commandName, config, logger)
        commandVal.Field(i).Set(reflect.ValueOf(stmt))
    }
    return commands
}

func prepareCommand(db *sql.DB, command string, config config.Configuration,
        logger logging.Logger) *sql.Stmt {
    filename, found := config.GetString("sql:commands:" + command)
    if !found {
        logger.Panicf("Config does not contain location for SQL command: %v",
            command)
    }
    data, err := os.ReadFile(filename)
    if err != nil {
        logger.Panicf("Cannot read SQL command file: %v", filename)
    }
    statement, err := db.Prepare(string(data))
    if (err != nil) {
        logger.Panicf(err.Error())
    }
    return statement
}
```

The openDB function reads the database driver name and connection string from the configuration system and opens the database before calling the loadCommands function. The loadCommands function uses reflection to get a list of the fields defined by the SqlCommands struct and calls the prepareCommand for each one. The prepareCommand function gets the name of the file that contains the SQL for the command from the configuration system, reads the contents of the file, and creates a prepared statement, which is assigned to the SqlCommands field.

Defining the Seed and Initialization Statements

For each feature required by the Repository interface, I need to define a SQL file that contains the query and define a Go method that will execute it. I am going to start with the Seed and Init commands. The Seed command is required by the Repository interface, but the Init function is specific to the SqlRepository struct and will be used to create the database schema. Add a file named sql_initseed.go to the models/ repo folder with the contents shown in Listing 36-15.

Notice that all the queries used by the repository use the methods that accept a context.Context argument (ExecContext, QueryContext, etc.). The platform created in Chapters 32–34 passes Context values to middleware components and request handlers, so I have used them when querying the database.

Listing 36-15. The Contents of the sql_initseed.go File in the models/repo Folder

```go
package repo

func (repo *SqlRepository) Init() {
    if _, err := repo.Commands.Init.ExecContext(repo.Context); err != nil {
        repo.Logger.Panic("Cannot exec init command")
    }
}

func (repo *SqlRepository) Seed() {
    if _, err := repo.Commands.Seed.ExecContext(repo.Context); err != nil {
        repo.Logger.Panic("Cannot exec seed command")
    }
}
```

To create the SQL commands these methods use, create the sportsstore/sql folder and add to it a file named init_db.sql with the content shown in Listing 36-16.

Listing 36-16. The Contents of the init_db.sql File in the sql Folder

```sql
DROP TABLE IF EXISTS Products;
DROP TABLE IF EXISTS Categories;

CREATE TABLE IF NOT EXISTS Categories (
    Id INTEGER NOT NULL PRIMARY KEY,        Name TEXT
);

CREATE TABLE IF NOT EXISTS Products (
    Id INTEGER NOT NULL PRIMARY KEY,
    Name TEXT, Description TEXT,
    Category INTEGER, Price decimal(8, 2),
    CONSTRAINT CatRef FOREIGN KEY(Category) REFERENCES Categories (Id)
);
```

This file contains statements that drop and re-create Categories and Products tables. Add a file named seed_db.sql to the sportsstore/sql folder with the content shown in Listing 36-17.

Listing 36-17. The Contents of the seed_db.sql File in the sql Folder

```
INSERT INTO Categories(Id, Name) VALUES
        (1, "Watersports"), (2, "Soccer"), (3, "Chess");

INSERT INTO Products(Id, Name, Description, Category, Price) VALUES
        (1, "Kayak", "A boat for one person", 1, 275),
        (2, "Lifejacket", "Protective and fashionable", 1, 48.95),
        (3, "Soccer Ball", "FIFA-approved size and weight", 2, 19.50),
        (4, "Corner Flags", "Give your playing field a professional touch", 2, 34.95),
        (5, "Stadium", "Flat-packed 35,000-seat stadium", 2, 79500),
        (6, "Thinking Cap", "Improve brain efficiency by 75%", 3, 16),
        (7, "Unsteady Chair", "Secretly give your opponent a disadvantage", 3, 29.95),
        (8, "Human Chess Board", "A fun game for the family", 3, 75),
        (9, "Bling-Bling King", "Gold-plated, diamond-studded King", 3, 1200);
```

The file contains INSERT statements that create three categories and nine products, using values that will be familiar to anyone who has read any of my other books.

Defining the Basic Queries

To complete the repository, I have to work through the methods required by the Repository interface, defining a Go implementation of that method and the SQL query that it will use. Add a file named sql_basic_methods.go to the models/repo folder with the content shown in Listing 36-18.

Listing 36-18. The Contents of the sql_basic_methods.go File in the models/repo Folder

```go
package repo

import "sportsstore/models"

func (repo *SqlRepository) GetProduct(id int) (p models.Product) {
    row := repo.Commands.GetProduct.QueryRowContext(repo.Context, id)
    if row.Err() == nil {
        var err error
        if p, err = scanProduct(row); err != nil {
            repo.Logger.Panicf("Cannot scan data: %v", err.Error())
        }
    } else {
        repo.Logger.Panicf("Cannot exec GetProduct command: %v", row.Err().Error())
    }
    return
}

func (repo *SqlRepository) GetProducts() (results []models.Product) {
    rows, err := repo.Commands.GetProducts.QueryContext(repo.Context)
    if err == nil {
        if results, err = scanProducts(rows); err != nil {
            repo.Logger.Panicf("Cannot scan data: %v", err.Error())
            return
        }
```

```
        } else {
            repo.Logger.Panicf("Cannot exec GetProducts command: %v", err)
        }
        return
}

func (repo *SqlRepository) GetCategories() []models.Category {
    results := make([]models.Category, 0, 10)
    rows, err := repo.Commands.GetCategories.QueryContext(repo.Context)
    if err == nil {
        for rows.Next() {
            c := models.Category{}
            if err := rows.Scan(&c.ID, &c.CategoryName); err != nil {
                repo.Logger.Panicf("Cannot scan data: %v", err.Error())
            }
            results = append(results, c)
        }
    } else {
        repo.Logger.Panicf("Cannot exec GetCategories command: %v", err)
    }
    return results
}
```

Listing 36-18 implements the GetProduct, GetProducts, and GetCategories methods. To define the functions that scan Product values from the SQL results, add a file named sql_scan.go to the models/repo folder with the content shown in Listing 36-19.

Listing 36-19. The Contents of the sql_scan.go File in the models/repo Folder

```
package repo

import (
    "database/sql"
    "sportsstore/models"
)

func scanProducts(rows *sql.Rows) (products []models.Product, err error) {
    products = make([]models.Product, 0, 10)
    for rows.Next() {
        p := models.Product{ Category: &models.Category{}}
        err = rows.Scan(&p.ID, &p.Name, &p.Description, &p.Price,
            &p.Category.ID, &p.Category.CategoryName)
        if (err == nil) {
            products = append(products, p)
        } else {
            return
        }
    }
    return
}

func scanProduct(row *sql.Row) (p models.Product, err error) {
```

```
    p = models.Product{ Category: &models.Category{}}
    err = row.Scan(&p.ID, &p.Name, &p.Description, &p.Price, &p.Category.ID,
        &p.Category.CategoryName)
    return p, err
}
```

The scanProducts function scans values when there are multiple rows, while the scanProduct function does the same thing for results with a single row.

Defining the SQL Files for the Basic Queries

Now comes the process of defining the SQL files for each query. Add a file named get_product.sql to the sportsstore/sql folder with the content shown in Listing 36-20.

Listing 36-20. The Contents of the get_product.sql File in the sql Folder

```
SELECT Products.Id, Products.Name, Products.Description, Products.Price,
    Categories.Id, Categories.Name
FROM Products, Categories
WHERE Products.Category = Categories.Id
AND Products.Id = ?
```

This query produces a single row containing the details for a product with a specified Id. Add a file named get_products.sql to the sportsstore/sql folder with the content shown in Listing 36-21.

Listing 36-21. The Contents of the get_products.sql File in the sql Folder

```
SELECT Products.Id, Products.Name, Products.Description, Products.Price,
    Categories.Id, Categories.Name
FROM Products, Categories
WHERE Products.Category = Categories.Id
ORDER BY Products.Id
```

This query produces rows for all the products in the database. Next, add a file named get_categories.sql to the sportsstore/sql folder with the content shown in Listing 36-22.

Listing 36-22. The Contents of the get_categories.sql File in the sql Folder

```
SELECT Categories.Id, Categories.Name
FROM Categories ORDER BY Categories.Id
```

This query selects all of the rows in the Categories folder.

Defining the Paged Queries

The methods for paged data are more complex because they have to perform one query for a page of data and query one to get the total number of available results. Add a file named sql_page_methods.go to the sportsstore/models/repo folder with the content shown in Listing 36-23.

Listing 36-23. The Contents of the sql_page_methods.go File in the models/repo Folder

```go
package repo

import "sportsstore/models"

func (repo *SqlRepository) GetProductPage(page,
        pageSize int) (products []models.Product, totalAvailable int) {
    rows, err := repo.Commands.GetPage.QueryContext(repo.Context,
        pageSize, (pageSize * page) - pageSize)
    if err == nil {
        if products, err = scanProducts(rows); err != nil {
            repo.Logger.Panicf("Cannot scan data: %v", err.Error())
            return
        }
    } else {
        repo.Logger.Panicf("Cannot exec GetProductPage command: %v", err)
        return
    }
    row := repo.Commands.GetPageCount.QueryRowContext(repo.Context)
    if row.Err() == nil {
        if err := row.Scan(&totalAvailable); err != nil {
            repo.Logger.Panicf("Cannot scan data: %v", err.Error())
        }
    } else {
        repo.Logger.Panicf("Cannot exec GetPageCount command: %v", row.Err().Error())
    }
    return
}

func (repo *SqlRepository) GetProductPageCategory(categoryId int, page,
        pageSize int) (products []models.Product, totalAvailable int) {
    if (categoryId == 0) {
        return repo.GetProductPage(page, pageSize)
    }
    rows, err := repo.Commands.GetCategoryPage.QueryContext(repo.Context, categoryId,
        pageSize, (pageSize * page) - pageSize)
    if err == nil {
        if products, err = scanProducts(rows); err != nil {
            repo.Logger.Panicf("Cannot scan data: %v", err.Error())
            return
        }
    } else {
        repo.Logger.Panicf("Cannot exec GetProductPage command: %v", err)
        return
    }
    row := repo.Commands.GetCategoryPageCount.QueryRowContext(repo.Context,
        categoryId)
    if row.Err() == nil {
        if err := row.Scan(&totalAvailable); err != nil {
            repo.Logger.Panicf("Cannot scan data: %v", err.Error())
        }
```

```
    } else {
        repo.Logger.Panicf("Cannot exec GetCategoryPageCount command: %v",
            row.Err().Error())
    }
    return
}
```

To define the main SQL query used by the GetProductPage method, add a file named get_product_page.sql to the sportsstore/sql folder with the content shown in Listing 36-24.

Listing 36-24. The Contents of the get_product_page.sql File in the sql Folder

```
SELECT Products.Id, Products.Name, Products.Description, Products.Price,
    Categories.Id, Categories.Name
FROM Products, Categories
WHERE Products.Category = Categories.Id
ORDER BY Products.Id
LIMIT ? OFFSET ?
```

To define the query used to get the total number of products in the database, add a file named get_page_count.sql to the sportsstore/sql folder with the content shown in Listing 36-25.

Listing 36-25. The Contents of the get_page_count.sql File in the sql Folder

```
SELECT COUNT (Products.Id)
FROM Products, Categories
WHERE Products.Category = Categories.Id;
```

To define the main query used by the GetProductPageCategory method, add a file named get_category_product_page.sql to the sportsstore/sql folder with the content shown in Listing 36-26.

Listing 36-26. The Contents of the get_category_product_page.sql File in the sql Folder

```
SELECT Products.Id, Products.Name, Products.Description, Products.Price,
    Categories.Id, Categories.Name
FROM Products, Categories
WHERE Products.Category = Categories.Id AND        Products.Category = ?
ORDER BY Products.Id
LIMIT ? OFFSET ?
```

To define the query that determines how many products are in a specific category, add a file named get_category_product_page_count.sql to the sportsstore/sql folder with the content shown in Listing 36-27.

Listing 36-27. The Contents of the get_category_product_page_count.sql File in the sql Folder

```
SELECT COUNT (Products.Id)
FROM Products, Categories
WHERE Products.Category = Categories.Id AND Products.Category = ?
```

Defining the SQL Repository Service

To define the function that will register the repository service, add a file named `sql_service.go` to the `sportssstore/models/repo` folder with the content shown in Listing 36-28.

Listing 36-28. The Contents of the sql_service.go File in the models/repo Folder

```
package repo

import (
    "sync"
    "context"
    "database/sql"
    "platform/services"
    "platform/config"
    "platform/logging"
    "sportsstore/models"
)

func RegisterSqlRepositoryService() {
    var db *sql.DB
    var commands *SqlCommands
    var needInit bool
    loadOnce := sync.Once {}
    resetOnce := sync.Once {}
    services.AddScoped(func (ctx context.Context, config config.Configuration,
            logger logging.Logger) models.Repository {
        loadOnce.Do(func () {
            db, commands, needInit = openDB(config, logger)
        })
        repo := &SqlRepository{
            Configuration: config,
            Logger: logger,
            Commands: *commands,
            DB: db,
            Context: ctx,
        }
        resetOnce.Do(func() {
            if needInit || config.GetBoolDefault("sql:always_reset", true) {
                repo.Init()
                repo.Seed()
            }
        })
        return repo
    })
}
```

The database is opened the first time a dependency on the `Repository` interface is resolved so that the commands are prepared only once. A configuration setting specifies whether the database should be reset every time the application starts, which is useful during development, and this is done by executing the `Init` method, followed by the `Seed` method.

Configuring the Application to Use the SQL Repository

Listing 36-29 defines the configuration settings that specify the locations of the SQL files. The code that loads these files will panic if these files cannot be loaded, so it is important to ensure that the paths specified match those used to create the files.

Listing 36-29. Defining Configuration Settings in the config.json File in the sportsstore Folder

```
{
    "logging" : {
        "level": "debug"
    },
    "files": {
        "path": "files"
    },
    "templates": {
        "path": "templates/*.html",
        "reload": true
    },
    "sessions": {
        "key": "MY_SESSION_KEY",
        "cyclekey": true
    },
    "sql": {
        "connection_str": "store.db",
        "always_reset": true,
        "commands": {
            "Init":                  "sql/init_db.sql",
            "Seed":                  "sql/seed_db.sql",
            "GetProduct":            "sql/get_product.sql",
            "GetProducts":           "sql/get_products.sql",
            "GetCategories":         "sql/get_categories.sql",
            "GetPage":               "sql/get_product_page.sql",
            "GetPageCount":          "sql/get_page_count.sql",
            "GetCategoryPage":       "sql/get_category_product_page.sql",
            "GetCategoryPageCount": "sql/get_category_product_page_count.sql"
        }
    }
}
```

The final change is to register the SQL repository so that it is used to resolve dependencies on the Repository interface and comment out the statement that registered the temporary repository, as shown in Listing 36-30.

Listing 36-30. Changing the Repository Service in the main.go File in the sportsstore Folder

```
...
func registerServices() {
    services.RegisterDefaultServices()
    //repo.RegisterMemoryRepoService()
    repo.RegisterSqlRepositoryService()
```

```
    sessions.RegisterSessionService()
    cart.RegisterCartService()
}
...
```

Compile and execute the project and use a browser to request http://localhost:5000, and you will see data that is read from the database, as shown in Figure 36-3.

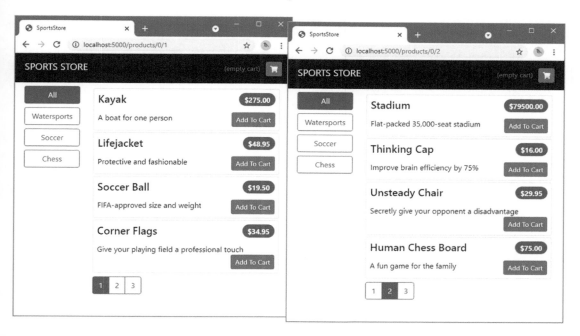

Figure 36-3. *Using data from the database*

Summary

In this chapter, I continued the development of the SportsStore application by adding support for the shopping cart and replacing the temporary repository with one that uses a SQL database. I continue the development of the SportsStore application in the next chapter.

CHAPTER 37

SportsStore: Checkout and Administration

In this chapter, I continue the development of the SportsStore application by adding a checkout process and starting work on the administration features.

■ **Tip** You can download the example project for this chapter—and for all the other chapters in this book—from https://github.com/apress/pro-go. See Chapter 2 for how to get help if you have problems running the examples.

Creating the Checkout Process

To complete the store experience, I need to let the user check out and complete an order. In this section, I will extend the data model to describe shipping details and create handlers to capture those details and use them to store an order in the database. Most e-commerce sites would not simply stop there, of course, and I have not provided support for processing credit cards or other forms of payment. But I want to keep things focused on Go, so a simple database entry will do.

Defining the Model

To define the type that will represent a user's shipping details and product selections, add a file named order.go to the models folder with the content shown in Listing 37-1.

Listing 37-1. The Contents of the order.go File in the models Folder

```
package models

type Order struct {
    ID int
    ShippingDetails
    Products []ProductSelection
    Shipped bool
}
```

© Adam Freeman 2022
A. Freeman, *Pro Go*, https://doi.org/10.1007/978-1-4842-7355-5_37

```
type ShippingDetails struct {
    Name string `validation:"required"`
    StreetAddr string `validation:"required"`
    City string `validation:"required"`
    State string `validation:"required"`
    Zip string `validation:"required"`
    Country string `validation:"required"`
}

type ProductSelection struct{
    Quantity int
    Product
}
```

The Order type defines a ShippingDetails field, which will be used to represent the customer's shipping details and which has been defined with struct tags for the platform validation feature. There is also a Products field, which will be used to store the products and quantities the customer has ordered.

Extending the Repository

The next step is to extend the repository so that it can be used to store and retrieve orders. Add the methods shown in Listing 37-2 to the repository.go file in the sportsstore/models folder.

Listing 37-2. Adding Interface Methods in the repository.go File in the models Folder

```
package models

type Repository interface {

    GetProduct(id int) Product

    GetProducts() []Product

    GetProductPage(page, pageSize int) (products []Product, totalAvailable int)

    GetProductPageCategory(categoryId int, page, pageSize int) (products []Product,
        totalAvailable int)

    GetCategories() []Category

    GetOrder(id int) Order
    GetOrders() []Order
    SaveOrder(*Order)

    Seed()
}
```

Listing 37-3 shows the changes required to the SQL file that which create new tables for storing order data.

Listing 37-3. Adding Tables in the init_db.sql File in the sql Folder

```
DROP TABLE IF EXISTS OrderLines;
DROP TABLE IF EXISTS Orders;
DROP TABLE IF EXISTS Products;
DROP TABLE IF EXISTS Categories;

CREATE TABLE IF NOT EXISTS Categories (
    Id INTEGER NOT NULL PRIMARY KEY,        Name TEXT
);

CREATE TABLE IF NOT EXISTS Products (
    Id INTEGER NOT NULL PRIMARY KEY,
    Name TEXT, Description TEXT,
    Category INTEGER, Price decimal(8, 2),
    CONSTRAINT CatRef FOREIGN KEY(Category) REFERENCES Categories (Id)
);

CREATE TABLE IF NOT EXISTS OrderLines (
    Id INTEGER NOT NULL PRIMARY KEY,
    OrderId INT, ProductId INT, Quantity INT,
    CONSTRAINT OrderRef FOREIGN KEY(ProductId) REFERENCES Products (Id)
    CONSTRAINT OrderRef FOREIGN KEY(OrderId) REFERENCES Orders (Id)
);

CREATE TABLE IF NOT EXISTS Orders (
    Id INTEGER NOT NULL PRIMARY KEY,
    Name TEXT NOT NULL,
    StreetAddr TEXT NOT NULL,
    City TEXT NOT NULL,
    Zip TEXT NOT NULL,
    Country TEXT NOT NULL,
    Shipped BOOLEAN
);
```

To define some seed data, add the statements shown in Listing 37-4 to the seed_db.sql file in the sportsstore/sql folder.

Listing 37-4. Adding Seed Data in the seed_db.sql File in the sql Folder

```
INSERT INTO Categories(Id, Name) VALUES
        (1, "Watersports"), (2, "Soccer"), (3, "Chess");

INSERT INTO Products(Id, Name, Description, Category, Price) VALUES
        (1, "Kayak", "A boat for one person", 1, 275),
        (2, "Lifejacket", "Protective and fashionable", 1, 48.95),
        (3, "Soccer Ball", "FIFA-approved size and weight", 2, 19.50),
        (4, "Corner Flags", "Give your playing field a professional touch", 2, 34.95),
        (5, "Stadium", "Flat-packed 35,000-seat stadium", 2, 79500),
        (6, "Thinking Cap", "Improve brain efficiency by 75%", 3, 16),
        (7, "Unsteady Chair", "Secretly give your opponent a disadvantage", 3, 29.95),
        (8, "Human Chess Board", "A fun game for the family", 3, 75),
        (9, "Bling-Bling King", "Gold-plated, diamond-studded King", 3, 1200);
```

1017

```
INSERT INTO Orders(Id, Name, StreetAddr, City, Zip, Country, Shipped) VALUES
        (1, "Alice", "123 Main St", "New Town", "12345", "USA", false),
        (2, "Bob", "The Grange", "Upton", "UP12 6YT", "UK", false);

INSERT INTO OrderLines(Id, OrderId, ProductId, Quantity) VALUES
        (1, 1, 1, 1), (2, 1, 2, 2), (3, 1, 8, 1), (4, 2, 5, 2);
```

Disabling the Temporary Repository

The temporary repository created in Chapter 35 no longer defines all the methods specified by the Repository interface. In a real project, I typically switch back to the memory repository when adding a new feature, like orders, and then switch back to SQL once I understand what is required. But, for this project, I am simply going to comment out the code that creates the memory-based service, as shown in Listing 37-5, so that it doesn't cause a compiler error.

Listing 37-5. Commenting Code in the memory_repo.go File in the models/repo Folder

```
package repo

import (
//    "platform/services"
    "sportsstore/models"
    "math"
)

// func RegisterMemoryRepoService() {
//     services.AddSingleton(func() models.Repository {
//         repo := &MemoryRepo{}
//         repo.Seed()
//         return repo
//     })
// }

type MemoryRepo struct {
    products []models.Product
    categories []models.Category
}

// ...other statements omitted for brevity...
```

Defining the Repository Methods and Commands

The next step is to define and implement the new Repository methods and the SQL files on which they will rely. Listing 37-6 adds new commands to the struct used to load SQL files for the database.

Listing 37-6. Adding Commands in the sql_repo.go File in the models/repo Folder

```
package repo

import (
    "database/sql"
    "platform/config"
    "platform/logging"
    "context"
)

type SqlRepository struct {
    config.Configuration
    logging.Logger
    Commands SqlCommands
    *sql.DB
    context.Context
}

type SqlCommands struct {
    Init,
    Seed,
    GetProduct,
    GetProducts,
    GetCategories,
    GetPage,
    GetPageCount,
    GetCategoryPage,
    GetCategoryPageCount,
    GetOrder,
    GetOrderLines,
    GetOrders,
    GetOrdersLines,
    SaveOrder,
    SaveOrderLine *sql.Stmt
}
```

Defining the SQL Files

Add a file named get_order.sql to the sportsstore/sql folder with the content shown in Listing 37-7.

Listing 37-7. The Contents of the get_order.sql File in the sql Folder

```
SELECT Orders.Id, Orders.Name, Orders.StreetAddr, Orders.City, Orders.Zip,
    Orders.Country, Orders.Shipped
FROM Orders
WHERE Orders.Id = ?
```

This query retrieves the details of an order. To define the query that will get details of the products that were ordered, add a file named get_order_lines.sql to the sportsstore/sql folder with the content shown in Listing 37-8.

Listing 37-8. The Contents of the get_order_lines.sql File in the sql Folder

```
SELECT OrderLines.Quantity, Products.Id, Products.Name, Products.Description,
    Products.Price, Categories.Id, Categories.Name
FROM Orders, OrderLines, Products, Categories
WHERE Orders.Id = OrderLines.OrderId
    AND OrderLines.ProductId = Products.Id
    AND Products.Category = Categories.Id
    AND Orders.Id = ?
ORDER BY Products.Id
```

To define the query that will get all the orders in the database, add a file named get_orders.sql to the sportsstore/sql folder with the content shown in Listing 37-9.

Listing 37-9. The Contents of the get_orders.sql Folder in the sql Folder

```
SELECT Orders.Id, Orders.Name, Orders.StreetAddr, Orders.City, Orders.Zip, Orders.Country,
Orders.Shipped
FROM Orders
ORDER BY Orders.Shipped, Orders.Id
```

To define the query that will get all the product details associated with all orders, add a file named get_orders_lines.sql to the sportsstore/sql folder with the content shown in Listing 37-10.

Listing 37-10. The Contents of the get_orders_lines.sql File in the sql Folder

```
SELECT Orders.Id, OrderLines.Quantity, Products.Id, Products.Name,
    Products.Description, Products.Price, Categories.Id, Categories.Name
FROM Orders, OrderLines, Products, Categories
WHERE Orders.Id = OrderLines.OrderId
    AND OrderLines.ProductId = Products.Id
    AND Products.Category = Categories.Id
ORDER BY Orders.Id
```

To define the statement that will store an order, add a file named save_order.sql to the sportsstore/sql folder with the content shown in Listing 37-11.

Listing 37-11. The Contents of the save_order.sql File in the sql Folder

```
INSERT INTO Orders(Name, StreetAddr, City, Zip, Country, Shipped)
VALUES (?, ?, ?, ?, ?, ?)
```

To define the statement that will store details of a product selection associated with an order, add a file named save_order_line.sql to the sportsstore/sql folder with the content shown in Listing 37-12.

Listing 37-12. The Contents of the save_order_line.sql File in the sql Folder

```
INSERT INTO OrderLines(OrderId, ProductId, Quantity)
VALUES (?, ?, ?)
```

Listing 37-13 adds configuration settings for the new SQL files.

Listing 37-13. Adding Configuration Settings in the config.json File in the sportsstore Folder

```
...
"sql": {
    "connection_str": "store.db",
    "always_reset": true,
    "commands": {
        "Init":                   "sql/init_db.sql",
        "Seed":                   "sql/seed_db.sql",
        "GetProduct":             "sql/get_product.sql",
        "GetProducts":            "sql/get_products.sql",
        "GetCategories":          "sql/get_categories.sql",
        "GetPage":                "sql/get_product_page.sql",
        "GetPageCount":           "sql/get_page_count.sql",
        "GetCategoryPage":        "sql/get_category_product_page.sql",
        "GetCategoryPageCount": "sql/get_category_product_page_count.sql",
        "GetOrder": "sql/get_order.sql",
        "GetOrderLines": "sql/get_order_lines.sql",
        "GetOrders": "sql/get_orders.sql",
        "GetOrdersLines": "sql/get_orders_lines.sql",
        "SaveOrder": "sql/save_order.sql",
        "SaveOrderLine": "sql/save_order_line.sql"
    }
}
...
```

Implementing the Repository Methods

Add a file named sql_orders_one.go to the sportsstore/models/repo folder with the content shown in Listing 37-14.

Listing 37-14. The Contents of the sql_orders_one.go File in the models/repo Folder

```
package repo

import "sportsstore/models"

func (repo *SqlRepository) GetOrder(id int) (order models.Order) {
    order = models.Order { Products: []models.ProductSelection {}}
    row := repo.Commands.GetOrder.QueryRowContext(repo.Context, id)
    if row.Err() == nil {
        err := row.Scan(&order.ID, &order.Name, &order.StreetAddr, &order.City,
            &order.Zip, &order.Country, &order.Shipped)
        if (err != nil) {
            repo.Logger.Panicf("Cannot scan order data: %v", err.Error())
            return
        }
        lineRows, err := repo.Commands.GetOrderLines.QueryContext(repo.Context, id)
        if (err == nil) {
            for lineRows.Next() {
```

```
            ps := models.ProductSelection {
                Product: models.Product{ Category: &models.Category{}},
            }
            err = lineRows.Scan(&ps.Quantity, &ps.Product.ID, &ps.Product.Name,
                &ps.Product.Description,&ps.Product.Price,
                &ps.Product.Category.ID, &ps.Product.Category.CategoryName)
            if err == nil {
                order.Products = append(order.Products, ps)
            } else {
                repo.Logger.Panicf("Cannot scan order line data: %v",
                    err.Error())
            }
        }
    } else {
        repo.Logger.Panicf("Cannot exec GetOrderLines command: %v", err.Error())
    }
} else {
    repo.Logger.Panicf("Cannot exec GetOrder command: %v", row.Err().Error())
}
return
}
```

This method queries the database for an order and then queries again for details of the product selections associated with that order. Next, add a file named sql_orders_all.go in the sportsstore/models/repo folder with the content shown in Listing 37-15.

Listing 37-15. The Contents of the sql_orders_all.go File in the models/repo Folder

```
package repo

import "sportsstore/models"

func (repo *SqlRepository) GetOrders() []models.Order {
    orderMap := make(map[int]*models.Order, 10)
    orderRows, err := repo.Commands.GetOrders.QueryContext(repo.Context)
    if err != nil {
        repo.Logger.Panicf("Cannot exec GetOrders command: %v", err.Error())
    }
    for orderRows.Next() {
        order := models.Order { Products: []models.ProductSelection {}}
        err := orderRows.Scan(&order.ID, &order.Name, &order.StreetAddr, &order.City,
            &order.Zip, &order.Country, &order.Shipped)
        if (err != nil) {
            repo.Logger.Panicf("Cannot scan order data: %v", err.Error())
            return []models.Order {}
        }
        orderMap[order.ID] = &order
    }
```

```
    lineRows, err := repo.Commands.GetOrdersLines.QueryContext(repo.Context)
    if (err != nil) {
        repo.Logger.Panicf("Cannot exec GetOrdersLines command: %v", err.Error())
    }
    for lineRows.Next() {
        var order_id int
        ps := models.ProductSelection {
            Product: models.Product{ Category: &models.Category{} },
        }
        err = lineRows.Scan(&order_id, &ps.Quantity, &ps.Product.ID,
            &ps.Product.Name, &ps.Product.Description, &ps.Product.Price,
            &ps.Product.Category.ID, &ps.Product.Category.CategoryName)
        if err == nil {
            orderMap[order_id].Products = append(orderMap[order_id].Products, ps)
        } else {
            repo.Logger.Panicf("Cannot scan order line data: %v", err.Error())
        }
    }
    orders := make([]models.Order, 0, len(orderMap))
    for _, o := range orderMap {
        orders = append(orders, *o)
    }
    return orders
}
```

This method queries the database for all the orders and their related product selections. To implement the final method, add a file named sql_orders_save.go to the sportsstore/models/repo folder with the content shown in Listing 37-16.

Listing 37-16. The Contents of the sql_orders_save.go File in the models/repo Folder

```
package repo

import "sportsstore/models"

func (repo *SqlRepository) SaveOrder(order *models.Order) {
    tx, err := repo.DB.Begin()
    if err != nil {
        repo.Logger.Panicf("Cannot create transaction: %v", err.Error())
        return
    }
    result, err :=  tx.StmtContext(repo.Context,
        repo.Commands.SaveOrder).Exec(order.Name, order.StreetAddr, order.City,
            order.Zip, order.Country, order.Shipped)
    if err != nil {
        repo.Logger.Panicf("Cannot exec SaveOrder command: %v", err.Error())
        tx.Rollback()
        return
    }
```

```
    id, err := result.LastInsertId()
    if err != nil {
        repo.Logger.Panicf("Cannot get inserted ID: %v", err.Error())
        tx.Rollback()
        return
    }
    statement := tx.StmtContext(repo.Context, repo.Commands.SaveOrderLine)
    for _, sel := range order.Products {
        _, err := statement.Exec(id, sel.Product.ID, sel.Quantity)
        if err != nil {
            repo.Logger.Panicf("Cannot exec SaveOrderLine command: %v", err.Error())
            tx.Rollback()
            return
        }
    }
    err = tx.Commit()
    if err != nil {
        repo.Logger.Panicf("Transaction cannot be committed: %v", err.Error())
        err = tx.Rollback()
        if err != nil {
            repo.Logger.Panicf("Transaction cannot be rolled back: %v", err.Error())
        }
    }
    order.ID = int(id)
}
```

This method uses a transaction to ensure that a new order and its related product selections are added to the database. If the transaction fails, then the changes are rolled back.

Creating the Request Handler and Templates

The next step is to define the request handler that will allow the user to provide their shipping details and check out. As noted at the start of this chapter, storing the order will complete the checkout process, although real online stores would prompt the user to provide payment. Add a file named order_handler.go to the sportsstore/store folder with the content shown in Listing 37-17.

Listing 37-17. The Contents of the order_handler.go File in the store Folder

```
package store

import (
    "encoding/json"
    "platform/http/actionresults"
    "platform/http/handling"
    "platform/sessions"
    "platform/validation"
    "sportsstore/models"
    "sportsstore/store/cart"
    "strings"
)
```

```
type OrderHandler struct {
    cart.Cart
    sessions.Session
    Repository models.Repository
    URLGenerator handling.URLGenerator
    validation.Validator
}

type OrderTemplateContext struct {
    models.ShippingDetails
    ValidationErrors [][]string
    CancelUrl string
}

func (handler OrderHandler) GetCheckout() actionresults.ActionResult {
    context := OrderTemplateContext {}
    jsonData := handler.Session.GetValueDefault("checkout_details", "")
    if jsonData != nil {
        json.NewDecoder(strings.NewReader(jsonData.(string))).Decode(&context)
    }
    context.CancelUrl = mustGenerateUrl(handler.URLGenerator, CartHandler.GetCart)
    return actionresults.NewTemplateAction("checkout.html", context)
}

func (handler OrderHandler) PostCheckout(details models.ShippingDetails) actionresults.
ActionResult {
    valid, errors := handler.Validator.Validate(details)
    if (!valid) {
        ctx := OrderTemplateContext {
            ShippingDetails: details,
            ValidationErrors: [][]string {},
        }
        for _, err := range errors {
            ctx.ValidationErrors = append(ctx.ValidationErrors,
                []string { err.FieldName, err.Error.Error()})
        }

        builder := strings.Builder{}
        json.NewEncoder(&builder).Encode(ctx)
        handler.Session.SetValue("checkout_details", builder.String())
        redirectUrl := mustGenerateUrl(handler.URLGenerator,
            OrderHandler.GetCheckout)
        return actionresults.NewRedirectAction(redirectUrl)
    } else {
        handler.Session.SetValue("checkout_details", "")
    }
    order := models.Order {
        ShippingDetails: details,
        Products: []models.ProductSelection {},
    }
    for _, cl := range handler.Cart.GetLines() {
```

```
        order.Products = append(order.Products, models.ProductSelection {
            Quantity: cl.Quantity,
            Product: cl.Product,
        })
    }
    handler.Repository.SaveOrder(&order)
    handler.Cart.Reset()
    targetUrl, _ := handler.URLGenerator.GenerateUrl(OrderHandler.GetSummary,
        order.ID)
    return actionresults.NewRedirectAction(targetUrl)
}

func (handler OrderHandler) GetSummary(id int) actionresults.ActionResult {
    targetUrl, _ := handler.URLGenerator.GenerateUrl(ProductHandler.GetProducts,
        0, 1)
    return actionresults.NewTemplateAction("checkout_summary.html", struct {
        ID int
        TargetUrl string
    }{ ID: id, TargetUrl: targetUrl})
}
```

This handler defines three methods. The GetCheckout method will display an HTML form that allows the user to enter their shipping details and will display any validation errors from previous attempts to check out.

The PostCheckout method is the target of the form rendered by the GetCheckout method. This method validates the data supplied by the user, and if there are errors, it redirects the browser back to the GetCheckout method. I use the session to pass data from the PostCheckout method to the GetCheckout method, encoding and decoding the data as JSON so it can be stored in the session cookie.

If there are no validation errors, the PostCheckout method creates an Order, using the shipping details provided by the user and the product details obtained from the Cart, which the handler obtains as a service. The Order is stored using the repository, and the browser is redirected to the GetSummary method, which renders a template that displays a summary.

To create the template for the shipping details, add a file named checkout.html to the sportsstore/templates folder with the content shown in Listing 37-18.

Listing 37-18. The Contents of the checkout.html File in the templates Folder

```
{{ layout "simple_layout.html" }}
{{ $context := .}}
{{ $details := .ShippingDetails }}

<div class="p-2">
    <h2>Check out now</h2>
    Please enter your details, and we'll ship your goods right away!
</div>

{{ if gt (len $context.ValidationErrors) 0}}
    <ul class="text-danger mt-3">
        {{ range $context.ValidationErrors }}
            <li>
                {{ index . 0 }}: {{ index . 1 }}
            </li>
```

```
        {{ end }}
    </ul>
{{ end }}

<form method="POST" class="p-2">
    <h3>Ship to</h3>
    <div class="form-group">
        <label class="form-label">Name:</label>
        <input name="name" class="form-control" value="{{ $details.Name }}" />
    </div>
    <div class="form-group">
        <label>Street Address:</label>
        <input name="streetaddr" class="form-control"
            value="{{ $details.StreetAddr }}" />
    </div>
    <div class="form-group">
        <label>City:</label>
        <input name="city" class="form-control" value="{{ $details.City }}" />
    </div>
    <div class="form-group">
        <label>State:</label>
        <input name="state" class="form-control" value="{{ $details.State }}" />
    </div>
    <div class="form-group">
        <label>Zip:</label>
        <input name="zip" class="form-control" value="{{ $details.Zip }}" />
    </div>
    <div class="form-group">
        <label>Country:</label>
        <input name="country" class="form-control" value="{{ $details.Country }}" />
    </div>
    <div class="text-center py-1">
        <a class="btn btn-secondary m-1" href="{{ $context.CancelUrl }}">Cancel</a>
        <button class="btn btn-primary m-1" type="submit">Submit</button>
    </div>
</form>
```

To create the template that is displayed at the end of the checkout process, add a file named checkout_summary.html to the sportsstore/templates folder with the content shown in Listing 37-19.

Listing 37-19. The Contents of the checkout_summary.html File in the templates Folder

```
{{ layout "simple_layout.html" }}
{{ $context := . }}

<div class="text-center m-3">
    <h2>Thanks!</h2>
    <p>Thanks for placing order #{{ $context.ID }} </p>
    <p>We'll ship your goods as soon as possible.</p>
    <a class="btn btn-primary" href="{{ $context.TargetUrl }}">
        Return to Store
    </a>
</div>
```

This template includes a link that will return the user to the list of products. The PostCheckout method resets the user's cart, allowing the user to start the shopping process again.

Integrating the Checkout Process

To allow the user to start the checkout process from the cart summary, make the changes shown in Listing 37-20.

Listing 37-20. Adding a Context Property in the cart_handler.go File in the store Folder

```
...
func (handler CartHandler) GetCart() actionresults.ActionResult {
    return actionresults.NewTemplateAction("cart.html", CartTemplateContext {
        Cart: handler.Cart,
        ProductListUrl: handler.mustGenerateUrl(ProductHandler.GetProducts, 0, 1),
        RemoveUrl: handler.mustGenerateUrl(CartHandler.PostRemoveFromCart),
        CheckoutUrl: handler.mustGenerateUrl(OrderHandler.GetCheckout),
    })
}
...
```

This change sets the value of the context property to give the template a URL for targeting the checkout handler. Listing 37-21 adds the link that uses the URL.

Listing 37-21. Adding an Element in the cart.html File in the templates Folder

```
...
<div class="text-center">
    <a class="btn btn-primary" href="{{ $context.ProductListUrl }}">
        Continue shopping
    </a>
    <a class="btn btn-danger" href="{{ $context.CheckoutUrl }}">Checkout</a>
</div>
...
```

Registering the Request Handler

Listing 37-22 registers the request handler so that it can receive requests.

Listing 37-22. Registering a New Handler in the main.go File in the sportsstore Folder

```
...
func createPipeline() pipeline.RequestPipeline {
    return pipeline.CreatePipeline(
        &basic.ServicesComponent{},
        &basic.LoggingComponent{},
        &basic.ErrorComponent{},
        &basic.StaticFileComponent{},
        &sessions.SessionComponent{},
        handling.NewRouter(
```

```
            handling.HandlerEntry{ "",   store.ProductHandler{}},
            handling.HandlerEntry{ "",   store.CategoryHandler{}},
            handling.HandlerEntry{ "", store.CartHandler{}},
            handling.HandlerEntry{ "", store.OrderHandler{}},
        ).AddMethodAlias("/", store.ProductHandler.GetProducts, 0, 1).
            AddMethodAlias("/products[/]?[A-z0-9]*?",
                store.ProductHandler.GetProducts, 0, 1),
    )
}
...
```

Compile and execute the project and use a browser to request http://localhost:5000. Add products to the cart and click the Checkout button, which will present you with the form shown in Figure 37-1.

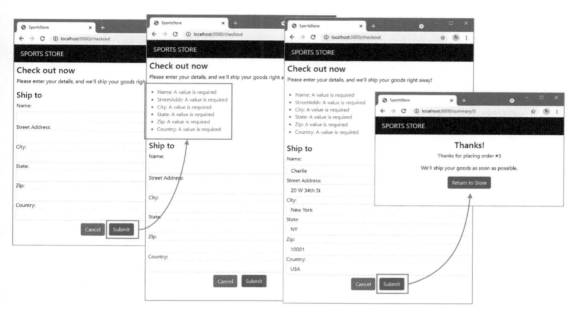

Figure 37-1. *The checkout process*

Creating Administration Features

The SportsStore application has a basic product listing and checkout process, and now it is time to create administration features. I am going to start with some basic templates and handlers that produce placeholder content.

Create the sportsstore/admin folder and add to it a file named main_handler.go with the content shown in Listing 37-23.

Listing 37-23. The Contents of the main_handler.go File in the admin Folder

```
package admin

import (
    "platform/http/actionresults"
    "platform/http/handling"
)

var sectionNames = []string { "Products", "Categories", "Orders", "Database"}

type AdminHandler struct {
    handling.URLGenerator
}

type AdminTemplateContext struct {
    Sections []string
    ActiveSection string
    SectionUrlFunc func(string) string
}

func (handler AdminHandler) GetSection(section string) actionresults.ActionResult {
    return actionresults.NewTemplateAction("admin.html", AdminTemplateContext {
        Sections: sectionNames,
        ActiveSection: section,
        SectionUrlFunc: func(sec string) string {
            sectionUrl, _ := handler.GenerateUrl(AdminHandler.GetSection, sec)
            return sectionUrl
        },
    })
}
```

The purpose of this handler is to display a template for the overall administration features, with buttons to move between different sections of functionality. Add a file named admin.html to the sportsstore/ templates folder with the content shown in Listing 37-24.

Listing 37-24. The Contents of the admin.html File in the templates Folder

```
{{ $context := . }}
<!DOCTYPE html>
<html>
<head>
    <meta name="viewport" content="width=device-width" />
    <title>SportsStore</title>
    <link href="/files/bootstrap.min.css" rel="stylesheet" />
</head>
<body>
    <div class="bg-info text-white p-2">
        <div class="container-fluid">
            <div class="row">
                <div class="col navbar-brand">SPORTS STORE Administration</div>
            </div>
```

```
            </div>
        </div>
        <div class="row m-1 p-1">
            <div id="sidebar" class="col-3">
                <div class="d-grid gap-2">
                    {{ range $context.Sections }}
                        <a href="{{ call $context.SectionUrlFunc . }}"
                            {{ if eq . $context.ActiveSection }}
                                class="btn btn-info">
                            {{ else }}
                                class="btn btn-outline-info">
                            {{ end }}
                            {{ . }}
                        </a>
                    {{ end }}
                </div>
            </div>
            <div class="col-9">
                {{ if eq $context.ActiveSection ""}}
                    <h6 class="p-2">
                        Welcome to the SportsStore Administration Features
                    </h6>
                {{ else }}
                    {{ handler $context.ActiveSection "getdata" }}
                {{ end }}
            </div>
        </div>
    </body>
</html>
```

This template uses a different color scheme to denote the administration features and displays a two-column layout with section buttons on one side and the selected administration function on the other. The selected feature is displayed using the handler function.

Add a file named products_handler.go to the sportsstore/admin folder with the content shown in Listing 37-25.

Listing 37-25. The Contents of the products_handler.go File in the admin Folder

```go
package admin

type ProductsHandler struct {}

func (handler ProductsHandler) GetData() string {
    return "This is the products handler"
}
```

Add a file named categories_handler.go to the sportsstore/admin folder with the content shown in Listing 37-26.

Listing 37-26. The Contents of the categories_handler.go File in the admin Folder

```
package admin

type CategoriesHandler struct {}

func (handler CategoriesHandler) GetData() string {
    return "This is the categories handler"
}
```

Add a file named orders_handler.go to the sportsstore/admin folder with the content shown in Listing 37-27.

Listing 37-27. The Contents of the orders_handler.go File in the admin Folder

```
package admin

type OrdersHandler struct {}

func (handler OrdersHandler) GetData() string {
    return "This is the orders handler"
}
```

To complete the set of handlers, add a file named database_handler.go to the sportsstore/admin folder with the content shown in Listing 37-28.

Listing 37-28. The Contents of the database_handler.go File in the admin Folder

```
package admin

type DatabaseHandler struct {}

func (handler DatabaseHandler) GetData() string {
    return "This is the database handler"
}
```

I will add access controls for the administration features in Chapter 38, but for now, I am going to register the new handlers so they can be accessed by anyone, as shown in Listing 37-29.

Listing 37-29. Registering the Administration Handlers in the main.go File in the sportsstore Folder

```
package main

import (
    "sync"
    "platform/http"
    "platform/http/handling"
    "platform/services"
    "platform/pipeline"
    "platform/pipeline/basic"
    "sportsstore/store"
    "sportsstore/models/repo"
```

```
    "platform/sessions"
    "sportsstore/store/cart"
    "sportsstore/admin"
)

func registerServices() {
    services.RegisterDefaultServices()
    //repo.RegisterMemoryRepoService()
    repo.RegisterSqlRepositoryService()
    sessions.RegisterSessionService()
    cart.RegisterCartService()
}

func createPipeline() pipeline.RequestPipeline {
    return pipeline.CreatePipeline(
        &basic.ServicesComponent{},
        &basic.LoggingComponent{},
        &basic.ErrorComponent{},
        &basic.StaticFileComponent{},
        &sessions.SessionComponent{},
        handling.NewRouter(
            handling.HandlerEntry{ "",   store.ProductHandler{}},
            handling.HandlerEntry{ "",   store.CategoryHandler{}},
            handling.HandlerEntry{ "", store.CartHandler{}},
            handling.HandlerEntry{ "", store.OrderHandler{}},
            handling.HandlerEntry{ "admin", admin.AdminHandler{}},
            handling.HandlerEntry{ "admin", admin.ProductsHandler{}},
            handling.HandlerEntry{ "admin", admin.CategoriesHandler{}},
            handling.HandlerEntry{ "admin", admin.OrdersHandler{}},
            handling.HandlerEntry{ "admin", admin.DatabaseHandler{}},
        ).AddMethodAlias("/", store.ProductHandler.GetProducts, 0, 1).
AddMethodAlias("/products[/]?[A-z0-9]*?", store.ProductHandler.GetProducts, 0, 1).
            AddMethodAlias("/admin[/]?", admin.AdminHandler.GetSection, ""),
    )
}

func main() {
    registerServices()
    results, err := services.Call(http.Serve, createPipeline())
    if (err == nil) {
        (results[0].(*sync.WaitGroup)).Wait()
    } else {
        panic(err)
    }
}
```

Compile and execute the project and use a browser to request http://localhost:5000/admin, which will produce the response in Figure 37-2. Clicking the navigation buttons in the left column invokes different handlers in the right column.

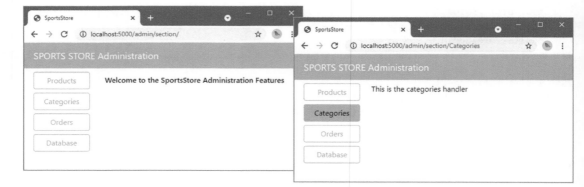

Figure 37-2. *Starting work on the administration features*

Creating the Product Administration Feature

The product administration feature will allow new products to be added to the store and existing products to be modified. For simplicity, I am not going to allow products to be deleted from the database, which has been created with foreign key relationships between tables.

Extending the Repository

The first step is to extend the repository so that I can make changes to the database. Listing 37-30 adds a new method to the Repository interface.

Listing 37-30. Defining a Method in the repository.go File in the models Folder

```
package models

type Repository interface {

    GetProduct(id int) Product
    GetProducts() []Product
    SaveProduct(*Product)

    GetProductPage(page, pageSize int) (products []Product, totalAvailable int)

    GetProductPageCategory(categoryId int, page, pageSize int) (products []Product,
        totalAvailable int)

    GetCategories() []Category

    GetOrder(id int) Order
    GetOrders() []Order
    SaveOrder(*Order)

    Seed()
}
```

1034

To define the SQL that will be used to store new products, add a file named `save_product.sql` to the sportsstore/sql folder with the content shown in Listing 37-31.

Listing 37-31. The Contents of the save_product.sql File in the sql Folder

```
INSERT INTO Products(Name, Description, Category, Price)
VALUES (?, ?, ?, ?)
```

To define the SQL that will be used to modify existing products, add a file named `update_product.sql` to the sportsstore/sql folder with the content shown in Listing 37-32.

Listing 37-32. The Contents of the update_product.sql File in the sql Folder

```
UPDATE Products
SET Name = ?, Description = ?, Category = ?, Price =?
WHERE Id == ?
```

Listing 37-33 adds new commands that will provide access to the SQL files for modifying product data.

Listing 37-33. Adding Commands in the sql_repo.go File in the models/repo Folder

```
package repo

import (
    "database/sql"
    "platform/config"
    "platform/logging"
    "context"
)

type SqlRepository struct {
    config.Configuration
    logging.Logger
    Commands SqlCommands
    *sql.DB
    context.Context
}

type SqlCommands struct {
    Init,
    Seed,
    GetProduct,
    GetProducts,
    GetCategories,
    GetPage,
    GetPageCount,
    GetCategoryPage,
    GetCategoryPageCount,
    GetOrder,
    GetOrderLines,
    GetOrders,
    GetOrdersLines,
```

```
    SaveOrder,
    SaveOrderLine,
    SaveProduct,
    UpdateProduct *sql.Stmt
}
```

Listing 37-34 adds the configuration settings that specify the location of the SQL files for the new commands.

Listing 37-34. Adding Configuration Settings in the config.json File in the sportsstore Folder

```
...
"sql": {
    "connection_str": "store.db",
    "always_reset": true,
    "commands": {
        "Init":                 "sql/init_db.sql",
        "Seed":                 "sql/seed_db.sql",
        "GetProduct":           "sql/get_product.sql",
        "GetProducts":          "sql/get_products.sql",
        "GetCategories":        "sql/get_categories.sql",
        "GetPage":              "sql/get_product_page.sql",
        "GetPageCount":         "sql/get_page_count.sql",
        "GetCategoryPage":      "sql/get_category_product_page.sql",
        "GetCategoryPageCount": "sql/get_category_product_page_count.sql",
        "GetOrder":             "sql/get_order.sql",
        "GetOrderLines":        "sql/get_order_lines.sql",
        "GetOrders":            "sql/get_orders.sql",
        "GetOrdersLines":       "sql/get_orders_lines.sql",
        "SaveOrder":            "sql/save_order.sql",
        "SaveOrderLine":        "sql/save_order_line.sql",
        "SaveProduct":          "sql/save_product.sql",
        "UpdateProduct":        "sql/update_product.sql"
    }
}
...
```

To use the SQL commands to implement the repository method, add a file named sql_products_save. go to the sportsstore/models/repo folder with the content shown in Listing 37-35.

Listing 37-35. The Contents of the sql_products_save.go File in the models/repo Folder

```
package repo

import "sportsstore/models"

func (repo *SqlRepository) SaveProduct(p *models.Product) {

    if (p.ID == 0) {
        result, err := repo.Commands.SaveProduct.ExecContext(repo.Context, p.Name,
            p.Description, p.Category.ID, p.Price)
        if err == nil {
```

```
        id, err := result.LastInsertId()
        if err == nil {
            p.ID = int(id)
            return
        } else {
            repo.Logger.Panicf("Cannot get inserted ID: %v", err.Error())
        }
    } else {
        repo.Logger.Panicf("Cannot exec SaveProduct command: %v", err.Error())
    }
} else {
    result, err := repo.Commands.UpdateProduct.ExecContext(repo.Context, p.Name,
        p.Description, p.Category.ID, p.Price, p.ID)
    if err == nil {
        affected, err := result.RowsAffected()
        if err == nil && affected != 1 {
            repo.Logger.Panicf("Got unexpected rows affected: %v", affected)
        } else if err != nil {
            repo.Logger.Panicf("Cannot get rows affected: %v", err)
        }
    } else {
        repo.Logger.Panicf("Cannot exec Update command: %v", err.Error())
    }
}
}
}
```

If the ID property of the Product received by this method is zero, then the data is added to the database; otherwise, an update is performed.

Implementing the Products Request Handler

The next step is to remove the placeholder response from the request handler and add the real functionality that will allow the administrator to see and edit the Product data. Replace the contents of the products_handler.go file in the sportsstore/admin folder with the content shown in Listing 37-36. (Make sure you edit the file in the admin folder and not the one in the store folder with a similar name.)

Listing 37-36. Adding Features in the products_handler.go File in the admin Folder

```
package admin

import (
    "sportsstore/models"
    "platform/http/actionresults"
    "platform/http/handling"
    "platform/sessions"
)

type ProductsHandler struct {
    models.Repository
    handling.URLGenerator
    sessions.Session
}
```

```go
type ProductTemplateContext struct {
    Products []models.Product
    EditId int
    EditUrl string
    SaveUrl string
}

const PRODUCT_EDIT_KEY string = "product_edit"

func (handler ProductsHandler) GetData() actionresults.ActionResult {
    return actionresults.NewTemplateAction("admin_products.html",
            ProductTemplateContext {
        Products: handler.GetProducts(),
        EditId: handler.Session.GetValueDefault(PRODUCT_EDIT_KEY, 0).(int),
        EditUrl: mustGenerateUrl(handler.URLGenerator,
            ProductsHandler.PostProductEdit),
        SaveUrl: mustGenerateUrl(handler.URLGenerator,
            ProductsHandler.PostProductSave),
    })
}

type EditReference struct {
    ID int
}

func (handler ProductsHandler) PostProductEdit(ref EditReference) actionresults.
ActionResult {
    handler.Session.SetValue(PRODUCT_EDIT_KEY, ref.ID)
    return actionresults.NewRedirectAction(mustGenerateUrl(handler.URLGenerator,
        AdminHandler.GetSection, "Products"))
}

type ProductSaveReference struct {
    Id int
    Name, Description string
    Category int
    Price float64
}

func (handler ProductsHandler) PostProductSave(
        p ProductSaveReference) actionresults.ActionResult {

    handler.Repository.SaveProduct(&models.Product{
        ID: p.Id, Name: p.Name, Description: p.Description,
        Category: &models.Category{ ID: p.Category },
        Price: p.Price,
    })
    handler.Session.SetValue(PRODUCT_EDIT_KEY, 0)
    return actionresults.NewRedirectAction(mustGenerateUrl(handler.URLGenerator,
        AdminHandler.GetSection, "Products"))
}
```

```
func mustGenerateUrl(gen handling.URLGenerator, target interface{},
        data ...interface{}) string {
    url, err := gen.GenerateUrl(target, data...)
    if (err != nil) {
        panic(err)
    }
    return url
}
```

The GetData method renders a template named admin_products.html with context data that contains the Product values in the database, an int value used to denote the ID of the Product the user wants to edit, and URLs that are used for navigation. To create the template, add a file named admin_products.html to the sportsstore/templates folder with the content shown in Listing 37-37.

Listing 37-37. The Contents of the admin_products.html File in the templates Folder

```
{{ $context := . }}
<table class="table table-sm table-striped table-bordered">
    <thead>
        <tr>
            <th>ID</th><th>Name</th><th>Description</th>
            <th>Category</th><th class="text-end">Price</th><th></th>
        </tr>
    </thead>
    <tbody>
        {{ range $context.Products }}
            {{ if ne $context.EditId .ID}}
                <tr>
                    <td>{{ .ID }}</td>
                    <td>{{ .Name }}</td>
                    <td>
                        <span class="d-inline-block text-truncate"
                            style="max-width: 200px;">
                                {{ .Description }}
                        </span>
                    </td>
                    <td>{{ .CategoryName }}</td>
                    <td class="text-end">{{ printf "$%.2f" .Price }}</td>
                    <td class="text-center">
                        <form method="POST" action="{{ $context.EditUrl }}">
                            <input type="hidden" name="id" value="{{ .ID }}" />
                            <button class="btn btn-sm btn-warning" type="submit">
                                Edit
                            </button>
                        </form>
                    </td>
                </tr>
            {{ else }}
                <tr>
                    <form method="POST" action="{{ $context.SaveUrl }}" >
                        <input type="hidden" name="id" value="{{ .ID }}" />
                        <td>
```

```
                              <input class="form-control" disabled value="{{.ID}}"
                                  size="3"/>
                          </td>
                          <td><input name="name" class="form-control" size=12
                              value="{{ .Name }}" /></td>
                          <td><input name="description" class="form-control"
                              size=15 value="{{ .Description }}" /></td>
                          <td>{{ handler "categories" "getselect" .Category.ID }}</td>
                          <td><input name="price" class="form-control text-end"
                              size=7 value="{{ .Price }}"/></td>
                          <td>
                              <button class="btn btn-sm btn-danger" type="submit">
                                  Save
                              </button>
                          </td>
                      </form>
                  </tr>
              {{ end }}
          {{ end }}
      </tbody>
      {{ if eq $context.EditId 0}}
          <tfoot>
              <tr><td colspan="6" class="text-center">Add New Product</td></tr>
              <tr>
                  <form method="POST" action="{{ $context.SaveUrl }}" >
                      <td>-</td>
                      <td><input name="name" class="form-control" size=12 /></td>
                      <td><input name="description" class="form-control"
                          size=15 /></td>
                      <td>{{ handler "categories" "getselect" 0 }}</td>
                      <td><input name="price" class="form-control" size=7 /></td>
                      <td>
                          <button class="btn btn-sm btn-danger" type="submit">
                              Save
                          </button>
                      </td>
                  </form>
              </tr>
          </tfoot>
      {{ end }}
</table>
```

This template produces an HTML template that contains all of the products, along with an inline editor for modifying existing products and another for creating new products. Both tasks require a select element that allows the user to choose a category, which is generated by invoking a method defined by the CategoriesHandler. Listing 37-38 adds this method to the request handler.

Listing 37-38. Adding Support for a Select Element in the categories_handler.go File in the admin Folder

```
package admin

import (
    "platform/http/actionresults"
    "sportsstore/models"
)

type CategoriesHandler struct {
    models.Repository
}

func (handler CategoriesHandler) GetData() string {
    return "This is the categories handler"
}

func (handler CategoriesHandler) GetSelect(current int) actionresults.ActionResult {
    return actionresults.NewTemplateAction("select_category.html", struct {
        Current int
        Categories []models.Category
    }{ Current: current, Categories: handler.GetCategories()})
}
```

To define the template used by the GetSelect method, add a file named select_category.html to the sportsstore/templates folder with the content shown in Listing 37-39.

Listing 37-39. The Contents of the select_category.html File in the templates Folder

```
{{ $context := . }}

<select class="form-select" name="category" value="{{ $context.Current }}">
    <option value="0">Select a category</option>
    {{ range $context.Categories }}
        <option value="{{.ID}}" {{ if eq $context.Current .ID }}selected{{end}}>
            {{.CategoryName}}
        </option>
    {{ end }}
</select>
```

Compile and execute the project, use a browser to request http://localhost:5000/admin, and click the Products button. You will see the list of products, which has been read from the database. Click one of the Edit buttons to select a product for editing, enter new values into the form fields, and click the Submit button to save the changes to the database, also shown in Figure 37-3.

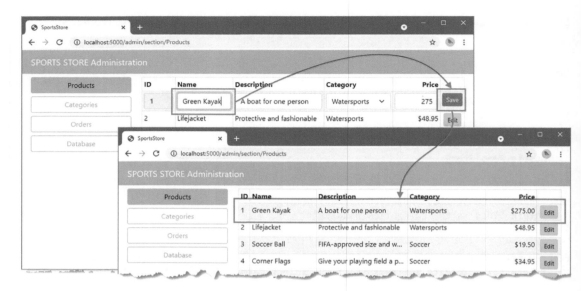

Figure 37-3. *Editing a product*

■ **Note**   The SportsStore application is configured to reset the database each time it is started, which means that any changes you make to the database will be discarded. I disable this feature when preparing the application for deployment in Chapter 38.

When no product is selected for editing, a form at the bottom of the table can be used to create new products in the database, as shown in Figure 37-4.

Figure 37-4. *Adding a product*

Creating the Categories Administration Feature

I am going to apply the basic pattern established in the previous section to implement the other administration features.

Extending the Repository

Listing 37-40 adds a method to the Repository interface that will store a Category.

Listing 37-40. Adding a Method in the repository.go File in the models Folder

```
package models

type Repository interface {

    GetProduct(id int) Product
    GetProducts() []Product
    SaveProduct(*Product)

    GetProductPage(page, pageSize int) (products []Product, totalAvailable int)

    GetProductPageCategory(categoryId int, page, pageSize int) (products []Product,
        totalAvailable int)

    GetCategories() []Category
    SaveCategory(*Category)

    GetOrder(id int) Order
    GetOrders() []Order
    SaveOrder(*Order)

    Seed()
}
```

To define the SQL that will be used to store new categories in the database, add a file named save_category.sql to the sportsstore/sql folder with the content shown in Listing 37-41.

Listing 37-41. The Contents of the save_category.sql File in the sql Folder

```
INSERT INTO Categories(Name) VALUES (?)
```

To define the SQL that will be used to modify existing categories, add a file named update_category.sql to the sportsstore/sql folder with the content shown in Listing 37-42.

Listing 37-42. The Contents of the update_category.sql File in the sql Folder

```
UPDATE Categories SET Name = ? WHERE Id == ?
```

Listing 37-43 adds new commands that will provide access to the SQL files.

Listing 37-43. Adding Commands in the sql_repo.go File in the models/repo Folder

```
...
type SqlCommands struct {
    Init,
    Seed,
    GetProduct,
    GetProducts,
    GetCategories,
    GetPage,
    GetPageCount,
    GetCategoryPage,
    GetCategoryPageCount,
    GetOrder,
    GetOrderLines,
    GetOrders,
    GetOrdersLines,
    SaveOrder,
    SaveOrderLine,
    SaveProduct,
    UpdateProduct,
    SaveCategory,
    UpdateCategory *sql.Stmt
}
...
```

Listing 37-44 adds the configuration settings that specify the location of the SQL files for the new commands.

Listing 37-44. Adding Configuration Settings in the config.json File in the sportsstore Folder

```
...
"sql": {
    "connection_str": "store.db",
    "always_reset": true,
    "commands": {
        "Init":                 "sql/init_db.sql",
        "Seed":                 "sql/seed_db.sql",
        "GetProduct":           "sql/get_product.sql",
        "GetProducts":          "sql/get_products.sql",
        "GetCategories":        "sql/get_categories.sql",
        "GetPage":              "sql/get_product_page.sql",
        "GetPageCount":         "sql/get_page_count.sql",
        "GetCategoryPage":      "sql/get_category_product_page.sql",
        "GetCategoryPageCount": "sql/get_category_product_page_count.sql",
        "GetOrder":             "sql/get_order.sql",
        "GetOrderLines":        "sql/get_order_lines.sql",
        "GetOrders":            "sql/get_orders.sql",
        "GetOrdersLines":       "sql/get_orders_lines.sql",
        "SaveOrder":            "sql/save_order.sql",
        "SaveOrderLine":        "sql/save_order_line.sql",
        "SaveProduct":          "sql/save_product.sql",
```

```
        "UpdateProduct":        "sql/update_product.sql",
        "SaveCategory":         "sql/save_category.sql",
        "UpdateCategory":       "sql/update_category.sql"
    }
}
...
```

To implement the new interface method, add a file named sql_category_save.go to the sportsstore/models/repo folder with the content shown in Listing 37-45.

Listing 37-45. The Contents of the sql_category_save.go File in the models/repo Folder

```go
package repo

import "sportsstore/models"

func (repo *SqlRepository) SaveCategory(c *models.Category) {
    if (c.ID == 0) {
        result, err := repo.Commands.SaveCategory.ExecContext(repo.Context,
            c.CategoryName)
        if err == nil {
            id, err := result.LastInsertId()
            if err == nil {
                c.ID = int(id)
                return
            } else {
                repo.Logger.Panicf("Cannot get inserted ID: %v", err.Error())
            }
        } else {
            repo.Logger.Panicf("Cannot exec SaveCategory command: %v", err.Error())
        }
    } else {
        result, err := repo.Commands.UpdateCategory.ExecContext(repo.Context,
            c.CategoryName, c.ID)
        if err == nil {
            affected, err := result.RowsAffected()
            if err == nil && affected != 1 {
                repo.Logger.Panicf("Got unexpected rows affected: %v", affected)
            } else if err != nil {
                repo.Logger.Panicf("Cannot get rows affected: %v", err)
            }
        } else {
            repo.Logger.Panicf("Cannot exec UpdateCategory command: %v", err.Error())
        }
    }
}
```

If the ID property of the Category received by this method is zero, then the data is added to the database; otherwise, an update is performed.

Implementing the Category Request Handler

Replace the contents of the categories_handler.go file in the sportsstore/admin folder with the code shown in Listing 37-46.

Listing 37-46. Replacing the Contents of the categories_handler.go File in the admin Folder

```
package admin

import (
    "sportsstore/models"
    "platform/http/actionresults"
    "platform/http/handling"
    "platform/sessions"
)

type CategoriesHandler struct {
    models.Repository
    handling.URLGenerator
    sessions.Session
}

type CategoryTemplateContext struct {
    Categories []models.Category
    EditId int
    EditUrl string
    SaveUrl string
}

const CATEGORY_EDIT_KEY string = "category_edit"

func (handler CategoriesHandler) GetData() actionresults.ActionResult {
    return actionresults.NewTemplateAction("admin_categories.html",
        CategoryTemplateContext {
            Categories: handler.Repository.GetCategories(),
            EditId: handler.Session.GetValueDefault(CATEGORY_EDIT_KEY, 0).(int),
            EditUrl: mustGenerateUrl(handler.URLGenerator,
                CategoriesHandler.PostCategoryEdit),
            SaveUrl: mustGenerateUrl(handler.URLGenerator,
                CategoriesHandler.PostCategorySave),
        })
}

func (handler CategoriesHandler) PostCategoryEdit(ref EditReference) actionresults.
ActionResult {
    handler.Session.SetValue(CATEGORY_EDIT_KEY, ref.ID)
    return actionresults.NewRedirectAction(mustGenerateUrl(handler.URLGenerator,
        AdminHandler.GetSection, "Categories"))
}

func (handler CategoriesHandler) PostCategorySave(
        c models.Category) actionresults.ActionResult {
```

```
    handler.Repository.SaveCategory(&c)
    handler.Session.SetValue(CATEGORY_EDIT_KEY, 0)
    return actionresults.NewRedirectAction(mustGenerateUrl(handler.URLGenerator,
        AdminHandler.GetSection, "Categories"))
}

func (handler CategoriesHandler) GetSelect(current int) actionresults.ActionResult {
    return actionresults.NewTemplateAction("select_category.html", struct {
        Current int
        Categories []models.Category
    }{ Current: current, Categories: handler.GetCategories()})
}
```

To define the template used by this handler, add a file named admin_categories.html to the sportsstore/templates folder with the content shown in Listing 37-47.

Listing 37-47. The Contents of the admin_categories.html File in the templates Folder

```
{{ $context := . }}
<table class="table table-sm table-striped table-bordered">
    <thead><tr><th>ID</th><th>Name</th><th></th></tr></thead>
    <tbody>
        {{ range $context.Categories }}
            {{ if ne $context.EditId .ID}}
                <tr>
                    <td>{{ .ID }}</td>
                    <td>{{ .CategoryName }}</td>
                    <td class="text-center">
                        <form method="POST" action="{{ $context.EditUrl }}">
                            <input type="hidden" name="id" value="{{ .ID }}" />
                            <button class="btn btn-sm btn-warning" type="submit">
                                Edit
                            </button>
                        </form>
                    </td>
                </tr>
            {{ else }}
                <tr>
                    <form method="POST" action="{{ $context.SaveUrl }}" >
                        <input type="hidden" name="id" value="{{ .ID }}" />
                        <td>
                            <input class="form-control" disabled
                                value="{{.ID}}" size="3"/>
                        </td>
                        <td><input name="categoryname" class="form-control" size=12
                            value="{{ .CategoryName }}" /></td>
                    <td class="text-center">
                            <button class="btn btn-sm btn-danger" type="submit">
                                Save
                            </button>
                        </td>
                    </form>
```

```
                </tr>
            {{end }}
        {{ end }}
    </tbody>
    {{ if eq $context.EditId 0}}
        <tfoot>
            <tr><td colspan="6" class="text-center">Add New Category</td></tr>
            <tr>
                <form method="POST" action="{{ $context.SaveUrl }}" >
                    <td>-</td>
                    <td><input name="categoryname" class="form-control"
                        size=12 /></td>
                    <td class="text-center">
                        <button class="btn btn-sm btn-danger" type="submit">
                            Save
                        </button>
                    </td>
                </form>
            </tr>
        </tfoot>
    {{ end }}
</table>
```

Compile and execute the project, use a browser to request `http://localhost:5000/admin`, and click the Categories button. You will see the list of categories, which has been read from the database, and can edit and create categories, as shown in Figure 37-5.

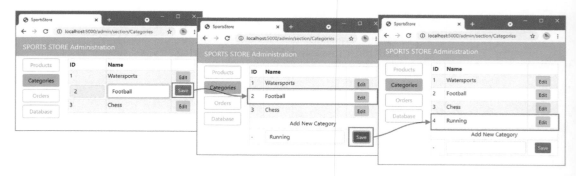

Figure 37-5. *Managing categories*

Summary

In this chapter, I continued the development of the SportsStore application by adding a checkout process and starting work on the administration features. In the next chapter, I complete those features, add support for access control, and prepare the application for deployment.

CHAPTER 38

SportsStore: Finishing and Deployment

In this chapter, I complete the development of the SportsStore application and prepare it for deployment.

Tip You can download the example project for this chapter—and for all the other chapters in this book—from https://github.com/apress/pro-go. See Chapter 2 for how to get help if you have problems running the examples.

Completing the Administration Features

Two of the four administration sections defined in Chapter 37 are not yet implemented. I define both of these features at the same time in this section, reflecting the fact that they are simpler than the product and category features.

Extending the Repository

Two new repository methods are required to complete the administration features, as shown in Listing 38-1.

Listing 38-1. Adding an Interface in the repository.go File in the models Folder

```
package models

type Repository interface {

    GetProduct(id int) Product
    GetProducts() []Product
    SaveProduct(*Product)

    GetProductPage(page, pageSize int) (products []Product, totalAvailable int)
```

```
GetProductPageCategory(categoryId int, page, pageSize int) (products []Product,
    totalAvailable int)

GetCategories() []Category
SaveCategory(*Category)

GetOrder(id int) []Order
GetOrders() Order
SaveOrder(*Order)
SetOrderShipped(*Order)

Seed()
Init()
}
```

The SetOrderShipped method will be used to update an existing Order to indicate when it has been shipped. The Init method corresponds to a method name already defined by the SQL implementation of the interface and will be used to allow the administrator to prepare the database for first use after it has been deployed.

To define the SQL that will be used to update existing orders, add a file named update_order.sql to the sportsstore/sql folder with the content shown in Listing 38-2.

Listing 38-2. The Contents of the update_order.sql File in the sql Folder

```
UPDATE Orders SET Shipped = ? WHERE Id == ?
```

Listing 38-3 adds a new command so that the SQL defined in Listing 38-2 can be accessed in the same way as the other SQL statements.

Listing 38-3. Adding a New Command in the sql_repo.go File in the models/repo Folder

```
...
type SqlCommands struct {
    Init,
    Seed,
    GetProduct,
    GetProducts,
    GetCategories,
    GetPage,
    GetPageCount,
    GetCategoryPage,
    GetCategoryPageCount,
    GetOrder,
    GetOrderLines,
    GetOrders,
    GetOrdersLines,
    SaveOrder,
    SaveOrderLine,
    UpdateOrder,
    SaveProduct,
    UpdateProduct,
    SaveCategory,
```

```
    UpdateCategory *sql.Stmt
}
...
```

Listing 38-4 adds a configuration setting that specifies the location of the SQL required for the new command.

Listing 38-4. Adding a Configuration Setting in the config.json File in the sportsstore Folder

```
...
"sql": {
    "connection_str": "store.db",
    "always_reset": true,
    "commands": {
        "Init": "sql/init_db.sql",
        "Seed": "sql/seed_db.sql",
        "GetProduct": "sql/get_product.sql",
        "GetProducts": "sql/get_products.sql",
        "GetCategories": "sql/get_categories.sql",
        "GetPage": "sql/get_product_page.sql",
        "GetPageCount": "sql/get_page_count.sql",
        "GetCategoryPage": "sql/get_category_product_page.sql",
        "GetCategoryPageCount": "sql/get_category_product_page_count.sql",
        "GetOrder": "sql/get_order.sql",
        "GetOrderLines": "sql/get_order_lines.sql",
        "GetOrders": "sql/get_orders.sql",
        "GetOrdersLines": "sql/get_orders_lines.sql",
        "SaveOrder": "sql/save_order.sql",
        "SaveOrderLine": "sql/save_order_line.sql",
        "SaveProduct":          "sql/save_product.sql",
        "UpdateProduct":        "sql/update_product.sql",
        "SaveCategory":         "sql/save_category.sql",
        "UpdateCategory":       "sql/update_category.sql",
        "UpdateOrder":          "sql/update_order.sql"
    }
}
...
```

To implement the repository method, add a file named sql_order_update.go in the sportsstore/ models/repo folder with the content shown in Listing 38-5.

Listing 38-5. The Contents of the sql_order_update.go File in the models/repo Folder

```
package repo

import "sportsstore/models"

func (repo *SqlRepository) SetOrderShipped(o *models.Order) {
    result, err := repo.Commands.UpdateOrder.ExecContext(repo.Context,
        o.Shipped, o.ID)
    if err == nil {
        rows, err :=result.RowsAffected()
```

```
            if err != nil {
                repo.Logger.Panicf("Cannot get updated ID: %v", err.Error())
            } else if rows != 1 {
                repo.Logger.Panicf("Got unexpected rows affected: %v", rows)
            }
        } else {
            repo.Logger.Panicf("Cannot exec UpdateOrder command: %v", err.Error())
        }
    }
```

Implementing the Request Handlers

To add support for managing orders, replace the content of the orders_handler.go file in the sportsstore/ admin folder with the content shown in Listing 38-6.

Listing 38-6. The New Contents of the orders_handler.go File in the admin Folder

```
package admin

import (
    "platform/http/actionresults"
    "platform/http/handling"
    "sportsstore/models"
)

type OrdersHandler struct {
    models.Repository
    handling.URLGenerator
}

func (handler OrdersHandler) GetData() actionresults.ActionResult {
    return actionresults.NewTemplateAction("admin_orders.html", struct {
        Orders []models.Order
         CallbackUrl string
    }{
        Orders: handler.Repository.GetOrders(),
        CallbackUrl: mustGenerateUrl(handler.URLGenerator,
            OrdersHandler.PostOrderToggle),
    })
}

func (handler OrdersHandler) PostOrderToggle(ref EditReference) actionresults.ActionResult {
    order := handler.Repository.GetOrder(ref.ID)
    order.Shipped = !order.Shipped
    handler.Repository.SetOrderShipped(&order)
    return actionresults.NewRedirectAction(mustGenerateUrl(handler.URLGenerator,
        AdminHandler.GetSection, "Orders"))
}
```

The only change that will be allowed on orders is to change the value of the Shipped field, indicating that the order has been dispatched. Replace the content of the database_handler.go file with the content shown in Listing 38-7.

Listing 38-7. The New Contents of the database_handler.go File in the admin Folder

```go
package admin

import (
    "platform/http/actionresults"
    "platform/http/handling"
    "sportsstore/models"
)

type DatabaseHandler struct {
    models.Repository
    handling.URLGenerator
}

func (handler DatabaseHandler) GetData() actionresults.ActionResult {
    return actionresults.NewTemplateAction("admin_database.html", struct {
        InitUrl, SeedUrl string
    }{
        InitUrl: mustGenerateUrl(handler.URLGenerator,
            DatabaseHandler.PostDatabaseInit),
        SeedUrl: mustGenerateUrl(handler.URLGenerator,
            DatabaseHandler.PostDatabaseSeed),
    })
}

func (handler DatabaseHandler) PostDatabaseInit() actionresults.ActionResult {
    handler.Repository.Init()
    return actionresults.NewRedirectAction(mustGenerateUrl(handler.URLGenerator,
        AdminHandler.GetSection, "Database"))
}

func (handler DatabaseHandler) PostDatabaseSeed() actionresults.ActionResult {
    handler.Repository.Seed()
    return actionresults.NewRedirectAction(mustGenerateUrl(handler.URLGenerator,
        AdminHandler.GetSection, "Database"))
}
```

There are handler methods for each of the operations that can be performed on the database, which will allow the administrator to jump-start the application after the application has been prepared for deployment later in this chapter.

Creating the Templates

To create the template used to manage orders, add a file named admin_orders.html to the sportsstore/ templates folder with the content shown in Listing 38-8.

Listing 38-8. The Contents of the admin_orders.html File in the templates Folder

```
{{ $context := .}}

<table class="table table-sm table-striped table-bordered">
    <tr><th>ID</th><th>Name</th><th>Address</th><th/></tr>
    <tbody>
        {{ range $context.Orders }}
            <tr>
                <td>{{ .ID }}</td>
                <td>{{ .Name }}</td>
                <td>{{ .StreetAddr }}, {{ .City }}, {{ .State }},
                    {{ .Country }}, {{ .Zip }}</td>
                <td>
                    <form method="POST" action="{{$context.CallbackUrl}}">
                        <input type="hidden" name="id" value="{{.ID}}" />
                        {{ if .Shipped }}
                            <button class="btn-btn-sm btn-warning" type="submit">
                                Ship Order
                            </button>
                        {{ else }}
                            <button class="btn-btn-sm btn-danger" type="submit">
                                Mark Unshipped
                            </button>
                        {{ end }}
                    </form>
                </td>
            </tr>
            <tr><th colspan="2"/><th>Quantity</th><th>Product</th></tr>
            {{ range .Products }}
                <tr>
                    <td colspan="2"/>
                    <td>{{ .Quantity }}</td>
                    <td>{{ .Product.Name }}</td>
                </tr>
            {{ end }}
        {{ end }}
    </tbody>
</table>
```

The template displays the orders in a table, along with details of the products that each contains. To create the template used to manage the database, add a file named admin_database.html to the sportsstore/templates folder with the content shown in Listing 38-9.

Listing 38-9. The Contents of the admin_database.html File in the templates Folder

```
{{ $context := . }}

<form method="POST">
    <button class="btn btn-danger m-3 p-2" type="submit"
            formaction="{{ $context.InitUrl}}">
        Initialize Database
```

```
    </button>
    <button class="btn btn-warning m-3 p-2" type="submit"
            formaction="{{ $context.SeedUrl}}">
        Seed Database
    </button>
</form>
```

Compile and execute the project, use a browser to request `http://localhost:5000/admin`, and click the Orders button to see the orders in the database and change their shipping status, as shown in Figure 38-1. Click the Database button, and you will be able to reset and seed the database, also shown in Figure 38-1.

Figure 38-1. *Completing the administration features*

Restricting Access to the Administration Features

Granting open access to the administration features simplifies development but should never be allowed in production. Now that the administration features are complete, it is time to make sure they are available only to authorized users.

Creating the User Store and Request Handler

As I explained previously, I do not implement a real authentication system, which is difficult to do securely and is beyond the scope of this book. Instead, I am going to follow a similar approach to the one I took with the `platform` project and rely on hardwired credentials to authenticate a user. Create the `sportsstore/admin/auth` folder and add to it a file named `user_store.go` with the content shown in Listing 38-10.

Listing 38-10. The Contents of the user_store.go File in the admin/auth Folder

```go
package auth

import (
    "platform/services"
    "platform/authorization/identity"
    "strings"
)
```

```
func RegisterUserStoreService() {
    err := services.AddSingleton(func () identity.UserStore {
        return &userStore{}
    })
    if (err != nil) {
        panic(err)
    }
}

var users = map[int]identity.User {
    1: identity.NewBasicUser(1, "Alice", "Administrator"),
}

type userStore struct {}

func (store *userStore) GetUserByID(id int) (identity.User, bool) {
    user, found := users[id]
    return user, found
}

func (store *userStore) GetUserByName(name string) (identity.User, bool) {
    for _, user := range users {
        if strings.EqualFold(user.GetDisplayName(), name) {
            return user, true
        }
    }
    return nil, false
}
```

To create the handler for authentication requests, add a file named auth_handler.go to the sportsstore/admin folder with the content shown in Listing 38-11.

Listing 38-11. The Contents of the auth_handler.go File in the admin Folder

```
package admin

import (
    "platform/authorization/identity"
    "platform/http/actionresults"
    "platform/http/handling"
    "platform/sessions"
)

type AuthenticationHandler struct {
    identity.User
    identity.SignInManager
    identity.UserStore
    sessions.Session
    handling.URLGenerator
}
```

```
const SIGNIN_MSG_KEY string = "signin_message"

func (handler AuthenticationHandler) GetSignIn() actionresults.ActionResult {
    message := handler.Session.GetValueDefault(SIGNIN_MSG_KEY, "").(string)
    return actionresults.NewTemplateAction("signin.html", message)
}

type Credentials struct {
    Username string
    Password string
}

func (handler AuthenticationHandler) PostSignIn(creds Credentials) actionresults.
ActionResult {
    if creds.Password == "mysecret" {
        user, ok := handler.UserStore.GetUserByName(creds.Username)
        if (ok) {
            handler.Session.SetValue(SIGNIN_MSG_KEY, "")
            handler.SignInManager.SignIn(user)
            return actionresults.NewRedirectAction("/admin/section/")
        }
    }
    handler.Session.SetValue(SIGNIN_MSG_KEY, "Access Denied")
    return actionresults.NewRedirectAction(mustGenerateUrl(handler.URLGenerator,
        AuthenticationHandler.GetSignIn))
}

func (handler AuthenticationHandler) PostSignOut(creds Credentials) actionresults.
ActionResult {
        handler.SignInManager.SignOut(handler.User)
    return actionresults.NewRedirectAction("/")
}
```

The GetSignIn method renders a template that will prompt the user for their credentials and displays a message that is stored in the session. The PostSignIn method receives the credentials from the form and either signs the user into the application or adds a message to the session and redirects the browser so the user can try again.

To create the template to let users sign into the application, add a file named signin.html to the sportsstore/templates folder with the content shown in Listing 38-12.

Listing 38-12. The Contents of the signin.html File in the templates Folder

```
{{ layout "simple_layout.html" }}

{{ if ne . "" }}
    <h3 class="text-danger p-2">{{ . }}</h3>
{{ end }}

<form method="POST" class="m-2">
    <div class="form-group">
        <label>Username:</label>
```

```
            <input class="form-control"  name="username" />
        </div>
        <div class="form-group">
            <label>Password:</label>
            <input class="form-control" name="password" type="password" />
        </div>
        <div class="my-2">
            <button class="btn btn-secondary" type="submit">Sign In</button>
        </div>
</form>
```

This template prompts the user for their account name and password, which is posted back to the request handler.

To allow the user to sign out of the application, add a file named signout_handler.go to the sportsstore/admin folder with the content shown in Listing 38-13.

Listing 38-13. The Contents of the signout_handler.go File in the admin Folder

```
package admin

import (
        "platform/authorization/identity"
        "platform/http/actionresults"
    "platform/http/handling"
)

type SignOutHandler struct {
    identity.User
    handling.URLGenerator
}

func (handler SignOutHandler) GetUserWidget() actionresults.ActionResult {
        return actionresults.NewTemplateAction("user_widget.html", struct {
            identity.User
            SignoutUrl string}{
                handler.User,
                mustGenerateUrl(handler.URLGenerator,
                    AuthenticationHandler.PostSignOut),
            })
    }
```

To create the template that will let the user sign out, add a file named user_widget.html to the sportsstore/templates folder with the content shown in Listing 38-14.

Listing 38-14. The Contents of the user_widget.html File in the templates Folder

```
{{ $context := . }}

{{ if $context.User.IsAuthenticated }}
    <form method="POST" action="{{$context.SignoutUrl}}">
```

```
        <button class="btn btn-sm btn-outline-secondary text-white" type="submit">
            Sign Out
        </button>
    </form>
{{ end }}
```

Listing 38-15 adds the user widget to the layout used for the administration features.

Listing 38-15. Adding a Widget in the admin.html File in the templates Folder

```
...
<div class="bg-info text-white p-2">
    <div class="container-fluid">
        <div class="row">
            <div class="col navbar-brand">SPORTS STORE Administration</div>
            <div class="col-6 navbar-text text-end">
                {{ handler "signout" "getuserwidget" }}
            </div>
        </div>
    </div>
</div>
...
```

Configuring the Application

Listing 38-16 adds a configuration setting that specifies a URL that will be used when a request is made for a restricted URL, which provides a more useful alternative to returning a status code.

Listing 38-16. Adding a Configuration Setting in the config.json File in the sportsstore Folder

```
{
    "logging" : {
        "level": "debug"
    },
    "files": {
        "path": "files"
    },
    "templates": {
        "path": "templates/*.html",
        "reload": true
    },
    "sessions": {
        "key": "MY_SESSION_KEY",
        "cyclekey": true
    },
    "sql": {
```

```
        // ...setting omitted for brevity...

    },
    "authorization": {
        "failUrl": "/signin"
    }
}
```

The specified URL will prompt the user for their credentials. Listing 38-17 reconfigures the request pipeline so the administration features are protected.

Listing 38-17. Configuring the Application in the main.go File in the sportsstore Folder

```go
package main

import (
    "sync"
    "platform/http"
    "platform/http/handling"
    "platform/services"
    "platform/pipeline"
    "platform/pipeline/basic"
    "sportsstore/store"
    "sportsstore/models/repo"
    "platform/sessions"
    "sportsstore/store/cart"
    "sportsstore/admin"
    "platform/authorization"
    "sportsstore/admin/auth"
)

func registerServices() {
    services.RegisterDefaultServices()
    //repo.RegisterMemoryRepoService()
    repo.RegisterSqlRepositoryService()
    sessions.RegisterSessionService()
    cart.RegisterCartService()
    authorization.RegisterDefaultSignInService()
    authorization.RegisterDefaultUserService()
    auth.RegisterUserStoreService()
}

func createPipeline() pipeline.RequestPipeline {
    return pipeline.CreatePipeline(
        &basic.ServicesComponent{},
        &basic.LoggingComponent{},
        &basic.ErrorComponent{},
        &basic.StaticFileComponent{},
        &sessions.SessionComponent{},
```

```
authorization.NewAuthComponent(
    "admin",
    authorization.NewRoleCondition("Administrator"),
    admin.AdminHandler{},
    admin.ProductsHandler{},
    admin.CategoriesHandler{},
    admin.OrdersHandler{},
    admin.DatabaseHandler{},
    admin.SignOutHandler{},
).AddFallback("/admin/section/", "^/admin[/]?$"),

handling.NewRouter(
    handling.HandlerEntry{ "",  store.ProductHandler{}},
    handling.HandlerEntry{ "",  store.CategoryHandler{}},
    handling.HandlerEntry{ "", store.CartHandler{}},
    handling.HandlerEntry{ "", store.OrderHandler{}},
    // handling.HandlerEntry{ "admin", admin.AdminHandler{}},
    // handling.HandlerEntry{ "admin", admin.ProductsHandler{}},
    // handling.HandlerEntry{ "admin", admin.CategoriesHandler{}},
    // handling.HandlerEntry{ "admin", admin.OrdersHandler{}},
    // handling.HandlerEntry{ "admin", admin.DatabaseHandler{}},
    handling.HandlerEntry{ "", admin.AuthenticationHandler{}},
).AddMethodAlias("/", store.ProductHandler.GetProducts, 0, 1).
    AddMethodAlias("/products[/]?[A-z0-9]*?",
        store.ProductHandler.GetProducts, 0, 1),    )
}

func main() {
    registerServices()
    results, err := services.Call(http.Serve, createPipeline())
    if (err == nil) {
        (results[0].(*sync.WaitGroup)).Wait()
    } else {
        panic(err)
    }
}
```

Compile and execute the application and use a browser to request http://localhost:5000/admin. When prompted, authenticate as user alice with password mysecret, and you will be granted access to the administration features, as shown in Figure 38-2.

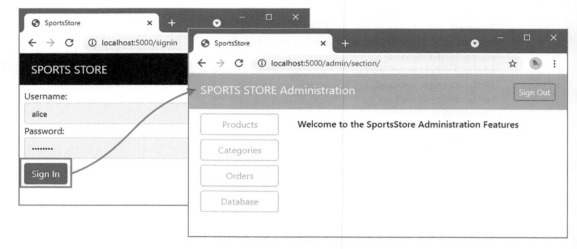

Figure 38-2. *Signing into the application*

Creating a Web Service

The final feature I am going to add is a simple web service, just to show how it can be done. I am not going to use authorization to protect the web service, which can be a complex process that depends on the type of clients expected to require access. This means that any user will be able to modify the database. If you are deploying a real web service, then you can use cookies in much the same way as I have done in this example. If your clients don't support cookies, then JSON Web Tokens (JWTs) can be used, as described at https://jwt.io.

To create the web service, add a file named rest_handler.go to the sportsstore/store folder with the content shown in Listing 38-18.

Listing 38-18. The Contents of the rest_handler.go File in the store Folder

```
package store

import (
    "sportsstore/models"
    "platform/http/actionresults"
    "net/http"
)

type StatusCodeResult struct {
    code int
}

func (action *StatusCodeResult) Execute(ctx *actionresults.ActionContext) error {
    ctx.ResponseWriter.WriteHeader(action.code)
    return nil
}
```

```
type RestHandler struct {
    Repository models.Repository
}

func (h RestHandler) GetProduct(id int) actionresults.ActionResult {
    return actionresults.NewJsonAction(h.Repository.GetProduct(id))
}

func (h RestHandler) GetProducts() actionresults.ActionResult {
    return actionresults.NewJsonAction(h.Repository.GetProducts())
}

type ProductReference struct {
    models.Product
    CategoryID int
}

func (h RestHandler) PostProduct(p ProductReference) actionresults.ActionResult {
    if p.ID == 0 {
        return actionresults.NewJsonAction(h.processData(p))
    } else {
        return &StatusCodeResult{ http.StatusBadRequest }
    }
}

func (h RestHandler) PutProduct(p ProductReference) actionresults.ActionResult {
    if p.ID > 0 {
        return actionresults.NewJsonAction(h.processData(p))
    } else {
        return &StatusCodeResult{ http.StatusBadRequest }
    }
}

func (h RestHandler) processData(p ProductReference) models.Product {
    product := p.Product
    product.Category = &models.Category {
        ID: p.CategoryID,
    }
    h.Repository.SaveProduct(&product)
    return h.Repository.GetProduct(product.ID)
}
```

The StatusCodeResult struct is an action result that sends an HTTP status code, which is useful for web services. The request handler defines methods that allow one product and all products to be retrieved using GET requests, new products to be created using POST requests, and existing products to be modified using PUT requests. Listing 38-19 registers the new handler with a prefix of /api.

Listing 38-19. Registering a Handler in the main.go File in the sportsstore Folder

```
...
handling.NewRouter(
    handling.HandlerEntry{ "",  store.ProductHandler{}},
    handling.HandlerEntry{ "",  store.CategoryHandler{}},
    handling.HandlerEntry{ "", store.CartHandler{}},
    handling.HandlerEntry{ "", store.OrderHandler{}},
    handling.HandlerEntry{ "", admin.AuthenticationHandler{}},
    handling.HandlerEntry{ "api", store.RestHandler{}},
).AddMethodAlias("/", store.ProductHandler.GetProducts, 0, 1).
    AddMethodAlias("/products[/]?[A-z0-9]*?",
    store.ProductHandler.GetProducts, 0, 1),
...
```

Compile and execute the project. Open a new command prompt and execute the command shown in Listing 38-20 to add a new product to the database.

Listing 38-20. Adding a New Product

```
curl --header "Content-Type: application/json" --request POST --data '{"name" : "Jet
Engine","description": "Paddling is hard work", "price":650, "categoryid":1}' http://
localhost:5000/api/product
```

If you are using Windows, open a new PowerShell window and run the command shown in Listing 38-21.

Listing 38-21. Adding a New Product in Windows

```
Invoke-RestMethod http://localhost:5000/api/product -Method POST -Body  (@{ Name="Jet
Engine"; Description="Paddling is hard work"; Price=650; CategoryId=1 } | ConvertTo-Json)
-ContentType "application/json"
```

To see the effect of the change, run the command shown in Listing 38-22.

Listing 38-22. Requesting Data

```
curl http://localhost:5000/api/product/10
```

If you are using Windows, run the command shown in Listing 38-23 in a PowerShell window.

Listing 38-23. Requesting Data in Windows

```
Invoke-RestMethod http://localhost:5000/api/product/10
```

You can also use a browser to see the effect of the change. Request `http://localhost:5000/admin`. Authenticate as the user `alice` with the password `mysecret` and click the Products button. The last table row will contain the product created using the web service, as shown in Figure 38-3.

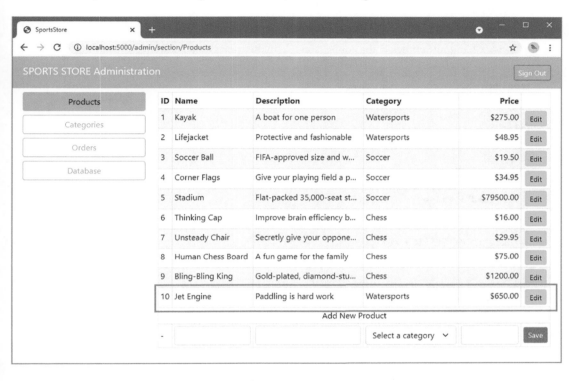

Figure 38-3. *Checking the effect of a database change*

Preparing for Deployment

In this section, I will prepare the SportsStore application and create a container that can be deployed into production. This isn't the only way that a Go application can be deployed, but I picked Docker containers because they are widely used and because they suit web applications. This is not a complete guide to deployment, but it will give you a sense of the process to prepare an application.

Installing the Certificates

The first step is to add the certificates that will be used for HTTPS. As explained in Chapter 24, you can create a self-signed certificate if you don't have a real certificate available, or you can use the certificate files from the GitHub repository for this book (which contain a self-signed certificate that I created).

Configuring the Application

The most important change is to change the application configuration to disable features that are convenient during development but that should not be used in deployment, as well as to enable HTTPS, as shown in Listing 38-24.

Listing 38-24. Changing Settings in the config.json File in the sportsstore Folder

```json
{
    "logging" : {
        "level": "information"
    },
    "files": {
        "path": "files"
    },
    "templates": {
        "path": "templates/*.html",
        "reload": false
    },
    "sessions": {
        "key": "MY_SESSION_KEY",
        "cyclekey": false
    },
    "sql": {
        "connection_str": "store.db",
        "always_reset": false,
        "commands": {
            "Init": "sql/init_db.sql",
            "Seed": "sql/seed_db.sql",
            "GetProduct": "sql/get_product.sql",
            "GetProducts": "sql/get_products.sql",
            "GetCategories": "sql/get_categories.sql",
            "GetPage": "sql/get_product_page.sql",
            "GetPageCount": "sql/get_page_count.sql",
            "GetCategoryPage": "sql/get_category_product_page.sql",
            "GetCategoryPageCount": "sql/get_category_product_page_count.sql",
            "GetOrder": "sql/get_order.sql",
            "GetOrderLines": "sql/get_order_lines.sql",
            "GetOrders": "sql/get_orders.sql",
            "GetOrdersLines": "sql/get_orders_lines.sql",
            "SaveOrder": "sql/save_order.sql",
            "SaveOrderLine": "sql/save_order_line.sql",
            "SaveProduct":          "sql/save_product.sql",
            "UpdateProduct":        "sql/update_product.sql",
            "SaveCategory":         "sql/save_category.sql",
            "UpdateCategory":       "sql/update_category.sql",
            "UpdateOrder":          "sql/update_order.sql"
        }
    },
    "authorization": {
        "failUrl": "/signin"
    },
```

```
"http": {
    "enableHttp": false,
    "enableHttps": true,
    "httpsPort": 5500,
    "httpsCert": "certificate.cer",
    "httpsKey": "certificate.key"
}
}
```

Make sure that the values you specify for the `httpsCert` and `httpsKey` properties match the names of your certificate files and that the certificate files are in the `sportsstore` folder.

Building the Application

Docker containers run Linux. If you are running Windows, you must select Linux as the build target by running the commands shown in Listing 38-25 in a PowerShell window to configure the Go build tools. This isn't required if you are running Linux.

Listing 38-25. Setting Linux as the Build Target

```
$Env:GOOS = "linux"; $Env:GOARCH = "amd64"
```

Run the command shown in Listing 38-26 in the `sportsstore` folder to build the application.

Listing 38-26. Building the Application

```
go build
```

■ **Note**   If you are a Windows user, you can return to a normal Windows build with the following command: `$Env:GOOS = "windows"; $Env:GOARCH = "amd64"`. But don't run this command until you have completed the deployment process.

Installing Docker Desktop

Go to docker.com and download and install the Docker Desktop package. Follow the installation process, reboot your machine, and run the command shown in Listing 38-27 to check that Docker has been installed and is in your path. (The Docker installation process seems to change often, which is why I am not being more specific about the process.)

■ **Note**   You will have to create an account on docker.com to download the installer.

Listing 38-27. Checking the Docker Desktop Installation

```
docker --version
```

Creating the Docker Configuration Files

To create the Docker configuration for the application, create a file named Dockerfile in the sportsstore folder with the content shown in Listing 38-28.

Listing 38-28. The Contents of the Dockerfile in the sportsstore Folder

```
FROM alpine:latest

COPY sportsstore /app/
COPY templates /app/templates
COPY sql/* /app/sql/
COPY files/* /app/files/
COPY config.json /app/
COPY certificate.* /app/

EXPOSE 5500
WORKDIR /app
ENTRYPOINT ["./sportsstore"]
```

These instructions copy the application and its supporting files into a Docker image and configure its execution. The next step is to create an image using the instructions defined in Listing 38-28. Run the command shown in Listing 38-29 in the sportsstore folder to create a Docker image.

Listing 38-29. Creating an Image

```
docker build  --tag go_sportsstore .
```

Ensure that you have stopped all other instances of the application and run the command shown in Listing 38-30 to create a new container from the image and execute it.

Listing 38-30. Creating and Starting a Container

```
docker run -p 5500:5500 go_sportsstore
```

Give the container a moment to start and then use a browser to request https://localhost:5500, which will produce the response shown in Figure 38-4. If you have used a self-signed certificate, then you may have to pass through a security warning.

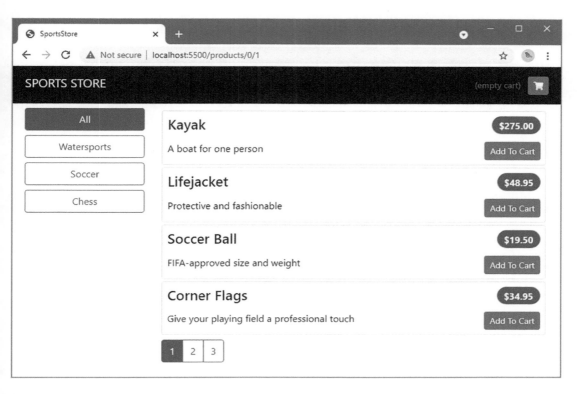

Figure 38-4. *Running the application in a container*

The application is now ready for deployment. To stop the container—and any other container that is running—run the command shown in Listing 38-31.

Listing 38-31. Stopping Containers

```
docker kill $(docker ps -q)
```

Summary

In this chapter, I completed the SportsStore application by finishing the administration features, configuring authorization, and creating a basic web service, before preparing the application for deployment using a Docker container.

That's all I have to teach you about Go. I can only hope that you have enjoyed reading this book as much as I enjoyed writing it, and I wish you every success in your Go projects.

Index

© Adam Freeman 2022
A. Freeman, *Pro Go*, https://doi.org/10.1007/978-1-4842-7355-5

Printed by Printforce, the Netherlands